CLIMATE RATIONALITY

Most environmental statutes passed since 1970 have endorsed a pragmatic or "precautionary" principle under which the existence of a significant risk is enough to trigger regulation. At the same time, targets of such regulation have often argued on grounds of inefficiency that the associated costs outweigh any potential benefits. In this work, Jason Johnston unpacks and critiques the legal, economic, and scientific basis for precautionary climate policies pursued in the United States and, in doing so, sheds light on why the global warming policy debate has become increasingly bitter and disconnected from both climate science and economics. Johnston analyzes the most influential international climate science assessment organizations, the US electric power industry, and land management and renewable energy policies. Bridging between sound economics and climate science and climate law and policy, this pathbreaking book shows how the United States can efficiently adapt to a changing climate while radically reducing greenhouse gas emissions.

Jason Scott Johnston is the Henry L. and Grace Doherty Charitable Foundation Professor of Law and Director of the Olin Program in Law and Economics at the University of Virginia Law School. He has been awarded a Bosch Fellowship at the American Academy of Berlin and a Simon Fellowship at the Property and Environment Research Center. Johnston has also served on the Board of the American Law and Economics Association, at the Searle Civil Justice Institute, and with the Law and Social Science Grant Review Panel of the National Science Foundation. His research has appeared in journals such as the *Journal of Law, Economics and Organization* and the *Yale Law Journal*, and he is the editor of *Institutions and Incentives in Regulatory Science* (2012).

Climate Rationality

FROM BIAS TO BALANCE

JASON SCOTT JOHNSTON
University of Virginia Law School

CAMBRIDGE
UNIVERSITY PRESS

University Printing House, Cambridge CB2 8BS, United Kingdom

One Liberty Plaza, 20th Floor, New York, NY 10006, USA

477 Williamstown Road, Port Melbourne, VIC 3207, Australia

314–321, 3rd Floor, Plot 3, Splendor Forum, Jasola District Centre, New Delhi – 110025, India

103 Penang Road, #05–06/07, Visioncrest Commercial, Singapore 238467

Cambridge University Press is part of the University of Cambridge.

It furthers the University's mission by disseminating knowledge in the pursuit of education, learning, and research at the highest international levels of excellence.

www.cambridge.org
Information on this title: www.cambridge.org/9781108415637
DOI: 10.1017/9781108234917

First published 2021

A catalogue record for this publication is available from the British Library.

Library of Congress Cataloging-in-Publication Data
NAMES: Johnston, Jason Scott, author.
TITLE: Climate rationality : from bias to balance / Jason Scott Johnston, University of Virginia Law School.
DESCRIPTION: Cambridge, United Kingdom ; New York, NY : Cambridge University Press, 2021. | Includes bibliographical references and index.
IDENTIFIERS: LCCN 2021027121 | ISBN 9781108415637 (hardback) | ISBN 9781108401753 (paperback) | ISBN 9781108234917 (ebook)
SUBJECTS: LCSH: Climatic changes – Law and legislation – United States. | Greenhouse gas mitigation – Law and legislation – United States. | Global warming – Government policy – United States. | Renewable energy sources – Law and legislation – United States. | Liability for environmental damages – United States | Environmental law – United States. | BISAC: LAW / Environmental | LAW / Environmental
CLASSIFICATION: LCC KF3819 .J64 2021 | DDC 344.7304/633–dc23
LC record available at https://lccn.loc.gov/2021027121

ISBN 978-1-108-41563-7 Hardback
ISBN 978-1-108-40175-3 Paperback

Contents

Figures

Acknowledgments

This book could not have been written without the support of a University of Virginia Law School Research Chair (in my case, the Armistead M. Dobey Professorship). I have received helpful comments from many people regarding the ideas in this book, too many to acknowledge particular contributions without risking inadvertently forgetting some. I thank my family and friends for their support – and patience. Any mistakes that I have made regarding anything said in this book are of course my sole responsibility.

1

Introduction and Overview

Ever since the passage by Congress of the great wave of late twentieth century federal environmental statutes, two competing normative principles have shaped the debate over how federal regulatory agencies should implement the statutory command to protect the environment. On the precautionary principle, regulation of an environmental risk is justified whenever there is some credible scientific evidence of a potentially "significant" risk of irreversible harm to human health or the natural environment. On the competing principle, that of economically efficient regulation, risks to health or the environment should be regulated only if the benefits of a particular regulatory intervention – reducing such significant risks – outweigh its costs – which often include the creation of new, equally significant and equally irreversible risks.

Most of the federal environmental statutes passed by Congress since 1970 have endorsed what may be called a pragmatic precautionary principle. Under such a principle, the existence of a significant risk is enough to trigger regulation but the scope of the regulation and its stringency depend not just on the magnitude of the risk reduction but also the costs imposed. Pragmatic precautionary statutes do not require that federal environmental regulations be justified on the grounds that their benefits exceed their costs. However, by longstanding executive order, agencies such as the federal Environmental Protection Agency must prepare regulatory impact analyses (RIAs) that analyze the benefits and costs of proposed regulations, with such RIAs reviewed by the Office of Information and Regulatory Affairs within the Office of Management and Budget.

With regulations implementing pragmatic precautionary statutes subjected routinely to review on cost-benefit grounds, as the EPA has continually tightened emission standards and broadened the activities and substances covered by such standards over the last several decades, the same story has been repeated over and over again: the EPA defends new regulations as necessary to lower health or environmental risk, and regulatory targets argue that the costs of the regulation outweigh any potential benefits.

Climate change regulation has become the most dramatic instance of the battle between the precautionary call for risk reduction regulation and arguments for a more balanced consideration of both the costs and benefits of regulation. The field of climate science has since the late 1970s produced studies demonstrating that the increasing concentration of atmospheric greenhouse gases (GHGs) (primarily carbon dioxide, CO_2) in the lower atmosphere (troposphere) may generate future surface temperature increases large enough to cause serious and indeed potentially catastrophic harm to future generations of humans. As most of the increase in atmospheric CO_2 is due to fossil fuel use to produce electricity and power transportation in industrialized nations, such fossil fuel use is easily identified as a target for precautionary regulation. But fossil fuels – coal, oil, and natural gas – are in a very real sense the foundation for modern civilization. As Smil (2017) recounts, everything from modern medicine to the information technological revolution has been built on fossil fuel energy. Actions to end the use of fossil fuels as a source of energy, to decarbonize western economies, are likely to impose costs that dwarf the cumulative cost of all previous, conventional environmental regulations. The precautionary principle says little if anything about how such costs should be weighed in designing policy. But, given the highly uncertain and unpredictable future impacts of rising atmospheric GHG concentrations and the unprecedented cost of reducing GHG emissions, any rational regulatory response to curbing human GHG emissions must surely closely scrutinize the case for decarbonization. The purpose of this book is to provide precisely such an examination.

One response to such a proposed examination is that any such critical scrutiny is unnecessary, the reason being that moving from fossil fuels to various forms of renewable energy – decarbonizing the US economy – is actually not such a big deal at all. As then-Secretary of State Kerry asked rhetorically back in 2014, even if it turns out the climate change risks are lesser than many people fear, "'what's the worst that can happen"[1] from ending the use of fossil fuels? In Part I of this book, I provide an answer. Precautionary US climate policy has already cost lives, damaged the environment, and increased costs for the basic life necessities, such as electricity, in ways that are felt most acutely by the poorest American households.

US precautionary climate policy has had three primary facets: subsidies and mandates for the use of renewable power, common law litigation against CO_2-emitting firms, and federal regulations promulgated during the Obama administration intended to increase the cost of mining and burning coal to generate electricity so drastically that coal-fired power plants would disappear from the US electricity system.

In Chapter 2, I begin my explication of precautionary US climate policy with a discussion of the key cases and the regulatory finding, the Endangerment Finding, that opened the door to Obama administration climate change regulation under the Clean Air Act. I begin in this way because the story of how the Obama administration went about regulating greenhouse gas emissions under the Clean Air Act (CAA) displays all of the major themes in precautionary climate policy. As I summarize in Chapter 2, even after Congress amended the CAA in 1977 and 1990, that law was all about reducing local air pollutants that were not only annoying but believed to cause increases in mortality. Congress had added a few provisions of the law dealing with international air pollution, and it added an entire Title of the law that implemented the 1987 Montreal Protocol's ban on ozone-depleting chlorofluorocarbon refrigerants (CFCs). But although several bills that would have amended the CAA to actually cover GHG emissions had been introduced over the years, such a bill never passed.

Frustrated by the George W. Bush administration's failure to regulate GHG emissions, a group of states and environmental groups sued, arguing that the CAA regulated GHG emissions and the EPA was legally required to decide whether such emissions endangered human health or welfare. In *Massachusetts* v. *EPA*,[2] the Supreme Court accepted this argument. In an opinion written by Justice Stevens that resonates with fear over imminent doom to America from changing climate – doom supported, he said, by assertions about climate change that federal government climate change science bureaucrats had made in sworn affidavits – the Court interpreted the CAA using techniques of statutory interpretation that for the most part were quite mainstream. To nonlawyer readers, these techniques may well seem bizarre and also surely wrong on a very basic common-sense level: the Court ended up concluding that a statute that regulates air pollution and which Congress had tried but failed many times to amend to also regulate GHG emissions actually never needed to be amended, because it already did regulate GHG emissions.

The Obama administration quickly proceeded to find that GHG emissions were "reasonably likely to endanger human health or welfare." Along with the Court's decision in *Massachusetts* v. *EPA* that CO_2 is an "air pollutant," this finding, known as the Endangerment Finding, opened the door to a raft of Obama-era EPA regulations that required reductions in CO_2 emissions under the CAA. The Endangerment Finding was upheld in court. The finding and its success in court vividly display several of the core features of precautionary climate policy. The finding relied entirely on climate change science assessment reports done by government climate change science agencies, primarily the Intergovernmental Panel on Climate Change (IPCC) and the US Global Change Research Program (USGCRP). The EPA's Endangerment Finding is quite literally a very long summary of such reports, primarily IPCC assessment reports. When a large group of plaintiffs challenged the Endangerment Finding in court, in *Coalition for Responsible Regulation* v. *EPA*,[3] the DC Circuit Court of Appeals engaged in no serious review of the science underlying the EPA's finding. Impressed by what it said was the participation of thousands of scientists from across the world in the production of IPCC assessment reports, that court simply accepted everything that the IPCC said as truth. Moreover, the court said, the word "endanger" as used in the CAA mandates a highly precautionary regulatory approach. Together with the court's own confessed very limited or nonexistent climate science expertise, this "precautionary" standard itself required that the court simply defer to whatever the EPA said was true (actually what the EPA said the IPCC said was true) about climate science.

As I trace out in subsequent chapters in Part I, the extreme judicial deference given to the EPA's Endangerment Finding – essentially, to the IPCC assessment report that it summarizes – has been the rule, with no exceptions, when the physical, statistical, or social scientific basis for any EPA climate change-related regulation has been challenged in court. Administrative lawyers and legal scholars know this, but I believe that most of my nonlawyer readers do not and therefore this point cannot be overemphasized: federal courts have failed completely to engage in any actual serious review of whether the supposed scientific basis for a climate change regulation is as strong, and typically one-sided, as the EPA (or other agencies) say it is. They do not look to see whether there is any scientific work contradicting what the EPA proclaims to be the scientific "consensus." Even more shockingly, federal judges, who do believe that they have expertise in crafting procedural rules for trials and appeals that are both fair and effective in getting at truth, have virtually never inquired into the procedures by which IPCC assessment reports are produced and disseminated. Instead, judges have uncritically accepted public relations statements about IPCC procedures. This is a complete abdication of the constitutional responsibilities of Article III, life-tenured judges.

Federal judges have punted in this way in reviewing all sorts of federal environmental regulations, and to the extent that they have a justification other than their lack of expertise, it typically is that the statute is "precautionary." By invoking this term, courts are actually invoking the same precautionary principle justification given for a whole raft of environmental regulations across the world. In Chapter 3, I explain the origins of this principle and its application to justify the European Union's ban on hormone-treated US and Canadian beef and to justify the international ban on CFCs. The precautionary principle itself says only that evidence of a serious and irreversible risk justifies regulation of the risk. Although a ban on the risky activity is the most direct type of precautionary regulation, the principle itself contains no guidance on what such regulation should look like. What the principle does say is that even scant scientific evidence of an actual risk can justify both some sort of risk regulation and a program of sustained government expenditure on research into the risk. As a practical matter, precautionary risk regulation depends upon politics. As a stylized fact, advocates of precautionary regulation stress the benefits of such regulation – the dire risks potentially avoided – while tending to minimize the costs. How this plays out in detail depends upon the outcome of what is primarily a political-economic contest between those who believe they will benefit from precautionary regulations and those who bear the costs.

The remainder of Part I therefore provides a detailed account of how American precautionary climate regulation has worked out in practice. I begin with the raft of Obama-era federal regulations targeting coal and cars. The first such regulation was a direct consequence of the EPA's Endangerment Finding, new standards for automobile mileage. Other regulations soon followed. Regulations promulgated under federal environmental statutes other than the CAA greatly increased the regulatory compliance costs of the coal mining industry, so much that their cumulative effect might well have been to end the industry. New air pollution regulations under the CAA, most importantly regulations requiring decreased mercury emissions, imposed massive new compliance costs on the coal-fired electric power industry. The final set of regulations, culminating in what was called the Clean Power Plan, had the goal of reducing CO_2 emissions from the electric power industry by terminating the combustion of coal to generate electricity.

This assault, explicated in Chapters 4, 5, and 6, caused serious harm. One form of harm was to the US constitutional structure, in which Congress, not the EPA, passes laws. The EPA promulgated regulations so at odds with statutory language supposedly justifying them that it made itself into the legislature. The Supreme Court ultimately rejected some of these arguments. For example, the CAA says that firms emitting more than 250 tons of covered air pollutants have to comply with permitting and certain other emission reduction requirements. But millions and millions of businesses emit more than 250 tons of CO_2 and so the businesses, never before covered under the CAA, would have faced multimillion dollar compliance and permitting costs. This would have politically killed the EPA's attempt to regulate GHG emissions under the Clean Air Act. So the EPA tried just to rewrite the CAA to say that for GHG emissions, the programs only applied to firms emitting more than 100,000 tons per year. In *UARG* v. *EPA*,[4] the Court said that the EPA could not act as the legislature to rewrite the statute. Relatedly, when the EPA said that it could determine that power plant mercury emission reductions were "appropriate" without even considering the cost of such reductions, the Court in *Michigan* v. *EPA*[5] said that such an interpretation was irrational and reversed the agency.

Judicial resistance, however, was spotty, succeeding in slowing the EPA's regulatory grab only when the agency had gone so far in extending its reach that its regulations could not be justified by any plausible reading of the statutes they supposedly implemented. With its auto mileage standards, the EPA, not Congress, put itself in charge of automobile fuel economy. With its Clean Power Plan, the EPA threatened to take control over state electric power systems. Such moves represented an attempt by unelected federal bureaucrats to put themselves in charge of a national system of GHG regulation that they themselves had created, a system that Congress had not established through legislation. The EPA represented the interests of people who perceived themselves to be winners from GHG emission reduction regulations. Consideration of the interests of those harmed by such regulations, which would have found a voice in Congress, are simply not the EPA's job to consider.

True to the precautionary principle, in its rulemakings, the EPA systematically exaggerated the benefits flowing from its congeries of GHG emission reduction regulations while completely neglecting many important costs. The EPA's new automobile mileage standards caused an increase in the price of used cars and new large, high-powered, and safe cars. Thus the EPA's war on automobile GHG emissions forced the poorest Americans to choose between more expensive used big cars and new small, fuel-efficient cars that had low prices but which, as has long been known, are much more dangerous in a crash with larger vehicles. The EPA's attack on coal-fired power plants meant the closure of hundreds of power plants and the permanent loss of tens of thousands of high-paying jobs in the coal-fired power industry. Added to this was the indirect loss of many more hundreds of thousands of jobs. A large body of work shows that prolonged unemployment increases mortality and reduces long-run future earnings. Yet in the cost-benefit analysis that the EPA is required to do for each of its major regulations, that agency does not attempt to quantify the social harm from such mass, regulation-induced layoffs. With its rules attacking the coal-fired power industry, the EPA not only systematically and massively underestimated plant closures and job losses, but following its standard procedures, did not even attempt to quantify the social costs of job loss.

These regulations evidence the precautionary principle at work. There was never any mystery as to the Obama administration's intent: it was to end the use of coal as an energy source for electric power, and, if possible, to end gasoline-fueled automobiles. With the EPA's promulgation of the Clean Power Plan (CPP) in 2015, this goal became explicit: the Clean Power Plan aimed to eventually convert the entire US electric power system to one based solely on electricity generated by solar and wind farms and hydropower. The CPP anticipated that the EPA would oversee state regulators as they attempted to effectuate this fundamental transformation in the American energy and transportation systems. But the EPA has no experience regulating the electric power industry. States are responsible for such regulation. Moreover, without some economically realistic substitutes available, a ban on ostensibly risky activities that have been as crucial to the US economy and society as coal and cars would have been not only politically unacceptable, but obviously catastrophic.

For this reason, the Obama-era climate change program coupled the regulatory attack on cars and coal with dramatic increases in subsidies for renewable electricity and electric cars. In many cases, these federal subsidies were built upon an already existing federal structure of subsidies for renewable energy that had been passed during the precautionary panic over American reliance on imported oil that arose during the 1970s in the aftermath of the OPEC oil embargo. That panic, of course, has turned out to be completely irrational. Once freed by deregulation, market incentives have stimulated the technological revolution called fracking that has made the United States one of the world's leading oil and natural gas producers. Regardless, over several decades, Congress has enacted a series of laws subsidizing renewable power, and in the aftermath of the Great Recession of 2007–2009, those laws plus some new ones were used to substantially increase subsidies for wind and solar power.

Combined with laws in many states that mandate that their electric utilities buy a certain fraction of their electricity from wind and solar power producers, Obama-era federal renewable power subsidies succeeded in quickly increasing the amount of electricity provided by wind and solar. Increasing the share of renewable power on an electricity system, however, turns out to be a complex and costly endeavor. The reason is that wind and solar power is intermittent, available only when the wind blows or the sun shines. On an electricity supply system (commonly called a grid), supply must be perfectly and continuously balanced with demand (called load). Failure to achieve such balance can result in damage to equipment and, in the extreme, to power blackouts affecting entire regions and lasting days. Adding substantial amounts of electricity from intermittent wind and solar to a power grid while ensuring the reliability of electricity supply can be very costly, in that additional electricity generating capacity must be paid for but held in reserve to cover periods when wind and solar are not available.

Chapter 7 explains why this is so. Among the things revealed by the chapter is that increasing wind and solar power on a grid actually increases the demand for easily dispatchable electric power generation (dispatchable in that it can be turned on and off, as it were, quickly and at relatively low cost) from natural gas-powered generators. Wind farms in particular are typically located in remote areas and require massive new investments in high voltage transmission lines to connect them to centers of electric power demand. As shown in Chapter 8, which follows, while it is possible to achieve relatively high levels of renewable power penetration and also ensure grid reliability, the costs are substantial. States that have high renewable power shares have high electricity prices. The cost of electricity and other utilities makes up a higher share of household income, the poorer the household. In this way, policies, such as state Renewable Portfolio Standards, that mandate high shares of renewable power impose costs that are disproportionately borne by the poor.

And these are not the only costs. Chapter 8 describes in some detail a list of present-day environmental harms caused by wind and solar farms and by hydropower projects. Grid scale wind and solar farms consume enormous amounts of land and cause a whole series of alleged harms to nearby landowners. Wind turbines and solar panels are made from materials that cannot be recycled and which must be disposed of in landfills at the end of their relatively short 20–30 year lifetimes. Wind and solar farms kill birds and bats in astounding numbers. In an effort to protect and restore natural aquatic ecosystems and fisheries, environmentalists have for decades opposed new hydropower projects and sought to remove old dams. State RPS laws very often call instead for expanding old hydropower facilities and building more dams.

In a nutshell, the raft of Obama-era regulations targeting coal and cars and subsidizing renewables have harmed the present-day environment and imposed costs disproportionately on poor households. But such regulations are not the costliest manifestation of precautionary US climate policy. The costliest, and most completely irrational, aspect of US climate policy is the decades-old attempt to use common law litigation as a means of assessing climate change damages against fossil fuel companies, electric utilities, and other firms whose activities have generated GHG emissions. I discuss such lawsuits in Chapter 9. These lawsuits typically allege that GHG emissions constitute a public nuisance. I argue that on purely legal grounds, the public nuisance theory cannot be applied to GHG emissions. On broader policy grounds, such lawsuits represent an attempt to completely bypass the democratic process by allowing states and environmental groups who have nothing to lose from the decarbonization of the US economy to force decarbonization on people who will bear all the costs but are not even parties to the lawsuits. Public nuisance suits are the perfect precautionary tool, for if they ever succeed, they would allow the costs of GHG emission reduction requirements to be completely ignored.

Chapter 9 completes Part I. My hope is that the content of Part I will have persuaded the reader that the precautionary climate change policies pursued thus far in the United States have been extremely costly along many dimensions that range from harm to the rule of law to harm to the present-day environment and poor households. A reader might well agree with this assessment and yet respond by arguing that whatever the costs may be, precautionary climate policy is fully justified by the potentially catastrophic costs of not pursing such a policy. This is the essence of precautionary policy: something, anything must be done and done now, to avert potentially catastrophic and irreversible future harm.

The obvious question to ask someone making this argument is how they are so sure that virtually any cost of reducing GHG emissions is justified by the potential harm risked by failing to make such reductions. Another way to put this is to say that given what we have seen are the enormous potential costs of rapid GHG emission reduction, a rational policy response would seem to require some assessment and consideration of the probability that such costs might be incurred incorrectly, in the sense that the actual climate change risk does not justify costs of such magnitude at such point in time.

To assess this risk of error, a rational policy analyst must undertake some evaluation of the evidence supporting the precautionary case for GHG emission reduction. This evidence consists primarily of physical science work involving the extent of climate change to date and its possible causes, and evidence on how climate can be expected to change in the future under alternative GHG emission paths. As it is such evidence that supports precautionary policy responses including even common law litigation, to fail to evaluate the evidence is essentially to undertake a policy without any consideration of whether it might be wrong. This is an irrational approach to any human choice.

Testifying on the basis of my own personal experience, even raising this possibility – that one take a critical look at the climate science case for precautionary climate policy – enrages precautionary policy advocates. They immediately raise a host of objections to such a critical look. Perhaps the most basic is that nobody can evaluate anything about climate science except climate scientists themselves, and as there are already two government sponsored organizations – internationally, the Intergovernmental Panel on Climate Change (IPCC), and nationally, the United States Global Change Research Program (USGCRP) – that have produced climate science assessments in a group effort engaged in by thousands of scientists from across the world, there is literally nothing more to do. Were one to insist, and not defer to these organizations, then precautionary climate policy advocates bring out rather more insidious arguments. They argue that surveys have shown that all scientists agree that radical and costly decarbonization is scientifically justified, and so there literally is nothing more to learn or say. Even worse, they argue that the only kind of people who question anything about climate science are bad, evil people, either greedy corporations or corrupt scientists who are in their pay.

In Chapter 10, which begins Part II to this book, I address these final two arguments – the existence of scientific consensus and the ad hominem argument. I discuss the ad hominem first. It has very often been made by politicians and the media, but the surprising thing that the reader may not know is that it is a staple rhetorical tool of climate scientists who advocate for precautionary climate policy (I refer to such scientists as climate science advocates). However often it may be made, the ad hominem argument is logically fallacious, and I explain why this is so in Chapter 10. As I also explain there, the argument from consensus as indicating the truth of the consensus opinion relies upon intuition about group agreement formalized in a mathematical theorem (the Condorcet Jury Theorem) that holds only under circumstances that do not pertain when it comes to climate science. Actual empirical findings about climate change science consensus have been generated using methods of determining consensus about climate science – searches by the consensus seeker in scientific article abstracts, and surveys of scientists – that are methodologically invalid for a large number of reasons.

Dispensing with the ad hominem and consensus objections to thinking critically about climate science still leaves unaddressed the objection that as a formal science assessment organization involving peer review by thousands of scientists, the IPCC has already done the assessment. Faith in the IPCC, however, is faith in its process. In Chapters 11 and 12, I provide a history of how the IPCC and, (secondarily) the USGCRP evolved and describe their structure and the process by which they produce assessment reports. These organizations were from their inception political, not scientific institutions. The purpose of each was to produce and compile scientific evidence supporting international, United Nations-coordinated policies on climate change (in the case of the IPCC) and (in the case of the USGCRP) to provide a continuing justification for congressional funding to government science agencies. As for how the IPCC assesses science (about which much more is made public than for the USGCRP), that process does not actively involve "thousands" of scientists. Rather, it engages a few dozen highly committed climate scientist advocates who write the chapters that comprise IPCC assessment reports. They write those reports free of any obligation to respond in any way to outside review comments, and thus have complete discretion to choose among competing scientific work which typically consists in part, if not large part, of work that they or their co-authors have produced. The scientists who have headed prominent US climate science organizations, such as NASA's Goddard Institute for Space Studies, have for decades been outspoken advocates for precautionary climate policy, so outspoken that they have established a tradition of "hottest temperature ever" reports about even individual months, knowing full well that climate change is defined not by a hot month or year, but rather by changes in thirty-year averages of climate variables like temperature and precipitation.

Chapters 13–15 actually do the unthinkable by discussing the substance of climate science. I say "unthinkable," but of course climate science has been argued back and forth in the blogosphere (with NASA GISS scientists as active participants) for many years. One problem with this debate has been that it tends to center on the latest scientific study said to support, or weaken, the case for dangerous climate change. People go back and forth about one study. There is no attempt to contextualize studies within a larger body of literature. I provide some context to my discussion here by focusing on what seem to be three crucial scientific questions for the design of a more rational climate policy: first, the reliability of recent observations of climate variables like temperature, sea level change, and the frequency of extreme weather events and how recent trends in these variables compare to past trends; second, whether the only explanation for industrial era (post-late nineteenth century) temperature is an increase in atmospheric CO_2 caused by humans, or whether the literature shows that other forces are known to play a role; and, finally, how future climate is projected from computer models and reconstructions of far distant paleoclimate.

It is of course possible that as a mere economist, I have made some errors in my interpretation of climate science. But the only pieces of scientific knowledge that I do describe on my own, as it were, are things that are taught in high school (or should be taught there). These are far from the scientific frontier. For things that are on or close to the scientific frontier, my goal is just to report on what I have found in the literature. And, to be quite clear, what I have looked for are not studies that confirm conclusions in IPCC assessment reports. Those reports talk about such studies in great detail. I have looked for studies by clearly accomplished researchers that have appeared in peer-edited science journals but which are either completely ignored or dismissed in often highly misleading ways by the IPCC. My purpose is not to determine whether these studies are in some sense "correct." That is beyond my expertise. Rather, it is to reveal the existence of a substantial body of peer-edited scientific work that raises serious questions about many popularly held beliefs about climate science that are crucial to policy design. Due in large part to the active propaganda campaign carried out by climate scientist activists with assistance from the media, these questions have *not even been asked*. But for climate policy to be rational, it must be based upon a critical consideration of all relevant scientific evidence, both that which supports a very high risk of very serious harm from future climate change, and that which cautions that the risk may be much less serious.

Such studies contain a number of highly policy-relevant findings. First, as to what has been happening with the climate, there seems no doubt that by increasing the atmospheric concentration of CO_2, human CO_2 emissions have played a role in increasing temperatures. However, there seems just as little doubt that surface temperature measurements still reported about in GISS's "hottest ever" announcements are biased upward. The recent increase in surface temperature is much bigger than the temperature increase in the lower atmosphere and in the oceans, where about 90 percent of the additional heat from higher CO_2 is felt. Over the longer time scale of the last 2000 years, recent temperatures are higher, but not clearly higher than during the medieval warm period that lasted roughly from A.D. 900 to 1200. For extreme weather events such as hurricanes, droughts, and heat waves, the evidence shows no recent upward trends relative to what has been observed historically. As for sea level, as measured by tide gauges, due to vertical land movements, at some coastal locations in the world, it is rising, at others falling; recent satellite measurements are themselves affected by errors measured in centimeters, and while some scientists think these have been fixed to the point where tiny changes in the rate of change of sea level – at the level of 1–2 mm per year – can be confidently declared, other scientists clearly believe that the fuzziness of even such satellite measurements precludes confident statements about sea level change.

As for the causes of recent and past climate change, computer climate models do not constitute a testable hypothesis about the role of CO_2. Climate modeling groups themselves say that the models are "tuned" to reproduce industrial era warming or other climate states. What this means is that computer code consisting of equations approximating key unknown climate processes, like how clouds respond to a CO_2-induced temperature increase, are chosen in whatever way is necessary to get the model's simulated temperature change to match observations. The one clearly testable hypothesis about CO_2-induced global warming generated by such models – that it should be greater in the tropical troposphere than on the tropical surface by a certain amount – has not been confirmed. Nor has increasing CO_2 led to increasing temperatures, as such models predict, over the past 12,000 years.

Perhaps even more importantly, in its policy-driven focus on CO_2 as the be-all and end-all, the IPCC has ignored alternative explanations for recent observed surface temperature trends in some regions of the world that are well established by the scientific literature. During the latter part of the twentieth century, land development and conversion to urban and suburban use has been a ubiquitous phenomenon in the United States and across the world. Such land conversion is known to increase surface temperatures, especially at night. It is clearly a real cause of temperature increase at the regional level. Yet because it is regional, and cannot be explained by global computer models, the IPCC ignores it. Similarly, black carbon or soot emissions from burning coal in home fireplaces and stoves, and burning biomass more generally, are known to be very powerful climate-warming aerosols. Scientists say that it may be responsible for most of the highly publicized late twentieth century warming observed in the Arctic. But because its effects are regional, and cannot be captured by global climate models, and cannot be put into a CO_2 equivalent metric for use by international climate negotiators, the IPCC has ignored it. Thus has the political mission of the IPCC – to provide information useful to climate policy negotiators – completely swamped its supposed scientific focus.

The most harmful impact of the IPCC science production complex has been its propagation of future climate projections. These projections have been based partly on global climate models, but recent work that actually looks empirically at data about industrial era climate change indicates that climate sensitivity – the increase in temperature caused by an increase in atmospheric CO_2 – is likely much lower than climate models project. Inferences from long ago global climate, paleoclimate – climate over the past millions of years – are generally inconclusive about the causal relationship between atmospheric CO_2 and temperature. And yet the IPCC may give more weight to inferences from paleoclimate in its forthcoming 2021 AR6, for the simple reason that computer climate models are getting worse, not better, at reproducing climate. The most recent generation of such models fails to simulate paleoclimate and generates future climate projections that even climate modelers perceive as implausible. Finally, the most highly publicized IPCC projection of all – which in the United States motivated the political program known as the Green New Deal – is its 2018 projection that global temperature increases of 1.5–2.0C are unavoidable unless massive cuts in CO_2 emissions are made before 2030. But this is not even a scientific projection. It is actually a projection about changes that need to be made in CO_2 emissions relative to an assumed rate of growth of CO_2 emissions *that would otherwise occur.* That rate of growth assumes, completely contrary to recent changes in developed country economies and emissions, that countries will not only grow very quickly, but do so while becoming even more dependent upon coal.

With these clarifications about climate science in hand, Part III of this book moves on to what are primarily economic questions: the measurement of the future harm from CO_2-induced climate change, and adaptation to such future climate change. Economists use the term social cost of carbon (SCC) to describe their estimate of the future harm from climate change. Such estimates rest on computer model projections of future climate. For this reason, computer model projections of future temperature increases that are now known to likely be too high themselves generate estimates of the SCC that are too high. In addition, the key relationship in such models is how temperature impacts economic performance. But this key relationship is not derived from economic first principles. It is inferred in a very informal way from statistical studies of how past temperatures (and other climate variables) have impacted productivity in various economic sectors, especially agriculture, and how temperature affects other measures of human well-being, such as health and disease. These studies suffer from a systematic flaw, which is that they consider too limited a set of explanatory variables. By focusing solely on climate, this econometric work overestimates the deleterious effects of climate change on human economies and societies.

An even bigger problem with computer-generated estimates of the SCC is that such estimates hinge entirely on very pessimistic assumptions made by such models regarding the ability of human economies and societies to adapt to changing climate. In the final two chapters of the book, I look to economic history and economic theory for lessons about the key institutional determinants of such adaptation. The tremendous increase in American agricultural productivity during the twentieth century itself represented an adaptation to changing climate. As settlement moved westward, American farmers succeeded in growing wheat and corn in climates that were, on average, 4–5C different than the regions from which they had migrated, with precipitation patterns that deviated by even more. Agricultural adaptation proceeded from hybridization – spurred at first by experiences with the great droughts of the 1920s and 1930s – to mechanization and irrigation. Central to such adaptation were private property rights that created rewards for those who developed and sold new adaptations. During the latter half of the twentieth century, far from the farm, air conditioning transformed American workplaces and homes. Not only did workplace productivity increase, but heat-related morality in America fell precipitously.

It may be objected that however effective was adaptation in the developed US, adaptation in developing countries is far less likely. Experience in the African Sahel provides evidence to the contrary. The famine that struck the African Sahel in the early 1970s was blamed on poor agricultural practices supposedly endemic to less-developed regions. A closer look shows that such farmers had dealt with drought successfully throughout the twentieth century, and that it was the destruction of indigenous forms of individual and collective property rights by French colonial administrators that led to famine. When traditional forms of property rights were restored, the Sahel greened once again.

In the concluding chapter, I set out some guidelines for policy that I believe follow from this book's analysis. I discuss only policies impacting three questions: adaptation to changing climate, reduction of US GHG emissions, and the production of climate science. When it comes to the first question, policy design begins by realizing that adaptation to changing climate has always occurred and is unavoidable. Recent climate science work has established definitively that climate will continue to change, on varying time scales, regardless of what happens with anthropogenic CO_2 emissions. The policy question is how best to encourage efficient adaptation to changing climate. Here, the clear lesson of my earlier analysis is that the market creates private incentives for efficient adaptation – in business, those who adapt prosper, those who do not, fail. The problem with climate adaptation in the United States has been that through a system of ex ante subsidies and ex post disaster relief, not only is adaptation discouraged, but land development in risky places is encouraged. Such policies should be discontinued.

Climate science has clearly revealed that climate changes for reasons that have nothing to do with human GHG emissions. Indeed, especially on the regional scale, climate changes simply because the climate system is highly nonlinear – climate changes because of the mathematical structure of the system, not because anything is "done" to the system. Granted, future climate may change because of continuing large increases in GHG emissions from other countries, in particular China. Policies undertaken by the Chinese Communist Party (CCP) are opaque; CCP leaders tout China's commitment to "green" energy, and yet both within China and across the world, the CCP is financing and building tens of thousands of megawatts worth of coal-fired power plants.[6] The CCP's GHG emission reduction policy will continue to be chosen to advance that party's Communist agenda, and it seems fanciful to believe that US GHG emission reduction policy will have any impact on how the CCP chooses to integrate GHG emission reduction policy into that larger agenda.

The fact that climate will change no matter what the United States does with its GHG emissions does not mean that America should not have a GHG emission reduction policy. The point of this book is merely to inform such a policy choice. The analysis presented in this book may best be thought of as providing a framework of analysis and body of information that, while highly relevant to the design of such a policy, has thus far been ignored in the precautionary panic over climate change. Through a haphazard process driven by political economics, the United States has already fallen into a de facto GHG emission reduction policy, one that combines subsidized renewable power with increased use of now cheap natural gas to provide electricity when renewable power is not available. US environmentalists, however, continue their assault on natural gas, seemingly unaware that an electricity system with high penetration of renewables can only provide reliable power if there is some source of readily dispatchable power, a source such as natural gas-powered turbines. As it is, America's evolving renewables–natural gas-based power system has had the even more harmful effect of eliminating the potential market for nuclear power. Yet nuclear power has zero GHG emissions, is very low cost, and – relative to wind and solar – causes very little present-day environmental harm. Opposition to nuclear power, sometimes led by the same environmental groups waging the counterproductive assault on natural gas, is itself perhaps the preeminent manifestation of the deleterious consequences of the precautionary principle. Nuclear power should be encouraged. Not with subsidies, for it is the raft of renewables subsidies and mandates that has gotten the United States into its present energy supply predicament. All that need be done is to eliminate the subsidies and mandates for wind and solar power. Free to compete, nuclear will win.

This book reveals that a fundamental cause of failure in climate policy to date has been the failure to set up an institutional structure within which both sides of the climate policy debate are presented and fully considered. The EPA was by design and still is an advocacy agency. Its mission is to marshal scientific and economic evidence supporting more environmental regulation, regardless of cost. The IPCC was also intentionally created to be an advocacy agency, finding scientific evidence supporting international climate policy interventions. There is no similar agency or body, either domestically or internationally, to present the other side of scientific and economic questions. US federal courts have completely failed to audit scientific and policy conclusions of the EPA and IPCC, exhibiting a degree of deference that is inconsistent with their constitutional existence as a separate branch. The project of justifying a much less deferential role for US courts must be left for another book and another day. Also left for another day must be the project of designing institutions for the assessment of regulatory science that objectively assess both sides of contested scientific issues rather than advocate in favor of science supporting particular policy interventions. What I am able to conclude now, however, is that the climate assessments produced by IPCC and the USGCRP constitute biased science advocacy rather than the balanced, objective consideration necessary for rational policy design.

Notes

1. As quoted in the Wall Street Journal editorial, "What's the Worst that Can Happen?"A14, May 12, 2014.
2. 549 U.S. 497 (2007).
3. 684 F.3d 102 (DC Cir. 2012).
4. 134 S.Ct. 2427, 2443 (2014).'s.
5. 135 S.Ct. 2699 (2015).
6. See Steven Inskeep and Ashley Westerman, Why Is China Placing a Global Bet on Coal, NPR, April 29, 2019, available at https://www.npr.org/2019/04/29/716347646/why-is-china-placing-a-global-bet-on-coal; Jude Clemente, Coal Isn't Dead. China Proves It, Forbes, January 23, 2019, available at https://www.forbes.com/sites/judeclemente/2019/01/23/coal-is-not-dead-china-proves-it/#5799281065fa; Institute for Energy Research, Is Coal in China Dead?, April 6, 2018, https://www.instituteforenergyresearch.org/fossil-fuels/coal/coal-dead-china/.

PART I

The Costs of Precautionary Policy

2

The Endangerment Game

As I explain shortly, the United States Congress has never enacted climate change legislation. After Congress failed to do so yet again in 2009, the Obama administration EPA began to issue regulations imposing GHG emission limits. But regulations implement statutes passed by Congress, and as Congress had repeatedly failed to pass legislation imposing limits on GHG emissions, one might well wonder how the EPA found the legal authority to promulgate any regulations limiting GHG emissions.

The answer is that the Supreme Court, not Congress, created that legal authority by virtually rewriting the Clean Air Act (CAA) in a case titled *Massachusetts* v. *EPA*.[1] In what was a huge surprise to most legal observers, the Supreme Court decided that a collection of environmental groups and states had legal standing to challenge the EPA's failure to regulate GHG emissions, that GHG emissions were a pollutant regulated under the CAA, and that the EPA was legally required to determine whether GHG emissions were "reasonably likely to endanger human health or welfare." Immediately after federal climate legislation failed in 2009, the Obama administration made this so-called endangerment determination, opening the door to regulating GHG emissions under the CAA.

As we shall see, regulating GHG emissions under the CAA was only part of the Obama-era attack on cars and coal, the two largest sources of such emissions in the United States. For example, a raft of new regulatory requirements – ranging from occupational safety rules requiring enhanced monitoring of coal dust in mines to new requirements on how coal dust waste may be disposed – increased the cost of mining and burning coal to generate electricity. But CAA regulations imposed such massive costs on coal-fired power plants as to amount almost to a death blow to them.

I begin with the Endangerment Finding not just because regulation of GHG emissions under the CAA was of such great practical importance. Both *Massachusetts v. EPA* and the litigation over the Endangerment Finding provide introductions to the key justifications for the Obama-era GHG regulatory program, justifications that I shall critically examine in the remainder of this part of the book.

I CONGRESSIONAL INACTION ON CLIMATE CHANGE AND THE CLEAN AIR ACT

A *Congress Has Often Considered, but Never Passed GHG Legislation*

In a story described in detail later, during the 1980s key international institutions, led by the United Nations Environmental Program, facilitated both the production of climate science and a movement for international political action on climate change. This culminated in the 1992 United Nations Framework Convention on Climate Change (UNFCCC). During the presidency of George H. W. Bush, the United States became a party to the UNFCCC. That international convention, however, marked the beginning and end of the participation of the United States as an actual party to international climate treaties.

The Clinton administration of 1992–2000 actively participated in international climate treaty negotiations pursuant to the UNFCCC, pushing for emission limits that were "realistic and achievable." It disagreed with the European Union countries both over that group's goal of a 15 percent reduction in GHG emissions relative to 1990 levels by 2010 and also over its insistence that all EU countries be treated as a single entity (or bubble) for GHG emission purposes. The Kyoto Protocol met many of the Clinton administration's demands – such as the United States committing to only a 7 percent reduction by 2010 relative to 1990 emissions and an international GHG emissions trading mechanism[2] – and in 1997, President Clinton actually signed the Kyoto Protocol.

However, six months before the UN climate conference in Kyoto, by a vote of 95–0, the US Senate passed the Byrd-Hagel Resolution declaring that it was the sense of the Senate that the United States should not sign any GHG emission reduction treaty "unless the protocol or other agreement also mandates new specific scheduled commitments to limit or reduce greenhouse gas emissions for Developing Country Parties within the same compliance period, or ... would result in serious harm to the economy of the United States."[3] Given this resolution (which directly contradicted the basic Kyoto structure that developed countries should move first to reduce GHG emissions), the Clinton Administration did not submit the Kyoto agreement to the Senate for advice and consent.

In 2001, in the midst of a US economic recession, President George W. Bush declared that he too would not submit Kyoto for ratification. It would not be until 2015 that an American president, Barack Obama, would sign another international climate agreement. President Obama signed the Paris Climate Agreement – finalized at the twenty-first convention of the parties to the 1992 UNFCCC and viewed as the successor to the expired Kyoto agreement – but that agreement too was never presented to the US Senate for ratification. In 2017, President Trump withdrew the United States from the Paris Agreement.

Domestically, Congress has never passed comprehensive US climate change legislation. Back in 1993, even with a Democratic House and Senate, President Clinton's proposed BTU tax – a rough version of a tax on carbon dioxide emissions – was whittled down by the Senate to just a 4 cent per gallon gasoline tax.[4] Clinton's more comprehensive Climate Change Action Plan (CCAP) was also introduced in 1993, but with the epochal Republican victory in the midterm elections (taking both chambers of Congress for the first time since the 1950s), the Clinton administration had to fight even to retain spending on energy efficiency measures.[5] With a Republican House and Senate and the Clinton administration enmeshed in the Monica Lewensky affair investigations that eventually led to Clinton's impeachment by the House, the Clinton administration's domestic climate initiatives effectively ended in 1998.

In 1999, a group of Republican senators introduced the "Energy and Climate Policy Act of 1999," which would have allocated $200 million per year for research to develop new technologies to reduce GHG emission, created a new Office of Global Climate Change at the Department of Energy, and strengthened the voluntary reporting of greenhouse gas reductions under various provisions of the Energy Policy Act (a law that I discuss later). That law did not pass.

During the George W. Bush presidency, three comprehensive climate bills were introduced in the US Congress. None succeeded.[6] The McCain-Lieberman Climate Stewardship Act,[7] first introduced in the Senate in 2003, eventually came to the floor in 2005 but failed 59–37, with ten Democrats voting against it. Other comprehensive climate bills never made it to a full floor vote. The Global Warming Pollution Reduction Act of 2007,[8] introduced by Senators Boxer of California and Sanders of Vermont, died in committee. Despite strong support from the newly elected Obama administration and a House and Senate both controlled by the Democratic party, the American Clean Energy Security Act of 2009 was barely approved by the House (219–212) and was never even voted on in the Senate.[9]

In the watershed election of 2010, both the House and Senate came under Republican control. After the failure of the American Clean Energy Security Act of 2009 to pass in a Democratic-controlled Congress, faced with a Republican-controlled Congress after 2010, the Obama administration pursued the policy of mandatory GHG emissions reductions through regulatory action, primarily by interpreting very old, traditional environmental statutes to cover the quite different issue of reducing GHG emissions.

B *The Clean Air Act: A Brief Introduction*

The Clean Air Act was passed by Congress in 1963 and significantly amended by Congress in 1965, 1970, 1977, and 1990. By 1970, US public opinion strongly favored reducing air and water pollution. Public opinion was strong because the incredible growth in postwar US manufacturing – the index of industrial production more than tripled between January, 1946 and January, 1970[10] – brought not only affluence and leisure time for outdoor recreation but also badly polluted air and water. Democratic senator Gaylord Nelson proclaimed April 22, 1970 to be the world's first "Earth Day" and to make sure the first Earth Day was an effective mass movement, he enlisted a group of organizers with strong backgrounds organizing protests against the Vietnam War.[11] The effort succeeded in convincing Congress that Earth Day marked a mass grassroots movement in favor of cleaning up the American environment. Senator Edmund Muskie made federal environmental legislation a cornerstone of his bid for the Democratic presidential nomination, and not a single senator voted against the 1970 Clean Air Act that Muskie sponsored and President Nixon signed.[12]

Up until the 1970 CAA, air pollution control had been a state and local responsibility. This made sense, because circa 1970, air and water pollution were understood to be local problems. When even the most strident environmentalists, such as Robert Kennedy Jr., look back on the 1970 Earth Day, they remember local pollution. According to Kennedy, "I remember what it was like for Earth Day. I remember when the Cuyahoga River burned, with flames that were eight stories high. I remember the Santa Barbara oil spill in 1969 that closed virtually all the beaches in Southern California. I remember when they declared Lake Erie dead. I remember that I couldn't swim in the Hudson or the Charles or the Potomac when I was growing up. I remember what the air smelled like in Washington, DC, which wasn't even an industrial city, but it stank."[13] Spurred by local voters who were fed up with dirty air and unusable water, by 1970, states and localities had, in fact, already begun to clean up their air and water. But Congress found that states and localities faced too much political pressure to attract and keep heavy, polluting industry to enact any real, tough pollution laws, necessitating a federal role to clean up local pollution.

Reflecting the local character of air and water pollution problems as they were then perceived and the traditional state and local role in dealing with such problems, the 1970 CAA set up a regime of so-called cooperative federalism. Under this regime, the federal EPA was to set health-based standards for a small number of air pollutants, standards that were uniform across the country. These pollutants, called criteria air pollutants, are lead, particulates (dust particles) of various diameters, sulphur dioxide, oxides of nitrogen, ground-level ozone, and carbon monoxide. In addition (under Section 108 of the CAA), the EPA was to set standards for any air pollutant that in its judgment would "cause or contribute to air pollution which may reasonably be anticipated to endanger public health or welfare." Health-based (called "primary") standards for air pollution reduction were to set at a level "the attainment and maintenance of which in the judgment of the Administrator, based on such criteria and allowing an adequate margin of safety, are requisite to protect the public health."

Under the 1970 CAA's cooperative federalism system, the states and not the federal EPA had the job of figuring out how to reduce pollution from existing factories to meet these uniform national standards. Only for new factories was the federal EPA in charge of setting pollution reduction standards, with pollution required to be reduced to the level achievable by installing the best existing, feasible pollution reduction technology. As the Supreme Court affirmed multiple times, the EPA could not consider costs in determining the uniform primary standards – called National Ambient Air Quality Standards (NAAQS). As that Court also consistently held, the states were free to weigh costs in determining which air pollution reduction strategies to adopt for existing sources of air pollution.

This system applied to factories and other industrial sources of air pollution, called "stationary sources" under the 1970 CAA. That law adopted a quite different system for cutting air pollution from automobiles. Due to its unique topography and virtually total reliance on private automobile versus public transportation, smog had been a problem in California cities since the late 1940s, and for decades virtually every member of the California congressional delegation had pressed for federal air pollution controls. By the 1960s, air pollution from cars and trucks was perceived to be the main cause of smog. By that time, moreover, smog routinely afflicted not just California but US metro areas across the country.[14] This meant that a large number of congressional members faced voter pressure to do something about the smog problem. The automobile industry strongly preferred a single set of federal regulatory requirements for cutting air pollution from cars to what could have been 50 conflicting state requirements.

What emerged in the CAA amendments of 1965 was an air pollution control system for cars – called "mobile sources" under the CAA – that was quite different than that for factories and other stationary sources. The basic framework for federal regulation of air pollution was set out during this period, in Section 202 of the 1965 Clean Air Act. That provision required federal standards for air pollutants from autos if federal regulators found that auto emissions contribute to air pollution that endangers health or welfare. It specified that federal auto air pollution standards must attach "appropriate consideration to technological feasibility and economic costs."

The CAA of 1970 marked a major expansion in the federal role in air pollution control, but that law did not change the framework for regulating pollution from autos set up in 1965. Under Section 202 of the 1970 CAA, the EPA employs the same "reasonably be anticipated to endanger public health or welfare" standard to determine if any additional mobile source air pollutants from cars needed reduction. The EPA itself, not state regulators, sets the standard for pollution reduction. Reflecting the unique importance of automobile air pollution in that state, if the EPA approves, California alone can set tougher automobile emission standards than the federal standard (and other states can follow California, again if the EPA approves). The baseline federal standard was to "reflect the greatest degree of emission reduction achievable through the application of technology which the Administrator determines will be available for the model year to which such standards apply." For this reason, it is often said that car companies were subject to a "technology forcing" standard, with the EPA forcing them to adopt the air pollution reduction technology that it found would be "available" for a future model year. However, that same section of the CAA (Section 202(a)(3)(A)) instructed the EPA to give "appropriate consideration to cost, energy, and safety factors associated with the application of such technology." Essentially these same provisions were incorporated into Section 202 of the 1970 CAA.

To meet the auto industry's primary demand for a uniform federal air pollution standard for cars, the 1970 CAA still allowed only California to seek a waiver from the uniform federal standard in order to set its own auto emissions standards. If California is granted such a waiver, then other states may choose to adopt the California standards.[15] That law sets up what seem to be tough standards that California has to meet in order to get such a waiver: the EPA must find that California's auto emission standards are at least as protective as the federal standards, and also that California faced "compelling and extraordinary circumstances."[16] However, in the more than five decades since its passage, the EPA has never denied a request from California for a waiver to enact its own standards for pollutants such as carbon monoxide, fine particulates, and oxides of nitrogen.

Within a few years after the enactment of the CAA of 1970, the United States faced the first, 1973–4 Arab oil embargo. With gasoline at first rationed and then doubling in price in less than a year,[17] price inflation accelerated and the United States fell into recession. In the midst of dour economic times, states did little to implement the federal NAAQS, and many major metropolitan areas had not come close to meeting the NAAQS by the original statutory deadline of 1975. After the Supreme Court interpreted the CAA to mean that plants would have to begin shutting down in areas of the country that had failed to attain the NAAQS,[18] Congress responded in 1977 by amending the CAA, pushing back until at least 1982 the date by which air quality regions were to meet the NAAQS.

The 1977 amendments gave the states more time to get into compliance, but they also sought to make federal pollution requirements tougher and easier to enforce. The law significantly federalized pollution reduction requirements for existing factories by requiring that they adopt all "reasonably available" pollution control technologies, with the EPA, and not the states, determining which technologies were reasonably available. In heavily polluted areas, new or modified large factories had to install the very best new pollution reduction technology (meeting a new federal standard of the lowest achievable emission rate). Recognizing that these tough technological standards for manufacturing in the heavily polluted rust belt areas of the country would create an incentive for business to relocate to the much less developed south and west, Congress also created a new program in 1977 called Prevention of Significant Deterioration or PSD, which required the installation of costly pollution reduction technologies in new factories located in regions where federal pollution standards were already being met.

Another aspect of the 1977 CAA amendments was for decades little discussed but is important background in understanding the historical context of the Obama-era assault on coal that I discuss in detail in a later chapter. Before the Arab oil embargo, the US electricity generating industry had been moving steadily away from coal as an energy source, burning more and more oil. This long-term shift was motivated in large part by state and local air quality regulations passed during the 1950s and 1960s that limited and in some cases actually banned the use of coal. The Arab oil embargo and then-limited US oil production made oil a much more expensive and much riskier energy source, so much so that a major goal of President Carter's 1977 National Energy Plan was to convert oil-burning electricity generating plants over to coal.[19] In 1974, coal-burning electricity generating facilities had in fact already been exempted under certain circumstances from pollution reduction requirements imposed by states under the CAA, and among all large sources of air pollution, coal-burning electric utility generating facilities were notable for their failure to reduce air pollution.[20] In the 1977 amendments, Congress gave the EPA the discretion to give extra time for electricity plants converting to coal, even when they were located in badly polluted, so-called non-attainment areas.[21]

More generally, under the 1977 amendments, new large coal-burning electricity generating units were required to reduce their emissions of sulfur dioxide and other criteria pollutants by adopting the "best technological system of continuous emission reduction that has been demonstrated adequately (taking into consideration the cost of achieving the reduction and any health and environmental impacts and energy requirements)." This so-called BSER standard required such plants to use a technological method of control, such as a scrubber (electrostatic precipitator) on the smokestack, rather than by using an alternative fuel such as low sulfur coal. Famously inefficient, Congress imposed the scrubber requirement for classical political economic reasons: without it, coal-burning electricity generators would have switched to low-sulfur coal from Wyoming and similar states, decimating high-sulfur eastern coal-producing states such as Kentucky and West Virginia.

When Congress amended the CAA in 1977, it still viewed air pollution as a local problem. The amendments responded to what were becoming the recognized realities of air pollution reduction: first, that air pollution reduction brought both local benefits and local costs and that local costs would be higher in older, developed areas of the country if industry could move to less developed regions where costly air pollution controls were not required; and, second, that even if pollution controls were required in less developed areas, as a political matter, heavily polluted states were very reluctant to impose tough standards on existing industry.

Consistent with the law's focus on local air pollution, up until 1990, the Clean Air Act mostly ignored pollution that crossed state lines. It is true that in Section 110(a)(2)(E) (which has come to be called the "good neighbor" provision), the 1970 CAA required states to include "adequate provisions for intergovernmental cooperation" concerning interstate air pollution in their own implantation plans,[22] and that in the

1977 amendments, this provision was toughened to require that state implementation plans be "adequate" to "prohibi[t] any stationary source within the State from emitting any air pollutant in amounts which will ... prevent attainment or maintenance [of air quality standards] by any other State."[23] As the Supreme Court observed recently,[24] however, this language "regulated only individual sources that, considered alone, emitted enough pollution to cause nonattainment in a downwind State," and "[b]ecause it is often impossible to say that any single source or group of sources is the one which actually prevents attainment downwind ... the 1977 version of the Good Neighbor Provision proved ineffective." Only in 1990 did Congress require that state implementation plans "contain adequate provisions ... prohibiting ... any source or other type of emissions activity within the State from emitting any air pollutant in amounts which will ... contribute significantly to nonattainment in, or interfere with maintenance by, any other State with respect to any [NAAQS]."[25]

Beginning in the 1990s, the EPA began to invoke the CAA's "good neighbor" provision to require state implementation plans to include emission reductions to curb interstate air pollution. The main type of interstate pollution targeted in these efforts, however, was traditional ground level ozone. So-called ozone precursors – various hydrocarbons and nitrogen oxides that interact with sunlight to form ozone – were the pollutants to be controlled. All of these were traditional pollutants long regulated under the CAA, and the pollution problem under attack was local air pollution, with the only difference from earlier CAA regulatory efforts being that by the 1990s, it was recognized that local air pollution was affected by emissions in upwind states.

Congress actually focused on another regional air pollution problem in the 1990 amendments, acid rain. Since the 1977 amendments, many people had become concerned that sulfur dioxide and nitrogen oxide pollution from coal-burning power plants in the Midwest was precipitating back to the earth as highly acidic rainfall in the northeastern United States. In the 1990 amendments, Congress enacted a plant-specific cap on emissions of these pollutants from power plants, with the cap declining over time but each plant given the option of either reducing its emissions or buying permits to emit freed up by other plants that had lower costs of emission reduction and had reduced their own emissions by more than that legally required. Between 1990 and 2000, over 300 plants located mostly in the Midwest were required to comply with this new cap and trade program. Importantly, these requirements did not apply to many of the oldest coal-burning electricity generating plants that had been built in the mid-1970s to provide energy security and which had been repeatedly exempted from CAA.

Responding to environmental groups' complaint that even the provisions of the CAA as amended in 1977 were not being enforced, the CAA amendments of 1990 added a new permit program. Under Title V of the 1990 amendments,[26] major sources of air pollution – factories and other facilities that emitted 250 tons per year or more of air pollutants covered under the CAA (with a lower 100 ton per year threshold for certain specific sources) – were required to have a permit document setting out all of the source's pollution reduction obligations and to file periodic reports identifying the extent to which it was in compliance with those obligations.

Congress has not amended the Clean Air Act since 1990. There is only one section of the Clean Air Act that addresses international air pollution, section 115. That section was included (as Section 105) in the original 1965 Clean Air Act, retained when Congress amended the CAA in 1970, amended in 1977, and has been unchanged since.[27] Section 115 creates the authority for the EPA to cooperate with other countries in negotiating agreements when the EPA finds that pollution from the United States is harming another country and the other country would reciprocally respond if its own pollution was harming US citizens. From the available evidence, it seems clear that in addressing international air pollution in 1965, Congress was thinking about local air pollution that spilled over to or from American cities on the Canadian or Mexican borders and was primarily concerned that no pollution abatement requirements be imposed on US firms that would not likewise be imposed across the border. For example,[28] during House consideration of the law, one member asked what would happen if pollution from the Buffalo, New York area spilled over to Fort Erie, Ontario. He was assured that "before they could proceed to bring about any program to deal with the subject they would have to be in agreement for reciprocal treatment." In the forty-plus years since it became part of the CAA, the EPA has never negotiated an international pollution agreement under Section 115.

In 1990 Congress also amended the CAA to address a specific international environmental issue, the so-called ozone hole. Pushed by US chemical companies that had already developed chemicals that substituted for ozone-depleting chlorofluorocarbons (CFCs) for use in air conditioning units and similar appliances, the US in fact led the international effort for very rapid decreases in CFC emissions.[29] This effort culminated with the United States becoming a party to the 1987 Montreal Protocol on Substances that Deplete the Ozone Layer. In 1990, Congress added Title VI to the Clean Air Act, a set of provisions[30] entitled "Stratospheric Ozone Protection" that phased out the use of CFCs and other gases that were deemed to be contributing to a potentially dangerous depletion of stratospheric ozone.

II THE NEW, OLD CLEAN AIR ACT: *MASSACHUSETTS* V. *EPA* AND THE PERILS OF EXPANSIONIST STATUTORY INTERPRETATION

During the Bush administration, a group of environmental interest groups and states such as Massachusetts and Rhode Island petitioned the EPA to make a determination under Section 202 of the CAA of whether GHG emissions could "reasonably be anticipated to endanger public health or welfare." As discussed above, such a finding would trigger the EPA's obligation under that same section to promulgate new emission standards for automobiles. As will be explained in more detail later, by finding that GHG emissions are an "air pollutant" under the CAA, a Section 202 Endangerment Finding was a pathway to legally required regulation of GHG emissions under several other provisions of the CAA.

From my discussion of the CAA, it should seem obvious that the CAA has nothing to do with regulating GHG emissions. The law was passed to create a federal role in curbing local air pollution problems such as smog. That role was extended, and logically so, to encompass a federal role in setting standards to curb local air pollution caused by pollution in distant upwind states. For decades, tougher federal air pollution standards have been justified primarily by reductions in the probability of premature mortality that have been statistically estimated to result from lower atmospheric concentrations of various pollutants such as ozone or fine particulate matter (particles of dust less than 2.5 microns in diameter). GHGs such as carbon dioxide are not a constituent of smog, and they can directly contribute to health problems only if people are exposed to them in far higher concentrations than those even possible in the atmosphere. For example, carbon dioxide – the main GHG targeted by Obama-era regulations – is a colorless and odorless gas that is produced by respiration, fermentation and combustion and so is a natural constituent of the earth's atmosphere. It is about 1.5 times heavier than air and in the earth's atmosphere, and normal indoor room air, CO_2 makes up about .04 percent of the air. Carbon dioxide becomes toxic to people only if its concentration level in air exceeds 5 percent, which is 12,500 percent higher than its typical concentration level.[31] Concentration levels above this threshold occur only under extremely unusual conditions, such as when a large amount of dry ice is rapidly warmed in small room.

Of course the plaintiffs in *Massachusetts* v. *EPA* were not petitioning for the EPA to regulate carbon dioxide because of its potential to be acutely toxic at extremely high concentrations. Nor were they arguing that long-term exposure to realistically elevated concentrations of carbon dioxide can cause the kind of premature death to chronic disease that is the primary adverse health effect from exposure to CAA criteria pollutants such as carbon monoxide. They were arguing that the EPA had to regulate carbon dioxide under the CAA because the continuing accumulation of human-generated (anthropogenic) GHGs in the earth's atmosphere could change the earth's climate, and such climate change could "reasonably be anticipated to endanger public health or welfare." The task facing the plaintiffs in *Massachusetts* v. *EPA* was to somehow convince the Court that the CAA actually required the EPA to make such a finding.

Were one to interpret the CAA in the light of even the abbreviated history I have presented above, the common sense response to the argument that the EPA had to make a finding as to whether GHG emissions could reasonably endanger public health or welfare would be that Congress meant for the EPA to make such findings only for possible contributors to local or perhaps regional air pollution problems and that as GHGs have nothing to do with air pollution problems, the CAA did not apply and the EPA did not have to make such a finding. But courts do not interpret statutes in light of common sense understandings of what statutes are about gleaned from broad reading and research. They interpret statutes by interpreting the precise language of the statute. Members of Congress do not write statutes. Nor do their typically very young and inexperienced staffers. Statutes are written by lawyers, to be interpreted by lawyers according to an arcane set of interpretive principles and rules that I teach every year to my law students. These interpretive principles and rules often conflict, and no one has ever demonstrated that they actually help anybody predict how courts will interpret statutes. Even worse, in Alice-in-Wonderland fashion, they can be used to argue that statutes mean things that no one who actually wrote the statute would ever imagine.

Such was the outcome in *Massachusetts* v. *EPA*. Like many statutes, the CAA defines many of the words that it uses. In particular, the CAA defines "air pollutant" as "any air pollution agent or combination of such agents, including any physical, chemical, biological, radioactive (including source material, special nuclear material, and byproduct material) substance or matter which is emitted into or otherwise enters the ambient air."[32] The most striking thing about this definition is that it is virtually a tautology, defining "air pollutant" as "any air pollution agent or combination of agents." To know what counts as an air pollutant under the CAA's definition, one would need to know what Congress meant by air pollution. Unfortunately, the definitions section of the CAA does not define air pollution.

Courts employ various approaches to figure out what Congress means by a word or term that it uses in statutes but does not define in those statutes. Often the first thing courts do is to look to an ordinary dictionary, like Merriam-Webster or American Heritage, for the dictionary or plain meaning of the term. If the plain meaning seems consistent with how Congress is using the term in the statute, then courts will stick with that. According to the American Heritage dictionary, "pollution" means the "contamination of soil, water or the atmosphere by discharge of harmful substances." According to Merriam-Webster, "pollution" means the "act of polluting," where to "pollute" means "to make physically impure or unclean" or to "contaminate (an environment) especially with man-made waste." These dictionary meanings are completely consistent with what the CAA is about: reducing the discharge of harmful man-made waste products that make the atmosphere "impure or unclean." After all, the law is called the *Clean* Air Act, and virtually every one of its provisions is concerned with a regulatory regime to control airborne waste products, whether from factory smokestacks or automobile exhaust pipes.

Yet these dictionary definitions don't completely answer the question of whether discharging GHGs constitutes pollution. Merriam-Webster doesn't tell us whether GHG emissions make the environment physically impure or unclean, and the American Heritage doesn't tell us what makes a substance harmful. The answer would depend upon what Congress was targeting in the CAA. To discern this, a court would typically look to the statute itself for guidance. The CAA provides precisely such guidance, because Congress specifically listed some pollutants of concern – so-called criteria pollutants, for which the EPA was to set national uniform air quality standards. The six criteria air pollutants are ozone (which causes smog), particulate matter of various sizes, sulfur dioxide (SO_2), carbon monoxide (CO), nitrogen dioxide (NO_2), and lead. Congress did not specifically list carbon dioxide, methane, or other GHGs as criteria pollutants. This doesn't mean that Congress thought GHG emissions were not air pollutants, but the pollutants that are specifically mentioned by Congress provide a guidepost or benchmark. A court would typically ask whether GHGs are sufficiently similar to the criteria pollutants – in terms of their harmfulness – that the Congress that passed the CAA would have considered them to be air pollutants.

In his opinion for the majority, Justice Stevens did not take such an approach. Instead, he simply declared that the statutory definition of air pollutant was "unambiguous" and "embraces all airborne compounds of whatever stripe." This is, first of all, simply not true, because as we've just seen, the statutory definition of air pollutant hinges on the undefined term "air pollution agent." It is, secondly, absurd. For Congress didn't pass the Clean Air Act so that the EPA could regulate any airborne chemical compound. That would mean regulating almost everything, including all of the natural constituents of the earth's atmosphere, and since human beings emit CO_2 as a waste gas, such a broad understanding of air pollutants could convert the CAA into a statutory basis for the EPA to regulate human population. Finally, if Congress had provided such a virtually limitless definition of the things that constitute air pollutants, then certainly it would have wanted the EPA to exercise some discretion to narrow things down a bit to those compounds that are actually harmful, and it would have wanted courts to defer to the agency's judgment.

To this final argument, made in dissent by Justice Scalia, Justice Stevens replied that "no party to this dispute contests that greenhouse gases both 'enter the ambient air' and tend to warm the atmosphere. They are therefore unquestionably 'agents' of air pollution."[33] Here, Justice Stevens himself did in 2007 what, as we have just seen, Congress for over forty years chose not to do by defining an "agent of air pollution" as anything that "warms the atmosphere." In so doing, he even admitted that "the Congresses that drafted Section 202 might not have appreciated the possibility that burning fossil fuels could lead to global warming," that is, that Congress never actually intended to regulate GHGs. But then Stevens said that these Congresses did understand that "without regulatory flexibility, changing circumstances and scientific developments would render the Clean Air Act obsolete. The broad language of Section 202 (a)(1) reflects an intentional effort to confer the flexibility necessary to forestall such obsolescence." In other words, by setting out a basically empty definition of "air pollutant" dependent entirely on the meaning of "air pollution agent," Congress left it to a federal judge to overrule the EPA and decide more than forty years later that global warming was an air pollution problem dealt with by the Clean Air Act.

Uniquely among all recent retirees from the Supreme Court, Justice Stevens was an active political commentator after his retirement, repeatedly calling for the repeal of the Second Amendment right to bear arms and castigating Justice Bret Kavanaugh as unfit for the Court.[34] But all Supreme Court justices have political preferences. Justice Stevens' ability to rewrite the CAA shows the danger when Congress passes statutes with broad and poorly crafted terms. Justice Stevens' interpretive approach in *Massachusetts* v. *EPA* is by no means unusual. Indeed, it was predictable. But it has major consequences for the structure and operation of the federal government. In *Massachusetts* v. *EPA*, an unelected Supreme Court did what Congress had repeatedly decided not to do: write a federal law regulating GHG emissions. The signal sent to future Congresses by such a result is that if any law is passed, the Supreme Court may well interpret that law to apply to activities that not only were never anticipated by the enacting Congress, but which Congress has repeatedly declined to address legislatively. As argued and evidenced by Rodriguez and Weingast (2007),[35] such a prospect makes passing a law much riskier for members of Congress.

The Bush administration's fallback to the argument that GHG emissions were not air pollutants under the CAA was that in its judgment, regulating GHG emissions under the CAA was a bad idea for various policy reasons. The problem with this argument was that the relevant provision of the CAA, Section 202, doesn't outline anything that would give the EPA the authority to decide not to make an endangerment determination simply because it didn't like the legal consequences. Under Section 202, those legal consequences were clear: via the use of the word "shall," Section 202 requires that if the EPA makes an endangerment determination, then it must set emission standards for new cars.

Even with a vague and open-ended statute, the result in *Massachusetts* v. *EPA* could have been avoided. The Bush administration might well have succeeded if it simply argued that given its limited budget, it put other tasks ahead of making an endangerment determination.[36] To be sure, an even more direct approach would have been to simply find that GHG emissions were not "reasonably likely to endanger public health or welfare" within the statutory meaning of those terms. The Bush administration had, however, precluded itself from making such a finding. The EPA never denied that anthropogenic GHG emissions could contribute to climate change that affects human health or welfare. Indeed, in denying the petition to regulate under Section 202, the EPA specifically agreed with President George W. Bush's statement that "the federal government 'must address' climate change."[37]

The Bush administration had thus gotten itself into an impossible predicament. That administration had steadfastly refused to regulate GHG emissions, but somehow it had also committed itself to statements about GHG emissions and their effects that led to a legal finding under the CAA that regulation of GHGs was legally required. This predicament enabled the holding in *Massachusetts* v. *EPA*, which set the stage for the Obama administration's Endangerment Finding, which the Obama administration then used as the basis for its attack on coal. Understanding the origins of the Bush administration's climate change predicament is therefore crucial to understanding how the Obama administration was able to move forward to regulate GHG emissions under the CAA.

III THE "EPA" WAS NOT ACTUALLY THE DEFENDANT IN *MASSACHUSETTS V. EPA*

The first step toward such understanding is a fact that has long been obvious to many lawyers and Washington insiders but has only recently begun to figure in daily news: whatever may be the policy preferences of a particular presidential administration elected by American voters, those preferences may be far different than the preferences of federal bureaucrats who run executive agencies like the EPA. Executive agencies are responsible for implementing statutes passed by prior Congresses, but they are part of the executive branch, controlled ostensibly by presidential appointees.

The EPA is an executive branch agency that was created by the Nixon administration in 1970. Originally, a Nixon administration task force recommended the creation of a new Department of Environment and Natural Resources.[38] That agency would have absorbed the entire Department of the Interior's responsibilities in managing public lands and would also have been responsible for pollution reduction regulations. Including agencies such as the Bureau of Reclamation, the Soil Conservation Service, and the Army Corps of Engineers, Interior had traditionally been a land and resource development agency. Nixon originally supported the idea of creating a new agency that would have the responsibility for both resource development and environmental regulation. The thinking was that such an agency would make and insulate the president from making the politically tough tradeoffs between resource development and resource protection.

Fearing that resource development interests would dominate such an agency, environmental groups proposed instead a new agency, reporting directly to the president, with responsibility only for pollution control programs. That agency was to have responsibility for all types of pollution, with a "clear focus on environmental advocacy." As explained by Landy et al. (1994, 32), Nixon and others in his administration, none of whom were themselves actually that interested in environmental protection, supported the new environmental agency because as a "highly visible and innovative" action, it scored political points with the burgeoning environmental movement, and was a compromise between completely changing the agency structure – which faced opposition both from entrenched bureaucracies and the interest groups they served – and doing nothing. Thus, during the administration of a president who was far from an environmental protection supporter, the EPA was born as an advocacy agency, with responsibility only for identifying new benefits from pollution reduction, and no obligation to consider the costs of such reduction.

As has been well documented by political scientists,[39] career bureaucrats at the EPA are strongly committed to an agenda of environmental advocacy. With few exceptions (such as economists in the agency), they want more environmental regulation regardless of its costs. While the president appoints the top leadership of the EPA, they number at most in the dozens, versus literally of tens of thousands of career EPA bureaucrats. As a practical matter, due to enormous procedural costs imposed by the Civil Service Act, career bureaucrats at the EPA and other executive branch agencies cannot be fired. Career bureaucrats at the EPA produce material supporting and actually write regulations during pro-regulatory administrations such as those of Clinton and Obama. And while they cannot promulgate new regulations over the opposition of a presidential administration, these career bureaucrats have plenty of leeway to continuously produce all kinds of material – such as assessments of scientific literature – that provide a basis for potential future regulation.

Moreover, when the EPA is headed by political appointees who are themselves environmental activists, those appointees may work to establish the basis for future regulations. Such was exactly the case at the EPA during the Clinton administration. Once the prospect of US ratification of the Kyoto protocol had disappeared, Administrator Carol Browner directed the agency's General Counsel Jon Cannon to prepare a legal memorandum setting out the case for regulating GHG emissions under the CAA. This memorandum closely tracked the arguments made and accepted by the Court almost ten years later in *Massachusetts* v. *EPA*.

Thus when the George W. Bush administration took the helm of the EPA, it was steering a ship whose previous captain had prepared detailed instructions on how to head in a particular direction – to regulate GHG emissions under the CAA. Moreover, the ship's effectively life-tenured crew, with control over the day-to-day operations, was strongly committed to going where the previous captain wanted to go, not where the Bush 43 EPA administrator wanted to go. Political appointees in federal executive branch agencies are like temporary ships' captains. It is constitutionally true that the captain is in charge of the ship, but if the crew of life-tenured bureaucrats doesn't favor the captain's destination, they can make getting there awfully difficult.

This is essentially the situation that confronted the Bush administration with climate change. Faced with the Bush administration's opposition to their policy agenda, EPA career bureaucrats did not simply quietly sit by and watch. They went to the media with their complaints about the direction the Bush administration was taking. As observed by President Obama's former climate czar Jody Freeman in a law review article co-written with Harvard Law colleague Adrian Vermeule, these complaints didn't amount to anything like a detailed list of the costs to Americans of what the Bush administration was and wasn't doing, but instead centered on the charge that the administration was inappropriately and perhaps illegally "altering scientific reports, silencing its own experts, ... suppressing scientific information that was politically inconvenient" and "tampering ... with the global warming data reported by numerous federal agencies."[40] Indeed, in September, 2002, EPA staff had deleted a section on global warming from the EPA's annual report on air pollution rather than accepting White House revisions to that section. The revisions would have deleted material linking increases in global temperatures to human activity and included language "question[ing] climate change science." EPA staff wrote in an internal memorandum that the revised language would "no longer accurately represent the scientific consensus on climate change," and if published would target the EPA for "severe criticism from the science and environmental communities for poorly representing the science." As Freeman and Vermeule (2007) continue to recount, EPA staff also revealed to the media that during 2002 and 2003, a White House official "with no scientific training" had introduced scientifically unjustified "doubt and uncertainty" into federal agency reports on global warming.[41]

Complaints about Bush administration interference with climate science came from plenty of federal agencies in addition to the EPA. As Freeman and Vermeule (2007) tell the story, "scores of scientists in agencies such as the National Oceanic and Atmospheric Administration (NOAA) and EPA reported being pressured to delete references to climate change and global warming from official documents, including their communications with Congress." Perhaps most prominently, "James Hansen, the top climate scientist at the National Aeronautics and Space Administration (NASA), reported that the administration had tried to stop him from publicly calling for prompt reductions in greenhouse gases linked to global warming, and that officials from NASA headquarters had ordered the agency's public affairs staff to review his upcoming lectures, web postings, and interviews out of concern for 'coordination.'"[42] Thus, for several years prior to the Court's decision in *Massachusetts* v. *EPA*, the newspapers had steadily reported on the ongoing battle in which climate science experts from across a range of government agencies struggled valiantly to tell the truth about climate change but faced opposition from untrained politicians.

Writing not long after the Court's decision in *Massachusetts* v. *EPA*, Freeman and Vermeule[43] describe the state of climate science and policy as then perceived by liberal law legal scholars:

> [A] scientific consensus that had solidified over the last decade was gelling in the public's mind: global temperatures were in fact rising and contributing, among other things, to elevated sea levels and more intense hurricanes, and the rising temperatures were linked to human activity, specifically, the emissions of greenhouse gases from the burning of fossil fuels. In the few years before *MA* v. *EPA* reached the Supreme Court, the rate of publication of articles on global warming in major US newspapers and journals had increased dramatically. Scientists both within and outside government were becoming more vocal in calling for a policy

response, including federal regulation of greenhouse gas emissions. Indeed, as the Court considered *MA* v. *EPA*, the Intergovernmental Panel on Climate Change (IPCC) was preparing to release its fourth assessment report, which would state the scientific consensus on the warming trend and outline the potential risks of unmitigated greenhouse gas emissions more forcefully than ever before.

According to the lead attorney for the plaintiffs' Supreme Court petitioners in *Massachusetts* v. *EPA*, Georgetown law professor Heinzerling, plaintiffs' lawyers thought that their chances of success would be maximized if they pursued a relatively technical and narrow legal argument – that the EPA had applied the wrong legal standard in declining to regulate GHG emissions – thereby "disguising this breakthrough case about climate change as an ordinary administrative and statutory matter."[44] As Heinzerling says, "nobody was fooled" by this attempt to mask the significance of the case. I agree with Freeman and Vermeule that it would have been impossible for the justices who decided *Massachusetts* v. *EPA* not to know that many people were coming to believe in a "growing scientific consensus on climate change" and that there had been a swirl of accusations that the Bush administration was "trying to suppress and manipulate agency science."[45] The majority opinion frankly confessed that the Court had agreed to hear argument in the case because of the importance of the climate change issue,[46] and Justice Stevens' majority opinion rings with alarm over the dangers of climate change.

Indeed, Stevens' opinion begins with an abbreviated history of dramatic increases in measured atmospheric carbon dioxide even as early as 1970, when Congress passed the CAA. According to Justice Stevens, progressive increases in the scientific understanding of climate change culminated in a comprehensive 1991 assessment report by the Intergovernmental Panel on Climate Change (IPCC). The apparently misnamed Intergovernmental Panel was, according to Stevens, a "multinational scientific body" that, based on "expert opinions from across the globe," had concluded in 1991 that anthropogenic GHG emissions were increasing atmospheric concentrations of GHG gases resulting "on average in additional warming of the earth's surface" and in a second comprehensive report in 1995 concluded that the balance of the information then known "suggests there is a discernible human influence on global climate." A "discernible human influence" is not necessarily a harmful influence, but – in finding that the states had the constitutional right to act as plaintiffs in *Massachusetts* v. *EPA* – Stevens repeatedly cited the "unchallenged affidavits" from the plaintiffs' climate scientist expert Michael McCracken (who for a time headed the US Global Change Research Program) as supporting the proposition that "the harms associated with climate change are serious and well-recognized." Among the harms that Stevens found declared by these experts were a "precipitate rise in sea levels," "serious and irreversible changes in natural ecosystems," an "increase in the spread of disease," and rising ocean temperatures that "may contribute to the ferocity of hurricanes." As for the state of Massachusetts in particular, Stevens pointed to expert witness declarations that "sea levels rose somewhere between 10 and 20 centimeters over the twentieth century as a result of global warming," and "rising sea levels have already begun to swallow Massachusetts' coastal land," with Stevens concluding that "the severity of that injury will only increase over the coming century."

After recounting these harms from global warming, harms that the EPA never even attempted to refute, it no doubt seemed to Stevens that all the scientists already agreed that human GHG emissions causing global warming were reasonably likely to endanger public health or welfare. Telling the EPA to make such a finding formally imposed no great burden, because the Court was simply telling the EPA to endorse what was an obvious scientific "consensus."

IV THE EPA'S ENDANGERMENT DETERMINATION

If this is what former Justice Stevens was thinking, then he turned out to be completely correct. After comprehensive climate legislation failed in Congress, under the direction of then-Assistant EPA Administrator Lisa Heinzerling, the Obama administration moved with breathtaking speed in late 2009 to make its endangerment determination.[47] The main authors of the Endangerment Finding were a then-recent graduate of a science and policy program at MIT (Marcus Sarofin) and the owner-operator of the Washington, DC weather blog (Jason Samenow). It was approved by a committee chaired by long-time EPA senior staffers. None of these people had extensive publications (most none) in climate science, but the Technical Support Document for the Endangerment Finding – the actual explanation and justification for the finding – was reviewed by a group of "federal expert reviewers" including exceptionally prominent climate scientists such as Thomas Karl of NOAA, Gavin Schmidt of NASA, and Susan Solomon, also of NOAA. While most important EPA science assessments are reviewed by subcommittees of the EPA's Science Advisory Board that are comprised primarily of scientists from outside the federal government, the EPA's Endangerment Finding was not reviewed by its Science Advisory Board.[48]

Such review would not have been too difficult. As the Technical Support Document accompanying the 2009 Endangerment Finding itself states quite clearly, it relies "most heavily on existing, and in most cases, very recent synthesis reports of climate change science and potential impacts, which have undergone their own peer-review processes, including review by the US government."[49] These "synthesis reports" were produced by the US Climate Change Science Program (CCSP) and US Global Change Research Program (GCRP) and by the IPCC. Karl, Schmidt, and Solomon were lead authors on several of the synthesis reports produced by the IPCC, and also directly involved in the synthesis reports generated by the US CCSP and the US GCRP. Thus in reviewing the basis for the EPA's Endangerment Finding, Karl, Schmidt, and Solomon were reviewing their own work. They could hardly have said that the EPA was wrong to rely upon it.

The endangerment determination relies upon IPCC synthesis reports (primarily the fourth such report, issued in 2007) for its findings about the global effects of increasing atmospheric GHGs and both IPCC reports and reports by the US CCSP and GCRP for its findings about climate change impacts in the United States in particular. Carbon dioxide is not the only GHG, and the EPA actually defined six GHGs as an "air pollutant" in its Endangerment Finding. It did so by converting but all GHG "air pollutants" into their "carbon dioxide equivalent" in terms of global warming potential.[50] This is a relatively standard practice in international climate policy, but it is not a mere definitional technicality. As I explain in a later chapter, focusing only on "air pollutants" that can be converted into a carbon dioxide equivalent has extremely important policy consequences.

The first set of EPA findings has to do with changes in various climate variables and the role of human GHG emission in causing such changes. These conclusions include the following (citations to the relevant TSD page numbers where findings can be found are in parentheses):

1. Between 1750 and 2005, primarily anthropogenic increases in GHGs had a positive radiative forcing of about 2.3 W/m^2 with CO_2 being the strongest, at about 1.66, and this forcing had increased 20 percent between 1995 and 2005, the largest change for any decade in 200 years; (23)
2. Over the 1906–2005 period, global mean surface temperatures had risen about 1.3F, with an increase of .66F between 1910s to 1940s and .99F from the 1970s to the end of 2006, with average Arctic temperatures increasing at "almost twice the global average rate in the last 100 years, and although Arctic temperatures "have high decadal variability," with a warm Arctic period observed from the late 1920s to the early 1950s, that warming had a "different spatial distribution than the recent warming"; (27)
3. Even though "instrumental surface temperature records began in the late nineteenth century, when a sufficiently large global network of measurements was in place to reliably compute global mean temperatures," it can be said "with a high level of confidence," that global mean surface temperature "was higher during the last few decades of the twentieth century that during any comparable period during the preceding four centuries"; (31)
4. According to NOAA, in the United States, "average annual temperatures" are 1.25F higher than at the start of the twentieth century, with the rate of warming increasing from .13 per decade from 1901 through 2008 to .58F from 1979 through 2008, with the last 10 five-year periods beginning in 1998 being the warmest since 1901, and with the greatest temperature increases occurring in Alaska and the Northeast and the least in the Southeast; (32–33)
5. After "little change between AD 0 and AD 1900, global sea level is rising, at an average rate that has increased from .18 cm per year (as measured by tide gauges) between 1961 and 2003 to .31 cm per year (as measured by satellite) between 1993

to 2003, with a total twentieth century sea level rise about 17 cm"; measuring global sea level rise is subject to uncertainty due to the "adjustment in vertical land movements in tide gauge data and the proper accounting for instrumental bias and drifts in satellite altimetry data"; (35–36)

6. In the United States, sea level has been rising on average between .2 and .3 cm per year, but varies, with sea level rising as much as 1 cm per year in places like Louisiana where land is sinking and sea level falling in places like Alaska where land is rising; (37)
7. Arctic sea ice has been diminishing since the late nineteenth century, but at an accelerating rate of more than 4.1% during the period 1979–2008, setting a record September low in 2007 at 38 percent below the 1979–2007 average; Antarctic sea ice increased a statistically insignificant .9 percent over the period 1979–2008, and northern hemisphere snow cover as observed by satellite fell every month except November and December between 1966 and 2005; (38–39)
8. Trends in droughts and heavy rains show that "hydrological conditions are becoming more intense in some regions," even though "significant trends in floods and in evaporation and evapotranspiration have not been detected globally," but very dry areas have more than doubled in frequency since the 1970s due to a combination of ENSO events and surface warming; (39–40)
9. There is "clear temperature-driven extension of the growing season by up to two weeks in the second half of the twentieth century in mid and high northern latitudes, mainly due to an earlier spring, but partly due also to a later autumn; (41)
10. In the last 50 years, "cold days, cold nights, and frost have become less frequent, while hot days, hot nights, and heat waves have become more frequent," "more intense and longer droughts have been observed over wider areas since the 1970s', particularly in the tropics and sub-tropics," with such increased drought frequency linked to changes in sea surface temperatures, changes in atmospheric circulation and precipitation, and decreased snowpack and snowcover and it is "likely that there have been increases in the number of heavy precipitation events" even in those regions where there has been a reduction in total precipitation "consistent" with a warmer atmosphere's ability to hold more water vapor; (43)
11. There has "likely" been an increase in the frequency and intensity of strong low pressure systems over the Northern Hemisphere, but such changes are hard to detect due to changing observing systems, and "longer records for the northeaster Atlantic suggest that the recent extreme period may be similar in level to that of the late 19 century"; (43)
12. According to the US CCSP and Karl especially, recent decades in North America have experienced more "unusually hot days and nights, fewer unusually cold days and nights," more frequent heavy downpours, more severe

droughts, at least in some regions, even though there are "no clear trends for North America as a whole," and the "power and frequency of Atlantic hurricanes have increased substantially in recent decades... Outside the tropics ... the strongest storms are becoming even stronger"; (44)

13. Citing the IPCC as an unquestioned authority, the EPA says that since the IPCC's first assessment report in 1990 – which contained "little observational evidence of a detectable anthropogenic influence on climate – the IPCC has grown steadily more confident of such an influence. In 1995, the IPCC said that there was a "discernible" human influence on twentieth century climate, the IPCC's 2001 report said that "most of the observed warming over the last 50 years was likely due to the increase in atmospheric GHG concentrations," and the 2007 IPCC assessment report said that "most of the observed increase in global temperatures since the mid-twentieth century is very likely due to the observed increase in anthropogenic GHG concentrations"; (48)
14. Anthropogenic GHG emissions have "likely contributed to the recent decreases in Arctic sea ice extent," which itself has "been more rapid than projected by climate models," and it is "very likely" that such emissions have contributed to sea level rise during the latter half of the twentieth century." (52)

Turning to projected future climate change, the EPA's Endangerment Finding states the following:

1. Such projections are generated by computer models of climate, and in justifying reliance on such model projections, the EPA simply quotes the IPCC's 2007 report: "[C]onfidence in such models comes from their physical basis, and their skill in representing observed climate and past climate changes. Models have proven to be extremely important tools for simulating and understanding climate, and *there is considerable confidence that they are able to provide credible quantitative estimates of future climate change*, particularly at larger scales" (emphasis supplied); (63)
2. Until about 2020, because of the existing accumulation of GHGs in the atmosphere, the world is locked in to about a .4F (.2C) warming per decade, or about .8F by 2020; by the middle decades of 2045–2065, projected warming varies between 2.3 and 3.2F (1.3–1.8C), with the variation resulting due to varying assumptions about how fast different national economies grow and how much they reduce GHG emissions and also, importantly, the sensitivity of the climate to increases in atmospheric GHG emissions; for the same reasons for variation, by 2100, warming varies between 3.2 and over 7F (1.8C to over 4C); (64)
3. According to the IPCC's 2007 report, the most likely response of global average surface temperature to a doubling of atmospheric GHGs by 2100 is an increase in average global surface temperature of 4 to 8F (or 2 to 4.5C), there is only a 10 percent probability or less that the increase will be below 2.7F

(1.5C), but between a 5 and 17 percent probability that the temperature increase will be greater than 8.1F (4.5C); (66)

4. The IPCC projects that global sea level will rise between 7.1 and 23 inches (18–59 cm) by 2100 relative to 1980–1990, and even if GHG emissions were "stabilized," sea level would continue to rise for centuries "due to the time scales associated with climate processes and feedbacks"; (67)
5. The IPCC says that heat waves will become more intense, frequent, and long lasting, whereas cold spells are projected to "decrease significantly"; (73)
6. Precipitation intensity is expected to increase, and in particular, there is projected to be a "decrease in heavy precipitation in California to an increase in northern Rocky, Cascade, and Sierra Nevada mountain ranges"; it is "likely" that tropical cyclones will become more intense, with heavier precipitation and stronger winds, but "projections in frequency changes in tropical cyclones are currently too uncertain for confident projections"; (74–75)
7. According to a 2005 National Research Council report, abrupt climate changes that occurred during the earth's past – such as abrupt warming over Greenland of 8 to 16C during the last glacial period – "are not fully explained yet, and climate models typically underestimate the size, speed, and extent of those changes .... [A]brupt future changes cannot be predicted with confidence, and climate surprises are to be expected"; (76)
8. "Rapid disintegration of the Greenland Ice sheet" would raise sea level by 7 meters (23 feet), and it is "extremely likely" that the Greenland ice sheet has been experiencing accelerated mass loss since the 1990s, and it might take "hundreds of years to complete" a complete melting of the Greenland ice sheet requiring a "sustained warming in the range of 3.4 to 8.4F (1.9 to 4.6C); although there is no consensus on the "long-term future of the West Antarctic Ice Sheet or its contribution to sea level rise," a "collapse of the West Antarctic Ice Sheet would raise seas 16 to 20 feet (5 to 6 meters)." (77)

According to the EPA's summary of various assessment reports, there is a long list of very bad human consequences from these projected climate changes. Included in this list are the following:

1. As "exposure to heat is already the leading cause of weather-related deaths in the United States and more than 3,400 deaths between 1999 and 2003 were reported as resulting from exposure to extreme heat, ... given projections climate warming, heat-related morbidity and mortality are projected to increase globally," and when "assumptions about acclimatization and adaptation are included in models" estimates of heat-related mortality "attributable on extreme heat days are reduced but not eliminated"; (83)
2. The IPCC says that "climate change is expected to lead to increases in regional ozone pollution in the United States and other countries" due to a variety of mechanisms, such as an increase in NOx emissions due to more

lightning strikes, with the EPA finding that "climate change effects on ozone grow continuously over time, with evidence for significant increases emerging as early as the 2020s"; (89)

3. Although moderate climate change, with temperature increases of 1 to 3C, may have "net beneficial effects" for US agriculture, "further warming is projected to have increasingly negative impacts in all regions," with warming even increasing the risk of frost damage because milder winters "induce premature plant development and blooming, resulting in exposure of vulnerable young plants and plant tissues to subsequent late-season frosts"; elevated CO_2 levels are "expected to contribute to small beneficial effects on crop yields" and FACE (free air CO_2 enrichment) experiments have shown yield increases of up to 25 percent for some crops from a doubling of CO_2 levels relative to pre-industrial levels, "high temperatures, water and nutrient availability, and ozone exposure ... can significantly limit the direct stimulatory CO_2 reponses (with no citation provided for this final claim)"; (99–100)
4. It is "likely that anthropogenic warming has increased the impacts of drought over North America in recent decades," and across North America, due to population growth and economic development, "vulnerability to extended drought is ... increasing .... [I]ncreased runoff due to intense precipitation on crop fields and animal agriculture operations may result in an increased contribution of sediments, nutrients and pathogens in surface waters," and another "economic consequence of excessive rainfall is delayed spring planting, which jeopardizes profits for farmers paid a premium for early season production of high-value horticultural crops such as melons, sweet corn and tomatoes"; (101; 115)
5. As for wildfires, "several lines of evidence suggest that large, stand-replacing wildfires will likely increase in frequency over the next several decades because of climate warming," and in the western United States in particular, 6.7 times as much forested area burned between 1987 and 2003 as between 1970 and 1986, with an increase in burn duration of western wildfires from 7.5 to 37.1 days due to a spring/summer warming of 1.6F; (107)
6. While sea level rise varies across the US coastline, "cities such as New Orleans, Miami and New York are particularly at risk, and could have difficulty coping with the sea level rise projected by the end of the century under a heightened emissions scenario"; in New Orleans and vicinity, which is between 59 and 118 inches below sea level, a mid-range projection of a 48 cm increase in sea level would put the area 98 to 157 inches below sea level, so that the storm surge from a category 3 hurricane would be 20 to 23 feet above areas that were heavily populated in 2004; in the Arctic Ocean, "sea ice extent is expected to continue to decrease and may even disappear entirely during summer months in the coming decades"; (119-121)

7. Perhaps more generally, "very large sea level rises that would result from widespread deglaciation of Greenland and West Antarctic ice sheets imply major changes in coastlines and ecosystems, and inundation of low-lying areas .... Relocating populations, economic activity and infrastructure would be costly and challenging." (121)

The EPA's endangerment TSD concludes with a summary of regional climate change impacts across the United States and international impacts.[51] It breaks the United States down into eight regions (Northeast, Southeast, Midwest, Great Plains, Southwest, Northwest, Alaska, and Islands). For each region, the TSD summarizes projected changes in temperature and precipitation trends and then discusses the projected regional change in the frequency and severity of weather extremes such as drought and storms.

It must be stressed that the 29 findings supporting the EPA's Endangerment Finding that I have listed above is by no means complete. In particular, I have not mentioned the EPA's findings as to the effects of climate change on nonhuman species and ecosystems. But those effects are just as dire as what the EPA says will be the effects of climate change for humans. The EPA findings I have mentioned illustrate the general tenor of the EPA's Endangerment Finding: while there may be a few scientific quibbles here and there, the EPA says that according to a number of peer-reviewed, government-endorsed reports, climate change is already happening and will in all likelihood get worse in the future, with dire consequences for Americans.

V THE ENDANGERMENT FINDING IN COURT: THE POWER OF THE PRECAUTIONARY PRINCIPLE

As discussed above, the EPA's Endangerment Finding was the trigger for EPA regulation of GHG emissions from cars and trucks, coal-burning electricity generating plants, and a small number of other types of factories. As soon as the EPA promulgated these regulations, a large number of states and industry groups brought a lawsuit challenging both the regulations and the underlying Endangerment Finding. The legal and economic justifications for the EPA's GHG regulations will be explored in later chapters. But if the Endangerment Finding had been struck down by the courts, then all of the Obama-era GHG regulations would have been immediately invalidated. The courts did not strike down the Endangerment Finding, and the judicial reasoning upholding it clearly displays the precautionary principle in action.

The lawsuits challenging the EPA's endangerment determination were consolidated into a single case decided by the DC Circuit Court of Appeals, *Coalition for Responsible Regulation, Inc.* v. *EPA*.[52] The opinion in that case begins by simply declaring, without any citation of any authority, legal or scientific, that "[m]any scientists believe that mankind's greenhouse gas emissions are driving ... climate change. These scientists predict that global climate change will cause a host of deleterious consequences, including drought, increasingly severe weather events, and rising sea levels."[53] As this declaration indicates, as it was talking to a court that was already convinced that "many scientists" thought harmful climate change was being caused by human GHG emissions, the EPA did not face a very tough task in persuading the court that its Endangerment Finding was supported by adequate evidence.

The EPA's job was made even easier by the failure of the plaintiffs to make a sustained effort to rebut in detail EPA Endangerment Finding conclusions of the sort I have listed above. As the court said, "Industry Petitioners do not find fault with much of the substantial record EPA amassed in support of the Endangerment Finding."[54] With plaintiffs not making any serious attempt to introduce evidence that might contradict the substantive basis of the Endangerment Finding, the court in *Coalition for Responsible Regulation* only needed to address two arguments attacking the Endangerment Finding: that the EPA was wrong to rely upon the IPCC and other reports synthesizing climate science, and that even if that was not wrong, those reports revealed far too much scientific uncertainty for the EPA to find that "greenhouse gases in the atmosphere may reasonably be anticipated both to endanger public health and to endanger public welfare."

Before even addressing the first argument – that the EPA had failed to do its job by effectively delegating the endangerment determination to various assessment groups such as the IPCC – the DC Circuit stressed the quality of the "peer-reviewed" synthesis reports that the EPA relied upon. According to the court, "[t]hese peer-reviewed assessments synthesized thousands of individual studies on various aspects of greenhouse gases and climate."[55] When it did address the delegation argument, the court said[56] that the EPA did not delegate any decision-making, but instead

> ...simply did here what it and other decision-makers often must do to make a science-based judgment: it sought out and reviewed existing scientific evidence to determine whether a particular finding was warranted. It makes no difference that much of the scientific evidence in large part consisted of "syntheses" of individual studies and research. Even individual studies and research papers often synthesize past work in an area and then build upon it. This is how science works. EPA is not required to re-prove the existence of the atom every time it approaches a scientific question.

In the event that a reader was not convinced that the EPA was just following standard scientific practice in relying upon assessment reports and not trying to "re-prove the existence of every atom," the DC Circuit stressed that before it relied on the assessment reports, the EPA "evaluated the processes used to develop the various assessment reports, reviewed their contents, and considered the depth of the scientific consensus the reports represented." It was only after this evaluation that the EPA determined that the assessment reports "represented the best source material to use in deciding whether greenhouse gas emissions may be reasonably anticipated to endanger public health or welfare."[57]

The second argument by plaintiffs in *Coalition for Responsible Regulation* – that there was too much scientific uncertainty for the EPA's Endangerment Finding to be justified – raises two separate subsidiary legal questions. The first question is how deferential a court should be to an agency's determinations about the state of the relevant science. The second question is how much uncertainty about climate change and its effects – as determined by the EPA – is consistent with regulation under Section 202 of the CAA, given congressional intent in enacting that provision.

As to the degree of deference to be afforded by the court to the EPA's judgment about the science, the DC Circuit was quite clear, quoting one of its earlier decisions for the rule that "we give an extreme degree of deference to the agency when it is evaluating scientific data within its technical expertise" (internal quotation marks omitted).[58] Under this standard, although in reviewing "the science-based decisions of agencies such as EPA, [judges] perform a searching and careful inquiry into the facts underlying the agency's decisions," the court "will presume the validity of agency action as long as a rational basis for it is presented."[59] These apparently contradictory statements are actually a pretty standard way of stating what courts do in reviewing agency scientific determinations. Putting the two statements together, what the court is saying is that it will search carefully through the "facts" underlying the agency's evaluation of the science, but if it finds anything, even a single piece of evidence supporting the agency's interpretation of the science, then the agency's decision will be upheld as "rational."

This standard of review is important to understand, for as the *Coalition for Responsible Regulation* opinion itself said, it is so deferential that its application leads a court to reject an agency's interpretation of the science only if that interpretation is found to be literally irrational. To understand this standard, consider how it would work if applied to areas of life outside judicial review of agency science. If the standard were applied by a hospital review board evaluating even a fatal mis-diagnosis by a physician, then even if 99.95 percent of practicing physicians in the field would have disagreed, the mis-diagnosing doctor's decision would be upheld if there is any physician anywhere in the world who can be found who would have made the same diagnosis. If the standard were applied to a corporate board evaluating a bankruptcy-threatening strategic business decision by a corporate CEO, then the CEO's decision would be approved if there were any interpretation of the numbers the CEO had before her that was not completely irrational.

Given that my list of 29 findings in the endangerment TSD is only a partial list of the EPA's many findings about the reality and harmfulness of present and future climate change, and given that virtually all of the EPA's conclusions are unqualified by any discussion of contradictory evidence, it is hardly surprising that the *Coalition for Responsible Regulation* had no problem finding that the Endangerment Findings conclusions were not "irrational." According the court, there were three lines of evidence supporting the EPA's findings about climate change. First, there was "our 'basic physical understanding' of the impacts of various natural and manmade changes on the climate system," with the court especially impressed by "evidence that the past half-century of warming has occurred at a time when natural forces such as solar and volcanic activity likely would have produced cooling."[60] Second, the court was impressed by the historical estimate of "past climate change," studies placing "high confidence in the assertion that global mean surface temperatures over the last few decades are higher than at any time in the last four centuries" and showing "albeit with significant uncertainty, that temperatures at many individual locations were higher over the last twenty-five years than during any period of comparable length since 900 A.D."[61] Third and finally, the court found very persuasive the fact, as found by the EPA, that simulations with computer models of global climate – models built "on basic principles of physics and scientific knowledge about the climate" – had only "been able to replicate the observed warming by including anthropogenic emissions of greenhouse gases in the simulations."[62] All in all, according to the court there was plenty of evidence to support the EPA's finding that "human activity is contributing to increased atmospheric levels of greenhouse gases; and that the climate system is warming ... and that the 'root cause' of the recently observed climate change is 'very likely' the observed increase in anthropogenic greenhouse gas emissions."[63]

As to the evidence supporting the EPA's findings about the likely adverse impact of global warming on human health or public welfare – which is, after all, the legal finding that justifies GHG emission regulation under the Clean Air Act – the court in *Coalition for Responsible Regulation* was much less precise. According to the court, relying upon "substantial evidence," the EPA determined that "extreme weather events, changes in air quality, increases in food- and water-borne pathogens, and increases in temperatures are likely to have adverse health effects," that "climate change endangers human welfare by creating risk to food production and agriculture, forestry, energy, infrastructure, ecosystems, and wildlife," and that "the warming resulting from the greenhouse gas emissions could be expected to create risks to water resources and in general to coastal areas as a result of expected increase in sea level." In the midst of substantial evidence of such mayhem, the court noted almost as an afterthought that "EPA determined from substantial evidence that motor-vehicle emissions of greenhouse gases contribute to climate change and thus to the endangerment of public health and welfare."[64]

The court was careful to leave no doubt that its review of the scientific basis for the EPA's endangerment determination had been very limited and deferential. As the court said, "[i]n the end, [the plaintiffs] are asking us to re-weigh the scientific evidence before EPA and reach our own conclusion. This is not our role. As with other reviews of administrative proceedings, we do not determine the convincing force of evidence, nor the conclusion it should support, but only whether the conclusion reached by EPA is supported by substantial evidence when considered on the record as a whole . . . . When EPA evaluates scientific evidence in its bailiwick, we ask only that it take the scientific record into account 'in a rational manner' (quoting a 1981 DC Circuit opinion) . . . . Industry Petitioners have not shown that EPA failed to do so here."[65]

After finding that so much evidence justified the EPA's Endangerment Finding, and looking after all at a finding supported by a TSD that hardly mentions any uncertainty in the scientific literature, the only way that the court in *Coalition for Responsible Regulation* could have found that there was too much uncertainty about the "science" underlying the EPA's finding was if Congress had said in the Clean Air Act that a Section 202 Endangerment determination could be upheld only if the evidence supporting an Endangerment Finding has to be completely certain. Quite to the contrary, quoting an almost fifty-year-old DC Circuit opinion upholding an EPA Endangerment Finding for lead air emissions, the court said that "requiring EPA to wait until it can conclusively demonstrate that a particular effect is adverse to health before it acts is inconsistent with both the [CAA]'s precautionary and preventive orientation and the nature of the Administrator's statutory responsibilities."[66] Further quoting its own old lead emissions opinion, according to the *Coalition for Responsible Regulation* court, Section 202 is a statute that is "precautionary in nature" and "designed to protect the public health," and under such a law, when "the relevant evidence is 'difficult to come by, uncertain, or conflicting because it is on the frontiers of scientific knowledge,' EPA need not provide 'rigorous step-by-step proof of cause and effect' to support an Endangerment Finding. As we have stated before, 'Awaiting certainty will often allow for only reactive, not preventive, regulation.'"[67]

To the contrary, quoting another old DC Circuit opinion in the old lead emissions dispute, the court concluded that "the Section 202 endangerment standard requires a precautionary, forward-looking scientific judgment about the risks of a particular air pollutant, consistent with the CAA's 'precautionary and preventive orientation.' Requiring that EPA find 'certain' endangerment of public health or welfare before regulating greenhouse gases would effectively prevent EPA from doing the job Congress gave it in § 202(a) – utilizing emission standards to prevent reasonably anticipated endangerment from maturing into concrete harm."[68] According to the *Coalition for Responsible Regulation* court, Congress intended Section 202 to be a "precautionary" statute, aimed at preventing harm before it occurred, whenever there was a reasonable likelihood of endangerment. Moreover, Congress meant for the same precautionary test to be applied in the 202 context of endangerment from GHG emissions as it had been almost fifty years before in the context of health endangerment from airborne lead emissions. And under this precautionary test, regulation is justified whenever it is based on a "precautionary, forward-looking scientific judgment."

As one should have predicted, under this standard the DC Circuit upheld the EPA's decision not to reconsider its Endangerment Finding in light of new evidence brought to its attention by the plaintiffs. That new evidence consisted of new studies tending to contradict the EPA's Endangerment Finding and various "factual mistakes in the IPCC's assessment report resulting from the use of non-peer reviewed studies and several scientific studies postdating the Endangerment Finding."[69] As for mistakes, according to the court, there were only two actual mistakes in the EPA's Endangerment Finding. The mistakes didn't arise because the EPA mistakenly paraphrased IPCC assessment reports. They were mistakes in the IPCC reports themselves: an erroneous statement about the percentage of the Netherlands that is below sea level, and an overestimate of the rate at which Himalayan glaciers are receding. The EPA said that the mistakes were "tangential and minor" and didn't change the conclusions of the IPCC report. The court agreed and said that the IPCC had "corrected" the mistakes and in any event the EPA hadn't relied upon either of these mistaken statements in making its endangerment determination.[70] As for the new studies – such as a new study that plaintiffs said "contradicts EPA's reliance on a projection of more violent storms in the future as a result of climate change" – according to the court, "the study they cite only concerns past trends, not projected future storms" and "EPA considered the new studies on storm trends and concluded that the studies were consistent with the Endangerment Finding."[71] The court had no difficulty concluding that both IPCC assessment report mistakes and new studies contradicting IPCC conclusions in such reports were irrelevant to the legal validity of an EPA endangerment determination based primarily on such IPCC assessment reports.

To anyone who has tried to forecast anything – from the financial performance of a company to coming pro and college football game outcomes – the *Coalition for Responsible Regulation* court's apparent belief that past trends are irrelevant to the validity of projections about the future should be shocking. Unless what we observe in the past is irrelevant to what we predict for the future, given the EPA Endangerment Finding's heavy emphasis on the recent reality of rising temperatures and sea levels, whatever has been happening to the severity of tropical storms during such a period is obviously relevant to projections about what will happen to storm severity if temperature and sea level trends continue. That the court was so confident and comfortable in saying something so obviously untrue and illogical certainly helps one to understand the reason why the court said that it would defer totally to whatever the EPA had found, for it shows that an actual independent audit or review by judges is likely to be highly error-prone.

Coming within the context of the court's cavalier dismissal of mistakes in IPCC reports and new studies showing that the IPCC and the EPA might be wrong about future storm projections, the court's dismissal of storm trend evidence signifies two other important things. It indicates the court's understanding of the sort of "precautionary, forward-looking scientific judgment" that Congress told the EPA to make in finding Endangerment. Under this precautionary standard, the validity of an EPA judgment of Endangerment is unaffected by mistakes here and there and even by new studies indicating that some of the "forward-looking" projections may be wrong. The point of the precautionary standard in Section 202 is to "prevent" future harm from happening, and this preventive goal could not be served if the EPA stands around "[w]aiting for certainty." As long as there remains evidence supporting the main EPA findings that harm might occur, the judgment will not be upset by courts.

This was easy for the court to say in *Coalition for Responsible Regulation*, moreover, because the court had already said that the EPA had been pursuing standard scientific practice when it relied upon "peer-reviewed assessments" that "synthesized thousands of individual studies on various aspects of greenhouse gases and climate." Just as Justice Stevens in *Massachusetts* v. *EPA* had no doubt about the reality and harmfulness of human GHG emissions, faced with an EPA finding backed by "thousands" of studies interpreted by government-endorsed assessment organizations such as the IPCC, the *Coalition for Responsible Regulation Court* clearly thought that the scientific basis for the EPA's endangerment was about as close to being completely certain as any such finding could ever be.

VI WHAT THIS BOOK IS ABOUT: CRITICALLY ANALYZING THE KEY POLICY QUESTIONS RAISED, BUT UNANSWERED, BY THE EPA'S ENDANGERMENT FINDING AND ITS JUDICIAL APPROVAL

The court's opinion in *Coalition for Responsible Regulation* upholding the EPA's Endangerment Finding was, as I have discussed, enormously important, for once it got the seal of judicial approval, the Endangerment Finding became the basis for a whole series of Obama-era GHG regulations targeting GHG emissions under the Clean Air Act. As we shall see, while some of those regulations were struck down by courts, many were upheld. Moreover, while not strictly legally necessary to gain such judicial approval, in order to meet regulatory guidelines in place since the Reagan administration, the EPA enlisted economists to show that the benefits of regulations limiting GHG emissions were bigger than their costs. As I shall explain further in a later chapter, the cost-benefit analyses produced by EPA incorporate assumptions about both climate science and the costs of climate change – in particular regarding how humans adapt to climate change – that themselves reflect the same highly cautious, precautionary approach that in *Coalition for Responsible Regulation* the DC Circuit found to be the ultimate justification for the EPA's Endangerment Finding.

The DC Circuit court's opinion in *Coalition for Responsible Regulation* raises questions that are fundamental to evaluating US climate policy. The opinion defers to the EPA's findings about human GHG emissions and harmful climate change, but those findings are entirely based on assessments of scientific literature done by government-endorsed scientific assessment organizations, primarily the IPCC. The obvious question, completely unexplored by the DC Circuit, is whether the IPCC and similar organizations can be trusted to have produced objective and unbiased assessments of the scientific literature. In defending its endangerment decision against legal challenge, it was perfectly appropriate for the EPA to act as an advocate, marshalling whatever evidence relied upon supporting that decision. But if the assessments it reviewed were also advocacy documents – discussing and endorsing only that scientific evidence that supports something like an Endangerment Finding – then even if they discuss "thousands" of scientific papers, there is no reason to think that the assessments themselves could properly have been relied upon by the EPA. Of course, even if the EPA had gone beyond IPCC assessment reports, and actually reviewed and discussed particular scientific studies, including those that weaken the case for harmful anthropogenic warming, then it is possible that under its extremely deferential approach applying the preventive, precautionary standard, the DC Circuit would still have upheld the EPA's Endangerment Finding.

The extreme degree of deference given to the EPA by the *Coalition for Responsible Regulation* court was inextricably tied to its view that under Section 202 of the CAA, the EPA was required only to make a "precautionary, forward-looking scientific judgment." The court's decision that Section 202 regulation was "precautionary" influenced its view of every aspect of the case before it. Evidence tending to contradict the EPA's key findings was more or less irrelevant. And the court did not look for or evaluate such evidence. Far from it. Given that the EPA was making a "precautionary" assessment of the evidence, the court was extremely deferential to the EPA's interpretation of all the science.

Clearly, concluding that a statute is "precautionary" has major consequences for how regulations interpreting that statute will be reviewed by courts. But the *Coalition for Responsible Regulation* court does not explain what it actually means by a "precautionary" policy. It is to this task – of explaining and describing Obama era precautionary climate policy – that subsequent chapters turn.

Notes

1. 549 U.S. 497 (2007).
2. Royden (2002, 440–447).
3. S. Res. 98, 105th Congress (1997).
4. Royden (2002, 420).
5. Royden (2002, 428).
6. The following paragraph borrows from my discussion in Johnston (2014, 1613–1614).
7. S. 1151, 109th Cong. (2005).
8. 276. S. 309, 110th Cong. (2007).
9. 278. H.R. 2454, 111th Cong. (2009).

10. St. Louis Fed, U.S. Index of Industrial Production, available at https://fred.stlouisfed.org/series/INDPRO.
11. Eliza Berman, "Meet the Organizers of the Very First Earth Day," *Time Magazine*, April 22, 2015, available at http://time.com/3772160/earth-day/.
12. Jaime Fuller, "Environmental Policy Is Partisan. It Wasn't Always," *Washington Post*, June 2, 2014, available at https://www.washingtonpost.com/news/the-fix/wp/2014/06/02/support-for-the-clean-air-act-has-changed-a-lot-since-1970/?noredirect=on&utm_term=.ca12b14bac65.
13. PBS, *Frontline*, "The Legacy of the First Earth Day, 1970," available at https://www.pbs.org/wgbh/pages/frontline/poisonedwaters/themes/earthday.html.
14. See Krier and Ursin (1977) (telling the story of how smog emerged as a problem in California and how auto emissions were identified as the cause, leading eventually to a push for federal auto emission standards) and Bailey (1998) (showing how the history of attempts to enact federal auto emission standards tracked the spread of smog as a local pollution problem across metropolitan areas of the United States).
15. 42 U.S.C. §7507.
16. CAA §209(b(1)(B), 42 U.S.C. §7543(b)(1)(B).
17. Kimberly Amadeo, "OPEC Oil Embargo, Its Causes, and the Effects of the Crisis: The Truth About the 1973 Arab Oil Crisis," *the balance*, Nov. 6, 2018, available at https://www.thebalance.com/opec-oil-embargo-causes-and-effects-of-the-crisis-3305806.
18. Union Electric Co. v. EPA, 427 U.S. 246 (1976).
19. Executive Office of the President, the National Energy Plan 1–23 (1977).
20. Kramer (1978, 137).
21. Kramer (1978, 137–139).
22. §110(a)(2)(E), 84 Stat. 1681, 42 U.S.C. §1857c–5(a)(2)(E).
23. §108(a)(4), 91 Stat. 693, 42 U.S.C. §7410(a)(2)(E) (1976 ed., Supp. II).
24. EPA v. EME Homer City Generation, __ U.S. __, __ (2014).
25. 42 U.S.C. §7410(a)(2)(D)(i) (2006 ed.).
26. 42 U.S.C. §7661 et seq.
27. Clean Air Act Amendments and Solid Waste Disposal Act, Pub. L. No. 89–272 (1965). See Burger et al., Legal Pathways To Reducing Greenhouse Gas Emissions Under Section 115 Of The Clean Air Act (Jan. 2016) available at http://columbiaclimatelaw.com/files/2016/06/Burger-et-al.-2016–01-Reduce-GHG-Emissions-Under-Section-115-of-CAA.pdf.
28. Provided by Burger et al. (YEAR,8).
29. Wiener (1999, 772–773).
30. Codified at 42 U.S.C. §7671 et seq.
31. Permentier (2017).
32. 42 U.S.C. Section 7602(g).
33. Stevens majority opinion fn. 26.

34. Adam Liptak, Retired Justice John Paul Stevens Says Kavanaugh Is Not Fit for Supreme Court, New York Times, Oct. 4, 2018, available at https://www.nytimes.com/2018/10/04/us/politics/john-paul-stevens-brett-kavanaugh.html.
35. Daniel B. Rodriguez and Barry R. Weingast (2007), The paradox of expansionist statutory interpretations, 101(3) Northwestern University Law Review 1207–1255.
36. Adler (2007, 36).
37. Adler (2007, 37–38).
38. The following discussion is drawn from Landy et al. (1994, 31–33).
39. See in particular Figure 3 in Clinton et al. (2012, 348).
40. Freeman and Vermuele (2007, 61).
41. Freeman and Vermuele (2007, 55–56).
42. Freeman and Vermuele (2007, 56).
43. Freeman and Vermeule (2007, 60).
44. Heinzerling (2008, 6).
45. Freeman and Vermeule (2007, 60).
46. *Mass.* v. *EPA*, 127 S.Ct.1438, 1447(2007).
47. Endangerment and Cause or Contribute Findings for Greenhouse Gases Under Section 202(a) of the Clean Air Act ("Endangerment Finding"), 74 Fed. Reg. 66,496 (Dec. 15, 2009).
48. *Coalition for Responsible Regulation* v. *EPA*, 684 F.3d 102, 124 (DC Cir. 2012).
49. EPA, Climate Change Division, Office of Atmospheric Programs, Technical Support Document for Endangerment and Cause or Contribute Findings for Greenhouse Gases under Section 202(a) of the Clean Air Act 4, Dec. 7, 2009, available at https://www.epa.gov/sites/production/files/2016–08/documents/endangerment_tsd.pdf.
50. Endangerment and Cause or Contribute Findings for Greenhouse Gases under Section 202(a) of the Clean Air Act ("Endangerment Finding"), 74 Fed. Reg. 66,496, at *Id.* at 66,536–37, 66,519.
51. TSD Document Endangerment, supra note __ at 142–155.
52. 684 F.3d 102 (DC Cir. 2012).
53. 684 F.3d 102, 114.
54. 684 F.3d 102, 121.
55. 684 F.3d 102, 119.
56. 684 F.3d 102, 120.
57. 684 F.3d 102, 120.
58. 684 F.3d 102, 120, quoting Am. Farm Bureau Fed'n v. EPA, 559 F.3d 512, 519 (DC Cir. 2009).
59. 684 F.3d 102, 120.
60. 684 F.3d 102, 120.
61. 684 F.3d 102, 121.
62. 684 F.3d 102, 121, citing the Endangerment Finding at Endangerment Finding, 74 Fed. Reg. at 66,523.

63. 684 F.3d 102, 120–121.
64. 684 F.3d 102, 121.
65. 684 F.3d 102, 122.
66. 684 F.3d 102, 121, quoting *Ethyl Corp.* v. *EPA*, 541 F.2d 1, 28 (DC Cir. 1976).
67. 684 F.3d 102, 121, quoting *Ethyl Corp.* v. *EPA*, 541 F.2d 1, 25.
68. 684 F.3d 102, 121, quoting *Ethyl Corp.* v. *EPA*, 684 F.3d 102, 121.
69. 684 F.3d 102, 124.
70. 684 F.3d 102, 125.
71. 684 F.3d 102, 125.

3

The Precautionary Principle

What It Does and Doesn't Do

The *Coalition for Responsible Regulation* opinion did not explain what it meant by a "precautionary, forward-looking scientific judgment." As used by the court, the word "precautionary" actually has a special legal meaning originating in something called the precautionary principle. This chapter explains the origins and application of the precautionary principle underlying such a judgment.

The precautionary principle has been applied mostly outside the United States, but, as in *Coalition for Responsible Regulation*, federal courts have long interpreted the word "endanger" in federal environmental statutes to incorporate a precautionary rationale. Wherever it has been applied, the precautionary rationale triggers regulation based on fear of serious and irreversible future harm that is supported by little if any solid scientific evidence. The principle does not provide any rigorous guidance for how to design regulatory responses, but instead allows the regulatory choice to be determined by a political lobbying contest among competing interest groups. In the case of climate change regulation, the precautionary principle easily justifies virtually any regulatory response designed to reduce CO_2 emissions. Because the precautionary rationale weighs only the consequences of failing to regulate stringently enough, it provides no criteria for choosing among alternative climate policies. Perhaps even more seriously, by both justifying regulation on the basis of thin scientific evidence and yet calling for a research program to justify regulation, the precautionary principle paradoxically means that for regulatory purposes, science is settled as soon as it provides a minimal justification for regulation.

I ORIGINS OF THE PRECAUTIONARY PRINCIPLE

In its German name of *Vorsorgeprinzip*, the precautionary principle originated in the 1970s in the context of German legislation to reduce air pollution that was believed to be responsible for acid rain damaging German forests. As translated by Boehmer-Christiansen (1994):

> The principle of precaution commands that the damages done to the natural world (which surrounds us all) should be avoided *in advance* and in accordance with opportunity and possibility. Vorsorge further means *the early detection of dangers to health and environment by comprehensive, synchronised (harmonised) research, in particular about cause and effect relationships... . [I]t also means acting when conclusively ascertained understanding by science is not yet available.* Precaution means to develop, in all sectors of the economy, technological processes that significantly reduce environmental burdens, especially those brought about by the introduction of harmful substances (Emphasis supplied)

According to Percival (2006, 24), the ideas captured in the above definition that "environmental harm should be foreseen before it occurs" and that "scientific uncertainty should not be an obstacle to taking sensible preventive measures," were not new and had indeed been incorporated into law as early as the Swedish Environmental Protection Act of 1969. Percival paraphrases, however, and this paraphrasing eliminates what is most striking about the precautionary principle.

As translated by Boehmer-Christiansen, this very early formulation of the precautionary principle both dictates a program of "comprehensive, synchronized" research and "acting when conclusively ascertained understanding by science is not yet available." These two mandates seem inconsistent. The point of a "comprehensive" program of scientific research would seem precisely to be to achieve "conclusively ascertained understanding by science" of the risks potentially to be regulated. But the precautionary principle says that action should be taken even before "conclusively ascertained scientific understanding" has been achieved. One might well ask what is the point of a comprehensive program of scientific research if regulatory action is to be taken regardless of whether such a program has generated scientific understanding.

What has become perhaps the most quoted version of the precautionary principle is the much less wordy and more focused definition provided as Principle 15 of the 1992 Rio Declaration on Environment and Development. According to Principle 15:[1]

> In order to protect the environment, the precautionary approach shall be widely applied by States according to their capabilities. Where there are threats of serious or irreversible damage, lack of full scientific certainty shall not be used a reason for postponing cost-effective measures to prevent environmental degradation.

Another version of the precautionary principle was set out in 1998 in a statement following a conference at the Wingspread Center in Wisconsin of activist scientists, environmental groups, and government representatives. This so-called Wingspread Statement reads as follows:

> When an activity raises threats of harm to human health or the environment, precautionary measures should be taken even if some cause and effect relationships are not fully established scientifically.[2]

The Rio Declaration's statement of the precautionary principle clarifies that the trigger for action is found in "threats of serious or irreversible damage." If such threats are somehow evidenced, then the "lack of full scientific certainty" is not a reason for postponing costly regulatory action. More precisely, the Wingspread Statement clarifies that even if the causal connection between the activity and the threatened harm is not "fully established scientifically," as long as there is some reason to think that the activity threatens harm to human health or the environment, some kind of precautionary measures are justified.

The Rio Declaration's definition of the precautionary principle has been influential in how that principle has been applied in international, European Commission, and World Trade Organization law (Zander 2010, 169). Since the early 1980s, the European Union has banned the importation of hormone-treated meat from the United States. The United States has complained that this is a disguised protectionist measure, which is illegal under World Trade Organization (WTO) provisions. The EU has responded that its ban is allowed under provisions of the WTO Sanitary and Phytosanitary (SPS) agreement that allow imports to be restricted on the basis of health or safety concerns provided that there is a scientific basis for so doing.[3] The SPS agreement requires that there be a risk assessment of some sort before trade restrictions are imposed on grounds of health or safety. But the WTO Appellate Body has ruled that the precautionary principle is reflected in several parts of the SPS agreement. Under that principle the WTO Appellate Body has said a country can rely on non-mainstream scientific opinion to justify a product ban, especially if the risk is "perceived as life-threatening and imminent" (Zander 2010, 47). Indeed, in the first EC versus US hormone ban case to be decided by WTO institutions, the WTO Appellate Body held that even though the EC's own scientific expert had said that there was no scientific evidence showing that the hormones were harmful, the opinion of a single scientific expert that there was a 1/1,000,000 excess risk caused by one particular hormone was sufficient evidence of a "possible" risk to justify the ban (Zander 2010, 59).

In European law, the precautionary principle has been even more powerful in lowering the requirements of scientific proof of a risk justifying regulation. Well before the Treaty of Maastricht, the European Court of Justice upheld a Dutch ban on the importation from other EU countries of milk products that was justified only by the Dutch assertion that there might possibly be an as-yet unidentified risk to some consumers from some hazily identified non-pathogenic micro-organisms in pasteurized milk. By 2000, following widespread public panic and severe criticism of EU food regulation in the aftermath of the late-1990s discovery of so-called mad cow disease in British beef, the European Commission (EC) issued a statement clarifying how the precautionary principle applies to justify regulation. Under that clarification, precautionary regulation was appropriate "where scientific evidence is insufficient, inconclusive or uncertain and there are indications through preliminary objective scientific evaluation that there are reasonable grounds for concern [of] potentially dangerous effects on the environment, human, animal, or plant health" (Zander 2010). Left unexplained is what is meant by "preliminary objective scientific evaluation" indicating "reasonable grounds for concern."

As the precautionary principle was first articulated in Sweden, it seems reasonable to think that the Swedish law may have generated relatively precise guidance of when such "grounds for concern" over a "serious or irreversible" risk actually exist. Instead, according to Zander (2010, 168), "guidance in Swedish legislation and case law relating to levels of proof in cases of scientific uncertainty is so scarce that it makes any conclusions hypothetical at best." But one thing is clear about the Swedish precautionary principle in action: after a regulator establishes a "reasonably well-founded suspicion of a risk" – sometimes called a "presumable" risk – the burden of proof switches over to the proponent of the risky action (think here a chemical manufacturer, for example) to show "that detriment need not be feared," or "as far as possible based on the current state of scientific research... the suspicion is unfounded" (Zander 2010, 170).

In practice, the EC has required regulators to provide very little evidence to satisfy the burden of showing "reasonable grounds for concern" in order to justify regulation. In 1998, the WTO's Appellate Body struck down the EC's ban on hormone-treated US and Canadian beef because the EC's scientific studies completely failed to address the supposed risk that justified the ban – the risk of carcinogenic or genotoxic harm from hormone residues in meat.[4] In response, the European Commission funded seventeen new studies on the effect of hormone residues in meat on human health. The EU Scientific Committee on Veterinary Measures relating to Public Health issued opinions in 1999, 2000, and 2002 reviewing these studies, and on the basis of these studies, in 2003 the EC promulgated Directive 2003/74/EC permanently banning the importation of meat from animals treated with oestradiol-17β (a form of estrogen).

In 2007 the European Food Safety Authority Panel on contaminants in food found that "epidemiological data provide convincing evidence for an association between the amount of red meat consumed and certain forms of hormone-dependent cancers." That panel also found, however, that "[w]hether hormone residues in meat contribute to this risk is currently unknown."[5] In 2008 that same panel reconvened and found that the EC had failed to produce any scientific evidence demonstrating the genotoxicity of oestradiol-17β or that residues of that hormone in meat lead to an increased risk of cancer or adverse immunological or developmental effects.[6] The expert opinions reviewed by the panel were consistent: while there clearly was evidence that at large enough doses, oestradiol-17β could be genotoxic, "the EC has not identified the potential for adverse effects on human health of residues of oestradiol found in meat from treated cattle," with no epidemiological studies of people consuming meat from hormone-treated cattle versus untreated cattle and no showing by the EC that "genotoxicity and cell proliferation would be induced by levels found in meat residues added to pre-existing levels occurring in exposed humans." Indeed, one expert concluded that "none of the information provided by the European Communities demonstrates the potential for adverse effects in humans of any of the six hormones in meat from cattle in which they are used for growth promotion purposes at the levels to which those consuming such meat would be exposed."[7]

The EC's position essentially was that no such evidence needed to be presented to justify its ban. According to the EC, the existing evidence showed that "the higher the exposure to residues from these hormones, the greater the risk is likely to be." The fact that people "may be exposed to multiple sources of hormones and hormone residues, via several intake routes, as well as from endogenous production of some of these hormones" made it "virtually impossible to assess all cumulative and synergistic effects that may arise from all potential exposure patterns." The EC conceded that "no quantitative estimate of risk related to residues in meat could be presented," but since the existing evidence showed that "no threshold exists for the risk from oestrogen metabolites," no quantitative evidence was needed.[8] Under the precautionary principle, the EC interpreted expert evidence that there is no evidence establishing a causal connection as showing continuing uncertainty about the existence of such a connection, and such uncertainty itself then justified a continuing ban. Thus under the EC's version of the precautionary principle, very general evidence of even a potential risk is sufficient to justify banning an activity, and the failure of ongoing research to find any evidence of the precise risk justifying the ban is irrelevant to whether it should continue.

II THE PRECAUTIONARY PRINCIPLE AS THE RATIONALE FOR THE EPA'S ENDANGERMENT FINDING

There is nothing in US law that explicitly adopts the precautionary principle. On the other hand, the basic precautionary regulatory framework – authorizing regulation, up to and including a ban on an activity, unless the proponent of the activity can prove that it is in some sense "safe" – can be found in some areas of US law. As Sachs (2011, 1307–1308) observes, the US regime for drug regulation under the Food, Drug, and Cosmetic Act (FDCA) prohibits drugs from being marketed unless the manufacturer can produce clinical trial and other evidence showing that the drug is both safe and efficacious. As pointed out by Applegate (2000, 420), under the Federal Insecticide and Rodenticide Act (FIFRA), similar (although far less intensive) approval process is required before pesticides can be sold and used in agriculture.

In its basic structure, however, the CAA is very different than the laws regulating new drugs and pesticides. It is true that under the 1990 amendments to the CAA, a big new industrial plant owner must show that the plant will be in compliance with applicable federal air pollution regulatory requirements in order to get a CAA permit (under Title V of that law). But while prudent to get (to avoid fines), a plant owner can build and operate a plant before getting such a permit. More generally, the CAA sets up pollution reduction requirements for existing sources of pollution. It does not say that all existing sources of pollution have to shut down until their owners can show that they meet pollution reduction requirements. It does say that whether pollution has to be reduced at all depends upon whether it imposes a risk to human health and/or the environment. It is by interpreting the trigger for pollution reduction requirements under two particular provisions that the courts have put the precautionary principle into the Clean Air Act.

The key word that courts interpreted to put the precautionary principle in the CAA is the word "endanger." Back in the very early days of the CAA, the EPA phased out the use of lead in auto gasoline under language found in Section 211(c)(1)(A) of the CAA authorizing that agency to "control or prohibit" any fuel additive that "will endanger the public health or welfare." In *Ethyl Corp.* v. *EPA* (1976),[9] the District of Columbia Circuit Court held that this language authorized the EPA's lead phase-out. Here is how that court reasoned to the conclusions that language allowing the EPA to control gasoline additives mandated a precautionary approach:

> [E]ndanger means something less than actual harm. When one is endangered, harm is threatened; no actual injury need ever occur. Thus, for example, a town may be "endangered" by a threatening plague or hurricane and yet emerge from the danger completely unscathed. A statute allowing for regulation in the face of danger is, necessarily, a precautionary statute. Regulatory action may be taken before the threatened harm occurs; indeed, the very existence of such precautionary legislation would seem to demand that regulatory action precede, and, optimally, prevent, the perceived threat. As should be apparent, the "will endanger" language of Section 211(c)(1)(A) makes it such a precautionary statute.[10]

As the Supreme Court explained in *Massachusetts* v. *EPA*, the provision at issue there, Section 202 of the CAA, had once been essentially the same as the fuel additive provision, Section 211, in that it mandated that the EPA regulate emission of tailpipe pollutants "which endangers the public health or welfare." However, Congress had amended Section 202 in 1977 to its present form, requiring that the EPA set standards for any tailpipe pollutant that "may reasonably be anticipated to endanger the public health or welfare." The Court in *Massachusetts* v. *EPA* said that with this change, Congress gave its full approval to the language in the *Ethyl Corp.* saying that the CAA "and common sense ... demand regulatory action to prevent harm, even if the regulator is less than certain that harm is otherwise inevitable."[11]

In justifying its precautionary reading of Section 202 of the Clean Air Act, the EPA relied on one other very old opinion interpreting the statutory word "endanger" to authorize a precautionary approach to environmental regulation. *In Reserve Mining Co.* v. *EPA*, the Eighth Circuit court of appeals had upheld the district court's injunction against Reserve Mining's continuing discharge of taconite mine tailings – a form of asbestos – into Lake Superior. That case involved a provision of the federal Clean Water Act giving the EPA the authority to take actions to abate discharge of pollutants into the waters of the United States that "endanger... public health or welfare."

It might seem that in cases involving lead and asbestos, the precautionary interpretation of "endanger" was overkill. After all, lead and asbestos are known to cause harm. In *Ethyl Corp.*, it was uncontested that lead is not naturally present in the human body and that in sufficiently high concentrations, it can cause neurologic damage, and that lead concentration in the atmosphere over major US cities was thousands of times higher than over the mid-Pacific. Although it was decided almost 50 years ago, in the *Reserve Mining* case there was clear scientific evidence that inhalation of asbestos fibers could cause a variety of long latency period diseases, such as mesothelemia.

However, in both *Ethyl Corp.* and *Reserve Mining*, there was actually very little evidence that the precise emissions at issue in those cases could actually cause harm. As for the harmful effects of lead in auto emissions, according to a study by Carothers (2015, 703–710) only in the early 1970s had studies been done on the health effects of the low concentrations of lead found in ambient air. In the 1975 *Ethyl Corp.* litigation, the EPA presented to that court only a single study finding that lead absorption levels resulting from exposure only to ambient air were inducing neurological disorders such as hyperactivity and impaired fine motor coordination in children. A 1972 National Academy of Sciences panel had in fact concluded that there was no information available on the causal impact of auto lead emissions on such behavioral problems. In *Ethyl Corp.*, the EPA's primary causal justification for eliminating lead from gasoline was that "urban children are particularly threatened by lead additives in that they are prone to ingest lead emissions that have fallen to the ground and mixed with dust."[12] The EPA did not argue that lead in gasoline was primarily responsible for lead in ground level urban dust. Instead, it produced only evidence that as many as 25 percent of "all preschool children living in substandard housing'[13] had elevated lead levels and epidemiological studies finding a "consistent relationship between lead in air and lead in blood" in different US metropolitan statistical areas.[14] The court conceded that the EPA's causal hypothesis was "admittedly not proved as fact." Under the lax precautionary proof requirements, however, it was enough that the EPA's causal story was "consistent with known information."

In *Reserve Mining*, the evidence that the defendant's taconite tailings actually posed a risk of harm was similarly thin. The Eighth Circuit said that the evidence that exposure to asbestos from drinking water drawn from Lake Superior was "comparable" to exposures found to cause gastrointestinal cancer in asbestos workers was of "dubious accuracy" and "evidentially weak." An expert said that even if the calculations of how exposures from drinking water compared to exposures among asbestos workers were accurate, "he would conclude only that the risk was non-negligible."[15] All the experts who testified said that tissues sampled from recently deceased Duluth residents "were virtually free of any fibers which could be attributed to the Reserve discharge."[16] The court found that such evidence showed only that "ingestion of asbestos fibers poses some risk to health, but to an undetermined degree," with "the best that can be said" being only that "the existence of this asbestos contaminant in air and water gives rise to a reasonable medical concern for the public health."[17] Even though the court conceded "it cannot be forecast that the rates of cancer will increase from drinking Lake Superior water or breathing Silver Bay air," the "reasonable medical concern for public health" sufficed to meet the legal "endanger" standard.

In justifying the legal basis of its Endangerment Finding, the EPA relied primarily on the reasoning in the *Ethyl* opinion, quoting it at length and noting the *Reserve Mining* opinion as well.[18] The EPA pointedly noted that in *Ethyl*, the court rejected "the argument that the EPA had to show that such harm was 'probable'" and instead had "made it clear that determining endangerment entails judgments involving both the risk or likelihood of harm and the severity of the harm were it to occur." Carothers (2015) is clearly correct that in comparison with the evidence on low level lead exposure circa 1975, "the body of evidence on the impact of GHGs on climate change when EPA issued its endangerment finding in 2009 is huge." As she says, the EPA was able to rely on expert syntheses of "thousands" of individual studies on various aspects of climate change and GHGs done by the IPCC, the US Global Climate Research Program, and the National Research Council (Carothers 2015, 710–711).

Responding to criticism from commentators, the EPA stressed that the precautionary principle did not shift the burden of proof over "to opponents of endangerment to show safety or no endangerment." As for the EPA's burden of proof, looking to the legislative history of the 1977 modification of Section 202, the EPA said Congress had authorized the EPA to "weigh risks and make projections" in determining endangerment.

III THE PRECAUTIONARY PRINCIPLE AND CLIMATE CHANGE POLICY CHOICE: AN INDUCTIVE APPROACH

The precautionary principle itself contains no formal criterion for how the principle guides policy choice. Such a criterion would consist, for example, of a rule recommending the choice of whatever policy generates the highest expected net benefits – benefits in terms of reduced risk minus the cost of the risk reduction. Or, alternatively, a rule could require – as do many US federal environmental statutes – that a policy is acceptable as long as it generates a certain minimum level of risk reduction. The precautionary principle is much less specific even than this. The only policy guidance in the principle itself is the recommendation that among equally effective policies to reduce or eliminate an irreversible and serious risk, the cheapest should be chosen. But this guide, called cost-effective policy choice, rarely applies, for the simple reason that there rarely are several equally effective policies.

Without any such formal criterion, one might look to the stylized facts of actual examples of the precautionary principle in action. I have already discussed one of these, the EU ban on Canadian and US beef. Another, probably more well-known regulatory application of the precautionary principle is the Montreal Protocol of 1987. This is an international treaty that bans the use of chlorofluorocarbon (CFC) refrigerants. CFCs absorb ultraviolet radiation and release chlorine atoms, which react with ozone in the stratosphere to form chlorine monoxide and also hydrogen chloride, that latter of which can produce more free chlorine, and so more ozone loss. As we shall see later, stratospheric ozone is very good at absorbing harmful UV-B shortwave radiation from the sun. Although at the time of the Montreal Protocol, the only evidence of a loss of stratospheric ozone was in the stratosphere over the Antarctic, according to Jacobs (2014, 161–171) it was believed that this ozone-depleting chain of reactions would occur at all latitudes of the globe. On this basis, a very large global increase in skin cancer and eye cataracts was predicted to result from CFC-caused ozone depletion, and the Montreal Protocol banned the use of CFC refrigerants.

The European ban on US and Canadian beef and the Montreal Protocol's ban on CFCs have several things in common. They both involved bans on activity for which there was relatively thin evidence of a potentially serious and irreversible risk. In addition, neither of these two precautionary bans was very costly. In the case of the European ban on US and Canadian beef, the market response has been to shift out the demand for more expensive European beef relative to what it would have been had it faced competition from cheaper US and Canadian beef. European consumers pay more for their beef because of the ban. But beef is still available for purchase and consumption in Europe. The ban on US and Canadian beef was not a ban on all beef. The Montreal Protocol's ban on the use of chlorofluorocarbon (CFC) refrigerants was even less costly. Major US and European chemical companies were ready to produce refrigerants that substituted almost perfectly for CFCs, so that actual cost of the Montreal Protocol was quite small.

The beef and CFC precautionary bans succeeded not just because they imposed relatively small costs. There were clear winners from both: European beef producers, and the large international chemical companies that produced CFC substitutes. Given small costs and clear beneficiaries from these bans, it is relatively easy to see why the countries could agree to take the precautionary principle's advice to "err on the side of caution and prevent activities that may cause serious or irreversible harm" (Barton 1998, 547). It is easy to "err on the side of caution" when there are clear economic winners from erring on the side of caution and the cost of error – banning an activity that is not as risky as feared – is not high.

The beef and CFC bans thus do provide some guidance when it comes to precautionary climate policy – look for winners from policies designed to reduce GHG emissions. But on the cost side, reducing GHG emissions is quite unlike banning beef or CFCs. Responding to the threat of GHG-induced climate change by banning or in some other way quickly eliminating the use of fossil fuels as a source of energy for human economy and society amounts to proposals to radically transform such societies and economies. As Smil (2017, 295) summarizes, the "prodigious energy stores" from fossil fuels have provided the basis for the rapid industrialization and urbanization, expansion and acceleration of transportation, "enormous" advances in agricultural productivity, and growth in communication and information capabilities that define the contemporary developed world. The costs of radically transforming a fossil fuel-based economy are several orders of magnitude larger than the cost of banning CFCs or US and Canadian beef.

This suggests several working hypotheses about the American precautionary response to climate change risk. With costs that dwarf those caused by any previous instance of precautionary regulation, one would expect the advocates of precautionary responses to the risks of climate change to exaggerate the benefits and minimize the costs of such responses. Moreover, any policy that imposes costs on some people cannot succeed unless there are also clear and identifiable policy beneficiaries. This aspect of the precautionary principle is most vividly displayed by the EU beef ban, which directly benefited European beef producers, but an even more direct way to create identified beneficiaries is by subsidizing activities that will replace a banned or phased out risky activity. This is especially likely to be true with US climate change policies, as unlike the EU beef ban, reducing US CO_2 emissions imposes costs on US firms and households who elect the politicians ultimately responsible for such policies, not foreign firms and households.

One does not, however need to speculate about precautionary climate policy. As we've seen, Obama-era regulation of GHG emissions under the CAA was justified by the precautionary principle. As we will see shortly, other regulatory actions taken by the Obama administration to reduce GHG emissions under other environmental statutes were similarly justified by the precautionary principle. And regulatory efforts to reduce GHG emissions are only part of the story of America's de facto climate policy. America's litigation system, under which juries can impose massive damages on corporate defendants with only the most speculative evidence that the defendant's activities risk harm, is perhaps the perfect institution for sanctioning activities deemed to risk serious and irreversible harm. As we shall see, such litigation came well before the Obama-era regulatory effort to reduce GHG emissions. Also coming well before that effort were a number of federal laws that subsidized renewable energy alternatives to fossil fuel-fired electricity generation and to gasoline-powered automobiles. Many of these laws were passed in a national panic over insecure energy that arose during the 1970s in the aftermath of the OPEC oil embargo of 1973–1974. These early subsidies for renewables turned out to be based on the increasingly unrealistic premise that the United States would forever be dependent on imported oil – as of 2019, the United States was one of the top three oil exporting nations – but they provided the basis for additional laws, all adding up to a large increase in renewable energy subsidies intended to lower US CO_2 emissions. Subsequent chapters explore all of these responses – regulation and litigation to penalize CO_2 emitting activities as well as subsidies for renewables.

Notes

1. UN General Assembly, Report of the UN Conference on Environment and Development, Annex I, RIO DECLARATION ON ENVIRONMENT AND DEVELOPMENT, A/CONF.151/26 (Vol. I)
(Rio de Janeiro, 3–14 June 1992), available at https://www.un.org/documents/ga/conf151/aconf15126-1annex1.htm.
2. The Wingspread Statement on the Precautionary Principle, Sci. & Env. Health Network (Jan. 1998), available at
3. For a more sustained discussion, see Renée Johnson, The U.S.-EU Beef Hormone Dispute, CRS Report R40449, Jan. 14, 2015, available at https://fas.org/sgp/crs/row/R40449.pdf.
4. Bernard Hoekman and Joel Trachtman, Continued Suspension: EC–Hormones and WTO Disciplines on Discrimination and Domestic Regulation. Appellate Body Reports: Canada/United States – Continued Suspension of Obligations in the EC – Hormones Dispute, WT/DS320/AB/R,WT/DS321/AB/R, 7, adopted 14 November 2008.
5. Opinion of the Scientific Panel on Contaminants in ghe Food Chain on a Request from the European Commission Related to Hormone Residues in Bovine Meat and Meat Products. Question N° EFSA-Q-2005–048, Adopted on 12 June 2007, The EFSA Journal (2007) 510, 1–62, 62.
6. WTO, Canada-Continued Suspension of Obligations in the EC – Hormones Dispute, Report of the Panel, WT/DS321/R, March 31, 2008, available at https://docs.wto.org/dol2fe/Pages/FE_Search/FE_S_S006.aspx?Query=(@Symbol=%20wt/ds321/r*%20not%20rw*)&Language=ENGLISH&Context=FomerScriptedSearch&languageUIChanged=true#.
7. Ibid.
8. WTO, Canada-Continued Suspension of Obligations in the EC – Hormones Dispute, Report of the Panel 225.
9. 541 F.2d 1 (DC Cir. 1976).
10. 541 F.2d 1, 13.
11. 549 U.S. 497, 506 n.7 (2007)
12. *Ethyl Corp.* at 43.
13. *Ethyl Corp.* at 40.
14. *Ethyl Corp.* at 42.
15. *Reserve Mining* at 517.
16. *Reserve Mining* at 520.
17. *Reserve Mining Co.* v. *EPA*, 514 F.2d 492, 520 (8th Cir. 1975).
18. See 74 Fed. Reg. at 66506–66507.

4

The EPA's Newfound Role in Regulating Automobile Mileage

As described in Chapter 2, after Congress failed to pass climate change legislation in 2009, the Obama administration EPA moved very quickly to find that GHG emissions from autos and light trucks were reasonably likely to endanger human health or welfare. This – the Endangerment Finding – then provided the legal basis for a number of subsequent regulations promulgated under the Clean Air Act. Most directly, the EPA first imposed GHG emission limits for cars (using the same section of the CAA under which the Endangerment Finding had been made). In so doing, the EPA arrogated to itself the job of setting mileage standards for cars and light trucks, a job that Congress had explicitly given to a very different agency, the National Highway Transportation Safety administration, that had a very different historical mission. Moreover, the automobile mileage standards set under the Obama administration's so-called tailpipe rule were essentially the standards that California and some northeastern states had imposed on themselves. In this way, the tailpipe rule reversed the CAA structure, with California regulators, not federal regulators, determining national auto emission standards. The net result of the tailpipe rule was an increase in mileage far less than advertised, and higher automobile prices that were mostly felt by poor and middle income households.

I THE CLEAN AIR ACT BARGAIN

Recall that if the Supreme Court had refused to find that GHG emissions were an "air pollutant" under the CAA, then the EPA would not have had to make a finding as to whether auto GHG emissions were "reasonably likely to endanger" human health or the environment. Because the Court did find that GHG emissions were an "air pollutant" within the meaning of that law, the EPA could potentially justify its GHG regulations under a number of provisions of the CAA. The CAA represented a bargain among different regions and interest groups who expected various costs and benefits from air pollution reduction. It was a bargain that met with unanimous approval by both the Senate and the House when amendments were passed in 1970. Later amendments to the law made in 1977 and 1990 passed almost with unanimous approval – 73–7 in the Senate and 326–49 in the House for the 1977 amendments and 89–10 in the Senate and 401–25 in the House for the 1990 amendments. Notably, positions on the law were not predictable based on party affiliation. For example, the 10 Senators voting against the 1990 amendments were half Democrat and half Republican. Thus the Clean Air Act, in its 1970, 1977, and 1990 amendments, came about as close to a universally acceptable deal as one can imagine.

The virtually universal acceptance of the CAA bargain within Congress was especially true for the provisions of that law that required cuts in pollution from cars and trucks. To recall the discussion from Chapter 2, by 1970, many large metropolitan areas across the US had a smog problem that was perceived as caused primarily by auto exhaust. Yet as of 1970, the manufacture of autos and auto parts was concentrated in just three states – Michigan, Indiana, and Ohio. The likely costs of requiring auto manufacturers to install costly technologies to reduce auto pollution was not only an increase in auto prices, but some reduction in auto industry employment and profitability. The latter two costs, unemployment and reduced profitability, were concentrated in just the three states that were home to the auto industry. Such costs were of little concern to the vast majority of states and localities with auto pollution problems and hence posed no political obstacle to tough auto pollution regulations in such places.

With few auto-related jobs and no automobile company corporate presence, California began to regulate auto exhaust emissions in 1966. When Congress authorized federal auto tailpipe emission regulation in the Clean Air Act, it allowed California but only California to require tougher auto tailpipe emission standards than the federal standards.[1] And in order to get the federal EPA's permission to set its own standards (more technically, to get a "waiver" of federal preemption), California had to show that its standards were at least as tough as the federal standards and were necessary to cope with "compelling and extraordinary" circumstances.[2] Once California is given such a waiver, other states can adopt California standards, but only California standards. With only this so-called California exception, the CAA represented a bargain under which the auto industry effectively agreed to reduce pollutants in exhaust but was freed from potentially even more costly, not to say varying, state and local regulations.

II HOW THE CAA ACHIEVED REDUCTIONS IN AUTOMOBILE AIR POLLUTION BY INCREASING CO_2 EMISSIONS

If one understands just the basics of the CAA approach to reducing air pollution from automobile exhaust, it is very, very difficult to see how the 1970 Congress that passed the CAA could have intended that law to cover automobile CO_2 emissions. To understand why this is so, we need to review some basics of air pollution from cars.

Burning a pure hydrocarbon fuel is a chemical reaction between oxygen and the hydrocarbon, which releases only CO_2 and water. It is true that the gasoline used by automobiles is not a pure hydrocarbon, but instead a mixture of about 150 different chemicals plus additives. Still, if all gasoline fuel is actually burned – complete combustion is achieved – then the chemical byproducts will be limited to heat, CO_2, water vapor, and nitrogen. The fuel mixtures necessary to start a car engine or accelerate prevent cars from achieving complete combustion, and this means that a variety of chemical by-products result from running an auto engine. These by-products include carbon monoxide, oxides of nitrogen, and various volatile organic compounds (chemical compounds such as formaldehyde and benzene, which easily evaporate into the air because they have a low boiling point). When they interact with sunlight, such volatile organic compounds produce ground level ozone, a key component of urban smog.

As we have seen, Los Angeles was the first city in the country with a major smog problem, and (as explained by Krier and Ursin [1978]) way back in the early 1950s, the state of California funded research into the causes of smog and what could be done about it. Such funding paid off when Eugene Houdry invented the catalytic converter. A catalytic converter is a dense honeycomb structure through which auto exhaust gases pass before being emitted out of the tailpipe. The honeycomb structure is ceramic material coated with chemical catalysts (such as platinum). These catalysts interact with the exhaust gas, with one catalyst breaking up oxides of nitrogen into nitrogen and oxygen, and the other adding oxygen to turn poisonous carbon monoxide into CO_2 and to turn various other incompletely combusted hydrocarbons into CO_2 and water.[3]

Houdry's catalytic converter was described in colorful terms in a 1955 *Popular Science* article.[4] The reason that it was not immediately applied to automobile engines was because back then, tetraethyl lead was added to all auto gasoline to prevent so-called engine knocking, and lead in auto exhaust coated the catalysts in Houdry's catalytic converter and prevented the auto exhaust gases from reacting with the metal catalysts. But catalytic converters were installed to clean the exhaust of forklifts and similar vehicles that ran on unleaded gasoline because engine noise was of no concern. By 1970, catalytic converter technology had been around for almost two decades.

In Section 202(a)(3)(A)[5] of the CAA, Congress told the EPA to set standards for "emissions of hydrocarbons, carbon monoxide, oxides of nitrogen, and particulate matter" that "reflect the greatest degree of emission reduction achievable through the application of technology which the Administrator determines will be available for the model year to which such standards apply, giving appropriate consideration to cost, energy, and safety factors associated with the application of such technology." This standard is sometimes called a best available technology (or BAT) standard. When Congress promulgated this standard, it wasn't just hoping that some new air pollution reduction technology could be found. The catalytic converter was already well known to Congress in 1970 as an available technology to reduce auto pollution. By 1973, the EPA had required that by the 1975 model year, all new cars had to be equipped with catalytic converters. At the same time, the EPA naturally banned lead from gasoline, since catalytic converters do not work with leaded gasoline.

As is evident from this description, catalytic converters that reduce automobile air pollution also generate CO_2, the primary GHG targeted by regulators. Moreover, as mentioned gasoline combustion in an auto engine, like the combustion of any hydrocarbon, has three direct products: carbon dioxide, water, and heat. As these two facts show, the technologies used to reduce pollution from cars not only do nothing to reduce CO_2 emissions from cars but sometimes actually increase such emissions. The only way to reduce CO_2 emissions from cars is to reduce the amount of gasoline burned by cars.

III THE SLOW EVOLUTION OF NHTSA'S FEDERAL CAFÉ AUTOMOBILE MILEAGE STANDARDS

In other words, the only tool open to the EPA to actually reduce CO_2 emissions from cars under Section 202 of the CAA was to mandate improved automobile mileage. The problem with this particular regulatory approach was (and is) that Section 202 of the CAA says nothing about automobile mileage standards, and from 1970 until 2009 the EPA had never even attempted to mandate improved automobile mileage as a "technology" for reducing automobile air pollution under Section 202.

Congress imposed automobile mileage standards – or as they are known more precisely, Corporate Average Fuel Economy (CAFÉ) standards – not in the CAA but in the Energy Policy and Conservation Act of 1975 (EPCA).[6] Passed in the "energy crisis" hysteria that followed the first Arab Oil embargo, EPCA required the secretary of transportation to set CAFÉ standards at the "maximum feasible average fuel economy level for such model year." Congress passed EPCA not to reduce GHG emissions from cars, but to increase domestic oil supply and reduce oil imports, conserve and manage energy demand, and establish programs to cut US vulnerability to disruptions in international oil supply.[7] Under the express terms of EPCA, Congress gave the job of setting mileage standards to the National Highway Transportation Safety Administration (NHTSA), an agency within the Department of Commerce whose primary focus was auto safety. By structure and design, NHTSA is a very different agency, with a very different mission, than the EPA.

Whereas even beginning law students know that the EPA is an environmental agency, when I ask my students if they know what NHTSA is or does, the vast majority say they have no idea. The few that do answer say they think that NHTSA does auto recalls. This is actually correct. Since the mid-1970s, NHTSA focused on recalling cars that had safety-related defects. However, as explained by Mashaw and Harfst (1987, 263), when NHTSA was created by the National Traffic and Motor Vehicle Safety Act of 1966, that agency was intended by Congress to "force the technology of automobile safety design." Up until 1974, NHTSA did promulgate some auto safety regulations. Much like the EPA, the NHTSA rules that actually became operational merely required car companies to use "off-the-shelf technologies, many of which were already in widespread, if not universal use." Thus the rules had "extremely modest technology-forcing effects." After the mid-1970s, NHTSA abandoned even this "modest" attempt to force auto safety technology development and pursued its auto safety mission solely with periodic recalls.

In 1975, NHTSA's responsibilities expanded to include setting CAFÉ standards under EPCA. EPCA requires that NHTSA consider three primary factors in setting CAFÉ standards: (i) technological feasibility; (ii) economic practicability; (iii) the need of the United States to conserve energy.[8] EPCA nowhere tells NHTSA to consider the environmental impact of its CAFÉ standards.

Under the factors that it is allowed to consider, NHTSA proceeded very slowly and cautiously to increase mileage requirements, increasing the standard only from 20.2 mpg in 1992 to 20.7 mpg in 1995. Even this was too much for Congress. From 1995 until 2002, Congress froze CAFÉ standards by including a provision in the appropriations bills for each year that prohibited NHTSA from using any funds even to propose CAFÉ standards that were different than the standards of the previous year.[9]

During this period, CAFÉ compliance was determined by measuring the harmonic sales-weighted average of the fuel economy of the cars sold by each manufacturer (Klier and Linn 2010). The standards had a differential impact on US, Japanese, and German auto companies. By increasing their sales of lighter, more fuel efficient cars (while also increasing sales of light duty trucks, a category that includes SUVs), the US automakers responded to consumer demand for larger, heavier vehicles while just meeting the fleet-wide fuel economy standards. Japanese manufacturers achieved better mileage than the standards required.

EPCA allows car companies to pay a fine rather than comply with the CAFÉ standards. Only in 1997 did NHTSA raise the penalty from the 1978 level of $50.00 per vehicle per mpg to $55 per vehicle per mpg. The penalty has not been adjusted for inflation and has remained at $55 per vehicle per mpg (Shiau et al. 2009, 814–828). Over the 1983–2002 period, the smaller volume foreign makers of heavy, high horsepower cars such as BMW and Mercedes paid fines rather than comply and paid fines for non-compliance adding up to about $600 million between 1983 and 2002 (Klier and Linn 2010). This aggregate fine was trivial to such carmakers' bottom line: in 2010 alone, BMW's global earnings before interest and taxes were about 4.9 billion Euros.[10] The shift of domestic producers to selling lighter and/or less powerful cars increased the (residual) demand for high powered cars made by foreign (fine-paying) automakers and also gave slack to Japanese auto manufacturers to sell more large cars. Profits of foreign carmakers went up.

By making cars lighter and less powerful, by the late 1980s, automakers achieved a dramatic increase in fleet-wide miles per gallon (mpg) (Klier and Linn 2010). However, empirical work by economists has uniformly shown that consumers value power above fuel economy,[11] and to meet consumer preferences, between the late 1980s, and 2007, automakers took advantage of improvements in power train technology to increase power and weight while keeping fleet-wide mpg roughly constant.[12] Consumers switched en masse to light trucks – i.e., SUVs – that had lower CAFÉ mileage standards. Between 1980 and 2004, light truck sales increased from only 20 percent of all vehicles sold to over 51 percent. Moreover, while the average fuel economy of the actual US auto fleet increased by 6.5 percent, the average horsepower of new cars increased by 80 percent and the average horsepower of light-duty trucks by 99 percent (Knittel 2011). As found by Shiau et al. (2009, 815) and Jacobsen (2013, 174), because consumers switched en masse to light trucks, actual average fuel economy increased very little between 1980 and 2004, even though both the car and light truck fleets had long met CAFÉ standards.

Reacting to the stalled progress in increasing auto fuel economy between the late 1980s and early 2000s, in the Energy Independence and Security Act (EISA) of 2007, Congress mandated that auto manufacturers achieve a higher CAFÉ standard of 35 mpg level by 2020. The higher mileage standard, however, came along with a change in how average fleet-wide mileage is measured. Under the 2007 revisions (so-called CAFÉ II), each vehicle model has a mileage standard that is determined by its footprint (the square area equal to wheelbase times track width). The mileage standard for each carmaker in each year is equal to the (expected) sales-weighted average of the mileage standards for the different vehicles it sells. In what one might not incorrectly perceive to be a protectionist outcome, small footprint cars in which Japanese manufacturers specialize have much higher mileage requirements – around 40 mpg – than the large footprint cars that generate most of the profits for American car companies (with an mpg standard of a bit over 30 mpg).

NHTSA constructed the footprint-based CAFÉ standards based on its own engineering estimates of the cost-effective fuel economy levels that could be achieved for each footprint (Whitefoot and Skerlos 2012, 402–411). The idea behind footprint based fuel economy standards was apparently to take away the incentive for carmakers to comply with new, higher CAFÉ standards just by redesigning a car to have a smaller footprint, rather than by developing new technologies that improved mileage. But NHTSA did not consider whether the footprint based system might create an incentive for carmakers to expand the footprint just to lower mileage requirements.[13] Researchers who did study this question found that, provided that consumers have any significant preference for bigger vehicles and do not demand extremely high acceleration capability, the footprint based mileage standards would increase sales-weighted average vehicle size increases by 2–32 percent and cut gains in mileage by between 1–4 mpg (Whitefoot and Skerlos 2012).

IV HOW CALIFORNIA, AND THE GREAT RECESSION, GOT THE EPA A ROLE IN SETTING CAFÉ STANDARDS

In 2004, before Congress mandated increased auto mileage in the 2007 EISA, the Air Resources Board of the state of California had promulgated its own automobile GHG standards. California's standards required a 30 percent reduction in auto emissions relative to 2009 emissions by 2016, a reduction that translates into a mileage standard of 37 mpg (Freeman 2011, 349n37). Thus California had set a mileage standard that exceeded the standard under the 2007 EISA and became effective much sooner. Moreover, unlike the federal CAFÉ standards, which as just discussed became based on a model's footprint under the 2007 EISA, California's auto GHG standards were weight-based, with lighter, smaller cars and trucks having a higher effective mileage requirement (rising to 43 mpg by 2016) than larger cars and trucks.[14] A weight based system was perceived as effectively favoring carmakers who sell lots of small, light cars and was opposed by US automakers (Freeman 2011, 355).

Until the Obama administration, California's automobile GHG standards had not taken effect, because the George W. Bush administration did not grant California the Clean Air Act waiver that would have allowed California to set its own standards. The US auto industry supported this refusal. The auto industry also challenged California's auto GHG standards in court. As explained earlier, the only way to reduce GHG emissions from automobiles is to increase mileage, and in several lawsuits,[15] the auto industry argued that under EPCA, only NHTSA – and not the states – had the authority to set auto mileage standards.

The statutes that assign regulatory authority to NHTSA – the National Traffic and Motor Vehicle Safety Act of 1966 and the 1975 EPCA – assign no regulatory authority at all to the EPA. There is a reason for this. The EPA is not an auto safety agency and none of the statutes that it administers are addressed to the national policy of conserving energy. To be sure, energy conservation may be a means of achieving the overriding goal of the many statutes that the EPA does administer – reducing pollution – but the EPA has no expertise in energy conservation. Nor does it have any expertise in understanding the fundamental tradeoff between safety and energy conservation that arises when CAFÉ standards are increased. This tradeoff arises because automakers can only meet tougher CAFÉ standards by including more small and light cars in the fleet of cars that they sell. More small cars are required because there are technological limits to the ability of carmakers to increasing the fuel efficiency of larger, heavier cars that carry more people and cargo and accelerate more quickly – the two features that consumers have valued most highly for decades.

Given the very distinct and different roles played over the decades by the EPA and NHTSA, there is a very good chance that even if the auto industry failed to persuade the courts that EPCA had preempted the state fuel economy standards that were the only way for California (or any other state) to reduce auto GHG emissions, it might well have succeeded in persuading the courts that the CAA gave neither the EPA nor any state environmental agency the legal authority to set fuel economy standards as a way of reducing automobile CO_2 tailpipe emissions.

The Obama administration had publicly committed itself to granting California a waiver to set its own auto GHG emission standards under the Clean Air Act. After the Endangerment Finding was upheld, the auto industry thus not only faced the certain prospect of federal auto GHG emission standards, it also faced the prospect of confronting two potentially conflicting automobile GHG emission standards, the California standard – which by 2007 had been adopted by eleven other states – and a federal standard. It was against this backdrop – the threat that California would be given a waiver to begin enforcing its own auto GHG emission standards – that the Obama administration, the California Air Resources Board, and the auto industry negotiated for new, tougher CAFÉ standards.

As of 2009, the American auto companies were in no position to drive a hard bargain with the EPA or any other federal government agency. To fend off impending bankruptcy, the George W. Bush and Obama administrations invested about $80 billion in GM, Chrysler, and many of their auto-parts suppliers. At one time, the federal government owned 60 percent of GM's stock. By the time the government sold off all its shares in 2013, it had lost $10.5 billion on its investment in GM and $1.2 billion on its investment in Chrysler.[16] Back in 2009, GM and Chrysler were completely dependent on the federal government for their very existence and in no position to resist demands by the Obama administration and the twelve California GHG emission standard states that they increase the fuel efficiency of their vehicles in order to reduce such emissions.

The stage was set for a bargain[17] under which the EPA and NHTSA, with California's agreement, jointly set new corporate average fuel economy (CAFÉ) standards as the Section 202 tailpipe GHG emissions standard. Finalized in May, 2010, the tailpipe rule set a CAFÉ standard of 35.5 mpg to be met not by 2020, as the 2007 EISA had required of its 35 mpg standard, but by 2016, as California required.[18] As the tailpipe rule essentially followed California, that state unsurprisingly agreed to treat compliance with the new federal auto GHG emissions rule as compliance with California's GHG emissions rule. Given California's agreement, which ensured that car companies would not face conflicting state and federal GHG emission standards, it is perhaps just as unsurprising that all of the major auto companies formally committed not to challenge in court the federal tailpipe rule or any waiver that might be granted to California to set its own standards (Freeman 2011, 345).

Just two weeks after the final tailpipe rule was promulgated in 2010, President Obama issued a Presidential Memorandum telling the EPA and NHTSA to extend such standards to model years 2017–2025. In 2012, proclaiming that they were "building on the success of the first phase of the National Program for these vehicles for model years 2012–2016," the EPA and NHTSA did just that, setting a 2017–2025 new GHG emission-limiting CAFÉ standard.[19] Relative to previous CAFÉ standards – which were unchanged for cars for almost 30 years – the 2012 rule set extremely aggressive future CAFÉ standards. NHTSA's fleet-wide estimated required CAFÉ levels for passenger cars was to increase from around 40 in 2017 to over 55 mpg in 2025, with fleet-wide required CAFÉ levels for light trucks (a category that, to recall, includes SUVs) was to increase from 29 mpg in 2017 to over 39 mpg by 2025.[20]

Professor Freeman of Harvard Law School, who served as the Obama administration's climate head when it negotiated this automobile GHG emissions deal, has called it a "rather ingenious" way to set national policy.[21] Ingenious perhaps, but also an almost complete inversion of the actual bargain struck by Congress in the CAA. Throughout Section 202 of the Clean Air Act, Congress referred to the specific pollutants – such as carbon monoxide and nitrogen oxides – in auto exhaust that it wanted to reduce through the use of well-known technologies such as the catalytic converter. Virtually every member of Congress agreed to this regulatory system, because even by 1970, virtually every metropolitan area in the United States had a smog problem traceable to auto exhaust pollutants. California had the worst problem, and was allowed over the years to impose tougher requirements for cars sold in California. Congressional representatives from the small number of states that housed the auto industry were able to negotiate some delays in the timing of when that industry had to install the requisite known technologies, but that is about all they got.

Consider, by contrast, the 2009 auto GHG emission regulations. Those had already been adopted by a small minority of eleven states. No state or locality has or could ever have a localized GHG pollution problem – as described in more detail later, CO_2 is mixed throughout the troposphere. It directly causes no harm to humans. Based on congressional voting on the several failed bills that would have explicitly regulated GHG emissions, it seems clear that representatives in both chambers from the vast majority of states and districts would have voted against any piece of legislation that did what the 2009 federal auto GHG emissions regulations did. Only a small minority of eleven states viewed those regulations as generating net benefits. And yet their will prevailed. By adopting automobile GHG emission limits – in the form of enhanced fuel economy standards – by regulation, the Obama administration bypassed a democratic process that would have allowed a voice to those industries and regions of the country that viewed the cost of such standards as outweighing the benefits. This is the essence of precautionary policy.

V THE TAILPIPE RULE'S EXAGGERATED BENEFITS AND REGRESSIVE COSTS

In 2011, an economic study estimated that assuming average rates of technological progress, just to meet the 2016 Obama standard, consumers would have to curtail purchases of trucks and SUVs and buy small, high-mpg cars. The required change in car purchase behavior would be drastic, as the US car/truck mix would have to shift back to its 1980 level while the weight and power increases since 1980 would need to be cut by 25 percent. Without such drastic changes in buying behavior, with a constant car/truck mix, the weight and power gains that automakers had achieved would have to be cut by 50 percent (Knittel 2011).

This dire prediction did not account for the ability of carmakers to comply with tougher CAFÉ standards by increasing average model footprint. A study of the feasibility of manufacturers' meeting the ambitious Obama administration 2025 CAFÉ standards found that by increasing average vehicle footprint, six out of ten CAFÉ vehicle categories (or classes) could comply without any reduction in horsepower, and more generally that "increasing the footprint of their vehicles in production will make them less dependent on technological progress and require smaller changes to the existing characteristics of the fleet" (Ullman 2016, 100).

According to a comprehensive report by the EPA, only this final prediction – that footprint would increase – is borne out by the evidence. Footprint increased by about 2 percent between 2008 and 2017.[22] However, despite the 2010 tailpipe rule and the even more aggressive 2017–2025 CAFÉ standards promulgated in 2012, vehicle power and weight have increased. Between 2009 and 2017, the average horsepower increased, reaching 233 in 2017, its highest level since 1975, while at 4094 pounds, average weight in 2017 was the highest since 2004. At 48.3 percent, the truck production share of all vehicles produced was at its highest share since 1975. Similarly, 0 to 60 acceleration, a vehicle attribute highly valued by consumers, reached an all-time record, with an average 2017 acceleration (0 to 60 in 8 seconds) almost twice as fast as in 1975 (0 to 60 in 15.6 seconds).

All of these changes were made to meet consumer demand. The cost of meeting consumer demand was that even the 35.5 mpg CAFÉ standard that applied to model year 2016 for cars was not met. For 2017 sedans and wagons, the average fuel economy was only 30.3 mpg, while for 2017 car SUVs – a type that did not even exist until 1995 but which had over 11 percent of the market by 2017 – average fuel economy was only 26.2.[23] The failure to meet the CAFÉ standard was nothing new. According to DOT's Bureau of Transportation Statistics,[24] although by 2016 the CAFÉ standard for cars was at 37 mpg, versus 27.5 in 2006, the actual average mpg achieved by cars on the road in the US in 2016 was only 22.3 mpg versus 20.4 in 2006. Thus, a roughly 36 percent increase in the CAFÉ standard corresponded to a 10 percent increase in actual mpg on the road Although repeatedly falling short of the CAFÉ standard, fuel economy levels have steadily increased and are now the highest ever achieved. That automakers were able to achieve even these levels of fuel economy is testimony to technological progress. It has been estimated that over the 2011–2013 period, increasingly widespread use of turbocharged engines in particular led to annual gains in fuel efficiency of around 1.7 percent for cars and light trucks (Ullman 2016).

These gains were not free. The Obama administration 2012 CAFÉ standards are estimated to have cost between $15 and $30 billion (Metcalf 2019, 916–929). The costs are not imposed uniformly across all types of cars and trucks. If a car company sells more large footprint, large horsepower, and therefore poor mpg vehicles, it must sell an even greater number of small footprint, high mpg cars to be in compliance with CAFÉ standards and avoid paying fines. The prices of big footprint, low mpg cars and trucks therefore includes what amounts to a tax on poor mileage. The prices of small footprint, high mileage cars is lower than they would be without CAFÉ standards, because selling more above average mileage cars lowers the cost to a car company of meeting the CAFÉ standard. Another way to see this, modeled formally by Jacobsen (2013, 148–187), is that car companies lower the prices of high mpg cars that help them meet CAFÉ standards and increase the prices of low mpg cars.

Such price effects amount to a tax on inefficient, low mileage vehicles and a subsidy for efficient, high mileage vehicles (see Levinson 2016).[25] Davis and Knittel (2019) find subsidies as big as $395 for a 2012 Honda Civic 1.8 liter car and even bigger for some relatively high mileage trucks (e.g. the Chevy Silverado is found to get a $1,312 subsidy). With this pattern of subsidies and taxes, one would guess that the cost of tougher CAFÉ standards is primarily borne by wealthier consumers who tend to buy high performance luxury vehicles that are low mileage relative to their footprint. Davis and Knittel (2019) indeed find that when one takes into account how car and truck purchase choices vary with income, the average tax as a share of income increases with income, with the bottom 70 percent of car buyers by income actually getting a subsidy rather than paying a tax.

But this is just the market for new cars. As analyzed first by Jacobsen (2013), when the price of new cars increases, demand for new cars falls and consumers wait longer before buying a new car. This reduces the supply of used cars. As low income households buy more used cars (and vice versa with respect to new cars), the indirect effects of CAFÉ standards in reducing the supply and increasing the price of used cars is felt mainly by lower income households. When Davis and Knittel (2019) took account of the impact of CAFÉ standards on the used car market, they found that CAFÉ standards have a strongly regressive impact, effectively increasing car prices and taxing households in the bottom half of the income distribution, with very little impact on those in the top half. Davis and Knittel (2013) conclude that low income households experience a loss of welfare as a percent of income that is three times that suffered by high income households.

Looking more broadly at drivers and their passengers, it has long been known that the injury rate in a car collision is much lower for drivers and passengers of large, heavy vehicles than for drivers and passengers in smaller, lighter cars. (For example, at .043, the injury rate over the period 2002–2010 for a GMC Yukon 4WD vehicle was less than one-third of the injury rate for a Nissan Altima.[26]) Although large vehicles are safer for their own occupants, some studies find that they increase the harm suffered by the occupants of a smaller, lighter car involved in a collision.[27] Recent work finds that a CAFÉ standard may actually reduce fatal collisions by shifting the auto fleet away from large SUVs and other light trucks (Jacobsen 2011). Yet these findings generally do not control for crash rate, owner characteristics, distance driven, or type of heavy vehicle. When such factors are observed and controlled, some types of SUV have been found to have the lowest casualty rate of any vehicle (Keall and Newstead 2008, 954–963).

The largest and most high powered SUVs are precisely the types of vehicle whose price goes up the most due to CAFÉ standards and demand for which is concentrated among higher income households. In this way, on the margin, the CAFÉ standard puts wealthier households in heavy, high powered, fuel inefficient but safe vehicles, and poorer households in fuel efficient but smaller vehicles. On the margin, therefore, CAFÉ standards make the deadly big car–little car crashes stories where high income households are protected, and low income households are put at risk.

Notes

1. CAA § 209(b)(1), 42 USC. § 7543(b)(1) (2006) provides that state tailpipe emission standards are preempted by federal standards except for "any State which has adopted standards ... for the control of emissions from new motor vehicles or new motor vehicle engines prior to March 30, 1966 ..."
2. CAA § 209(b)(1)(B), 42 USC. § 7543(b)(1)(B).
3. For a very clear explanation of this process, see Chris Woodford, Catalytic converters, Explain that Stuff, available at https://www.explainthatstuff.com/catalyticconverters.html. Last updated: September 7, 2019.
4. Jacob Roberts, Clean Machine, Distillations, Jan. 12, 2015, available at https://www.sciencehistory.org/distillations/clean-machine.
5. 42 USC. §7521(a)(3)(A).
6. Pub. L. No. 94–163, 89 Stat. 871 (1975).
7. H.R. REP. NO. 94–340 at 1(1975), *reprinted in* 1975 USC.C.A.N. 1762, 1763.
8. 49 USC.A. § 32902(f).
9. Request for Comments; National Academy of Science Study and Future Fuel Economy Improvements, Model Years 2005–2010, 67 Fed Reg. at 5768.
10. See Statista, Global EBIT of BMW Group from 2006 to 2018 (in million Euros), available at https://www.statista.com/statistics/264344/global-ebit-of-bmw-group-since-2006/.
11. See, for example, Klier and Linn (2012, 204–205); Jacobsen (2013, 174–175).
12. For details on and estimates of the quantitative significance of various technologies that allowed carmakers to shift the technological relationships between weight and fuel economy and horsepower and fuel economy, see Knittel (2011, 3373–3386).
13. US National Highway and Traffic Safety Administration, 2006. Average Fuel Economy Standards for Light Trucks, Model Years 2008–2011. Federal Register 49 CFR 523–537, May 22.
14. DieselNet, California: Light Duty Vehicles: GHG Emissions 2009–2016, available at https://www.dieselnet.com/standards/us/ca_ghg.php, "(1) for passenger car/light-duty truck 1 (PC/LDT1) category, including passenger cars and

light-duty trucks below 3,750 lbs equivalent test weight (ETW); and (2) for light-duty truck 2 (LDT2) category, including light trucks between 3,751 lbs ETW and 8,500 lbs gross vehicle weight (GVW). In addition, medium-duty passenger vehicles (MDPVs) from 8,500 to 10,000 lbs GVW were included in the LDT2 category for GHG emission standards."

15. For a list of some such suits, see Freeman (2011, 358, n. 107).
16. Peter Weber, The US auto bailout is officially over. Here's what America lost and gained, The Week, Dec. 10, 2013, available at https://theweek.com/articles/454749/auto-bailout-officially-over-heres-what-america-lost-gained.
17. My description of the terms of this deal is drawn from Freeman (2011, 362–365).
18. EPA and NHTSA, Light-Duty Vehicle Greenhouse Gas Emission Standards and Corporate Average Fuel Economy Standards; Final Rule, 75 Federal Register 25324 (May 7, 2010).
19. EPA and NHTSA, 2017 and Later Model Year Light-Duty Vehicle Greenhouse Gas Emissions and Corporate Average Fuel Economy Standards; Final Rule, 77 Federal Register 62624 (October 15, 2012).
20. EPA and NHTSA, 2017 and Later Model Year Light-Duty Vehicle Greenhouse Gas Emissions and Corporate Average Fuel Economy Standards, supra at 62639.
21. Freeman (2011, 365).
22. EPA, The 2018 EPA Automotive Trends Report: Greenhouse Gas Emissions, Fuel Economy, and Technology Since 1975, p. 32, EPA-420-R-19–002 (March, 2019).
23. EPA, The 2018 EPA Automotive Trends Report at 33.
24. DOT, Bureau of Transportation Statistics, Average Fuel Efficiency of Light Duty Vehicles, available at https://www.bts.gov/content/average-fuel-efficiency-us-light-duty-vehicles.
25. Arik Levinson, Energy Efficiency Standards are more Regressive than Energy Taxes, NBER Working Paper No. 22956, December, 2016, available at http://www.nber.org/papers/w22956.
26. 28 (10) Highway Loss Data Institute Bulletin, Injury Odds and Vehicle Weight Comparison of Hybrids and Conventional Counterparts (Sept. 2011).
27. See the discussion in Jacobsen (2011, 105–109).

5

"It Will Bankrupt You" – Using Environmental Regulations to End the Mining and Use of Coal in America

In early 2008, then-presidential candidate Barack Obama described his climate change regulatory agenda by saying that "if somebody wants to build a coal-fired [electricity generating] plant they can. It's just that it will bankrupt them."[1] After his election, President Obama made good on his promise.

The Obama administration conducted a multi-pronged assault on the use of coal in America. This assault had the clear goal of ending the mining and use of coal: a ban on coal, the classic precautionary response to a triggering risk. This assault consisted of two prongs. The first prong attacked coal-burning power plants indirectly by promulgating regulations to drive up the cost of mining coal. Most significant among these was a new occupational safety and health rule requiring that coal miners be given costly real-time monitors of their exposure to coal dust. The second prong of the Obama administration assault on coal involved a direct attack on coal-burning power plants. Primarily, this regulatory effort took the form of wide-ranging regulatory action under the CAA. While regulations requiring targeting CO_2 emissions from coal-burning power plants were the core element, by targeting other kinds of air pollution from coal-burning plants, in particular mercury, additional CAA regulations drove up the costs of coal-burning plants even higher.

In this chapter, I describe the first part of the Obama-era assault on coal. This part of the Obama-era program did not go after GHG emissions directly. Instead, a variety of regulations were promulgated, under a variety of statutes including but not limited to the CAA, all of which increased the cost of coal mining and burning coal to generate electricity. These regulations had several things in common: the benefits they generated were highly speculative; the methods by which benefits were estimated would likely never have withstood serious critical inquiry had they ever been subjected to such; and many actual costs such as lost jobs are the kind of costs that the EPA simply does not attempt to quantify.

This chapter opens up the hood, as it were, and gets into substantial detail regarding what the EPA's technical documents said about the costs and benefits of its regulations. I compare what the EPA said not only to what the regulated industries said in litigating against such regulations at the time, but to other evidence that was available at the time that the EPA promulgated its regulations or which has become available since. Not only did the EPA consistently and substantially underestimate the costs and overstate the benefits of its regulations, but in some cases – such as with its rule targeting mercury emissions from coal-burning power plants – the EPA argued that it did not even need to *consider* the costs of its regulations. These costs, however, included the permanent loss of tens of thousands of high-paying jobs, a loss that was regionally concentrated and which was catastrophic to many local economies. Economic work has established that permanent job loss causes permanent harm, not only in the form of reduced lifetime earnings but in the form of reduced life expectancy. That the EPA did not even consider such harm, and indeed tried to avoid any consideration of any costs of its mercury emissions reduction rule, is a stark illustration of the policy bias generated by the precautionary principle's focus only on one kind of risk and one kind of harm. While one might have hoped that some other institution – perhaps the federal courts – would have forced the EPA into a more balanced deliberation, this did not occur. The courts overruled only the EPA's most obviously absurd legal interpretations of the statutes under which it promulgated regulations. The courts consistently failed to conduct even the most superficial audit of the technical basis for the EPA's regulations, thus ensuring that only one side of the story – the EPA's – would influence the design of precautionary regulation.

I OBAMA-ERA REGULATIONS TARGETING COAL MINING

A *Ending Mountaintop Mining*

I begin with the Stream Protection Rule, a regulation promulgated by the Office of Surface Mining (OSM) within the Department of Interior during the dying days of the Obama administration in late 2016. The Stream Protection Rule required that during mountaintop and other surface mining, costly steps were to be taken to ensure that nearby streams were not polluted, and after such mining, the mountaintop be restored essentially to the same topographic and vegetative state it had started with. Mountaintop mining involves quite literally blasting off the entire top of a mountain in order to get at coal buried up to 400 feet underneath the surface. The monitoring and reclamation required by the Obama administration rule was generally understood to be sufficiently costly that if enforced, it would have ended mountaintop mining, especially by smaller mine operators in central Appalachia (West Virginia, Ohio, and Kentucky).[2] It was rescinded in February, 2017 by bicameral vote of Congress under the Congressional Review Act.

The Stream Protection Rule was never enforced, but it is worth discussing, albeit briefly, as it illustrates a pattern in the Obama-era EPA regulations targeting coal that we shall see in much more drastic form with some of the regulations affecting coal-burning power plants. The Stream Protection Rule would have effectively banned mountaintop mining. This is something that some environmental groups had long sought. But Congress never banned mountaintop mining. Instead, the EPA banned mountaintop mining, and it did so by promulgating a rule whose benefits were barely quantified, and whose costs seem to have been greatly underestimated.

As for the benefits, the Obama-era OSM itself estimated that the primary benefit of the rule in Appalachia – to preserve and enhance streams damaged by mountaintop mining – was small indeed, as only 174 stream miles out of a total of 126,000 stream miles in Appalachia would have improved stream water quality due to the rule.[3] To improve these 174 miles of stream – a bit more than 1/1000th of total Appalachian stream miles – the OSM estimated that over the 2020–2040 study period, surface mines in Appalachia would incur annual costs of $26 million, or roughly 32 percent of the $81 million cost estimated to be incurred by all US coal mines.[4] It should be noted that this $26 million was calculated using a 7 percent discount rate. I shall explain such discount rates in more detail in a later chapter, but for present purposes what is key to see is that using a 7 percent discount rate, $1 in compliance costs incurred in, for example, 10 years, only counts as about $0.44. Using a more realistic discount rate, such as 3 percent, the annual compliance cost of the Stream Protection Rule to Appalachian coal mines would have been around $50 million. Over the 20 year period that OSM used to calculate the impacts of the rule, these realistically discounted costs would total about $1 billion.

According to OSM, the rule would cost Appalachian mine workers as many as 500 jobs and $21 million in income in any given year, but averaged over the entire 20 year period and discounted at the high rate of 7 percent, this would average out to only a loss of 77 jobs and over $6 million per year. Again, with a more realistic discount rate, the average income loss would be over $10 million per year, or about $200 million over the 20 year period.

Despite this, according to OSM, the net effect of the rule on employment would be strongly positive – to the tune of 143 jobs and $12 million in income – because the rule would actually create new jobs in surface and stream reclamation and improvement.

B *The Coal Dust Rule*

In May, 2014, the Labor Department's Mine Safety and Health Administration (MSHA) promulgated a new rule that lowered the permitted level of coal dust in mines from 2.0 to 1.5 milligrams per cubic meter of air (mg/m^3) and required that coal mine operators use a brand new air sampling device to sample the level of coal dust at mines much more frequently than had been previously required.[5] Under the rule, the new device would sample the air surrounding a miner for an entire working shift, which typically lasted 10 hours rather than the 8 hours previously assumed by the MSHA. Mine operators would be cited for violations and required to take corrective action if a single sample during a single shift measured above the

1.5 mg/m^3 standard. Such actions to fix the problem would be deemed adequate by the MSHA only if and when the mine operator produced five valid samples that complied with the standard and MSHA approved new dust control measures at the mine, which would become permanent obligations of the mine.

According to the MSHA, by providing continuous, real-time measurements of coal dust, the rule requiring the new device – called a "continuous personal dust monitor" or CPDM – would allow mine operators to "make immediate adjustments... to suppress, divert, or capture the generated dust."[6] The MSHA noted that the "vast majority of miners' exposures" were below the new standard, but for those mines that were found to be out of compliance, mine operators would lower the level of coal dust to exactly the required standard of 1 mg/m^3.[7] As up to 70 percent of air samples for one type of mine – longwall tailgate – were above the new standard, the MSHA estimated that up to 102 cases of black lung (coal worker pneumoconiosis or CWP) per 1000 miners working 45 years in such a mine would be prevented by age 73.[8] In dollar terms, the MSHA estimated annual average benefits for miners in all types of coal mines of between $128 million and $158 million.[9]

Even for underground mines, these benefits swamped the $36–40 million annual average discounted cost of the rule estimated by the MSHA. The vast majority, $25 million, of this cost to underground mines came from buying and using the new CPDM sampling devices. By contrast, MSHA estimated that the cost of fixing violations averaged only $300,000.

The coal industry vigorously disputed these figures. Rather than a seemingly minor change aimed at more accurate monitoring of coal dust levels in mines, industry argued that the Coal Dust Rule was a major change that would entail hugely expensive changes to mine operations. It was undisputed by either the industry or the agency that for decades, compliance was determined by the measurements taken bimonthly in five monthly samples from a particular mine occupation and one from a particular location. If the average of the samples for the occupation or the single location sample exceeded the dust standard, then the mine operator was cited for a violation and required to fix (abate) the violation.[10] The new rule would base compliance on the real-time measurement during a single sample over a work shift.

Industry outside experts reported that because dust concentrations vary randomly over the course of a typical mining shift day, to ensure that they were always in compliance – which now would be measured continuously – mine operators would need to install costly engineering controls to get dust levels down to .4 (40 percent) of the new legal limit.[11] MSHA's own sampling data revealed random variability in dust levels at a specific location over the course of a workday, and it recognized "that ventilation currents found in mines can produce widely varying results or seemingly poor precision between two identical side-by-side instruments."[12] The agency ignored these known facts and simply assumed – with no explanation – that mines could somehow get their dust levels down to precisely the new standard of 1 mg/m^3.

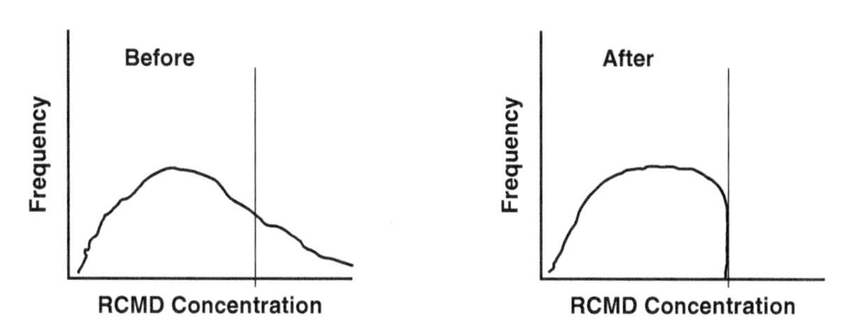

FIGURE 5.1. EPA Assumed No Overcompliance with the New Coal Dust Rule

The actual graphical depiction of this assumption presented by the agency in justifying its final rule is reproduced above:[13]

To anyone at all familiar with any type of pollution control, the MSHA's Figure III-2 (Figure 5.1 above) will be shocking. Even the best pollution control technologies cannot produce a distribution of actual observed pollution levels that truncates at a particular value, as does the right hand panel in Figure 3.1. Of course, the MSHA never said that such a distribution of actual levels was really possible. The agency just assumed that this was true, and in fact confessed that this assumption was "artificial and extremely conservative" and was "deliberately designed to avoid overestimating the effect of applying a single sample exposure to every individual shift [precisely what the rule does], in the absence of any data establishing what the effects would actually be."[14] In other words, with no data, the agency simply assumed that mines could easily and cheaply perfectly comply with the new rule.

As for the cost of correcting violations, the MSHA relied again simply on an assumption, in this case that mine operators could rectify excessive coal dust levels at particular locations "during the shift, between shifts, or an maintenance shifts" without any "delay in production." According to the industry experts, far from being a such minor problem, to be corrected even between shifts, mine operations would sometimes be shut down in order to fix coal dust violations at particular locations. An industry expert estimated that the cost of delayed production caused by the need to correct a single sample showing dust levels above the standard would be "$1.6 billion in early years of the rule, declining in later years but still reaching $221 million per year."[15] By contrast, MSHA assumed that the total cost to underground mine operators of abating violations of the standard would be only $300,000.[16] Thus the agency's abatement cost estimate was a little more than 1/1000th of just one component of abatement cost as estimated by the mining company's expert. While one expects differences between the cost estimates of an agency and an industry it regulates, differences on this level – three orders of magnitude – lend credence to the mining industry's characterization of the Coal Dust Rule as based on so many "wishful assumptions" as to amount to assuming an "alternate reality" completely at odds with the actual economic and operational reality faced by coal mine operators.

The mining industry provided crucial background facts, completely omitted by the MSHA, that suggested the benefits of the Coal Dust Rule were completely illusory.[17] Murray Mining called the agency's attention to a study it commissioned of the epidemiological evidence MSHA had relied on in crafting the Coal Dust Rule. The study was done by three experts in black lung disease, all of whom were senior officials at the National Institute for Occupational Safety and Health (NIOSH) when NIOSH developed its own black lung program.[18] NIOSH's own 40-Year Review of black lung disease noted that the disease was much more prevalent in central Appalachia than in any other coal mining region, but also found that "the increased prevalence [of what was believed to be black lung disease] was not explained by the measured levels of dust exposures." As for what did explain the higher prevalence of black lung in central Appalachia, it is known that many central Appalachian miners work in small, confined mines where they cut a lot of silica-containing quartz rock. One of the authors of the Critical Review commissioned by Murray, Robert Glenn, former director of NIOSH's Division of Respiratory Disease Studies, opined that "the far likelier cause of the observed illnesses in the studied miner populations was silicosis," not black lung.

If this is true, then the Coal Dust Rule likely has zero benefits. Defying the most basic obligation of a federal regulatory agency, despite the fact that the coal industry raised these crucial points during the comment period on the proposed rule, the MSHA completely failed to respond to them. When the industry challenged the final Coal Dust Rule before the Eleventh Circuit in *American Mining Congress v. MSHA*,[19] that court completely failed to seriously consider the mining industry's core objections to the rule. Recall that the industry argued that when the new, lower 1 mg/m^3 standard was combined with continuous, one shift testing for violations, violations would be frequent just because of random variations in the concentration of coal dust at different mine locations and could only be eliminated with costly engineering fixes that lowered the average level far below the standard. The court's response to this was a non-response. It quoted an earlier opinion to the effect that there was "no perfect sampling method," and stated that "MSHA's rule reflects knowledge of this imperfection, as well as a detailed understanding of improvements – both technological and in the standards for collection by operators – that make single-shift sampling sufficiently 'accurate' as to satisfy the statutory standard."[20] Whether or not deliberate, this completely mischaracterizes the mining industry's objection to the new single shift sampling rule. That objection was not that the new sampling was not accurate, but that random variations in the level of coal dust in air are inevitable and taking a single reading during a single shift as evidence of a violation was nonsensical.

That the Eleventh Circuit would not seriously consider the industry's objections was an inevitable consequence of its decision to adopt an extremely deferential standard in reviewing the mining agency's regulation. At the outset of its opinion, the court clearly stated that "We do not sit in judgment of what evidence is indeed 'best' or whether the proposed rule is 'feasible' under the statute." Instead, the court explained, "we believe it appropriate to 'give an extreme degree of deference to the agency when it is evaluating scientific data within its technical expertise.'"[21] The court quoted an old Supreme Court opinion[22] for the proposition that "when specialists express conflicting views, an agency must have discretion to rely on the reasonable opinions of its own qualified experts even if, as an original matter, a court might find contrary views more persuasive." Under this deferential standard, it was enough for the MSHA to assert that the Coal Dust Rule was feasible and had benefits. The court uncritically accepted this assertion.

One might think that when Congress passed the Administrative Procedures Act in 1947 and specifically said that agency regulations can be reviewed by the federal courts, it did so because courts would actually fully assess objections to such regulations, rather than simply accept whatever the agency said. The Eleventh Circuit offered two justifications for the extreme deference it gave to the MSHA. First, that court said, if it was not so deferential, then it would put itself in the "unenviable – and legally untenable – position of making for itself judgments entrusted by Congress to MSHA." I consider this argument in a bit more detail later in this part, but the fundamental objection can be put quite simply: if Congress wanted agencies such as MSHA to have unbridled discretion in making regulatory judgments then it could have written the courts completely out of the process, rather than writing them into it, as is the explicit point of the Administrative Procedure Act.

Perhaps aware that it had gone too far in saying that Congress had given the MSHA completely unreviewable discretion, the Eleventh Circuit ended up relying squarely on the precautionary principle to justify its decision to accept whatever the agency said about the Coal Dust Rule. The court said that "the Mine Act evinces a clear bias in favor of miner health and safety." As the court continued, the agency's "duty to use the best evidence and to consider feasibility are appropriately viewed through this lens and cannot be wielded as counterweight to MSHA's overarching role to protect the life and health of workers in the mining industry."[23] In other words, by invoking the precautionary words that its rule was necessary to protect "miner health and safety," the MSHA got a free pass on whether or not the evidence supporting the rule was credible and whether the rule was even feasible.

By adding to the costs of mine operators, the Coal Dust Rule was a small piece of the Obama-era attack on coal. In this way, the rule indirectly helped the provider of the coal-fired power substitute, the renewable power industry. But there was a much more direct winner from the Coal Dust Rule: Thermo Fisher Scientific, the company that owned the propriety technology that provided the basis for the new CPMD monitors required by the MSHA. That company had a very active regulatory cheerleading squad, bureaucrats within the very same National Institute of Occupational Safety and Health (NIOSH).

As we have just seen, NIOSH issued reports on coal dust and black lung disease. But it did much more than simply study coal dust and black lung. The NIOSH blog bemoans[24] that "until recently, underground coal miners and mine operators had little way of knowing – in real time – if miners were being exposed to hazardous levels of respirable coal dust during their shifts." Such real-time knowledge would matter very much if miners got black lung from short periods of exposure to high levels of coal dust. But that isn't how black lung works. It is a chronic condition, caused by years and years of breathing in coal dust in mines. In this light, it is not clear why NIOSH, a supposedly expert agency, was so worried about the inadequacy of five-day samples taken at different points in a year. But there has to be some problem that justified what NIOSH then reports, its "collaboration" with an "instrument manufacturer" to develop the CPDM, a device that would reduce from weeks "to minutes" the process of reporting coal mine dust violations to the MSHA. The device was not generic, but rather highly specific, "the PDM3700, a certified and commercially available CPDM... based on a proprietary technology known as the tapered element oscillating microbalance (TEOM) originally developed as a fixed-site environmental particulate mass monitor by Rupprecht and Patashnick Co., Inc., Albany, NY" but then adapted to "smaller sampling devices that could be worn safely underground" by NIOSH, working in collaboration with Thermo Fisher Scientific, the successor company of the Albany, New York firm that invented the underlying technology.

Thermo Fisher Scientific is a publicly traded company with a market capitalization of about $51 billion in 2014 that has since risen to over $140 billion. Back in 2014, on its website, Thermo Fisher praised both NIOSH and the MSHA as "continually developing programs to identify risks, monitor dust levels, and implement strategies and technologies to reduce exposure" to coal dust.[25] It then explained how it had been working with NIOSH for 16 years to develop the CPDM, justifying the device as a response to evidence that "following a long decline... CWP [black lung] is on the rise in certain areas of the United States." Here, Thermo Fisher's blog for its new product almost perfectly echoed the MSHA in defense of mandating the use of Thermo Fisher's new product, including the agency's indifference to evidence that any increase in black lung had been confined to Appalachian mines and seemed uncorrelated with coal dust levels. But the precautionary principle imposes few if any evidentiary requirements. All one needs is a possible risk and a political or economic winner from risk regulation, and in Thermo Fisher Scientific, the MSHA found a big, powerful firm that was a clear winner from regulations requiring use of the CPDM.

II USING THE CLEAN AIR ACT TO INCREASE THE COSTS OF COAL-FIRED ELECTRIC POWER

The Endangerment Finding made legally possible the Obama EPA's regulations cutting GHG emissions under the CAA. Those regulations, culminating in the Clean Power Plan of 2015, were central to that agency's attack on coal-fired power plants. But they were not the only regulatory sticks aimed at coal that the Obama EPA promulgated under the authority of the CAA. Before explaining in some detail the many serious harms threatened by the Clean Power Plan, I briefly discuss two early Obama EPA regulatory initiatives that together significantly added to the cost of generating electricity from coal. While my main focus is the Obama EPA's regulation designed to cut mercury emissions from power plants, I begin with an economically less significant prelude, regulations justifying additional spending to reduce air pollution from power plants by the need to reduce interstate air pollution.

The Obama EPA began its assault on coal under the CAA by responding to a court decision leaving in place but ordering some changes in the George W. Bush EPA's attempt to deal with the problem of interstate ozone pollution as required by the so-called good neighbor provision of the CAA. To recall, that provision requires states to impose additional pollution reductions on those plants whose emissions are "contributing significantly" to the inability of downwind states to meet national ambient air quality standards. By the early 2000s, the EPA had identified oxides of nitrogen and sulfur dioxide emissions from power plants in the midwestern and eastern regions of the United States as significant contributors to the failure of eastern US states to meet the air quality standards for, respectively, ozone and fine dust particles (fine particulates). The George W. Bush administration (hereafter referred to as the Bush administration) came up with a new, market-based approach to achieving additional reductions in these pollutants sufficient to improve air quality in downwind states. This program was called the Clean Air Interstate Rule (CAIR).

CAIR was intended to generate additional reductions in two main air pollutants, oxides of nitrogen and sulfur dioxide. I say additional reductions because the reduction of sulfur dioxide (SO_2) and oxides of nitrogen (NO_x) has been a primary goal of the CAA from the beginning. By 2005, when the Bush administration promulgated CAIR, the technologies for reducing both SO_2 and NO_x pollution from coal-burning power plants were well established. Given that a major objective of the Obama EPA was to require increasing use of such expensive pollution reduction technologies, it is important to briefly explain why coal combustion generates so much pollution and how these technologies work.

Coal consists of pulverized and pressurized decayed remnants of plants that grew millions and millions of years ago. It is a relatively dirty source of energy. To put it more objectively, coal is chemically complex. It consists not only of carbon, but also hydrogen, oxygen, nitrogen, and sulfur and a variety of other elements found in the ancient forest floors where coal was formed. Because coal is so complex, a variety of by-products result when coal is burned. By-products include hydrogen, ammonia, sulfur dioxide, carbon monoxide, benzene, and other hydrocarbon gases. Other elements that coal contains, such as mercury, aluminum, and arsenic, adhere to the fine particles of fly ash that is created when coal is burned.[26] Trace amounts of other elements found in coal, such as chlorine and fluorine, combine with hydrogen during coal combustion to form similarly tiny amounts of hydrogen fluoride and hydrogen chloride gases.

Electrostatic precipitators are a very old way to get suspended particles out of the exhaust gas from combustion processes. They were patented in the United States in 1908 and first used on a large commercial scale in 1910 to collect lead and zinc oxide fumes at the Balaklala smelter in northern California (White 1957, 168). Electrostatic precipitators work by passing dirty exhaust (or flue) gas in a factory smokestack first over a highly negatively charged metal plate and then over a highly positively charged plate. As opposite charges attract, after becoming negatively charged, particles in the flue gas are attracted to and stick to the positively charged plates. The particles are then cleaned off the positively charged plates.

Baghouses are another means of eliminating particulate or dust pollution from coal combustion. They are also used to remove dust from the exhaust emitted by a whole range of other industrial processes in a variety of industries ranging from pharmaceutical manufacture to food processing. Baghouses work by passing exhaust gas up through long, cylindrical bags made out of special fabric engineered to withstand very high temperatures. Particles accumulate on the fabric and then are shaken or blown off.

Electrostatic precipitators and baghouses remove particles. Sulfur dioxide and other acid gases are removed from power plant exhaust via a process known as flue gas desulfurization (FGD), also called scrubbing. So-called wet scrubbing involves spraying sulfur dioxide-laden flue gases with a wet, highly alkaline limestone slurry solution in an absorber unit. The slurry solution reacts with the sulfur dioxide to produce CO_2 and gypsum, which can be sold. By the mid-2000s, about 85 percent of the scrubbers installed in the United States used this wet scrubbing process.[27] Wet scrubber technology is highly effective. The Obama EPA reported in 2011 that such technology can remove 96 percent of SO_2 and at least 99 percent of other acid gases emitted by coal-burning plants, such hydrogen fluoride.[28]

An alternative to scrubbing for removing SO_2 is a process called dry sorbent injection (DSI). In the DSI process, an alkaline powdered material (such as calcium carbonate) is injected into the exhaust gas stream. It reacts with SO_2 and other acid gases, yielding a particulate product that can then be removed either by an electrostatic precipitator or a baghouse.

Another pollutant generated by coal combustion are various oxides of nitrogen (NO_x). Through a relatively complex chain of chemical reactions, in the presence of sunlight, such oxides of nitrogen interact with volatile organic compounds (various hydrocarbons) to form ground level (tropospheric) ozone.[29] They are therefore called ozone precursors. Coal combustion generates NO_x emissions as a by-product because there is nitrogen both in the coal and in air. NO_x emissions from coal-fired power plants can be cut by altering the combustion process itself (as by super-heating the air) or by installing systems that reduce NO_x from the combustion exhaust gases. The most common such system is called selective catalytic reduction (or SCR). In SCR, ammonia is injected into the flue gas where it combines with NO_x and a catalyst to form water and nitrogen. SCR systems can reduce NO_x levels by 90 percent (compared to only 40 percent for selective noncatalytic reduction), lowering NO_x emission rates to under 0.01 lbs/mmBtu.[30]

By targeting about 3000 (mostly) coal-fired power plants, the Bush CAIR aimed to reduce annual SO_2 emissions in 23 states and seasonal NO_x emissions in 25 states by very large amounts, respectively 73 percent for SO_2 and 61 percent for NO_x (from 2003 levels). The EPA projected that these large pollution reductions were to be accomplished primarily through the installation of new pollution control equipment: by 2015, 64 GW of scrubbers for SO_2 control and an additional 34 GW of selective catalytic reduction technology (SCR) on existing coal-fired generation capacity for NO_x control.

To put these numbers into perspective, and to provide information for future discussions about electricity in this book, note that a gigawatt (GW) of electric power is 1000 megawatts (MW), which in turn is equal to 1000 kilowatts (KW). An average US household consumes about 12,000 KW hours (KWh) of electricity per year. Dividing out the 8760 hours of the year (24 x 365), the average household consumes all the electricity produced by a 1.4 KW power plant producing at 100 percent capacity 24 hours a day 365 days a year. Scaling up, a 1.4 MW power plant produces enough power for 1000 average US households, and a 1.4 GW plant (again producing at 100 percent of capacity 24 hours a day 365 days a year) produces enough power for 1,000,000 households. Hence when the EPA said that the Bush CAIR would lead to the installation of new scrubbers on 64 GW worth of power and 34 GW worth of new selective catalytic reduction, it was saying that the CAIR rule would cause the installation of new pollution reduction equipment on plants providing electricity to tens of millions of US households.

Such additional control would, the EPA projected, cost \$2.4 billion in 2010 and another \$3.6 billion in 2015.[31] The EPA cautioned that these cost estimates were likely too high, because the Bush administration's CAIR allowed power plants to comply with new pollution reduction requirements by buying pollution permits from other plants. CAIR built on tradeable pollution permit regimes for both SO_2 and NO_x that were already in place. For NO_x, back in 1998, in what was called the "NO_x SIP call," the EPA had capped power plant NO_x emissions in certain upwind states, but had allowed states within the upwind, polluting region to trade permits to emit.[32] The NO_x trading program required 21 eastern states to submit plans to reduce their NO_x emissions from more than 2,500 plants (Schmalensee and Stavins 2017, 65). The NO_x trading program was challenged in court, primarily on the ground that in determining which plants in upwind states were "significant" contributors to downwind state pollution problems and so had to meet the new NO_x cap, the EPA had illegally considered the cost of reducing NO_x emissions.

The courts did not strike down the NO_x regional trading program.[33] The program was highly effective, with 99 percent of the plants complying and regional NO_x

emissions falling by about 74 percent (from around 1.9 million tons in 1990 to less than 500,000 tons by 2006). It was also highly efficient, as abatement costs over the 1999– 2003 period were estimated to be only 40 to 47 percent of what they would have been under a conventional regulatory regime that did not allow trading or banking (Schmalensee and Stavins [2017, 65]).

In Title IV of the CAA, Congress created the more well-known cap and trade program, for acid rain–causing SO_2 emissions. Title IV's tradeable permit regime set national and plant-specific caps on power sector SO_2 emissions. The caps declined over time, and applied beginning in 1995 to the biggest 236 coal-burning plants and to all 3,200 fossil fuel–fired power plants in the United States by the year 2000 (Schmalensee and Stavins 2017, 61–63). If one looks online, one can still see today (in Table A of Section 404 of Title IV), the facility-specific SO_2 limits that were to be met by 1995 (so-called Phase I limits). For example, in the state of Georgia, Section 404 listed five plants, each with a specified number of generating units and SO_2 emission limits for each generating unit. Title IV gave great flexibility to power plants in determining how to meet the cap. They could burn low sulfur coal from the western United States, install scrubbers, or buy permits to emit SO_2 from plants that had reduced their emissions even below their caps.

As explained in Schmalensee and Stavins (2017), economists have long known that such tradeable pollution permit schemes are the most efficient way to achieve any given level of aggregate pollution reduction. Title IV was both highly effective and efficient. Between 1990 and 2004, a period when electricity generation from coal-fired plants increased by 25 percent, SO_2 emissions from fossil-fuel fired power plants decreased 36 percent. These large SO_2 reductions were achieved at a cost estimated to be between 15 percent and 90 percent lower than they would have been under regulations requiring the installation of pollution control technologies. Schmalensee and Stavins (2017, 62).

Under the Title IV program, power plants were allowed to save (or "bank") pollution permits that they had not needed to use because they cut their SO_2 emissions by more than the law required. The Bush administration's CAIR cut the number of such banked allowances that could be used (by 50 percent in 2010 and 65 percent in 2015), but even with these reduced numbers, the EPA expected that the use of banked allowances to comply with CAIR's emission reduction goals would be a "significant compliance strategy." It was for this reason that the EPA said that its estimation of the cost to power plants of complying with CAIR was likely an overestimate.[34]

At the state level, one can think of the winners and losers from CAIR as consisting of three groups. First are upwind states in the midwestern area, exemplified by Missouri, Arkansas, Texas, and also Illinois, Indiana, and Ohio. For such states, the additional reductions in SO_2 and NO_x required by CAIR imposed costs on their utilities, passed on to their citizens, with small benefits. Next are states such as Pennsylvania, Georgia, and Virginia. CAIR imposed costs on some power producers and consumers in such states but may also have generated benefits to people living in the eastern portions of the state. The final group are mid-Atlantic and northeastern states running from North Carolina to Maine. For these states, CAIR imposed few costly new pollution reduction requirements while conferring the benefit of reductions in SO_2 and NO_x generated in upwind states.

In *North Carolina* v. *EPA*,[35] a group of downwind states and environmental groups brought suit alleging that CAIR did not do enough to reduce SO_2 and NO_x emissions. The court agreed, holding essentially that the regional trading program allowed by CAIR did not ensure sufficient pollution reduction in every upwind polluting state whose plants "contributed significantly" to pollution problems of downwind states. This holding, of course, would have invalidated the entire NO_x trading program. It thus represented an interpretation of "contributed significantly" that while straightforward enough – "contribute significantly" seems to require regulation of upwind pollution that causes significant pollution problems downwind, no matter how costly it might be to reduce such pollution – struck at the heart of a very effective program. Perhaps recognizing this, the *North Carolina* v. *EPA* court left the CAIR program in place, but ordered the EPA to fix it.

This the Obama administration did with startling and arguably illegal alacrity.[36] As recounted by the American Bar Association, in August, 2010, the Obama EPA published its 1,300 page redo of CAIR (a rule called the Cross State Air Pollution Rule, or CSAPR, and then simply the Transport Rule). The 1,300 page rule was accompanied by thousands of pages of technical support documents that set out the various quantitative models of key things such as how pollutants are transported downwind. During the sixty day comment period, the EPA announced and made three revisions to such key models, and also changed its methods for allocating pollution permits to individual plants under the program. All of these changes affected the pollution caps that applied to upwind states and plants, often substantially reducing – toughening – their pollution caps, sometimes indeed cutting them in half. As a result of the changes the EPA made, some states, such as Texas, were included in programs that they were not even in in the proposed rule.

The EPA did not follow standard – and likely legally required – practice by issuing a supplemental proposed rule showing these impacts. It didn't even agree to extend the comment period, as requested by dozens of parties, including several upwind states. Yet so frenzied was the EPA's pace that such additional time might well not have mattered, because the same day that the EPA issued the final rule, it also issued a proposal to revise it by expanding the number of states required to reduce their plants' summer season NO_x reductions. In October 2011, the EPA said it would need to revise the rule further to fix errors in pollution caps caused by errors in its underlying data and modelling assumptions. Without such fixes having even been finalized, the EPA required that its new SO_2 and NO_x emission reduction requirements would take effect January 1, 2012, less than five months after publication of the final rule (with the summertime ozone NO_x reductions required by May, 2012).

In the CAA, the good neighbor provision is addressed to states. It tells the EPA that in their own pollution reduction plans, the states must ensure that they reduce pollution that is significantly contributing to pollution problems in downwind states. As a fallback, the EPA can promulgate its own plan for a state (called a Federal Implementation Plan) if the state fails to come up with a plan that meets with EPA approval. In the case of its Transport Rule, the EPA skipped the first step, issuing the regulations replacing CAIR as a federal plan without first giving the states an opportunity to design their own plans. The EPA determined everything: the pollution reduction necessary not only for each state but for every plant within each state. As we will see, this centralized approach was a harbinger of things to come, for when it came time to officially and explicitly end coal-burning power plants with its Clean Power Plan, the Obama EPA simply paid no respect to principles of federalism, overwhelming state authority rather than trying to use state expertise to design smart and efficient regulation.

However rushed and arguably illegal the process by which it promulgated its federal plan for reducing interstate SO_2 and NO_x pollution, the EPA defended its rule as continuing steps already taken under CAIR.[37] In the short run, meaning 2012, NO_x emissions would fall, the EPA said, primarily because selective catalytic reduction (SCR) would be run year round, instead of just during the summertime ozone season. Also by 2012, the Transport Rule – as CSAPR was called in its final incarnation – would cause additional reductions in SO_2 and other fine particulate emissions by requiring the "sustained operation" of all existing scrubbers, some of which might not operate without its new rule. As for the longer term, the EPA said that by 2014 SO_2 emissions would fall even more because its rule would cause plants in states that would not otherwise have been regulated to install 5.9 GW of new FGD and 3 GW of new dry sorbent injection (DSI). Even in 2014, however, the EPA said that most of the reduction in SO_2 and NO_x would occur because equipment already required by CAIR would be operated more often (25 GW of scrubbers for SO_2 reduction and the year-round operation of an additional 5 GW of selective catalytic reduction technology [SCR] for NO_x control on existing coal-fired generation capacity).

In light of the relatively marginal impact of the Transport Rule relative to CAIR, the EPA unsurprisingly predicted that the Rule would have very small impact on employment in the electric power industry. Using a model, Morgenstern et al. (2002), that I discuss in some detail below, the EPA said that Transport Rule would lead to an expected *increase* of 700 jobs in coal-fired power plants, but this was not statistically significant as the 95 percent confidence interval ranged from -1,000 to +3,000.[38] That is, using the Morgenstern et al. (2002) model, the EPA found no statistically significant non-zero impact on employment in plants that continued in operation after the Transport Rule.

The EPA estimated that coal-fired plants with a capacity of 4.8 GW would be retired due to the rule, adding another 2,700 lost job years. However, while stating this figure, the EPA cautioned that the net loss of jobs would likely be far lower, saying that "utilities are expected to have the need to fill over two thousand additional job slots to operate the pollution controls needed to meet the requirements of the Transport Rule .... While it is not possible to determine how many of these workers from particular coal retirements could be employed to operate the new pollution controls, it is likely that a significant portion of them could find gainful employment at nearby units." Thus according to the EPA, even the 2,700 lost jobs due to coal-fired plant closures might be illusory, so that on net the Transport Rule would have no (statistically significant) impact on jobs in coal-fired power plants.[39]

III THE MERCURY AND AIR TOXICS STANDARDS (MATS)

The good neighbor provision that provided the legal justification for CAIR and the Obama EPA's Transport Rule is one of only three places in the CAA where the federal EPA is given authority allowing it to impose tougher environmental requirements on existing industrial plants. A second provision that creates such authority is Section 112, which authorizes the EPA to regulate hazardous air pollutants. In Section 112, the 1970 CAA required the EPA to promulgate emission standards providing "an ample margin of safety for to protect the public health" for any "air pollutant to which no ambient air quality standard is applicable and which in the judgment of the Administrator may cause, or contribute to, an increase in mortality or an increase in serious irreversible or reversible incapacitating, illness." Under the regulatory scheme of Section 112 as enacted in 1970, once the EPA produced a list of such hazardous air pollutants, it was required (under Section 112(b)(1)(B)) to promulgate an emission standard for such a pollutant unless information was presented at a public hearing showing that pollutant was "clearly" not a hazardous pollutant. Under Section 112, as standards for hazardous air pollutants were to be based solely on the federal EPA's expert determination of how to eliminate increases in mortality, there was no role for the states under Section 112. Again, as the risks were specific to particular pollutants and not place specific, it was the federal EPA, the specialist in health risk assessment, to which Congress assigned sole regulatory responsibility under Section 112.

As of 1990, the EPA had failed to list any hazardous air pollutants under Section 112. This failure was widely ascribed to the purely precautionary language of Section 112. That language seemed to require that once any pollutant was listed because the EPA found it could "cause, or contribute to, an increase in mortality or an increase in serious irreversible or reversible incapacitating, illness," then "a no-risk standard must be set regardless of cost" (Rugh 2003, 201). For hazardous air pollutants with "no known safe level," the use of Section 112 could create regulations "so harsh that major segments of the economy would be adversely impacted."

In 1990, Congress reacted to the EPA's decades-long inaction under Section 112 by rewriting that section to completely change the CAA system of hazardous air pollution regulation. Instead of a pollutant-by-pollutant determination of risk, the 1990 Amendments to the CAA required technology-based maximum achievable control technology (MACT) standards for industrial category sources of hazardous air pollutants (with risk-based tightening of the standards possible).[40] There was a clear rationale for a hazardous air pollution regulatory system that told the EPA to find feasible ways of reducing such pollutants from entire industrial categories: the EPA had been setting such standards for over a decade and had thereby acquired the experience and expertise to set such standards.

With one exception, the EPA was to set such standards for all major sources of hazardous pollutants (those emitting more than 25 tons of such hazardous pollutants or more than 10 tons of a single such pollutant) and also for sources that emitted smaller quantities but were still determined by the EPA to raise a "threat of adverse effects to human health or the environment." The one exception was for coal-fired power plants.

Pollution from coal-fired power plants was a major focus of the 1990 amendments. Indeed, perhaps the most famous of those amendments was the Title IV SO_2 acid rain trading program that I have discussed. In 1990, Congress specifically exempted hazardous emissions from coal-fired power plants from the Section 112 hazardous pollutants system. The reason was that up until 1990, when it added the Title IV acid rain trading provision, Congress and the EPA did not allow coal-burning power plants to reduce their SO_2 emissions by burning low sulfur coal. Instead, in a somewhat infamous[41] move designed to prop up the market for high sulfur eastern coal that was mined in parts of Illinois, Kentucky, and Ohio, the EPA interpreted Congress as requiring all coal-burning power plants to install scrubbers. The scrubbing system sufficiently reduces SO_2 in the exhaust from coal-burning power plants that such plants could burn high sulfur coal and still meet federal SO_2 standards. But scrubbers reduce not only SO_2, but also many other pollutants, some of which would be considered hazardous under Section 112, that are emitted by coal-burning power plants.

Indeed, if we go down the list of potentially hazardous air pollutants in coal combustion exhaust, almost all of them are removed by one of the technologies used to reduce other, conventional pollutants. Heavy metals such as arsenic and chromium attach to coal ash and so are removed by electrostatic precipitators and baghouses that capture fine particles of all types. Acid gases are removed by wet or dry scrubbing.

Power plant mercury emissions are not as completely removed by standard pollution reduction technologies used in coal-fired power plants. Some of the mercury that is emitted when coal is burned binds to the coal ash and so is removed by the dust removal equipment – baghouses and electrostatic precipitators – that coal-burning facilities operate anyway. Mercury is also emitted in its elemental form. The remainder of the mercury can be oxidized by injecting carbon or a halogen into the exhaust gas, and the oxidized mercury compound can then be removed either with a wet scrubber or by a process known as activated carbon injection (ACI).

Having experienced over two decades of studies and debates about scrubbers and SO_2 pollution from coal-burning power plants, by 1990 Congress knew that conventional pollution technology would remove the vast majority of the hazardous air pollutants from coal combustion exhaust. For this reason, in Section 112, Congress said that before regulating any hazardous pollutant from a coal-burning power plant under Section 112, the EPA had to do a study of whether any hazardous air pollutants from coal-burning plants could be "reasonably anticipated" to raise "hazards to public health." The EPA was to regulate hazardous air pollutants from coal-burning power plants only if it concluded after such a study that such regulation was "appropriate and necessary."[42]

IV THE TWISTING AND LEGALLY SHAKY ROAD TO THE OBAMA-ERA MERCURY RULE

Way back in 1997, during the Clinton administration, the EPA did such a study of hazardous air pollutants (HAPs) from coal-burning power plants. It concluded that mercury emissions from such plants were the hazardous air pollutant "of greatest potential concern." The EPA did not, however, find that regulation was appropriate and necessary, but rather concluded that "[f]urther research and evaluation are needed to gain a better understanding of the risks and impacts of utility mercury emissions."[43] For two other HAPs from coal-fired plants – dioxin and arsenic – the EPA found, in an early 1998 report, that there was a "potential concern" but that the substantial uncertainty about the impact of such emissions necessitated "further study."[44]

No one has ever asserted that mercury emissions from power plants pose a risk to humans because of the amount of mercury contained in the air that people breathe. The risk from mercury arises solely because after mercury-containing power plant exhaust circulates in the atmosphere for some months, it eventually comes back to the earth (largely in rainfall), thereby getting into soil and water. Anaerobic bacteria that live in lakes, rivers and oceans, and also some sediments and soils essentially eat the mercury, creating methylmercury as a by-product (Hamdy and Noyes 1975, 424–432). Such methylmercury then gets into plankton and vegetation, which are eaten by various aquatic organisms, which are in turn eaten by fish, which may be eaten by humans. Human consumption of such fish is the primary means by which humans are exposed to methylmercury that originated in power plant mercury emissions.

As the EPA reported in its 1997 study, power plant mercury emissions, then estimated at 51.5 tons – and by 2011 down to only about 29 tons – are a small fraction of the 2000 tons of mercury emissions for which humans are responsible. After its study, the EPA asked the National Academy of Sciences to report on whether the small amount of methylmercury that could be traced to power plant mercury emissions could be harmful, and asked coal-fired power plants to measure the amount of mercury in the coal they burned and in their exhaust gases.

Before any of this data was collected and fully analyzed, the political bell tolled on the Clinton administration. On its way out the door, in December 2000, the Clinton EPA published what it called a "notice of regulatory filing" concluding that regulation of mercury emissions from coal-burning power plants was "appropriate and necessary" under Section 112. This "notice" didn't say anything about how much mercury emissions needed to be reduced, but this was unsurprising, because the notice made no attempt to quantify how much methylmercury in fish comes from power plant mercury emissions. The only opportunity for public comment on the EPA's "filing" finding that regulation of mercury emissions from coal-burning power plants was "necessary and proper" was a single public meeting that the EPA held in Chicago, Illinois in June, 2000.[45]

It is a basic principle of administrative law that before a federal administrative agency issues any kind of pronouncement – whether it calls it a regulation, or something else, like a "policy statement" or "guidance document" – that is intended to have the force of law, then it must first provide notice and an opportunity for public comment. A court must invalidate any agency rule issued without such an opportunity for public comment. The Clinton EPA had made its "filing" about mercury emissions from coal-burning power plants without going through the public comment process. Clinton EPA Administrator Browner justified skipping the legally required public comment requirement by characterizing the December, 2000 notice as simply a "finding" that would be followed by actual implementing regulations that would themselves be subject to such public comment.[46]

In a brief and cursory opinion, the DC Circuit Court of Appeals agreed,[47] saying that under another part of Section 112,[48] Congress did not permit a court to review the EPA's determination that power plant mercury emissions needed to be regulated until after the EPA had decided how to regulate them. This likely reflected the congressional sense that the EPA would proceed by issuing both a determination that power plant mercury emissions needed to be regulated and the regulations themselves at the same time. It surely assumed that both the decision to regulate and the regulations would have gone through the full legally required public notice and comment process.

The Bush EPA actually did the follow-up studies required to determine whether mercury emissions from power plants risked human health by affecting methylmercury levels in fish. It concluded that given the reductions in mercury emissions generated by all the other pollution control devices on power plants (including those required by new Bush administration rules designed to cut interstate SO_2 and ozone) the remaining mercury emissions in fact did not cause a hazard to public health.[49]

One might assume that the DC Circuit would have now been very deferential to the EPA's decision, after a full study, that regulating mercury under Section 112 was not "necessary and appropriate." Quite to the contrary, in a 2008 opinion, *New Jersey*

v. *EPA*,[50] the DC Circuit now said that the EPA's earlier "notice" announcing that power plant mercury emissions needed to be regulated had the force of law, and for this reason could not be undone by the EPA unless it went through a cumbersome process found in yet another part of Section 112.

This decision was quite obviously incorrect. Congress made it difficult for the EPA to remove an entire industrial sector from hazardous air pollution regulation, but only under the assumption that the EPA had actually *regulated* that sector. It would be nonsensical for Congress to have set forth a number of findings that the EPA had to make to deregulate hazardous air pollution by an industry when the EPA had said only that it was *planning* on regulating the industry.

It is worth pausing for a moment to consider the upshot of the DC Circuit's decisions on EPA mercury rule decisions over the years from Clinton to Obama. Through these decisions, the DC Circuit effectively allowed the Clinton EPA to use a last minute non-binding and nonfinal "notice," which was never subject to public comment and unreviewable by the courts, to commit the EPA to regulate mercury emissions as Section 112 hazardous air pollutants. In that its decision was neither subject to public comment and participation beforehand nor reviewable by the courts afterwards, the EPA was thereby given completely unchecked power in making a decision to regulate an entire industrial sector, one which Congress had specifically otherwise exempted from separate hazardous air pollution regulations.

V THE MATS RULE: SPECULATIVE BENEFITS SUFFICE WHEN COSTS ARE NOT CONSIDERED

The Obama administration was committed to imposing on the coal-burning electricity industry every costly regulation it could find in the statute books. With help from environmental groups – who got a federal trial court to order the EPA to regulate mercury emissions by 2011, thus forestalling challenge by the power industry – this is just what it did. Before regulating power plant mercury emissions, the Obama EPA required every coal-burning power plant to provide a year's worth of data on its emissions testing since 2005 and on the chemical constituents of the coal burned. According to the power industry trade group,[51] it cost power companies over $100 million to comply with the EPA's data request. The cost was apparently imposed simply to impose more costs on the industry, as the EPA had barely even received this information when it went forward with promulgating and finalizing its mercury emissions rule.

The Obama EPA's mercury rule (called the mercury and air toxics standard, or MATS, because although primarily focused on mercury, the rule also covers some of the other hazardous air pollutants emitted by coal-fired power plants mentioned earlier) required that coal-burning power plants install additional pollution control technologies, such as the activated carbon injection (ACI) process described above, together with the installation of new fabric filters to improve the efficiency of mercury removal by that process and by dry scrubbing. By installing these new controls, the coal-burning power industry was to reduce its annual mercury emissions from 29 to 6 tons, or by 79 percent per year.[52]

According to the Obama EPA, the finding that such regulation was "necessary and appropriate" was fully met by evidence that the mercury rule would generate benefits in the billions of dollars. By far the biggest estimated benefits came not from any health benefits of reducing methylmercury, but from the reduction in fine dust pollution (called fine particulate pollution) attendant upon installing the enhanced pollution reduction equipment I just described. The EPA estimated the health benefits of reducing mercury were only between $4 and $6 million, benefits that were far smaller than roughly $11 billion in social costs from the rule.[53] Indeed, according to the EPA's own analysis, the costs of the mercury rule outweighed benefits by at least a ratio of 1833 to 1. However, at between $59 to $140 billion, the additional benefits of reducing fine dust particles – called "PM2.5 related co-benefits" in the table – clearly swamp the social costs of the rule.

A longstanding presidential order (which originated in President Reagan's Executive Order 12866) required the EPA to do a cost-benefit analysis of the mercury MACT rule. For regulations with an economic impact of $100 million or more, this executive order adds an additional layer of interaction within the executive branch, as the EPA produces the required cost-benefit analysis (called a Regulatory Impact Analysis) and that analysis is then reviewed by the White House Office of Management and Budget.

Executive Order 12866's cost-benefit requirement does not (and constitutionally cannot) change what Congress required in the CAA, or any other statute for that matter. The vast majority of federal environmental statutes do not in fact say that the EPA can promulgate only those regulations that meet a cost-benefit test. For decades, environmental groups have argued that not only has Congress not required environmental regulations to be cost-benefit justified, but in such statutes, Congress actually prohibited the EPA from using cost-benefit analysis to set pollution reduction standards.

The issue came to a head in *Entergy Corp.* v. *Riverkeeper Inc.*[54] That case was decided in 2009, just as the Obama administration was gearing up its Endangerment Finding and other regulations targeting coal-burning power plants. It too involved EPA regulation of power plants, one setting an environmental standard for power plant cooling water intakes. As I explain in a bit more detail below, whether the energy source is the combustion of coal or natural gas or instead nuclear fission, thermal power plants generate electricity by boiling water to create steam that spins turbines. The steam has to be cooled back into water before it can be reused or disposed of, and power plants accomplish this by sucking cooler water out of nearby water bodies and running the cooler water back through the plant. In the process of intaking this cooling water, power plants cause the death of fish and other aquatic organisms.

Entergy Corp. v. *Riverkeeper Inc.* challenged EPA regulations affecting over 500 power plants that provided about 53 percent of America's electricity generation capacity.[55] In these regulations, the EPA said that while these existing power plants should aim to install technologies reducing the intake water system kill of fish and other organisms by 85 to 90 percent, specific plants could get variances from this standard if they were able to show either that the costs of compliance were "significantly greater than" the costs considered by the agency in setting the standards, or that the costs of compliance "would be significantly greater than the benefits of complying with the applicable performance standards."[56] The environmental group plaintiffs argued that by requiring that the EPA set a standard based on the "best technology available for minimizing adverse environmental impact," Congress in the Clean Water Act[57] (the statute at issue there) had precluded the EPA from using a cost-benefit test in deciding whether to grant variances.

The Clean Water Act is a long and complicated statute. However, its core water pollution standard[58] requires firms to reduce pollution in their wastewater by installing the "best available technology economically achievable." In *Entergy*, the environmental plaintiffs argued that because the Clean Water's Act's intake water standard by contrast said nothing about the standard being "economically achievable," and instead mandated the "best technology for minimizing the adverse environmental impact," the EPA could not employ any kind of cost-benefit test in granting variances from its new cooling water intake standard.

The Supreme Court majority in *Entergy* disagreed, observing that in its over thirty year history of setting cooling water intake standards, the EPA had consistently considered costs in some way or another. As Justice Scalia's opinion observed, in conceding that the "best technology available standard" did not require the EPA to set a standard forcing power plants to "spend billions to save one more fish or plankton," even the environmental group plaintiffs had to admit that the EPA could use "at least some cost-benefit analysis" in setting such standards.[59]

The *Entergy* opinion merely allowed the EPA to consider and weigh regulatory compliance costs against benefits when regulating under a statutory provision that said nothing explicit about economic costs. Like the key statutory language in *Entergy*, the CAA test for whether the EPA is to regulate mercury emissions under Section 112 of the Clean Air Act – that such regulation was "necessary and appropriate" – does not explicitly say that the EPA is allowed to consider and weigh costs against benefits. The Obama EPA took this to mean that, in determining that regulation of power plant mercury emissions was "necessary and appropriate," it did not even need to *consider* the costs of such regulation, let alone weigh costs against regulatory benefits. As the EPA interpreted Section 112 of the CAA, regulation of power plant mercury emissions was "necessary" because they were not "adequately addressed" by other, existing CAA regulations.[60] And the only thing the EPA needed to conclude that it was "appropriate" to regulate power plant mercury emissions was evidence that such emissions posed "an identified or potential hazard to public health or the environment." Moreover, according to the EPA, the statutory trigger that regulation be "appropriate" did not "allow for the consideration of costs in assessing whether hazards to public health or the environment are reasonably anticipated to occur based on EGU emissions." As the EPA explained, "[h]ad Congress intended to require the Agency to consider costs in assessing hazards to public health or the environment associated with EGU HAP emissions, it would have so stated."[61] Thus, the EPA said that congressional failure to specifically authorize the EPA to consider costs in determining whether to regulate mercury emissions under Section 112 meant that it was free to ignore them.

It would be hard to think of a purer form of the precautionary principle in action. According to the EPA, provided that they weren't already being reduced, even a potential public health hazard made reductions in power plant mercury emissions appropriate. The cost of achieving such reductions was, according to the EPA, simply irrelevant to determining whether the reductions were appropriate.

To be sure, "appropriate" is a different regulatory standard than the "best available technology" standard that the Court in *Entergy* had said allows the EPA to consider and balance costs against benefits. But Congress did specifically mention cost in specifying when hazardous air pollutants from power plants should be regulated, telling the EPA that when it did its study of mercury emissions from such plants, it was to consider "the health and environmental effects of such emissions, technologies which are available to control such emissions, and the costs of such technologies."[62] Especially in light of what the Court said in *Entergy*, one might have well have predicted that the EPA's position that it could regulate power plant mercury emissions without even considering cost might well have fared poorly before the Supreme Court.

This is exactly what happened. In 2015, in *Michigan* v. *EPA*, the Court was presented both with the EPA's own Regulatory Impact Analysis – showing that regulatory costs were almost two thousand times the actual health benefits from reducing power plant mercury emissions – and the EPA's argument that this was legally irrelevant, because it did not have to consider costs at all. The Court said that "one would not say that it is even rational, never mind 'appropriate,' to impose billions of dollars in economic costs in return for a few dollars in health or environmental benefits." Completely ignoring costs, said Justice Scalia's majority opinion, would be flatly inconsistent with longstanding regulatory practice, under which "[a]gencies have long treated cost as a centrally relevant factor when deciding whether to regulate." Relying on Justice Breyer's partial concurrence and dissent in *Entergy*, Scalia continued that for the EPA to completely ignore cost would fly in the face of the "the reality that too much wasteful expenditure devoted to one problem may well mean considerably fewer resources available to deal effectively with other (perhaps more serious) problems."[63]

Justice Scalia's characterization as irrational of the EPA's position on the irrelevancy of costs may well have been provoked by the Obama administration Justice Department's remarkable position, taken during oral argument before the Court, that even if the EPA were to find "that the technologies needed to eliminate" power plant mercury emissions "do even more damage to human health" than the mercury emissions, "it would *still* deem regulation appropriate." As Scalia concluded, "Consideration of cost reflects the understanding that reasonable regulation ordinarily requires paying attention to the advantages *and* the disadvantages of agency decisions, [and] [n]o regulation is 'appropriate' if it does significantly more harm than good."[64] Here, Justice Scalia is not endorsing a strict principle that regulatory benefits must exceed regulatory costs, but rather a minimal test for rational regulation: that the regulator considers both the cost of erroneously failing to regulate – what the EPA is happy to consider, the benefits of regulation – and the cost of erroneously regulating – the compliance and other costs of regulation.

It was easy for the EPA to respond to the Court's instruction to consider costs.[65] Recall that as estimated by the EPA, the costs of the mercury rule were $11 billion. This was far less than the floor $59 billion minimum benefit that the EPA estimated its mercury rule would bring about by reducing the emission not of mercury but of fine dust particles (fine particulates). The EPA's justification for including the benefits from reducing fine particulates was that the new pollution control technology required to reduce mercury emissions – such as the installation of new fabric filters to improve the efficiency of mercury removal by activated carbon injection and by dry scrubbing – would create a reduction in fine dust particles above and beyond that which the EPA was already about to require separately.

Including such so-called co-benefits from reducing fine dust particles was to vastly overestimate the benefit of reducing mercury. The EPA was already in the process of promulgating separate regulations to reduce fine particulates, and if the additional pollution control technology required by the mercury rule was so efficient at lowering fine particulates, the EPA should have required it under its regulation of fine particulates. Moreover, EPA officials knew that the Endangerment Finding, which had been finalized two years previously, was the prelude to other CAA regulations designed to completely eliminate coal-burning power plants. Before such plants would even be able to comply with the mercury rule, they would likely be closed, with zero emissions of fine particulates or any other pollutant.

VI THE MATS RULE: EXAGGERATING BENEFITS AND UNDERESTIMATING COSTS

A detailed analysis of whether there were actually *any* fine particulate co-benefits from the mercury rule is beyond the scope of this book. My own view, set out at length in Johnston (2019), is that the studies that the EPA has relied upon as establishing an actual causal relationship between higher level of airborne fine particulates and increased mortality suffer from far too many obvious but serious methodological problems for anyone to reasonably conclude that such a causal relationship exists. Still, the key point to see here is that it was only by including the co-benefit from reducing fine particulates that the EPA could claim that the benefits of the mercury rule exceeded its costs. This was because not even the EPA could plausibly argue that the health benefits of reduced mercury emissions were at all substantial.

EPA estimated that power plants emitted 29 tons of mercury in 2011. To put this in perspective, as of 2003, almost a decade earlier, mercury emissions from coal burning in China had reached 257 tons (Wu et al. 2006), almost ten times the 2011 emissions from U.S. coal-fired plants. For that same year, Seigneur et al (2004, 557) estimated that natural mercury emissions from the oceans (which, to be sure, include some re-emission of anthropogenic mercury emissions) were between 2200 and 2800 tons. If we add in natural mercury emissions from vegetation burning and volcanic eruptions (also from Seignur et al. 2004, 557), we see that EPA's estimated 2011 U.S. power plant mercury were likely 100 times smaller than natural mercury emissions and ten times smaller than Chinese mercury emissions from coal.

Recall that humans are not exposed to elemental mercury, but to methylmercury formed by bacterial decomposition of mercury. The main health concern regarding human exposure to methylmercury is the effect of high blood levels of methylmercury in a pregnant mother on the neurological development of the human fetus she carries. Few human populations consume enough fish to generate very high levels of methylmercury in the blood of pregnant women, but there are a few populations – people who live in the Faroe and Seychelles Islands, and some American Cree Indian tribe members – who do. A number of studies have looked at the statistical relationship in these populations between neurological functioning in children and the mercury blood levels of their mothers while pregnant. A review of these studies by Spurgeon (2007, 307) summarized that these studies had reported "contradictory" and "inconsistent" results. More precisely, Spurgeon explains, while some neurologic test scores on children (tested at ages ranging from as early as two weeks up to twelve years) decreased in a statistically significant way with the mother's exposure to methylmercury, others, including the biggest study, of Seychelles Island children, found either no associations between test scores and maternal exposure or a positive association – higher maternal methylmercury levels were correlated with better neurological functioning in children.

With such fragmentary evidence of any adverse effect of human health of exposure to methylmercury, it is perhaps unsurprising that even in 2016, when the EPA responded to the *Michigan* v. *EPA* opinion by actually considering costs, the highest monetized health benefit it was able to report having found in new studies was only $3.7 billion.[66] By itself, this was still less than the $10 billion in costs that the EPA reported, and had the EPA not included the "co-benefits" from reducing fine dust particles, the cost-benefit analysis of its mercury rule would have tipped decidedly in the negative direction.

The EPA's estimate of the costs of its mercury rule was subject to much less discussion and consideration, whether by the Court or by the EPA. But for several reasons, the EPA's estimate of the impact of its mercury rule on the closure (called retirement) of coal-burning power plants and on employment in the coal-burning power plant industry was truly shocking.

According to the EPA, the MATS rule would cause the retirement by 2015 of only 4.7 GW of coal-fired power plant generating capacity.[67] This number was derived from the EPA's so-called Integrated Planning Model (IPM). As described by the EPA, this is "a multi-regional, dynamic, deterministic linear programming model of the electric power sector" that the EPA uses to generate forecasts going out as far as 2050 of how the EPA's environmental regulations affect everything from changes in generating capacity [to] emission control strategies ... of over 15,000 electricity generating units."[68] I describe this in more detail below, but the key idea behind the EPA's planning model is that power plants attempt to minimize their cost of being available to provide electricity when demanded, but regulations, among other things, such as fuel costs, affect power plant cost. The EPA's model is designed to allow quantification of how its regulations change power plant operator behavior.

The National Research Council has described the EPA's IPM as a "proprietary model."[69] Since the EPA is a taxpayer-funded federal regulatory agency, it seems impossible that the EPA could actually treat its Integrated Planning Model as something that it owns and to which it may exercise full rights to exclude others. And yet I have discovered no study by any non-EPA economist or engineer actually running the EPA's IPM model to rigorously explore whether its predictions have actually been confirmed. Nor have I seen the actual computer code for this model posted anywhere online. Even finding and analyzing the output of the EPA's Integrated Planning Model is not easy. It's even difficult to identity model output, as the EPA describes model output using an arcane, non-standard terminology that seems to be unique to its own regulatory universe. The EPA runs its model for the current status quo world, without a particular new regulation, producing what it calls a "base case parsed file," and then runs the model with the new regulations in place, producing what it calls a "policy parsed file." Of course, the key question is always how a regulation changes behavior compared to the world without the regulation. But the EPA does not produce a single file where it compares the "base" and "policy" cases. To figure this out, a person has to do the comparison across the two files produced by the EPA.

For the 2011 MATS rule, the EPA's base case assumed that coal-burning power units had already installed the additional pollution control technology necessary to comply with the Cross State Air Pollution Rule (CSAPR). When one compares the capacity reduction due to early retirements of coal-burning power plants that the EPA projected in this base case with the capacity reduction its model predicted would result from the MATS rule, one indeed finds only an additional 4.7 GW (4700 MW) due to the MATS rule.[70]

However, when one compares EPA projected retirement of coal-fired electricity generating capacity to what was known and what then actually occurred, the results are shocking. Throughout 2011 and 2012, major power companies were announcing that due to the additional compliance costs imposed by the MATS rule (additional, that is, to the new costs imposed by the CSAPR rule), they would be closing dozens of coal-fired generating units by 2015 and often sooner. For example,

- Duke Energy shut down all the coal-fired units at its W. C. Beckjord station in Ohio, removing 862 MW of power production and killing 120 jobs;
- FirstEnergy retired nine coal-fired power generating units in Ohio, Pennsylvania, Maryland, and West Virginia, removing about 3,300 MW of electric power, and costing 630 jobs;[71]
- GenOn, which reported a net loss of $189 million in 2011, shut eight coal-fired power plants in Ohio and Pennsylvania, eliminating over 3,600 MW of generating capacity and 455 jobs and also closed its Potomac River, Virginia coal-fired plant, removing another 1,100 MW of generating capacity;
- In Michigan, Consumers Energy closed seven coal-fired generating units, removing 950 MW of electricity generating capacity and around 250 jobs;[72]
- AEP, which reported that it would cost more than $6 billion to comply with the MATS (and CSAPR) rules,[73] retired more than 6,000 MW at 11 power plants in seven states across the Midwest and South, with most plant closings in Ohio and West Virginia. In total, AEP had approximately 570 positions that were affected by upcoming generating unit retirements;[74]
- Dominion Resources closed its 717 MW capacity coal-fired power plant in Chesapeake and one unit at its 1,257 MW capacity Yorktown plant, costing 145 jobs at the Chesapeake plant and dozens more of the 127 people employed at the Yorktown plant;[75] another cost was the loss of the $7.4 million in taxes that the Chesapeake plant paid to the city of Chesapeake in 2010 and most of the most of the $2.4 million in taxes that Dominion paid to York; in Massachusetts, Dominion closed its 747 MW Salem Harbor Power Station, causing the loss of 150 jobs and more than $4 million in taxes each year that had been paid to the town of Salem;[76]
- Also in Michigan, DTE Energy closed its St. Clair, Trenton Channel, and River Rouge power plants. The St. Clair plant employed 230 people and had a capacity of 1,425 MW.[77]

The closure of particular generating units should not be confused with the closure of an entire power station. For example, in 2016, Consumers Energy of Michigan closed all of the coal-burning units at its J. C. Weadock plant near Bay City, Michigan, leaving operational only the adjacent D. E. Karn plant, seen in the photo displayed as Figure 5.2.[78] The oil and natural gas Karn generating units are still operational today, while the Karn coal-fired units are in the process of being closed.

With this clarification, when we add up just the reported unit closures that I've listed above, we see that just these reported coal-fired power generating unit closures alone caused the loss of over 16 GW of power generation. This is almost four times more than the EPA's IPM model projected *for the entire country*.

FIGURE 5.2 Consumers Energy Karn Power Plant

More systematic evidence indicates that the MATS rule (on top of the CSAPR requirements) actually caused even more severe loss of coal-fired electricity generating capacity. In 2012, the Institute for Energy Research added to the coal-fired unit closures predicted by the EPA's IPM model all of the closures that utility companies had announced publicly. They got a figure of 34 GW of lost capacity.[79] Virtually all of these plant closures were in the Eastern Interconnection electricity transmission region. By 2013, researchers the Oak Ridge National Laboratory found that in that region alone, 221 generating units with a capacity of 29 GW had been or were being retired.[80] These two estimates are very close, and it seems clear that around 30 GW of coal-fired generation capacity was retired or planned for retirement by 2013.

This 30 GW of power producing capacity lost by 2013 was only a fraction of what was to come. By 2014, the EIA projected that power plants with a total generating capacity of 60 GW of electricity would retire by 2020. The EIA noted that the EPA would begin to enforce the mercury rule in 2016, and the EIA projected that by that year, 90 percent of projected coal-fired plant retirements would occur. It included such projected closures even if the plant owners and operators had not yet reported to the EIA that they planned such closures.[81]

The very next year, EIA reported that 13 GW of coal-fired power plants would be closed in 2015, with the retiring plants concentrated in Ohio, West Virginia, and Kentucky, and Indiana, removing more than 8 GW of power plant capacity.[82] EIA explained that "[t]he large number of coal-fired generator retirements is primarily because of the implementation of the Environmental Protection Agency's Mercury and Air Toxics Standards (MATS) this year," as "some power plant operators have decided that retrofitting units to meet the new standards will be cost-prohibitive and are choosing to retire units instead."

By 2018, the Energy Information Administration reported that the closure of coal-fired power plants increased by about 400 percent between 2011, when the mercury rule was finalized, and 2012[83] As that agency reported, between 2011 and 2017, over 46 GW of coal-fired power plants were retired from service. Compliance with the mercury rule was required by 2016, and about 23 GW of coal-fired power plants were retired just over the 2015–2016 period.

As the EIA also reported,[84] the retirement of coal-fired plants was concentrated in the Eastern Interconnection region. According to the EIA, as of October, 2017, the Eastern Interconnection – one of the three US regional wholesale electricity transmission networks – had over 70 percent of all US electricity generating capacity. Over the 2011–2017 period, about 44 GW of coal-fired power generating capacity – over 90 percent of the total US retirement of 46 GW of coal-fired power plants capacity – occurred in the Eastern Interconnection. This 44 GW of retired coal capacity represented 19 percent of the Eastern Interconnection's coal-fired generating capacity.

According to the EIA, the coal-fired units that were retired to avoid compliance with the mercury rule were generally smaller, older plants that operated at a lower capacity. EIA reported that the plants that were retired in 2013 had an average capacity of 158 MW and had been operated at only 24 percent of capacity. As EIA reported, these closed plants were much smaller and operated at a much lower capacity than the average operating coal-fired power plant at the time, which had a capacity of 261 MW and operated at 60 percent of capacity (or, in electric power industry lingo, had a capacity factor of 60 percent). Two years later, an electric power industry trade publication reported that the average capacity of coal plants retired in 2015 was a bit smaller, at 133 MW (versus an average capacity then of 278 MW).[85] The EPA itself had forecast in 2011 that the average size of retired coal-burning plants would be 129 MW, operating at an average capacity factor of 54 percent.[86]

There is a ready economic explanation for why the EPA's mercury rule disproportionately led to the closure of small plants. The impact of the fixed cost of installing new pollution control equipment, such as that required by the mercury rule, decreases as the total quantity of sales over which the average is computed increases. For example, a $100 fixed cost spread over 100 units sold increases average cost by only $1; if the firm sells only 20 units, average cost is increases by $5 per unit sold. Power plants with relatively low electricity production capacity – in particular, those less than 200 MW – have a relatively small denominator over which to average the fixed costs of additional pollution control. Even worse, such plants were operating well below capacity – with a capacity factor of only 24 percent in 2013. As I explain below, such older, smaller plants operate at low capacity factors because they have relatively high marginal cost of producing power and can profitably sell power only at high demand (high load, in electric power industry lingo) periods. With a low capacity factor, the older, smaller plants had very small quantities of sold power over which to spread the large fixed cost of installing more pollution reduction controls.

Because it was concentrated in small units averaging around 130 MW capacity, the loss of roughly 50 GW (5000 MW) of coal-fired electricity generating capacity due to the MATS (and CSAPR) rule entailed the closure of a large number of generating units. According to the 2013 Oak Ridge labs study, these EPA rules caused the closure of 221 units producing 29 GW of power by that year. These smaller, older units generally required proportionately more workers to operate and maintain than do newer and larger plants (that is, more workers per MW of capacity). From my list of specific closures given above, we see that the retirement of 16 GW coal-fired generation capacity from such units meant the loss of 2,500 jobs. Were we to scale this up to the roughly 50 GW that EIA estimated was lost by 2018, we get a rough estimate that at least 7,500 jobs in coal-fired power plants were lost due to regulation-induced unit closures.

Such jobs were generally very high paying. According to the Bureau of Labor Statistics' most recent report, the mean wage in the electric power generation, distribution, and transmission industry is over $81,000 per year.[87] As a source of high paying jobs and reliable tax revenue, the closed coal-burning power plants had historically had an enormous economic footprint in the communities in which they were located. DTE's St. Clair plant was estimated to provide 350 total jobs and $37.5 million in earnings to its home county.[88] When Consumer Energy closed its B. C. Cobb plant in Muskegon, Michigan, that city lost $3 million in annual tax revenues.[89] When Duke Energy closed its W. C. Beckjord plant, the village of New Richmond, Ohio's school district lost $1.7 million and its police and fire departments lost 40 percent of their annual budget.[90] Dominion Energy's closure of its Chesapeake units cost that city $7.4 million in taxes and closure of its coal-burning units at York cost that city a large fraction of the $2.4 million in taxes that Dominion paid to York. When Dominion closed its Salem Harbor Power Station in Massachusetts, the town of Salem lost over $4 million in annual taxes.

These jobs will likely not come close to being made up by jobs in the new electricity generating units that replace the retired coal-fired units. To replace the lost electric generating capacity due to the closure of coal-fired units, US utilities have primarily turned to natural gas-fired generation. They have been proposing to build and building massive new natural gas-fired plants. For example, in Michigan, DTE plans a $1 billion 1,150 MW plant in the same county where its closed coal-fired units were located. In eastern Ohio, Kallanish Energy is building a $1.6 billion 1,875 MW natural gas-fired plant. In 2014, Dominion Energy opened its new $1.1 billion, 1,370 MW natural gas-fired Warren County plant. Natural gas-fired plants also provide very high paying jobs. But in general, natural gas-fired plants require far fewer employees to run. GenOn (now NRG) managed to switch its Shawville, Pennsylvania plant from coal to natural gas, continuing to produce hundreds of MW of power, but the plant became a peaking plant – one operated only during periods of peak electricity demand – and its employment fell from 73 jobs to 40. Similarly while according to AEP "several" of its employees at retired coal-fired units managed get keep their jobs after those plants were switched to natural gas, "it takes a much smaller number of employees to operate a natural gas plant – 25 or so for a good-size natural gas plant versus well over 100, sometimes nearly 200, for a good-size coal unit." The difference in labor demand is even starker when one compares old coal units to the newest natural gas plants. While it takes 800 employees to operate Exelon's 2,300 MW coal-fired Limerick Generating Station in Pottstown, Pennsylvania, it will only require 30 people to operate the 1,480 MW natural gas-fired Lackawanna natural gas-fired plant that Invenergy LLC is building only two hours distant, and which will compete in supplying power to the same wholesale market.[91] Thus it would seem that only a small fraction, perhaps only 10–20 percent, of the high paying jobs in coal-fired electricity generating units will be offset by similarly high paying jobs in new or converted natural gas-fired units.

According to the Regulatory Impact Analysis (RIA) that the EPA did for its 2011 MATS rule, the EPA was not at all sure about the impact of the rule on employment in the coal-fired electricity generating industry, estimating that employment might decrease by 15,000 per year, but that it might actually *increase* by as many as 30,000 workers. In the end, the EPA expected that the rule would actually generate an *increase of 8,000 jobs* in the coal-fired power plant industry.[92]

Using different methodology (its IPM model), the EPA predicted that some jobs might be lost due to plant closures, but since it only predicted the loss of 4.7GW worth of coal-fired capacity, it estimated only 2,500 lost job years lost due to plant closures.[93] Note that using the same ratio of jobs lost to capacity retired that the EPA used to get its figure of 2,500 jobs lost and applying it to the 50 GW capacity lost by 2018 as reported by the EIA, we would have not 2,500 jobs, but 25,000 high paying jobs in coal-burning power plants due to the MATS rule.

We get an even larger number of lost jobs if we use the data from my illustrative plant closures presented earlier. That list recounts 1.8 GW of plant closures that caused 2,720 lost jobs. Extrapolating that ratio of jobs lost to GW closed, the 50 GW of plant closures caused by the EPA's MATS rule would have cost 76,160 jobs. Even if average salary was only $50,000 – far less than BLS data suggest – and even the average worker at one of the closed plants had only 10 years more to work before retirement, the EPA's MATS rule would have caused the loss of $38 billion in earnings to workers in retired coal-fired power plants.

Even had the EPA taken the time to calculate lost earnings due to the MATS rule, the EPA could probably have found a big net increase in earnings. The reason is that the EPA's 2011 RIA estimated that in the short run, compliance period, its MATS rule would actually *create an additional 46,000 jobs* in industries that manufacture pollution reduction equipment. Thus, in stark contrast to the roughly 7,500 short-run job loss in coal-burning power plants and likely 25,000 jobs lost due to plant retirements one can infer from existing data, the EPA's 2011 RIA for the MATS rule concluded that the rule could increase employment by tens of thousands of jobs!

The EPA used different methods to get its various jobs numbers. The jobs lost due to plant closure and created in the pollution reduction equipment industries came from its IPM. Its basic number of the job impact of the rule on still-operating coal-fired plants was derived via a different approach. The EPA estimated that the annual cost of complying with the MATS rule by installing, maintaining, and operating new pollution control equipment would be $9.6 billion (in 2007 dollars). To obtain the MATS rule's net impact on employment, it simply multiplied this rule by 1.55 (after discounting back to 1987 dollars).[94] It then divided this dollar number by its estimate of average cost in the coal-burning power plant industry.

The EPA's justification for this highly simplistic approach was a single study, by Morgenstern et al. (2002). Morgenstern et al. (2002) is an empirical study that tries to capture three key effects of new pollution control regulatory requirements. The first and most direct effect is that by increasing costs, such requirements increase prices and reduce demand for the regulated firm's product, which means the firm needs to hire less labor. The second effect comes about because rules such as the MATS rule – that require firms to make a large capital investment, in installing expensive pollution control equipment – may actually end up requiring firms to hire more labor just to maintain the same output. The third and final effect is that – as we have seen concretely with the coal dust monitoring rule discussed earlier – new pollution reduction regulatory requirements mean increased demand for pollution reduction products and for the workers who make them.

Morgenstern et al. (2002) attempt to estimate these various effects by looking at the impact of environmental regulatory requirements in four industries – pulp and paper, plastics, petroleum refining, and iron and steel – measured at four points of time, the years 1979, 1983, 1988, and 1991. They do not, however, include as an explanatory variable any particular regulatory change such as the MATS rule, or any of the other major changes in regulatory requirements that the EPA has imposed since the CAA was first enacted in 1970. Their variable measuring environmental "regulation" is simply annual operating expenses (plus capital depreciation) incurred for pollution abatement equipment. They assume that regulations affect individual plants in proportion to their total costs, so that an extra dollar of pollution abatement expenditure for an industry increases a given plant's total costs by an amount equal to the plant's total costs divided by the industry's total costs. They get a very rough number for net jobs actually created (or lost) by regulation by dividing total labor spending by an industry-specific measure of average cost.

The key focus of modern econometric methods is to identify effects that are truly causal, as opposed to being mere statistical correlations. The problem facing an industry level study that does not measure discrete changes in regulatory requirements such as Morgenstern et al. (2002) is precisely that of distinguishing actual causal effects from mere correlation. Bigger plants have higher pollution abatement expenses, and also employ more workers, thus spending more money on labor. Other things equal, there is therefore a positive correlation between pollution reduction expenditure and labor expenditure. This does not mean that there is therefore a fixed causal relationship whereby an increase in a particular plant's pollution reduction expenditure by $1 million causes an increase in employment derived by multiplying $1 million by 1.55. Obscured by the analysis in Morgenstern et al. (2002) is that different plants within a given industry differ radically in how they are impacted by pollution reduction requirements (Smith et al. 2011, 20–22).

Beginning in the early 2000s, around the same time as the Morgenstern et al. (2002) study, economists have done a number of econometric studies estimating the impact of environmental regulations on employment using methods designed to carefully isolate the causal impact of such regulations. These studies have compared the change in employment (or other economic measures, such as labor productivity) in industries or plants subject to stringent environmental regulation and those that were not. Variation in the stringency of environmental regulations arises in part because, as I have described before, the CAA imposes costlier pollution control requirements on plants located in heavily polluted nonattainment areas than it does in cleaner attainment areas. It also arises because under the so-called good neighbor provision that I have also described earlier, plants located in upwind states that contribute to air pollution in downwind states have to install extra pollution control equipment. Finally, and most obviously perhaps, in a given county or state, plants in low polluting industries have lower pollution control costs than plants in dirtier industries.

Studies using these sources of variation across plants and counties in the costliness of pollution control to statistically identify the impact of environmental regulations on employment levels, wages, and labor productivity have consistently found big negative effects.

- Greenstone (2002, 1175–1219) compared changes in manufacturing activity and employment in nonattainment counties with attainment counties. He found that in the first 15 years after Congress passed the CAA (which included around 10 years during which the EPA actually enforced the differential regulatory requirements), the stringent pollution reduction requirements in nonattainment counties cost those counties (relative to attainment ones) approximately 590,000 jobs, $37 billion in capital stock, and $75 billion (1987 dollars) of output.

- The 1990 amendments to the CAA initiated the regulation of coarse dust particle air pollution (called PM10). Some US counties were instantly out of compliance with the new PM10 air quality standards, and some plants had to install new pollution control equipment to reduce their emissions of such particles. Walker (2013, 1737–1835) looked at how particular plants and particular workers were affected by these new regulatory requirements. He found an immediate and lasting impact of new regulations on employment and earnings in the affected plants, with employment levels five years after the regulatory change 15 percent lower than they would otherwise have been, and earnings for an average worker nine years later 20 percent lower in (discounted present) value.
- Around the same time, Curtis (2014)[95] employed a somewhat coarser methodology to explore the impact of the EPA's 2003 initiation of tougher regulation of power plant nitrous oxide emissions as part of the good neighbor requirement to reduce ozone formation in downwind states. This program (called the NO_x Budget Program) had been estimated by Palmer et al. (2001)[96] as costing (primarily coal-burning) electric utilities over $2 billion per year. Using the energy intensiveness of an industry as a proxy for the likely cost to it of this new regulatory program, Curtis (2014) found that relative to the least energy intensive industry, the new regulatory program would cost about 110,000 jobs.

The studies are directly relevant to the likely impact of the MATS rule on jobs and earnings. The reason is that whether under the 1977 amendment (Greenstone), or the 1990 amendments (Walker), or the EPA's 2003 NBP (Curtis), all of the differential regulatory regimes studied required the installation of additional pollution control equipment in some plants but not others. The MATS rule (together with the CSAPR) did functionally the same thing, requiring coal-fired electricity generating units to spend more money on filtering out particulates, reducing NO_x emissions (through catalytic or noncatalytic reduction), and (in the case of mercury) installing a new type of scrubber (dry sorbent injection). Based on what is known about the impact of new pollution reduction requirements on jobs, one would have predicted that the MATS rule would have led to substantial job losses and earnings reductions in the coal-burning power plant sector.

The employment impacts of the MATS rule were in fact likely far greater than what one would inferred from existing studies of environmental regulation and jobs and from the number of plant closures. The reason is that the Morgenstern et al. (2002) analysis is what economists call a partial equilibrium analysis, one that looks only at the effects of the MATS rule on employment in the coal-burning power plant industry. By shutting down 40 GW or more of coal-burning power generation

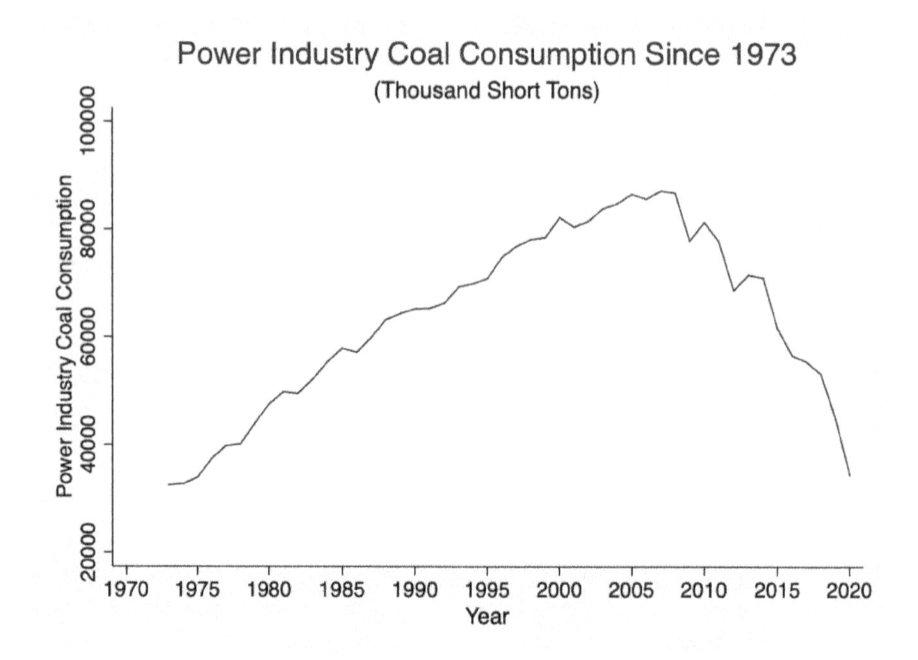

FIGURE 5.3 Power Industry Coal Consumption since 1973

capacity and causing the installation of massively expensive pollution reduction equipment at plants that stayed online, the MATS rule had big upstream and downstream employment effects.

Upstream, by reducing power plant demand for coal, the MATS rule reduced employment in the coal mining industry. The MATS rule was of course not the only thing influencing electricity generating companies to move away from burning coal. As shown EIA data depicted by Figure 5.3,[97] steep drops in US electricity sector coal use (consumption) began as early as 2009.

The drop in power sector demand for coal closely follows the massive decline in natural gas prices from a peak of $12.69 per million Btu in 2008 to $2.17 - per million Btu in 2012.[98] However, as one can see from Figure 5.4, natural gas prices have had no distinct trend since 2012, averaging a little above $3 per million Btu over the period 2012–2017, and yet the power sector's demand for coal has continued to fall.

Downstream, by increasing electricity prices, the MATS rule reduced employment in manufacturing industries by increasing electricity costs and prices charged by such employers. Smith et al. (2013)[99] estimated that when both the decrease in coal demand and coal mining employment and the reduction in manufacturing employment are considered, the MATS rule would lead to the loss of labor income equivalent to 180,000 jobs.

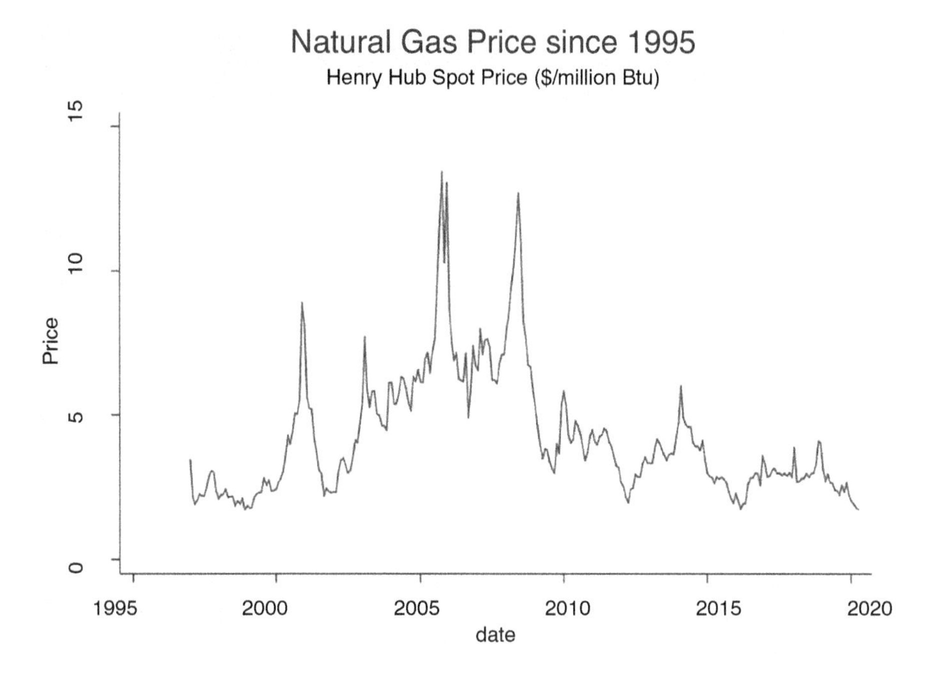

FIGURE 5.4. Natural Gas Prices Since 1995

To be sure, this estimate that the MATS rule caused the loss of labor income equal to 180,000 jobs is the result of one particular general equilibrium model of economy-wide impacts. This might not be the best model, and other models could generate different estimates. But the key point to see is that the EPA did not even *attempt* to estimate the economy-wide jobs impacts of the MATS rule. And even in estimating the employment impact within the coal-fired electricity generating industry, the EPA relied on a single model whose methods and findings differ dramatically from the standard approach now taken to estimate the impact of environmental regulations on jobs.

VII WHAT THE EPA DID NOT CONSIDER: THE SOCIAL COSTS OF JOB LOSS

For decades, economists have known that workers who lose their jobs suffer long periods of unemployment and, especially when they have to switch industries, have to accept jobs with substantially lower earnings than their lost jobs paid.[100] Aside from layoffs during periods of secular economic recession, the most significant reason for job loss is closure of a plant (Farber, 2004). Chan and Stevens (2001) find that the consequences of job loss for workers older than 55 are especially severe, with 40 percent of men and 45 percent of women over 55 still looking for a job fully two years after becoming unemployed. More recent work by Davis and von Wachter (2011, 1–55) looking at younger male workers less than 50 years of age who lost their jobs over the period 1980 to 2005 found that mass layoffs reduced earnings over the following 20 year period by an amount equal to 1.7 years-worth of pre-job loss earnings. This was an average. Workers who lost their jobs during periods when the unemployment was 8 percent or higher – such as that which prevailed over the period 2008–2012 – suffered an even bigger loss of future earnings equal to 2.8 years of pre-unemployment wages.

Other work finds that the costs of job loss are not limited to prolonged unemployment and permanent reductions in future earnings. Sullivan and von Wachter (2009, 1265–1306) find that long term male workers unemployed during the mid-1980s not only suffered increased unemployment and a 15–20 percent drop in long-run earnings, but – partly as a result of the earnings reduction – a 50–100 percent jump in mortality for the years immediately following job loss and a long term, persistent 10–15 percent increase in their death rates. If continued beyond the 25 year period studied by Sullivan and von Wachter, they conclude that such an increase in mortality rate implies a loss of life expectancy of 1–1.5 years. The most recent few years' earnings, moreover, rather than longer average earnings, seem to be most strongly associated with mortality, with a 10 percent decrease in average earnings over a five year period associated with a 38 percent increase in workers' (instantaneous) death rate (Sullivan and von Wachter 2009, 133–138). A similar impact of job loss in increasing mortality and reducing life expectancy has been found in Sweden (Eliason and Storrie 2009, 277–302).

Economists have not attempted to uncover precisely how it might be that unemployment increases mortality, but epidemiologists have. What they have discovered (as summarized, for example, by Dooley et al. [1996, 449-465] and, more recently, Catalano et al. [2011, 431–450]) is that unemployment not only leads to a variety of unhealthy behaviors such as excessive alcohol consumption and tobacco use, but also consistent and significant increases in the damaging stress hormone cortisol and decreased immune function. And such adverse health impacts on job losers cascades through the generations. A large body of work (see, for example, Kalil and Wrightman [2011, 57–78]) shows that both because of lost income and psychological stress, parental job loss negatively impacts both the short- and long-run educational achievement and attainment of children. This negative effect of unemployment is especially pronounced for African-American families, where parents have lower average wealth and experience unemployment more often.

Perhaps the most important thing to understand is that even for regulations with the potentially large impacts on employment as the MATS rule, the EPA does not actually consider the costs of lost jobs in its formal cost-benefit analysis. It breaks out employment impacts separately, and despite the substantial body of work just surveyed that attaches dollar estimates to the lost earnings and numerical estimates of the decreased life expectancy that prolonged unemployment causes, that is the end of the EPA's treatment of employment effects in its RIAs. According to Ferris and McGartland (2013, 172–179) – who serve respectively as an EPA economist and Director of the EPA's National Center for Environmental Economics – in analyzing the impact of its regulations, EPA economists assume that the economy is at full employment and workers have no cost of transitioning between jobs. If this is true, then environmental regulations by assumption cannot have any employment impacts. In such a world, the engineers and plant operators who worked in coal-fired power plants that were retired due to the MATS rule costlessly found jobs that are just as good.

Empirically, this is not what happened in the coal-fired power industry. Ferris and McGartland (2013, 173–176) recognize that the full employment, zero transition cost world is unlikely to be a realistic assumption. Yet they defend the practice of ignoring employment costs in environmental regulations in the EPA's formal cost-benefit analyses on the ground that if employment impacts were considered, then it might be that those impacts are so big that their analysis would conclude "that policymakers should (or should not) regulate on the basis of employment impacts instead of environmental quality." From the point of society as a whole, this is of course precisely what we would want: if environmental benefits from a regulation are swamped by the harm the regulation does to workers, then the regulation should not be promulgated.

From the EPA's point of view, by contrast, such a result would be intolerable. Remember that as I explained in Chapter 2, the Nixon administration faced a choice in creating a new environmental agency between an agency that would consider and trade off the full costs of reducing pollution against the benefits and an agency that was an advocacy agency, responsible only for finding and justifying new types of pollution reduction opportunities. The Nixon administration chose the latter type, and the EPA is that agency. With some justification, the EPA can say that it is not its job to spend resources on the kinds of complex economic analysis that is required to come up with reliable estimates of the equilibrium employment impacts of its regulations, where equilibrium means the impact of regulations on employment – taking account of the full range of direct and indirect effects. Such effects include not only the adverse effects on earnings and mortality from job loss that I have already discussed, but labor market benefits, such as increased jobs in the pollution reduction equipment sector, reduced sick days due to improved air quality, and a host of other impacts that one might find.

The argument against taking into account such myriad positive and negative indirect impacts has some persuasive force when it is applied to regulations that have relatively small, limited employment effects. But it has considerably less force when applied to a regulation, such as the MATS rule, that led to the closure of hundreds of power plants and the loss of thousands of high paying jobs, effects that were highly concentrated in geographic regions of the country with unemployment rates that as of 2012 had only very recently fallen below the 10–12 percent level they had been at since the Great Recession began in 2007. To put it mildly, as do Ferris and McGartland (2013 175), under such conditions, cost-benefit analysis may "appropriately include the aggregate monetized value of net employment changes." A rule like the EPA's MATS, that caused mass plant closures and job loss in an already economically depressed region of the country, epitomizes the kind of regulation that carries very high "transition" costs – prolonged periods of unemployment that cause permanent lost earnings and significant increases in mortality rates.

All of these costs pertain just to unemployment. As we have seen above, coal-fired power plants were generally located in relatively small towns and rural or exurban areas. For the communities in which they were located, coal-fired power plants closed by the MATS rule had been crucial taxpayers, providing the funding for everything from schools to police. When they closed, entire communities suffered losses that no one has attempted to quantify.

Even aggregated, these costs are surely an underestimate of the cost of the MATS rule. That regulation was only a small piece of a regulatory agenda with the explicit goal of eliminating entire American industries – coal mining and coal-fired electricity generation. The kind of cost-benefit analysis done by the EPA has never been designed to estimate the dollar harm from such massive, catastrophic economic change.

Notes

1. Erica Martinson, Uttered in 2008, Still Haunting Obama, Politico, April 5, 2012, https://www.politico.com/story/2012/04/uttered-in-2008-still-haunting-obama-in-2012-074892.
2. William Yeatman, Congress should Eliminate Obama's Stream Protection Rule, Competitive Enterprise Institute, January 31, 2017, available at https://cei.org/blog/congress-should-eliminate-obamas-stream-protection-rule.
3. Industrial Economics Inc., Final RIA of the Stream Protection Rule at 7–10, November, 2016, available at https://www.regulations.gov/document?D=OSM-2015-0002-0194.
4. Final RIA for the Stream Protection Rule at ES-30.
5. Mine Safety and Health Administration, Lowering Miners' Exposure to Respirable Coal Mine Dust, Including Continuous Personal Dust Monitors, 79 Fed.Reg. 24,814 (May 1, 2014) (codified at 30 C.F.R. pts. 70, 71, 72, 75, 90).
6. Lowering Miners' Exposure to Respirable Coal Mine Dust, supra at 79 Fed. Reg. 24,871.
7. US Department of Labor, Mine Safety and Health Administration Office of Standards, Regulations, and Variances, Preliminary Regulatory Economic Analysis For Lowering Miners' Exposure to Respirable Coal Mine Dust Including Continuous Personal Dust Monitors, Proposed Rule 16, RIN 1219-AB64, September 2010.
8. Mine Safety and Health Administration Office of Standards, Regulations, and Variances, Preliminary Regulatory Economic Analysis For Lowering Miners'

Exposure to Respirable Coal Mine Dust Including Continuous Personal Dust Monitors (Coal Dust Rule Preliminary Economic Analysis) at 16.

9. Coal Dust Rule Preliminary Economic Analysis, Table III-5 pp. 23-24.
10. W.R. Reed et al., A Company-Perspective Cost Analysis of the Personal Dust Monitor (PDM), Centers for Disease Control, NIOSH, https://www.cdc.gov/niosh/mining/UserFiles/works/pdfs/acpca.pdf.
11. *Murray Energy* v. *Sec'y DOL*, 912 F.3d 843 (11th Cir. 2016), Brief for Petitioner 51, 2014 WL 3766636, at
12. Murray Energy, Brief for Petitioner, supra note 11 at 47.
13. The F appears 79 Fed. Reg. 24,852.
14. Murray Energy Brief for Petitioner, supra note 11 at 46.
15. Murray Energy Brief for Petitioner, supra note 11 at 51 and following.
16. See MSHA Preliminary Economic Analysis, supra note 7, Table V-2.
17. *Murray Energy* v. *Sec'y of Labor*, Brief for Petitioners at 61-63.
18. John F. Gamble et al., A Critical Review of the Scientific Basis for MSHA's Proposal for Lowering the Coal Mine Dust Standard (Critical Review), I-COMM-57-7; see also I-COMM-76-5.
19. *National Mining Association* v. *Sec'y US Dept of Labor*, 812 F.3d 843 (11th Cir. 2016).
20. *National Mining Association* v. *Sec'y of Labor* at 872.
21. *National Mining Association* v. *Sec'y of Labor*, at 866.
22. *Marsh* v. *Oregon Nat. Res. Council*, 490 US 360, 378, 109 S.Ct. 1851, 1861, 104 L. Ed.2d 377 (1989)
23. *National Mining Association* v. *Sec'y US Department of Labor*, at 872.
24. Continuous Personal Dust Monitor, Posted on February 3, 2017 by Steven Mischler, PhD, and Valerie Coughanour, MA, MFA, available at https://blogs.cdc.gov/niosh-science-blog/2017/02/03/pdm/.
25. Alan Matta, Working the Coal Mine – Avoiding Dust Inhalation, Thermo Fisher Scientific, Dec. 9, 2014, available at https://www.thermofisher.com/blog/mining/working-in-the-coal-mine-avoiding-dust-inhalation-2/.
26. Coal, Chemistry Explained, available at : http://www.chemistryexplained.com/Ce-Co/Coal.html#ixzz6FAkeBiWx.
27. USEPA (United States Environmental Protection Agency). 2004. Air Pollution Control Technology Fact Sheet. Washington, DC: USEPA.
28. US Environmental Protection Agency Office of Air Quality Planning and Standards Health and Environmental Impacts Division, Regulatory Impact Analysis for the Final Mercury and Air Toxics Standards 2-8, EPA-452/R-11-011, December 2011.
29. National Research Council (1991, 24-26).
30. EPA, Regulatory Impact Analysis for the Final Clean Air Interstate Rule 6-7, EPA-452/R-05-002 March 2005, available at https://www3.epa.gov/ttn/ecas/docs/ria/transport_ria_final-clean-air-interstate-rule_2005-03.pdf.

31. EPA, RIA for the Final Clean Air Interstate Rule at 7-5.
32. NO_x SIP Call, 63 Fed. Reg. 57,356, 57,359 (Oct. 27, 1998).
33. *Michigan* v. *E.P.A.*, 213 F.3d 663 (DC Cir. 2000), *Appalachian Power Co.* v. *E.P.A.*, 249 F.3d 1032 (DC Cir. 2001).
34. EPA RIA for the Final Clean Air Interstate Rule at 8-15.
35. 531 F.3d 896 (DC Cir. 2008), *reconsidered at*, 550 F.3d 1176 (2008).
36. The following is drawn from ABA, The Cross-State Air Pollution Rule and EPA's Rush to Regulate, Jan. 1, 2012, available at https://www.americanbar.org/groups/environment_energy_resources/publications/trends/2011_12/january_february/cross_state_air_pollution_rule_epas_rush_regulate/.
37. EPA, Regulatory Impact Analysis (RIA) for the final Transport Rule 256-258, Docket ID No. EPA-HQ-OAR-2009-0491 (2011), available at https://www.epa.gov/csapr/cross-state-air-pollution-final-and-proposed-rules.
38. EPA, Regulatory Impact Analysis (RIA) for the final Transport Rule 287-290, Table 8-7 at 297.
39. EPA, Regulatory Impact Analysis (RIA) for the final Transport Rule at 379.
40. For more on the Section 112 system of hazardous air pollutant regulation created by the 1990 amendments, see Mank (1994, 267).
41. Classically described in considerable detail by Ackerman and Hassler (1981, 18–41).
42. The relevant provision concerning power plants is Section 112(n)(1)(A).
43. EPA, Mercury Study Report to Congress, Vol. 1 (Dec. 1997), EPA-HQ- OAR-2009-0234-3054.
44. EPA, Study of HAP Emissions from EGUs – Final Report to Congress, Vol. 1 at 7-7 (Feb. 1998), EPA-HQ-OAR-2009-0234-3052
45. 85 Fed. Reg. 25,894.
46. See 65 Fed. Reg. 79,829, 79,830.
47. In *Utility Air Regulatory Group* v. *EPA*, No. 01-1074, (DC Cir. 2001).
48. 42 USC Section 7412(e)(4).
49. See 70 Fed. Reg at 16,007-16,008, 16,011-16,020.
50. 517 F.3d 574 (DC Cir. 2008).
51. *White Stallion Energy Center LLC* v. *EPA*, Joint Brief of State, Industry and Labor Petitioners, No. 12-1177, Document No. 1401252 (DC Cir. 2012).
52. EPA, National Emission Standards for Hazardous Air Pollutants From Coal- and Oil-Fired Electric Utility Steam Generating Units and Standards of Performance for Fossil-Fuel-Fired Electric Utility, Industrial-Commercial- Institutional, and Small Industrial- Commercial-Institutional Steam Generating Units (EPA, Mercury Rule), 76(85) Fed. Reg 24,976, 25,073, Table 21 (May 3, 2011).
53. EPA, Mercury Rule at 76 Fed. Reg. 25078
54. 129 S.Ct. 1498 (2009).
55. 129 S.Ct. at 1504.
56. *Entergy Corp.* v. *Riverkeeper, Inc.*, 129 S.Ct. at 1505.

57. 33 USC § 1326(b).
58. 33 USC § 1311(b)(1)(A).
59. *Entergy Corp.* v. *Riverkeeper Inc.*, 129 S.Ct. at 1510.
60. 76 Fed. Reg. 24,987-24,988.
61. 76 Fed. Reg, 24,989.
62. § 7412(n)(1)(B).
63. *Michigan* v. *EPA*, 135 S.Ct. 2699, 2707 (2015).
64. *Michigan* v. *EPA*, 135 S.Ct. at 2708.
65. Environmental Protection Agency, Supplemental Finding That It Is Appropriate and Necessary To Regulate Hazardous Air Pollutants From Coal- and Oil-Fired Electric Utility Steam Generating Units, 81(79) Fed. Reg. 24,420, April 25, 2016.
66. Environmental Protection Agency, Supplemental Finding That It Is Appropriate and Necessary to Regulate Hazardous Air Pollutants from Coal- and Oil-Fired Electric Utility Steam Generating Units, at 24,441.
67. EPA, Regulatory Impact Analysis for the Final Mercury and Air Toxics Standards 3-17, EPA-452/R-11-011, December, 2011.
68. EPA, EPA Integrated Planning Model – EPA Applications, Revised June 6, 2014, available at https://cfpub.epa.gov/si/si_public_record_report.cfm?Lab=OAP&dirEntryId=74919.
69. National Academy of Sciences, National Research Council Consensus Study Report, Models in Environmental Decision Making 50, Box 2-1 (2007).
70. EPA, IPM Analysis of the Final Mercury and Air Toxics Rule (MATS), https://www.epa.gov/airmarkets/ipm-analysis-final-mercury-and-air-toxics-standards-mats. The base case and policy case parsed spreadsheets are available on the website for this book at __
71. Sam Batkins and Catrina Rorke, Regulations Eliminate More Than 1,850 Jobs, American Action Forum, March 22, 2012, available at https://www.americanactionforum.org/research/regulations-eliminate-more-than-1850-jobs/.
72. Dave Alexander, Consumers Energy Announces Cobb Plant to Close Down by 2015, Dec. 2, 2011, available at https://www.mlive.com/business/west-michigan/2011/12/consumers_energy_announces_bc.html (reporting the loss of 116 jobs at this plant); Tom Henry, Coal Fired Power Plant in Monroe County closes Next Week, Toledo Blade, April 8, 2016, available at https://www.toledoblade.com/business/2016/04/08/Coal-fired-plant-in-Monroe-Co-closes-next-week/stories/20160407368 (reporting that 71 employees of the J.R. Whiting plant would lose their jobs); from Lindsey Knake, Consumers Energy plans to begin demolition of J.C. Weadock Plant on Saginaw Bay in Hampton Township in 2016, October 30, 2013, https://www.mlive.com/news/bay-city/2013/10/consumers_energy_to_demolish_w.html, I have estimated that 1/5 of the total employment at the Karn-Weadock facility lost their jobs as a result of the closure

of just the Weadock facility, which provided about 1/5 of the facility's total generating capacity.

73. Sam Batkins and Catrina Rorke, Regulations Eliminate More Than 1,850 Jobs, American Action Forum, March 22, 2012, available at https://www.americanactionforum.org/research/regulations-eliminate-more-than-1850-jobs/.
74. Power, Supporting Coal Power Plant Workers Through Plant Closures, May 3, 2016, available at https://www.powermag.com/supporting-coal-power-plant-workers-plant-closures/.
75. Peter Frost, Dominion plans to shutter Yorktown and Chesapeake power plants between 2015 and 2022, Daily Press, September 1, 2011, available at https://www.dailypress.com/news/dp-xpm-20110901-2011-09-01-dp-nws-yorktown-dominion-20110901-story.html.
76. Sean Teehan, Salem Power Station scheduled to close by June, 2014, Boston Globe, May 12, 2011.
77. Anderson Economic Group, Economic Impact of the St. Clair Power Plant, Sept. 12, 2017, available at https://www.andersoneconomicgroup.com/Portals/0/St.%20Clair%20Econ%20Impact%20Report_9-12-2017.pdf.
78. Photo reproduced with permission from Consumers' Energy.
79. Institute for Energy Research, Impact of EPA's Regulatory Assault on Power Plants: new Regulations to Take 34 GW of Electricity Generation Offline and the Plant Closing Announcements Keep Coming, April 20, 2012.
80. Penn N. Markham, Yilu Liu and Marcus Young, Environmental Regulation Impacts on Eastern Interconnection Performance, Oak Ridge National Laboratory, Energy and Transportation Sciences Division, July 2013, ORNL/YM-0000/00. It is worth noting that this Oak Ridge report verifies the closure of all the units in my list of announced or reported closures.
81. US EIA, AEO2014 projects more coal-fired power plant retirements by 2016 than have been scheduled, Feb. 14, 2014, available at https://www.eia.gov/todayinenergy/detail.php?id=15031.
82. US EIA, Scheduled 2015 capacity additions mostly wind and natural gas; retirements mostly coal, March 10, 2015, available at https://www.eia.gov/todayinenergy/detail.php?id=20292#tabs_SpotPriceSlider-2.
83. EIA, Almost all power plants that retired in the past decade were powered by fossil fuels, Dec. 19, 2018, available at https://www.eia.gov/todayinenergy/detail.php?id=37814. Data source, US Energy Information Administration, Form EIA-860M, *Preliminary Monthly Electric Generator Inventory*.
84. EIA, Almost all power plants that retired in the past decade were powered by fossil fuels, supra note 83.
85. Power Magazine, Supporting Coal Power Plant Workers Through Plant Closures, May 3, 2016, available at https://www.powermag.com/supporting-coal-power-plant-workers-plant-closures/.

86. EPA, Regulatory Impact Analysis for the Final Mercury and Air Toxics Standards 6-11 to 6-12, Office of Air Quality Planning and Standards Health and Environmental Impacts Division, EPA-452/R-11-011, December 2011.
87. US BLS, Occupational Employment and Wages, May 2019
    51-8013 Power Plant Operators, available at https://www.bls.gov/oes/current/oes518013.htm#ind.
88. Anderson Economic Group, Economic Impact of the St. Clair Power Plant, Sept. 12, 2017, available at https://www.andersoneconomicgroup.com/Portals/0/St.%20Clair%20Econ%20Impact%20Report_9-12-2017.pdf
89. Closure of Consumer Energy's B.C. Cobb Plant would mean loss of millions in taxes, Dec. 2009, https://www.mlive.com/business/west-michigan/2009/12/closure_of_consumers_energys_b.html.
90. Kristin Rover, Duke Energy retires coal units at Beckjord Claremont Sun, April 4, 2014, https://www.clermontsun.com/2014/09/04/duke-energy-retires-coal-units-at-beckjord/.
91. Russell Gold, Utility Jobs Lost as New Power Plants Need Fewer Workers, Wall Street Journal, Jan. 6, 2018, available at https://www.wsj.com/articles/utility-jobs-shrink-as-new-power-plants-need-fewer-workers-1516021200.
92. EPA, Regulatory Impact Analysis for the Final Mercury and Air Toxics Standards 6-11 to 6-12, Office of Air Quality Planning and Standards Health and Environmental Impacts Division, EPA-452/R-11-011, December 2011.
93. EPA, RIA for the Final MATS Rule at 6A-8.
94. EPA, RIA for the Final MATS Rule at 6-6 fn. 5.
95. E. Mark Curtis, Who Loses Under Power Plant Cap-and-Trade Programs?, NBER Working Paper No. 20808, December, 2014, available at https://www.nber.org/papers/w20808.
96. Karen Palmer, Dallas Burtraw, Ranjit Bharvirkar, and Anthony Paul, Restructuring and Cost of Reducing NO_x Emissions in Electricity Generation, RFF Discussion Paper 01/10.
97. Data come from EIA, Energy Annual, at https://www.eia.gov/totalenergy/data/annual/.
98. EIA, Henry Hubb Natural Gas price, available at https://www.eia.gov/dnav/ng/hist/rngwhhdm.htm.
99. Anne E. Smith et al, February 2013, Estimating Employment Impacts of Regulations: A Review of EPA's Methods for Its Air Rules 28, NERA, February 2013, available at https://www.uschamber.com/sites/default/files/documents/files/020360_ETRA_Briefing_NERA_Study_final.pdf.
100. See, for example, Farber (2004, 69-117).

6

The Clean Power Plan, the Rule of Law, and the EPA's Takeover of State and Regional Electricity Systems

All of the rules aimed at coal mines and coal-burning electric utilities discussed in the previous chapter were just a prelude to what the Endangerment Finding had made possible – EPA regulations under the CAA that were intended to end the American coal-burning power industry forever. As we have seen, Congress passed the CAA to create federal standards for dealing with local air pollution problems, and then amended it twice, attempting to deal with the newly recognized interstate air pollution problems of acid rain and ground level ozone, and also giving the federal EPA a significantly bigger role. The accumulation of CO_2 in the global atmosphere is a problem completely unlike either local or interstate air pollution. Because the CAA was simply not written to deal with the problem of rising atmospheric CO_2 concentration, it was not easy for the EPA to find language in that statute that arguably justified concrete steps to regulate GHG emissions. Even the tailpipe rules discussed earlier – promulgated under the very same section of the CAA that contains the Endangerment trigger – required the EPA to assume an unprecedented role in setting CAFÉ standards. It turned out to be even more difficult for the EPA to use the Endangerment Finding as a pathway to regulations cutting GHG emissions from the coal-fired power industry.

This chapter describes the torturous path followed by the Obama-era EPA in regulating such emissions under the CAA.

I REGULATING GHG EMISSIONS FROM NEW PLANTS UNDER THE PSD PROGRAM

To adopt, for a moment, the language of environmental law advocacy, the "challenge" facing the Obama EPA was in trying to figure out how to regulate GHG emissions from power plants and factories under the CAA in way that would survive legal challenge. The seriousness of this "challenge" becomes apparent as soon we recall how the CAA is structured. The core provisions of the law work by having the EPA set health-based National Ambient Air Quality Standards (NAAQS), which are to be achieved primarily by having all new factories and plants install pollution reduction technologies.

In regulating GHG emissions under the CAA, the EPA did not proceed by setting a NAAQS for GHG emissions. The reason is that for policy purposes, it is universally accepted that the atmospheric concentration of GHGs is geographically uniform. For this reason, regulating GHGs by first setting a NAAQS for GHGs would have caused every region in the country to be either out of attainment with the NAAQS or in attainment with the NAAQS. Either way, every major source of GHG emissions in the entire country would have been subject to technology-based emission requirements. If the EPA set a NAAQS for GHGs that was above the status quo atmospheric concentration level, so that every air quality in the United States would have been in attainment, then every factory (in 28 listed industrial categories) with GHG emissions of 100 tons or more per year would have been required to use the best available control technology (BACT) in order to get a permit under the PSD program for attainment areas. If, on the other hand, the EPA set the NAAQS for CO_2 below the current atmospheric CO_2 concentration level, then every air quality region in the country would have been in non-attainment, and any new source of CO_2 emission anywhere in the country would be allowed only if there was an offsetting reduction of CO_2 emissions by some other source in the same air quality region and the new factory met the toughest technology-based standard in the entire CAA, the lowest achievable emissions rate (LAER).[1]

While the costs of setting a low GHG ambient air quality standard would have been nationally catastrophic – literally prohibiting any new factory or plant that would increase CO_2 emissions, which is virtually every factory or plant – even setting a high GHG standard would have entailed massive, nationwide costs under the PSD program. In addition, new air quality standards have for decades been justified by the EPA with epidemiological evidence showing that excess mortality would decline with tougher standards. Such epidemiological evidence does not exist to support a GHG NAAQS, regardless of whether it might be lower or higher than the current atmospheric concentration level.

For all these reasons, rather than trying set and the defend in court NAAQS for GHG emissions from factories, the EPA decided to proceed directly to regulating CO_2 emissions under the CAA's technology-based pollution standards. The EPA could do this because those standards apply to factories that emit an "air pollutant."[2] The Supreme Court clearly held in *Massachusetts* v. *EPA* that GHG emissions are an "air pollutant" under the CAA. Hence the EPA could regulate them under statutory sections that applied to emissions of an "air pollutant." The key regulatory programs invoked by the EPA were the PSD program for attainment regions, and the Title V permit requirement.

To recall, PSD technology-based pollution reduction requirements apply to any "major stationary source" that begins actual construction on a new facility or undertakes a "major modification" in an area designated as attainment or unclassifiable for a NAAQS. It might seem that since it applies only to attainment regions with relatively clean air, the PSD program would have been inadequate to really get at all factories and plants emitting CO_2. However, under the language of the CAA, the PSD permitting requirements apply in any region that is in attainment for either sulfur dioxide or particulates (dust), or which meets the NAAQS standard for any air pollutant.[3] As early as 1987, *every* region in the United States had met the NAAQS for at least one pollutant. Indeed, the only region that approached a complete failure to meet the NAAQS was the South Coast Air Basin in California, which had met only the sulfur dioxide standard.[4] Thus even by the late 1980s, for purposes of triggering the technology-based standard of the PSD program, the entire United States was sufficiently in compliance with national air quality standards. The PSD program had become a regime of nationally uniform technology-based air pollution reduction requirements.

But the fact that the PSD requirements would apply to GHG emitters everywhere in the United States actually caused a huge problem for the Obama EPA. As the EPA itself reported, by 2014, there were only about 800 applications per year for PSD permits. Because the PSD requirements apply to any emitter of more than 250 tons of a CAA pollutant, covering GHG emissions under the PSD program would mean that about 82,000 such applications would be required. Just the cost of administering the PSD program would increase from $12 million to $1.5 billion – a 125 fold increase. Even worse, covering GHG emissions under the Title V permit program that applies to pollution sources emitting 100 tons or more of a covered air pollutant would increase the number of required permit holders from 15,000 to 6,000,000, with covered "emitters" including tens of thousands of small businesses and even some large households (Miller 2011, 1403). According to the EPA, annual administrative costs for the Title V permit program would increase from $62 million to $21 billion, and the tens of thousands of small businesses and even households now covered by Title V permits would face permitting costs of $147 billion.[5] Such increases in regulatory cost and burden were uniformly viewed as completely infeasible from a political point of view.

One is tempted to add that such an increase in regulatory scope and cost under the CAA must also surely have been illegal. Indeed, the EPA itself argued that such an outcome would be "contrary to congressional intent," and would "severely undermine what Congress sought to accomplish."[6] If one accepts these contentions – that including GHG emissions under the language of the CAA would frustrate Congress' intent in passing the CAA and undermine that law's purpose – then it would seem that one must conclude that GHG emissions are not "pollutants" under the CAA. One would conclude, in other words, that it is absurd to think that GHG emissions are regulated under the CAA.

But remember that in *Massachusetts* v. *EPA*, the Supreme Court had said that GHG emissions *are* simply another "air pollutant" regulated just like any other "air pollutant" under the CAA. How the Court could have interpreted the CAA in a way that led directly to such results is actually quite a deep question going to the reliability of the Court's methods for interpreting statutes. My own view is that *Massachusetts* v. *EPA* shows that the Court's current methods for interpreting statutes – looking extremely narrowly at a particular small part of a statute, such as the definition of "air pollutant" provided in the CAA, without paying sufficient attention to how the regulatory scheme created by the statute was intended to work – generate an unacceptably high probability of such absurd results.

Whether this is so is an important, and unresolved, question about different methods courts use to interpret statutes. But for practical purposes, all that mattered for the Obama EPA's program of regulating GHG emissions under the CAA was that while that effort was based on the Court's decision that GHG emissions are an "air pollutant" covered under the CAA, it would have meant political death to that effort if the EPA had declared that virtually every business in the country now had costly CAA compliance obligations.

Logically enough, the EPA simply rewrote the CAA to say that even though GHG emissions were an "air pollutant," GHG emitters were required to comply with the PSD and Title V requirements only if their GHG emissions were at least 100,000 tons per year (with the threshold possibly going down to 50,000 tons after 2013).[7] To be clear, the express language of the CAA says that GHG emitters have to comply with PSD and Title V requirements if their GHG emissions exceed 250 tons per year. The Obama EPA said that as this would lead to absurdly costly and virtually universal compliance obligations for American business, only factories emitting more than 100,000 tons per year had to comply.

This was too much for the Supreme Court. The EPA's PSD and Title V GHG regulations were challenged in *Utility Air Regulatory Group* v. *EPA*. The Court did not concede in that case that it had created the entire problem by saying that GHG emissions are an "air pollutant." In the entire history of the Supreme Court, one can discover few instances in which the Court admitted that its own prior decision had been responsible for absurd and unintended results. What the Court said was that the EPA was wrong to say that it was required by the CAA to apply the onerous PSD technology-based standards and costly Title V permitting requirements to any factory with GHG emissions above the statutory threshold. Interestingly, the EPA was wrong, said Justice Scalia's majority opinion, not because of something that the CAA actually explicitly says. Rather, according to Justice Scalia, the EPA was wrong because the EPA's view "would place plainly excessive demands on limited governmental resources" and "would bring about an enormous and transformative expansion in the EPA's regulatory authority without clear congressional authorization. . . . We expect Congress to speak clearly if it wishes to assign to an agency decisions of vast 'economic and political significance.'"[8]

Having scolded the EPA for taking *Massachusetts* v. *EPA* too literally, the Court in *UARG* v. *EPA* then scolded the agency even more harshly for rewriting the clear statutory regulatory triggers of 100 and 250 tons of GHG to read 100,000 tons. As Justice Scalia lectured:[9]

> an agency has no power to "tailor" legislation to bureaucratic policy goals by rewriting unambiguous statutory terms. . . . It is hard to imagine a statutory term less ambiguous than the precise numerical thresholds at which the Act requires PSD and Title V permitting. When EPA replaced those numbers with numbers of its own choosing, it went well beyond the bounds of its statutory authority.

The two parts of Justice Scalia's *UARG* v. *EPA* admonishment of EPA are arguably consistent: the EPA must adopt a reasonable interpretation – one that does not vastly expand its own jurisdiction and the economic burdens of regulation on industry – when it is interpreting a somewhat general statutory term such as "air pollutant," but it may not simply rewrite a specific statutory term such as the 250 and 100 ton triggers for PSD and Title V regulatory obligations. Conversely, one could argue that Scalia's view that "air pollutant" was a vague term subject to the EPA's reasonable interpretation was inconsistent with Justice Stevens' opinion for the majority in *Massachusetts* v. *EPA* that GHG emissions were clearly included among "air pollutants." There the Court had no problem in saying that GHG emissions were an "air pollutant" even though – unlike every other covered pollutant – GHGs are specifically mentioned nowhere in the regulatory provisions of the CAA.

In functional terms, none of this mattered very much. From a functional point of view, the EPA actually won *UARG* v. *EPA* because the Court held that it was perfectly reasonable for the EPA to regulate GHG emissions from factories and plants that already had to comply with the PSD program's technology-based standards and Title V permitting because their emissions of standard air pollutants exceeded the 250 and 100 ton thresholds. As the federal government itself conceded that such sources of air pollution generated 83 percent of US GHG emissions from factories[10] (including virtually all coal-burning electricity generating plants), just by upholding the extension of permit and technology-based pollution reduction requirements to GHG emissions from big polluters that were already regulated, the Court would in effect give the EPA virtually all the regulatory authority it actually needed.

In an almost offhand way, the Court did just that. It stated without qualification that "applying BACT to greenhouse gases is not so disastrously unworkable, and need not result in such a dramatic expansion of agency authority, as to convince us that EPA's interpretation is unreasonable." After all, the Court said, the only thing being talked about in the case was the EPA "moderately increasing the demands EPA. . . can make of entities already subject to its regulation. And it is not yet clear that EPA's demands will be of a significantly different character from those traditionally associated with PSD review."[11] Here, the Court seems to think that just as there are technologies for reducing air pollution from a given factory, so too are there technologies for reducing GHG emissions from a given factory. This is false. To understand why it is that the regulation of GHG emissions is indeed of "a completely different character" than cutting air pollution, one needs to have in hand some concrete facts about how factories and power plants reduce air pollution.

There are two crucial aspects about the technologies used to reduce pollution from coal-burning facilities. The first is that they are old, dating from the early to mid-twentieth century. It is true that the CAA forced polluters to incur the cost of installing these technologies. But it is not true that the CAA somehow incentivized the development of completely new and previously unknown technologies. The second aspect is that many, if not most, of the air pollution reduction technologies called for by the CAA generate CO_2. This was well known and understood at the time the CAA was passed. Thus in a very real sense, in the CAA, Congress intended both to reduce air pollution and also to increase CO_2 emissions. As near I have been able to discover, when they decided that CO_2 emissions were an "air pollutant" under the CAA, the Justices of the Supreme Court were completely ignorant of the fact that technologies that the CAA required or anticipated as a means of reducing air pollution generally do so by increasing CO_2 emissions.

Environmental lawyers typically have two responses to this line of argument. The first response is that the CAA allows polluters to reduce their pollution in a number of different ways. If they can reduce air pollution some other way than by installing costly pollution reduction technology at the exhaust stage, they are free to do so. Hence, this argument goes, the CAA did not anticipate let alone cause an increase in CO_2 emissions. The second point is an argument in the alternative, that even if the CAA anticipated pollution reduction technologies that increase CO_2 emissions, there are now available similar technological fixes for the CO_2 emission problem.

The first point – that the CAA does not require that polluters adopt particular pollution reduction technologies – is true in only a very limited sense. It is true that various provisions of the CAA allow the EPA to mandate ways other than technology adoption to reduce pollution. But the CAA also imposes many restrictions on such non-technological fixes. For example, the George W. Bush administration proposed allowing a tradable pollution reduction credit system for reducing NO_X emissions in the Rust Belt and Northeast. But the courts struck this down as barred by the language of the CAA. Another example is provided by the history of how the CAA treats sulfur dioxide emissions from coal-burning electric utilities. From 1970 until 1990, the CAA did not allow such plants to reduce their SO_2 emissions by burning low sulfur coal mined in western states such as Wyoming, but required such plants to reduce their emissions by installing scrubbers. It is widely agreed that Congress did this in order to preserve the market for eastern high sulfur coal, mined in states such as West Virginia and Illinois. Only in 1990 did Congress amend the CAA to allow coal-burning electric utilities the flexibility to reduce SO_2 emissions by burning low sulfur coal or, in the alternative, to buy SO_2 emission permits from utilities that had reduced their SO_2 emissions by even more than the law required. These are exceptions to the rule: for the most part, the CAA requires factories to install particular pollution reduction technologies.

II AT COMMERCIAL SCALE, CARBON CAPTURE AND STORAGE IS ECONOMICALLY INFEASIBLE AND COMPLETELY UNLIKE THE POLLUTION REDUCTION TECHNOLOGIES REQUIRED UNDER THE CAA

Although the Obama-era EPA argued consistently to the contrary, on a number of dimensions, the technological approach to lowering CO_2 emissions – carbon capture and sequestration (or CCS) – is completely unlike conventional air pollution reduction technologies. The most fundamental differences flow from the basic fact that there simply is no technological means of converting CO_2 in industrial exhaust from fossil fuel combustion into some other, completely benign, gas. This is a matter of basic chemistry. As explained earlier, when a fossil fuel is combusted CO_2 is a direct product. Since CO_2 cannot be eliminated as a result of fossil fuel combustion, the only kind of technological approach to CO_2 emissions into the atmosphere is to route those emissions elsewhere. This is the idea behind what is called carbon capture and sequestration (CCS).

Carbon capture has actually been in use for years.[12] The oil and gas industries have used carbon capture for decades as a way to enhance oil and gas recovery. The CO_2 is captured and returned underground, where it is used to re-pressurize oil fields, allowing more oil to be pumped out of the ground. For existing industrial processes that burn coal for fuel, including electric power generation, CO_2 is separated from the exhaust gas and captured. This process is similar to air pollution scrubbers, in that a filter containing a chemical solvent absorbs CO_2. These absorbers are housed in their own separate, towering smokestack type buildings. The solvent is then heated, releasing water vapor and leaving behind concentrated CO_2.

This is where the similarity with conventional air pollution ends. While it is true that the sludge from SO_2 scrubbers must itself be transported away and disposed of, in terms of the amount of energy required, the process of transporting away and disposing of CO_2 is orders of magnitude more costly. In order to be transported away – back underground, typically – the CO_2 has to be compressed and pushed through a pipeline. This compression and transportation process takes a lot of energy. Like the CO_2 recovered from oil and gas drilling, the CO_2 filtered out of a coal-burning plant's exhaust is typically injected into underground rock formations. The long term fate of the injected CO_2 depends upon the kind of underground rock formation into which it is injected. When injected into basalt, the CO_2 eventually converts back into limestone rock. When injected into different rock, such as sandstone, it is unknown how the CO_2 might move within the rock formation, whether the CO_2 will leak out eventually, and if so, when. It is also possible to inject CO_2 under the ocean floor. The Sleipner offshore gas field owned by the Norwegian state corporation Statoil has been injecting CO_2 under the sea floor since 1996.

Breaking the chemical bond between CO_2 and the chemical solvent that absorbs it is very energy intensive (requiring 3,900–4,200 KJ/kg of CO_2) (Anderson and

Newell 2004, 109–142). Indeed, the whole CO_2 removal process – from capture and separation to transport and storage – takes a tremendous amount of energy. In order to capture, transport, and store 90 percent of its CO_2 emissions, a (bituminous) coal-burning electric utility has to consume 21–44 percent more energy per MWh of net electricity produced (Rubin et al. 2015, Table 2). That is, other things held constant, such a plant has to burn 21–44 percent more coal. Together, reduced plant efficiency and the capital costs for CO_2 capture have been estimated to increase the levelized cost of electricity produced by a coal-burning plant by between 46 and 69 percent.[13]

These costs are orders of magnitude higher than the cost to a coal-burning electricity plant of retrofitting flue gas desulfurization scrubbers, the kind of air pollution reduction technology required under the CAA. According to the EPA,[14] as of 2002, capital costs for SO_2 scrubbers had decreased by over 30% since the beginning of the 1990s, and for plants bigger than 400 MW electric utility generating facilities, the then-current capital cost for SO_2 scrubbers applied to electric utilities was reported to be approximately $100-$250/kW, with operating and maintenance between $2-$8/kW and an annual cost of $20-$50/ kW. A 2004 estimate for coal-burning power plants owned by Allegheny Power that was filed with the SEC put the capital cost of retrofitting scrubbers at bit higher, at $300/kW.[15] Using the conservative, higher estimate, the capital cost to install scrubbers at a 1,000 MW plant (a bit below average for the United States as of 2018) would be $300,000,000. Assuming that plant operates 54 percent of the time (the average for the United States in 2017), the average daily output of such a plant is 1,000 MW x .54 x 24 hours = 12,960 MWh. Over the course of an entire year, such a plant would produce 4,730,400 MWh. Dividing the $300,000,000 capital cost of scrubbers by total annual power output, the capital cost of installing scrubbers would add about $63/MWh to the cost of power.

Coal-burning plants last a long time. For example, as of 2004, when Allegheny Power was considering installing scrubbers at all of its plants, the average age of its operating fleet of plants was 41 years. Assuming (conservatively) plant life of 50 years, this illustrative levelized (plant lifetime) capital cost of scrubbers was about $1.25/ MWh. As of 2018, the Institute for Energy Research estimated the levelized cost of building and operating a coal-fired electric power plant at $41/MWh.[16] Inflating the 2004 estimate of scrubber cost at our illustrative electric power plant system to 2018 dollars (which results in an increase in levelized capital cost from $1.25/MWh to (1.33)$1.25 or $1.66/MWh), the levelized capital cost of installing scrubbers is still only $1.66/$41 or about 4 percent of the total levelized cost of electricity from coal-burning plants.

This 4 percent addition to the cost of electricity caused by installing flue gas sulfurization is not even comparable to the 46 to 69 percent increase in (levelized) cost caused by installing CCS. The relative cost increase caused by CCS is between roughly 1200 and 1700 percent of the relative cost increase due to installing scrubbers. And the cost of CCS has not been decreasing. According to one recent estimate, the levelized cost of CCS for the new generation of coal-burning electric utility generating plants in the United States ranges from $100 to $150/MWh.[17] These costs are multiples of the current cost of electricity from such plants. There are so high that very few existing coal-burning electric utility generating plants can be retrofitted with CCS. This is detailed in a recent Oxford University report. According to Caldecott, Kruitwagen, and Kok (2016), for a CCS retrofit to be feasible at a coal-burning electric utility plant, it must be (i) less than 20 years old, (ii) have relatively low CO_2 emissions (less than 1t CO_2/MWh), (iii) have a generating capacity of at least 100 MW, and (iv) in order to avoid prohibitive transport costs, be within 40 kilometers of a "suitable" or "highly suitable" underground injection site (sedimentary basins or contingent margins with well understood geology).[18] With all of these requirements, it is perhaps not surprising that of the 100 largest coal-fired electric utility providers in the world, 65 percent had *no plants* – zero – that could be retrofitted with CCS. Of the 23 largest coal-burning electric utilities in the United States, the vast majority – 18 or 78 percent – had no plants that were deemed "retrofittable" for CCS. No US utility had more than 25 percent of its plants that were deemed retrofittable.[19]

The likely extreme commercial infeasibility of CCS has been known for a long time. Back in 2007, former ExxonMobil CEO Lee Raymond commented that while the oil and gas industry had been pumping CO_2 back underground to repressurize fields for a long time, "to go from that, quickly, to massive carbon sequestration for a power plant is a whole different animal." As Raymond emphasized then, the problem has always fundamentally been one of scale: "if you tried to inject all the supercritical CO_2 that came from all the coal-fired power plants you end up moving more… liquids than the oil and gas industry moves today, just for CO_2. So it is a huge, huge undertaking. And, again, people – this gets into a lot of the infrastructure issues, people just assume that that can happen. You can't assume that's going to happen. And the cost is going to be very, very significant."[20]

Developments since 2007 have proven that Raymond was correct about the infeasibility of commercial scale CCS. Despite this, governments around the world have wasted billions of dollars on pilot projects trying to find a way to change the dismal economic facts of CCS. In the UK, a £1 billion competition to develop CCS was cancelled in 2015. In the United States, FutureGen was funded in the hope that it would to build the first coal-fueled power plant with zero CO_2 emissions. Like other new CCS projects, FutureGen was not a traditional coal-burning power plant, but a coal gasification plant, also called an Integrated Gasification Combined Cycle (IGCC) plant. Such plants combust coal, oxygen, and steam to form a mixture of carbon monoxide (CO) and hydrogen (H_2) that is called syngas (synthetic gas). The syngas is then reacted with steam and various catalysts to form a mixture of hydrogen and CO_2. The syngas is burned, like natural gas, to drive turbines the produce electricity. The CO_2 is separated and then, as with capture from traditional coal-fired plants, compressed, transported, and stored (Anderson and Newell 2004, 118).

The FutureGen plant was to have a 275 MW capacity, enough to provide electric power to 150,000 homes. When costs exceeded $1.8 billion with the plant still nowhere near being operational, President Bush pulled federal support, despite the loss of $50 million in federal grants.

Even more infamous, perhaps, is the failure of the Kemper CCS project in Mississippi. In 2010, Southern Company obtained regulatory approval for and began construction on a 582 MW coal gasification plant in Kemper, Mississippi. Combining coal gasification along with CO_2 capture, transport, and storage is a complicated and costly process. The Kemper project was beset by a raft of problems:[21] the plant was to burn lignite coal, a dirty and low energy content coal that was to be mined locally, but such coal had been sitting in piles for too long and therefore became too wet; heat lining in the gasification units was poorly installed and had to be fixed; finally, tubes that were supposed to be used to cool the gas failed. Many of these may seem small, but they added up to continually increase the cost of the project far above initial estimates. It may be unfair to use the widely quoted initial cost for the plant of $2.8 billion, as that apparently did not include the cost of the CO_2 transport pipeline, or the cost of building a new coal mine to supply the plant, but when cost estimates began to top $7 billion and state regulators made clear that Southern Company would not be allowed to capture cost overruns in higher prices, in 2017 the company killed the Kemper CCS project. Despite having received almost $400 million in federal grants, Kemper was turned into a natural gas-fired electricity generator.[22] By 2019, Southern was not only facing a Justice Department investigation into what happened to this massive amount of taxpayer money, but was incurring expenses to reclaim the land at the adjacent lignite coal mine. Southern reported that along with compliance and safety costs, plus property taxes for the mine and gasifier, its ongoing costs for the Kemper CCS project would be approximately "$11 million for the remainder of 2019 and $2 million to $6 million annually in 2020 through 2023." All of these costs incurred for a plant that will never happen.

III THE CLEAN POWER PLAN

After the Supreme Court's decision in *UARG* v. *EPA* upholding the application of GHG emission limits to factories and electricity generating facilities that already had to meet PSD requirements, in October, 2016, the EPA actually specified what these PSD standards would be. As CCS was by then known to be infeasible for such plants, there simply was no GHG emission standard based on a pollution reduction technology. The PSD standard actually required by the EPA was underwhelming: for the largest and most significant GHG emission sources, the EPA required enhanced energy efficiency. That is, such plants were supposed to reduce their GHG emissions by burning less coal per unit of power generated.[23]

By October, 2016, however, the GHG emission reduction requirements imposed by the EPA under the CAA's PSD program had already been rendered largely irrelevant. The reason is that by 2016, the EPA had promulgated a set of regulations called the Clean Power Plan. In accordance with President Obama's 2013 "Climate Action Plan," the Clean Power Plan (CPP) aimed not only to end the construction of new coal-burning power plants, but also to terminate as quickly as possible the use of existing coal-burning power plants.

The Clean Power Plan was promulgated only through yet another aggressive interpretation of the CAA by the EPA. So aggressive was this interpretation that the Clean Power Plan might well have been declared illegal, as an unreasonable interpretation of the CAA, had the Court ever had the opportunity to pass on the issue. But the Court never got the opportunity, as the Trump administration rescinded the Clean Power Plan.

Even though the Clean Power Plan was never implemented, it perfectly epitomized precautionary policy. Unlike the federal CAA and its 1977 and 1990 amendments, whose structure clearly expresses the interest of those states, regions, and private groups that bore both the costs and garnered the benefits of reducing air pollution, the Clean Power Plan expressed the interests of a minority of states and groups, those who expected to benefit from the elimination of coal-burning electric utility generation while bearing few if any costs. The Clean Power Plan was not federal legislation passed by a majority vote. It was a regulatory program promulgated by an agency, the EPA, whose mission is to represent the interests of those who benefit from regulation. In other words, the Clean Power Plan was the perfect expression of precautionary policy, designed to eliminate a potentially distant but serious risk with little attention to immediate costs.

Unlike regulations under the PSD program – which covered only new power plants or major upgrades to existing power plants – the CPP covered not only new fossil fueled power plants but existing fossil fueled power plants. It was promulgated under Section 111 of the CAA. Section 111(b) gave the EPA the authority to set air pollution standards for all new factories and plants (stationary sources in the language of the CAA). Under Section 111(b), the EPA regulates new factories in industries that emit air pollution that the EPA judged to "cause, or contributes significantly to, air pollution which may reasonably be anticipated to endanger public health or welfare." This is precisely the same standard for air pollution standards for cars under Section 202 of the CAA. Like that provision, it authorizes the EPA to regulate "air pollution," not particular types of air pollution – such as sulfur dioxide. Thus under the Court's determination in *Massachusetts* v. *EPA* that GHG emissions are a form of "air pollution," Section 111(b) provided a legal basis for the EPA to regulate GHG emissions from new power plants.

But Section 111(b) does not authorize federal regulation of any "air pollutant" from an *existing* power plant. Section 112 authorizes federal regulation of hazardous air pollutants from existing plants, and as we have seen, the EPA managed to kill off about 50 GW of coal-fired power plants with its MATS rule under section 112. But even the Obama EPA realized that regulating GHG emissions as a "hazardous air pollutant" was impossible. The emissions that the EPA has regulated as "hazardous air pollutants" are all waste gases or particles that even at the quantities emitted from a single plant can cause acute harms to the health of people living near the plant, things such as hydrogen chloride, benzene, or asbestos. As we have seen, there are no acute health effects from CO_2 emissions, nor even chronic health effects at any atmospheric concentration. Regulating GHG emissions under Section 112 was not an option for the EPA.

Under the interstate air pollution provision of the CAA (Section 126) the EPA's Transport Rule had usurped state regulatory authority over interstate NO_x and SO_2 emissions and imposed large additional costs on existing coal-burning power plants. But GHG emissions could not even arguably be considered covered by Section 126.

This left only one provision in the entire Clean Air Act that the Obama EPA could interpret as giving it the authority to regulate GHG emissions from existing coal-burning plants. Section 111(d) of the CAA tells the EPA to promulgate regulations establishing procedures for states to follow in regulating air pollution from "any existing source for any air pollutant (i) for which air quality criteria have not been issued. . . or emitted from a source category which is regulated under [section 112, the hazardous air pollutant section] but (ii) to which a standard of performance under this section would apply if such existing source were a new source." This provision is not a model of clarity, but it seems to authorize the EPA to require states to regulate air pollutants that are not hazardous and not criteria air pollutants (such as sulfur dioxide) but that are emitted by factories that emit at least one kind of hazardous air pollutant regulated under Section112. In the 2011 MATS rule, the EPA had decided that coal-burning electric power plants do emit hazardous air pollutants that are regulated under Section 112. As CO_2 is not an air pollutant that Congress specifically listed in the CAA, but is only an "air pollutant" because the Supreme Court had said so 37 years after the CAA was passed in its *Massachusetts* v. *EPA* decision – Section 111(d) looked to be just the sort of statutory authority that the EPA needed to regulate CO_2 emissions from existing power plants.

The problem for the EPA was that over the many decades of practice under the CAA, the EPA had hardly ever regulated anything under Section 111(d), and when it had, it applied very traditional technology-based air pollution reduction standards, indeed, the same sort of standards that it applied to new factories under Section 111 (b). This made perfect sense, as Section 111 says that the EPA should set pollution reduction standards that "reflect the degree of emission limitation achievable through the application of the best system of emission reduction [or BSER] which (taking into account the cost of achieving such reduction and any non-air quality health and environmental impact and energy requirements) the Administrator determines has been adequately demonstrated." Up until the Clean Power Plan, all the regulations that the EPA had promulgated under Section 111(d) had been based on technologies for reducing end-of-stack air pollution at particular categories of industrial facilities.

For example, phosphate fertilizer plants emit a number of Section 108 criteria pollutants such as particulates, Section 112 hazardous air pollutants such hydrogen fluoride, and also gaseous fluoride not in the form of hydrogen fluoride. Most legal scholars believe that the purpose of Section 111(d) was indeed to capture things like gaseous fluoride – not a criteria pollutant like SO_2 or NO_x – not a hazardous pollutant, but still a pollutant to reduce. When the EPA set limits under Section 111(d) on the emissions of various pollutants from phosphate fertilizer plants, it determined the BSER for such plants by surveying the performance of plants in the industry. The EPA decided that for phosphate fertilizer plants, the best systems of emissions reduction for fluorides and particulates are different types of precipitators and entrainment separators and baghouses with physical filters.[24]

As another example of Section 111(d) emission limits, consider sulfuric acid mist from sulfuric acid plants. Such mist includes liquid mist and also sulfuric trioxide and sulfuric acid vapor. In 1977, the EPA promulgated Section 111(d) emission guidelines for sulfur mist emissions from existing sulfuric acid plants. The EPA had already promulgated standards for sulfur dioxide and acid mist emissions at new sulfuric acid plants that set the required level of pollution reduction as that achievable by using either dual absorption or scrubbing as a BSER. Taking cost into consideration, as the Section 111 BSER allows, in 1977 the EPA set the emission limits for acid mist at such plants at those levels that it felt could be achieved without excessive financial impact given the cost of adding vertical panel or horizontal dual pad mist eliminators to different types of plant.[25]

In these two examples, EPA guidelines for state emission standards under Section 111(d) were calculated by surveying emission reductions achieved by installing the best systems for reducing emissions at existing facilities, where those systems were traditional end-of-the pipe techniques for reducing air pollution, often some form of chemical or physical precipitation process (that converted air pollution into a solid waste streams). Were these examples expanded to include *all* EPA guidelines promulgated under Section 111(d) over the past forty years, the pattern would remain the same: except for methane gas from solid waste landfills (which the EPA allowed to be flared off, lest they accumulate and trigger massive and potentially locally catastrophic explosions), in setting emission limits for existing sources under Section 111(d), the EPA has targeted for regulation locally hazardous air pollutants and has established emission limit guidelines for states that are based on the best system of end-of-the pipe emission reduction then in use.

As we have seen, there is no commercially feasible "system" for either eliminating or capturing and storing CO_2 emissions from coal-fired power plants. So how was the EPA's Clean Power Plan to reduce CO_2 emissions from coal-fired power plants in a way even arguably consistent with the ostensible legal authority for that Plan, Section 111(d) of the CAA?[26] According to the EPA (in its 2014 proposed rulemaking), as it had "done in previous CAA Section 111d rulemakings," in determining what constituted BSER for reducing CO_2 emissions from coal-burning power plants (or electric utility generating units, or EGUs, in the EPA's lingo), the EPA "considered the types of strategies that states and owners and operators of EGUs are already employing to reduce the covered pollutant." These strategies, according to the EPA, "reflect the fact that, in almost all states, the production, distribution, and use of electricity can be, and is, undertaken in ways that accommodate reductions in both pollution emission rates and total emissions." A bit more concretely, the EPA came up with two ways that it believed "can and are being" implemented to reduce CO_2 emissions at EGUs: first, reducing the emissions at particular EGUs by improving the efficiency of their operations, and, second by "varying the utilization levels."

To be sure, reducing emission of a pollutant by increasing the efficiency of plant operations was not unprecedented as a BSER. Section 101 of the CAA says that among that law's purposes is to "encourage" and "promote" federal actions for pollution prevention. Win-win approaches to setting emission limits – whereby emissions are improved while cutting costs – were in fact a hallmark of the era of "smart" or "performance-based" regulation that the EPA and the states experimented with during the 1990s and early 2000s. However, as the EPA itself said in its June, 2014 proposed rulemaking, improving the efficiency of coal-burning EGUs generates at most a 4 to 6 percent reduction in CO_2 emissions.

With such limited emission reductions through better plant efficiency, the EPA was left with two recommendations for the states as to what constituted the BSER for reducing CO_2 emissions at power plants. In its 2014 proposed CPP, the EPA recommended that "for purposes of expressing the BSER" for coal-burning power plants, the states employ two categories of "broad-based, cost-effective, long-term strategies to reduce CO_2 emissions." These two strategies were state regulatory initiatives designed to (i) shift electricity production to other types of EGUs with lower or zero CO_2 emissions and (ii) cut the demand for electricity by encouraging "energy efficiency." As for traditional pollution reduction technology, the EPA admitted that even if it was technologically possible, CCS was much too costly to be BSER (at around \$83 to \$150 per ton of CO_2) for existing coal-fired power plants.[27]

During the comment period on the EPA's 2014 proposed rule, abundant evidence was submitted that energy conservation programs – employed most ambitiously in states such as California – are not very effective. In the final CPP, therefore, the EPA dropped the energy conservation strategy. Aside from the minor CO_2 emission reductions that could be achieved by increasing plant efficiency, the final CPP relied only on the first strategy: that states should shift electricity production from coal to natural gas-fired plants, and in the longer run, from coal and natural gas to renewables such as wind and solar.

The CPP illustrates several features of the precautionary principle in action. First, like the EPA's attempt to rewrite the CAA by changing the numeric threshold for PSD and Title V regulation and determining that reduction of power plant mercury emissions was appropriate regardless of how much such reduction cost, the EPA's view that the "best system" for reducing GHG emissions from coal-fired power plants was the elimination of such plants represented an assumption by the EPA of lawmaking authority that is constitutionally vested in Congress, not any regulatory agency. Second, although characterized as mere "guidance" to states on how they should aim to increase the share of zero CO_2-emission, renewable power in their electric power systems, the CPP represented an imminent threat that states that failed to comply with such guidance would have their regulatory authority supplanted by the federal EPA. Since unlike state regulators, the EPA has no statutory obligation to consider any costs of increasing the share of renewable energy, such centralization of state power system regulation in the EPA would have meant regulation free from any legal obligation to consider costs. Those costs could well have been substantial, for the EPA has no expertise in regulating the electric power sector, where the costs of regulatory mistakes are likely to be enormous and potentially catastrophic. And yet as with its other rules targeting coal, the EPA's analysis severely underestimates this and other costs of the Clean Power Plan.

IV THE CLEAN POWER PLAN AND THE EPA AS LAWMAKER OF LAST RESORT

Just as the EPA tried to rewrite the CAA to create a threshold level of pollution for regulating power plant CO_2 emissions under the PSD and Title V programs that was orders of magnitude higher than the precise numerical thresholds that Congress had actually written into the statute, so too did the EPA attempt in the Clean Power Plan to completely revise the meaning of the statutory "best system of emission reduction." True, unlike the precise numerical thresholds triggering PSD regulation under the CAA, Congress did not define what it meant by "best system of emission reduction" that is "adequately demonstrated." However, decades of regulatory practice had established that the "best system of emission reduction" under Section 111 of the CAA meant something like the precipitators, catalytic reducers, and baghouse filters that the EPA had required phosphate fertilizer plants to install to reduce their emissions of fluoride and particulate waste products. Such technologies perfectly fit one of the no fewer than *twelve* context-dependent definitions of "system" given by the Oxford English Dictionary (OED) – "a set of objects or appliances arranged or organized for some special purpose, as parts of a mechanism, components of an interdependent or interconnecting assembly or network." Such a reading is completely consistent with everything found elsewhere in the text of the 1970 CAA, and also with common sense: Congress told the EPA to base standards for emissions reduction on the reductions achieved by the best emissions reduction mechanism "adequately demonstrated."

Courts use the label "plain meaning" for such a sensible, dictionary-based interpretation of "system." This interpretation is to be contrasted with the EPA's contention in the Clean Power Plan that the best "system" for reducing carbon dioxide emissions from power plants is a haphazard congeries of state laws and regulations aimed at requiring states to get more of their electricity from renewable power sources. State electricity regulation can indeed be described as a regulatory "system" but only in the sense of a "system" of "government, or religion, or philosophy," as the OED puts it. In the fifty years since the passage of the 1970 CAA, no one even tried to argue that a "system of government" is what Congress required when it told the EPA in the CAA to determine the best "system" of emission reduction.

The only thing that the kind of "system" that the EPA called for the states to implement under the Clean Power Plan had in common with the Clean Air Act is that with the Clean Air Act, Congress clearly intended to create a federal environmental regulatory "system." However, that "system" was one under which the federal EPA was to identify, for particular industrial source categories, the best practical, mechanical system for reducing air pollution emissions. It was not a system in which the EPA was to play a central role in regulating the production and distribution of electricity from different power sources.

The EPA itself recognized the weakness of its position that the "best system of emission reduction" for power plant GHG emissions was for states to move their systems for producing and distributing electricity toward a heavy reliance on wind and solar sources of power.

The EPA's justification for such a radical interpretation of BSER given in the final CPP rule was purely precautionary. The EPA noted that in Section 101 of the CAA, Congress had endorsed "pollution prevention" as a goal, and had even defined pollution prevention as "the reduction or elimination, through *any* measures, of the amount of pollutants produced or created at the source." But as the EPA itself recognized, Congress had not simply announced the goal of reducing pollution reduction and then left the EPA to decide how to accomplish such a goal. Members of Congress negotiated and bargained over how the EPA would be allowed to accomplish that goal.

The long and complex CAA represents the terms of that congressional deal. According to the EPA,[28] "Climate change has become the nation's most important environmental problem," and the country had reached "a critical juncture to take meaningful action to curb the growth in CO_2 emissions and forestall the impending consequences of prior inaction." As the only way to reduce CO_2 emissions at existing power plants, the EPA continued, was to switch to renewables ("or far more expensive measures such as CCS"), "interpreting the 'system of emission reduction' provisions in CAA section 111(d)(1) and (a)(1) to allow the nation to meaningfully address the urgent and severe public health and welfare threats that climate change pose is consistent with what the CAA was designed to do." In other words, the threats posed by climate change are so severe that interpreting "best system of emission reduction" to mean a nationwide switch to renewable power was a linguistically and legally reasonable interpretation.

As with virtually every question involving the interpretation of the CAA to authorize the EPA to regulate CO_2 emissions, environmental law scholars were actually much more sanguine than was the EPA itself about its chances of persuading a court that the "best system" for reducing CO_2 emissions at power plants consisted of state regulations that shifted power production to renewables. Freeman and Spence, for example, argued that the EPA's view that requiring states to shift electricity production to renewables was the "best system" for reducing CO_2 emissions at power plants was "entirely plausible based on the plain meaning" of the CAA and was a "sensible interpretation in light of the interconnected nature of the electricity system and the unique characteristics of carbon dioxide emissions" (Freeman and Spence 2014, 41). Purely as a matter of how judges and lawyers interpret statutes, Freeman and Spence's "plain meaning" contention is simply wrong. Even more troubling, and more indicative of the harm caused by the precautionary principle, is their second argument, that the "interconnected nature of the electricity system and the unique characteristics of carbon dioxide emissions" somehow justified the EPA's interpretation of the CAA.

As for the first point, one must understand that courts do not interpret entire statutes. They interpret particular words in provisions of statutes, such as the "best system of emission reduction" in Section 111(d). In this process, "plain meaning" refers to the operative words used in the particular provision of the statute being interpreted. Unless it can be shown that the plain meaning of the statutory provision at issue is somehow badly inconsistent with the overall purpose of the statute, the plain meaning is the end of the interpretive process. But while courts routinely speak about the purpose of a statute such the CAA, statutes as a whole are not understood to have a "plain meaning."

The second argument made by Freeman and Spence to justify the EPA's incredible interpretation of "best system of emission reduction" to mean new state electric power generation "systems" is a dangerous application of the precautionary principle. It is far from clear what Freeman and Spence mean when they say that "the interconnected nature of the electricity system and the unique characteristics of carbon dioxide emissions" somehow justifies the EPA's interpretation. Rather than providing any further explanation of exactly what they might have meant by vague generalities such as the "interconnected nature" and "unique characteristics," the bulk of Freeman and Spence's essay consists of an argument that because of increasing ideological polarization, Congress is hopelessly deadlocked and incapable of passing legislation to address urgent public policy problems requiring a legislative solution. They argue that given the impossibility of a congressional response, the urgency of the climate change problem virtually required the EPA to interpret the CAA to create a new federal climate change program.

After 2010, both chambers of Congress were controlled by Republicans, and it was indeed impossible for President Obama to enact virtually any legislation. Freeman and Spence are far from the only scholars who argued during this period that whether in the form of executive orders or agency regulations, aggressive de facto lawmaking by the executive branch was a national imperative. Political scientists supported this argument with data purportedly demonstrating congressional paralysis. This line or argument and analysis, however, suffers from two fatal flaws.

The first is that it is completely at odds with reality. According to counts done by the Pew Research Center (reproduced as Figure 6.1 below), although there may have been a slight downward trend since 1989, the number of substantive laws passed by Congress has remained roughly constant. The 442 bills that Pew designed as substantive passed by the 115th Congress over the period 2017–2019 was about average for the post-1998 period and exceeded the number of such bills passed in the late 1990s. What the Pew numbers show is not a downward trend in congressional laws passed due to paralysis, but cycles in which lots of laws are passed when one party controls both chambers and relatively few laws are passed when control is split.

Especially when it comes to climate change, the second and perhaps more fundamental flaw in the congressional paralysis justification for agency lawmaking is that there is no universal agreement as to whether a problem is so "urgent" that federal legislation to address it is required. Some empirical efforts by political scientists to evidence the paralysis hypothesis actually demonstrate this. Binder (2015, 21), for example, finds evidence that Congress is "dysfunctional" in congressional failure to legislate on issues addressed by unsigned (that is, editorial board) editorials in the *New York Times*. Lots of people do not agree with *New York Times* editors about which issues should be addressed by Congress and which should not. The failure of Congress to act on issues that the *New York Times* editors feel is urgent is hardly evidence of congressional dysfunction.

Freeman and Spence are thus wrong about ideological polarization causing a general paralysis of Congress, but they are partially correct about congressional

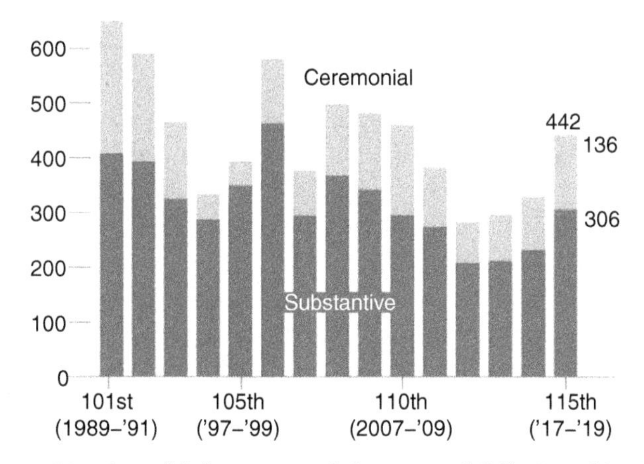

FIGURE 6.1 Number of Substantive and Ceremonial Bills Passed by Congress

voting on federal climate change legislation. Such voting does in part, but only in part, reflect ideological and party polarization around the issue. Economists have done empirical studies exploring the factors that determine how members of Congress have voted on the climate change bills that have actually made it to a floor vote. One such study, by Cragg et al. (2012, 1640), found that congressional ideology – a unidimensional liberal versus conservative score based on voting on environmental legislation – is statistically significant in explaining congressional voting on the 2009 American Clean Energy Security Act whose failure prompted the Obama administration's regulatory assault on coal. Ideology is highly correlated with party affiliation, and by around 2000, if not sooner, federal environmental regulation had become a party "brand" issue, with Republicans opposed to costly new environmental regulations and Democrats supporting them. Social psychologists (see Kahan [2012, 255]) have found that among all environmental issues, climate change is especially polarizing along ideological lines.

Moreover, as I have argued previously (Johnston 2014, 1613–1617) and as my discussion here thus far has indicated, the non-ideological benefits and costs of costly actions to reduce CO_2 vary dramatically across states. Back in 1970, federal air and water pollution legislation gave residents of industrialized US localities the benefit of cleaner air and water while cutting, at least on the margin, the cost to them in terms of lost jobs and local tax revenue caused by expensive pollution reduction requirements. The cost of reducing American CO_2 emissions by cutting the use of coal to generate electricity is by contrast severely concentrated on states that have historically relied upon coal-fired power plants for their electricity (and the costs were even steeper in states that also had substantial coal mining). As of 2002, for example, both Wyoming and West Virginia got over 95 percent of their electric power from coal-fired power plants. Another 18 states got over half of their electricity from coal-fired plants. Given that the cost of electricity is a crucial determinant of where firms locate manufacturing plants, any program to increase the cost of electricity generated by coal-fired plants threatened potentially severe loss of manufacturing jobs in states reliant on coal for their electricity.

By contrast, as of 2002, there were 9 states in which coal-fired power plants provided less than 25 percent of the state's electricity. For these states, a federal law increasing the cost of electricity from coal-fired plants would not only have little impact on electricity prices, it would actually put them at a competitive advantage relative to coal dependent states.

What seems to explain the pattern of congressional voting on climate change legislation is that the relative cost to a state or district from eliminating coal-fired power is highly correlated with the political party of that state's congressional representatives. Senators and representatives who belong to the environmentally conservative Republican party overwhelmingly come from states and districts (mostly in the American South and Midwest) that bear the brunt of the cost of ending coal-fired power production. Senators and representatives who belong to the environmentally liberal Democratic party disproportionately represent states and districts that get huge fractions of their electric power from hydropower (Oregon, Washington, and California) or nuclear power (New Hampshire, New Jersey, New York, and Vermont). Since around 2000, there have been very few instances where a US senator's political party affiliation and ideology does not line up with the costs their state can expect to incur from the elimination of coal-fired electric power.

Thus as a purely positive, meaning explanatory matter, congressional failure to pass federal climate change legislation doesn't reflect some kind of general congressional dysfunction or paralysis. It instead reflects the complexity and cost as well as the highly ideological nature of the problem of reducing US CO_2 emissions. Given the distribution of the cost of reducing coal-fired power production in the manner undertaken by the Obama-era EPA, it seems inconceivable that Congress would have ever passed legislation authorizing such an approach.

V INSTALLING THE EPA AS THE NATION'S CHIEF ELECTRIC POWER SECTOR REGULATOR

Freeman and Spence's argument that the EPA's CPP was legally justified by the "interconnected nature of the electricity system" was a response to the anticipated argument that with the Clean Power Plan, the EPA had "exceeded its traditional regulatory authority to regulate air pollution and is now improperly interfering with the state's energy mix" (Freeman and Spence 2014, 41). This was true. From all the evidence, the real point of the CPP was to make the EPA the de facto chief regulator of the entire US electric power system, overriding traditional state regulation as well as existing federal regulation by other agencies.

Perhaps the strongest evidence that the main point of the Clean Power Plan was to put the EPA in charge of the energy source mix of national energy production is the otherwise seemingly strangely modest goals that the Plan set for increasing renewable energy.

The heart of the final CPP regulations was a "guideline" for states to increase the amount of electric power that they get from renewables. While the CPP supporting technical documents argue that such a shift was possible at reasonable cost, the EPA is not an electric power regulator. Yet under Section 111(d), the EPA would have the authority to directly regulate GHG emissions from power plants if a state failed to come up with a plan that the EPA approved, and through such a threat, the EPA would indeed have been dictating whether states had adopted the "best system" for moving to renewables.

What is perhaps most surprising about the Clean Power Plan is the relatively modest nature of its core recommendation – that states lower power sector CO_2 emissions by shifting electricity production to low or zero CO_2 emission energy sources. The CPP called for reductions in power sector CO_2 emissions and power sector use of coal that at most amplified existing trends. As for total CO_2 emissions, the CPP called for a nationwide reduction of 30 percent in 2030 power sector CO_2 emissions relative to 2005 emission levels.[29] However, according to the EIA, power sector CO_2 emissions in 2015 when the CPP was finalized were only 5% higher than such emissions way back in 1990. And 2015 power sector CO_2 emissions were actually 12% *lower* than 2005 emissions.[30] With 2018 power sector CO_2 emissions roughly the same as 2015 emissions, were the 2005–2018 linear trend in power sector CO_2 emission reductions simply extrapolated out to 2030, *that baseline trend would itself lead to about a 25% reduction relative to 2005*. When it proposed the CPP in 2014, the EPA forecast a baseline trend under which power sector CO_2 emissions would fall only 5 percent by 2030. Relative to that forecast, the EPA could say that the CPP generated a significant additional reduction of 25 percent (in absolute terms) or 500% percent relative to the baseline.[31] *But the EPA's baseline forecast was off probably by about 500%*. Relative to the observed trend, the CPP would have generated only a 25% additional reduction.

Similarly modest was the EPA's recommendation that states increase the fraction of power coming from natural gas. In its 2014 CPP proposed rule, the EPA said that even in 2030, coal and natural gas would "remain the two leading sources of electricity generation, with each providing more than 30 percent of the projected generation."[32] Already by 2020, one can see that this prediction was far off the mark. As can be seen in Figure 6.2 below, electricity generation from natural gas has been increasing since the early 1990s. In 1990, coal-fired power plants accounted for a bit over half of all US electricity production, with natural gas-fired plants generating only about 12% of US electricity. By 2010, coal was down to 45% of US electricity, while natural gas had risen to 24%. If one simply extrapolated these trends another 20

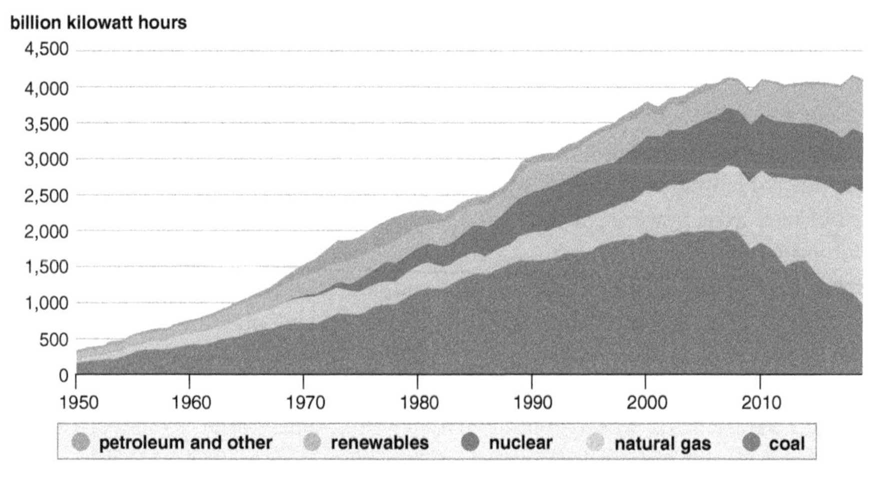

FIGURE 6.2 US Electricity Generation by Source, 1950–2019 (from EIA)

years, out to 2030, one would predict that by 2030, natural gas would account for about half of US electricity, with coal probably no more than 40%. But such an extrapolation would have greatly overestimated the staying power of coal even without the CPP. By 2019, coal-fired power plants accounted for only 22% of US electricity production, with natural gas the most important energy source, providing 37% of US electric power.[33] Were these trends to continue, even without the CPP, by 2030 coal-fired plants would likely provide only a little more than 10% of US electric power, with natural gas likely providing 50% or more of all US electricity, thus completely reversing the relative importance of coal and natural gas back in 1990 and proving completely wrong the EPA's 2014 baseline predictions about coal versus natural gas.

As for increases in electric power from renewable energy, the EPA set interim goals for the period 2020–2023 and then final 2030 goals. For the interim 2020–2023 goals, the EPA simply required that generation capacity from renewable energy sources would continue to increase at the average increase in capacity realized over the period 2010–2014. Over the period 2023–2030, the EPA required that renewable capacity increase at the maximum rate realized over the 2010–2014 period.[34] The EPA then distributed these required increases in renewable energy-based electricity over the three interstate electricity transmission regions of the United States – the Eastern, Western, and Texas networks. Later in this book, these networks will be discussed in a bit more detail. The main point for present purposes is that the vast majority of the increase in renewable electric power called for by the EPA was to occur in states that make up the Eastern Interconnection region – 69 percent by 2020, falling only to 62 percent by 2030. The remaining increase in renewable power was initially to occur mostly in the Western Interconnection region but eventually more evenly there and in Texas – with 22 percent of the renewable power increase in the Western and 8 percent in Texas by 2020 and with Texas increasing to 15 percent of the national renewable capacity increase by 2030.[35]

In its 2014 proposed rule, the EPA set renewable energy goals for each state, rather than for the three vast regional electrical transmission interconnections that I describe in the next chapter. State goals elicited hundreds of critical comments from people who actually run the US electricity system. Their basic point was that electric power markets do not stop at state lines. As will be explained in more detail shortly, generators sell electricity into wholesale markets that are linked across state lines by high voltage transmission lines. As an engineering matter, a state doesn't need to build more renewable power facilities within its borders to be able to use more renewable power. If renewable power provides a greater share of the total electricity flowing through the wholesale transmission network that the state accesses, then renewable power will constitute a greater share of the power actually consumed in the state. For states on a wholesale network to meet renewable energy goals, states just need to cooperate somehow to find a way to get more renewable power supplied to the wholesale networks that they share.

Even though the EPA abandoned the state-specific renewable energy goals in the final CPP rule, the state goals in its proposed rule are indicative of the actual state-by-state changes in renewable power use that the final 2015 CPP would have forced. I say "forced" because the CAA provision that the EPA said authorized the CPP, Section 111(d), requires that if a state fails to submit a plan, or fails to submit one meeting with the EPA's approval, then the EPA must come up with its own plan.[36]

As of 2015, at least 12 states did not have any state law requiring that a certain percentage of electricity supplied come from renewables. Such states faced the imminent prospect of the federal EPA mandating such requirements. These states had some things in common. For example, eight of these twelve states were in the southern United States. But in other ways they were very different. For example,[37] while as of 2012 Nebraska got 73 percent of its electricity from coal- and oil-burning generators, South Carolina got only 29 percent of its power from such sources. But both Nebraska and South Carolina got significant shares of their power from sources that do not emit CO_2 – with Nebraska getting 21 percent from nuclear- and wind-powered facilities, and South Carolina getting 55 percent of its power from nuclear. Indeed, as of 2012, some states that had their own renewable portfolio standards were doing far worse on the renewable power front than states without any state law renewable energy requirement. For example, Maryland, with a state RPS law, got only 2 percent of its power from renewables, whereas Idaho got 16 percent of its power from renewables even without any state law requirement.

These examples are indicative of the more general pattern emerging at the state level from the EPA's 2014 proposed CPP. Under that pattern, the EPA set renewable power goals for 2030 that were weaker than the goals that the states with the most ambitious renewable power laws had set for themselves to meet even sooner (typically by 2020 or 2025) than 2030. Indeed, in some cases – such as Maine, Iowa, and Minnesota – the EPA's 2030 renewable power goal was actually lower than the fraction of renewable power consumed by the state in 2012. For these states, even with its bizarre state-level renewable power goals, the CPP did not ask for states to do more than they had already committed to do by law. However, for the 12 states that did not have any state law renewable power requirement, the CPP would have raised the specter of an imminent takeover by the federal EPA of the state's electricity system.

The disparate impact across states was not clearly disclosed in the final CPP's regional approach, but given that the vast majority of the increase in renewable power called for by the final CPP was concentrated in the Eastern Interconnection region – where most of the states without RPS laws are found – such states would have reasonably seen the final CPP as threatening the future takeover of their electricity systems by the EPA.

VI UNDERESTIMATING AND DOWNPLAYING THE CPP'S POTENTIALLY CATASTROPHIC COSTS

Prominent constitutional scholars such as the progressive Laurence Tribe of Harvard argued that such a federal EPA takeover of state electric utility infrastructure would be unconstitutional under the 10th Amendment. But if it occurred, putting the federal EPA in charge of revamping state electricity systems could well have been catastrophic. The reason is that the operation of the electricity system is complex and requires expertise that the EPA's own CPP rulemaking clearly revealed that the EPA does not possess. The CPP mandated changes to state power systems to deliver purported climate change benefits for which the EPA could claim credit, but it generated costs that the EPA minimized or ignored. The biggest potential cost – from a loss of electric system reliability with a higher risk of regional electric power blackouts that cause billions of dollars in harm to health and the economy – was one for which the EPA was simply not responsible. The CPP created a host of new regulatory burdens for the state regulators, utilities, and transmission system operators who actually are responsible for power systems. As far as the risks and costs from such burdens, according to the EPA, they simply weren't the EPA's problem.

As I shall shortly explain, in promulgating the final CPP, the EPA was more than willing to admit that it had neither the responsibility nor the expertise to ensure that states could meet the CPP's zero carbon, renewable energy goals while still ensuring electrical system reliability. But as illustrated by the other Obama-era EPA regulations I've discussed in this part, the EPA has routinely been in the business of estimating job losses caused by its regulations. One might have hoped that the EPA's estimate of job losses from the CPP would at least be as good as its estimate for the MATS rule, for example. This hope was not met. In estimating employment impacts of the CPP, the EPA did not attempt to apply the Morgenstern et al. (2002) approach. Instead, it derived employment impacts on both the coal and natural gas-fired power plant industries by using its own IPM plus data from various secondary sources. To derive jobs lost due to the retirement of coal-fired plants, the EPA estimated the capacity lost due to plant retirements and then used its own estimate of per plant operating and maintenance employment. The EPA estimated that only between 6 and 7 percent of coal-fired capacity and roughly 0 percent of natural gas-fired capacity would be retired by 2020. But by 2030, after the CPP had fully kicked in, the EPA estimated that between 11 and 16 percent of coal-fired capacity would be retired. Even for 2030, the EPA predicted no change in existing combined cycle natural gas-fired power production, but it did forecast that "[d]ue largely to the electricity demand reduction attributable to the demand-side energy efficiency improvements," there would be a massive fall – of between 38 and 68 percent – of new natural gas-fired plant capacity that would otherwise be built.[38] Using its average per plant employment estimates, the EPA ended up estimating that by 2030, the CPP would lead to the loss of 14,700 job years in coal-fired power plants and 3,700 job years in natural gas-fired plants, not to mention 13,900 lost jobs in the coal mining sector.[39]

As mentioned earlier, by 2019 the CPP had been rescinded and replaced by the Trump administration. However, by 2019 it was clear that the EPA had severely underestimated job losses in coal-fired power plants. Relative to 2015, about 16 percent of coal-fired capacity had already been lost by 2018.[40] In the EPA's base case (that is, no CPP) estimate, it expected zero change in coal-fired capacity all the way through to 2030. With coal-fired capacity declining so quickly even without states under a binding CPP mandate to eliminate it, the decline would surely have been much larger with the CPP in effect. In the CPP, the EPA had also forecast that without the CPP, there would be no change in new combined cycle natural gas-fired capacity. This too was wildly wrong: combined cycle natural gas-fired capacity increased by about 10 percent between 2015 and 2018. Since the EPA's forecast of the jobs impact of the CPP is relative to what it projected would occur in a world without the CPP, the fact that the world without the CPP has been so radically different than the EPA expected implies that its forecasted impact of the CPP was also likely radically off.

While the EPA's wildly incorrect forecast of job changes in coal and natural gas-fired power plants is noteworthy, the most striking feature of the EPA's RIA for the final 2015 CPP was not its likely big underestimate of the jobs lost due to the CPP. It was the fact that most of the EPA's 2015 CPP analysis was about the huge number of new jobs that the CPP would create in the energy conservation industry. Recall that a big difference between the final CPP and the CPP as proposed by the EPA in 2014 is that the EPA dropped energy conservation measures as one of the prongs by which states could cut their CO_2 emissions. And yet in estimating the employment impacts of the final, 2015 CPP, the EPA spent most of its time estimating the new jobs that would be created in the "demand side energy efficiency" sector. As defined by the EPA, this industry included everything from weatherization of low income housing to green building projects and state and local government-funded energy conservation programs. According to the EPA, energy efficiency spending of whatever sort generated between 2 and 3 new jobs per $1 million of spending. Even though state energy efficiency programs of this sort were not part of the final 2015 CPP, the EPA reported that somewhere between 52,000 and 83,000 new jobs would somehow result from the CPP by 2030. By estimating the jobs created by something that was not even part of the final CPP, the EPA was able to report a job creation number that swamped the roughly 18,000 jobs that the EPA had forecast the CPP eliminate in the coal and natural gas-fired power industries by that same year.

As I explained earlier in my discussion of the MATS rule, the EPA and other federal agencies are not required by OMB cost-benefit guidelines to put dollar numbers on the total social cost of jobs lost due to EPA regulations. The job loss figure is somewhat obscure and more an afterthought to formal EPA cost-benefit analysis. When the CPP was proposed, there were few comments on the EPA's estimated job losses. By contrast, the proposed CPP elicited a flood of formal comments and published editorials in which state public utility owners and regulators shouted the alarm that in many states, the proposed CPP could have catastrophic impacts on electrical system reliability.

In the final CPP, the EPA admitted that it found this criticism to be "compelling, and "thanks in no small part" to such comments, had made sure that the CPP guidelines to states "reflect the paramount importance of ensuring electrical system reliability."[41] Reliability may have been of "paramount importance," but the EPA made clear that reliability was not its responsibility. Based not on its own expertise regarding electrical system operation – which it did not claim to have – but instead on "substantial input from experts in the energy field," the EPA's final CPP added a "requirement . . . for states to demonstrate that they have considered electric system reliability in developing their state plans."[42] To provide time for states to be able to figure out how to meet the EPA's zero carbon, renewable energy power sector transformation while still ensuring electrical system reliability, the final CPP extended the date for interim state compliance from 2020 to 2022, divided up the next eight years into two-year periods with their own interim goals, and added a new requirement that states demonstrate that "they have considered electric system reliability in developing their state plans." The final CPP also provided a so-called safety valve allowing modification of CO_2 emission standards in the event of an "unforeseen, emergency situation that threatens reliability."[43]

To summarize all of this, to ensure that EPA-imposed renewable energy requirements did not jeopardize the reliability of state electricity supply, the states – not the EPA – had to devote resources to producing a series of plans and reports to the EPA on how they were managing to reduce power sector GHG emissions while ensuring system reliability. Such reports would be due every two years, but electrical system reliability was clearly to take a back seat to the renewable energy goal. Only in "unforeseen, emergency" cases could a state possibly get the EPA to grant it a "short term modification" of power sector GHG emission standards.

This was all the EPA had to say about electrical system reliability in the final CPP. From what the EPA had to say, one can't discern how the EPA's proposal to massively increase the usage of renewable power and reduce reliance on coal-fired generation could even possibly create a problem for electric system reliability. To understand these issues requires a basic understanding of how the US electric power system works, how it is regulated, and how an increased share of power from solar and wind in particular affect the operation and reliability of the power system. Such an understanding is also necessary to evaluate the other side of precautionary climate change initiatives, federal and state laws mandating or subsidizing the use of wind and solar.

Notes

1. My discussion here relies upon Miller (2011, 1389).
2. In 42 USC §7602(j)(2010), for example, the CAA defines a major stationary source as any facility that emits or could emit 100 tons per year or more of any "air pollutant."
3. Under 42 USC §7471, the PSD program applies to areas that either i) cannot be classified as violating primary and secondary air quality standards for both sulfur dioxide and particulate matter, 42 USC §7407(d)(1)(d)(D), or ii) have air quality better than any other NAAQS or if information does exist to determine that a violation of a standard is occurring, 42 USC §7407(d)(1)(d)(E).
4. See EPA, 52 Fed Reg 24,683 (July 1, 1987) and 40 CFR §81.305 (1987).
5. *Utility Air Regulatory Group* v. *EPA*, 134 S.Ct. 2427, 2443 (2014).
6. 134 S.Ct at 2443.
7. 134 S.Ct. at 2437.
8. 134 S.Ct. at 2444.
9. 134 S.Ct. at 2445.
10. 134 S.Ct. at 2438.
11. 134 S.Ct. at 2448–2449.
12. The following is taken from Debra Ronca, How Carbon Capture Works, How Stuff Works, available at https://science.howstuffworks.com/environmental/green-science/carbon-capture4.html.
13. See Rubin et al. (2015, Table 2). An earlier estimate of an 80 percent increase in cost is provided in Anderson and Newell (2004, 109–42).
14. EPA-CICA Fact Sheet, Flue Gas Desulfurization, supra note __ at p.2.
15. Stone and Webster Management Consultants, Inc., Evaluation of Emission Compliance at Allegheny Energy Electric Generating Units, December 1, 2004, available at https://www.sec.gov/Archives/edgar/data/1233563/000091957404003493/d531509_ex99-5.txt.
16. Thomas F. Stacy and George S. Taylor, The Levelized Cost of Electricity from Existing Generation Sources, Institute for Energy Research Table 1, p. 5, June, 2019, available at https://www.instituteforenergyresearch.org/wp-content/uploads/2019/06/IER_LCOE2019Final-.pdf,
17. Lawrence Irlam, Global Costs of Carbon Capture and Storage, Fig. 1 p. 5, Global CCS Institute, June, 2017 Update, available at https://www.globalccsinstitute.com/archive/hub/publications/201688/global-ccs-cost-updatev4.pdf.
18. Ben Caldecott, Lucas Kruitwagen, and Irem Kok, Carbon Capture and Storage in the Thermal Value Chain, in COP21 and the Implications for Energy, 105 Oxford Energy Forum 50, 53 (May 2016).
19. Caldecott, et al., Carbon Capture and Storage in the Thermal Value Chain, supra note __ at 54.

20. From Carbon Capture: Expensive Pipe Dream or "Holy Grail" Climate Investigations Centeron March 6, 2019 available at https://climateinvestigations.org/carbon-capture-sequestration-ccs/.
21. Toby Lockwood, The Kemper County CCS project – what went wrong and what next?, One: Only Natural Energy, Oct.–Dec. 2017, available at https://www.onlynaturalenergy.com/the-kemper-county-ccs-project-what-went-wrong-and-what-next/.
22. Megan Geuss, Department of Justice opens investigation into failed carbon-capture plant, Ars Technica, May 2, 2019, available at https://arstechnica.com/tech-policy/2019/05/department-of-justice-opens-investigation-into-failed-carbon-capture-plant/.
23. EPA, Revisions to the Prevention of Significant Deterioration (PSD) and Title V Greenhouse Gas (GHG) Permitting Regulations and Establishment of a Significant Emissions Rate (SER) for GHG Emissions Under the PSD Program, 40 CFR Parts 51, 52, 60, 70 and 71, 81 Fed. Reg. 68110, 68133, [EPA–HQ–OAR–2015–0355; FRL–9951–79– OAR], RIN 2060–AS62 (Oct. 3, 2016).
24. See Pacific Environmental Services, Background Report AP-42 Section 6.10 Phosphate Fertilizers, Prepared for US Environmental Protection Agency OAQPS/TSD/EIB, Research Triangle Park, NC 27711, 1–96 available at http://www.epa.gov/ttnchie1/ap42/ch08/bgdocs/b08s05.pdf.
25. EPA, Final Guideline Document: Control of Sulfuric Acid Mist Emissions from Existing Sulfuric Acid Production Units, EPA-450/2–77-019, September, 1977 at I-4 to I-8.
26. 79 CFR 34,830 et seq.
27. 79 CFR 34,856 to 34,857.
28. EPA, Carbon Pollution Emission Guidelines for Existing Stationary Sources: Electric Utility Generating Units, 80 Fed. Reg. 64,662, 64,774–64,775, October 23, 2015.
29. 79 Fed. Reg. 34,832.
30. EIA, US Energy-related Carbon Dioxide Emissions 2018, available at https://www.eia.gov/environment/emissions/carbon/.
31. See Brattle Group, Policy Brief: EPA's Proposed Clean Power Plan: Implications for States and the Electric Industry, June, 2014, available at http://www.ksg.harvard.edu/hepg/Papers/2014/EPAs%20Proposed%20Clean%20Power%20Plan-Implications%20for%20States%20and%20the%20Electric%20%20%20.pdf
32. Ibid.
33. Data available at EIA, Electricity Explained, available at https://www.eia.gov/energyexplained/electricity/electricity-in-the-us.php.
34. EPA, Technical Support Document (TSD) for Carbon Pollution Guidelines for Existing Power Plants: Emission Guidelines for Greenhouse Gas Emissions from Existing Stationary Sources: Electric Utility Generating Units, Greenhouse Gas

Mitigation Measures, Docket ID No. EPA-HQ-OAR-2013–0602, August 3, 2015, 4–1 to 4–5.

35. EPA Technical Support Document, note 44 supra, Table 4–6, p. 4–7.
36. For a detailed explanation of how this legal requirement would have applied in the CPP context, see Daniel P. Selmi, Federal Implementation Plans for Controlling Carbon Emissions from Existing Power Plants: A Primer Exploring the Issues, Sabin Center for Climate Change Law, Columbia University, May 2015, available at https://web.law.columbia.edu/sites/default/files/microsites/climate-change/selmi_-_fip_primer_0.pdf.
37. For the state renewable power goals in the 2014 proposed CPP, see EPA, Technical Support Document, GHG Abatement Measures 3–14 (June 10, 2014), available at http://www2.epa.gov/sites/production/files/2014-06/docuyments/20140602tsd-ghg-abaterment-measures.pdf. For state RPS goals and 2012 renewable power consumption, see individual State websites.
38. EPA, RIA for the Final Clean Power Plan Table 3–12, at 3–31.
39. EPA, RIA for the Final Clean Power Plan Table 6–4, at 6–24.
40. EIA, US natural gas-fired combined-cycle capacity surpasses coal-fired capacity, April 10, 2019, available at https://www.eia.gov/todayinenergy/detail.php?id=39012.
41. EPA, Carbon Pollution Emission Guidelines for Existing Stationary Sources: Electric Utility Generating Units, Final Rule, 80 CFR 64,662, October 23, 2015 at 64,669.
42. 80 Fed. Reg. 64,676.
43. EPA Carbon Pollution Emission Guidelines, Final Rule, 80 CFR at 64,669, 64,671, 64,676, 64,948.

7

Renewable Power and the Reliability and Cost of Electricity

In order to understand and evaluate any proposal, such as the Obama EPA's Clean Power Plan, to shift American electricity generation to rely more heavily on renewable power, one must first understand the basics about how the US electricity system works. As we shall see in this chapter, moving to a higher share of renewable power while ensuring the reliability of electricity supply is far from trivial. The cost of a system with a high renewable power share is far greater than the cost of simply building and operating wind and solar farms. It includes not only the costs of building new transmission lines, and upgrading transmission stations and substations, but also the cost of electricity from rapidly dispatchable power sources such as natural gas turbines that can provide power when solar and wind power are unavailable. Together, these costs cause high electricity prices in systems with high renewable power penetration. Moreover, as shown by the 2017–2019 California wildfires, if the cost of moving to a high renewable power share squeezes out more mundane but necessary electricity system investments in things such as maintaining existing transmission and distribution lines, the results can be catastrophic.

I *US Electric Power System and Its Regulation:* A *Capsule Explanation*

The electric power system in the United States has three stages: generation (or production), wholesale transmission, and distribution.

A Generation

Electricity consists of moving electrons that can be described by both the frequency and amplitude of the current. In a battery or solar cell, the electrons are always moving in the same direction, from a negatively charged terminal to a positively charged terminal. This is called direct current. Power plants produce alternating current (AC) electricity, an oscillating current that looks like a sine curve and flows back and forth, changing direction. Power plants in the United States produce an

AC current that oscillates at a frequency of 60 cycles per second. AC current is used in the electric power system for a number of reasons. It is easier to convert AC to direct current (DC) than vice versa, and big power plants produce AC current naturally, plus the long distance electricity transmission lines require AC power to operate. Power plants produce three phases or sine waves of electricity carried by three wires (plus a fourth wire that uses the ground as the negative terminal) simultaneously. The three sine waves are offset by 120 degrees. By synchronizing the three sine waves of electricity with a 120 degree offset, one of the waves is always near its peak. In this way, a constant voltage of power is supplied.

Power plants produce this oscillating electricity by spinning a giant turbine. The energy to spin the turbine can come from a variety of sources. With hydropower, water is funneled from behind dammed up reservoirs through narrow channels (called penstocks) where it spins propeller-like turbines. Wind farms consist of turbines with giant blades that capture energy from wind. In a coal-powered generation facility, pulverized coal is burned in a boiler, generating steam that spins the blades of huge turbines.

With water, wind, and coal-fired thermal power, the turbines are then connected by a shaft to an electromagnet inside copper coils. As students in high school learn, as a magnet spins when surrounded by wires, electricity is created.

When natural gas is burned to generate electricity, the process by which the turbine is spun is somewhat different. In a natural gas turbine, air is taken in and compressed, then combusted with natural gas, and the high velocity gas produced by combustion itself spins the turbine. In a simple gas turbine, the process stops there. In a combined cycle natural gas-fired plant, the hot gases that are created by natural gas combustion are not wasted but used to boil water to create steam and, as with a coal-fired plant, the steam can then be used to spin another turbine. The waste heat from natural gas combustion can also be used to heat industrial plants, or even used to heat homes. When this is done, it is called natural gas cogeneration.

Whether water, wind, coal, or natural gas is used as a fuel, power plants that produce electricity by spinning turbines generate AC electricity. While there are some solar-powered thermal power plants that use heat to spin turbines, as will be explained soon, these have not proved to be practical. Today, solar power is predominantly produced from photovoltaic (PV) cells. Although the ability to produce electricity using the PV effect was first realized using selenium wafers in 1883, by the mid-1950s, it was discovered that silicon wafers were more effective and solar cells now are made from silicon. Silicon has a crystalline structure, and in the presence of small amounts of phosphorous (adding a positive charge) and boron (adding a negative charge) silicon electrons are destabilized by sunlight and move through a solar cell. This DC (unidirectional) electricity then flows through wires to a solar inverter where it is converted into the AC electricity that is used in the power system. Unlike the other energy sources described – water, wind, coal, and natural gas – solar electricity is not produced by spinning turbines. The importance of this will be explained momentarily.

The electrical power produced by a plant is expressed in watts (W). By Ohm's Law, this power can be transmitted on lines at varying levels of voltage (V) but the lower the voltage, the higher must be the current (in amps) carried by the line. The higher the current carried by the line, the bigger and more expensive is the line and the greater the power loss during transmission. To reduce such costs, when it comes out of a power plant (or solar inverter), the voltage of the AC electricity is increased by transformers to (typically) around 350,000 volts. At this voltage, power moves for distances up to 300 miles through three relatively small lines connected by the high steel towers. One can see such lines throughout the world.

B *The Operation of the Interstate Electricity Transmission System: Understanding Power Dispatch and Balancing*

Power cannot be used at the very high voltages at which it is transmitted. At power substations, transformers are used to step-down (lower) voltage levels below 10,000 volts. These lowered voltages are then distributed by a bus, and these buses (which may be thought of as the hub of a wheel) send the electricity to local distribution stations. The local distribution stations step down the power further (to 7200 volts) and distribute this electricity across various distribution lines. Some of the power at this voltage is directly sent to large commercial users. The power that comes into subdivisions and shopping malls on local distribution lines is also at this voltage, and single lines are then split off to deliver one phase power at 7200 volts. Transformers serving a few houses then step down the power further, to the 240 volts that is the norm for US electrical service. The 240 volts is delivered to homes by two 120 volt lines (plus a ground wire) that deliver two-phase power (so people can use both 120 and 240 volt appliances). In electricity system lingo, the power usage of businesses and households is called the system "load" or demand.

1 The Development and Regulation of the US Interstate Electricity Transmission Grid

As explained in Joskow's (2005) excellent summary history, until the 1990s, the nascent interstate electricity transmission system was completely owned and operated by large vertically integrated utilities that generated, transmitted, and ultimately distributed electricity to retail customers. In this context, vertical integration means that a utility owns and operates the entire electric system, from generation, through long distance transmission, to distribution to ultimate consumers. During their early years, from 1879 to 1907, vertically integrated electric utilities were regulated only by cities, which had the authority to grant or deny them licenses to run electric lines along public thoroughfares. This system was highly inefficient, leading to a mass of

FIGURE 7.1 Power Lines in New York City, circa 1890

duplicative power lines put up by competing utilities. Such a mass is depicted in Figure 7.1 below, a photo of the mass of power lines in New York City around 1890.

Beginning in 1907 in New York and Wisconsin, states transferred regulation of electric utilities from municipalities to state public utility commissions. By 1914 most (twenty-seven) states had followed New York and Wisconsin in establishing state public utility commissions (Jarrell 1978, 269–295). Eventually it came to be widely agreed that such state regulation was required because the integrated utilities were natural monopolies – free from competition because the large sunk, fixed costs of building and operating a system meant that whichever provider captured the market could not be profitably dislodged. State public utility commissions were to control the behavior of electric utility monopolies by regulating retail electricity rates and electric services to protect the public interest and ensure efficient and reliable delivery of electric service.

Even in the early twentieth century, vertically integrated electric utilities would sometimes cooperate to build and operate transmission lines that crossed state lines. For example, in 1917, the Narragansett, Rhode Island Electric Lighting Company entered into a twenty year contract to supply all of the electricity demanded by the Attleboro, Massachusetts Steam and Electric Company.[1] By 1920, through complex holding company structures, large regional vertically integrated electric utilities dominated the US electricity market. The 1935 Public Utility Holding Company Act broke these companies up and mandated that they could not operate across state lines. Yet as electricity demand surged in the post-World War II boom, such utilities routinely cooperated to develop regional transmission systems. In such systems, transmission lines are used to interconnect power flowing through transmission systems powered by generators located in various states.

This interconnected system equated demand (or load) and supply across entire regions. In this system, huge power plants were located close to necessary resources – in particular, rivers and lakes that provided cooling water – but often far from load centers such as large metropolitan areas. The problem of the cost of long distance transmission was solved by transmitting very high voltage (as we've seen, up to 340,000 volts today) but low (60 Hz) frequency current. By Ohm's Law (and the definition of power as voltage times current in amps), resistance (loss) is proportional to the square of the current. Thus very high voltage low current transmission lines minimized the cost of long distance transmission. It allowed utilities to realize the tremendous economies of scale realized by producing power from high capacity generators. During the 1960s, retail electricity rates fell from 3 cents/KWh to 2.5 cents/KWh (Brennan et al. 1996, 23–35).

Before the 1990s, such utilities had no obligation to open up the use of their long distance transmission lines and they bundled the generation, transmission, and distribution prices into a single price. Only through antitrust litigation did local municipal and co-op power distributors force the utilities to unbundle transmission so that distributors could shop for power across geographically proximate transmission providers (Joskow 2005). Once utilities opened up their transmission lines, they became subject to regulation by the Federal Energy Regulatory Commission (FERC, which assumed tasks under the Federal Power Act of 1935 previously performed by the defunct Federal Power Commission). FERC regulated the terms and rates charged by utilities for power they transmitted to distributors.

By the late 1960s, vertically integrated utilities subject only to regulation by state public utility commissions formed power pools and loosely coordinated in the interstate transmission of electricity. The Federal Power Commission warned in 1964 that the nascent regional electricity transmission systems would need to be better coordinated to ensure a reliable electric supply. Before any such coordination effort was begun, on November 19, 1965, thirty million people from Canada to New Jersey lost electricity in an event known ever since as the Northeast blackout of 1965. Congressional investigations followed, and in order to avert an intrusive government regulatory response (Nevius 2020, 1–6), in 1968 the large investor-owned utilities formed a national reliability council called the North American Electric Reliability Corporation (NERC).

Originally comprised of twelve regional reliability councils (Nevius 2020, 5–6), the number of such councils shrank down to eight by 2010, and then in 2011, NERC replaced such regional councils with what are called “reliability assessment areas.” There are eighteen such areas, depicted in Figure 7.2.[2] Within the United States, those councils set reliability standards for three regionally interconnected AC transmission networks – the Western Interconnection and the Texas Interconnection (which are the green and yellow regions in Figure 7.2), and the Eastern Interconnection (the remaining US councils).

Even with the formation of regional reliability organizations, as of the early 1990s, the US wholesale power market was still dominated by the decades-old vertically integrated utilities. During the 1990s, this changed quickly. The first step in opening

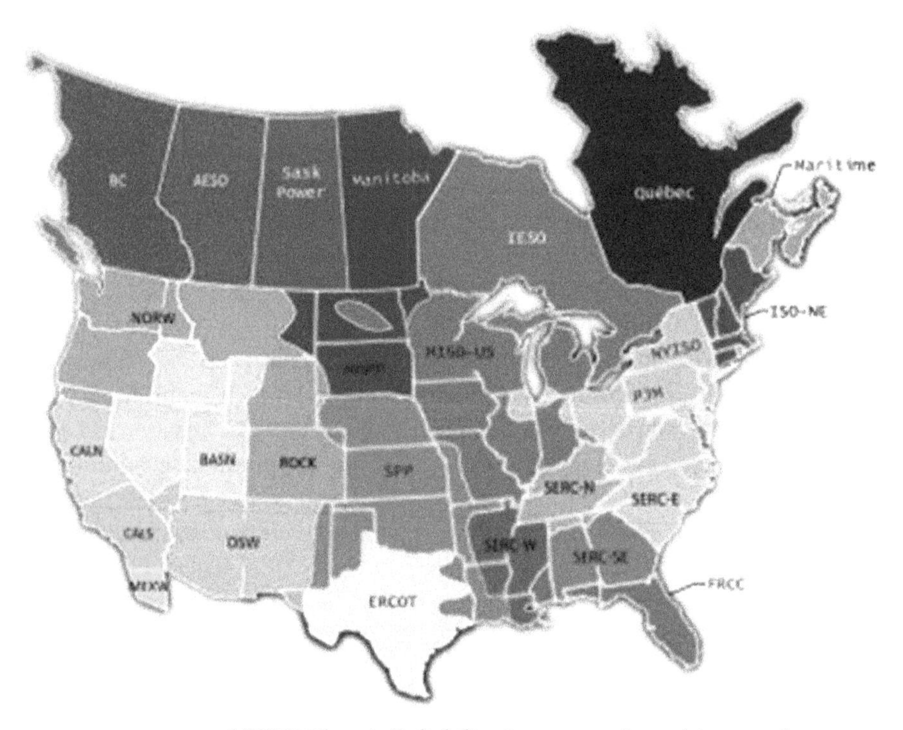

FIGURE 7.2 NERC Electric Reliability Assessment Areas (since 2011)

up the market for wholesale power was the Public Utility Regulatory Policy Act of 1978. Passed during the energy crisis years of the late 1970s – when the oil embargo of 1973–1974 and repeated OPEC price hikes triggered congressional efforts to assure US energy security – PURPA required utilities to buy power from natural gas cogeneration plants and small hydroelectric and other renewable generators. By the early 1990s, about 60 GW of power from providers that qualified under PURPA had come online in New England, New York, New Jersey, Pennsylvania, California, and Texas (Joskow 2005, 102).

With PURPA as the impetus, FERC issued orders designed to encourage the growth of independent power producers – independent, that is, of any vertically integrated utility. In the Energy Policy Act of 1992 (APAct92), Congress allowed both utilities and non-utilities to own generation facilities and gave FERC the authority to require utilities to sell transmission services to power producers. It took some time – and two 1996 FERC orders – for transmission services to really be made available to power producers on a scale sufficient to develop regional US wholesale power markets. But by the late 1990s, three existing northeastern power pools – California, several midwestern states, and Texas – had created the first regional transmission organizations (RTOs) and Independent Service Organizations (ISOs). In 1999, FERC encouraged utilities to transfer the operation (but not the ownership) of regional transmission networks to these organizations.

The current regional wholesale transmission authorities are actually displayed in Figure 7.2. That figure, for example, displays PJM for the mid-Atlantic, NYISO for New York, ISO-NE for New England, and MISO for parts of the Midwest, all of which are independent system operators. Some such system operators and regional transmission authorities – such as ERCOT in most of Texas – are also the unique balancing authority in their region – the authority responsible for balancing power demand (load) with supply (generation). In other regions, such as the PJM and MISO regions, there has been a consolidation of balancing authorities. The West – which includes all of the green shaded areas in Figure 7.2 other than California – is highly decentralized, with a large number of balancing authorities.

Subject to FERC regulatory authority, these RTOs and ISOs are responsible for virtually every aspect of transmission market operation – they establish prices for transmission services and decide how transmission revenues are distributed back to owners and also regulate transmission expansion projects. Practices vary across regions. For example, generators in some regions pay the full cost of connecting new generation facilities to the transmission network (their direct cost plus any indirect costs necessitated by adding power), in others, only part of the cost (Joskow 2005, 111–113). Importantly for purposes of my discussion of renewable power to come, in some states, utilities did not transfer control over transmission to an ISO or RTO. In particular, transmission is bundled with generation – and still operated by vertically integrated utilities – in the Northwest, Southwest, and Southeast. (For a list of bundling by state, see Sugimoto 2019, 314–315.) More generally, in states where vertically integrated utilities subject to state cost-of-service regulation dominate, the utilities act as balancing authorities. In states that through deregulation have created competition among generators, ISOs and RTOs coordinate and control power system operation.[3]

2 Ensuring Reliability on the Grid by Matching Generation with Load

The key task of such RTOs and ISOs is to ensure a reliable supply of electricity across these vast interconnected transmission systems. Reliability requires matching – at the level of seconds or fractions of seconds – the amount of electricity produced (generation) with the amount of electricity demanded (load). In more precise terms, such matching means that transmission network operators must ensure that the grid frequency is maintained as close to the frequency standard as possible. In the United States, the standard grid frequency is 60 Hz. If load exceeds the amount of power generated into the system, then transmission frequency declines. (Intuitively, there is not enough push – or active power – to maintain the current at sufficient frequency.) If generation exceeds load, then frequency increases. As explained by UK biomass power company Drax,[4] "just a 1% deviation from system frequency (50 Hz in the UK) begins to damage equipment and infrastructure." If, for example, a heat wave generates sudden electricity demand in a system served by a single generator, then other things equal, the generator will slow down (think of your car engine slowing down as the car encounters a hill to climb). The generator's slower turning means lower frequency and also lower voltage. If these go too low, the generator can be seriously damaged as it is out of sync with the turbine.

Spikes in system demand (load) caused by heat waves can often be predicted at least a few days in advance. What cannot be so well predicted are random failures of transmission lines and generators. The Northeast blackout of 1965, which caused the loss of power to 30 million people in the northeastern United States, Ontario, and Quebec, happened when a faulty relay tripped a 230,000 volt transmission line running from an Ontario hydroelectric plant to serve loads in Toronto. When the transmission line tripped off, power was shifted to other lines heading into Toronto, overloading them and causing them to trip off, with the power then redirected to transmission lines in western New York state. These were already heavily loaded and so immediately tripped off too, causing the entire Northeastern transmission network to break up into islands, within virtually all of which load and generation were out of balance, causing them all to shut down[5]

In July, 1977, New York City was blacked out for two days. That blackout was caused by a series of lightning strikes, the most serious of which caused two 345,000 volt transmission lines to be tripped, leading to shutdown of generation at the Indian Point nuclear plant and the overloading of other transmission lines that eventually led to a cascading failure.

Finally, the biggest recent US blackout of all, affecting 50 million people in Canada and the midwestern and northeastern United States, occurred in August, 2003 when 21 power plants shut down in just three minutes. The blackout was caused by overgrown trees coming into contact with transmission lines carrying power from FirstEnergy Corporation's Eastlake, Ohio power plant, a loss of transmission that caused a massive frequency imbalance and quickly shut down that plant.[6]

The social costs of blackouts are substantial. The 1977 New York City blackout occurred in the evening of July 13 during a summer heat wave. As darkness fell on the first night of the blackout, widespread looting and arson broke out across four of New York's five boroughs. By the end of the blackout some 26 hours later, New York had suffered 1,037 fires, of which 60 were major, 1,809 incidents of property damage, 2 deaths, and injuries to 436 police officers, 204 civilians, and 80 firefighters.[7] There were 3,000 arrests for looting (compared to a 24 hour norm for total arrests of 600). In the areas worst hit by looting and vandalism, 82 sanitation trucks and 4,000 workers were needed to clean-up the garbage and refuse created. Including the damage caused by looting and arson, a 1978 study commissioned by the US Department of Energy estimated that the blackout had cost New York businesses $290 million, which is equivalent to about $1.1 billion in 2020 dollars.

The 2003 blackout affected not just a single city but heavily industrialized and populated metropolitan areas on both sides of the US–Canadian border. About 50 million people lost power. Unlike the 1965 and 1977 blackouts, there was no mass looting or property destruction during the 2003 blackout. However, estimates of the economic cost of the blackout done shortly after its occurrence ranged from a low of $4.5 billion to somewhere between $6 and $10 billion ($13 billion in 2020 dollars) with most of the loss taking the form of lost income to workers and investors.[8] In Ohio alone, some 12,300 manufacturing companies – about 55 percent of all Ohio manufacturers – lost an average of $88,000 each. Unlike the 1967 and 1977 blackouts, adverse health effects from the 2003 blackout have been quantified. For New York City alone, Anderson and Bell (2012, 189–193) estimate that the blackout increased both accidental deaths somewhere between 28 and 287 percent and also increased total mortality by 28 percent, causing about 90 excess deaths. As Anderson and Bell (2012, 3) explain, disease-related mortality increased for a variety of reasons – people were trapped in subways and elevators, many food stores and pharmacies were closed, and some power-related medical equipment failed. As these estimates are for New York alone, which represented at most 20 percent of the total population affected, excess deaths over the entire region affected by the 2003 blackout may well have been around 500.

Such blackouts result from generating plants and transmission lines tripping off to avoid damage due to frequency imbalance. In a very real sense, they represent cascading frequency imbalances. As explained in a 2011 technical report from the National Renewable Energy Lab by Ela, Milligen, and Kirby,[9] small variations in system frequency are smoothed out by utilizing the inertial energy of spinning generators themselves, whose speed of rotation adjusts to changes in load.[10] Such a response rebalances generation and load but at a lower frequency than the nominal or standard value. The system remains vulnerable to further disturbances (e.g., a further increase in load due to a generator outage), and to get the frequency back up to the nominal or standard value, more spinning generators that are synchronized to the grid frequency but not operating at their full capacity (in electric utility lingo, these would be said to be operating at capacity factors significantly below one) must be kicked in. This reserve capacity is supplemented by further, slower-responding reserve capacity to return the system to frequency stability.

Virtually every component of the electric power system – generation, load, and transmission line availability – is subject to unpredictable variation (Ela et al. 2011, 1). The additional generating capacity that is made available to maintain the active power through the system if generation falls or load increases (sudden load declines have not empirically been a problem) is called the operating reserve capacity of an electrical supply system. At the regional level, NERC defines reserve margin as maximum available capacity minus expected peak demand, all divided by expected peak demand.[11] Maintaining reserve generating capacity is expensive – it may be thought of as having invested money in power plants that are operated below their capacity just to ensure that they are available in an emergency.

3 Minimizing the Cost of Electricity through Merit Order Dispatch

Ensuring a balance between electricity generation and load is one of the primary day-to-day jobs of transmission system operators. In so doing, they attempt to minimize the cost of providing electricity. More precisely, system operators attempt to minimize the cost of providing electricity to meet demand (load) subject to the constraint that system frequency is balanced continuously during the day and that sufficient reserve capacity is available to meet peaks in load. The process of determining which generators are providing power to the system at any given point in time is called economic dispatch.[12]

In the electricity business, the cost-minimizing approach to determining which power plants to use on a given day is called merit (or rank) order dispatch. In the merit order dispatch, system operators try to use the lowest-priced generators (with price to supply power sometimes set via an auction process or sometimes not) while taking account of constraints on power production faced by different types of generators. These constraints include how quickly a particular type of generator can increase output, its maximum and minimum output levels, and the minimum time a generator must be run once it is started.[13]

The way in which merit order dispatch minimizes generation cost is displayed in Figure 7.3. The figure depicts merit order dispatch to supply a fixed (price inelastic) demand given by the vertical line D.

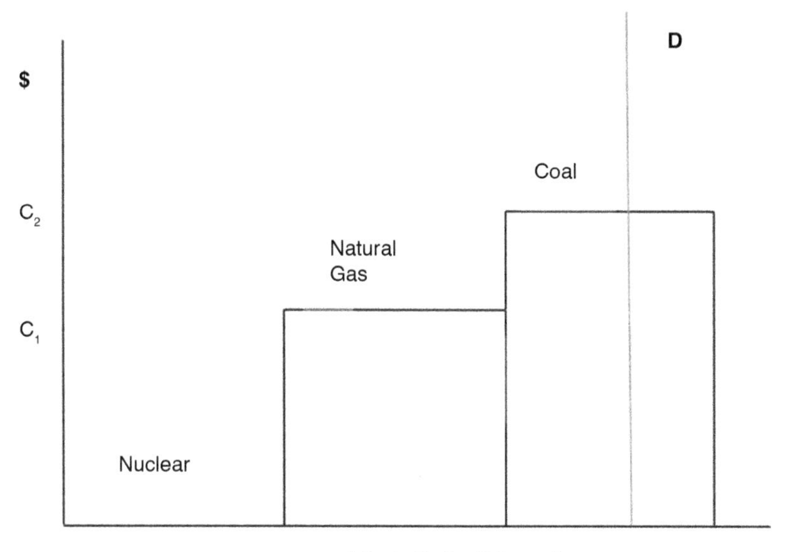

FIGURE 7.3 Merit Order Dispatch

In the figure, electricity from nuclear fission is supplied first because it has zero marginal cost. As depicted, power from natural gas is dispatched next, as it has a marginal cost of C_1. Finally, at its marginal cost is C_2, power from a coal-fired plant is dispatched. The length of the horizontal line for each source is the capacity of the plant. As depicted, nuclear and natural gas produce up to their maximum or nameplate capacity – meaning they produce with a capacity factor of 1 – while the coal-fired plant has a capacity factor significantly less than 1 but more than .5.

Figure 7.3 does not depict the price at which power is sold. RTOs and ISOs operate markets for wholesale power supply and demand for their designated area, including both day-ahead and hourly markets. Markets where vertically integrated utilities manage the grid are similar in that through a variety of contracts, utilities do not necessarily buy power produced by generators that they own but try to minimize the cost of purchased power. Regardless of whether an ISO or RTO or instead a vertically integrated utility is managing the market, the market price is the price necessary to induce supply from the marginal provider. In the figure, this is C_2, the price demanded by the coal-fired generator. Such a price is far higher than the 0 marginal cost of the nuclear provider and also the marginal cost C_1 of the natural gas-fired plant, providing net revenues that – if high enough to cover fixed costs – can make these low cost providers very profitable.

Under merit order dispatch, generators with the lowest prices for supplying power are called upon first to supply the minimum or base demand (load) in the system. Such base load units run continuously and produce electricity at a roughly constant rate throughout the day. Because they have essentially zero variable (and marginal) cost of producing power but cannot be switched on and off quickly (or at any time interval without enormous costs), nuclear plants are base load power suppliers. Hydroelectric dams and geothermal-fueled power plants also have very low variable costs and so, where available, provide base load power. Natural gas- and coal-fired power plants have higher variable costs (as they have fuel costs that may increase with the amount of fuel consumed), but some (especially highly efficient combined-cycle natural gas plants) may have low enough costs to provide base load power.

Demand for power predictably peaks at certain times during the day (such as late afternoon and early evening) and on certain days (such as when air conditioning use increases on hot days and heating demands increase on cold days). For a generator to be a candidate to supply peak load power, it must be available relatively quickly, and capable of being turned on and off at a cost that is non-prohibitive. Fuel flow and hence the speed of natural gas- and oil-powered generators can be adjusted continuously, as can the flow of water through a hydropower sluice gate. For this reason, these types of generators are typically used for peak load power.

In between base load and peak load generation fall what are called intermediate or load following generating units. These are power plants whose generation levels can be continuously adjusted during the day to follow changes in load that occur during the day. Not all types of power plants can be used to supply fluctuating demand. Nuclear generally cannot be used for load following. Indeed, only one nuclear plant in the United States – the Columbia River Generating Station in the Pacific Northwest – has the capability of varying the amount of power it produces so as to be able to follow load during the day or to respond to peak loads. The newest light water reactor nuclear plants, such as those used in France – which gets 75 percent or more of its power from nuclear – are much more flexible, with continuous power output adjustments possible (down to 50 percent of capacity) over 24-hour periods.[14] Today in the U.S., however, the ideal load following electric power plants are either hydropower facilities or combined cycle natural gas plants. Natural gas-fired turbines can be shut down and started up quickly and at relatively low cost and, like hydropower, within limits, the speed (frequency) of natural gas-fired turbines can be varied continuously simply by controlling gas flow and other parameters.[15]

As this discussion suggests, while once true, the merit order of coal and natural gas depicted in Figure 7.3, with coal cheaper than natural gas and therefore coming online before natural gas, is no longer the case.[16] Natural gas prices have remained low, while due primarily to the raft of Obama-era regulations I have described, the price of electricity from coal-burning plants has increased. Thus today, natural gas is typically cheaper than coal. Price is not the only reason for the increased competitive advantage of natural gas. The traditional concepts of base, peak, and intermediate electricity loads have been altered by demand-side measures designed to conserve electricity usage. Such measures have been designed to lower average, minimum, and maximum electricity demands by allowing continuous management of demand. Such continuous management has tended to make it necessary for more and more power supply to follow load. Natural gas is an ideal load following power source; large capacity coal-fired plants cannot be used for load following.

II *The Impact of Increasing the Share of Renewable Power on Power System Cost and Reliability*

Increasing the share of renewable power (primarily solar and wind) has two basic impacts on the electric power system. Renewables affect reliability because they do not provide inertial power that can be used to continuously balance grid frequency. Second, because they are intermittent sources of power – available only when the sun shines or the wind blows – increasing the share of renewables paradoxically increases the amount of non-renewable reserve power that must be held back as reserve capacity to guarantee reliability and continuous operation. The cost of such additional reserve capacity is a cost of increasing the share of renewable power on the grid.

A *Electrical System Reliability with an Increasing Renewable Share*

Consider first the impact of renewables on grid frequency stability and reliability. Conventional coal- or gas-powered synchronous generators connect to the electrical power system and deliver an active power response proportional to the rate of change of frequency (or "RoCoF" for short, as it is called in the electrical engineering literature) in the system. The large rotating mass of a synchronous generator provides rotating inertia that can continue to operate through small voltage and frequency deviations caused by faults and failures. Solar PV and wind turbines do not connect synchronously to the grid. They connect to the grid using a power interface called an inverter (or convertor). PV systems connect via an inverter because they have to convert DC power to AC power. Fixed speed wind turbines do provide an inherent inertial stabilization of power system frequency, but variable speed wind turbines are much more common and these connect to inverters that convert the current generated by their non-synchronous and varying rotation into a sine wave compatible with the grid.[17]

Frequency stability, to recall, is necessary to avoid potentially cascading tripping of system components that can lead to mass power outages (blackouts) (Tielens and Van Hertem 2016, 1004). With enough spinning, rotational power on a grid, adding renewable power that makes little or no contribution to reserve inertial power capacity does not affect the system's ability to maintain frequency stability. Indeed, when renewable generation is a relatively low fraction of total system power production, adding renewables to the generation mix can actually enhance the flexibility of the system, because some gas-fired units may not be providing power but are still online.

Grid reliability problems arise, however, when the fraction of power supplied by wind and solar rise above a certain level. In a comprehensive discussion of the role of inertia on power systems, Tielens and Van Hertem (2016, 1007) explain that "in a system with high penetration of converter connected generation [that is, renewables], not only loss of main, but also major power imbalances" can cause high frequency change rates [RoCoF] above relay settings, causing cascading disconnection of generation that can eventually lead to widespread power outages. Even short of such catastrophic events, increasingly common rapid fluctuations in frequency due to high renewable penetration can cause an increase in wear and tear on generators, cutting the expected lifetime of such units. As Wang et al. (2016, 10–16) say, the "most challenging periods" for maintaining grid stability with a high penetration of renewables are when there are few high spinning generators online but high load that is being served by renewables. During such periods of relatively little synchronous power generation being supplied, there is lower system inertia and therefore much greater frequency variation caused by contingencies such as trees falling over transmission lines (Flynn et al. 2017).

In island power grids, such as Ireland or the UK, that are not connected to larger regional grids, the reliability problems caused by rising shares of variable renewable power must be directly addressed. Such island systems cannot rely on synchronous generation elsewhere on a larger regional grid to ensure frequency stability and hence system reliability. Discussing such island systems, Flynn et al. (2017) note the need to keep frequency swings within prescribed limits itself sets a limit to the fraction of renewable power that can be utilized. They go on to recommend that once wind annual penetration exceeds 10 percent, a whole variety of stability measures – including changes in grid stability codes, "changes in operational practice and electricity market structures" – may all become necessary. By 2017, variable renewable power (virtually all wind) provided 25 percent of Ireland's electricity.[18] The stability of the Irish grid has been ensured despite a rapidly rising share of wind power in large part by imposing what is called a minimum synchronous generation (SG) requirement (Vithayasrichareron et al. 2017, 32–41). Also called a system non-synchronous penetration (SNSP) requirement, this means that a certain minimum amount of conventional spinning generation on the system must be retained in reserve to ensure stability.

Unlike Ireland, most of the other jurisdictions that have achieved very high usage of variable renewable power are part of large, interconnected grids. Renewables (primarily wind and solar) provided about 47 percent of Danish electricity in 2019,[19] 40 percent of German electricity in 2018,[20] and about 27 percent in California, but all of these jurisdictions' systems are part of much larger regional or international grids. As a fraction of the total electricity produced on the relevant regional or international grid, the variable renewable shares produced by these states is small.

In Europe, for example, there are five synchronous electricity grids. These are shown below in Figure 7.4.[21] As one can see from that figure, Denmark is part of the

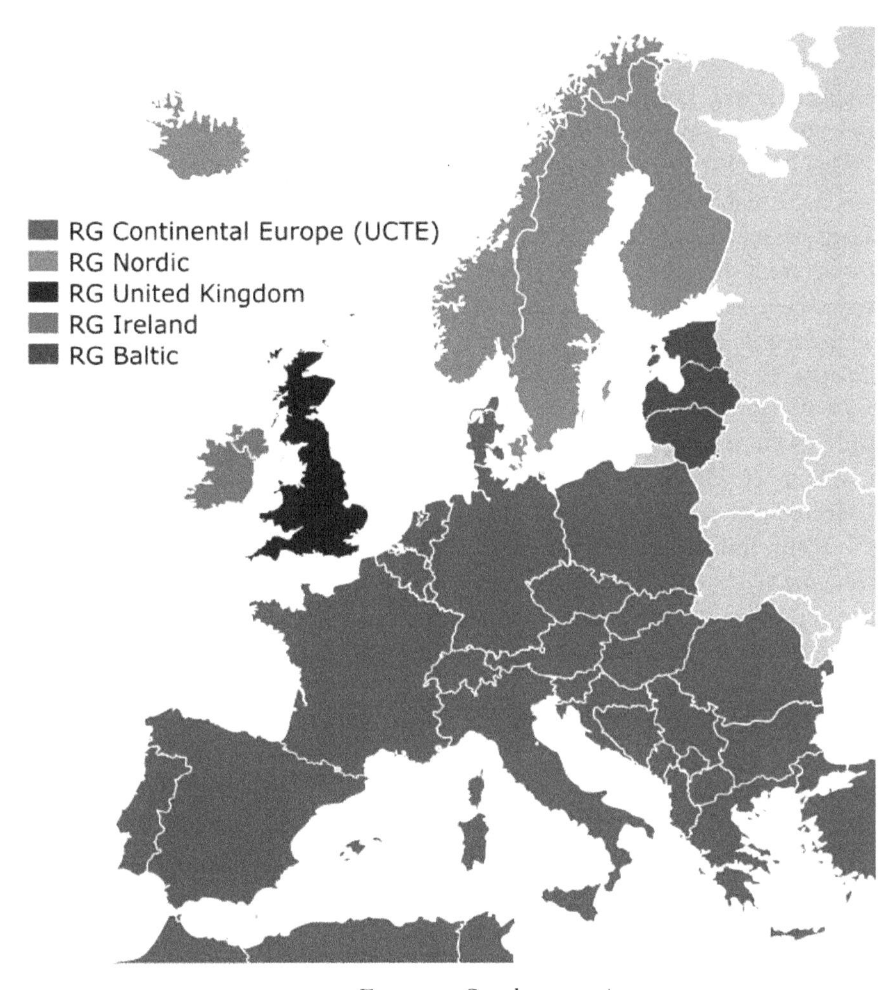

FIGURE 7.4 European Synchronous Areas

largest of these, RG Continental Europe (UCTE). Wind supplied 41 percent of Danish electricity load in 2018, but Denmark's installed wind capacity of 5.7GW is only 3 percent of the total installed wind capacity of 179 GW for Europe as a whole.[22] Europe's 179 GW installed wind generation capacity is in turn only 19 percent of total installed European grid generating capacity, meaning that Denmark's 5.7 GW of installed wind is only .6 percent of total European installed generating capacity. Denmark is so small that it could not only get all of its electricity from wind but build out enormous wind generation capacity for export (as it is trying to do) without affecting the stability of its own power supply. As Kroposki (2017) points out, countries and states that are "part of larger synchronous AC grids" can both export excess renewable power out to the grid and "rely on the overall system for stability support." Depending on pricing, national or state electricity systems that get a high fraction of their electricity from wind or solar power that they produce within their boundaries may free-ride on the grid stability provided by synchronous spinning generation located elsewhere on the grid.

Countries that are not part of large synchronous grids have much greater reliability assurance problems. The United Kingdom is one such country. On August 9 2019, a large lightning storm knocked out a UK transmission line, and simultaneously with the lightning strike, two generators shut down, a 737 MW wind farm off the Yorkshire coast and a natural gas-fired 244 MW steam turbine in Cambridgeshire. This caused an immediate drop in system frequency. With all of the available reserve generating capacity employed, frequency was restored, only to be lost again when another 210 MW gas turbine at the Cambridgeshire plant suddenly shut down. At that point, with frequency below operating levels, load (power demand) to about 1.1 million people was eliminated.

According to a report by the UK Electrical System Operator,[23] while the offshore wind farm initially reacted correctly to the lost transmission trip by immediately reducing generation, when transmission was restored, the wind farm did not ramp power back up, but instead shut down both active and reactive power. According to the wind turbine manufacturer, the turbine controllers did not function properly, leading to a large decrease in voltage at the wind farm causing the turbines to shut down. The first Cambridgeshire plant's natural gas steam turbine was tripped off at the time of the lightning strike, but was then followed for unknown reasons by the loss of another natural gas turbine. Grid frequency was restored by quickly ramping up generation from other natural gas cogeneration plants and by releasing water from two pumped storage facilities, and within about 45 minutes from the time of the lightning strikes power had been fully restored.[24]

Significantly, this power outage occurred on a day when wind was providing a large fraction of system generation, at one point reaching 67 percent. With wind such a huge percentage of generation mix, there was very little synchronous generation already online to provide frequency-stabilizing inertial power. Although not discussed by the UK ESO, the fact that all available reserve capacity had been brought online, leaving no capacity left to cover the loss of the final Cambridgeshire natural gas turbine, is at least suggestive of a shortage of reserve synchronous generation capacity.

B *The True Cost of Intermittent Variable Renewable Power*

A consequence of the increasing share of renewable power affecting grid reliability is that, from the point of view of an entire grid, the cost of increasing the share of variable renewable power is significantly greater than the cost of simply building and operating solar PV facilities and wind generation farms. Other than its inability to supply inertial stabilizing power, the crucial feature of renewable electricity generation is that it is intermittent (or variable). When the sun is not shining and the wind is not blowing, solar and wind power are not being generated. When solar and wind power are being generated, they produce power at zero marginal cost – unlike natural gas and coal, the wind and sun provide free energy.

If electricity could be stored at the scale needed by an entire grid, the fact that the wind and solar power is intermittent would be much less important. Power could be produced by wind and solar facilities and then stored until needed. But such storage does not exist and likely will not exist for the foreseeable future.

Batteries are one way to store power. And certainly, and obviously, there have been some great successes in improving lithium ion battery storage at the scale needed for automobiles. However, the existing attempts to supply battery storage at levels useful at the scale necessary to help with grid level power and load matching have proven to be completely uneconomic. Tesla's LiIon installation was brought online to help with the 2016 South Australia blackout, but it costs $275,000 per MWh. The Tesla PowerWall v2 provides power at a cost of $496/MWh. Finally, power supply in 2018 from Florida Power and Light's Babcock Ranch 10 MW battery for four hours cost $375/MWh.[25] Even in New England, with the most expensive retail electricity in the United States as of March, 2020 at $200/MWh,[26] battery provision of power to the grid is clearly uneconomic. In addition to cost, there are a number of serious safety risks from grid scale lithium-ion storage,[27] and although alternatives such as manganese-hydrogen batteries have shown promise,[28] no existing potential candidate battery types currently provide safe, low cost, long life-cycle, and reliable storage at grid scale.

The other way to store energy produced by solar and wind is to use the power such facilities produce to pump water into reservoirs, where it can then be released when needed to drive turbines. Pumped storage essentially uses excess wind and /or solar power when available to store water to produce hydropower when the wind and/or solar power is unavailable. Pumped storage has limited feasibility, as it can only be undertaken where hilly terrain creates possible reservoirs for storage. Even where feasible, it is enormously expensive. The largest pumped storage facility in the world is in Bath County, Virginia, construction of which was completed in 1985. It has an electricity generation capacity of 3,000 MW but cost (in 2014 terms) $4.1 billion.[29] Assuming a roughly average capacity factor of .28, this $4.1 billion investment was necessary to provide daily power of 4,800 MWh/day from an 800 MW solar facility to a city of only 160,000 people (assuming half the power is used to fill the storage facility every day). Finally, for very high renewable penetration, the size of the pumped storage reservoir would need to be enormous. To buffer against multi-week wind droughts that occur during the European winter, a European grid with high renewables penetration would require pumped storage equal to 10 percent of annual European electricity load. The entire existing European pumped storage capacity falls short of this.[30]

With storage infeasible, wind and solar are inherently intermittent. This fundamental characteristic of renewable power – zero marginal cost when available, but uncertain availability based on the time of day and the weather at a particular point in time – radically changes the problem of dispatching generation so as to minimize the cost of reliably producing power (merit order). We can see this looking back at Figure 7.3, and supposing that it depicts a day and time when there is both robust demand and actual availability of wind or solar power so that wind or solar, and not nuclear, is the zero marginal cost power provider. Under these conditions, if price is determined competitively, price is likely to be equal to the bid price of the marginal supplier, in this case coal, bidding a bit above its cost of C_2. At this price, the zero marginal cost wind or solar provider earns significant revenue.

But the zero marginal cost renewable provider may well be unable to supply power during the period of robust demand. Electricity load varies during the day and over the course of a week. Such variation is depicted in the EIA figure reproduced as Figure 7.5 below. This gives electricity load for the week of July 13, 2013 on the mid-Atlantic PJM interconnection in the United States.[31]

As indicated by Figure 7.5, 24-hour load is especially variable during a hot summer month such as July in the mid-Atlantic region of the United States, where the demand for air conditioning increases from the morning to the evening and then declines. In other months, demand is generally much flatter, with much less of a daytime peak, and in the wintertime, demand actually falls during the morning hours.

Moreover, demand patterns differ across regions. This is shown by Figure 7.6, which is taken directly from the EIA's Hourly Electricity Grid Monitor for the day June 8, 2020.[32] As Figure 7.6 shows, the total demand as well as the fluctuation of demand varies across regions of the United States. The mid-Atlantic, midwestern, and southeastern regions have the highest and most variable daily demand, with demand much lower and much less variable in less populous and less industrialized regions such as New England.

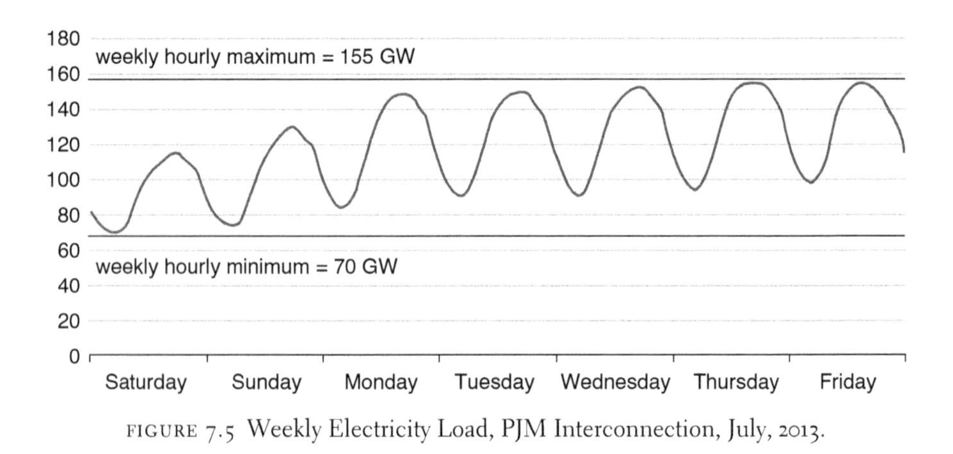

FIGURE 7.5 Weekly Electricity Load, PJM Interconnection, July, 2013.

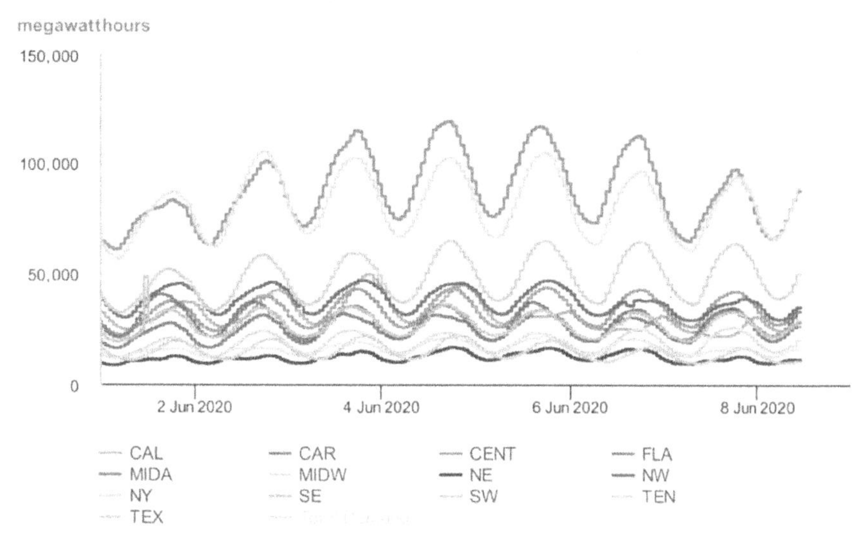

FIGURE 7.6 US Electricity Demand by Region, June 1–8, 2020

Renewable wind and solar power is not always available when electricity demand peaks. We can see this in Figure 7.7 below, which is also taken directly from the EIA's Hourly Electricity Grid Monitor for the week of June 1–8, 2020.

When we consider Figure 7.7, several points emerge. At the national level, we see that nuclear power is providing a steady baseload, with both natural gas and coal, and where available hydropower, providing load following power at relatively high levels. After these three sources, relatively little power needs to be supplied by other sources. Solar provides very little power, but the natural daily cycle of solar – available during the day, but not at night – does follow fairly closely the typical pattern of daily load. Wind does not follow the daily pattern of demand. Quite the opposite, wind generation tends to peak at night, when load is low, and it also undergoes multi-day cycles, sometimes remaining at low or high levels for days (Figure 7.7 shows such a multi-day cycle, with wind providing almost zero MW of power during the afternoons of June 3 and June 4 but then rising to provide 50,000 MW or more over the entire June 6–8 period).

Thus although both wind and solar have zero marginal cost of providing electricity, their actual value in supplying power to the grid varies greatly.[33] Especially in sunny, dry regions, such as California and the Southwest, solar is a reliable source of very low cost electricity during precisely those periods of the day when demand is high. Wind, by contrast, has more unpredictable availability but predictably is most abundant during nighttime low demand (off-peak) hours.

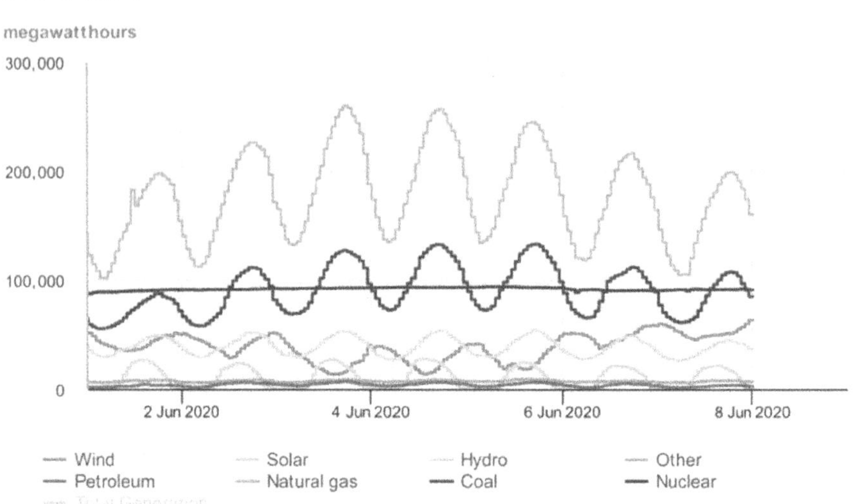

FIGURE 7.7 US Electricity Generation by Source June 1–8, 2020

These basic facts about wind and solar power have a number of consequences for the cost of providing reliable electricity. More precisely, the availability of zero marginal cost wind and solar at certain times pushes the supply curve out during those times, generally lowering the marginal cost and hence market price determined by the marginal electricity provider when wind and solar is available. I've shown this in Figure 7.8, which has precisely the same demand curve as Figure 7.3 but with market supply conditions changed so that such a high quantity of zero marginal cost solar is available (but nuclear is now not available) up to the effective capacity of S_C.

As the figure shows, this zero marginal cost solar has (literally) pushed coal out of the supply picture, and made low cost natural gas the marginal supplier. The natural gas-fired marginal supplier now gets a lower price, of C_1, and also is operating at a lower capacity factor – that is, most of the horizontal distance it could supply is not supplied – versus the capacity factor of (close to) 1 with which it operated prior to the introduction of the huge supply of zero marginal cost solar.

Now imagine what will happen when solar is not available. Under such conditions, with demand fixed at D, the natural gas facility depicted in the figure will operate at full capacity (it will be our first generator online, which can be visualized by moving the natural gas "box" all the way so that it begins at 0 MWh). Its capacity is insufficient to meet the entire load D, and additional facilities will need to be brought online to make up the huge shortfall caused by the unavailability of solar. Our natural gas facility depicted will be the lowest cost and first in merit order

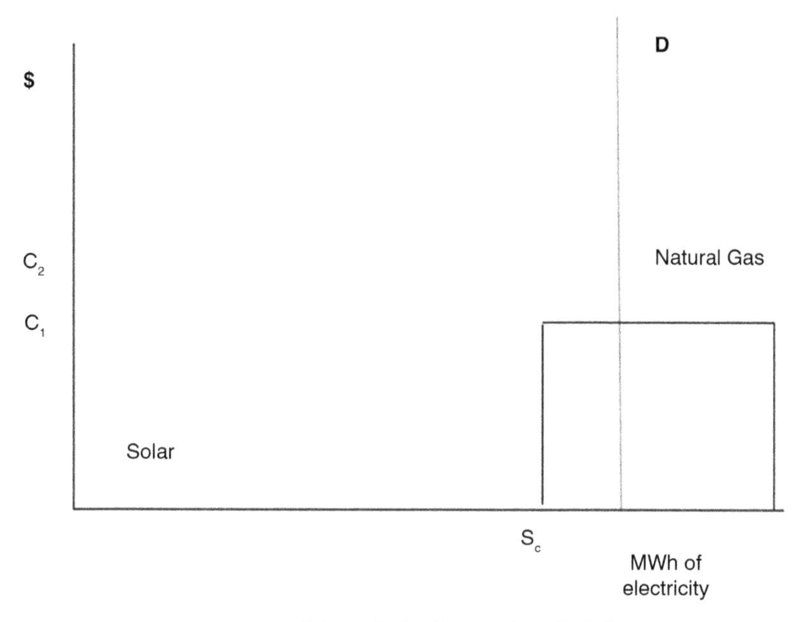

FIGURE 7.8 Merit Order Dispatch with Solar

inframarginal provider of power at such times, with a series of high cost providers (boxes in the figure) arrayed in ascending order to the right.

California is the US state that has had the most rapid increase in solar power provision, and by using results from Bushnell and Novan (2018), we can be more specific about the impact of increasing solar penetration on the electricity market. As Bushnell and Novan (2018, 6) report, from 2012 to 2017, the amount of utility-scale solar capacity installed in California increased from .6 to 10 GW. Solar power is available only between 8 am and 7 pm, peaking in availability around noon. Noontime solar generation in California grew by 1,000 percent between 2012 and 2016 (from 640 MW to over 6,400 MW). As solar is zero marginal cost power, it serves the market when available, and the real time (versus one day forward) price for electricity likewise fell dramatically between 2012 and 2016 during the hours when solar is available. Bushnell and Novan (2018) estimated that increased solar power output reduced noontime prices by 35 percent between 2012 and 2016 (from $34.25 to $22.05).

1 The Costs of Intermittent Wind and Solar Power: Increased Need for Dispatchable Reserve Capacity

However, Bushnell and Novan (2018) also found that the increase in solar power production led to around 20 percent increases in electricity prices during the 6 and 7 am and 6 and 7 pm hours of the day. During these periods when solar was not available, electricity was supplied by natural gas turbine-driven power plants. Among natural gas-fired plants, gas turbines operate at the highest heat rates and burn the most natural gas. They are in a sense wasting a good deal of the energy produced by combusting gas and are therefore the most expensive type of natural gas-fired plant. Gas turbine plants are costly and relatively inefficient because they do not attempt to do anything with the heat generated by burning natural gas to spin a turbine, neither using it to produce more electricity from steam (which is what natural gas steam turbine plants do) or using the heat directly in industrial applications (which is what combined cycle plants do). Precisely because they are simple, however, gas turbines can be brought up to full output in as little as ten minutes (Bushnell and Novan 2018, 17), and are the easiest plants to turn on and off to provide power when solar polar is unavailable. Benson and Majumdar (2016)[34] project that if California continues to rely mainly on solar to reach its goal of getting 50 percent of its electricity from renewables by 2050, not only will it be literally over-generating solar power during the middle of the day (about 23 percent of the time), but it will need to have available at least 10 GW of natural gas power plants to provide power during the high load early evening (4–6 pm) hours when not enough solar is available.

Thus in the specific case of California, the rapid addition of massive amounts of solar power had precisely the kind of price effects that one would predict from Figure 7.8. Looking at the power supply net of nuclear (which in California provides a constant baseline amount of power at virtually all times), solar massively pushed out the daytime supply curve, lowering the price received by the marginal daytime providers – in California, a mix of natural gas cogeneration, large hydropower, plus coal-fired power imported from outside the state. This reduced the profitability of such relatively low marginal cost daytime power providers. Paradoxically, as Bushnell and Novak (2018, 21–22) explain, for the highest marginal cost providers who only operate during hours when solar is offline and prices are the highest – natural gas turbines in California – the expanded penetration of solar power had little or no impact on profitability.

Figure 7.9 below depicts daily average solar irradiance across the United States for the period 1998–2016.[35] As one can see from that figure, most of California gets high levels of solar irradiance and is an ideal place for solar power. In other places, solar power is not so reliably available even during the core noontime hours. I am aware of no econometric study of the impact of solar penetration on hourly electricity prices outside California. However, in places where solar is less reliably available but dominating the market and generating very low prices when it is available, the need for quickly dispatchable power must increase.

Dispatchable providers provide a very real service to the grid as a whole by keeping power production capacity, which is often unused because outbid by zero variable cost solar but which is critical to ensuring generation and load balance during times

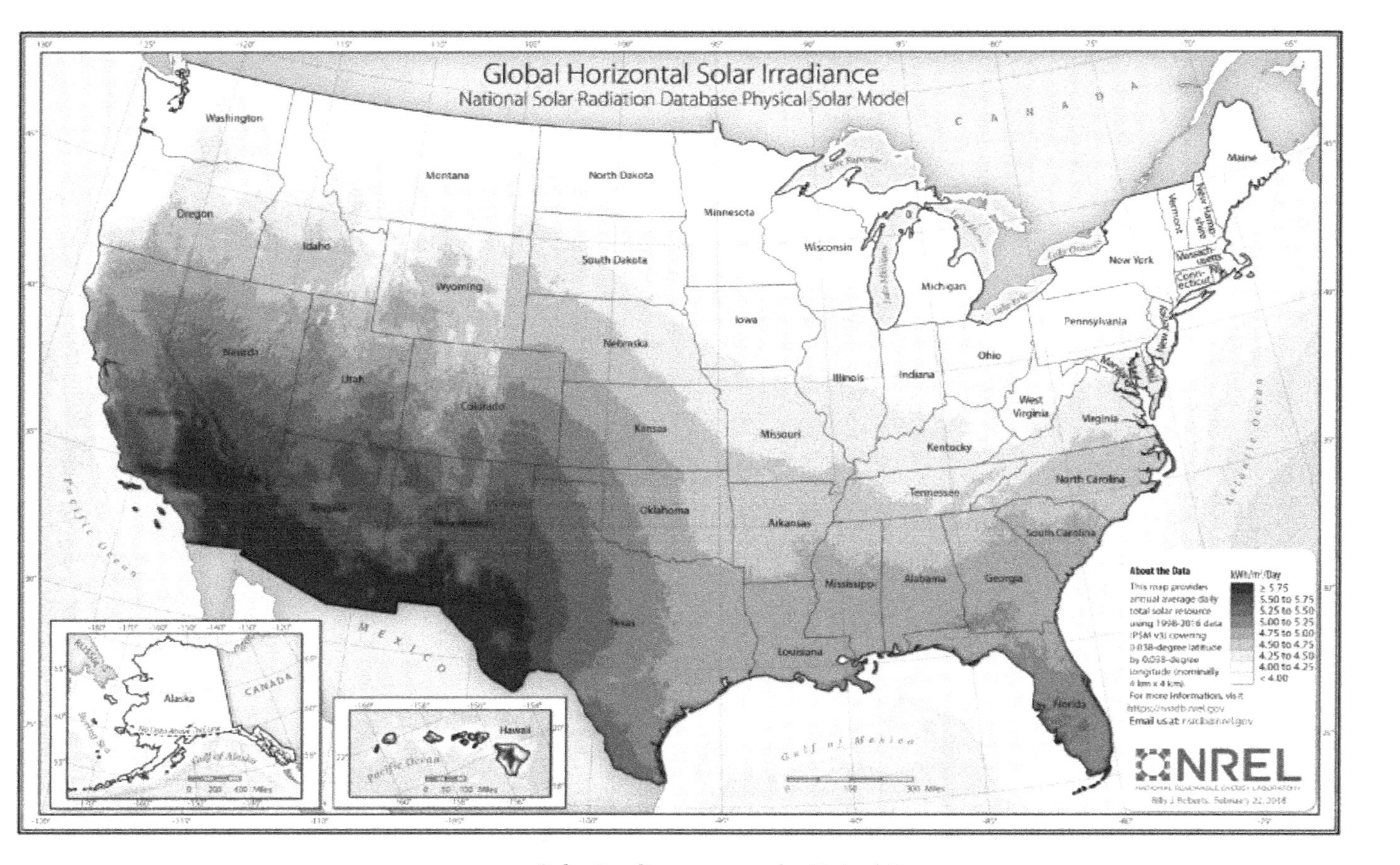

FIGURE 7.9 Solar Irradiance across the United States

when solar and/or wind are unavailable. Such reserve capacity may be actually "in the money" generating revenue only a small fraction of total hours of the year. As Joskow (2011, 160)[36] pointed out, "if prices during these few critical hours are too low, then the net revenues will be inadequate to support the efficient quantity and mix of generating capacity; that is, there will be underinvestment in generating capacity, too many hours when capacity is fully utilized, too much reliance on non-price rationing, and too high a probability of a network collapse." In other words, the impact of zero variable cost solar on the problem of least cost power dispatch also means that the profitability of dispatchable reserve capacity falls, ultimately decreasing incentives to invest in such capacity.

As in my example, the addition of wind and solar to a grid's power generation capacity, however, generally lowers prices. Solar is available during the 8 am – 7 pm daytime period and depresses price during those hours. Although highly variable, when wind is available, it often depresses prices during off-peak nighttime hours. In California, wind is not nearly as significant as solar. Even during the peak hours of wind availability (between around 9 pm and 5 am), wind electricity generation only increased about 50 percent or less in California between 2012 and 2016 (Bushnell and Novan 2018, 30). However, as discussed earlier, wind is the dominant source of renewable power in Germany. Using German data, Gerster (2016, 271–289) has run simulations indicating that if wind were to reach an 80 percent share, money losing off-peak hours of power sold by German coal-burning plants would jump between 18 percent to 77 percent, a result that would "threaten the financial viability of conventional plants." Germany is far from getting 80 percent of its power from wind. But as we've seen, with around 40 percent from wind, Germany has one of the highest penetrations of renewable power in the world. Since at least 2015, that country has struggled with the issue of how to ensure that sufficient coal – or, now that the country has phased out coal, natural gas – capacity exists.

There are two ways that reserve capacity can be financed. One, called an energy-only market, allows prices for power to rise to very high levels during periods when additional capacity is needed to avert power failures. This method relies on the prospect of such potentially high but unpredictable prices as an incentive for generators to hold spare capacity. The other, called a capacity market, involves contractual payments to generators to provide certain quantities of capacity whenever the future spot price of power rises above a fixed price. (For a detailed discussion of the differences between these two approaches, see Cramton et al. 2013, 27–46). Germany has repeatedly eschewed both the energy only and capacity market approach, and many utility industry executives project that Germany will soon endure electricity shortages and periodic blackouts.[37]

Regardless of how the problem of financing reserve dispatchable capacity is dealt with, the basic fact is that the creation of such necessary but often unused or out-of-the-money capacity is a direct consequence of increasing the share of renewable power on a grid. This cost must be added to the levelized cost of renewable electricity to get the true cost of renewable power.

This is an extremely important point to understand. The most commonly quoted figures for the levelized cost of wind and solar power – generated by organizations ranging from the investment bank Lazard, to the renewable energy media cheerleader Bloomberg, to the EIA itself – do not even attempt to estimate and include the dispatchable power capacity cost of renewable power.[38] One must remember that a levelized cost figure for renewable solar or wind just averages over facility expected lifetime power output the capital cost of building the facility plus the facility's lifetime maintenance and operational expenses. Levelized cost does not include the cost that solar and wind intermittency imposes on dispatchable generation.

When Stacy and Taylor (2019, 15)[39] did estimate the capacity cost imposed on dispatchable natural gas-fired power plants by wind and solar, they found (using 2018 prices) that the levelized cost of wind increased by 36 percent, from $66 to $90/MWh, while the levelized cost of solar increased by 29 percent, from $69 to $89/MWh. Whereas Stacy and Taylor found that levelized cost of wind and solar when this capacity cost was not included was about the same as nuclear and hydro (but at $66–67/MWh still far above the levelized cost of $19/MWh for combined cycle natural gas), *with capacity cost included, the roughly $90/MWh cost of wind and solar was far above the levelized cost of any other power supplier* (other than a conventional natural gas combustion turbine, which is so expensive that it can provide only peaking power). In an analysis of solar power penetration in the Tucson, Arizona grid, Gowrisankaran et al. (2016, 1187–1234) found that with 20 percent solar penetration, operating reserves equal to 35 percent of load were optimally required, with the cost of capacity required because of predictable solar intermittency making up over 50 percent ($46 out about an $82 base) of the total cost of solar generation. As Gowrisankaran et al. (2016) observe, if the capital cost of building solar facilities continues to fall, the intermittency cost of solar will make up a bigger and bigger share of the total cost of solar.

2 The Cost of Intermittent Wind and Solar Power: Additional Transmission Lines

From the point of view of the total cost of providing reliable electricity, there is a final and very significant cost of increasing the share of renewable power. This is the cost of building new transmission lines to connect renewable power generators to the grid. New transmission capacity represents a very large, lumpy (fixed cost) investment. When it allows the transmission of relatively low cost power to distant sites of power demand such as big cities and metro areas, such large, lumpy investments can make both generators and ultimate power users better off – transmission line developers get large loads sufficient to more than cover their costs, while power users get lower prices than would otherwise be available. The low prices come about because when the new long distance transmission line is built, economies of scale are realized as more and more generators hook into the transmission line through spur lines. In addition, congestion is reduced on existing transmission lines. But such investments are risky. There is an incentive to build and operate generators located closer to load centers before construction of long distance transmission lines has been completed. Investments in transmission capacity will not be made without assurances that they will not be preempted by new generation, or transmission, elsewhere on the grid.

For all of these reasons (established more formally by Joskow and Tirole 2005, 233–264), transmission capacity will not be competitively supplied at anywhere near optimal levels, and incentives both to invest in new transmission capacity and to maintain existing capacity depend upon decisions made by dispatch and reliability decisions that are made by system operators (the ISOs and RTOs discussed earlier). This is the economic justification for the fact that in the US system, ISOs and RTOs in fact are both in charge of power dispatch and also regulate investments in and maintenance of transmission capacity.

The existing transmission network was originally designed around the location of very large conventional power plants. As the number of such plants has increased, new bulk (high voltage) transmission lines have been built, and many such plants have been connected to the grid via less expensive spur lines. Wind plants in particular have created a demand for new transmission capacity.

To see why, observe first that the best places for wind and solar power generation are, unsurprisingly, places with reliable wind and sunshine. As shown in Figure 7.10,[40] the very best US region for onshore wind is central Wyoming, with the High Plains region from North Dakota all the way down to central and western Texas comprising the largest region of reliably high winds. (Offshore, as we can see from that same figure, both the east and west coasts have a rich wind resource.) Unlike the solar resource, which as we have seen in the earlier figure (Figure 7.9 above) is located precisely where many big cities such as Denver, Phoenix, and Los Angeles are found, the best US areas for onshore wind are very far from most major load centers. For wind power generated in the High Plains to have value, new transmission lines have had to be built.

As reported by the University of Texas Energy Institute (Andrade et al. 2016), as of around 2010, for a not insubstantial number of wind projects in the United States, at around $6.2 million, the average cost of building new transmission lines was over half of the total project cost. Texas has undertaken by far the largest expansion of transmission capacity of anywhere in the United States designed to connect distant renewable power sites with load centers. Under legislation passed in 2005, the Texas public utilities commission identified prime wind resource development areas (called Competitive Renewable Energy Zones or CREZ) in west Texas. At a cost ultimately of $6.8 billion, by 2014 Texas had financed the construction of 3,600 miles of 345,000 volt transmission lines connecting 18.5 GW of new wind energy production in west Texas to load centers in northern (Dallas) and eastern and southeastern (Austin, San Antonio, and Houston) parts of the state.

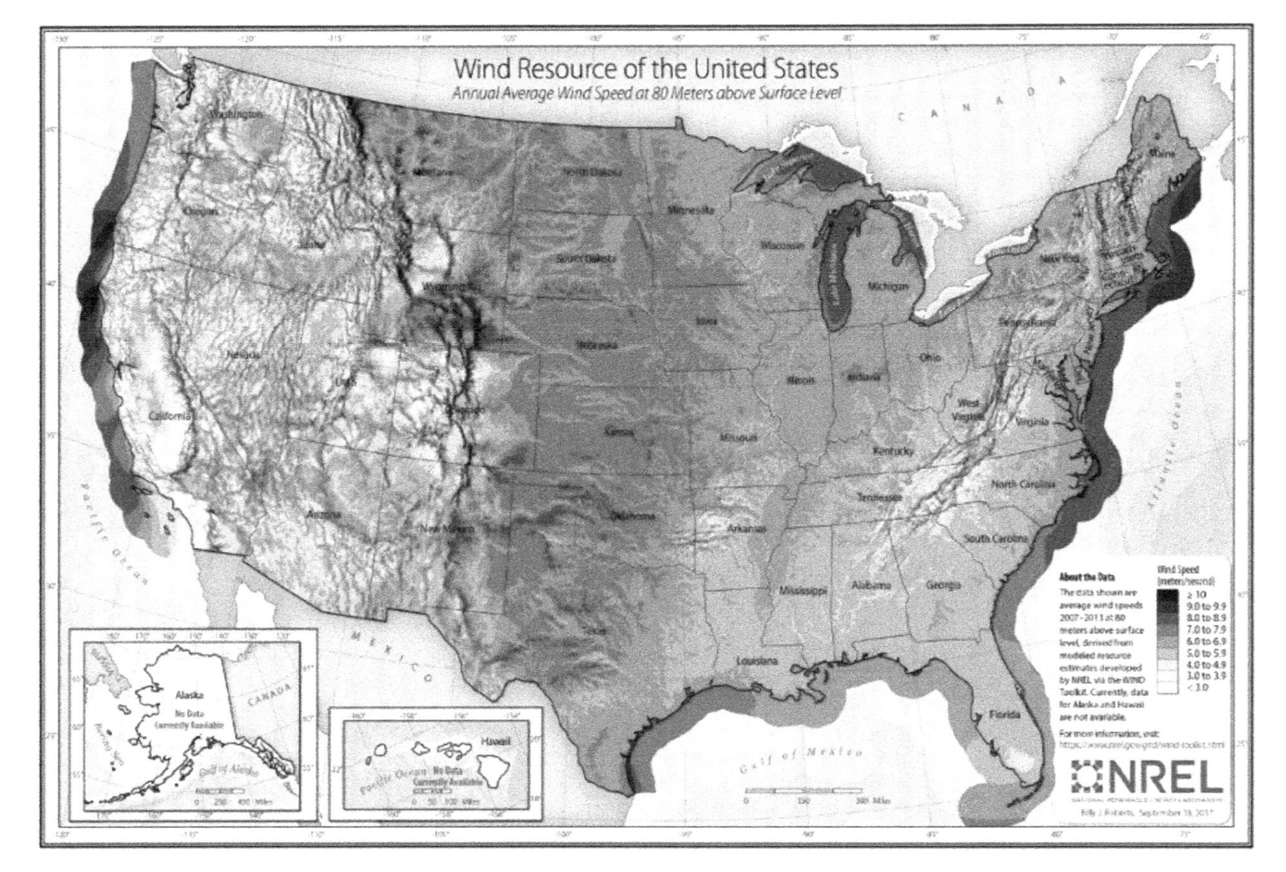

FIGURE 7.10 US Average Wind Speed at 80 Meters above Ground

The vast expansion in transmission capacity brought about by Texas' CREZ program not only brought new wind power production online, effectively increasing supply to load centers, but also reduced congestion (and also perhaps market power exercise) that had effectively increased prices. LaRiviere and Lu (2018) calculate that the value of the (primarily off peak) price drop from increased supply on wholesale power markets in Texas was $500 million per year. Against this, however, must be balanced the $6.8 billion cost of the transmission line expansion, a cost that is passed on by ERCOT, the Texas RTO, to all Texas electricity consumers. In addition, Texas wind farms, like other wind power producers, benefited from a federal production tax credit for renewable power development.

The tax credit will be discussed further in the next chapter. For present purposes it is worth noting that LaRiviere and Lu (2018) estimate the value of the production tax credit to wind farms brought online due to the CREZ at around $600 million per year, or 12 percent of the total US value of the wind production tax credits. Thus while west Texas wind has lowered wholesale off-peak electricity prices, Texas electricity consumers – not wind farm developers – paid the $6.8 billion cost of the new transmission lines that created the market for this wind power. And power developers not only got free new transmission capacity but a subsidy worth $600 million per year. As LaRiviere and Lu conclude, the wholesale off-peak price drop it generated cannot be taken to imply that the Texas CREZ transmission capacity investment was socially worth its costs: that depends entirely on how one values whatever pollution and CO_2 emission reduction was generated by the transmission and wind power expansion.

3 Increasing Intermittent Power at the Cost of System Safety and Reliability: The PG&E Saga

One of the oldest public utilities in the United States, Pacific Gas and Electric, provides electricity to millions of customers in northern California. Facing a new California state law mandating that utilities get 20 percent of their power from renewables such as wind and solar and geothermal (which is relatively abundant in California due to the highly seismically unstable Owens Valley fault region) by 2020, beginning in 2008, PG&E undertook a highly ambitious program to ramp up its reliance on solar power. Back in 2008, PG&E got only about 11 percent of its power from renewables, but it immediately began entering into very long term, 20–30 year contracts with solar farm developers.[41] So aggressive was PG&E in acquiring solar power that by late 2017, three years ahead of the deadline set by the California law, PG&E could announce that fully 33 percent of its power came from renewables.[42] The contracts PG&E had made with solar power providers over the period since 2008 paid prices to some such providers – such as the $197 per MWh received by Con Edison, the owner of the Copper Mountain Solar Project in Nevada – that ended up being many multiples of the market prices only 10 years later ($25 to $30 in 2019). All in all, PG&E entered into about $30 billion worth of such long term solar power contracts.[43]

What PG&E did not spend money on was the maintenance of its existing transmission and distribution lines. During hot and windy Santa Ana conditions that prevailed during the fall (California summer) of 2017, overgrown trees fell on PG&E transmission and distribution lines, sparking 17 of the 21 major fires that hit the California wine growing region north of San Francisco, fires that killed 22 people and destroyed 3,256 buildings and homes. In November, 2018, a fire broke out in Butte County, in the Sierra foothills region of California. Called the Camp Fire, it eventually destroyed the entire town of Paradise, California, killing 85 people and burning 18,793 homes and buildings. Its cause was traced to a "worn-out, ancient" PG&E transmission tower hook and to a tree falling on a PG&E distribution line.[44]

Following the catastrophic fall, 2018 wildfires, PG&E accelerated its line inspection process. It discovered 10,000 problems, including damaged transmission towers and leaking transformers on substations. It quickly repaired about 1,000 immediate safety risks, but was still working through over 3,700 additional needed repairs when the fall, 2019 fire season began.[45] With its lines still so vulnerable, PG&E avoided causing even more fires during fall, 2019 only by turning off the power to 800,000 people for the better part of a week. According to its CEO, the utility said in October, 2019 that it could take 10 years – until 2030 – before such blackouts are "really ratcheted down significantly."[46]

Faced with some $30 billion in expected damage liability for the 2017 and 2018 fires, in 2019 PG&E filed for bankruptcy. By late spring, 2019, the bankruptcy court allowed PG&E to renegotiate to lower the prices on some of the $34 billion worth of long term solar power contracts.[47] A year later, by June, 2020, PG&E had pled guilty to 84 criminal counts of involuntary manslaughter, and agreed to pay over $13 billion into a victim's compensation fund. It was allowed to leave bankruptcy and granted future access to a new $21 billion California state wildfire victims compensation fund.

PG&E had known for some time that its 18,500 miles of transmission lines were badly in need of repair and replacement. A consulting firm hired by PG&E back in 2010 reported that it couldn't even determine the age of about 6,900 transmission towers, but of those it could date, nearly 30 percent, or more than 3,500, were installed in the 1900s and 1910s and 60 percent of PG&E's towers were built between 1920 and 1950. PG&E got itself in the position of having 90 percent of its transmission towers over half a century old by repeatedly delaying transmission line upgrades. Even after getting the 2010 consultant's report, PG&E repeatedly delayed upgrades of some of its oldest transmission lines in favor of spending billions of dollars on substation upgrades.[48]

To understand why PG&E neglected line maintenance and upgrading in favor of projects such as substation upgrades, the key thing to know is that PG&E is a vertically integrated utility regulated by the California Public Utilities Commission (CPUC). Everything from the investments it makes to the rates it charges consumers are controlled by the CPUC. During the 2010–2017 period, PG&E was doing what the CPUC was telling it to do: investing billions of dollars to create a so-called Smart Grid in California. In a 2011 report required by the CPUC, the utility promised that its "Smart Grid Deployment Plan is not just a plan, it represents a fundamental change to the way PG&E uses technology to serve its customers and operate its business."[49] As PG&E explained in the plan required by a 2008 CPUC regulation, the point of the Smart Grid was to "integrate wind and solar supplies to give customers more clean and renewable energy" and to "support more widespread customer adoption of rooftop solar as well as 'smart charging' programs that encourage the use of zero-emission electric vehicles while helping protect the safety and reliability of the energy grid."

As PG&E reported to the CPUC, the primary goals of its Smart Grid investments were to "improve the ability to match energy supplies and energy demand while maintaining the reliability of the grid and increasing the use of renewable energy to meet statutory requirements," and to "integrate large-scale renewables into the grid."[50] In developing the Smart Grid, PG&E consulted not with the kind of prosaic contracting firms responsible for line maintenance, but with renewable power advocates such the Environmental Defense Fund (EDF), the Silicon Valley Leadership Group, the GridWise Alliance, and the Center for Democracy and Technology.

PG&E's Smart Grid investments were mammoth. During its 2014 fiscal year, PG&E reported investing around $620 million in the program;[51] one year later, it reported investing even more, $828 million,[52] thus putting its Smart Grid investments at right about $1.5 billion for just two years. As late as late September, 2017, just before the devastating wine country fires broke out, PG&E still reported investing about $234 million in the Smart Grid program.[53]

The largest components of this investment went to digitizing transmission substations. This digitization of grid system control might have happened eventually anyway, but it was made an absolute imperative by the need to manage the vast amount of intermittent and highly variable solar power that PG&E had brought online through contracts and its own development.[54] One might well say that even if PG&E was investing billions in the Smart Grid, it could still have invested whatever it took to upgrade and maintain its transmission lines. This would be true if the CPUC were guaranteed to grant every rate request made by PG&E. But as I discuss below, California already has among the highest electricity prices in the United States. There is nothing to suggest that the CPUC would have granted additional rate increases needed to cover the cost of transmission line maintenance. Quite to the contrary, the CPUC clearly made the Smart Grid its priority, requiring annual reports from PG&E on how it was doing with Smart Grid investment. The CPUC imposed no similar reporting requirement for PG&E transmission line maintenance and upgrading expenditures. The answer to the question of why PG&E spent so little on transmission line maintenance, and so much on the Smart Grid would seem to be simple: because the Smart Grid, and not transmission line maintenance, was what the California state assembly and the CPUC cared about.

III THE CLEAN POWER PLAN AND THE GRID

With this chapter's discussion of how an increasing share of renewable power is likely to impact the US electric supply system in hand, we are now in a better position to evaluate the EPA's plans for transforming states' generation mix via its CPP.

The proposed CPP elicited a flood of comments from state utility regulators, utilities, and ISOs and RTOs, the organizations actually responsible for operating the grid. According to North American Electric Reliability Corporation (NERC), the EPA's model – the same IPM that it used for every regulation affecting the power plant industry – simply assumed that there was "adequate transmission capacity… to deliver any resources located in, or transferred to, the individual regions" and assumed also that since most regions had capacity above their minimum required reserve capacity (target reserve margins), the retirement of coal-fired power plants would simply come out of reserve capacity (NERC 2014, 18). Additionally, since most regions currently have capacity above their target reserve margins, the EPA assumed most of the retirements are absorbed by a reduction in excess reserves over time.

My discussion in this chapter has explained why big increases in renewable power, especially wind, require big investments in new transmission lines such as that undertaken by Texas. In justifying its CPP, the EPA said precisely the opposite, that there was plenty of transmission capacity in the various regions. NERC, the organization responsible for the reliability of the nation's power supply, entirely disagreed with the EPA. Confirming the analysis of this chapter, NERC (2014, 20) explained that:

> The CPP analysis assumes that adequate transmission capacity is available to deliver any resources located in, or transferred to, the region. Given the significant changes and locations anticipated to occur in the resource mix, it is likely that additional new transmission, or transmission enhancements, will be necessary in some areas. New transmission lines will be required to transport the amount of renewable generation coming online, particularly in remote areas, and that creates additional timing considerations. Further, as replacement generation is constructed, new transmission may be needed to interconnect new generation. Mitigating transmission constraints identified from the proposed EPA regulations in a timely way, consistent with CPP targets, presents a potential reliability concern.

As NERC (2014, 20, 24) further elucidated, the additional renewable power production required by the CPP amounted to "well over twice the energy currently supplied by VERs [variable energy resources, or producers]… and would be dominated mostly by new wind." To support so much new wind power, "the power industry would need to invest heavily to expand transmission capacity to access more remote areas with high-quality wind resources. Given the natural wind variability in these locations, incremental wind project resources would have relatively low capacity factors (20–35 percent) that would require complex financial decisions to support transmission capacity." Nothing in the EPA's CPP rule or supporting documents even hints at such financial consequences.

Given that the planning of new, high voltage transmission lines could not even begin until the states had come up with their own compliance plans (or, as would have happened in many cases, the EPA had written its own plan for a state) and that it typically takes 5–15 years to actually build such new lines, NERC (2014, 22) advised the EPA that its proposed 2020 deadline did not "provide enough time to develop sufficient resources to ensure continued reliable operation of the electric grid by 2020. To attempt to do so would increase the use of controlled load shedding and potential for wide-scale, uncontrolled outages." NERC's bottom line: as proposed, the EPA's CPP required major new investments in transmission capacity that could not have been completed by the scheduled compliance date, and without additional transmission capacity, "wide-scale, uncontrolled" power outages were likely.

As for the impact of the CPP on reserve capacity required to ensure grid reliability, NERC made the same set of points that I have worked through earlier in this chapter. As it said, "as the penetration of variable generation increases, maintaining voltage stability can be more challenging." And with respect to wind in particular, NERC explained that "wind projects will significantly increase the demand for reactive power and ramping flexibility," and "ramping flexibility will increase cycling on conventional generation and often results in either increased maintenance hours or higher forced outage rates – in both cases, increased reserve requirements may result." NERC ended by calling for additional studies of the impact of the CPP on grid reliability, which it said should be a "foundational" piece of any power sector transformation.

The EPA did respond to NERC (and other organizations') comment that the EPA's time frame for the renewables transition was too quick. Indeed, the EPA said[55] that it addressed the "reliability implications" pointed out by such organizations by giving the states more time to comply. As discussed earlier, the EPA did not actually extend the final 2030 full compliance deadline, but just broke the 2022–2030 period into a series of two-year compliance assessments. According to the EPA, these were supposed to "provide more time for planning, consultation, and decision making in the formulation of state plans and in EGUs' [power plants'] choices of compliance strategies." In addition, the EPA required states "to consult with relevant ISOs/RTOs and/or planning/reliability authorities during plan development, and to document recommendations in their plans." In sum, the EPA's response to concerns about its command that most states vastly increase the share of power from renewables was purely procedural – to give the states more time and to tell them to do something they would do anyway, consult with grid operators.

Entirely missing from the EPA's CPP and the RIA that accompanied it is any real response to the substantive points that NERC made about the impact of high levels of renewable penetration on the cost and reliability of electric power. According to the EPA, states like California and countries such as Germany had increased renewable power shares "without negative impacts to reliability" by taking "low cost measures."[56] Indeed, the EPA proclaimed that as proven by the use of wind power in several regional grids during the record cold winter of 2018, "renewable energy can contribute to reliable system operation." The multiple failures at the UK wind facility off Yorkshire in 2019 have proven far too sanguine the EPA's blithe proclamation in 2015 that the newest wind plants "meet a higher standard and far exceed the ability of conventional power plants to 'ride-through' power system disturbances" caused by the "break down" of conventional power plants. As for the need for new transmission capacity, whereas NERC said big increases in transmission capacity would be necessary to connect the EPA's planned massive increase in wind power to the grid, the EPA said that lots of transmission lines – such as that being used to convey power from First Solar's Moapa solar farm to Los Angeles – could simply be switched from delivering coal-fired power to delivering solar or wind. And according to the EPA, whatever new transmission capacity was needed was actually "within historical investment magnitudes," and even less than what the Obama-era Department of Energy had called for in its own plans for massive increases in solar.

Nowhere in the EPA's CPP (or the RIAs accompanying it) is there any analysis of the very real problems for electric system reliability and cost raised by high levels of renewable energy. Rather than explaining and analyzing how and why increasing levels of renewable power can create reliability problems, the EPA simply dismissed such problems as more or less nonexistent. It never discussed in any detail at all how electric power systems would have to be modified to ensure reliability with high levels of renewables, and it never analyzed in any detail the cost of such major changes. The CPP was intended to transform the US electricity system, but as far as the EPA was concerned, its role was limited to legally compelling the transformation. Responsibility for the costs and consequences of the transformation were not EPA's problem.

Notes

1. This contract was at issue in the famous case *Public Utilities Commission of Rhode Island* v. *Attleboro Steam & Electric Company*, 273 US 83 (1926).
2. Figure 2, depicting Regional Entities and Regional Councils NERC Long-Term Reliability Assessment Areas (2010 forward) is reproduced from EIA, Form EIA-411 Data, available at https://www.eia.gov/electricity/data/eia411/#tabs_NERC-1.
3. EPA, TSD for the Final CPP, supra note __ at 3–1 to 3–2.
4. Drax, The great balancing act: what it takes to keep the power grid stable, June 8, 2018, available at https://www.drax.com/technology/great-balancing-act-takes-keep-power-grid-stable/.

5. Gregory S. Vassell, Northeast Blackout of 1965, IEEE Power Engineering Review 4-8, 5, January, 1991. See also History, The Great Northeast Blackout, available at https://www.history.com/this-day-in-history/the-great-northeast-blackout.
6. History, Blackout Hits Northeast, August, 2003, available at https://www.history.com/this-day-in-history/blackout-hits-northeast-united-states.
7. Jane L. Corwin and William T. Miles, Impact Assessment of the 1977 New York Blackout 14, SCI Final Report, tSC1 Project 5236-100, Department of Energy, July, 1978, https://pdfs.semanticscholar.org/edbe/8276761c5043e2058507ef0b2f6c5357746a.pdf?_ga=2.51497897.1287372661.1592321856-938104366.1592321856.
8. Patrick L. Anderson and Ilhan K. Geckil, Northeast Blackout Likely to Reduce US Earnings by $64 billion, AEG Working Paper 2003-2; Electricity Consumers Council, the Economic Impacts of the August 2003 Blackout, February 9, 2004.
9. Erik Ela, Michael Milligan, and Brendan Kirby, Operating Reserves and Variable Generation, NREL, Technical Report 5, NREL/TP-5500-51978 August 2011. Contract No. DE-AC36-08GO28308.
10. As explained by Seneviratne and Ozansoy (2016, 661), primary system frequency control is also provided by generator governors. Together, inertial support and primary frequency control schemes such as governors are called ancillary services.
11. EIA, Reserve electric generating capacity helps keeps the lights on, June 1, 2012.
12. For further discussion of economic dispatch showing the problem mathematically, see Kirschen and Strbac, (2019, 155–167).
13. Report on Security Constrained Economic Dispatch By The Joint Board for the PJM/MISO Region 5-6, Federal Energy Regulatory Commission Docket No. AD05-13-000, May 24, 2006.
14. Nuclear Economics Consulting Group, Flexible Nuclear Power, NECG Commentary #12, September 24, 2015.
15. US EIA, Electricity explained: Electricity generation, capacity, and sales in the United States, available at https://www.eia.gov/energyexplained/electricity/electricity-in-the-us-generation-capacity-and-sales.php.
16. For evidence on how the falling price of natural gas has displaced coal-fired power generation, see Fell and Kaffine (2018, 90–116).
17. This is explained by Kroposki (2017, 831–832) and Flynn et al. (2017).
18. Sustainable Energy Authority of Ireland, Renewable energy in Ireland, 2019 Report, available at https://www.seai.ie/publications/Renewable-Energy-in-Ireland-2019.pdf.
19. Renewables Now, Wind meets record 47% of Denmark's power demand in 2019, available at https://renewablesnow.com/news/wind-meets-record-47-of-denmarks-power-demand-in-2019-682219/.

20. Sven Egenter, Renewables hit record in Germany in H1 2019, outlook uncertain, June 26, 2019, Clean Energy Wire, Renewables available at https://www.cleanenergywire.org/news/renewables-hit-record-germany-h1-2019-outlook-uncertain.
21. Source: Map of European Transmission System Operators Organizations (Regional Groups) Continental Europe, Nordic, Baltic, Great Britain and Ireland/Northern Ireland (former UCTE, UKTSOA, NORDEL, ATSOI, IPS/UPS), available at https://commons.wikimedia.org/wiki/File:ElectricityUCTE.svg, original upload date 20 November 2006. This file is licensed under the Creative Commons Attribution-Share Alike 3.0 Unported license, with permission is granted to copy, distribute and/or modify this document under the terms of the **GNU Free Documentation License**, Version 1.2 or any later version published by the Free Software Foundation; with no Invariant Sections, no Front-Cover Texts, and no Back-Cover Texts. A copy of the license is included in the section entitled *GNU Free Documentation License*.
22. Wind Europe, Wind energy in Europe in 2018: Trends and statistics 7-10, available at https://windeurope.org/wp-content/uploads/files/about-wind/statistics/WindEurope-Annual-Statistics-2018.pdf.
23. UK National Grid Electrical Systems Operator, Technical Report on the events of 9 August 2019, September 12, 2019, available at https://www.nationalgrideso.com/document/152346/download.
24. Watt-Logic, What caused the UK's power blackout and will it happen again?, August 12, 2019, available at http://watt-logic.com/2019/08/12/august-2019-blackout/.
25. These examples are provided by Rud Istvan, Grid Scale Battery Storage, Watts up with That, available at https://wattsupwiththat.com/2019/04/05/grid-scale-battery-nonsense-2019/.
26. EIA, Electric Power Monthly, available at https://www.eia.gov/electricity/monthly/epm_table_grapher.php?t=epmt_5_6_a.
27. Rosewater and Williams (2015, 460–471).
28. Chen et al. (2018, 428–435).
29. Philp Dowd, A Solar Power Plant vs. A Natural Gas Power Plant: Capital Cost – Apples to Apples, Watts up with That, April 1, 2016, available at https://wattsupwiththat.com/2016/04/01/a-solar-power-plant-vs-a-natural-gas-power-plant-capital-cost-apples-to-apples/.
30. See Heide et al. (2010, 2483–2489); Gimeno-Gutiérrez and Lacal-Arántegui (2013).
31. Reproducing the figure from EIA, Electricity Demand Patterns Matter for Valuing Electricity Supply Resources, August 27, 2013, available at https://www.eia.gov/todayinenergy/detail.php?id=12711.
32. Available at https://www.eia.gov/beta/electricity/gridmonitor/dashboard/electric_overview/US48/US48.

33. For further demonstration of this point, see Joskow (2011, 238–241).
34. S. Benson and A. Majumdar, On the Path to deep decarbonization: Avoiding the solar wall, Stanford University, available at https://energy.stanford.edu/from-directors/path-deep-decarbonization-avoiding-solar-wall.
35. Figure source: NREL, Global Horizontal Solar Irradiance, available at https://www.nrel.gov/gis/assets/images/solar-annual-ghi-2018-usa-scale-01.jpg.
36. For further discussion of this see Joskow (2008, 159–170).
37. Julian Wettengel, Gas industry calls for capacity market debate as Germany exists nuclear and coal, Clean Energy Wire, February 11, 2020, available at https://www.cleanenergywire.org/news/gas-industry-calls-capacity-market-debate-germany-exits-nuclear-and-coal;

    Benjamin Wehrmann, Capacity market debate resurfaces as Germany may need gas to replace coal, Clean Energy Wire, March 5, 2019, available at https://www.cleanenergywire.org/news/capacity-market-debate-resurfaces-germany-may-need-gas-replace-coal;
38. Some recent estimates of the levelized cost of electricity from alternative energy sources generated by these sorts of organizations can be found on Wikipedia, Cost of Electricity by Source, available at https://en.wikipedia.org/wiki/Cost_of_electricity_by_source.
39. Thomas F. Stacy and George F. Taylor, The Levelized Cost of Electricity from Existing Generation Resources, Institute for Energy Research, June, 2019.
40. Figure source: NREL, Wind Resource of the United States, available at https://www.nrel.gov/gis/assets/images/wtk-80m-2017-01.jpg.
41. Ilana DeBare, PG&E plans big investment in solar power plants, SF Chronicle, August 15, 2008, available at https://www.sfgate.com/business/article/PG-E-plans-big-investment-in-solar-power-3199510.php.
42. PG&E, PG&E Clean Energy Deliveries Already Meet Future Goals, February 20, 2018, available at https://www.pge.com/en/about/newsroom/news details/index.page?title=20180220_pge_clean_energy_deliveries_already_meet_future_goals.
43. Ivan Penn and Peter Eavis, PG&E Bankruptcy Could Deal Blow to Its Solar-Power Suppliers' Finances, New York Times, Jan. 17, 2019, available at https://www.nytimes.com/2019/01/17/business/pge-bankruptcy-solar-power.html.
44. These facts are taken from the court's opinion in US v PG&E, No. CR 14-0175 WHA, Document No. 1186 (N.D. Cal, April 29, 2020).
45. Katherine Blunt and Russell Gold, PG&E Makes Thousands of Repairs After Inspections, WSJ, July 15, 2019, available at https://www.wsj.com/articles/pg-e-makes-thousands-of-repairs-after-inspections-11563243514.
46. Richard Gonzalez, California Can Expect Blackouts For A Decade, Says PG&E CEO, NPR, October 18, 2019, available at https://www.npr.org/2019/10/18/771486828/california-can-expect-blackouts-for-a-decade-says-pg-e-ceo.

47. Peg Brickley, PG&E Can Pull out of Green Power Deals, June 10, 2019, available at https://www.wsj.com/articles/pg-e-wins-ruling-allowing-it-to-pull-out-of-power-contracts-11559997507.
48. The discussion in this paragraph is drawn from Katherine Blunt and Russell Gold, PG&E Knew Aging Grid Was Fire Risk, July 11, 2019, available at https://www.wsj.com/articles/pg-e-knew-for-years-its-lines-could-spark-wildfires-and-didnt-fix-them-11562768885?mod=article_inline.
49. Pacific Gas and Electric Utility Company, Smart Grid Deployment Plan 2011–2020, Smart Grid Technologies Order Instituting Rulemaking 08-12-009 California Public Utilities Commission, Appendix A: PG&E's Smart Grid Deployment Plan 2 (June 2011), available at https://www.pge.com/includes/docs/pdfs/shared/edusafety/electric/SmartGridDeploymentPlan2011_06-30-11.pdf.
50. PG&E Smart Grid Deployment Plan: Executive Summary Page 5.
51. Annual Report of Pacific Gas and Electric Company (U 39 E) on Status of Smart Grid Investments Pursuant to Ordering Paragraph 15 OF D. 10-06-047, pp. 81–82 (October, 2014).
52. Pacific Gas and Electric Company Smart Grid Annual Report – 2015 October 1, 2015.

    Smart Grid Technologies Order Instituting Rulemaking 08-12-009 California Public Utilities Commission pp. 72-73, available at https://www.pge.com/includes/docs/pdfs/myhome/edusafety/systemworks/electric/smartgridbenefits/AnnualReport2015.pdf.
53. Pacific Gas And Electric Company Smart Grid Annual Report – 2017 Date For Submission: September 29, 2017 Smart Grid Technologies Order Instituting Rulemaking 08-12-009 California Public Utilities Commission 75-76, available at https://www.pge.com/pge_global/common/pdfs/safety/how-the-system-works/electric-systems/smart-grid/Annual-Report-2017.pdf.
54. See, for example, GE's webpage on Advanced Energy Management Systems, where the need for such systems due to higher renewables penetration is cast as a major selling point, https://www.ge.com/digital/applications/transmission/advanced-energy-management-system-aems
55. EPA, RIA for the Final CPP at 7-11.
56. EPA, CPP Final Rule, 80 Fed. Reg. 64,809-64,810.

8

Renewable Power Subsidies and Mandates

Harming Today's Environment and Punishing the Poor

I GOOD FOR SPECIAL INTERESTS, BAD FOR THE ENVIRONMENT: THE UNHAPPY HISTORY OF FEDERAL LEGISLATION MANDATING FUEL CHOICE FOR POWER GENERATION

As we have seen, the CPP represented a decision by the EPA that the EPA should assume the job of transforming the energy basis of the US electric power industry away from fossil fuels and toward renewables. Congress did not give the EPA this task. To the contrary, as we have seen, for half a century, since the creation of the EPA in 1970, the EPA's role in regulating the electric power generation industry has been limited to imposing pollution reduction requirements. On several occasions, however, Congress has passed laws directly mandating the use of particular fuels, both by power plants, and by automobiles. The history of these laws displays two patterns: the EPA has never been given a primary role, and typically was given no role, in implementing them; more importantly, such laws have virtually always had perverse effects, causing environmental harm rather than averting it.

As discussed earlier, since World War II, coal has been the major fuel source for US electricity generation. During the late 1960s, electricity generation from petroleum-burning generators soared. Petroleum's share of US electricity production actually doubled, from 6 to 12 percent, between the years 1960 and 1970.[1] The rise of petroleum corresponded to a quite abrupt flattening of electricity production from coal. This was not a coincidence. During the 1960s, midwestern rust belt and northeastern states and cities passed laws and ordinances mandating that because of the local air pollution from coal, power plants had to switch to less polluting fuels.

The rise of petroleum as a fuel for generating electricity ended when, due to the oil embargo of 1973–1974, oil prices tripled. This created severe problems in the electricity market, as state electric utility regulators did not allow utilities to raise the rates they charged to fully cover these dramatic cost increases. After the second wave of oil price increases in the late 1970s, Congress reacted, first by passing the Power Plant and Industrial Fuel Use Act of 1978.

A *The Fuel Use Act of 1978*

Natural gas is far cleaner than coal. Per million Btu generated, CO_2 emissions from burning natural gas to generate electric power are only about 50–60 percent of those from burning coal to generate such power.[2] Air pollutants from burning natural gas are also much lower. In 2011, for example, when natural gas-fired plants produced 24 percent of US electric power, versus 44 percent produced by coal – so that coal-fired plants produced almost twice as much power as natural gas-fired plants – coal-fired plants generated 10 times the NO_x emissions and over 8 times the fine and coarse particulate emissions generated by natural gas-fired plants. Moreover, the combustion of natural gas does not generate sulfur dioxide emissions; in the power sector, virtually all sulfur dioxide emissions (98 percent to be more precise) come from coal-fired plants.[3]

In the Fuel Use Act of 1978, Congress actually prohibited new power plants from using oil or natural gas as a primary energy source and required that all existing oil or gas-powered power plants convert to coal (Gordon 1979, 873). Given that natural gas combustion generates far less CO_2 and also far fewer air pollutants than coal, it is from today's perspective passing strange, but environmentalists of the late 1970s actually supported using the Fuel Use Act to force power plants to burn coal instead of natural gas. According to Yandle,[4] then a member of the President's Council on Wage and Price Stability, "At the time, a strange bedfellow, the 1970s environmental community, celebrated with the coal lobby ... [and] argued that clean natural gas was too valuable to burn in bulk just to produce electricity. The coal lobby, like the bootlegger who profits when stores cannot sell liquor, must have loved it."

Electricity production did shift away from oil, as the percentage of electric power produced by oil- and gas-burning plants dropping from 30.3 percent in 1978 to 15.9 percent in 1985. And the key congressional goal of reducing the use of costly and insecure imported natural gas as fuel for electric power generation was largely achieved.[5] But ending the use of imported natural gas did not mean the end of natural gas in electricity production. Completely contrary to what Congress intended in the Fuel Use Act, but as a direct consequence of other legislation passed by Congress, natural gas came to supplant both oil and coal.

The shift to natural gas was in large part a product of federal legislation undoing decades-old federal regulation that had stunted the supply of US natural gas. Under the 1938 Natural Gas Act as interpreted by the Supreme Court, the Federal Power Commission regulated natural gas pipeline companies, which the Natural Gas Act took to be natural monopolies that were both price discriminating in natural gas prices and building too many pipelines (Pierce Jr. 1982, 66). By the late 1960s, the natural gas regulatory system was not only enormously complex, but characterized by regulated prices for gas from new wells that discouraged new production. According to Pierce, writing in 1982, by that time there was "no longer serious doubt that regulation of gas producer prices was the dominant factor responsible for the gas shortage that caused significant economic dislocations in the United States from 1969 through 1978" (Pierce Jr. 1982, 69). Simply put, the Federal Power Commission was regulating and capping both producer and interstate natural gas prices at levels that were below market clearing levels.

Congress responded to this problem – which it, along with the Federal Power Commission and the Supreme Court, had in a very real sense created – by legislating in the Natural Gas Policy Act of 1978 to gradually deregulate interstate natural gas prices. By 1985, FERC (which as we have seen, replaced the Federal Power Commission) deregulated all categories of natural gas sales that were still subject to price controls. In response to deregulation, by the late 1980s, interstate pipeline mergers had led to the creation of regional and national natural gas transportation markets fed by a national network of supply sources.[6] The end result was that by the mid-1980s, congressional intent in the 1978 Fuel Use Act to encourage power plants to burn coal had run into the new market reality of cheap and increasingly abundant natural gas that was produced domestically, not by OPEC.

In addition, not only did coal face new competition from natural gas, but, as Yandle recounts, "concerns about 'dirty' coal had taken center stage, while natural gas was even more plentiful, and the price was low." As Yandle continues, "[w]ith coal lobbyists working to keep their favored position, environmental organizations now allied with natural gas lobbyists." The coal industry in 1986 blocked a bill to repeal the Fuel Use Act because it did not provide language requiring new power plants to be "coal capable," that is able to burn coal when they were built. In 1987, when much of the Fuel Use Act was repealed, the coal industry succeeded only in retaining an amended provision that provided that no new baseload power plant could be built that was incapable of being converted to coal or another "alternate fuel"[7] (where the "alternate fuel" category included synthetic natural gas from coal but excluded natural gas).[8]

Importantly, throughout its relatively abbreviated lifespan, the 1978 Fuel Use Act was implemented by the Department of Energy. The EPA did not promulgate regulations under the law, and was afforded only a secondary role, given a right in some cases to submit early comments on proposed Fuel Use Act regulations.[9] The Fuel Use Act represents an instance where Congress directly intervened to mandate the use of particular energy sources by the electric power sector. Not only was the law based on future projections that turned out to be wildly incorrect, it had little or no impact on the energy source for future electricity generation, and, perhaps most importantly, in this single instance where Congress legislated to force utilities to change their fuel for electricity generation, Congress gave the EPA only a minor advisory role.

B *The Paradox of PURPA*

In responding to OPEC-driven oil price increases, Congress passed two other laws in 1978 that represent attempts to change how electricity was generated. Unlike the

Fuel Use Act of that same year, which mandated the use of coal, these laws sought to encourage the production of renewable power. In the Energy Tax Act of 1978,[10] Congress provided a 10 percent tax credit to companies that generated such power. In the Public Utilities Regulatory Policies Act (PURPA) of that same year, Congress required utility monopolies that controlled transmission and distribution to connect to their lines and buy power provided by small renewable power generators (and also natural gas cogeneration plants). PURPA capped the price that utilities had to pay to such providers at the cost of new generation that was avoided by getting power from generators who "qualified" under PURPA (cogenerators and small renewable power providers).

As discussed briefly earlier, PURPA was an important step in opening up transmission lines to new power producers that were not owned by vertically integrated utilities (so-called independent power producers). It reflected not only the congressional goal of making the US electricity system independent of OPEC-induced oil price shocks, but also a large body of economic work that had built up during the 1970s arguing that even though transmission and distribution did continue to be natural monopolies, electric power generation was no longer a natural monopoly and could be competitively supplied.

FERC, in coordination with state public utility commissions, had regulatory responsibility for implementing PURPA. FERC interpreted PURPA's requirement that utilities buy power from new, nonutility generators at a price below their avoided cost of new capacity as prohibiting utilities from considering "whether the benefits of purchasing power from qualifying facilities exceeded their costs." Many state public utility commissions required utilities to buy all of the power offered by small renewables producers and other "qualifying facilities," and in some states, utility commissions and FERC set "avoided cost" at the tremendously high cost of building a new nuclear plant or starting up a mothballed coal-fired plant, or the highest cost power plant on the grid, a plant typically brought on line last, during peak load periods (Brennan et al., 1996, 31).

PURPA had been especially generous to new hydropower projects. Small hydropower projects were exempt from FERC licensing requirements, and PURPA authorized special loans to convert old dams to hydroelectric production. In the 1980 Energy Security Act, Congress expanded PURPA's special treatment for small hydropower projects by increasing the ceiling on qualifying small projects to 30 MW. In the Crude Oil Windfall Profits Tax Act of that same year, Congress provided an additional 11 percent tax credit, on top of the existing 10 percent investment tax credit, to such qualifying small hydroelectric facilities (Cole 1986, 648).

The end result of all these federal laws was that new small hydropower projects were exempt from FERC licensing, guaranteed to sell all the power they produced, and recipients of a 21 percent tax credit. Unsurprisingly, this mix of subsidies and mandates led to a rapid increase in the number of small hydropower projects.

The year before PURPA, 1977, FERC received just nine permit and thirty license applications for small hydropower projects. In 1979, FERC processed 101 such permit and license applications. After the additional tax credit was added to the mix in 1980, REFC received over 500 applications for preliminary permits, and the next year, when the licensing exemption program took full effect, FERC processed 177 applications for exemptions and 1,800 permit applications. In 1982, FERC processed 475 exemption applications (Cole 1986, 648). Between 1979 and 1985, FERC got 6,100 applications for hydropower developments, two times the number it had received in the previous 60 years.[11]

PURPA's various benefits, plus the federal subsidies, had a big impact. In a 1987 report, FERC estimated that other things equal, PURPA benefits could have led to the construction of an additional 274 dams producing about 2,400 MW of electricity. As these numbers indicate, FERC projected that PURPA would incentivize very small projects, with an average capacity of less than 10 MW. This was consistent with the fact that of the 931 projects licensed since PURPA's passage – almost half of all 2,007 US hydro projects that FERC knew about in 1988 – 90 percent of the hydro projects built since 1978 had capacity less than 15 MW.[12]

The dams incentivized by PURPA may not have produced much power – the 2,400 MW generated by the 274 dams that FERC projected would be built because of PURPA could have been produced by just 10 small natural gas-fired plants – but they had big negative environmental impacts. Typical of the small new dams incentivized by PURPA was the Columbia Falls Dam in Maine. The dam was only 9 feet tall and 350 feet long, and was built by a local landowner between 1981 and 1983 at cost of only $250,000. Despite its small size and limited power production, the dam had a very harmful environmental impact, ending an already dwindling Atlantic salmon migration on the Pleasant River. Even with PURPA benefits and federal subsidies, the dam was never profitable, and in 1990, faced with costs of at $80,000 to repair a fishway to allow migrating salmon to pass, the dam was torn down.[13]

The Columbia Falls Dam was typical of many others. As early as 1984, the US Fish and Wildlife Service issued a report (Rochester et al. 1984) listing a number of typical adverse environmental impacts from PURPA-style small hydro-projects. These included adverse impacts on water quality, alteration of river flow regimes and stream habitats, elimination of habitats suitable for fish, amphibians and reptiles, and other riparian-dependent species, damage to terrestrial habitats due to runoff from road building and transmission line clearance, and long-term changes in river flow regime and contribution to ground water.[14] By the mid-1980s, the adverse environmental consequences of dams had become a key focus for environmental groups. In 1986, Congress responded by passing the Electric Consumers Protection Act (ECPA). Among other things, the 1986 ECPA amended PURPA Act by imposing a moratorium on PURPA benefits to new dam projects and requiring thereafter that small hydro projects could get PURPA benefits only if they had no substantial impact on the environment and complied with requirements imposed by state fish and wildlife agencies.

In 1992, American Rivers, Trout Unlimited, and American Whitewater formed the Hydropower Reform Coalition, a group founded to work to restore recreational and environmental value to rivers dammed up to produce hydroelectric power. For thirty years, this group has had dam removal as perhaps its core goal, and has succeeded in spurring the removal of 1,199 dams since its first major dam removal, the 1999 removal of the Edwards Dam on the Kennebec River in Maine.[15]

Regardless of whether or not one supports dam removal (I do), the key point to see is that in its precautionary panic to increase US energy security, Congress enacted a series of bills that strongly incentivized the construction or transformation (to hydroelectric generation) of thousands of environmentally harmful hydropower projects.

C *Filling the Desert with Panels: The Rise of Renewables Subsidies from the 1990s to the 2009 Stimulus*

As extended and expanded over the years, the Energy Policy Act of 1992[16] directly targeted renewable power. That law authorized the creation of a ten year, inflation-adjusted Production Tax Credit (PTC) for wind, solar, geothermal, and other renewable power. The credit – a reduction of tax liability, and so equivalent to a subsidy for renewable power – started out in 1994 at 1.5¢ per kWh ($15 per MWh) and by 2018 had risen to $24 per MWh. The PTC was first supposed to expire after five years, in 1999, but Congress renewed it for two years. Since that first renewal in 2001, through language in a variety of bills – some having to do explicitly with energy, and some, like the Working Families Tax Relief Act of 2004, relatively unrelated to energy – Congress has renewed the PTC ten times. Beginning in 2016, when Congress extended the PTC for yet another five years, the PTC for wind projects was to fall by 20 percent per year. In the latest renewal, coming in the Taxpayer Certainty and Disaster Tax Relief Act of 2019, the tax credit for solar projects has been eliminated, but the PTC for wind remained at 60 percent for projects begun in 2019 but fell to 0 for projects begun in 2020 or later.

As can be seen in the EIA figure reproduced as Figure 8.1,[17] wind farms essentially did not exist until the passage of the PTC. As pointed out by the Department of Energy (DOE),[18] over the years since its creation, when the PTC lapsed before congressional renewal, investments in new wind projects shut down. This has been shown rigorously by Metcalf (2009, 15429), who found that during the three periods during the 2000s when Congress allowed the PTC to go out of effect, investment in new wind generating capacity collapsed. Less formally, we can see this in Figure 8.1: the periods of PTC lapse in 2000, 2002, 2004, and 2013 are times when wind capacity did not increase. Given these numbers, it seems fair to say that on a national scale at least, the US wind energy is entirely a creature of federal subsidies.

The other federal subsidy for wind comes in the form of accelerated depreciation. Depreciation is the amount of a capital investment that can be taken as an annual

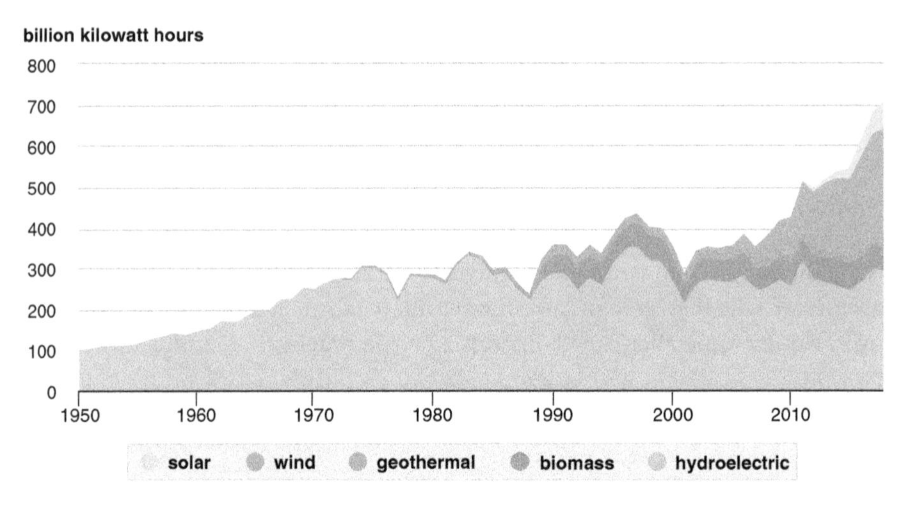

FIGURE 8.1 Renewable Electricity Generation by Source (EIA)

expense that lowers net profits and therefore (since taxes are paid on net profits) a company's tax bill. As I discuss shortly, wind turbines last 25–30 years. The standard way to depreciate a capital investment lasting 25–30 years would be to take 1/25 (or 1/30) of the investment amount as an expense in each year. Congress allowed wind project developers to depreciate wind farm investments over a much shorter period of only 5–6 years. The December, 2017 tax reform bill went even further, allowing 100 percent depreciation of both new and used wind farm equipment. (See DOE 2019, 70.) By increasing the amount of investment that can be expensed by up to 500 percent, such accelerated depreciation greatly reduces short-term after-tax profits – sometimes generating a loss that can be carried ahead to reduce taxes in future years – and thus incentivizes wind project construction.

Called by some the most important piece of federal energy legislation since the 1930s, the Energy Policy Act of 2005 actually had few provisions dealing with renewable power.[19] It did, however, create the Solar Investment Tax Credit, which allows a tax credit for residences and businesses of 30 percent of the cost of installing a solar energy system. Section 1703 of the EPA of 2005 also authorized the DOE to federally guarantee up to 80 percent of the total cost of new clean energy projects that cannot obtain private funding.

Two years later, in the 2007 Energy Independence and Security Act (EISA), for the first time in two decades, Congress raised passenger car and light truck fuel economy (CAFÉ) standards from 27.5 miles per gallon to 37.5 miles per gallons, with the new standards to be met by 2020. In 2007, actual fleetwide fuel economy and the new tougher standard came along with subsidies. Congress created a federal $7,500 federal tax credit for plug-in electric vehicles (phasing out after 200,000 sales per manufacturer). Sections 16(a) and (b) of the EISA authorized the DOE to award up to $25 billion in loans for Advanced Technology Vehicles Manufacturing (ATVM). Under this loan program, auto manufacturers and parts suppliers get direct loans to construct new US factories or to retrofit existing factories to produce vehicles that achieve at least 25 percent higher fuel economy than model year 2005 vehicles of similar size and performance.[20]

The 2007 EISA had two other important provisions for federal funding of renewable energy. That law was one of the ten congressional extensions of the renewables production tax credit. It also mandated the use of biofuels in automobile gasoline. In particular, the 2005 the EPA created a federal Renewable Fuels Standard that required increasing amounts of ethanol in automobile gasoline. The RFS ethanol mandate was further toughened by the 2007 EISA.

In October, 2008, in the Cantwell-Ensign Clean Energy Tax Stimulus Act of 2008 (which was part of the Emergency Economic Stabilization Act of 2008, the law that created the Troubled Assets Relief Program [TARP]), Congress renewed the production tax credit (PTC) for wind, geothermal, and most other forms of renewable power and the investment tax credit (ITC) for solar power projects.

October, 2008 was also of course roughly in the middle of the Great Recession. Because tax credits only have value if the beneficiary has taxable income, the 2008 congressional renewal of the PTC and accelerated deprecation didn't help the renewable power industry by much – electricity demand, and renewable power revenues, fell drastically during the Great Recession. As explained by Aldy (2012, 12), for a new solar or wind energy firm that did not yet have any income, such tax credits could only be taken advantage of by forming a partnership with an equity investor – a large financial corporation such an insurance company or investment bank – with taxable income against which the credit could be claimed. With the onset of the financial crisis in 2007, the volume of such so-called tax equity capital fell by more than 50 percent.

In 2009, the American Reinvestment and Recovery Act (ARRA) came to the rescue of the renewable power industry. With over $400 billion in spending and spending obligations, the ARRA, often called the 2009 stimulus bill, was at the time the largest spending bill in US history. The 2009 stimulus bill included more than $90 billion in support of clean energy activities, with $25 billion for renewable power generation, $18 billion in financing high-speed rail and[21] mass transit, $6 billion for advanced vehicles, fuels, and battery development, and over $10 billion for grid modernization and increases in capacity (Aldy 2012, 8). It thus marked the zenith of federal funding for renewable power.

To be more precise, the stimulus bill helped renewable power in three ways.[22] First, it extended the PTC for three years. Second, it created a grant program and a loan program targeted at encouraging new renewable power plants. The so-called 1603 grant program allowed a developer of a renewable electricity power plant to choose among the PTC, a 30 percent ITC (for solar), or a cash grant equal to 30 percent of investment costs. Third, at a cost of $6 billion, the stimulus bill's

Section 1705 loan program guaranteed loans, thereby lowering borrowing costs, for commercial renewable power developers.

It has been estimated that the Section 1603 grant program led to an increase of about 2,400 MW of wind capacity during 2009 (about 25 percent of the new capacity that year) that would not otherwise have occurred. Under the Section 1705 loan program, the federal government guarantees that if the borrower defaults, then the government pays the balance of the loan. In most federal loan guarantee programs, such as the Section 1703 program under the 2005 EPA, the lender has to pay an upfront loan guarantee fee back to the government (which is ultimately paid in part by the borrower who gets the guarantee). The federal guarantee reduces loan risk, and has been estimated (by Aldy) to cut recipients' borrowing costs by about 14 percent. For the Section 1705 program, however, Congress appropriated $2.4 billion so that the government paid the fee for the loan guarantee that it itself made.

It may well be true that the Section 1705 program "did not have a meaningful impact on the US power sector."[23] However, it was definitely attractive to certain very large solar power developers. DOE paid $16 billion in Section 1705 loan guarantees between 2009 and 2012 with $10.3 billion in loan guarantees (64 percent of the total) going to four very large companies, NRG Energy, NextEra Energy Resources, LLC (a Fortune 200 company, with the project Desert Sunlight), Abengoa Solar, a Spanish multinational, and Prologis (Project Amp), a global real estate investment trust owning warehouses across the United States.[24] Commenting on the subsidies in 2011, the CEO of NRG commented that "I have never seen anything that I have had to do in my 20 years in the power industry that involved less risk than these projects. . . . It is just filling the desert with panels."[25] NRG fully took advantage of the 2009 stimulus money. In addition to the $3.8 billion NRG got in Section 1705 loan guarantees, various NRG companies (such as Green Mountain Energy and Reliant Energy Tax Retail LLC) got at least 39 Section 1603 grants, with NRG and its affiliates getting at least $5.2 billion in loan guarantees.[26]

"Less risk" to private solar project developers did not mean less risk to society. By 2015, many of the projects that had received Section 1705 loan guarantees had failed, and companies that had received such guarantees, from the small – the now notorious Solyndra, a start-up that received a federally guaranteed $528 million loan that it never repaid – to the huge – the Spanish multinational Abengoa with almost $3 billion in federally guaranteed loans that it could not repay – were in bankruptcy.[27]

A final step taken by Congress with the 2009 stimulus was to keep the ATVM program going by appropriating $7.5 billion to cover the risk of default on up to $25 billion in ATVM loans. Since the start of the program, DOE has awarded $8.4 billion in loans to five companies, Fisker, Ford, Nissan, Tesla, and the Vehicle Production Group. Fisker and the Vehicle Production Group defaulted on their DOE loans and went into bankruptcy. Only Tesla has paid off all of its DOE loans, finishing payments in 2013, nine years ahead of schedule.[28]

If we include loans made to automobile manufacturers under the ATVM program, between 2009 and 2012, the congeries of loans, loan guarantees, and grants authorized by the 2009 stimulus bill provided $35 billion to renewable power or low GHG emission cars. With 2009 stimulus programs adding to the federal subsidy total, it has been estimated[29] that in 2010 federal financial support for wind power was at $57/MWh and for solar power at $260/MWh. As stimulus funding declined, these amounts also gradually fell over the 2010–2013 period. However, as of 2013, the wind and solar subsidies still stood respectively at $15/MWh and $43/MWh. Over that same period, coal-based electricity plants received subsidies $0.5-$1/MWh, hydrocarbons $1/MWh, and nuclear $1–2/ MWh. Thus over the entire 2010–2013 period, federal subsidies for solar and wind electricity generation dwarfed those for coal, hydrocarbons, and nuclear.

Over a longer period of time, federal subsidies for renewable energy have rapidly grown even as federal subsidies for fossil fuels have declined. This is shown in Figure 8.2[30] for tax credits, which as the previous discussion indicates can fairly be described as the main federal tool for subsidizing renewables. Such tax credits reduce federal tax revenue and therefore like other programs that reduce federal tax revenues, such as accelerated depreciation schedules and full current year expensing of capital investments, fall into the category of tax expenditures. As one can see from the figure,[31] tax expenditures on renewable energy steadily increased from 2006 to 2013 before falling off with the expiration of the 2009 stimulus.

Figure 8.3 looks at a shorter period of time, since 2010, but includes all forms of federal financial support for all stages of electricity generation – production through distribution. As one can see, even with the expiration of the DOE loan guarantee programs, as recently as 2016, at 42 percent, federal financial support for renewable electricity through direct expenditures and tax expenditures made up the largest share of federal spending on electricity.

It may well be objected that however large and oftentimes wasteful they may have been, the federal renewables subsidies over the last 30 years are but a drop in the

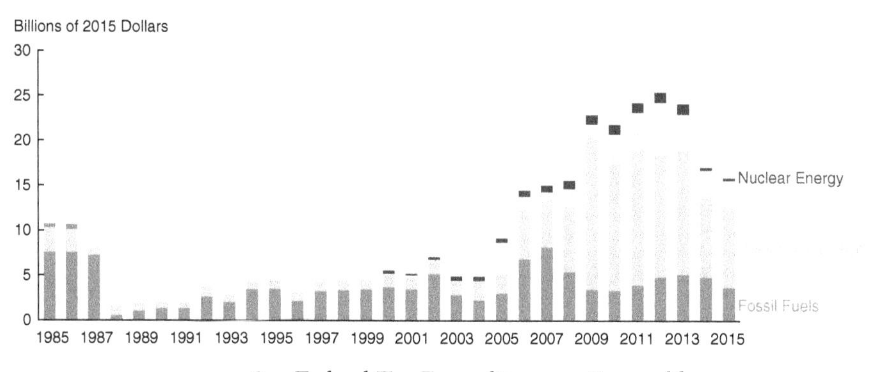

FIGURE 8.2 Federal Tax Expenditures on Renewables

Year and Support Type	Coal	Refined Coal	Natural Gas and Petroleum Liquids	Nuclear	Renewables	Electricity– Smart Grid and Transmission	Conversation	End Use	Total	Share of Total Subsidies and Support
2010										
Direct Expenditures	48	–	83	69	5,732	4	3,226	6,264	15,427	41%
Tax Expenditures	506	187	2,883	999	8,913	63	3,511	1,055	18,119	48%
Research and Development	320	–	10	177	844	566	704	97	2,718	7%
DOE Loan Guarantee Program	–	–	–	292	296	22	4	1,113	1,728	5%
Total	**875**	**187**	**2,976**	**1,537**	**15,785**	**655**	**7,446**	**8,530**	**37,992**	**100%**
share of Total	**2%**	**0%**	**8%**	**4%**	**42%**	**2%**	**20%**	**22%**	**100%**	
2013										
Direct Expenditures	77	–	388	38	8,716	9	872	3,349	13,450	46%
Tax Expenditures	801	10	2,345	1,155	5,683	219	657	2,081	12,951	44%
Research and Development	216	–	64	197	864	887	517	189	2,934	10%
DOE Loan Guarantee Program	–	–	–	–	–	–	–	–	–	–
Total	**1,094**	**10**	**2,796**	**1,390**	**15,264**	**1,115**	**2,046**	**5,619**	**29,335**	**100%**
share of Total	**4%**	**0%**	**10%**	**5%**	**52%**	**4%**	**7%**	**19%**	**100%**	
2016										
Direct Expenditures	19	–	111	40	909	11	234	3,391	4,716	31%
Tax Expenditures	906	–	(940)	160	5,316	160	560	2,653	8,816	59%
Research and Development	337	–	56	164	456	49	189	200	1,451	10%
DOE Loan Guarantee Program	–	–	–	–	–	–	–	–	–	–
Total	**1,262**	**–**	**(773)**	**365**	**6,682**	**220**	**983**	**6,244**	**14,983**	**100%**
share of Total	**8%**	**–**	**(5%)**	**2%**	**45%**	**1%**	**7%**	**42%**	**100%**	

FIGURE 8.3 Energy Specific Federal Financial Support, 2010, 2013, and 2016 (millions of dollars)

bucket when compared with the decades of subsidies received by oil and natural gas. It is true that the oil industry has long been benefited from various federal subsidies. The Oil Depletion Allowance, which allows a percentage of the value of an oil field to be deducted each year from the income on such a field, thereby reducing taxes, has been around since 1913. Some other oil subsidies, such as accelerated depreciation, are not unique to the oil industry. Renewable power gets them too. Subsidies for the oil industry differ in one fundamental way from subsidies for renewables. Historically, the problem for the oil industry has been too much production, causing not only a decline in the long term value of oil fields by depressurizing them too quickly, but also market oversupply that often led to ruinous price collapse. The oil subsidies were an unnecessary and undesirable gift to a small number of oil producers that if anything exacerbated the chronic problem of oversupply. Subsidies to renewables, by contrast, have literally created renewable power supply. Without the subsidies, renewable power might still be provided in some places, but at much lower quantities.

II THE NEGLECTED ENVIRONMENTAL HARM FROM RENEWABLE POWER PROJECTS

Solar and wind power installations may indeed reduce CO_2 emissions, but they have a number of serious adverse consequences for the environment. Such projects may be thought of trading off certain present day environmental and human costs for a potential reduction in the risk of future climate change damages. As one would expect by this point in my survey of the Obama-era precautionary policies, the vast renewables subsidies just surveyed were enacted without any serious consideration of the present day environmental and human harm caused by those renewable energy projects. And the Obama administration implemented them by ignoring or waiving legal requirements that they at least be considered.

In 2009, before the renewable subsidies kicked in, hydropower was by far the biggest renewable power source, producing 275 million MWh of electricity, versus only 75 million MWh produced by wind. By 2019, wind had overtaken hydropower, producing 300 MWh of electricity, versus about 260 million MWh from hydropower.[32] Thus while hydropower production slightly declined over the decade, wind power exploded, increasing by 400 percent. Given the rapid growth and significance of wind power in US electricity production, I focus my discussion of the serious but largely ignored environmental and human costs of renewable power by explaining some of the most important adverse consequences of wind projects. I then discuss two examples of how these consequences were deliberately ignored during the post-Great Recession renewable subsidies binge. I conclude with a similar but more abbreviated discussion of solar.

A *Land*

The first and most direct present day cost of renewables subsidies is the land area that consumed by subsidized projects. To understand how the amount of land required for wind power is estimated, one must first know the basics about wind turbines. A wind turbine, such as one of those shown in Figure 8.4, consists of a tubular steel tower at the top of which is a hub with three attached rotors (blades). Behind the blades is a pod-shaped "nacelle," which houses the shaft, gearbox, generator, and controls. When wind strikes the blades, the kinetic force of the wind rotates the blades, turning a shaft that spins a turbine. As with power from steam or water, the spinning turbine produces electricity that runs down a cable in the tower and which connects to the grid after being suitably transformed in frequency. A wind farm or facility consists of a large number of such turbines. A portion of one such wind farm, located in Power County, Idaho (in the heart of one of the best US wind regions), is depicted in Figure 8.4.[33]

The Power County, Idaho wind turbines are big but not atypical. Since 2012 US wind turbines have been big, with an average tower height of almost 300 feet with 150 foot rotor blades. The construction of such massive wind turbines was one of the consequences of the renewable power subsidy binge; such large turbines were rare before 2006.[34] Each wind turbine has a rated power production capacity. Excluding California, which has a large number of decades-old wind turbines with an average capacity rating of only .79 MW, as of 2019, the average wind turbine capacity in the remaining top US wind power states (Texas, Iowa, and Oklahoma) was about 1.8 MW.[35] This is a bit bigger than the US average. As of April, 2020, according to data available on the relatively new, state-of-the-art US Wind Turbine Database,[36] there were 63,794 turbines with a rated capacity of 105,085 MW in the US, for an average turbine capacity of 1.65 MW.[37]

FIGURE 8.4 Power County, Idaho Wind Farm

As we have seen in earlier discussions of electric power production, rated capacity is not the same as actual power production. Wind turbines produce power only when the wind is blowing between roughly 10 and 55 miles per hour and only when they are not down for maintenance. Wind turbine power production is roughly proportional to the rotor diameter multiplied by average wind speed. As with other sources of electric power, the capacity factor of a wind turbine is the amount of electricity a wind turbine produces in a given time period (typically a year) relative to its maximum or nameplate power production capacity.[38]

About 300 million MWh of electricity were produced from wind in 2019.[39] If we divide out the hours (24 hours times 365 days), this amount of electricity is equivalent to a 34,250 MW generator producing at 100 percent of capacity every hour of every day. According to the US Wind Turbine Database, US wind capacity is 105,085 MW. Using this figure for total stated capacity, across the entire year, US wind is operating at a capacity factor of 33 percent (34,250/105,085). Such a capacity factor means that over the course of a typical year, an average-sized 1.65 MW wind turbine actually produces what a .54 MW turbine would produce if it operated every hour of every day at full production capacity. With 100 such turbines put together to comprise a wind farm, we would have a wind farm with a capacity of 165 MW but operating with a 33 percent capacity factor and therefore capable of producing 54 MW x 24 x 365 MWh of power per year.

As commented recently by Miller and Keith (2019), "there is no well-established method to compute the area of each wind power plant." Like any spinning blade, wind turbines generate a wake, an area of suppressed wind downwind of the turbine. The amount of land devoted to each wind turbine in a wind farm is determined primarily by the need to keep turbines far enough apart so that the one turbine is not operating in the wake of another. If we think of wind turbines in a wind farm as points, then the Veroni polygon is the smallest area around each point that does not interfere with other points.[40] By computing the Veroni polygon for each wind turbine identified in the state-of-the-art US Wind Turbine database, Miller and Keith (2019) assumed efficient installation of wind turbines, and using this method, estimated that on average, a US wind turbine in 2016 produced .9 W per square meter of land. Hence to produce 900 W or .9 MW, an average US wind turbine uses up one square kilometer of land. For a wind farm to produce 9 MW of power, it would need 10 square kilometers of land. To produce 90 MW of electricity, a wind farm uses 100 square kilometers of land.

Miller and Keith (2019) also came up with an average wind power installation capacity factor of 35 percent, which is very close to the 33 percent that I derived simply by dividing total 2019 wind turbine electricity production by nameplate capacity. They find that the US wind power capacity factor has been increasing since 2010, with the capacity factor from 2010 to 2016 of 37 percent, versus about 32 percent for the period 1984–2009. Despite increasing capacity factors, Miller and Keith (2019) find no significant trend in wind farm power density – the electricity output per square meter of land. As they explain, the reason why power density has stayed constant even as capacity factors have increased is that capacity factors have increased even as capacity densities have fallen. What this seems to indicate is that even with better turbine design, in order to increase the capacity factor of each wind turbine, wind farm developers have been reducing the number of turbines installed per square kilometer. Consistent with an average power density of about .9 MW per square kilometer, the average installed capacity of a US wind farm was (of 2016) 2.7 MW per square kilometer (one can check this; a capacity factor of .35 yields .94 MW of power output per square kilometer for 2.7 MW average capacity per square kilometer).

To see how these numbers translate into the total amount of land consumed by wind farms, we can look back to recall that as of 2019, the total US wind capacity was 105,085 MW. Using the 2.7 MW per kilometer squared capacity density found by Miller and Keith (2019), one finds that wind farms currently occupy about 39,000 square kilometers of land area. This is a tiny fraction of the 9,326,410 square kilometer land area of the United States; to be precise, only about 4/10 of one percent. By comparison, the 300 million MWh of electricity produced by wind farms represented 7 percent of the 4.1 billion MWh of electricity consumed in the United States in 2019.[41] Using 4/10 of one percent of US land area for a zero CO_2 source of 7 percent of US electricity may seem like a pretty efficient use of land.

Were wind to make up a greater share of US electricity production, however, these numbers would quickly change. Miller and Keith (2019) estimate that wind power plants of 100–200 square kilometers, with power densities of only about .5 W per square meter of land, are "most illustrative" of what could "be achieved by replicating existing wind plants in adjacent regions with similar wind resources." A future wind power density of .5 W per square meter of land is 56 percent of the average wind power density estimated by Miller and Keith (2019). Using this figure for future wind power density, assuming suitable land is available, to triple the share of electricity production from wind would require about 209,000 square kilometers of land.

This is a huge land area, a little bit bigger than the land area of the state of Nebraska (at 200,346 square kilometers, the sixteenth largest state) and a little smaller than area of Kansas (at 213,096 square kilometers, the fifteenth largest state).[42] It is also significantly bigger (by about 60,000 square kilometers) than the combined land area of the eastern US states of Maryland, Delaware, New Jersey, Connecticut, Massachusetts, Rhode Island, Vermont and New Hampshire.

Future wind power land requirements are based on the current land requirements required by the wind power density of .9 W per square meter estimated by Miller and Keith (2019). That estimate is consistent with previous model-based estimates that large scale wind power density would be below 1 W per square meter. But as Miller and Keith (2019) also point out, it is much smaller than earlier estimates that had

B *Species Kill*

In a 2015 survey article, Dai et al. (2015, 912) reported estimates that in an average year, wind turbines kill 234,000 birds. A more recent estimate for the year 2012 presented by Gibson et al. (2018, 928) puts the number of birds killed by US turbines at a much higher 573,000. Birds die by colliding with rotating blades, towers, and other structures at wind farms. Of course, birds are killed by lots of human activities. Millions of birds are killed every year in collisions with cars and cats kill billions of birds per year (Gibson et al. 2018). However, depending on where they are located, wind turbines have an especially savage impact on particular bird species.

As Dai et al. (2015) summarize, wind farms located on ridges and upwind slopes – especially good locations for reliable winds – and those located near bird migration routes kill the most birds. Due perhaps to their foraging or flight behavior, a number of raptors, including golden eagles, red-tailed hawks, and kestrels, are especially susceptible to being killed by wind turbines. Of 573,000 birds killed by wind turbines in 2012, 83,000 were raptors (Gibson et al. 2017, 928). Nearly half (46 percent) of all bird collisions with wind turbines are estimated to have occurred in California. Especially lethal is the 5,400 wind turbine facility at Altamont Pass, which kills an estimated 2,700 birds per year, of which 1,100 are raptors. Among the raptors killed were 67 golden eagles, at least 25 percent of which had migrated from more than 100 kilometers away (Gibson et al. 2018, 929). As Gibson et al. state, the number of migrating golden eagles killed suggested that "this single facility has continental-scale impacts."

Studies have also explored which wind turbine attributes are most strongly statistically associated with bird mortality. An older study, Loss (2013),[45] studied only turbines that are much smaller than those now typical, with rotor heights less than 80 meters, but they found that mortality increased ten-fold as rotor height increased from 36 to 80 meters. More recently, Thaxter et al. (2017) found that bird mortality increased exponentially as turbine size fell below 1 MW capacity.

Bats too are especially susceptible to wind turbines. Nearly a quarter of bat species are routinely killed by wind turbines (Dai et al. 2015). Surveying results from a number of different studies, Arnett et al. (2016, 309), report estimated cumulative wind turbine bat fatalities in the USA and Canada of from 0.8 to 1.7 million over a 12-year period 2000 to 2011 and an estimated 888,000 bats kill at wind facilities in the US. While both local and migratory bat species are at risk from wind turbines, a study in the Appalachian Mountains by Pylant et al. (2016) found that of the two bat species killed most often, 57 percent of the eastern red bats killed were migratory and 99 percent of the hoary bats killed were migratory. Plyant et al. (2016) interpreted such a large kill of migratory bats as indicating that wind turbine bat kill could imperil the hoary bat species. The hoary bat species suffers the highest proportion, 38 percent, of bat fatalities at North American wind farms, and consistent with Plyant et al. (2016), the median expert prediction reported by Frick et al. (2017) was that been used to calculate the land needs for wind power expansion. The World Fund, for example, estimated that power densities as high as 808 W per square n were obtainable in the windiest 10 percent of the United States. This estimate is plausible. But the Miller and Keith (2019) estimate is also much smaller t potentially plausible estimates of 1.4–1.7 W per meter squared for the Uni States by other investigators. Miller and Keith (2019) point to two reasons for t discrepancy: the earlier estimates of higher obtainable power densities were n based on actual observations but simply assumed power densities between 2 and times the installed capacity density actually found in US wind installations; sec ondly, earlier estimates were inconsistent with known atmospheric constraints or the maximum amount of kinetic energy potentially found in wind.

The land area requirements for wind power may well increase even beyond the projections in Miller and Keith (2019). The reason is that because the best, windiest locations have already been developed, future wind turbines will increasingly be located in places with relatively low wind speeds. To produce power at such low wind locations, wind project developers have steadily increased wind turbine tower height and rotor diameter (blade length). The share of wind turbine towers in the 90–100 meter range has steadily increased, reaching 45 percent in 2018, and whereas in 2009, no turbines had rotors bigger than 100 meters in diameter, by 2018, turbines with rotors bigger than 110 meters accounted for 87 percent of the market. In 2018, fully 30 percent of wind turbines had rotors over 120 meters in diameter.[43] By 2019, the median total height of wind turbines (including tower and rotors) seeking permits was nearly 500 feet.[44]

Increasing rotor diameter and tower height have not coincided with an increase in the capacity of the generators spun by wind turbines. Quite the opposite. To ensure that wind turbines are producing power as often as possible, even when winds are slight, thereby boosting capacity factors, wind turbine developers have combined taller towers and bigger blades with constant or even declining capacity generators. They have lowered the ratio of maximum generator capacity to the circular area swept out by the rotor blades. For the US wind turbine system as a whole, this ratio, called the specific power of a wind turbine, fell by about 50 percent between 1999 and 2018 (from 395 W/m2 among projects installed in 1998–1999 to 230 W/m2 among projects installed in 2018). Importantly, these massive, 500 foot high, but lower power wind turbines have become widely used even in US locations with relatively high average winds.

Should these trends continue, the American landscape will increasingly be dominated by gigantic wind turbines occupying two football fields of sky but whose rotors are spinning very, very slowly as they reliably generate small amounts of electric power. Each such massive turbine will need much more land area than the average turbine generating the estimates provided by Miller and Keith (2019), and since each will produce much less power, wind farms will need to consist of many more turbines, consuming much more land, than they have in the past.

wind turbine mortality would reduce the hoary bat population by 90 percent within the next 50 years and increase the probability of hoary bat extinction by 22 percent.

Wind turbines located on ridge lines are especially lethal for bats, with forested ridge line locations the worst for bats (see Dai et al. 2015, 913 discussing studies). Barclay (2007, 381–387) found that whereas increasing tower height had little impact on bird fatalities, bat mortality increased exponentially as tower height went above 65 meters. More recently, although Thaxter et al. (2017) did not include a measure of tower height, tower height has until recently been correlated with turbine capacity, and Thaxter et al. (2017) found that mortality for bats increased as turbine capacity increased from 1.2 to 2.5 MW. At the time of the Thaxter (2017) study, such high capacity turbines also typically had very high towers and large diameter rotors.

It is important to point out that the current trends in wind farm development discussed in the previous section imply that the harm to birds and bats from wind farms will likely increase. The newest generation of wind turbines have very high towers, well over 100 meters, and huge rotor diameters sometimes approaching or exceeding 120 meters. Based on the evidence of wind turbine harm to birds and bats discussed in this section, it seems more than likely that the new generation of wind farms will cause an increase in bat kills and perhaps bird kills as well.

C *Global Warming*

A decade ago, Wang and Prinn (2010, 2053–2061) used a three dimensional climate model of the type used for future IPCC climate projections and found that getting 10 percent of global 2100 energy from onshore wind would lead to "global scale" changes in the atmospheric circulation pattern and increase global temperatures by 1°C. More recent work by Miller and Keith (2018) shows that the impact of wind farms on surface temperatures is more nuanced. At the level of its rotors, now about 100 meters, a wind turbine captures kinetic energy and slows winds. This creates a bigger gradient between winds at the surface and at rotor level, increasing the mixing between surface air and air above. During the daytime, the additional mixing generated by wind turbines is relatively minor, as daytime convection is already driving air up to 1,000–3,000 meter levels. But in the typical US location, the nighttime 100–300 meter boundary layer is quite stable. As Miller and Keith (2019) explain, wind turbines have an influence extending up to 500 meters, and during the nighttime – when wind farms are most active in supplying power – due to both rotor air mixing and reduced wind speed, turbines bring warmer air down to the cooler surface level, increasing nighttime surface temperatures. In a model assuming uniform wind arm capacity density of .5 W per squared meter across the United States, Miller and Keith (2018) predicted if the entire 2018 US electricity demand were met with wind, US surface temperatures would increase by .24C. Such an increase in nighttime surface temperatures had also been found in at least seven satellite studies of temperatures before and after construction of (or on and off) wind farms in four US states. The magnitude of the warming seems to be uncertain – three studies of a very large Texas wind farm had found an average increase of .29C in nighttime temperatures at the surface after creation of the wind farm whereas for the same farm, Miller and Keith's (2018) model predicted a nighttime warming of .66C two meters above the surface – but nighttime warming seems to be a clear consequence of wind farms.

It is true that such wind farm – induced warming affects regional surface temperatures, rather than global tropospheric temperatures. On this ground, it might be downplayed as not relevant to the central problem of climate change. However, as I discuss in some detail later, climate science agencies have for decades reported surface temperatures to the public as reliable evidence of climate change. If widespread wind farms themselves significantly increase such surface temperatures, then at the very least this effect would need to be removed from reported temperature change for such reports to be a reliable indicator of actual climate change.

D *Wind Farms and Human Health and Welfare*

As we've seen, wind turbines have been getting bigger and bigger. A standard vintage 2018 wind turbine stands over 300 feet tall, with blades carving out a gigantic circle with a radius of almost 400 feet. And of course a wind power facility consists of not one or two but dozens and even hundreds of such turbines. Such large installations are industrial complexes that completely change the character of the local area in which they are located.

The first such change is the most obvious – the loss of the aesthetic value of undeveloped landscapes. We can see a dramatic illustration of this loss in the two photos of Figure 8.5. Both photos depict Stirling Castle in Scotland, one of the most iconic and culturally significant landmarks in the entire country. The first, top photo, Figure 8.5(a), is the vista from the castle before the installation of the Braes O'Doune windfarm. The bottom photo, Figure 8.5(b), shows the vista as altered by some (not all) of the wind turbines comprising that farm. The pictures[46] speak for themselves.

One might respond that in the United States, massive windfarms have typically been placed in relatively remote areas, not right across valleys from iconic historic sites. West Texas, the US region of most rapid windfarm development, is indeed relatively lightly populated. But the scope and scale of utility scale windfarms is such that their aesthetic impact stretches for miles. The small town of Sweetwater, Texas, about 180 miles west of Fort Worth, not only hosts the Sweetwater Wind Farm, a 585 MW wind farm with 392 wind turbines, but lies within Nolan County, which hosts over 1,300 wind turbines.[47] As described in journalistic accounts, rather than watching the sun set over unspoiled canyons, Nolan County ranch owners now

FIGURE 8.5(A) The view from Stirling Castle Scotland before the Braes O'Doune Wind Farm

FIGURE 8.5(B) The view from Stirling Castle Scotland after the Braes O'Doune Wind Farm

watch as the skyline becomes a sea of blinking red lights that sit atop wind turbines to warn aircraft, with the crackling of 340,000 volts of electricity through transmission lines clearly audible.

Not all wind farms are as remotely located as those in Texas. Iowa, for example, has a large number of wind farms, most of which are located on farm land near residences and towns. Industrial wind farms are precisely that, industrial facilities with the same kinds of negative impacts that industrial plants of all types typically have on nearby residents and landowners. As surveyed by Krekel and Zerrahn (2017, 221–238), economic studies of the impact of wind turbines on real estate values have consistently found that turbines decrease real estate prices of nearby properties by between 2 and 16 percent. Krekel and Zerrahn (2017) relatedly find that the construction of wind turbines in Germany caused a significant decline in the well-being of residents living within 4,000 meters (about 2.5 miles) of turbines, with the negative effects lasting for years after turbine construction.

Based on the allegations in dozens of lawsuits that have been filed across the world, nearby residents' biggest complaint about wind turbines is the noise. Wind turbines generate two kinds of noise: aerodynamic noise as the blades pass through the air, generating a random, relatively high frequency sound, and mechanical noise caused by the turbines' gears and other internal parts. Such mechanical noises can be damped out but become more serious, the bigger is the turbine (Dai et al. 2015, 914). It is known that chronic exposure to noise can cause not only headaches, irritability, and fatigue, but also arterial constriction and weakening of the immune system. Dozens of lawsuits have been filed alleging that such noise-induced health harms make wind turbines common law nuisances.[48] Across the world, they have almost always been settled, often for millions of dollars paid to residents.[49]

E *Wind Turbines Live Forever: As Waste*

The expected lifetime of a wind turbine is said to be 25–30 years, but many older wind farms, such as the Ponnequin Wind Farm on the border of Colorado and Wyoming, are being closed before they reach even 20 years of operation. When wind turbines have worn out, their many parts need to be disposed of or recycled. While it is claimed that 90 percent of a wind turbine's parts can be recycled, this is not true of their biggest parts – the blades. Wind turbine blades are made of fiberglass-fiber or carbon-fiber reinforced plastics. They cannot be recycled. The huge blades – as we have seen, at least around 250 feet long – are typically cut up into smaller pieces and trucked to landfills. Crushing equipment at most US landfills is too small to crush the giant blades, even after they are cut up into pieces, and there are very few landfills in the United States that have the capacity to serve as waste dumps for used wind turbine blades. It has been estimated that 720,000 tons of such blades will need to be disposed of over the next 20 years.[50] With an average landfill size of about 600 acres (as estimated by NASA in 2001 using satellite altimetry), it would take about 1,200 landfills just to handle the wind turbine blade wastes to come.

Decommissioning – that is, closing – a wind farm involves more than just getting rid of the giant blades. The entire turbine – blades, nacelle and its contents, tower – plus the turbine's base must be removed to a depth of 4 feet. The base or foundation for a large turbine often extends down 15 feet and cannot be fully removed. In Minnesota, Excel Energy is in the process of decommissioning the 134 turbines that comprised its Noble wind farm, a process that it estimates will cost $71 million (or $532,000 per turbine).[51]

F *Solar Is No Better*

As the vast majority of new US renewable power has come from new wind farms, I have focused my discussion of the environmental impacts of renewable power projects on wind farms. But solar farms too have many adverse environmental consequences. The typical solar facility consists of densely packed PV panels. The density doesn't change much with the overall size of the solar farm, and as estimated by Miller and Keith (2019) solar power density for solar farms of all capacities is between 5.6 and 7.5 watts per square meter. Power production from even the biggest solar PV facilities in the sunniest places – such as the Solar Star, Topaz Solar and Desert Sunlight farms in California – maxes out at about 550 MW. To produce this much power requires a large land area, ranging from 1,664 square kilometers (1,000 square miles) for Solar Star to 1,268 square kilometers (760 square miles) for Topaz Solar. By contrast, a modern 1,000 MW nuclear facility requires only 1 square mile.[52] Natural gas power plants of various types require on average about .343 acres per MW.[53] Thus a 1000 MW natural gas-fired plant (about the size of many recent new cogeneration plants) would require 343 acres, or a little more than ½ square mile. To be fair, the land requirements for nuclear power include the land lost by mining uranium ore, the raw material from which uranium oxide and enriched uranium is produced. Yet only .06 acres of land needs to be mined to obtain the enriched fuel required to generate 1000 MW (1 GW) of electricity from a nuclear plant.[54] Even including this land, nuclear's land requirements are relatively minimal.

In many ways, remote deserts – with guaranteed sunshine and no human neighbors to bother – are the ideal location for solar farms. But desert locations in the southwestern United States – America's prime solar territory – are also home to many endangered and threatened species. Arizona alone is home to 44 endangered and threatened species. In California, the Mojave Desert is home to the threatened desert tortoise. According to Rule (2014, 89), the Ivanapah solar plant in the Mojave desert – a solar powered thermal power plant that I discuss in more detail shortly – displaced at least 144 desert tortoises. Such displacement occurs just as much with solar PV facilities.

Like large scale wind farms, solar farms may have impacts on local and even global climate. Because solar PV panels absorb solar rays that would otherwise be absorbed by the earth's surface and reflected back as longwave radiation, their basic effect is to cool the surface air temperatures in the area where they are located (see Hu et al. 2016, 290–294). When plugged into climate models, large scale deployment of solar PV in desert areas ends up cooling and reducing precipitation in such deserts, but it also may lead to increases in temperature in urban areas, exacerbating urban heat island effects that I discuss in Part II.

Solar panels last about as long as wind turbines, 20–30 years. While the main constituent of a solar PV panel nowadays is silicon, many other highly toxic metals are used in such panels. As described by Leena and Hook (2015, 11818–11837), not only cadmium but even rarer metals such as indium, gallium, and ruthenium are important constituents of many solar technologies. Solar PV panels are mostly (up to 90 percent) glass, but that glass includes lead, antimony, and cadmium. Because the cost of recycling solar panels is greater than the value of the materials recovered through such recycling, solar PV panels are disposed of in landfills. In landfills, however, rainwater can wash out the cadmium and other toxic metals. Local environmentalists near the proposed location of a 6,350 acre solar farm meant to provide power to new Microsoft data centers in Fawn Lake, Virginia estimated that the facility's 1.8 million panels would contain 100,000 pounds of cadmium. As reported by Shellenberger (2018), the International Renewable Energy Agency (IRENA) in 2016 estimated there could be 78 million metric tons of solar panel waste by 2050.[55]

G A *Regulatory Free Pass: The Obama-era's Precautionary Approach to the Costs of Wind and Solar Farms*

The modern, late twentieth century American environmental movement was driven by the goal of preserving nature from development. That movement began with a mid-1950s battle over a proposal by the Bureau of Reclamation to construct Echo Park Dam on the Colorado River within Dinosaur National Monument. The dam was intended to store water for irrigation and for cheap hydroelectric power. It was opposed by environmentalists on the ground that its construction would mean the loss of an irreplaceable natural resource, Whirlpool Canyon on the Colorado, that was located in an ostensibly protected national monument area. Through a multi-pronged political and public relations campaign, the Sierra Club, led by David Brower, managed not only to stop the dam but to persuade Congress to amend the Colorado River Storage Project Act to prohibit dams in national parks and monuments.[56]

When passed in 1970, the CAA, which I have discussed at some length in earlier chapters, was not viewed as the American environmental movement's greatest early federal legislative success. That appellation would have been bestowed upon a different law, the 1969 National Environmental Policy Act (NEPA). NEPA was intended to ensure that federal infrastructure projects such as Echo Park Dam could not simply be pushed through regardless of their environmental consequences. With high minded purposes – including the promotion of "efforts which will prevent or eliminate damage to the environment and biosphere" and enrichment of man's "understanding of the ecological systems and natural resources important to the Nation" – NEPA required that before undertaking any project, federal agencies must consider the project's environmental impact.

Under regulations promulgated by the Council on Environmental Quality, in conducting such an environmental impact, federal agencies follow a three step process. First, they determine whether the project falls into a categorical exclusion from NEPA. Projects that are categorically excluded are those that the agency has determined do not individually or cumulatively significantly affect the quality of the human environment.[57] If not categorically excluded, the agency must prepare an environmental assessment, a relatively short (typically 100 pages or less) document determining only if the project likely has a significant impact on the environment. If the assessment determines that there is no significant impact, the process ends (although that finding can be challenged in court). If the agency finds a significant impact, then the agency must prepare a full environmental impact study. Such a study typically runs to hundreds or even thousands of pages and may take several years and millions of dollars to complete.

Under NEPA, the environmental impact of a project is understood broadly. The statute explicitly states that it seeks to assure "for all Americans safe, healthful, productive, and esthetically and culturally pleasing surroundings."[58] Thus federal agencies must consider visual, aesthetic impacts of projects before going forward.

As discussed, wind turbines are especially lethal to raptors such as golden and bald eagles. Although bald eagles were once officially protected as an endangered species, in the United States (but not Canada) both bald and golden eagle populations have recovered in recent decades. However, reflecting the cultural significance of both species, way back in 1940, the Bald and Golden Eagle Protection Act was enacted to specifically and specially protect both species. Under that law, it is illegal to "take" a bald or golden eagle, where taking is defined broadly to include "wound, kill, capture, trap, collect, molest, or disturb."[59]

In 2009, faced with evidence that wind turbines were clearly "taking" bald and golden eagles, the Obama-era US Fish and Wildlife Service (USFWS) promulgated regulations under which it granted permits for non-purposeful disturbance, injury, or killing of eagles if the take is incidental to an otherwise lawful activity and the take is "compatible with the preservation of the bald eagle and the golden eagle."[60] Under the 2009 regulations, wind farms granted permits for eagle takes would have to reapply every five years and show that their continued operation was consistent with eagle preservation.

For each such renewal application, the USFWS would have to comply with NEPA before granting a renewal. The entire 2009 eagle take regulation itself had to go through the NEPA process. It did not go far. The USFWS concluded that because it anticipated issuing only a conservative number of permits for such programmatic (that is, "recurring" and "occurring over a long time") eagle takes, the 2009 regulation would not have a significant impact on the environment.[61] Thus the USFWS never did a full environmental impact statement for its 2009 eagle take rule.

In the face of the massive increase in wind farm development and eagle kills brought about by the increase in wind subsidies under the 2009 stimulus, the USFWS asked the wind industry to voluntarily comply with measures that would reduce eagle kill. The wind industry's response was to complain that the five year eagle take permits granted by the 2009 regulation were too short. The industry wanted to be able to get a single permit at the time of project development that would last the entire 20–30 year expected lifetime of a wind farm.

In 2012, the Obama-era USFWS gave the wind industry everything it wanted, proposing a new regulation that would have extended the standard length of eagle take permits to 30 years. The USFWS was quite frank in stating that the purpose of the rule was to "facilitate the development of renewable energy and other projects that are designed to be in operation for decades," and explaining that the 30 year term was chosen "because industry has indicated it desires a longer permit." For this regulation, the USFWS did not even do an environmental assessment. It said that the 30 year rule was "categorically excluded" from the NEPA process because it was "strictly administrative."[62]

The USFWS's decision to completely bypass the NEPA process for its 30 year eagle take proposed rule was opposed by virtually everybody except the wind industry. Environmental groups, Indian tribes, and the USFWS's own staff demanded that the agency do a full EIS before finalizing its take rule. Instead, the USFWS finalized the 30 year eagle take rule without even doing an environmental assessment, modifying it only slightly to require that USFWS would review such 30 year permits every five years to determine whether eagle deaths were reaching a trigger point where various ill-defined protective measures needed to be implemented. Even though not everyone even in the wind industry agreed, the USFWS and the secretary of the Department of Interior (the agency that houses the USFWS) said that the rule would help wind developers "obtain financing" and thereby increase the number of permits granted for "longer term" wind projects.

In 2015, a federal trial court in the Northern District of California soundly rejected the USFWS's attempt to promulgate 30 year permits for wind turbine eagle kills without going through the NEPA process. The thirty year eagle kill permit, however, is indicative of the general approach to the environmental consequences of wind and solar projects taken by the Obama administration – ignore them, if possible, but in any event go full speed ahead with renewable power.

This was true even of unconventional renewable projects whose adverse environmental impacts were clearly foreseeable. An early post-stimulus project, Ivanpah

Solar Plant, received $1.6 billion in federal loan guarantees and $600 million in tax credits. It does not generate power from solar PV panels but instead uses five square miles of garage door-sized mirrors to generate tremendous heat from solar rays that is then used to produce steam in boilers atop 300 foot towers. The plant consumes about 5.6 square miles in an otherwise pristine area of the Mojave Desert that is part of the federally protected California Desert Conservation Area. Ivanpah occupies land that is home to the desert tortoise, a species listed under the federal Endangered Species list as threatened with extinction, and is part of a flyway for migrating birds. Ivanpah is only three miles from the Mojave National Preserve, which is part of the national park system.

Environmentalists were concerned about the Ivanpah plant's impact on the desert tortoise and migrating birds, and while the Bureau of Land Management (the federal agency responsible for the area) did go through the full NEPA process, it did so in virtually record time – less than two years – with most of its data supplied by the project developer. The project began operations in 2013. By 2016, federal biologists were reporting that about 6,000 birds per year were dying from collisions with the plant's tower or from being burned alive in the solar radiation concentrated and reflected by the plant's mirrors.[63]

In its final days, the Obama administration if anything stepped up its efforts to minimize and downplay the environmental costs of wind and solar projects. In December, 2016, the Obama BLM finalized a rule that would have created solar energy zones in which site specific environmental assessments under NEPA were not required. The agency announced plans for similarly vast areas of federal lands where wind farms could be developed without the need for site-specific environmental impact assessment.[64]

NEPA is a purely procedural statute. It forces agencies to consider the environmental impacts of their decisions but doesn't say how environmental impacts should affect those decisions. The Endangered Species Act (ESA), by contrast, is strongly substantive. Section 9 of the ESA prohibits private parties from "taking" an endangered or threatened species. What the Obama administration did to exempt wind farms from this "anti-take" provision of the ESA was even more egregious than what it did to speed the NEPA process for wind and solar farms.

In Section 10 of the original 1973 ESA, Congress allowed a private actor to take a member of a species only for scientific research and species propagation efforts that had been approved by the Fish and Wildlife Service. By 1981, Fish and Wildlife Service regulations had expanded the meaning of "take" under Section 9 to include private land development of species habitat that "actually kills or injures wildlife by impairing essential behavioral patterns." After the courts had made it clear that they would enforce this new regulatory definition in ways that allowed the FWS to actually regulate and limit private land development, Congress amended Section 10 to allow the FWS to permit private land development that harmed species habitat provided that the developer took measures to ensure that the development would not "jeopardize" the continued existence of the species. Eubanks (2015, 283) has shown that during the Clinton and George W. Bush administrations, the FWS issued about 600 such "incidental take permits" allowing development on about 48 million acres of private land.

As pointed out by a number of environmental law scholars (see, for example Nagle 2013, 96; Eubanks, 2015, 287), the ESA does not have a statutory exemption from its prohibition on taking an endangered species for projects that are self-declared pro-environment or "green projects." Like other private developments that significantly impact species habitat, such projects have to go through the lengthy and costly process of getting an incidental take permit under Section 10 of the ESA. Such delay and cost was antithetical to the Obama administration's goal of ramping up wind farm development as quickly as possible, and so that administration granted Section 10 scientific recovery permits to wind farms. Such permits, to recall, had been granted on a limited basis to allow the taking of individual members of a species so as to study the species in order to design recovery plans. Before the Obama era, they had been granted to private land developers only for the purpose of examining a potential development site for the presence of endangered species. For a number of large wind farms, the Obama FWS granted such scientific study take permits not so that wind farms could study their potential impact ahead of time, but in order to authorize killing of endangered species by wind turbines *that had already occurred* in violation of the ESA.

For example, as recounted by Eubanks (2015, 288–293), by the time it applied for a "scientific study" incidental take permit, the Fowler Ridge Wind Farm's turbines had already killed two and perhaps more endangered Indiana bats and the project's owners anticipated killing half a dozen more during the upcoming fall migration period. The only "scientific study" it was conducting was experimenting to see if it might kill fewer bats by changing wind turbine speeds. If a private developer of, say, a hospital project had killed such bats, it would have faced an order to immediately cease operations or else face potential criminal prosecution. The Obama FWS not only granted the Fowler Wind Farm a "scientific research" permit to kill bats, but repeatedly renewed that permit.

III STATE RPS LEGISLATION: THE MANY COSTS OF "RENEWABLE" POWER AS DEFINED BY SPECIAL INTERESTS

Beginning with Iowa in 1983, 36 states have passed laws requiring utilities to buy renewable power. As these laws generally specify that a certain percentage of total electric power purchased by such utilities must come from renewable power producers, they are called Renewable Portfolio Standards (RPS) laws. Iowa enacted the first RPS law in 1983, but most such laws were enacted between 1997–2000 and 2004–2009. There have been many revisions to state RPS laws. Since 2016, most changes have been in the direction of increasing the required renewable share.

While some increases have only modestly boosted the required renewables share – for example, Michigan and Maryland now aim for 15 and 25 percent by 2020 and 2021, respectively, other states such as New York now require 70 percent renewable power by 2030.[65] Even more recently – essentially, since the beginning of the Trump administration – another 9 states (California, Colorado, Hawaii, Maine, Nevada, New Mexico, New York, Virgini a, and Washington) have passed laws mandating or setting a goal of 100 percent renewable electricity by 2040 to 2050.

Among the 36 states with RPS laws, one can see several distinct patterns. First is a group of ten states (Arizona, Illinois, Indiana, Iowa, Montana, North Dakota, Oklahoma, South Carolina, South Dakota, and Wisconsin) that have minimal and effectively non-binding RPS requirements. As of 2019, virtually all of these states (the exception being North Dakota) far exceeded their renewable power goals.[66] At the other extreme are the 100 percent by 2050 states. As demonstrated in the previous chapter, these states have set a goal that would be obtainable only if other states sharing the same grid were to retain vast amounts of conventional, dispatchable power that could be used to balance load and generation and to provide power during the frequent periods when renewable power is unavailable. These states are similar to other states with the most ambitious renewable power goals: many have far to go to reach their goals. As of 2019, Connecticut, with a goal of 44 percent by 2030, actually got only 13 percent; Maryland, with a goal of 50 percent by 2030, actually got 17 per cent; New Mexico, with a goal of 40 percent by 2025, actually got 1 percent.

Comparing state RPS goals with what states say they have achieved, however, is an inaccurate and misleading way to discern the actual present day environmental impact, not to mention the impact on CO_2 emissions, of a state RPS law. State laws vary tremendously in what they consider to be "renewable" power. Generally, state RPS targets are highly tailored to the energy producing resources located within a state and are much less ambitious than they sound.

Take Vermont. Vermont counts power purchased from old and massive hydro-electric dams operated by Hydro-Quebec toward the renewable power mandate, and also counts power generated by biomass-fueled electric power plants.[67] In addition, Vermont electricity generators can meet their renewable power mandate either by providing renewable power or by buying credits generated by renewable power production elsewhere in New England, or by making what is called an "Alternative Compliance Payment" (ACP) the price of which is determined by the "environmental attributes" of electricity delivered by Hydro-Quebec. All in all, electricity providers in Vermont can meet 75 percent of Vermont's ambitious goal of being 90 percent renewable by 2050 either by buying ACPs or tradeable renewable credits purchased from old hydropower providers in nearby Maine.[68]

As for Maine, that state's RPS goal is 80 percent by 2030. It will probably meet that goal, as by 2018 Maine already got 75 percent of its electricity from renewable power sources. However, as with Vermont, a peek under the hood shows that what Maine counts as "renewable" energy production is not quite what one would expect. By

2019, Maine was getting between 20–25 percent of its electricity from burning biomass, with another 33 percent generated by small (less than 100 MW) and mostly old[69] hydropower projects.[70]

Like Maine's, several of the seemingly most aggressive state RPS laws are actually carefully crafted to impose minimal costs by favoring already existing power sources. Oregon's statute sets what sounds like an ambitious goal of 50 percent renewable power by 2040, but Oregon counts hydropower as renewable power. Since Oregon has historically gotten at least 50 percent of its electricity from huge, federally subsidized hydropower projects, with up to 90 percent from hydropower in especially wet years, Oregon's statutory goal requires the state to do nothing.[71]

A *The Environmental Costs of State RPS Laws*

Polls find that controlling for per capita income across states, Vermont and Maine residents – like those of many other New England and Northeastern states – are among the most supportive of stricter environmental regulations.[72] However, the RPS laws of these states incentivize electricity generation from power sources that are directly in conflict with traditional environmental goals. First, these RPS laws count electricity production from burning wood biomass as renewable production. Burning wood biomass generates potentially high concentrations of air pollutants such as carbon monoxide, a poison,[73] precisely the kind of air pollution that American environmental laws have sought to reduce for the past 40 years. Generating electricity by burning wood biomass counts as renewable electricity only because if a tree is planted and then burned, the carbon dioxide emissions from burning would be offset by the carbon dioxide taken in by the tree during its life. If the rate of growth of demand for such electricity is sufficiently high, however, then trees could not be planted and grown fast enough to satisfy the demand, meaning that the existing stock of trees would be depleted, generating net carbon dioxide emissions. Thus wood biomass is an electricity power source that certainly generates conventional pollution and can help reduce GHG emissions only if the rate of growth of electricity demand is low relative to the rate of growth of trees.

Second, Vermont, Maine, and Oregon count electricity generated by water stored behind dams as renewable power. As discussed earlier in this chapter, for decades, environmentalists and outdoorsmen have recounted how dams harm migratory fisheries (think shad and salmon), degraded and destroyed river ecosystems, and replaced scarce wilderness rivers with muddy reservoirs. Still today, environmental groups such as American Rivers aim to tear down and remove old dams.[74] Massive dams in the Columbia and Snake River basins in the Pacific Northwest supply Washington and Oregon with the cheapest electricity in the United States, but those dams have destroyed salmon runs and their removal is still on the wish list of many environmentalists.

Even worse, in Vermont and even more so in New York state, "renewable" hydroelectric power comes from Hydro-Quebec's La Grande Complex near James Bay. That project was strongly but unsuccessfully opposed by Canadian Cree and Inuit Indians and by Canadian environmental groups. To build the La Grande dam complex, Hydro-Quebec cut down approximately ten million trees, excavated 262,400,000 cubic meters of fill, changed the course of 5 rivers, and built five airports and hundreds of kilometers of roads to facilitate construction (Paregoi 1998, 157). Indian and environmental groups say that their dire predictions about the environmental consequences of the La Grande project have been more than realized. The Cree Indian tribe got millions of dollars in compensation, but they say that the fish they depend upon for food and commercial sales have been poisoned by mercury, their traditional hunting grounds turned into reservoirs, while the roads that were supposed to bring new jobs have instead brought only tribal alcoholism and drug addiction (Linton 1991, iii–iv).

The harm to Canada's environment from massive dam projects designed to satisfy US RPS–driven demand for renewable power may be accelerating. In 2019 in Labrador, state-owned Nalcor power completed Muskrat Falls, a $12.7 billion dam on the Churchill River, which drains the province's main watershed. With the expectation that massively expensive new transmission lines – New York City is planning to spend $3 billion and Maine $950 million on new transmission lines running north to Canada – will connect Canadian hydropower to eastern US load centers, Canadian hydropower developers expect to invest $100 billion, tripling their power output. The environmental cost of this will be tragic – Canada will have lost all of its wild, undammed rivers. Flooded will be ecosystems upon which Canadian tribes still depend for their livelihoods. According to a 2016 survey, all 22 future hydropower projects in Canada then planned were within 60 miles of at least one tribal community.[75]

B *The Impact of State RPS Laws on Renewable Power Capacity and Retail Electricity Prices*

While many states have defined their RPS laws so that traditional hydropower and even biomass burning count as renewable power, in other states, RPS targets have required and will continue to require additional big investments in wind and solar. Nevada, for example, aims to get 50 percent of its power from renewables by 2030, but that state still gets 66 percent of its power from natural gas.[76] As it has little water and thus no hydropower option, and for the most part is not in a high wind region, Nevada will need to increase its use of solar if it is to meet its RPS goal. New York has a goal of 70 percent renewable power by 2030, but it still gets 40 percent of its power from old, hybrid natural gas/petroleum-fired power plants, and overall gets over 90 percent of its power from such plants plus hydropower (largely imported from Quebec) and nuclear plants. Especially with planned retirement of nuclear plants, even with increased imports of Canadian hydropower, New York will need a massive expansion in wind power in order to meet its RPS goal.[77] New Mexico, which by statute now aims to be 100 percent renewable by 2045, is actually a national leader in its reliance on coal for electricity generation, still getting 40 percent of its electricity from coal-fired power plants. New Mexico's current plans include expansions in both renewable power and natural gas. As shown by California's experience, natural gas is the best current dispatchable power source in a high renewable penetration grid, but increasing natural gas capacity is not consistent with New Mexico's goal of 100 percent renewable power.[78]

According to one federally funded institute – the Lawrence Livermore Lab at UC Berkeley – of the 120 GW of RE capacity added in the United States since 2000, over half of the increase in renewable electricity capacity has been driven at least in part by state RPS requirements, with an even higher percentage, between 60 and 70 percent, being driven by state RPS laws over the period 2008–2014.[79] As can be seen by looking back at Figure 8.1, it is true the most rapid rate of increase in renewable electricity generation has occurred since about 2008, with wind generated power making up the vast majority of renewable electric power today.

However, when economists have looked closely – trying to isolate the effect of state RPS laws by comparing states with such laws to closely matched states without such laws – they have often found that in most states the passage of an RPS law had no statistically significant impact on renewable electricity generation capacity in the state. One study (Maguire and Munasib 2016, 486) of states that adopted RPS standards during the early period found that only in Texas did the RPS spur increased renewable generation capacity. This was likely because unlike other states – some of which, like Maine, set very high renewable targets but allowed them to be met from existing hydropower capacity – Texas required that specific amounts of renewable capacity be added. As mentioned above, moreover, Texas has its own power grid (ERCOT) and is not connected to the other two regional power grids in the United States. This means that Texas utilities can satisfy a renewable power mandate only by building or buying renewable power from within Texas.

As this last point suggests, for states other than Texas, renewable power can be provided by generators located in-state or by out-of-state generators who supply the same wholesale power network. The existence of tradeable renewable power permit markets within transmission regions such as New England makes it a bit more complicated to estimate precisely the extent to which state RPS laws have caused an increase in renewable power production. Greenstone and Nath (2019) did study renewable capacity changes at the regional level. They found that RPS passage led to statistically significant increases in wind and hydropower production (although in some formulations of the statistical relationship, the increase in wind capacity was not statistically significant).

It is worth noting that from the point of view of increasing renewable power usage within a regional network, it is irrelevant how much renewable generating capacity is installed within particular states. From the standpoint of economic efficiency, within a regional grid, renewable power, like other power, should be provided by the lowest cost providers. A trading scheme such as Vermont's, where utilities can either buy renewable power or buy credits generated by renewable power providers elsewhere in the same region – choosing whichever is cheaper – is a way of realizing such efficiencies. Some environmentalists[80] have criticized state RPS laws that allow utilities the option to buy credits instead of buying actual renewable power on the ground that under such schemes, there might be no actual increase in renewable power generating capacity within a state. This criticism is striking, for it suggests that at least to some supporters, state RPS laws may be about something more or other than just increasing the usage of renewable power.

While there seems still to be some uncertainty over whether state RPS laws actually have had a marginal impact in increasing state renewable power generation, there is less uncertainty regarding the impact of state RPS laws on state electricity prices. State RPS laws increase electric power providers' costs in two ways: by requiring them to buy potentially more expensive renewable power, and by requiring them to spend money connecting renewable power suppliers to the wholesale transmission and/or retail distribution network. Greenstone and Nath (2019) find that passage of a state RPS has a long lasting impact in increasing retail electricity prices by 11 percent, rising to 17 percent by 12 years after passage (by 1.3 cents per KWh, the retail unit of measure, rising to 2 cents per KWh, or $20 per MWh, the wholesale measure). It has been estimated that if natural gas prices remain low (so that renewable power to meet RPS law requirements is displacing cheaper natural gas), the incremental system cost of meeting current RPS goals in place in 29 states over the 2015–2050 period will be about $31 billion; if all states adopted RPS laws requiring even higher levels of renewable power, the cost could be as high as $194 billion (Wisser et al., 2017, 094023). With such big projected cost increases, it is perhaps unsurprising that even RPS laws requiring on average less than 5 percent have been found to have increased electric utility prices to consumers (Tra 2016, 184–189).

Texas presents a vivid illustration of the effect of state RPS laws on renewable power supply and prices and also the care that must be exercised in attempting to estimate the impact of state RPS laws on prices. Texas had essentially no renewable power in 1998. The following year, the Texas Public Utility Commission of Texas began to adopt rules for the state's renewable energy requirements, but it was not until 2005 that the state legislature enacted a law requiring the installation of a specific quantity of renewable generating capacity (5,880 megawatts, or about 5 percent of the state's electricity generating capacity) by 2015, with a goal of 10,000 megawatts of renewable capacity by 2025.[81] With the state building a new $7 billion transmission network to connect Texas wind farms in the west with population centers in the east, by 2009, Texas had already met the 2015 goal, relying almost entirely on wind power. By 2016, Texas produced more non-hydroelectric renewable

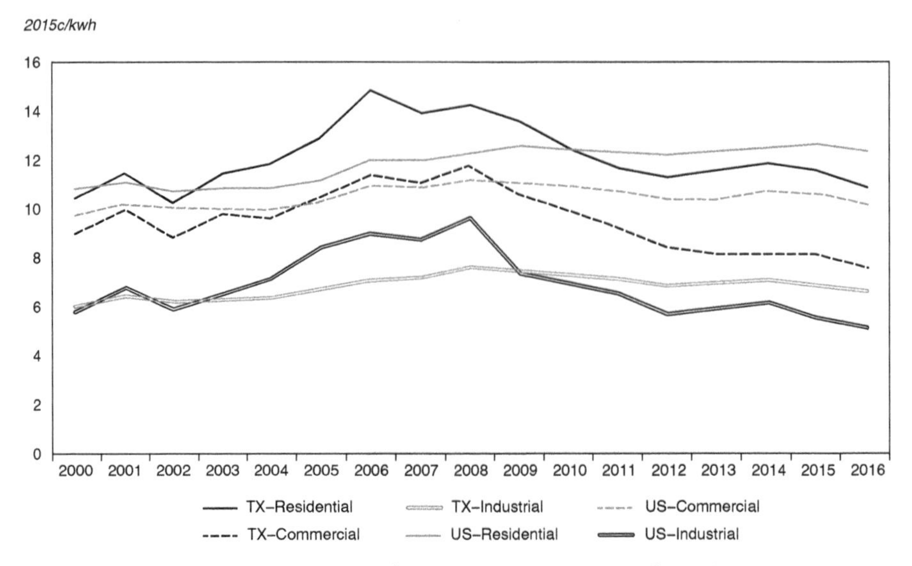

FIGURE 8.6 Texas Average Electricity Prices Compared to US Average

generation than any other state in the nation, producing one-fourth of all US wind-powered electricity.

Focusing just on residential electricity prices (the dark, Texas, and light, US average, solid lines in Figure 8.6[82]), Texas has gone from prices that were roughly at the US average between 1990 and 2002 to prices that were at times considerably above average US prices from 2003 to 2009 to prices slightly below the US average since 2009. From the figure, it is clear that the estimated impact of the Texas RPS law would depend upon the year one takes to mark the beginning of that law's effectiveness (1998, as in Maguire and Munasib [2018] or 2005, when the legislature toughened the law) and the period of time over which one estimates the effect (e.g., if one had truncated the sample studied about 2009, likely a direct impact would have been observed).

Determining the impact of state RPS laws on renewable generating capacity and electricity prices across different states is more complicated than the discussion thus far suggests. As indicated by my previous discussion, states vary a lot in what they consider to be "renewable" power. The state of Washington, for example, as of 2010 got only 4.6 percent from solar and wind combined but could report that 70 percent of its power came conventional hydropower, another "renewable" power source.[83] Washington's hydropower, from the federal Bonneville Power Project, has zero marginal cost of generation, and so its electricity is as cheap – less than 10 cents per kilowatt hour – as it is in oil-rich Louisiana and Oklahoma.[84] In California, which got about half of its 2018 power from various types of renewables, the electricity price is about 19 cents/kilowatt hour.[85] California's price would likely be even higher, but for the fact that it gets a very large share of its power from hydroelectric facilities, some of which are located in California (supplying widely varying amounts of power, depending on annual rainfall in California), but the most reliable of which are the zero marginal cost Pacific Northwest hydroelectric facilities that export power to California.[86]

In some states, electricity prices are high, but they are high not because the states rely so heavily on solar and wind but because they are simultaneously waging costly attacks on fossil fuels. To see how this plays out, take New England. California's retail electricity prices are high, but not as high as prices in the New England states: as of 2019, the only continental US states with prices above 20 cents per kilowatt hour were in New England (Connecticut, New Hampshire, Massachusetts, and Rhode Island, and Vermont was not far behind at 17 cents per KWh).[87] All five New England states have set goals of reducing state level GHG emissions by at least 75 percent by 2050. All five states have RPS laws, with the most ambitious, Maine and Vermont, calling for, respectively, 80 and 75 percent renewable power by 2030 and 2032.

As explained in the previous chapter, because renewable power is intermittent, the backup or base load power source is crucial in determining the actual cost, and retail electricity price impact of a shift to renewable power. Traditionally, the New England states got their base load power not from coal but from oil, which as recently as 2000 provided 34 percent of New England's electricity. ISO New England is the organization responsible for the New England high voltage transmission network and manages the wholesale power market in New England. It says that as of 2018, at 45 percent natural gas had become the dominant fuel source for New England's electric power. ISO New England projects that by 2025, natural gas will supply 65 percent of New England's electric power. According to that organization, by 2025, the remaining electric power generation will be derived 20 percent from hydro and nuclear and 11 percent from renewables.[88]

Obviously according to the organization that actually has the legal obligation to make sure that the New England electricity system works, that region's state RPS goals are not going to be met, and at least for next decade, natural gas will supply the overwhelming share of electric power in New England. A major reason that New England has such high electricity prices has been state and local level political opposition to constructing pipelines that would move cheap natural gas from Ohio and Pennsylvania, where it is recovered via fracking.[89] With constrained supply, natural gas prices in New England have spiked to extremely high levels during winter cold snaps, with prices at the natural gas hub serving Boston increasing from a norm of around a little less than $10 per million British thermal units (mmBtu) to more than $100 per mmBtu during a cold snap in early January, 2018.[90] As New England increasingly relies upon natural gas, continued successful political opposition to natural gas pipelines will require New England to rely on very expensive liquid natural gas. This will mean higher electricity prices, not directly because of the New England states' RPS laws, but because those laws are part of an attack on fossil fuels.

C *The Distributional Consequences of State Renewables Mandates and Natural Gas Supply Restrictions*

The 11–17 percent higher electricity prices that Greenstone and Nath (2019) estimate in states with RPS policies may not sound like much. But RPS policies are only one policy that influences state electricity prices. The states with the most aggressive renewables policies and also the most draconian approach to natural gas, such as California plus the New England states, have electricity prices that are somewhere between 50–80 percent higher than states that do not combine ambitious RPS goals with stringent policies toward coal and natural gas. This translates into a big difference in monthly electricity bills, with the average consumer, for example, paying about $197 per month in Massachusetts but only $98 in Missouri.

For households in the top 20 percent by income, these kinds of differences in electricity bills are barely felt. According to the Bureau of Labor Statistics 2018 Consumer Survey,[91] households in this income group spend only about 1 percent of their after-tax income on electricity. Even in the middle 60 percent of households by income, electricity costs amounted to only about 2.5 percent of total expenditures. However, the bottom 20 percent of US households ranked by income spent 9 percent of their after-tax income just on electricity. For these households, for whom electricity costs make up 900 percent more of their budget than such costs do for the top 20 percent, even increases in electricity costs in the 10–20 percent range mean that some other expenditure must be cut, or else borrowing increased. And a doubling of electricity costs – as would occur if such a household moved from Missouri to California – would mean a major sacrifice of some other form of expenditure.

Further perspective may be gained by adding in annual household expenditures for natural gas – used primarily for heating – and on utilities and fuels. Households in the bottom 20 percent of the income distribution spend another 23 percent of their after-tax income on these, which means that they spend 32 percent of their after-tax income on electricity, natural gas, and utilities and fuel combined. By contrast, households in the top 20 percent spend only 4.5 percent of their after-tax income on electricity, natural gas, and utilities and fuel. When these additional categories of spending are considered, we see that relative to the top 20 percent, the households in the bottom 20 percent of the income distribution spend about 800 percent more of their income on the basic needs – electricity and natural gas and utilities – whose prices are most directly affected by and most substantially raised by renewable energy policies.

These are highly regressive effects, where by regressive I mean tending to impose greater costs, the poorer is the household. State renewables mandates, like any other policy mandating the use of more expensive energy sources for electricity and heating and transportation (such as the CAFÉ standards discussed earlier, in Chapter 4), have regressive effects, punishing the poor, because these expenditures categories do not vary as much by income (have lower income elasticity, in economics lingo) as do other categories. For example, while the top 20 percent spend a tiny fraction of their after-tax income on electricity and natural gas compared to households in the bottom 20 percent, they spend almost three times as much on personal services as a share of after-tax income as do the poorest 20 percent. The poorest 20 percent can and do cut back on personal services. But they do not, and to some extent cannot, cut back on electricity and natural gas for heating, and it is precisely these expenditure categories whose prices are increased by renewables policies.

These regressive effects of renewables policies are magnified for minority households. Black and Hispanic households in the bottom 20 percent of income are often living in older, energy inefficient homes. A very recent study, Kontokosta et al. (2020, 89–105), finds that even within the same income group, minority households systematically spend a higher share of their after-tax income on electricity and other energy bills. Hence increases in electricity prices caused by state RPS laws disproportionately burden such households.

Notes

1. Based on data in EIA Annual Energy Review 2011, Table 8.2a, p. 224.
2. EIA, How much Carbon Dioxide is produced when different fuels are burned, available at https://www.eia.gov/tools/faqs/faq.php?id=73&t=11.
3. Emanuele Massetti, Marilyn A. Brown, Melissa Lapsa, Isha Sharma, James Bradbury, Colin Cunliff, Yufei Li, Environmental Quality and the US Power Sector: Air Quality, Water Quality, Land Use and Environmental Justice, Oak Ridge National Laboratory of the US Department of Energy, ORNL/SPR-2016/772, Jan. 4, 2017, available at https://www.energy.gov/sites/prod/files/2017/01/f34/Environment%20Baseline%20Vol.%202–Environmental%20Quality%20and%20the%20U.S.%20Power%20Sector–Air%20Quality%2C%20Water%20Quality%2C%20Land%20Use%2C%20and%20Environmental%20Justice.pdf.
4. Bruce Yandle, Yes, Sen. Warren, The System Is Rigged – By Congress, The Hill, Nov. 6, 2019, available at https://thehill.com/opinion/finance/469244-yes-sen-warren-the-system-in-rigged-by-congress.
5. See Gordon (1979, 874).
6. J. D. Steelman Jr., Deregulation of the Natural Gas Industry, Foundation for Economic Education, June 1, 1986, available at https://fee.org/articles/deregulation-of-the-natural-gas-industry/.
7. "Fuel Use Act Repealed." (1988, 323-24).
8. 42 U.S.C. §8302.

9. Under 42 U.S.C. §8411(f).
10. PL 95-618.
11. FERC, PURPA Benefits at New Dams and Diversions, Final Staff Report Evaluating Environmental and Economic Effects 1-2, Office of Hydropower Licensing, Docket No. EL87-9 (1987), available at https://play.google.com/books/reader?id=E9Nf42Kvo30C&hl=en&pg=GBS.SA2-PA12.
12. FERC, PURPA Benefits at New Dams and Diversions, supra note 11 at 1–19.
13. These facts are drawn from American Rivers, et al., Dam Removal Success Stories xiii (1999) available at https://www.michigan.gov/documents/dnr/dam success_513764_7.pdf.
14. From the full list as summarized in Proett (1987, 87).
15. Amy Souers Kober, Twenty years of dam removal successes – and what's up next: The lesson from the Kennebec after twenty years? Dam removal works, American Rivers, June 27, 2019, available at https://www.americanrivers.org/2019/06/twenty-years-of-dam-removal-successes-and-whats-up-next/.
16. 16 U.S.C. 46 §2601 et. seq. and 42 U.S.C. §13201 et seq.
17. Source: EIA, Electricity Explained, available at https://www.eia.gov/energyexplained/electricity/electricity-in-the-us-generation-capacity-and-sales.php.
18. DOE, Office of Energy Efficiency and Renewable Energy, 2018 Wind Technologies Market Report 70 (2018).
19. Mark Holt and Carol Glover, Energy Policy Act of 2005: Summary and Analysis of Enacted Provisions, CRS Report for Congress, March 8, 2006
20. Bill Canis and Brent D. Yacobucci, the Advanced Technology Vehicles Manufacturing (ATVM) Loan Program: Status and Issues, CRS Report R42064, Jan. 15, 2015, available at https://fas.org/sgp/crs/misc/R42064.pdf.
21. Veronique de Rugy, A Guarantee of Failure: Government Lending under Section 1705, Testimony to the House Oversight Committee, July 18, 2012, available at https://oversight.house.gov/sites/democrats.oversight.house.gov/files/documents/de-Rugy-Testimony.pdf.
22. The following discussion draws upon the explanation of the stimulus bill and renewable energy provided by one of its designers, Aldy (2012).
23. Aldy, (2012).
24. De Rugy, supra note 21 at 9.
25. Eric Lipton and Clifford Krauss, A Gold Rush of Subsidies in Clean Energy Research, New York Times, Nov. 11, 2011, available at https://www.goupstate.com/article/NC/20111111/News/605165708/SJ.
26. De Rugy, supra note 21 at 7.
27. Cassandra Sweet, High Tech Solar Projects Fail to Deliver, Wall Street Journal, June 12, 2015, available at https://www.wsj.com/articles/high-tech-solar-projects-fail-to-deliver-1434138485.
28. Canis and Yacobucci, supra note 20 at 5–6.

29. University of Texas Energy Institute, The Full Cost of Electricity, Federal Financial Support for Electricity Generation Technologies 4 (2017), available at https://energy.utexas.edu/sites/default/files/UTAustin_FCe_Subsidies_2018_April.pdf.
30. EIA, Direct Federal Financial Interventions and Subsidies in Energy in Fiscal Year 2016 9, April 2018, available at _.
31. University of Texas Energy Institute, supra note __ at 6.
32. EIA, Today in Energy, Wind has surpassed hydro as most-used renewable electricity generation source in US, February 26, 2020, available at https://www.eia.gov/todayinenergy/detail.php?id=42955.
33. Source: American Wind Energy Association, Free Use Wind Energy Image Gallery, available at https://www.awea.org/resources/free-use-wind-energy-image-gallery.
34. EIA, Wind Turbine heights and capacities have increased over the past decade, November 29, 2017, available at https://www.eia.gov/todayinenergy/detail.php?id=33912.
35. EIA, Texas ranks first in US installed wind capacity and number of turbines, July 31, 2019, available at https://www.eia.gov/todayinenergy/detail.php?id=40252.
36. Rand et al. (2020) describe this dataset as the "most comprehensive, accurate and complete description of a nation's wind infrastructure publicly available anywhere in the world."
37. See US Wind Turbine Database, available at https://eerscmap.usgs.gov/uswtdb/viewer/#3.37/33.65/-91.46.
38. American Wind Energy Association, Basics of Wind Energy, available at https://www.awea.org/wind-101/basics-of-wind-energy.
39. EIA, Wind explained Electricity generation from wind, March 23, 2020, https://www.eia.gov/energyexplained/wind/electricity-generation-from-wind.php.
40. For an application of Veroni polygons in optimizing wind farm efficiency – so-called Veroni tessellation – see Shapiro, et al. (2019, 2956).
41. EIA, What Is US Electricity Generation by Energy Source, available at https://www.eia.gov/tools/faqs/faq.php?id=427&t=3.
42. Thought Co. How Big Is Each State?, https://www.thoughtco.com/list-of-us-states-by-area-1435813.
43. Department of Energy, Office of Energy Efficiency and Renewable Energy, 2018 Wind Technologies Market Report 25, available at https://emp.lbl.gov/sites/default/files/wtmr_final_for_posting_8-9-19.pdf.
44. DOE 2018 Wind Technologies Market Report at 33.
45. Scott R. Loss, Tom Will, and Peter P. Marra, Estimates of bird collision mortality at wind facilities in the contiguous United States, 168 Biological Conservation 201–209 (2013).

46. Source for Figure 8.5(a): Flickr, available at https://www.flickr.com/photos/stirlingcouncil/5455709703/in/photolist-9j6Wqp-9Z8Pmz-9ZbVEu-5raRv-2TQfiC-9Z8Xyc-aecQFf-qBm9nL-54NHq-9ja4gC-c8dUHL-dKCX31-qn83Wt-9Z9hai-dKywT2-8qBeah-8m1kp2-oM2fgu-qDB8Wn-ouyT8v-ouy6aa-qn1g7d-oM2dJm-ouytyC-ouydhY-oM2bwA-oK24aN-6oW1Ja-vKPkg-asgEzk-9ja5xW-9ja5uC-9ja5Jy-9ja4x7-9ja46o-9j6Xii-9ja4k7-9j6VqH-9ja4Hs-9ja4Q1-9j6VQF-9ja54m-9ja61Q-9ja5T5-9ja4am-ukVZFh-qDoZtF-c1LaMf-ouzafF-oWqg16, source for Figure 8.5(b) is Alamy, available at https://www.bing.com/images/search?q=alamy+stirling+castle+with+wind+farm&qpvt=Alamy+sterling+castle+with+wind+farm&form=IGRE&first=1&scenario=ImageBasicHover.
47. Kristian Hernandez, An uncertain future for America's wind energy capital, Public Integrity, October 8, 2018, available at _.
48. See, for example, *New Creek Mountain Sportsman's Club* v. *New Creek Wind*, No.'s 2:18-cv-00111, 2:18-cv-00112, 2:18-cv-00113 (N.D. W.Va. 2018), National Wind Watch, Group to continue opposing wind turbines: Action filed in Allegheny County Circuit Court, Greg Larry, The Cumberland Times-News, June 27, 2020, available at www.times-news.com.
49. Jack Spencer, One Lawsuit Settled, But No Truce in Wind Energy Debate Michigan Capitol Confidential, January 31, 2015, available at _.
50. Christina Stella, Unfurling The Waste Problem Caused By Wind Energy, NPR, September 10, 2019, available at https://www.npr.org/2019/09/10/759376113/unfurling-the-waste-problem-caused-by-wind-energy.
51. Institute for Energy Research, the Cost of Decommissioning Wind turbines is huge, November 1, 2019, https://www.instituteforenergyresearch.org/renewable/wind/the-cost-of-decommissioning-wind-turbines-is-huge/.
52. DOE, The Ultimate Fast Facts Guide to Nuclear Energy 2 (2019), available at https://www.energy.gov/sites/prod/files/2019/01/f58/Ultimate%20Fast%20Facts%20Guide-PRINT.pdf.
53. Landon Stevens, The Footprint of Energy: Land Use of US Electricity Production, Strata, June, 2017 (using the median land use requirement figure from the Natural Gas Association), available at https://www.strata.org/pdf/2017/footprints-full.pdf.
54. See, How Much Land Is Needed to Mine Uranium Ore for nuclear plants?, The Freeing Energy Project, available at https://www.freeingenergy.com/math/uranium-nuclear-mining-land-acres-m128/.
55. Michael Shellenberger, If Solar Panels Are So Clean, Why Do They Produce So Much Toxic Waste, Forbes, May 23, 2018, available at https://www.forbes.com/sites/michaelshellenberger/2018/05/23/if-solar-panels-are-so-clean-why-do-they-produce-so-much-toxic-waste/#5f33a585121c.
56. George Mumford, Echo Park Dam and the Early Environmental Movement, Intermountain Histories, available at https://www.intermountainhistories.org/items/show/56?tour=7&index=0.

57. 40 C.F.R. §1508.4.
58. 42 U.S.C. § 4331(b)(2) (2006)
59. 16 U.S.C. §668c.
60. See 50 CFR §§22.3.
61. This discussion is drawn from *Shearwater* v. *Ashe*, 2015 WL 4747881 (N.D Cal. 2015).
62. The discussion in this paragraph is likewise based on the court's discussion in *Shearwater* v. *Ashe*.
63. On Ivanpah, see Louis Sahagun, This Mojave Desert solar plant kills 6,000 birds a year. Here's why that won't change any time soon, LA Times, September 2, 2016, available at https://www.latimes.com/local/california/la-me-solar-bird-deaths-20160831-snap-story.html, and David Danelski, Ivanpah solar plant, built to limit greenhouse gases, is burning more natural gas, The Press-Enterprise, January 23, 2017, available at https://www.pe.com/2017/01/23/ivanpah-solar-plant-built-to-limit-greenhouse-gases-is-burning-more-natural-gas/.
64. Department of the Interior, Bureau of Land Management, Competitive Processes, Terms, and Conditions for Leasing Public Lands for Solar and Wind Energy Development and Technical Changes and Corrections, 81(243) Federal Register 92,122, Monday, December 19, 2016.
65. National Conf. of State Legislatures, State Renewable Portfolio Standards and Goals 4/17/2020, available at https://www.ncsl.org/research/energy/renewable-portfolio-standards.aspx#:~:text=Details%3A%20In%202019%2C%20Maryland%20enacted%20legislation%20increasing%20its,annual%20percentage%20carveout%20up%20to%2014.5%25%20in%202030.
66. Energy.gov, Renewable Energy production by state, available at https://www.energy.gov/maps/renewable-energy-production-state?page=0%2C3 (data available for download on site).
67. Vermonters for a Clean Environment, Understanding Vermont's Energy Policies, March, 2018, available at http://www.vce.org/VCE_WhitePaper_UnderstandingVermont_EnergyPolicies_12March2018.pdf.
68. Vermonters for a Clean Environment, supra at 8.
69. See http://www.mainelegislature.org/legis/bills/bills_125th/chapters/PUBLIC413.asp.
70. EIA, Maine: State Profile and Energy Estimates, available at https://www.eia.gov/state/analysis.php?sid=ME.
71. EIA, Oregon, https://www.eia.gov/state/analysis.php?sid=OR.
72. Brian Kennedy, Public support for environmental regulations varies by state, Pew Research Center FactTank, Feb. 25, 2016, available at http://www.pewresearch.org/fact-tank/2016/02/25/public-support-for-environmental-regulations-varies-by-state/
73. EIA, Biomass Explained, available at https://www.eia.gov/energyexplained/index.php?page=biomass_environment.

74. American Rivers, Map of Dams removed since 1916, available at https://www.americanrivers.org/threats-solutions/restoring-damaged-rivers/dam-removal-map/.
75. Matt Hongoltz-Hetling, US demand for clean energy destroying Canada's environment, indigenous peoples say, The Guardian, June 22, 2020, available at https://www.theguardian.com/environment/2020/jun/22/us-clean-energy-demand-destroying-canadian-environment-indigenous-peoples-say.
76. EIA, Nevada, https://www.eia.gov/state/analysis.php?sid=NV
77. EIA, New York, available at https://www.eia.gov/state/analysis.php?sid=NY
78. EIA, New Mexico, https://www.eia.gov/state/analysis.php?sid=NM.
79. Galen Barbose, U.S. Renewables Portfoliio Standards: 2017 Annual Status Report 13, Lawrence Berkeley National Laboratory, July, 2017, available at https://emp.lbl.gov/projects/renewables-portfolio/.
80. See Vermonters for a Clean Environment, Understanding Vermont's Energy Policies, March, 2018, available at http://www.vce.org/VCE_WhitePaper_UnderstandingVermont_EnergyPolicies_12March2018.pdf.
81. EIA, Texas Profile Analysis, Jan. 2018, available at https://www.eia.gov/state/analysis.php?sid=TX.
82. Figure 8.6 reproduces Figure 1 from Hartley, et al. (2019, 2).
83. EIA, State Renewable Electricity Profiles, available at https://www.eia.gov/renewable/state/Washington/.
84. Electric Rate, Electric Rates by State, available at https://www.electricrate.com/electricity-rates-by-state/.
85. EIA, Electric Power Monthly, available at https://www.eia.gov/electricity/monthly/epm_table_grapher.php?t=epmt_5_6_a.
86. EIA, California, https://www.eia.gov/state/analysis.php?sid=NM.
87. Electric Rate, Electric Rates by State, available at https://www.electricrate.com/electricity-rates-by-state/.
88. ISO New England, Resource Mix, available at https://www.iso-ne.com/about/key-stats/resource-mix/.
89. State of the Markets Report 2015, FERC, March 2016. Available at: https://www.ferc.gov/market-oversight/reports-analyses/ st-mkt-ovr/2015-som.pdf.
    US Chamber of Commerce, What if? … Pipelines Aren't Built into the Northeast, 9-10, 14-15.
90. William Murray, New Englanders Have Only Themselves to Blame for Energy Price Spikes, Real Clear Energy, Jan. 17, 2018, available at https://www.realclearenergy.org/articles/2018/01/17/new_englanders_have_only_themselves_to_blame_for_energy_price_spikes.html.
91. Expenditures on electricity and after-tax income by decile are taken from the Bureau of Labor Statistics, 2018 Consumer Expenditure Survey, https://www.bls.gov/cex/2018/combined/decile.pdf.

9

Spinning the Tort Liability Roulette Wheel

Long before the Obama administration EPA's Endangerment Finding, early IPCC assessment reports (AR's) were a call to action for American tort lawyers. After all, the IPCC ARs attributed all sorts of human and environmental harms to climate change, and confidently linked climate change to anthropogenic CO_2 emissions. These reports thus established a causal connection between CO_2 emissions and harm. Such a causal connection held out the prospect of holding CO_2 emitters legally liable under American tort law for harm from climate change.

After it had become clear that the United States would not sign on to the Kyoto Protocol, American tort lawyers began filing lawsuits against firms that emitted CO_2, seeking to enjoin such emissions and/or to recover damages for the harm that such emissions had caused. Such suits continued throughout the Bush administration, and with the Trump administration's rollback of Obama administration federal GHG regulations and withdrawal from the 2015 Paris Climate Agreement, such tort suits returned to the courts and continue today.

In this chapter, I explain why as a matter of both policy and legal doctrine, conventional tort liability is completely ill-suited to the problem of climate change. Lawsuits seeking to impose tort liability on firms for the harm that can allegedly be traced to their CO_2 emissions have always had at best a tiny chance of success. Climate activists have nonetheless brought such suits in the hope that even a tiny chance of being found liable for billions of dollars in damages will terrorize major corporations in key industrial sectors into agreeing to the their demands and supporting federal climate change legislation. In this, the suits have been a great success.

I CLIMATE CHANGE AND COMMON LAW TORT LIABILITY: A BAD FIT

A tort is a civil (versus criminal) wrong. If the victim of a tort can prove the legal elements of the tort, then they can recover damages from the wrongdoer. The first element that the plaintiff is required to prove is that the injurer caused harm. For most torts, such as an auto accident, the victim must also show that the injurer at least acted negligently, meaning that the injurer did not take sufficient care to avoid the accident. In American tort law, true strict liability – where the injurer must compensate the victim regardless of how careful they were to avoid causing harm – is rare. Such strict (or absolute) liability is limited to situations where the injurer has engaged in an activity, such as setting off dynamite, that is dangerous no matter how much care is taken.

As described earlier, lots of activities, including human breathing, emit CO_2. And – aside from melting dry ice in a small closed room – no individual CO_2 emission causes harm to anybody. Because CO_2 emissions are a direct product of human life and the combustion of fossil fuels, such emissions cannot plausibly be viewed as somehow due to the emitter's lack of due care – the traditional conception of fault in tort law. With so many emitters of CO_2 and no direct harm caused by any such emission, it would seem that emitting CO_2 is not at all like causing personal injury or property damage by driving a car negligently.

Environmental law scholars have agreed that tort liability for CO_2 emissions does not fit well with traditional legal conceptions of such liability. But they have viewed this not as indicating that tort liability for climate change is a bad idea, but instead that tort law must be altered so that CO_2 emitters can be held liable. Douglas Kysar of Yale Law School, for example, argues that:

> [J]ust as automobile and product-caused accidents illuminated extended chains of responsibility in the twentieth century, climate change will challenge prevailing conceptions of wrongdoing in the twenty-first century. When even the most dystopian climate change scenario – such as the complete erasure of territorial homeland for distinct and long-lived civilizations, or the rendering of vast swaths of currently inhabited land unsuitable for human existence due to the threat of hyperthermia – fails to register as a responsibility of any actor anywhere, our principles of causal and moral attribution need to be rethought. As with earlier periods of societal evolution in response to suffering that is uncompensated, undeterred, and unrationalized, tort law will not be exempt from this necessity of reevaluation. Put bluntly, tort law will be forced to adapt or perish, much like life itself in a warming world. (Kysar 2011, 7).

What one sees in this passage from Kysar is a clear application of precautionary principle thinking. As a basis for his concern that climate change could make "vast swaths of currently inhabited land" so hot that they are "unsuitable for human existence," Kysar cites a peer-edited article discussing how increases in global mean surface temperature of 7C would mean that some places are no longer fit for human habitation, while a temperature increase of 11–12C would mean that most of the globe is no longer fit for humans.[1] There is no gainsaying that an increase of 7–12C in surface temperatures would be very bad. But as my climate science report below clearly shows, there is nothing in any IPCC assessment report or in the peer-edited literature even suggesting that temperature increases of anywhere near 7C are a likely consequence even of CO_2 doubling.

On the other hand, as my report also reveals, given uncertainty over positive feedbacks from CO_2-induced warming – the most powerful of which is increased water vapor in a warmer troposphere – climate models do not attach zero probability to such huge temperature increases. That is, such horrific futures cannot be ruled out as certainly impossible. From the precautionary point of view, the only thing one needs to "prove" to justify somehow regulating a potentially risky activity is that it is impossible to prove with *certainty* that a potentially catastrophic and irreversible harm is literally impossible (that is, that it occurs with zero probability). When Kysar concludes that traditional tort ideas about things like the need to prove that the defendant caused harm in a way that seemed at least somewhat blameworthy must be jettisoned, he is on firm precautionary ground. Faced with the potential end of the world, it may actually seem quite modest to say only that tort law itself needs to "adapt or perish."

But of course whatever precautionary vision of twenty-first century tort law might be dreamt up by "progressive" legal academics such as Kysar, to use tort law to attach liability for CO_2 emissions, actual practicing attorneys have to find a legal theory of liability that is at least potentially viable given the current state of the law.[2] The effort to find such a theory and bring tort suits against CO_2 emitters began very early, perhaps soon after the publication of the very short and inconclusive first IPCC AR in 1995. According to one 2010 journalistic account, as soon as he saw that the IPCC had opined in that report that there was a causal connection between "anthropogenic actions and the warming we are experiencing today," a lawyer named Matt Pawa began "working tirelessly to establish global warming as a 'public nuisance' under tort law, holding corporations accountable for their greenhouse gas pollution and forcing them to face their victims in court."[3] According to this same account, to pursue this theory, Pawa founded his own law firm, and spent "three years doing research to understand how this could be done, working with attorneys generals offices, and a lot of people who put a lot of thought and effort into it, and by 2004 we felt like we had found a way to connect all the dots and that's when we filed our first case." That case, *Connecticut et al.* v. *American Electric Power Co. et al.*, alleged that the defendants' CO_2 emissions constituted a public nuisance.

II THE RISE AND DECLINE OF PUBLIC NUISANCE

Broadly speaking, nuisance law attaches liability to land uses that cause harm to nearby landowners or the public. Under the law of private nuisance, if a landowner can persuade the court that an adjacent landowner's land use is a nuisance, the plaintiff can hold the adjacent landowner liable for damages (and possibly even persuade a court to enjoin the activity on the adjacent owner's land that is causing harm). The test varies from one state to another, but in most states, a court will find a private nuisance only if it finds that the harm caused was "serious" and also that the "gravity of the harm outweighs the utility of the actor's conduct."[4]

Private nuisance law applies to control land activities, such as operating a smoke-belching factory, that seriously interfere with an adjacent landowner's "use and enjoyment" of their land. The alleged congeries of harms said to result from rising atmospheric CO_2 levels, however, ostensibly impact virtually everyone anywhere on the planet. Indeed, one of the distinguishing features of emitting CO_2 is that as CO_2 eventually mixes throughout the atmosphere, the harm from any particular flow of CO_2 emissions may be felt by people located across the world. The scope of private nuisance law is far too narrow to provide a useful legal theory upon which to hold CO_2 emitters liable for such far-flung harm.

Another type of common law nuisance action, called public nuisance, provides a much more promising theory of liability. A public nuisance is defined as an "unreasonable interference with a right common to the general public." Under this intentionally vague test, common law courts are bestowed with enormous discretion to determine which activities have made an "unreasonable interference" with some "right" that is "common to the general public." Activities can be categorized as public nuisances if a court finds that they have caused a "significant interference with the public health, the public safety, the public peace, the public comfort, or the public convenience," and that the activity is "of a continuing nature or has produced a permanent or long lasting effect, and, as the actor knows or has reason to know, has a significant effect upon the public right."[5] Needless to say, as industrial firms have been emitting CO_2 since the late-nineteenth century dawn of the industrial revolution, and as the IPCC ARs have unremittingly broadcast the potential "significant" and "permanent or long lasting" harms to public health and public comfort that have been produced by the atmospheric buildup of CO_2 due to such emissions, CO_2 emissions would seem to be an ideal candidate for legal liability as a public nuisance.

A *A Very Short History of the Rise of Interstate Public Nuisance*

According to Novak (1996, 61), until the late nineteenth century, public nuisance was understood to encompass any use of property that injured the whole community, a category of "crimes and misdemeanors" that originally "encompassed almost the whole of modern tort law." Public nuisance was used as de facto means of regulating all kinds of locally undesirable land uses – noxious, polluting trades involving animals such as slaughterhouses, tanneries, liveries, and lard and tallow rendering factories; activities considered morally offensive such as brothels, gambling and dance halls, and theatres; and two serious local fire hazards, gunpowder and wooden buildings.[6] As a regulatory tool, early nineteenth century public nuisance was used to abate smoke and smells from factories, and also – through legal injunctive relief – to force the relocation of locally offensive trades from cities to their outskirts. Rising population and the growth of true urban centers in a sense created land use conflicts, by transforming the neighborhoods in which various noxious trades were located. Public nuisance was a legal tool for localities to cope with these changes. Whereas today, cities use local zoning ordinances to try to minimize and adjust to such land use conflicts in order to protect public health, in the first half of the nineteenth century, local prosecutors brought public nuisance actions (Novak 1996, 217–227).

After the civil war, state legislatures took an increasingly active role in public health regulation and essentially "disenfranchised localities (as well as private citizens) of common law powers to define and abate public nuisances" (Novak 1996, 243). Such state regulation rested on firm constitutional foundations, as state constitutions unquestionably conferred broad police power – the power to regulate private property and contracts so as to protect public health, safety, morals, comfort, and welfare generally. By the 1870s, state attorneys general had clearly established authority to seek injunctions against a wide range of alleged public nuisances. In the vast majority of late nineteenth century public nuisance actions, the attorneys general asked courts to enjoin private activities that were obstructing commerce by blocking rivers, streets, railroads, or ports.[7] Sometimes such actions involved what today would be called environmental harms of various sorts. Famously, for example, in *People* v. *Gold Run Ditch and Mining Co.*, the California Supreme Court upheld the authority of that state's attorney general to bring a public nuisance action to enjoin the defendant gold mining company from continuing its practice of annually discharging six hundred thousand cubic yards of cobbles, gravel, and sand mining waste into the north fork of the American River.[8] And with state legislatures much more active by this time, very often the public nuisance had been declared to be such in a statute. For example, a Pennsylvania court[9] upheld the authority of the state attorney general to sue to enjoin as a public nuisance the sale of liquor on Sunday. Such activity was straightforwardly a public nuisance; a state statute had prohibited it.

Under the basic contours of public nuisance law that emerged during this period, most individuals did not have a legal right to sue for public nuisance. Under the law then established and still in place today, a private individual can bring an action to abate a public nuisance only if that can prove to have suffered an injury "differing in kind and degree from those sustained by other members of the public."[10] And the power of nineteenth century state attorneys general to bring actions to curb public nuisances stopped at the border. When an activity caused harm across a state border – such as pollution from a factory smokestack – the state attorney general of the victim state had no power to use the victim state's public nuisance law to enjoin the out-of-state activity.[11]

With no state law remedy for pollution and other public nuisances that crossed state lines, the only potential legal remedy would have been federal. However, up until at least 1877, Supreme Court precedents had clearly established that under the federal constitution, Congress did not have police power regulatory authority. Indeed, in *United States* v. *DeWitt*,[12] the Court struck down a federal law that regulated the intrastate sale of illuminating oil made from petroleum on the then obvious ground that whereas the federal Constitution conferred the power on Congress to regulate interstate commerce, the federal Constitution did not create anything like a generalized federal police power.

And yet with rapid post-Civil War industrialization, by the late nineteenth century, interstate pollution was an unhappy reality. Eventually, two interstate pollution disputes reached the Supreme Court. The first, *Missouri* v. *Illinois* (1906)[13], was a direct consequence of pollution attendant upon the rapid late nineteenth century growth of the city of Chicago into a major metropolis. In order to deal with a horrendous sewage problem, in 1900, Chicago actually reversed the flow of the DesPlaines River so instead of its natural flow into Lake Michigan, where sewage accumulated on the lakeshore of Chicago, the DesPlaines was engineered to flow into the Illinois River, which flows away from Chicago and eventually into the Mississippi. Of course, Chicago's sewage didn't magically disappear. According to the city of St. Louis, it went downstream and contaminated that city's drinking water with the bacteria that caused typhoid fever. Observing that such an alleged nuisance – "a visible change of a great river from a pure stream into a polluted and poisoned ditch" – was one "which, if it arose between independent sovereignties, might lead to war," Justice Oliver Wendell Holmes Jr.'s majority opinion found that by explicitly extending the judicial power of the federal courts to controversies between states, the Constitution implied authority in the Court to resolve the dispute between Illinois and Missouri.

Holmes said that in exercising this constitutional authority the Court would only intervene in interstate pollution disputes of "serious magnitude, clearly and fully proved." Holmes didn't set out a standard, such as the balancing test found in private nuisance, for how courts were to decide if interstate pollution constituted a legally actionable interstate public nuisance. But Holmes did find it highly relevant that the "discharge of sewage into the Mississippi is to be expected," with the "practice of discharging into the river general along its banks." St. Louis itself discharged sewage into that river, and it conceded that such discharge was "proper within certain limits," but argued that Chicago had exceeded those limits.[14] Holmes's attention to what other cities and St. Louis itself were doing with their sewage suggests a kind of public nuisance reciprocity standard: the Court is unlikely to grant a remedy of any sort if the plaintiff state allows precisely the same conduct that it says is a public nuisance when done by the defendant state.

The bulk of Holmes's opinion is taken up with an overview of the evidence presented by the state of Illinois. This evidence was directed at showing that Chicago's sewage discharge didn't cause typhus in St. Louis. Illinois introduced evidence that because the DesPlaines was now drawing clean water from Lake Michigan, its reversal had actually improved water quality in the Illinois and Mississippi; that the level of typhus bacteria at the mouth of the Illinois had not increased and that whatever bacteria were found at that point likely did not survive all the way to St. Louis; and, finally, that most of the typhus bacteria found in the Mississippi at St. Louis came not from the Illinois but from the Missouri. In the face of such evidence, the Court found that St. Louis had failed to prove its case.

In the other seminal interstate public nuisance case, 1907's *Georgia* v. *Tennessee Copper Co.*,[15] the Court actually issued an injunction ordering a private defendant to curb "noxious" sulfur dioxide emissions from its copper smelter that were being carried by prevailing winds over the state of Georgia. The opinion, also written by Holmes, is notable for clarifying the difference between a private nuisance action, brought by a private landowner, and a public nuisance action, brought by the state suing in its "quasi-sovereign capacity" to protect the interest of its citizens in the air and land within its borders. Holmes stressed that when the states agreed to join the nation, they thereby gave up the right to "forcible abatement of outside nuisances," with the only remaining "alternative to force" being suit in which they presented reasonable demands for abatement of the nuisance to the Court. As for how such reasonable demands were to be balanced, Holmes emphasized that by "joining the union, States did not thereby sink to the position of private owners." With a state as a plaintiff, the Court would give less weight to the "calamity of a stop to defendant's business caused by enjoining it." The Court found that the proof was more than adequate to show that sulfur dioxide gas emitted by the defendant caused harm on a "considerable scale" to the forests and vegetable life if not public health within Georgia and therefore enjoined such emissions.

When one reads *Missouri* v. *Illinois* and *Georgia* v. *Tennessee Copper Co.* together, several themes become clear. First, there is no doubt that Justice Holmes viewed adjudication of interstate pollution disputes by the Court as the *only* way that such suits could be peaceably resolved. When these cases arose, it was universally understood not only that one state had no authority to regulate activities conducted in another state, but that the federal government lacked the constitutional police power authority to regulate generally to protect the environment, health, or safety. Moreover, when Justice Holmes spoke of how such interstate disputes might have "led to war" between sovereigns and stressed the need to provide an "alternative to force," he was not speaking metaphorically. At age 20, Holmes had interrupted his studies at Harvard to enlist in the Union forces. As a member of the 20th Massachusetts regiment, Holmes saw action and was shot through the chest at Ball's Bluff. After he returned to his regiment, Holmes was shot in the back of the neck and nearly killed at Antietam. In 1863, he was shot through the foot near Fredericksburg. As his three year enlistment period ended during the bloodbath of the 1864 battle of the Wilderness, Holmes wrote that "nearly every Regimental off[icer] I knew or cared for is dead or wounded."[16]

Holmes's father, the famous Boston physician and writer Dr. Oliver Wendell Holmes Sr., visited Antietam shortly after the battle there in search for his son. He published a story about his journey in the *Atlantic Monthly*. Many years later, when Holmes was appointed to the Supreme Court, to give readers a sense of who Holmes was, newspapers published excerpts from his father's story about his trip to Antietam. Holmes's most famous public address was not as a judge but as a veteran speaking on Memorial Day to the Grand Army of the Republic union veterans association in Keene, New Hampshire. When Holmes said that the Court was compelled to provide a forum for the adjudication of interstate pollution disputes, he spoke as one with a permanent memory of the catastrophic civil war that had resulted from interstate conflicts.

In addition to a very literal, rather than metaphorical, perception of the need to provide a legal remedy for interstate public nuisance so as to preclude armed conflict between states, Holmes's opinion in *Georgia v Tennessee Copper Co.* is notable for Holmes's relative indifference to the economic loss that the defendant firm might suffer if its pollution was enjoined. In a private nuisance case, a landowner can only get an injunction against a neighboring landowner's pollution if the court finds that the harm from the pollution is greater than the economic harm done by enjoining the polluting activity next door. Holmes suggested that such a balancing was inappropriate in interstate nuisance action brought by a state against a private firm.

This is quite different than the approach that Holmes took to balancing state interests in *Missouri* v. *Illinois*. And yet, according to Holmes, the evidence in the two cases was also radically different. As catalogued above, in *Missouri* v. *Illinois*, Holmes recited abundant evidence indicating that Chicago's sewage was not responsible for typhus far downstream in St. Louis. In *Georgia* v. *Tennesee Copper Co.*, Holmes found it to be completely clear that sulfur dioxide emissions from the defendant's smelter were causing substantial and serious harm in Georgia.

In the Supreme Court's interstate public nuisance jurisprudence, the dispute in *Tennessee* v. *Georgia Copper Co.* is an extreme outlier. The majority of interstate public nuisance disputes adjudicated by the Supreme Court have been between states, and in virtually all of those, the Court did not itself resolve the disputes but instead provided a framework for interstate bargaining that dragged on for years. Indeed, the dispute over the various environmental harms caused by the city of Chicago's reversal of the DesPlaines eventually expanded to include the states of New York, Michigan, and Wisconsin, which argued that the diversion had harmed Great Lakes navigation by lowering the levels of those lakes. That multistate dispute took decades to resolve.

In another similar interstate public nuisance case, 1921's *New York* v. *New Jersey*,[17] New York sought to stop New Jersey from executing a plan to dump sewage into New York Bay. That case too dragged on for decades. To quote the Supreme Court's final observation about that dispute:

> [T]he grave problem of sewage disposal presented by the large and growing populations living on the shores of New York Bay is one more likely to be wisely solved by cooperative study and by conference and mutual concession on the part of representatives of the States so vitally interested in it than by proceeding in any court however constituted.

As this quote indicates, by the early twentieth century, the Court was skeptical of the effectiveness of public nuisance suits and judicial mediation as a way to resolve disputes between the states involving pollution from one state that spilled across state lines.

B *The Rise of Federal Regulation and the Decline of Interstate Public Nuisance*

The Court was stuck in the role of mediating interstate public nuisance disputes, however, only because it had interpreted the Constitution in a way that meant Congress lacked the constitutional authority to regulate to resolve such disputes. As previously mentioned, under Supreme Court precedent, the federal Constitution did not (and still does not) give Congress a general regulatory police power. Up until the New Deal, the Court had also interpreted congressional authority to regulate under the Commerce Clause to mean that Congress could regulate interstate commerce. Under this interpretation, while Congress could regulate, for example, where and how bridges were constructed over navigable waters used for interstate commerce, it could regulate pollution of such waterways only if it could be shown that such pollution somehow affected interstate commerce.

The Commerce Clause explicitly gives Congress only the authority "to regulate Commerce with foreign Nations, and among the several States, and with the Indian Tribes." While one could argue that "Commerce ... among the several states" is actually broader than "interstate commerce," by the late nineteenth century, the Court had solidly read the Commerce Clause as meaning interstate commerce (Weiler 2019, 329). Under this interpretation, there would have been no constitutional authority for primary New Deal programs such as the Farm Security Administration and National Industrial Recovery Act that went far beyond merely regulating interstate commerce and instead directly regulated major industrial sectors. After initially finding New Deal programs to be without constitutional foundation, in the face of Roosevelt's threat to pack the Court, the Court backed down. In *Wickard* v. *Filburn*, 317 US 111 (1942), the Court went so far as to hold that the federal government could limit the amount of wheat grown by a farmer to feed the animals on his own twelve acre farm. That wheat was never put on the interstate market and indeed was deliberately withheld from interstate commerce, but the Court came up with the ingenious theory that Congress could regulate even activities that were wholly intrastate with a trivial tie to interstate commerce if the aggregate effect of such activities could have a substantial impact on interstate commerce.

On this theory (sometimes called the aggregation theory), almost any activity can be found to impact interstate commerce, meaning that almost any activity can be regulated by Congress. Whatever one may think of it – my own view is that it is the height of judicial sophistry – the aggregation theory gives Congress the authority to regulate pretty much any public nuisance one could imagine, both interstate and intrastate. Pollution, for example, is not commerce, but has all kinds of connections to interstate commerce: states clearly do compete to get polluting firms that are competing in interstate commerce to locate within their borders, so that commerce may directly generate pollution; interstate pollution may itself be generated as states compete to attract polluting industries that are located near state borders so as to externalize harm to other adjacent states.

Modern United States federal pollution regulation has all been constitutionally justified under the Commerce Clause. Under the expansive interpretation of congressional Commerce Clause authority, moreover, federal environmental regulation goes far beyond controlling pollution that is primarily interstate – and which therefore could have possibly been viewed as within the Court's interstate public nuisance jurisdiction – to include pollution that has primarily local impacts. Indeed, as argued earlier, the core concerns of the 1970 Clean Air Act and 1972 Clean Water Act were to improve local air and water quality. Congressional focus on interstate pollution came only later.

Still, the main point for present purposes is that once Congress passed statutes covering both local and interstate pollution, those statutes had functionally replaced the federal common law of interstate public nuisance as a means of controlling pollution. In *City of Milwaukee* v. *Illinois and Michigan* (1981)[18] Illinois and Michigan managed to persuade a federal trial court that pathogens and phosphorus in the sewage that Milwaukee dumped into Lake Michigan both posed a health hazard to lake waters used by Illinois residents for drinking and swimming and contributed substantially to the eutrophication of Lake Michigan. But the Supreme Court held that the 1972 Federal Water Pollution Control Act amendments had established "an all-encompassing program of water pollution regulation" that left no room for the federal courts to impose water pollution controls under the guise of the federal common law of interstate public nuisance.

Importantly, the Court explained that under the federal water pollution control law, the states of Illinois and Michigan had explicit statutory rights to participate in the process by which federal water pollution standards were set and permits granted for polluters in the city of Milwaukee and state permits written and granted, and the federal Environmental Protection Agency could veto any permit issued by a state pursuant to the federal regulatory scheme if it found that the waters of another state were affected. The federal agency had a right, moreover, to issue its own permit if negotiations between the polluting and victim states had reached a "stalemate." Passage of the federal law thus obviated a primary concern requiring a federal common law intervention – that a state harmed by pollution from another state would not have "any forum in which to protect its interests."[19] States bargained in Congress over legislation, and the forum for state bargaining over state pollution standards and permits for particular polluters was the federal agency, the EPA, that Congress had created, not the courts.

The state of Illinois responded to its defeat in the Supreme Court by changing its legal theory. In *Illinois* v. *Milwaukee*[20] it alleged not that such pollution was an interstate public nuisance under federal common law – for the Court had held that the federal Clean Water Act displaced the federal common law of interstate public nuisance – but that Milwaukee's sewage discharge was a public nuisance under Illinois law.

That theory was put to rest by the Seventh Circuit Court of Appeals. It held that a state court could not apply the law of a victim state to find that pollution generated by an out-of-state polluter was a public nuisance. As the court reasoned:[21]

> [A]llowing different states to apply their law of public nuisance to a single source of pollution would lead to chaotic confrontation between sovereign states. Dischargers would be forced to meet not only the statutory limitations of all states potentially affected by their discharges but also the common law standards developed through case law of those states. It would be virtually impossible to predict the standard for a lawful discharge into an interstate body of water. Any permit issued under the Act would be rendered meaningless. In our opinion Congress could not have intended such a result.

The Supreme Court declined to hear Illinois' appeal from its defeat in the Seventh Circuit.[22] This ended that case.

The Court, however, had failed to deliver its own opinion definitively resolving whether a state could use its own statutory or public nuisance law to impose tougher pollution standards on out-of-state polluters than were imposed by either the federal government or their home states.

With no such decision by the Court, several federal trial courts located outside the Seventh Circuit issued rulings that directly contradicted the Seventh Circuit's holding. To end this chaos, the Supreme Court finally took a case to explicitly set forth its agreement that states could not apply their own common law of nuisance to effectively regulate out-of-state polluters. In *International Paper Co.* v. *Ouelette* (1987)[23], the Court held that the federal Clean Water Act preempted a suit by a Vermont landowner on the shores of Lake Champlain alleging that wastewater discharges into that lake by a New York pulp mill constituted a nuisance under Vermont law.

Despite the fact that the CWA explicitly preserves an injured person's right to seek relief for injuries "under any statute or common law," the Court found that this did not mean that Vermont's common law of nuisance could be used to determine whether pollution by a New York pulp mill could be enjoined or sued for damages. The Court's opinion clarifies many of the fundamental issues that would arise were state public nuisance law allowed to supplement federal regulatory control over interstate pollution problems.

The Court began by explaining the system that Congress had set up in the Clean Water Act. According to the Court in the CWA, Congress recognized that the ultimate goal of "eliminating" water pollution could not be "achieved immediately" and "without incurring costs." In issuing permits determining allowable levels of pollution discharges, Congress told the federal EPA to consider a variety of factors including available technology for reducing such pollution, the competing public versus industrial uses of the waterway, and the types of pollutants. Source states – states where the polluter is located – had the right to set more stringent standards, but they too had to consider what levels of pollution reduction were technologically possible. The Court explained that Congress wanted to achieve "efficiency and predictability" in the permit-based federal water pollution reduction system.

Allowing any state affected by water pollution from a source in a different state to bring a public nuisance action under its own laws, the Court explained, would "undermine" the system that Congress had set up. Rather than "clear and identifiable" standards for water pollution reduction, polluting firms would be subject to potential damage liability and injunction under "vague" and "indeterminate" state nuisance law standards. In the particular dispute between New York and Vermont, the Court explained:

> If a New York source [of pollution] were liable for violations of Vermont law, that law could effectively override the [federal] permit requirements and the policy choices made by the source State. The affected State's nuisance laws would subject the point source to threat of legal and equitable penalties if the permit standards were less stringent than those imposed by the affected State. Such penalties would compel the source to adopt different standards and a different compliance schedule than those approved by EPA even though the affect State had not engaged in the same weighing of the costs and benefits.[24]

The Court concluded that it "would be extraordinary for Congress, after devising an elaborate permit system that sets clear standards, to tolerate common-law suits that have the potential to undermine this structure."

The *Illinois* v. *Milwaukee* and *IPC* v. *Ouelette* opinions together make completely clear the Court's view that federal environmental regulation itself represents a bargain among the states. Under the terms of this bargain, the federal EPA sets minimum required levels of pollution reduction, and only the states within whose borders sources of pollution are located can set tougher standards. The states who feel only the effects of pollution do not have a legal right to attack as a public nuisance and demand more pollution reduction from out-of-state sources than is required under the terms of the bargain struck in Congress.

From the point of view of economic logic, this makes perfect sense. The cost of reducing pollution is borne generally by four groups: workers – as firms may cut output and lay off workers when they must spend on costly pollution reduction technology; shareholders – to the extent that costly pollution reduction reduces profits; the municipality in which the polluting firms is located, as reduced profits mean reduced taxes to finance local public goods; and consumers, who pay higher prices that reflect the cost of pollution reduction. While some of these costs are widely distributed across states, the most humanly painful costs – lost jobs and lost local taxes – are felt in the state where the polluting firm is located. The voters in such a source state likely bear disproportionately the costs of a decision to promulgate even tougher pollution reduction standards than are required by the federal government. If they nonetheless decide to implement such tough standards, then we can be pretty sure that they also attach a very big benefit to pollution reduction.

No such inference can be drawn from the decision of one state, such a Vermont, to attack as a public nuisance pollution from a source in another state, such as New York. When that source is fully in compliance with federal and home state pollution reduction requirements, as was true in *IPC* v. *Ouelette*, the affected state is effectively trying to get an additional benefit – even more pollution reduction – than under the bargain struck in Congress. Yet Vermont bore none of the cost of such additional pollution reduction. To be more concrete, the International Paper mill in New York provided jobs and local tax revenues in New York, not Vermont. It polluted a shared water, Lake Champlain. Additional pollution reduction at the International Paper plant would provide the benefit to Vermonters of a cleaner Lake Champlain than required by the federal government and the state of New York, while costing Vermonters nothing.

Of course Vermonters, through that State's attorney general, would want International Paper to reduce its pollution, all the way to zero if possible. Every state would have precisely the same incentive to insist upon maximum pollution reduction at out-of-state sources of pollution that spills across the border. Every such state would get benefits but incur no costs, and every such state would claim that the pollution constituted a public nuisance under *its* laws. In most every such suit, the injured state could demonstrate that from the point of view of its citizens, the polluting firm generates only environmental costs, with no offsetting economic benefits such as jobs and local taxes. From the perspective of the injured state, virtually every out-of-state polluter that causes harm to public water (or air) resources but provides few benefits *is* a public nuisance. But as this is true for virtually every injured state, a system in which pollution reduction requirements are determined by the public nuisance laws of various injured states would be one that weighs only the harm from pollution, with no weight at all given to the cost of pollution reduction.

By giving de facto regulatory authority to a governmental entity focused solely on reducing harmful pollution, with no attention to the cost of such reduction, such a system epitomizes what I have defined as an irrational policy. It is, however, perfectly consistent with the precautionary principle. That principle says to regulate if there is any evidence that an activity risks potentially serious or irreversible harm. It pays at best lip service to the cost of regulation, recommending that a cost effective regulatory alternative be chosen.

A system of decentralized interstate pollution reduction – with victim states enjoining out-of-state polluters – would in practice likely give even more consideration to the cost of pollution reduction than the precautionary principle requires. For polluters would have every incentive to bargain around injunctions granted to victim states, agreeing to various pollution reduction steps in exchange for a lifting of such injunctions. Polluters, who pay the cost of pollution reduction, would have an incentive to choose least cost pollution reduction strategies.

As the Supreme Court recognized, the transaction costs of a decentralized victim state–determined interstate public nuisance regime would be enormous. Simple dyadic interstate nuisance disputes are atypical. With interstate air pollution, for example, states in the eastern United States would be suing and seeking injunctions against polluters located in upwind states including virtually the entire midwestern portion of the country. With Mississippi River pollution, the furthest downstream state, Louisiana, could likely find and target polluters in virtually every upstream state – Mississippi, Arkansas, Tennessee, Missouri, Illinois, Iowa, Wisconsin and Minnesota.

More troubling than high transaction costs, a victim state interstate public nuisance regime would leave unrepresented the interests of citizens of polluters' home states. After all, under US corporate law, the fiduciary duties of boards that control private polluting firms run solely to the shareholders of such firms. In bargaining to get out from under injunctions granted to victim states suing to protect their citizens from pollution, defendant firm boards would be risking liability were they to give weight to the effect of such bargains on their workers and citizens of the states within which they were located. Looking out for the best interests of shareholders only, the boards of polluting firms would, among other things, give relatively little attention to the impact of pollution reduction deals on employment.

However skeptical of Congress one may be, it at the very least provides a forum for the representation of the interests of all the citizens of a state. When it comes to interstate pollution problems, bargains struck by senators and representatives and finalized in federal legislation such as the Clean Water Act and the Clean Air Act give weight to a much broader set of citizens' interests in polluters' home states than would the deals between polluting firms and victim states in bargaining around public nuisance – based injunctions.

When it comes to interstate pollution in particular, both the Clean Air Act and Clean Water Act create systems in which the interests of both victim states and polluting states are represented. As the Court succinctly described the Clean Water Act's structure, that law created a "partnership" between the federal EPA and the source state – the state where the polluting activity is located. Such source states generally implement the federal pollution control permit program, and can regulate more stringently by requiring even greater pollution reduction in permits they themselves require. Source states also have substantial discretion to allow polluters to re-route their effluent so that instead of spilling into US waterways, it is piped into local, publicly owned sewage treatment works that treat wastewater before discharging it. As the Court also explained clearly, however, victim states have a "much lesser role" in regulating interstate water pollution under the CWA. This role is purely "advisory," with victim states afforded only a right to be notified before federal and source-state permits are granted and to object to terms of such permits. The source state must consider such victim state objections and comments, and the federal EPA administrator may fail to approve a source state permit if they find that the pollution will have an "undue impact" on interstate waters. But the victim state has no right to veto permits for source state polluters.

In the Clean Air Act, Congress also set up a system of shared federal and state responsibility in which downwind, victim states have only a minor role. As discussed earlier, under this system the federal EPA sets nationally uniform health-based local air quality standards, but states are responsible for coming up with State Implementation Plans (SIPs) to reduce pollution within their borders so as to meet the local air quality standards. With regard to interstate air pollution, Congress did require that state SIPs prohibit air pollution from in-state sources that "contribute significantly to nonattainment" of local air quality standards in a downwind state.[25] Downwind states can complain to the federal EPA that an upwind state is allowing levels of air pollution that are "significantly" affecting its own ability to meet national air quality standards.[26] But it is the federal EPA, and not a judge or jury in the victim state, that decides whether the upwind state is allowing enough pollution to contribute significantly to a downwind state's failure to meet air quality standards. And it is the federal EPA that may require the source state to adopt tougher air pollution standards and that may impose such standards on its own if the source state fails to comply. The downwind state is relegated to the role of lobbying the federal EPA.

Thus, under both the Clean Air Act and Clean Water Act, states play an important role in setting pollution reduction standards, but only in their capacity as the location of pollution sources. Under these federal statutory schemes, states have a much more limited role in their capacity as victims of pollution from upriver or upwind states. That role is essentially limited to complaining to and lobbying the federal EPA for more pollution control in upwind or upriver states. As it gives states only very limited bargaining power in their capacities as victims of pollution from other states, the scheme might at first seem surely to lead to too little pollution reduction. But states are both sources and victims of pollution, and for most types of pollution, the harm from pollution is localized within the state itself. When this is so, states internalize or capture the benefit when in-state sources reduce their pollution. As source state citizens bear most of the cost of pollution reduction, giving source states most of the bargaining power in determining how far to reduce pollution means that such states both bear the costs and reap the benefits of pollution reduction. Such a system is likely to lead to a regulatory outcome that meets the criterion for policy rationality that costs as well as benefits of pollution reduction be considered.

To summarize, the choice is between a decentralized, chaotic system in which interstate pollution reduction requirements are set by bargaining between victim states and the polluters they have enjoined as public nuisances under victim state common law, and a centralized system in which source states must meet pollution reduction requirements set by a federal regulatory agency and their own legislatures. Under a decentralized, victim state public nuisance system, the advocates for pollution reduction at out-of-state sources by definition bear none of the costs of such reduction. Their interest is simply in more pollution reduction, whatever the cost to source state citizens. In the centralized, federal system, by contrast, source states bargain as both sources and victims of pollution from firms within their borders. They are forced to balance the benefits against the costs of pollution reduction.

III CLIMATE CHANGE AS INTERSTATE PUBLIC NUISANCE

To summarize the previous discussion, from its central significance as a form of local land use regulation in the early nineteenth century, public nuisance enjoyed a short period of importance under the guise of federal common law as a mean of resolving interstate pollution problems that arose as a consequence of late nineteenth century and early twentieth century industrialization. That period ended, however, when late-twentieth century federal environmental regulation displaced the federal common law of interstate public nuisance.

Against this background, it should be clear that when the crusading attorney Matt Pawa, selected state attorneys general, and other activist attorneys and their funders began meeting to design and file lawsuits attacking CO_2 emissions as a climate change–causing public nuisance, they faced very long odds of ever actually succeeding with such a suit. The plaintiffs in the suit that was eventually filed, *AEP* v. *Connecticut*, included eight states – California, Connecticut, Iowa, New Jersey, New York, Rhode Island, Vermont, and Wisconsin – three nonprofit land trusts, and New York City. They sued four private electric power providers – American Electric Power Company, Inc., Southern Company, Xcel Energy Inc., and Cinergy Corporation – and the Tennessee Valley Authority, a public electric power provider. (By the time that the Supreme Court heard the case, the states of Wisconsin and New Jersey had pulled out of the lawsuit.)

The composition of the plaintiff and defendant groups matter for two reasons. The most important reason is that the six plaintiff states were suing a group of electric utility companies that did not provide power to the citizens of the plaintiff states and whose CO_2-emitting electricity generating plants were all located in other states. *AEP* v. *Connecticut* thus exemplified precisely the same situation that the Supreme Court had dealt with in *City of Milwaukee*: an attempt by a group of states to use the federal common law of public nuisance to impose emission reduction standards on out-of-state emitters. As the Court pointedly remarked, it had never held that a state could bring such an action to "abate any and all manner of pollution originating outside its borders."

By the time the *AEP* v. *Connecticut* case actually reached the Supreme Court, it was unnecessary for the Court to decide whether out-of-state CO_2 emissions were something that states could enjoin as contributors to climate change. The reason is that the Court had already interpreted the Clean Air Act to regulate GHG emissions, and the Obama administration had made its Endangerment Finding and had already promulgated new GHG emission reduction requirements for automobile tailpipe emissions. Thus there was already an incipient federal regulatory regime for CO_2 (and other GHG) emissions under the CAA. A direct and logical consequence of the Court's prior holding in *City of Milwaukee* was that as CO_2 emissions were already regulated under the CAA, federal common law interstate public nuisance actions against CO_2 emitters had been displaced.

The most important thing about this basis for the Court's decision is that it was not strictly dictated by *City of Milwaukee*. There, the Court was faced with the question of whether to allow interstate public nuisance actions targeting interstate water pollution that was already regulated by the federal EPA. In *AEP* v. *Connecticut*, the EPA had just begun regulating CO_2 emissions under the CAA, and it was far from clear how comprehensive such a regulatory regime would be. The *AEP* v. *Connecticut* Court could have said that the federal common law of interstate public nuisance is displaced only when Congress has enacted a comprehensive federal regulatory scheme delegating regulatory authority to the EPA and the EPA has "actually exercised its regulatory authority." The Court pointedly rejected this option, saying that "the critical point is that Congress delegated to EPA the decision whether and how to regulate carbon-dioxide emissions from powerplants; the delegation is what displaces federal common law." Given such delegation, the Court said even "were ... EPA to decline to regulate carbon-dioxide emissions altogether, ... the federal courts would have no warrant to employ the federal common law of nuisance to upset the Agency's expert determination." In short, because the Court had itself held in *Massachusetts* v. *EPA* that the CAA covered GHG emissions as an "air pollutant," federal common law interstate public nuisance actions seeking to reduce such emissions had been displaced.

Unlike the *City of Milwaukee* line of opinions, the *AEP* v. *Connecticut* opinion did not spend much time explaining precisely how and why federal common law interstate public nuisance actions regulating CO_2 emissions would interfere with federal regulation by the EPA. The Court did observe that such suits would have required that individual federal judges determine, in the first instance, what amount of carbon-dioxide emissions is "unreasonable, ... and then decide what level of reduction is "practical, feasible, and economically viable," decisions that would end up being made in "thousands or tens of thousands" of lawsuits against firms that were "large contributors" to global CO_2 emissions.[27] It does not take a fabulous imagination to see that the problems raised by regulating CO_2 emissions via such a flood of lawsuits would epitomize the harm from the precautionary approach.

As did *AEP* v. *Connecticut* itself, such suits would inevitably have involved states suing out-of-state utilities and other companies for CO_2 emissions that allegedly caused various harms from climate change to the states themselves. The plaintiff states (and environmental groups, if the Court eventually held that they had standing to bring suit) would be notable for internalizing only the potential benefits of CO_2 emission reduction. Their opinion of what constituted a "reasonable" reduction in CO_2 emissions would ignore the cost of such reductions. Of course they would be negotiating for a "reasonable" reduction with firms that did bear the direct costs of such emission reduction, but as stressed above, such private, profit-maximizing firms represent only the interests of their shareholders. Unrepresented by such firms are their employees and the many other employees of businesses who benefit from the firms' presence with the same state, citizens of such states, the localities within which firms pay taxes, and citizens of any other states who lose when such firms are made to incur potentially massive costs to reduce CO_2 emissions. The bottom line is not only that such lawsuits would involve the "chaos" of tens of thousands of negotiations, but those negotiations would have deliberately excluded the interests of hundreds of millions of people likely suffering very real and immediate harm from costly CO_2 emission reductions.

Suits would have been more than merely the perfect instrument of irrational climate policy. They would have faced a raft of serious and likely successful legal challenges. Of course the Court did not need to address such challenges in *AEP* v. *Connecticut*, because it held that CO_2 emission regulation under the CAA had displaced the federal common law of CO_2 emissions as interstate public nuisance. But in other global warming as public nuisance suits brought after *AEP* v. *Connecticut*, the courts have found a long list of terminal legal problems.

Joined by several well-known plaintiff law firms – many of whose attorneys had worked on the many lawsuits brought against tobacco companies – in 2009, in *Native Village of Kivalina* v. *ExxonMobil Corp.*,[28] Pawa sued a group of oil companies and electricity providers on behalf of Kivalina, a native village in Alaska. Located in northwest Alaska on a thin barrier island on the Chukchi Sea, Kivalina alleged that the defendants' CO_2 emissions had caused sea level increases due to melting ice and warmer temperatures that were slowly but surely submerging its island home and that such emissions were therefore an interstate public nuisance under federal common law. The trial court dismissed the case, holding that Kivalina did not even have standing to sue, as it could not show that its injury could be traced to any of the defendants' CO_2 emissions, and its injury was too remote geographically to those emissions. This decision was appealed, and the Ninth Circuit held that even though Kivalina was seeking damages – whereas the states in *AEP* v. *Connecticut* had sought to enjoin CO_2 emissions – Kivalina's suit too was displaced by CO_2 regulation under the CAA.[29]

A different, state law theory of liability was advanced in *Comer* v. *Murphy Oil USA, Inc.*[30] The cleanup from hurricane Katrina had barely begun when *Comer* was filed, and in it a group of lawyers based in New Orleans and Mississippi sued virtually every oil company one could imagine, alleging that their CO_2 emissions had caused Katrina, which had damaged the plaintiffs' property and therefore constituted a state law nuisance. The litigation dragged on for seven years before finally being dismissed by a federal trial court. According to the court, the *Comer* suit failed for several reasons:

- Under federal constitutional law, a plaintiff must produce evidence that it has suffered an actual injury that is "fairly traceable" to the actions of the defendants in order to have standing to even bring a suit. As described by the court, the plaintiffs' theory how defendants' CO_2 emissions had caused Katrina was that "the type of emissions released by defendants, when combined with similar emission released over a long time by innumerable manmade and natural sources across the planet, maybe have contributed to global warming, which may have caused sea temperatures to rise, which in turn may have caused glaciers and icebergs to melt, which may in turn have caused sea levels to rise, which may have strengthened Hurricane Katrina, which damaged plaintiffs' property." According to the court, this long causal chain was far too "tenuous" to establish standing to sue.[31]
- Even if the plaintiffs' harm was "fairly traceable" to defendants' CO_2 emissions, under Mississippi nuisance law, "a claim that defendants' emissions combined over decades or centuries with other natural and manmade gases to cause or strengthen a hurricane that caused damage to personal property is precisely the kind of remote, improbable, and extraordinary circumstance that is excluded from liability."[32]
- The determination of whether the defendants' emissions constituted a public nuisance would require deciding whether their emission levels had been unreasonable, but this would depend upon a "policy determination about the benefits and harms of energy products that are universally relied upon." Such a decision was not for judges to make, but for the EPA.[33]
- Given that Congress had already given the job of determining a reasonable level of CO_2 emissions to the EPA, the plaintiffs' state law nuisance claims "cannot be reconciled with the decision-making scheme enacted by Congress" and were therefore preempted by CAA regulation.[34]

IV BEYOND PUBLIC NUISANCE: CARBON DIOXIDE AS THE NEW NICOTINE

As discussed above, the Obama administration's aggressive use of the CAA to regulate CO_2 began soon after the 2009 Endangerment Finding. To the extent that lawsuits seeking judicial condemnation of CO_2 emissions as a public nuisance were viewed solely as a substitute for federal regulation, Obama administration

CO_2 regulation should have put an end to the global warming public nuisance lawsuits.

The global warming public nuisance lawsuits did stop, resuming when the 2016 election of Donald Trump as president brought a change in the EPA's approach to regulating CO_2 under the CAA. But even during the Obama administration, other lawsuits – based on even more legally implausible theories – were brought seeking damages for or injunctions to stop for harms allegedly done by CO_2 emissions. For climate activists, lawsuits against fossil fuel companies were clearly much more than just a substitute for federal regulation.

We know precisely how much more because of a remarkable "Workshop on Climate Accountability, Public Opinion, and Legal Strategies" held in June 2012, at the Scripps Institute of Oceanography in La Jolla, California (hereafter referred to simply as the 2012 Accountability Workshop). The workshop was organized by two nonprofit environmental interest groups, the Union of Concerned Scientists (the name is misleading, it is an environmental interest group, not some kind of scientific association or society) and the recently formed Climate Accountability Institute. As the Workshop Report explains, the organizers convened it in 2012 because they viewed that time as a "pivotal moment for climate change, with international agreement all but stymied and governmental action in the US largely stalled."[35] The purpose of the workshop is clear from the title of its summary report: "Establishing Accountability for Climate Change Damages: Lessons from Tobacco Control." What the organizers meant by "lessons" was whether and how the "drivers of change that eventually proved effective against the tobacco industry" could be applied to corporate CO_2 emitters.

Common law litigation was foremost among the "drivers of change" covered at the 2012 Accountability Workshop. Workshop "participants weighed the merits" of suing not only companies that emitted CO_2, such as electricity providers, but also coal, oil, and natural gas companies, so-called "carbon producers." Workshop participants viewed the tobacco litigation as having succeeded primarily because of the "front page news" publication of internal tobacco industry documents that depicted "the tobacco industry's lies to the public, its efforts to target children in its marketing campaigns, and its manipulation of the amount of nicotine in cigarettes to exploit their addictive properties." Participants at the Accountability Workshop pointed to the analogous possibility that climate litigation might uncover "incriminating documents" showing that the major fossil fuel companies had had "knowledge ... that the use of their products damages human health and well-being by contributing to dangerous anthropogenic interference with the climate system."[36] Workshop participants clearly understood that evidence of such knowledge would go far to establishing a wrong that cried out for justice.[37]

The end goal of litigation was to succeed in both "spurring action and engaging the public on global warming." Accountability Workshop participants stressed the "need to make conspiracy" among fossil fuel producers "prominent." As to the precise legal theories of liability to be advanced in court, workshop participants were eclectic. The most forceful legal attack would be to allege a civil violation of the federal RICO (Racketeer Influenced and Corrupt Organizations) statute. That statute, however, was passed to enable more effective prosecution of organized crime operations. It requires the plaintiff to show a "criminal enterprise" with at least two acts of racketeering. Even Richard Ayres, the veteran NRDC litigator who suggested the theory, recognized it was an extreme long shot, but he opined that even bringing a losing RICO action would "effectively change the subject to the campaign of deception practiced by the coal, gas, and oil companies."[38]

Other legal theories discussed at the 2012 Accountability Workshop constitute direct attacks on corporate speech and research funding. The possibility that fossil fuel producers might be sued for false advertising was suggested by Naomi Oreskes. A founder of one of the sponsoring organizations (the Climate Accountability Institute), Oreskes is a historian of science who in 2010 published an entire book, *Merchants of Doubt*, that consists of an ad hominem attack on scientists who had dared to question "the truth" on issues ranging from second-hand smoke to global warming. Later, I discuss ad hominem arguments in climate policy in more detail. But Oreskes was not the only workshop participant to support the idea of suing fossil fuel companies for false advertising. Another workshop participant, Joe Mendelson, the director of climate policy at the National Wildlife Foundation, said that false advertising lawsuits could "take on the coal industry's advertising campaign," and "might achieve a victory in terms of public education and engagement."[39]

Accountability Workshop participants also discussed a much more direct legal attack on speech, suits alleging as libelous "fossil fuel industry's attempts to discredit or silence atmospheric scientists." The report noted that climate scientist Michael Mann had already won such a libel suit in Canada, and attorney Pawa explained that the legal requirement of showing harm would easily be met in such suits, as "What could be more harmful than impugning the integrity of a scientist's reputation?"

A final legal theory discussed at the Accountability Workshop was that the CO_2 emissions of fossil fuel companies had violated the public trust in the atmosphere. Such suits have been a prominent part of the post-Trump climate lawsuit landscape, and I explain shortly how they not only represent an extreme form of precautionary policy but also face likely insuperable legal obstacles. At the 2012 Accountability Workshop, Mary Christina Wood, the University of Oregon law professor who pioneered these "atmospheric trust" lawsuits commented that they have the "promising" features of being filed by children as plaintiffs, could be filed in every state, thereby "highlight[ing] the local impacts of climate change," and as they relied on such a flexible legal cause of action, can target "states, tribes, the federal government, or corporations."[40]

What is very clear from the Accountability Workshop is that lawsuits were viewed as only part of an overall "campaign to identify key climate 'wrongdoers.'" Such a campaign was aimed both at moving public opinion, convincing people that "polluters did this and they need to clean this up," and "changing the narrative ...

in the international realm" from one that only holds nations responsible "for the carbon emitted by parties within their own borders."[41] Not only did workshop participants discuss legal strategies, they also considered how to tailor public communications to generate public outrage toward fossil fuel companies. Several leading cognitive psychologists explained recent social psychological findings on the determinants of attitudes toward climate change. Only one psychologist, Daniel Yakelovich, argued that lawsuits might not be the best way to communicate the workshop message of the need for action to a "confused, inattentive, conflicted public." Yet even he agreed that "a legal strategy focused on the industry's disinformation campaign could help advance public opinion on global warming, as it did in the case of tobacco."[42] There is no dissent in the Accountability Workshop report from the view that conspiracy and collusion should be the focus of both litigation and public relations campaigns.

Even in discussing the seemingly technical question of whether and how various harmful changes, such as rising sea level, could be attributed to the CO_2 emissions of particular companies, workshop participants repeatedly returned to the theme of conspiracy and collusion, the "close connections among climate change deniers, the fossil fuel industry, and even the tobacco companies." A participant by the name of John Mashey, whom the report describes as a "computer scientist and entrepreneur who has meticulously analyzed climate change deniers" was reported as having clarified the "extent of the collusion" by tracing "funding, personnel, and messaging connections between roughly 600 individuals and 100 organizations in the climate change denial camp." The Accountability Workshop report states that Mashey had discovered memos from a 1998 "climate denial plan ... involving most of the major oil companies."[43] On my reading, the main focus of the 2012 Accountability Workshop was to strategize about how to use lawsuits against fossil fuel companies to cause as widespread a public perception as possible that such companies had long known that their CO_2 emissions were causing identifiable harm to particular people and places, and not only hadn't done anything to cut such emissions but hid the truth from the public. The end goal was to paint such companies as clear moral wrongdoers.

A *The Tobacco-Inspired Plan in Action: Climate Change Litigation after the Obama Administration*

After the change in EPA regulatory policy regarding GHG emissions following the election of Donald Trump, some municipalities in California and New York that had voted overwhelmingly against him filed global warming public nuisance lawsuits. What is striking in these is the primacy given to the kind of conspiracy theories discussed and strategized about in the 2012 Accountability Workshop. The complaint in *City of New York* v. *BP* that was filed in 2017, for example, begins by alleging that the defendant oil companies' CO_2 emissions made up fully 11 percent of "all CO_2 and methane pollution from industrial sources since the dawn of the Industrial

Revolution," and that such emissions had caused climate change harms to the city including "inundation, erosion, and regular tidal flooding of its property."[44]

The claim that the defendants' emissions were responsible for 11 percent of all CO_2 and methane emissions since the industrial revolution (and, along with about 90 other fossil fuel producers, for fully 71 percent of all GHG emissions since 1988) is based on a single study[45] done by one of the three founders of the Climate Accountability Institute that co-sponsored the Accountability Workshop. I briefly discuss the methodology of that study below, but the point for present purposes is that most of the allegations in the complaint in *New York* v. *BP PLC* concerned not the defendants' emissions, but their wrongdoing in mounting a "public relations strategy" aimed at "downplaying the risks of climate change and promoting fossil fuel use despite the risks."[46]

According to the allegations in the *New York* v. *BP PLC* complaint, the defendant oil companies "knew decades ago that the fossil fuel products they produce and sell were altering the atmosphere and would cause a dire global warming problem," and even as they used this knowledge to "protect their own infrastructure, ... they told the public a very different story." New York alleged that as early as 1980, the defendants received a "scientific warning" that "global warming would cause catastrophic harms," but they "disregard[ed] the findings of their own internal scientists and scientific consultants, [and] re-committed themselves to fossil fuel exploration, production, marketing, and sales over the ensuing decades." Over the following years, "in an effort to protect their market, Defendants orchestrated a campaign of deception and denial regarding climate change. Defendants sponsored publicity campaigns using front groups and paid "scientific" mouthpieces – including some of the same scientists that the tobacco industry had used to downplay the risks of cigarettes – to discredit the mainstream scientific consensus on global warming and downplay the risks of climate change." According to New York, beginning "in earnest" in the 1990s, BP and other defendants began a "coordinated effort to discredit the science ... [and] Defendants and their agents and advocates have made the alleged 'uncertainty' of climate science their constantly-repeated mantra. The purpose of this campaign of deception and denial was to increase sales and protect market share." And according to New York, such a campaign to "discredit the science" still continues, as the defendants "misleadingly tell the public that the science of global warming is uncertain." According to the complaint in *New York* v. *BP PLC*, what made the defendant's fossil fuel production and sale activities really wrong was that they at first ignored the science, and then actually funded scientists whose work was an attempt to "discredit ... climate science" and to "misleadingly" convey to the public that "the science of global warming is uncertain."

It is clear from the report that 2012 "Workshop on Climate Accountability" participants pushed the strategy of emphasizing what fossil fuel companies supposedly knew about CO_2 and climate change but actively concealed because they believed that just such a strategy had been the key to litigation that succeeded in getting damages from tobacco companies. It would be wrong, however, to think that this litigation strategy originated only in 2012. After all, the participants in that workshop included attorneys such as Matt Pawa who had been bringing climate change litigation with similar allegations of conspiracy for many years. Back in 2008, in *Kivalina* v. *ExxonMobil*, for example, the complaint alleged that the defendants – who in that case included not just fossil fuel producers but also electricity providers – used "front groups, fake citizens organizations, and bogus scientific bodies" to try to convince the public that even if global warming caused some "ill effects, there is not enough scientific uncertainty to warrant action." Such evil "tactics" included the "funding and use of 'global warming skeptics,' i.e., professional scientific 'experts' (many of who are not atmospheric scientists)" who publish "marginal views expressing doubts about numerous aspects of climate change science" in places such as the "Wall Street Journal editorial page but rarely, if ever, in peer-edited scientific journals."[47] Thus at least from the 2008 *Kivalina* until today, climate public nuisance cases have been substantially if not primarily about attacking the defendants' efforts to encourage speech that dissented from "climate change science."

Another climate change litigation tradition that post-Trump cases such as *New York* v. *BP PLC*[48] and *City of Oakland* v. *BP PLC*[49] have carried on is that they have been quickly dismissed by the courts. The plaintiffs in these cases have attempted to plead facts that were sufficiently unlike the facts of cases such as *AEP* and *Kivalina* as to persuade the courts that somehow they had not been displaced (if federal common law) or preempted (if state common law) by regulation of CO_2 under the CAA. But they have not succeeded.

In *City of Oakland* v. *BP PLC*, California, on behalf of several of its cities, brought a state and federal public nuisance action against companies that had sold fossil fuels on international markets even after they knew that the "combustion of such fuels had contributed to the phenomenon of global warming."[50] The sale of such fuels and their subsequent combustion, it was alleged, had led to increased atmospheric CO_2 concentration, which was raising sea levels due to global warming, threatening grave harm to the plaintiff coastal cities.

By attacking the sale of fossil fuels on international markets, the plaintiffs actually succeeded in escaping the displacement of their suit by the CAA, for the trial court held that international sales and CO_2 emissions were outside the reach of the CAA and the US EPA. Plaintiffs had, however, gone too far. As the trial court reiterated, the Supreme Court had already said in *AEP* v. *Connecticut* that it was for Congress and the president, not the courts, to undertake the "balancing of policy concerns – including the harmful effects of greenhouse gas emissions, our industrialized society's dependence on fossil fuels, and national security" that entered into the decision about how to regulate GHG emissions. As the court continued, attacking the sale of fossil fuels worldwide raised a whole set of additional legal obstacles. The plaintiffs, the court explained, were trying to impose billions of dollars of liability under US tort law on foreign companies that had engaged in conduct that was not only entirely lawful in every foreign nation but actively supported by many such countries. Global warming, the court noted, was already the subject of a number of international treaties. As the court explained:

> [Q]uestions of how to appropriately balance these worldwide negatives against the worldwide positives of the energy itself, and of how to allocate the pluses and minuses among the nations of the world, demand the expertise of our environmental agencies, our diplomats, our Executive, and at least the Senate. Nuisance suits in various United States judicial districts regarding conduct worldwide are far less likely to solve the problem and, indeed, could interfere with reaching a worldwide consensus.[51]

The court therefore concluded that the plaintiffs had not overcome the strong general presumption against extraterritorial application of US federal common law and dismissed the federal common law of nuisance claims.

The claims in *New York* v. *BP PLC* were also clearly and quickly dismissed. Like the court in *City of Oakland* v. *BP PLC*, the *New York* v. *BP PLC* court said that given the clear international consequences of the claims against international fossil fuel sales and emissions, they were barred by the presumption against extraterritorial application of US law and by separation of powers principles that the executive was the branch of government with constitutional authority over the problem.[52]

B *Pursuing Irrational Policy while Stifling Dissent: The Many Harms of Climate Litigation*

As discussed above, suits alleging that there was somehow an unlawful conspiracy among CO_2 emitters to conceal what they knew about the harms from such emissions and to fund "skeptics ... expressing doubts about numerous aspects of climate change science" and "misleadingly tell[ing] the public that climate change science is uncertain" are not the only recent type of legal attack mounted in the US courts by climate activists. Activist attorneys have recruited child plaintiffs who (through their legal guardians) have sued as "citizen beneficiaries" of the "public trust" in the atmosphere, a trust that states[53] and the federal government[54] allegedly have violated by failing to take sufficiently aggressive steps to reduce CO_2 emissions. While some of these child climate lawsuits have been quickly dismissed by the courts on the sensible ground, among others, that climate change policy cannot constitutionally be made by a single trial court's view of how to best protect the atmosphere,[55] at least one federal trial judge was ready to hold a trial and assume such monarchical authority. In *Juliana* v. *United States*, Ann Aiken – a federal trial judge based in Eugene, Oregon – decided that the child plaintiffs had adequately alleged that the United States had violated the public trust by failing to reduce CO_2 emissions. In the late fall of 2018, Judge Aiken was preparing to hold a trial to adjudicate such a theory when the Ninth Circuit stayed the trial. On that same court's strong and highly unusual recommendation, Judge Aiken reconsidered an earlier decision and allowed the defendants to immediately appeal her ruling on the viability of the public trust theory to the Ninth Circuit.[56]

Prior to *Juliana*, no United States court had ever attempted to regulate any sort of alleged pollution of the atmosphere as a violation of the public trust. The child plaintiff public trust lawsuits rely on a legal theory that is even more tenuous than the public nuisance theory. But of course they feature children as plaintiffs suing on behalf of, among others, the children they might have. Surely one reason to include children as plaintiffs is to dramatize the impacts of climate change on future generations. However, as I discuss in Chapter 10 in more detail, another plausible reason to include children as plaintiffs in public trust suits is to deter any criticism of the people who have brought such suits. Criticizing children who sincerely believe certain things about the potential horrors of climate change on any grounds – as uninformed or naïve or whatever – can itself be labeled not only as mean and unfair but as yet another attempt to suppress the truth conveyed by climate science. Hence, enlisting children as plaintiffs in climate litigation is another way to disable criticism of such suits.

An even more direct legal attack on those who doubt or dissent from establishment climate science is to sue such dissenters for defamation. The most well known such defamation lawsuit was brought back in 2012 by Michael Mann, a prominent establishment climate scientist. Back in 1998 and 1999, Mann and colleagues produced a reconstruction of global average surface temperature going back 1,000 years. It showed no increase in temperatures until 1900, when there was an abrupt increase. The IPCC's 2001 Assessment Report prominently displayed this so-called "hockey stick" temperature reconstruction graph. But 2001 was the last year that the IPCC included Mann's temperature reconstruction. As I show below, a variety of more recent temperature reconstructions going back 2,000 years do not show temperatures sailing off to unprecedented levels during the twentieth century. They generally present a very different picture of temperatures over the last 1,000 years than Mann and colleagues reconstructed, showing not unprecedentedly high twentieth century temperatures but recent high temperatures that are around the same levels seen during the pre-industrial medieval warm period of roughly 800–1100 AD.

Scientific work challenging the methods used by Mann and colleagues to produce their hockey stick temperature reconstruction dates to 2005, when McIntyre and McKitrick published a paper showing the dependence of the Mann et al. reconstruction on tree rings from particular ancient pine trees and on particular statistical methods used to estimate the relationship between tree ring growth and temperature (McIntyre and McKitrick 2005, L03710). Not surprisingly, McIntyre and McKitrick's criticism elicited responses by Mann and others claiming to show that the hockey stick reconstruction was much more robust to things like the choice of tree rings to include as temperature proxies.

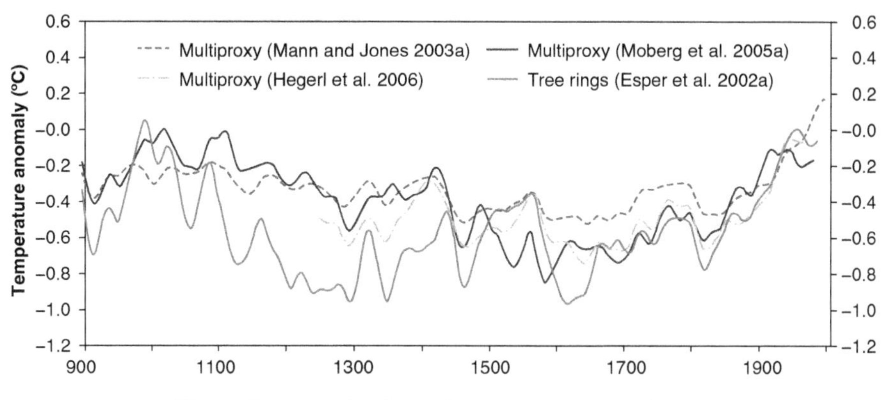

FIGURE 9.1 Alternative reproductions of temperatures over the past 2,000 years

As this suggests, the matter of the validity of the hockey stick graph quickly became quite controversial as a matter of science. Indeed, the National Academy of Sciences (2006) produced a National Research Council Report entitled *Surface Temperature Reconstructions for the Last 2,000 Years*. That report includes a graph, reproduced as Figure 9.1,[57] showing several different reconstructions of surface temperatures over the last 1,000 years. As one can see from the figure, of the three reconstructions that extend back the full 1,000 years, the Mann and Jones reconstruction (the red line) gives the lowest temperatures during the medieval warm period and the highest during the late twentieth century. Two other reconstructions, depicted by the green and purple lines, have temperatures during the peak of the medieval warm period (around 1,000 AD) that are right about at late twentieth century temperatures. Thus according to the NRC's review of the evidence as it was even back in 2006, while Mann's reconstructions showed late twentieth century temperatures at their highest levels in a millennium, other reconstructions did not.

Mann, to his credit, did not bring a defamation suit against scientists who had published work critiquing his own scientific work. His suit arose of out a much more highly publicized science and policy controversy ignited in 2009 when the email accounts of several establishment climate scientists were hacked and literally thousands of their emails made publicly available. This disclosure of email correspondence, dubbed "Climategate," revealed among other things correspondence between Mann and colleagues that suggested to some people that in reconstructing ancient temperatures, Mann and colleagues had made choices about what data to include and how to interpret that data that tended to suppress medieval warm period temperatures. The matter was taken seriously enough that Penn State, where Mann is a tenured faculty member, and the National Science Foundation, which had funded some of Mann's work, investigated charges that Mann had variously suppressed or falsified data to obtain the hockey stick.

None of these investigations found any wrongdoing by Mann and colleagues, but the matter did not end there. In 2012, an adjunct scholar named Rand Simberg at the conservative thinktank the Competitive Enterprise Institute (CEI) published a highly inflammatory post on CEI's website calling Mann the "Jerry Sandusky of climate science." Sandusky, a former Penn State assistant football coach, was convicted of molesting children in Penn State facilities. To settle claims that it intentionally and systematically covered up Sandusky's crimes, Penn State has paid out hundreds of millions of dollars to the molestation victims. Simberg also discussed the substantive, scientific criticisms of Mann's hockey stick reconstruction and quoted prominent meteorologists saying that Penn State's investigation of the charges against Mann had been less than thorough. Later that same year, the media figure Mark Steyn published an online article in the periodical *National Review* quoting and linking to Simberg's CEI post.

Mann brought suit in 2012 in a District of Columbia trial court alleging that he had been defamed by Simberg's post and by Steyn's quotation from and re-use of that post. The defendants sought to immediately dismiss Mann's suit on the ground that it violated the First Amendment to the US Constitution's guarantee of freedom of speech. Both the trial and the appellate court in the District of Columbia disagreed with the defendants, and the Supreme Court declined to hear the appeal on the constitutional question (it denied certiorari, to use the language of Supreme Court practice).

Justice Alito dissented from the Court's decision to deny certiorari. As his dissent clarified, what most people likely find really offensive about Simberg's post – likening Mann to a convicted child molester whose university studiously covered up his hideous crimes – cannot itself be legally defamatory. Defamation requires a false statement, and likening Mann to Sandusky is not itself a false statement. As Justice Alito aptly summarized the law, the First Amendment clearly and absolutely protects even a "pungently phrased expression regarding one of the most hotly debated issues of the day."[58] No one in the Mann defamation lawsuits disputed that climate change qualifies as high visibility and "hotly contested" public policy issue. And no one disputed that Mann has long been an active participant in the climate change public policy debate. Using offensive language to describe an opponent in a public policy debate is hardly unusual, and easily protected from liability by the First Amendment.

But Simberg and Steyn also accused Mann of wrongdoing, and scientific misconduct in the manipulation and torture of data. As Alito's dissent also explained, these statements might be interpreted to be an assertion of fact that could be proven in court to be false. The First Amendment does not protect such statements from liability. A moment's reflection, however, is enough to see that what counts as manipulation and torture of data rising to the level of actual scientific misconduct is a matter of opinion, not a simple on-off factual assertion. Alito would have granted certiorari precisely so that the Court could have set out guidance on when "such an expression of opinion on the quality of a work of scholarship relating to an issue of public concern" is protected by the First Amendment and when it is not. In his view, such guidance was most important in "cases involving disfavored speech on important political or social issues." According to Justice Alito, Mann's defamation action was "just such a case." As Alito explained further:

> Climate change has staked a place at the very center of this Nation's public discourse. Politicians, journalists, academics, and ordinary Americans discuss and debate various aspects of climate change daily – its causes, extent, urgency, consequences, and the appropriate policies for addressing it. The core purpose of the constitutional protection of freedom of expression is to ensure that all opinions on such issues have a chance to be heard and considered . . . the standard to be applied in a case like this is immensely important. Political debate frequently involves claims and counterclaims about the validity of academic studies, and today it is something of an understatement to say that our public discourse is often 'uninhibited, robust, and wide-open'" [concluding with a quote from *New York Times Co. v. Sullivan*, 376 US 254, 270 (1964)].

Justice Alito is clearly correct about the importance of the legal standard for determining when an opinion about the scientific merit of academic research "relating to an issue of public concern" can be false in the sense of triggering potential liability for damages for defamation. And he is also correct about the increasing significance of "claims and counterclaims about the validity of academic studies" to political debate.

As for Alito's second point, whatever misimpression may be conveyed by the media and some politicians, costly actions to reduce GHG emissions are predicated fundamentally on "academic studies" projecting that lowering GHG emissions today will reduce the probability (and magnitude) of future harm. The validity of such studies determines the risks from climate policy, both the potential harm from waiting too long to reduce or reducing GHG emissions too modestly, and the risk that enormous present-day human and environmental costs will be incurred by aggressively decarbonizing the industrial world with little if any future benefit. A legal outcome in which the validity of such studies cannot even be questioned without risking tort liability is one that attaches potential liability to precisely the sort of inquiry that rational policy requires.

The crucial insight contained in Alito's first point is that the Mann defamation action attacks *opinions* about Mann's research. Neither of the defendants made any direct factual assertions. They said that Mann had committed misconduct by manipulating and torturing the data. Whether data has been manipulated or tortured, however, is entirely a matter of subjective opinion. True, precisely what Mann did or did not do with his data would surely be relevant to an informed opinion about whether he manipulated or tortured it. But as of 2021, rare indeed is the empirical academic study in any field where the investigators have not had to make choices about which data to use and which to discard, choices reflecting their views about which data is free from measurement error and other problems and which is not. And as for choices about statistical methodology, those are not just common but inevitable in empirical work.

In the case of Mann's temperature reconstruction, he and his coauthors made choices about what sort of data to use as proxy measures for ancient temperatures (so ancient that there were no direct measurements). In particular, Mann et al. made choices about which tree ring datasets to include and which to exclude. The width of ancient tree rings, however, is only informative about ancient temperatures if one presumes a certain statistical relationship between temperature and annual tree growth. That relationship comes from modern times, when temperature, precipitation, and other growing season variables are precisely measured. The statistical estimation of the relationship between tree ring growth and temperature, for particular trees, is called calibration. The most important academic paper criticizing the original Mann et al. 1,000 year temperature reconstruction, by McIntyre and McKitrick (2005), indeed focuses its critique on the calibration methods used by Mann et al. and on the question of whether particular tree rings are crucial to Mann et al.'s temperature estimates.

To be sure, other researchers responded to McIntyre and McKitrick (2005) producing evidence that they interpreted as showing that Mann et al.'s original results were in fact robust with respect to which tree ring datasets are included and to statistical calibration methodology. (And McIntyre and McKitrick responded in turn to these). This is the scientific process at work. In none of these articles will one find any group of researchers saying that anybody has manipulated or tortured data. The reason is that these are scientifically meaningless terms. They have no place in a scientific paper. If asked whether or not Mann et al. had manipulated or tortured data, a scientist critical of Mann et al.'s methods would simply refuse to answer that question, and instead simply explain the problems they found with Mann et al.'s methods. A scientist who supports the methods used by Mann et al. should likewise refuse to opine on manipulation, but simply describe why they believe that Mann et al.'s methods were valid and reliable.

If scientists called as experts in the Mann defamation suit stick strictly to science – as they must, since they will be qualified to testify only as scientific experts – Mann should be unable to find any scientist willing to opine on the truth or falsity of claims that Mann manipulated or tortured data. Scientists could describe and critique the data selection choices Mann et al. had made and also the statistical methods they used to calibrate the relationship between temperature and tree rings. They could give their opinion as to whether the choices and techniques employed by Mann et al. are likely to be reliable and valid ways to estimate past temperatures. But that's all they could say.

The published allegations that Mann et al. had committed wrongdoing and scientific misconduct are likewise purely matters of opinion. Anybody can have an opinion about whether certain scientific practices constitute scientific misconduct or wrongdoing. Steyn and Simberg expressed the opinion that Mann was guilty of such behavior, but any reader of their online posts was completely free to discount their opinions entirely. After all, neither of these individuals has produced anything indicating that they have any ability to actually understand the various scientific criticisms of Mann el al.'s famous hockey stick temperature reconstruction. There are scientists, scientific organizations, and government and non-government institutions who support science who disagree with Steyn and Simberg. For example, recipients of grants for scientific research from the NSF such as Mann et al. may lose their grants if they are found to have engaged in "Research Misconduct," which the NSF defines as "fabrication, falsification, or plagiarism in proposing or performing research funded by NSF."[59] As mentioned, in the wake of Climategate in 2009, the NSF in fact conducted an investigation and found that Mann et al. had not engaged in misconduct as so defined.

Thus at least one ostensibly expert group, the NSF funding agency, clearly disagreed with Steyn and Simberg. But that is just another opinion. Steyn and Simberg never explicitly asserted that any particular person or organization had found that Mann had engaged in wrongdoing or scientific misconduct. Opinions cannot be legally defamatory unless, as Justice Alito explained, they are read as containing implied factual assertions. But under this standard, the question would be who precisely it was that Steyn and Simberg impliedly asserted believed that Mann was guilty of wrongdoing and misconduct. If one interpreted their remarks as saying, implicitly, that the NSF had found that Mann had engaged in "fabrication, falsification, or plagiarism," then their remarks would be false and defamatory. But such an interpretation is completely unwarranted. More plausibly, Steyn and Simberg were saying that some people with actual knowledge of the hockey stick controversy thought that Mann had committed scientific misconduct. Provided that some such people exist, their assertions were not defamatory.

Because the Supreme Court refused to clarify any of these legal questions, they will be resolved by a trial judge and a lay jury in a single jurisdiction – the District of Columbia. Thus a single judge and jury will determine whether organizations such as the CEI and *National Review* are liable for potentially millions of dollars in damages when they allow their employees to publicly criticize scientific work supporting the case for rapid and costly decarbonization policies. In this sense, common law defamation litigation – like common law litigation generally – is a lottery. The result depends upon the venue and jury that hears the action. What a DC jury might find defamatory could well be found truthful be a jury in, for example, Alabama.

One might well be undisturbed by this prospect, arguing that even if liability is random, depending on where the lawsuit is brought and who sits on the jury, a random risk of potential liability statements might cause those who publish on climate science and policy to be more careful to avoid outright falsity. Inasmuch as false statements mislead and confuse public debate, reducing their frequency may be viewed as socially desirable. This seems entirely reasonable to me, I must confess. The problem, however, is that while the jury in the Mann defamation action would likely hear all kinds of scientific experts testifying as to whether Mann et al. had committed scientific misconduct, the jury is far from expert and subject to a variety of well-known biases and limitations. As I discuss in the concluding chapter, a mountain of social psychological work shows that especially for people with a left-leaning or so-called "progressive" ideological view, climate change long ago ceased being about the science of GHG emissions and climate and became a moralized story about good people who want to save the planet by doing something about known GHG-caused climate change pitted against bad people who care only about making money today. It's hardly far-fetched to imagine that when given the opportunity provided by the Mann defamation action to finally punish with damages those who would criticize planetary scientific saviors, a jury composed of a majority of people holding this moralized worldview of climate change would be relatively indifferent to the legal distinction between assertions of fact versus opinion and to whatever evidence the defendants might present showing the truth of whatever factual assertions may have been implied by their allegations.

Of course, the jury might be composed mainly of people who don't view climate change as a battle between good and evil and such a jury might decide that the defendants statements were not defamatory. But this is precisely the problem with potential liability for engaging in or funding dissident views on climate science and policy: it makes potentially massive liability turn upon the whims of lay jurors. If the plaintiff gets lucky with the judge and jury, the plaintiff can win, and – by selecting where to file the case – plaintiff attorneys get to choose the odds of getting such a judge and jury. Contrast this with the traditional scientific process, where the validity and persuasiveness of competing theories and evidence is contested through the liability-free process of publishing articles setting forth those theories and evidence. "Winning" a long-running scientific debate involves persuading most scientists in the field that one's theory best explains the entire body of evidence; "winning" a defamation court case involves persuading a jury that the defendant's statements should – for whatever inchoate reason, as juries are not even legally permitted to explain the basis of their decision – be punished with potentially massive punitive damages.

Mann's defamation action has the virtue of attacking as false statements made outside the scientific arena. A more disturbing use of the courts is presented by a lawsuit filed by Stanford atmospheric chemist Mark Jacobson, who brought a defamation action against the National Academy of Sciences as publisher and the lead author of a scientific paper, Clack et al. (2017), that criticizes two scientific papers by Jacobson, Delucchi, Cameron et al. (2015) and Jacobson, Delucci, Bazouin et al. (2015). The scientific dispute centers around the argument by Jacobson et al. that it would be both technologically and economically feasible to convert the US electric supply system to rely solely on wind, solar, and hydropower.

This would require among other things a massive increase in hydroelectric power supply. As I discussed earlier, American environmentalists have opposed big new hydropower projects for decades, seeking to remove old dams, rather than make major changes to them in order to increase their power output. Clack et al. (2017, 6722–6727), a group of 21 environmental scientists, argued that while such a future was, with an unlimited budget, technologically possible, it would involve incredible cost and cause great present day harm to traditional environmental values.

What matters for present purposes is that rather than fighting out this dispute in the scientific literature, Jacobson brought a lawsuit seeking to punish his academic critics with $10 million in damages for disagreeing with him. As yet another indication of how where a lawsuit is filed is itself a strategic choice, Jacobson, based in California, brought the suit in the same court – the DC trial court – chosen by Mann for his defamation action. However friendly might be a DC jury to Jacobson's suit, DC has a statute allowing dismissal of defamation actions that are found by the court to be intended to stifle public debate. Jacobson dropped his suit when facing a motion to dismiss it under that statute, but his lawsuit already had an impact in silencing scientific and policy debate and dissent. After the lawsuit was filed, neither Jacobson nor Clack would speak directly with the media, referring reporters to their lawyers. One of Clack's co-authors reported that after the Jacobson lawsuit, "Even when I'm talking with other scientists in an on-the-record setting, I find myself being careful about that I say because there's the threat of legal action out there."[60] Thus insofar as the purpose of Jacobson's suit was merely to stifle criticism and scientific debate, it seems to have succeeded regardless of its legal merits.

C *What the Climate Change Lawsuits Omit: Challenging the "Science"*

Scientific and statistical evidence is at the heart of many legal disputes. In virtually any product liability case involving alleged harm from a drug or chemical product, for example, the plaintiff must introduce expert testimony supporting the allegation that the plaintiff's injuries have in fact been caused by use of or exposure to the defendant's product. And the defendant has a legal right to rebut this evidence with testimony by its own experts that exposure did not, in the relevant legal sense, cause the plaintiff's harm.

Climate change litigation such as the public nuisance cases is based on a very large number of crucial factual allegations. For example, the most recent lawsuits by cities on the west and east coasts of the United States allege that the defendants' CO_2 emissions are causing rising temperatures and sea levels, and that such changes will cause serious harm to these cities. As in any legal dispute, evidence for and against factual allegations such as these only is considered if the court first decides that the allegations, if true, might make out a legally valid claim. As I have described above, none of the climate change lawsuits has made it past this hurdle. All have been dismissed as legally flawed, and in none has any legal factfinder heard evidence pro and con the plaintiff's factual allegations.

Of course, as shown by the 2012 Accountability Workshop Report discussed earlier, a finding by a jury or judge of a causal link between fossil fuel CO_2 emissions and various harms from climate change was never the goal of climate change litigation activists. They viewed litigation just as one part of an overall strategy to identify climate "wrongdoers," thereby moving public opinion and shifting the narrative in the international political realm. A trial at which the plaintiffs and defendants would present conflicting expert evidence on whether the defendant fossil fuel companies' CO_2 emissions were the legal cause of temperature and sea level increases of some particular magnitude was never the main objective of climate change litigation activists.

This is not to say that the plaintiffs could not have found scientists willing to testify for them. Myles Allen, a leading IPCC establishment climate scientist and a participant in the 2012 Accountability Workshop, had published an article in 2004 claiming that simulations with general circulation climate models showed that the likelihood of the 2003 European heatwave had been vastly increased by human GHG emissions (Stott et al. 2004, 610). Around the same time, Allen editorialized on a method that he dubbed "probabilistic event attribution" (Allen 2003, 891). Under this approach – which he elaborated in a *University of Pennsylvania Law Review* article (Allen et al. 2007, 1353) written for a symposium that I organized – the increase in the risk of various weather events is quantified by running simulations with general circulation computer models. Run over potentially very long periods of thousands of years (so as to allow the system to fully incorporate all the effects of a "forcing" such as elevated CO_2), such simulations generate final or equilibrium distributions of climate variables such as summer average temperatures – that is, equilibrium climate states that are characterized by probabilities. By "probabilistic event attribution," Allen means that one can compare the model-generated probability of some event like the summer 2003 European heat wave in worlds with and without anthropogenically elevated atmospheric CO_2.

The first response of a competent defense attorney to an attempt to use Allen's "probabilistic event attribution" methodology to show that defendant fossil fuel companies' CO_2 emissions had "caused" things like sea level rise would be to searchingly question the reliability of the computer models that generate the event probabilities. I do this in Part II in some detail, where I simply report on what one finds published in the scientific literature and the IPCC's own reports regarding what computer simulations of climate do and don't do. Part II is a bit of a long haul (the gist of which is summarized in an introduction), but among other things, a defense attorney would surely point out that one cannot rely on a computer model's future climate projections unless that model can at the very least accurately reproduce past climate, and yet the computer models used by Allen et al. reproduce twentieth century climate change only by arbitrarily setting the numerical value of things such as the response of clouds to increasing atmospheric CO_2 – something that is not even close to being understood – so as to get the right temperatures. That is, the models do not actually reproduce twentieth century temperatures; rather, twentieth century temperatures are allowed to determine the numerical parameters that drive the models. Other things that a defense attorney should point out include the fact that the models run by Allen and colleagues focus entirely on external "forcings" of the earth's climate system (things like increasing atmospheric aerosols such as SO_2, variations in solar activity, and GHGs) and (at least in the main model runs thus far) do not incorporate the impacts of regional scale development and land use conversion that are known to increase surface temperatures. Another – but by no means the final – problem with the simulations that Allen et al. use to generate their "probabilistic event attribution" is that as run by Allen et al., the computer simulations do not incorporate black carbon or soot, a pollutant (and an atmospheric "forcing") that in some regions of the world is even more important in increasing temperatures than CO_2. These regions include the Arctic, where some scientists believe that black carbon is responsible for most of the much publicized twentieth century warming.

Surely these aspects of Allen et al.'s computer simulations would be highly relevant to a judge or jury's decision about the reliability of the probabilities these models attach to things like temperature increases and sea level rise. The model simulations, after all, would be the primary if not the sole basis for Allen's opinion. To be sure, none of the climate lawsuits proceeded to trial, so the reliability of computer climate model projections has never been tested through the full trial process. There has been at least one recent opportunity for lawyers to critically analyze the validity of the climate model projections, but that opportunity was not taken.

The opportunity was provided by a rather unusual climate science "tutorial" convened by US District Judge William Alsup, who presided over and in 2018 dismissed the City of Oakland public nuisance climate change litigation. At this May, 2018 tutorial, Judge Alsup allowed both the plaintiff and the defendants to bring in experts to educate him about climate change. Myles Allen was the primary expert for the plaintiff, which also brought in two other climate scientists. The defense, however, called no expert witnesses. The defense presentation of climate science was made solely by its lead litigation counsel, Theodore Boutrous. Mr. Boutrous is a highly skilled and famous litigator, who is renowned especially for his diligent appellate representation of media organizations and as a "crisis management strategist." There is nothing in his background to suggest, however, that Mr. Boutrous has any real familiarity with climate science or that he has the technical training to have come up to speed on the science in time to deliver a detailed explanation to the court. Despite this, Mr. Boutrous's attempt to overview climate science for the court makes up the bulk of the tutorial transcript (about 80 out of 190 pages, versus only 50 pages of testimony by Professor Allen). At no point in the transcript does Mr. Boutrous attempt to actually question any of the assertions made by any of the plaintiff's experts. And Mr. Boutrous called no expert witnesses; nowhere in Judge Alsup's climate tutorial can one find an expert scientist critically analyzing any of the many assertions made by the plaintiff's experts about climate change.

Yet many of these assertions represent opinions with which many highly credentialed climate scientists disagree. A central assertion to the court by Allen[61] is that the "fingerprint" of anthropogenic GHG-driven warming can be identified by fixing the external forcers of variation in total solar and volcanic activity within a climate model and then comparing observed warming with warming simulated by the model, with the difference being ascribed to the impact of anthropogenic GHGs. This assumes that the computer models have been validated by reproducing climate variables at both global and regional scales, and, as I discuss later in the book, many climate scientists do not believe that the models have been so validated. Donald Weubbles, a plaintiff expert testifying about various impacts of climate change on the United States, asserted[62] to the court that "temperatures now are well above anytime in the last 2,000 years." To see how shaky is this assertion, one can again look later in this book, where I present the set of 2,000-year temperature reconstructions that the IPCC displayed in its 2013 AR. Or one could look back where earlier in this chapter I presented the various 1,000-year temperature reconstructions displayed in the 2005 NRC report on the hockey stick controversy. Both of these show that recent temperatures may be returning to levels reached during the medieval warm period, not that they have clearly exceeded those levels.

With no experts called by the defense, there simply was no questioning of any of the assertions made by the plaintiff's experts in *California* v. *BP PLC et al.* One supposes that this was likely for strategic reasons, as Mr. Boutrous perhaps deemed that questioning anything said by any sort of climate scientist would cast his clients in a bad light with the broader public. If this was indeed the reason that the defense called no experts, then it was hardly unintended. After all, as explained by the 2012 Attribution Workshop participants – who included Professor Allen – a major goal of the CO_2-as-tobacco litigations was to liken fossil fuel producers to cigarette companies whose wrong was not just or even mainly in producing cigarettes, but in intentionally misleading the public about the risks of smoking. All of the climate change litigation has received extensive media coverage[63] so that the goal of using such litigation to publicly label various companies as wrongdoers – in large part because they allegedly funded scientific and policy dissenters – has been achieved. That the public relations impact of the climate change lawsuits would itself chill vigorous legal defense was clearly anticipated by one participant in the 2012 Attribution Workshop, Stanford Glantz.

A medical school professor at the University of California San Francisco, Glantz is described by his webpage as producing the first "major review" paper identifying secondary smoking as a cause of heart disease and the publisher of a book, *The Cigarette Papers*, "which has played a key role in the ongoing litigation surrounding the tobacco industry."[64] Glantz is described as a "tobacco control activist" who after obtaining his PhD in mechanics became a leader in the campaign to show harms from second-hand smoke. He published a famous paper purporting to show that the adverse cardiovascular effects of second-hand smoking were as large as the adverse effects from actually smoking and another paper purporting to show that hospital admissions for heart attacks in Helena, Montana fell after that city banned smoking in public buildings and outdoor areas.[65]

At the Climate Accountability Workshop, after some cautionary remarks from Myles Allen that calculations as to what portion of various adverse impacts, such as sea level rise, could be attributed to the "emissions caused by a single carbon-producing company" were "not complicated" but yet "easy to get wrong," Glantz "expressed enthusiasm" about the strategy of attributing particular harmful impacts to emissions from individual companies. He said that based on his "experience with tobacco litigation … I would be surprised if the industry chose to attack the calculation that one foot of flooding in Key West could be attributed to ExxonMobil. They will not want to argue that you are wrong and they are only responsible for one half-foot. That is not an argument that they want to have." For similar reasons, he said, tobacco companies have never challenged death estimates, noting "their PR people tell them not to do that, focusing instead on more general denial and other tactics."[66] Thus filing lawsuits was anticipated to deter vigorous and fine-grained defense in such suits.

This was not just due to the potentially negative public relations impact from challenging the plaintiffs' experts. In *California* v. *BP PLC*, the defendants, through Mr. Boutrous, may have been well advised merely as a matter of legal strategy to avoid mounting such a challenge. Judges are members of the public, and one of the most noteworthy aspects of Judge Alsup's opinion in that case was the great effort taken by the court in stressing that by no means did the judge have any doubts about the basic impacts of anthropogenic CO_2 emissions. To quote the opinion:

> "The issue is not over science. All parties agree that fossil fuels have led to global warming and ocean rise and will continue to do so, and that eventually the navigable waters of the United States will intrude upon Oakland and San Francisco";[67]
>
> "[I]t is true that carbon dioxide released from fossil fuels has caused (and will continue to cause) global warming";[68]
>
> "This order fully accepts the vast scientific consensus that the combustion of fossil fuels has materially increased atmospheric carbon dioxide levels, which in turn has increased the median temperature of the planet and accelerated sea level rise";[69]
>
> "In sum, this order accepts the science behind global warming. So do both sides."[70]

With the court so clearly convinced of some of the plaintiff's most basic allegations, the defense might well have correctly perceived significant legal risk in contesting any of the many assertions made by plaintiffs' experts that went well beyond such basics.

However, as my later overview of climate science shows, while it is beyond dispute that human activities have impacted global climate, they have done so in many ways beyond increasing atmospheric CO_2. In particular, the evidence is overwhelming that land use conversion and urbanization and the emission of black carbon (or soot) have substantially contributed to elevated surface temperatures in many regions of the world. The legal causation issue in cases such as *California* v. *BP PLC* is not whether human activities in general have impacted global climate, it is the *magnitude of the impact of the defendants' CO_2 emissions*. To estimate this magnitude, other influences must be measured and carefully controlled for in any kind of analysis that is done (statistical, computer 3D climate modeling or lower dimensional climate modeling). Precautionary climate science has failed to do this, precisely because it is precautionary, focusing on establishing evidence supporting regulatory interventions to reduce CO_2 emissions, rather than actually understanding and quantifying the full set of human influences on climate. As the defense in California v. BP PLC completely failed to present any of this, it ended up managing a climate tutorial that did not inform the court as to the real issues in the case.

Notes

1. This is from Kysar (2011, 7), citing Sherwood and Huber (2010, 9554).
2. For more information on legal remedies for global warming, see Grossman (2003, 1); Pawa (2005, 407); Drabick (2005, 503); Harper (2006, 661)
3. Amy Westervelt, The Man who Makes Greenhouse Polluters Face their Victims in Court, Attorney Matt Pawa has applied tort law to global warming and provoked groundbreaking rulings, InsideClimate News, June 22, 2010, https://insideclimatenews.org/news/20100622/man-who-makes-greenhouse-gas-polluters-face-their-victims-court.
4. Restatement 2d of Torts Section 826.
5. These factors are set out in the Restatement 2d of Torts § 821B (1979).
6. This can be found throughout Novak 1996, for example on pages 63, 71–81, 157–171, and 217–227.
7. These ran the gamut from a Michigan logging company's blocking most of the width of a river for two miles with logs, booms, piers, piles and timber, *Attorney General ex rel Muskegon Booming Co.* v. *Evart Booming Co.*, 34 Mich. 462 (1876), to
8. *People* v. *Gold Run Ditch and Mining Co.*, 66 Cal. 138, 4 P. 1152, 56 Am.Rep. 80 (1884).
9. *Wishart* v. *Newell et al.*, 4 Pa.C.C. 141 (1887).
10. *People* v. *Gold Run Ditch and Mining Co.*, 66 Cal. 138, 153 (concurring opinion).
11. *Pennsylvania* v. *Wheeling & B. Bridge Co.*, 13 How. 518, 14 L. Ed. 249 (1851).
12. *International Paper* v. *Ouelette*, 107 S.Ct. 805, 810–811.
13. 26 S.Ct. 268, 200 US 496 (1906).
14. 26 S.Ct. at 269.

15. 206 US 230 (1907).
16. Susan Mary-Grant, Oliver Wendell Holmes Jr., Essential Civil War Curriculum, available at https://www.essentialcivilwarcurriculum.com/oliver-wendell-holmes-jr.html.
17. 256 US 296, 313 (1921).
18. 451 US 304.
19. *City of Milwaukee* v. *Illinois and Michigan*, 101 S.Ct. 1784, 1797 (1981).
20. 731 F.2d 403 (7th Cir. 1984).
21. *Illinois* v. *Milwaukee*, 731 F.2d 403, 414 (7th Cir. 1984).
22. More precisely the Court denied certiorari at 105 S.Ct. 979 (1985).
23. 479 US 481.
24. 479 US 481, 495.
25. This requirement is found in Clean Air Act 110(a)(2)(D)(i)(I), also called the "good neighbor" provision.
26. The downwind state petition right is found in Clean Air Act Section 126(b).
27. *AEP* v. *Connecticut*, 131 S.Ct. at 2540.
28. 663 F. Supp. 2d 863 (N.D. Cal. 2009).
29. *Native Village of Kivalina* v. *ExxonMobil Corp.*, 696 F. 3d 849 (9th Cir. 2012).
30. 839 F. Supp. 2d 849 (S.D. Miss. 2012).
31. 839 F. Supp. 2d at 861–862.
32. 839 F. Supp. 2d at 867–868.
33. 839 F. Supp. 2d at 864–865.
34. 839 F. Supp. 2d at 865.
35. Climate Accountability Institute and Union of Concerned Scientists, Establishing Accountability for Climate Change Damages: Lessons from Tobacco Control, October, 2012, available at https://www.ucsusa.org/sites/default/files/attach/2016/04/establishing-accountability-climate-change-damages-lessons-tobacco-control.pdf.
36. Accountability Workshop Report at 9.
37. Accountability Workshop Report at 10.
38. Accountability Workshop Report at 13.
39. Accountability Workshop Report at 13.
40. Accountability Workshop Report at 14.
41. Accountability Workshop Report at 18.
42. Accountability Workshop Report at 24.
43. Accountability Workshop Report at 19.
44. *City of New York* v. *BP PLC*, Complaint, p. 4, Doc. No. 1 (Case No. 18-cv-00182-JFK S.D. N.Y. filed 01/09/18).
45. Richard Heede, Tracing Anthropogenic Carbon Dioxide and Methane Emissions to Fossil Fuel and Cement Producers, 1854–2010, Climatic Change, Jan. 2014.
46. *City of New York* v. *BP PLC*, Complaint p. 2. Subsequent quotes from the complaint come from pp. 2–5.
47. *Kivalina* v. *ExxonMobil*, complaint, p. 47.

48. The opinion dismissing this case is *City of New York* v. *BP PLC*, 325 F. Supp. 3d 466 (S.D. N.Y. 2018).
49. *City of Oakland* v. *BP PLC*, 325 F. Supp. 3d 1017 (N.D. Cal. 2018).
50. *City of Oakland* v. *BP PLC*, 325 F. Supp. 3d 1017, 1022 (N.D. Cal. 2018).
51. *City of Oakland* v. *BP PLC*, 325 F. Supp. 3d at 1026.
52. *City of New York* v. *BP PLC*, 325 F. Supp. 3d 466, 475–476 (S.D. N.Y. 2018). The court there also held, at 472–473, that New York's federal common law of public nuisance claims against CO_2 emitters had been displaced by Connecticut v. AEP.
53. *Kanuk* v. *State of Alaska Department of Natural Resources*, 335 P.3d 1088 (Alaska 2014).
54. *Juliana* v. *United States*, 217 F.3d 1224 (D. Ore. 2016).
55. *Kanuk* v. *State of Alaska DNR*, supra.
56. *Juliana* v. *United States*, slip opinion, 2018 Westlaw 6303774 (D. Ore. Nov. 21, 2018).
57. Figure 9.1 reproduces Panel C from Figure O-5, "Large-scale surface temperature variations since A.D. 900 derived from several sources" NRC (2006, pp. 16–17).
58. *National Review, Inc.* v. *Michael E. Mann*, *Competitive Enterprise Institute et. al.* v. *Michael E. Mann*, 589 US __ (2019) (Justice Alito, dissenting).
59. See NSF, Proposal and Award Policies and Procedure Guide, Chapter XII: Grant Administration Disputes and Misconduct, available at https://www.nsf.gov/pubs/policydocs/pappg19_1/pappg_12.jsp#XIIC.
60. Michael Hiltzik: A Stanford professor didn't just debate his scientific critics – he sued them for $10 million, L.A. Times, Nov. 21, 2017, available at https://www.latimes.com/business/hiltzik/la-fi-hiltzik-jacobson-lawsuit-20171121-story.html.
61. *California* v. *BP PLC et al.*, No C 17–6011 WHA, tutorial transcript at pp. 41–57.
62. Tutorial transcript at pp. 164–165.
63. Some representative articles include Felicity Barringer, Flooded Village Files Suit, Citing Corporate Link to Climate Change, NYT, Feb. 27, 2008, available at https://www.nytimes.com/2008/02/27/us/27alaska.html, Paul Webster, Is it time to hand global warming to the lawyers? The Toronto Star, April 29, 2007.
64. Available at https://tobacco.ucsf.edu/people/stanton-glantz-phd.
65. Glantz (2005, 2684–2698), and a study purporting to show a large reduction of people admitted to the hospital in Helena after that city banned smoking from public buildings and outdoor areas, "The Helena Study (Abstract)," Retrieved 2007–05-01.
66. Accountability Workshop Report at 19.
67. *California* v. *BP PLC*, 325 F. Supp. 3d at 1022.
68. Ibid. at 1023.
69. Ibid. at 1026.
70. Ibid. at 1029.

PART II

The Other Side of the Story

The Structure, Process, and Output of Climate Science Assessment Institutions and the Science They Neglect

10

But Is It True?

The Case for Taking a Critical Look at the Economic and Physical Science Underlying Estimates of the Benefits of GHG Emission Reduction

In this part of the book, I take a critical look at the beliefs about the state of scientific knowledge about climate change and its economic impacts that are commonly taken to support the precautionary policies explicated in Part I. Such an inquiry is necessary because a balanced and rational climate change policy must be based on both what is actually known and what is unknown about climate change and its impacts.

By a balanced policy I mean a policy that takes account of two types of errors that are possible when policies are chosen under conditions of uncertainty. The first type of error is often called a false negative – a failure to regulate when in fact there is actually a risk of serious and irreversible harm. The second of type of error is called a false positive – a decision to regulate a risk that is not realized.

The precautionary principle focuses solely on the cost of a false negative, potentially serious and indeed irreversible harm to human health or the environment that occurs because of a failure to regulate. It does not weigh the cost of false positives. But false positive may also be costly.

A false positive is a decision to regulate that turns out to have been wrong, in the sense that the probability of harm was smaller and/or the magnitude of the harm smaller than believed. The cost of false positive depends upon what kind of regulation is adopted. In the most well-known instances where regulation has been justified by the precautionary principle, the regulation is a ban on the risky activity. This is perhaps the simplest regulatory response – if something risks serious and irreversible harm, then ban it.

Such bans have costs. The costs were not large in the case of the Montreal Protocol's CFC ban and the European ban on Canadian and US beef. But as the previous part of this book has established, the combination of US policies aimed at effectively banning coal mining and use and subsidizing various renewable energy sources have caused substantial and in many cases irreversible harm. The Obama-era regulatory war on coal likely put hundreds of thousands of people out of work and decimated entire regional economies. Federal and state policies subsidizing or mandating the use of renewable power have harmed the present-day environment, increased electricity and automobile prices, and made the job of ensuring electric system reliability much more complex and costly. Economists know that sustained periods of unemployment kill. Ecologists know that gigantic wind farms kill birds and bats. What may seem to be purely economic costs of precautionary climate policy – higher prices for energy and transportation – disproportionately harm poorer households, for whom an increase in the price of things like electricity forces painful reductions in other expenditures on necessities of life.

Many people seem to have to the opinion that however serious may be these costs, there is zero probability that they were erroneously imposed. More precisely, many people have come to believe that that increases in CO_2 emissions will certainly cause serious and irreversible harm, meaning that there is a zero probability that any action taken today to reduce CO_2 emissions could turn out to be erroneous. It might seem that if one believes this, then precautionary regulation is a no-brainer.

As near as I can discern, the "many people" who believe that there is literally no risk of erroneous climate change regulation include virtually every American environmental law scholar (except, apparently, me). Such scholars have found the conclusions about climate science set out in Assessment Reports by the IPCC and the USGCRP (and the related US Climate Change Research Program or CCRP) to establish as a matter of complete certainty that human CO_2 emissions are responsible for all industrial era (post late nineteenth century) temperature increases and that continuing increases in CO_2 emissions will lead to far bigger and more harmful such changes in the future unless emissions were quickly reduced.

We can see this by looking at the views of several important environmental law scholars.

- Georgetown Law School Professor Lisa Heinzerling, who led the Obama administration's Endangerment Finding effort, had several years earlier written that "for a long time, climate change has been the exemplar for application of the precautionary principle" Heinzerling (2008, 452). Indeed, according to Heinzerling, even by 2008, "the scientific debate over whether climate change is happening, and whether it will hurt us, is over; the important questions are when it will get worse and by how much," questions to be analyzed under something called the "post-cautionary principle."
- In the process of criticizing cost-benefit analysis as a framework for analyzing alternative climate policies, way back in 2004 (when there had been only one full-scale IPCC assessment), Yale Law School Professor Douglas Kysar (2004, 567) suggested that a better approach would be one that "presumes an inalienable right held by each generation to the benefit of a minimally stable climate and a corresponding duty on the part of each preceding generation not to act in

a manner that jeopardizes the baseline level of climate stability." On this explicitly precautionary view, even the possibility of a future world in which climate is "severely and irreversibly disrupted" justifies cutting GHG emissions to a level at which such a catastrophic future world no longer seems plausible."

- While rejecting most versions of the precautionary principle, Harvard Law School Professor Cass Sunstein – who was the Obama administration's first head of the OMB office responsible for regulatory cost-benefit analysis – nonetheless way back in 2005 (Sunstein 2009, 27), described "general agreement that global warming is in fact occurring," with a "possibility" of a mean temperature increase of 4.5°C, with a "significant number of deaths from malaria," and up to $5 trillion in monetized costs.
- Finally, commenting in 2015 on EPA's invocation of the precautionary principle to justify its Endangerment Finding, Cal Berkeley Law School Professor Daniel Farber (2015, 1684) asserted without qualification that "scientific developments since the finding was made have only strengthened the conclusion that climate change is a threat to human health and welfare." According to Farber (2015, 1675), all kinds of serious and/or irreversible harm are now known to be potential consequences of climate change, including passing a tipping point where the earth's climate spins off into a world of heat or cold incompatible with human civilization, and irreversible mass die-off of nonhuman species.

Every one of the legal scholars just cited has no doubt about the potential harm from climate change, whether potentially catastrophic shifts in global climate, or "irreversible harm [that] could occur to ecosystems as their resilience levels are exceeded" with a wave of species extinctions "akin to the great extinction events in the geologic record" (Farber 2015, 1684). As Heinzerling (2008) pronounced shortly before leading the Obama administration's Endangerment Finding:

> According to the latest scientific research, we can expect the following in our warming world: disease carrying insects will alter their ranges, ... causing more widespread incidence of vector borne diseases such as malaria, ... crop productivity will decline, causing a concomitant increase in the risk of malnutrition, ... water supplies will decrease due to reduced snowpack and increased drought, storms will become more frequent and severe, threatening Katrina-like consequences for human health and welfare; diarrhoeal disease will increase due to floods and drought, cholera will grow more frequent due to higher water temperatures.

The IPCC and USGCR thus long ago succeeded in persuading at least one group – environmental law scholars, including several who held important jobs in the Obama administration – that a whole range of truly horribly harmful futures would happen unless the United States acted to quickly reduce its CO_2 emissions.

As we have seen, the EPA's Endangerment Finding was itself essentially a long summary of various conclusions reached by the IPCC and USGCRP. These conclusions were taken to be true to establish an unquestionable foundation for costly precautionary policy. With such overwhelming policy importance attached to what the IPCC and (albeit to a lesser extent) the USGCRP have said about climate change, a rational approach to climate policy – one that considers and weighs both types of potential error – requires that we investigate the basis for such faith in IPCC and USGCRP conclusions.

The next two chapters trace the evolution of international and US climate science institutions and unpack in some detail how those institutions actually go about assessing science. My focus in on the IPCC, as it has been much more open about how it produces its Assessment Reports. As we shall see, from their inception, these institutions have had a primarily political, not scientific purpose. The IPCC's structure and process ensures that it does not produce unbiased and objective assessments of various competing scientific paradigms and results, but rather – especially in the summaries that is publicizes to the press months before full reports are issued – champions scientific work that supports the policy preferences of the government representatives who compose the official Panel. And as for the primary US climate change assessment body – the US Global Change Research Program – its leaders have for decades been active decarbonization policy advocates, about as far from disinterested reporters on science as one could imagine.

One of the many harmful things that these climate science advocacy organizations have accomplished is, paradoxically, to make the science irrelevant. Work in social psychology that I discuss in more detail later in the book has solidly demonstrated that for many people, a package of stylized stories marketed by climate change science advocacy organizations with active support from the media have been accepted as the final truth and become a matter of faith. Adherents to this faith need hear nothing further from science. They know, as a matter of faith, that future climate change will be catastrophically bad. And they also know – thanks in part to the efforts of the groups behind the climate change litigation discussed in the previous part – that big fossil fuel companies and electric utilities are the culprits, the evildoers. With such beliefs supported, indeed inculcated by heavily funded professional organizations, it should be no surprise that for many people, climate change is a purely moral issue, with the righteous prepared to impose any cost, however great, on the greedy capitalists who are responsible for endangering the world. For such people, the destruction of fossil fuel–based modern industrial civilization seems to be the end goal, regardless of any precise calculation of the cost or benefit of so doing.

People who are not quite so fanatical in their belief that something must be done about climate change tend to think that some sort of balance should be struck between the potential future benefits of reducing present-day GHG emissions and the cost of such reductions. My hope is that after reading Part I of this book, such readers will appreciate that the present-day costs are real and substantial, and fall – at least in the case of the precautionary policies adopted in the United States –

disproportionately on poor households. The size of these costs, and their unfair distribution, provides more than enough reason to be as rigorous as possible in estimating the potential benefits from such costly present-day GHG emission reduction. From an economic point of view, the primary benefit from present-day GHG emission is the decrease in future harm from climate change. Since, as we have seen in Part I, CO_2 is by far the most important GHG from a policy point of view, economists have come to use the term the Social Cost of Carbon for the future harm from present-day CO_2 emissions.

Even a moment's thought reveals that the value of spending today to reduce climate change harm in the future depends entirely upon what the climate future is projected to be. If, for example, the future climate is projected to be 0.05°C warmer on average than today's climate, then an economic estimate that avoiding even such a small change would bring big future benefits would be counterintuitive and would have to marshal an enormous amount of evidence in its favor for anyone to take it seriously. If, on the other hand, present-day CO_2 reductions were being made to avoid a future climate that is projected to be, say, 5°C hotter than today, then one would expect that as big potential harm is to be feared and avoided, decarbonization of modern economies should proceed as swiftly as possible, regardless of the cost.

In this way, climate science – in particular projections about future climate under alternative future CO_2 emissions paths – is the foundation for SCC estimates that provide a basis for rational policy design. One cannot generate SCC estimates without using projections of how future atmospheric CO_2 concentrations translate into future temperatures. In turn, one cannot critically evaluate such SCC estimates – my task in this book – unless one critically analyzes the projections of future temperatures as a function of future atmospheric CO_2 levels that are used to generate SCC numbers.

Hence, while in Chapter 16, I explain and critically analyzes how economists have come up with SCC estimates, before that chapter, I take a critical look at the future temperature projections that drive SCC estimates. This order of presentation – first the science, then the economics – is necessary simply because the SCC estimates are driven in large part by borrowed climate model projections of future temperatures.

Almost as a matter of common sense, climate policy depends upon more than just projections of future climate. It has to depend upon the reliability of such projections. As we shall see, the primary basis for IPCC future climate projections are mathematical, computer models that generate a relationship between atmospheric CO_2 concentration and global average surface temperature. Like any model, the weight placed on a computer climate model projection must depend in part upon how and whether the model can explain past climate. When it comes to key climate variables – the main one being global average surface temperature – one needs first to know something about what is being measured and explained. And one needs to know whether there are competing explanations, and how they stack up against an explanation that attached primacy to atmospheric CO_2 concentration as a driver of global average temperature.

As we shall see, the US government has spent tens of billions of dollars subsidizing climate science. This investment has generated millions of pages of climate science research. My discussion of climate science is extremely brief, and focuses just on the three questions that are most policy relevant and which indeed have already repeatedly been advanced to support precautionary policies of all sorts, including common law liability: first, the things we have observed, industrial era temperature and (to a lesser extent) sea level measures and whether these observations are unusual in longer-term historical perspective; second, whether there are forces other than the buildup of atmospheric CO_2 that have contributed to observed changes that are significant in long-term perspective; and, third, the basis for future climate projections of these key climate variables that drive the SCC as estimated by economists.

Reflecting the fact that my own formal training and PhD is in economics and not any area of geophysics, my discussion of these three questions aims to be a report of work that one finds in the peer-edited climate science literature but which is neglected, or even completely ignored by the official climate science assessment organizations. I do not spend much time discussing climate science work that is endorsed by institutions like the IPCC. One can look at any one of hundreds of reports to find such a discussion. And I don't attempt to make any judgment about which body of scientific evidence is in some sense the most persuasive. This is beyond my expertise. My goal instead is merely to report on a large body of scientific work, published in peer-edited scientific journals, which raises questions that in most cases have simply not been addressed at all by the IPCC and similar institutions. Sometimes the IPCC and similar establishment climate science institutions completely ignore this work, and sometimes the IPCC reports dismiss such work on grounds that are so patently unpersuasive that I present them here for the reader to evaluate.

What I have found, and report about, is a large body of work that shows the following:

- While temperature has clearly increased in the latter part of the twentieth century, surface temperature measurements are highly unreliable and have since 1980 increased by much more than far more accurate measurements of tropospheric (lower atmosphere) and ocean temperatures since 1980.
- Although there are no instrumental measurements of climate variables before the mid- to late nineteenth century, and estimates of climate before than are very noisy "reconstructions" from various proxy measures of climate, such reconstructions show that temperatures and sea levels are probably similar to levels reaches at other points in the last 2,000 years; over historical scales ranging from decades to centuries, temperatures, and sea level and most

other climate variables – such as hurricanes and droughts – are not constant but cycle in what mathematicians call long memory processes.

- Such cycles are internal to the complex, nonlinear climate system, and while industrial era – post late nineteenth century – temperature increase seems clearly to be partly due to increased atmospheric CO_2, over longer periods, the causal relationship between CO_2 and global temperature has not been clearly established.
- Although minimized or ignored by official climate science assessment organizations, large body of scientific work shows that in some regions – most importantly the Arctic – black carbon or soot emissions are responsible for a major share of recently observed surface warming; a similarly large body of work shows that in other regions, pretty much anywhere on earth where there has been rapid economic development and land conversion to urban and suburban use, such regional land development has significantly raised measured surface temperatures.
- Computer climate models do not explain or predict industrial era temperature change, but rather are fit after the fact to reproduce observed temperatures, and such models are generally not able to reproduce internal climate cycles that operate at time scales ranging from decades to centuries.
- Given all this, the computer climate projections of future climate are not likely to be reliable, and seem increasingly at odds with evidence about long distant past climate (called paleoclimate).
- Perhaps most importantly, computer projections of future climate and especially projections about required CO_2 emission cuts are actually projections based entirely on assumptions about future economic conditions involving both national income and wealth and global CO_2 emissions; for this reason, the crucial hoped-for contribution from computer climate models that are sold as being based solely on physical science – guidance about how present-day CO_2 emission reduction policy translates into future temperatures based solely on physical science – is in fact determined by assumptions about future economic conditions and the CO_2 emissions of future economies.
- Finally, the one thing that does seem to be universally agreed upon is not only that temperature and climate more generally has always been subject to cycles ranging from decades to centuries, but that this will surely continue to be true, and with some amount of temperature increase expected to continue for many decades, adaptation to changing climate is inevitable.

For policy purposes, this final observation is the most important. My report on climate science reveals that climate has always cycled, making adaptation to climate inevitable. My explication of the SCC estimates that are hoped to provide the basis for balanced climate policy likewise reveals that the primary determinant of the SCC is what economists assume about the ability of economies to adapt to changing climate. If climate change – climate cycles – is inevitable, and adaptation to climate is the primary determinant of the SCC, then policies that impact the cost and success of economic adaptation to climate change become central to the climate change policy debate.

My explication of the SCC shows not only that SCC estimates are driven by assumptions about future adaptation but that the SCC estimates used by the Obama administration to quantify the benefits of its CO_2 emission reduction policies were based on very conservative assumptions about future adaptation in the United States, where I mean conservative in the sense that they assume that the United States and other developed modern economies had very limited ability to adapt to changing climate. In Chapter 16, I show that the assumptions about human adaptation that underlie SCC estimates are not just conservative but unrealistically so. That chapter looks to work in economic history. Such work has demonstrated the remarkable human ability to adapt to varying and changing climates. These case studies are buttressed by more recent quantitative work that gives some rough numerical sense of how adaptation can lower the cost and in some cases even allow benefits to be realized from climate change. In light of the demonstrated ability to adapt to varying and changing climates, SCC estimates based on the assumption that there is very little ability to adapt to climate change are revealed to be exceptionally pessimistic, an application of precautionary thinking rather than an antidote to such.

Obviously this part of the book is not very deferential to the story about climate science that is packaged and sold in Science Assessment reports by institutions such as the IPCC and the USGCRP. By uncovering the political origins of and explicating the process followed by the IPCC in producing such reports, the next two chapters defend such lack of deference: the IPCC and USGCRP do not present both sides of ongoing scientific work, they present the side that provides evidence supporting the policies favored by the politicians who provide funding to them. The next two chapters thus overcome an oft-made objection to anyone actually taking an independent look at the climate science driving policy – the IPCC (or USGCRP) have already reliably told us all we need to know about climate science. My explication of the institutional structure of the IPCC shows that while this may sometimes happen – some chapters in IPCC AR's may come close to being balanced assessments, rather than evidence marshaled for policy advocacy – the IPCC's structure and process is not set up to encourage such balance, but to ensure that only one side of ongoing scientific disputes is even presented.

Before undertaking my explication of the evolution and structure of what I shall refer to sometimes as the climate–science–industrial complex, I discuss two objections that are often raised in opposition to undertaking any independent look at anything involving climate science. These two objections may be summarized as follows:

- *Climate Science advocacy positions are consensus positions among climate scientists and therefore certainly true.* This argument tells the listener "every scientist agrees with this proposition, therefore it is true." This argument says that a policy maker has to defer totally when all scientists in the field agree. This argument says that it is pointless to try to think crucially about claims regarding climate science, because since every scientist agrees, the policy maker cannot find anything to contradict or question any particular expert opinion.
- *The argument ad hominem:* Any and all scientific work that does seem to deviate from the supposed consensus view should be completely discounted because all of the scientists who produce such work are either paid shills for the fossil fuel industry or otherwise morally bad and untrustworthy.

If one accepts either the scientific consensus argument or the ad hominem defense, then it would seem pointless to incur the energy and effort that I myself have incurred in thinking critically about climate science and economics, and perhaps equally silly for a reader to incur a (hopefully much) smaller measure of such energy and effort in reading what I have to say. Hence before taking a closer look at the government institutions that compose the climate–science–industrial complex, it is important to show what is wrong with both the consensus and ad hominem arguments in favor of complete deference.

I WHAT IS WRONG WITH THE AD HOMINEM ARGUMENT

If any professional person – be they a physical scientist, economist, lawyer, or policy maker – challenges what climate science advocates have to say, the first response of many climate activists is to furiously investigate whether the challenger has worked or is working for the fossil fuel or some related industry or is a conservative or libertarian or Republican or otherwise a very bad person. If the investigation reveals that the challenger is such a person, then this alone is taken as conclusive evidence that what the challenger has to say is likely false, not worth listening to, and should be completely ignored.

I take it that the reader does not need to be persuaded that this argument is commonly used by media and environmental activists, but what one may not know that it is actually used by academics with positions at very prestigious institutions. Indeed, in *Merchants of Doubt* (2010), a book that is not only widely praised by environmentalists but immediately preceded her appointment as a tenured professor of the history of science at Harvard University, Naomi Oreskes (and her coauthor Erik M. Conway) devoted a large number of pages to an ad hominem attack on several high profile dissenting climate scientists. As we have seen, Oreskes was one of the organizers of the 2012 litigation workshop, a primary purpose of which was to recast common law climate change litigation against fossil fuel companies as attacking the same sort of conspiracy among evil corporations that had succeeded in generating multi-billion-dollar payouts by tobacco companies. Oreskes and Conway (2010, 157–167) introduce Fred Singer, an established climate scientist who had been publishing articles in top science journals for decades, not as a climate scientist but as consultant to the tobacco industry in its effort to rebut what Oreskes and Conway believe to be the obvious and indisputably established serious health hazards of inhaling small amount of smoke from cigarettes being smoked by other people – so-called secondhand smoke. Singer's substantive work in climate science is not discussed. Rather, Oreskes and Conway (2010, 190–197) tell a story about how Singer took advantage of the illness of his coauthor and climate change hero Roger Revelle to alter their joint paper in ways of which Revelle would not have approved. Oreskes and Conway (2010, 193, 195) quote various people as saying that Singer was "not a very good scientist" and that such people were "still angry" about what they called "Singer's betrayal of Roger." Oreskes and Conway (2010, 203) introduce former Virginia state meteorologist and IPCC critic Pat Michaels as having "worked as a consultant . . . to a coal mining industry group to promote the idea that burning fossil fuels was good." Oreskes and Conway's (2010) book perfectly illustrates the ad hominem tactic: rather than attempting to rebut the substance of a dissenting scientist's argument, attack the scientist personally.

Why are ad hominem arguments effective at all? This question is far from rhetorical. To see why, try to imagine an ad hominem argument being mounted against a mathematician who has published a proof of a previously unproven but long known mathematical conjecture. Assume (as is actually true of many unproven mathematical conjectures) that there is no payoff other than fame for being able to prove the conjecture. In this sense, the conjecture is a matter of pure, abstract science.

Now suppose that there is evidence that our mathematician has previously worked for cigarette companies in some capacity. It is hard to imagine any mathematician or anybody else bringing up this this employment history as somehow relevant to the validity of our mathematician's proof. The proof either works or it doesn't. It is fully accessible to other mathematicians and they can verify whether each step in the proof is free of error and consistent with axioms and existing true theorems in the relevant field of mathematics. Our mathematician's employment history might be considered odious by some other mathematicians, but if they used it as evidence that her proof was wrong, they would be thought ridiculous and suspected of incompetence.

But now suppose that our scientist is not a mathematician but a climate scientist who publishes a paper containing evidence that computer climate models have failed to predict temperature and precipitation patterns that have been observed over the period 1998–2019. It is almost surely the case that ad hominem attacks calling attention to her past history working with cigarette companies would be mounted against our climate scientist and that they would be considered to be relevant. Evidence that the scientist had worked for cigarette companies would be argued to show that her work cannot be trusted and should be dismissed without serious consideration. The ad hominem is here used as a short cut to justify not trying to work through, understand, and then critique work by our scientist. But the scientific merit of the work can and should be independently evaluated without regard to the ad hominem evidence.

To see why, one needs only to see that it is just as easy to mount an ad hominem argument against climate science activists. Such scientists actively promote and support the policy goal of cutting GHG emissions as quickly as possible. Is it possible that such a scientist would actually publish a paper weakening the case for such regulation? If not, does this not imply that what is published by such as scientist has already been sifted through a filter allowing only some findings to be released and published? Even if the answer to this question is yes, that does not mean that we should not independently evaluate the merit of such a scientist's work. He or she might be right.

Perhaps even more seriously, the ad hominem argument replaces the traditional test for scientific value with a purely political test. Traditionally, the value of a scientific hypothesis is judged by its ability to actually explain observations. As I soon explain in more detail, in the climate change area, activists support only one hypothesis – that while things like volcanic eruptions and solar variation account for short run fluctuations, human CO_2 emissions are the sole cause of long-term industrial era temperature increase. As we shall see, there are competing hypotheses – not that increased atmospheric CO_2 has been irrelevant to the long-term observed temperature increase, but that other forces have also been at work – such as internal climate variability – and so CO_2 has caused less warming than originally believed. Rather than taking on such a competing hypothesis – as the best climate scientists have been doing – the ad hominem argument completely shifts away from science, to mount an essentially political attack on the scientist advancing the competing hypothesis. This subverts the scientific process.

II THE IRRELEVANCE OF CONSENSUS WHEN SCIENTISTS HAVE POLICY PREFERENCES

One of the most important and powerful true theorems in political science and social choice is called the Condorcet jury theorem. The theorem applies to situations where we are taking a decision by majority vote, and the correct decision depends upon the state of the world. For example (and the reason for the theorem's name), we can imagine a jury in a criminal trial voting on whether to convict, where conviction results if a majority of jurors vote for guilt. A correct majority jury vote decision is to convict when the defendant really did it and acquit when she did not. Condorcet's theorem says that if the probability that each juror gets the true state of the world correct is bigger than ½, then as the number of jurors gets bigger and bigger (and so too the majority required for conviction), the probability of a correct majority vote goes to 1.

There are a variety of ways to prove mathematically that Condorcet's theorem is true,[1] but what it says is actually quite intuitive. If all decision makers are more likely than not to get the state of the world correct, then the probability that the majority of the jurors are correct gets really high when it takes a lot of jurors to constitute a majority. Intuitively, the Condorcet theorem says that if scientists only report what they honestly believe their work has revealed to them about some contested state of the world, and they do actually have some, albeit imperfect, information about the world, then if a majority of lots and lots of scientists agree, they are probably correct.

I think it is this intuition that underlies the constant invocation of scientific consensus regarding climate change as proof of virtually any assertion to the effect that climate change will happen with future consequences that are very bad and is happening with already bad consequences. But the supposed consensus opinion among climate scientists has been identified using completely unreliable methods.

One method is for someone to survey the climate science literature for the proportion of articles that seem to agree with some statement about climate change. In one of the most widely cited such articles employing this method, Oreskes (2004, 1686) – whose book is discussed above briefly as an example of extended ad hominem attack – looked at articles in peer-reviewed scientific journals published between 1993 and 2003 whose abstracts contained the search keywords "climate change." She put the abstracts she surveyed into six categories. The first category included all abstracts that endorsed the statement in the IPCC's 2001 Assessment Report that human activities are "modifying" the atmospheric concentration of gases that "scatter or absorb" radiant energy and "most of the observed warming over the last 50 years is likely to have been due to the increase in greenhouse gas concentrations." According to Oreskes, 75 percent of the abstract fell into this category, "none of the papers" argued that "current climate change is natural."

Oreskes's article is often taken to show that 100 percent of scientists agree with something like the 2001 IPCC statement. Of course it doesn't do that. But more importantly, as I set out in the introduction, virtually no one disputes that (1) increases in atmospheric greenhouse gases lead to some increase in average surface temperature and that (2) over the course of the twentieth century, human activities have increased atmospheric greenhouse gases, and therefore (3) anthropogenic GHG emissions likely made some contribution to increasing average global surface temperatures over the course of the twentieth century. This is to say that everybody agrees with the first part of the IPCC's 2001 statement.

Whether a scientist agrees to the second part, that human activities are "likely" responsible for "most of the observed warming over the last 50 years" depends upon how one interprets "most." It could mean "more than 50%" or it could mean something like "a substantial fraction." For those who take it to mean something like "substantial fraction" the statement is close to being trivially true. For papers claiming "most" in the sense of "more than 50%" one would like to know more about the paper and the scientist: did the paper actually present the statistical work that would allow an expert conclusion that more than 50 percent of warming was due to anthropogenic GHG emissions? Or did the abstract just mean that anthropogenic emissions contributed to climate change? It is impossible to know.

To be sure, there have now been a number of other papers published in which the authors survey academic papers on climate science and conclude with a finding about the fraction that agree with some statement about climate change. Of these, the one paper by Cook et al. (2013, 024024) is probably the best known, because it generated the widely publicized number that 97 percent of climate scientists agree that anthropogenic GHG emissions are the "primary cause of recent warming." Cook et al. categorized abstracts from articles included in the ISI Web of Science over the period 1991–2012 using topic searches for "global warming" or "global climate change." For reporting purposes, they put the articles into three categories, those that endorsed the "consensus position" that "humans are causing global warming," those that did not take a position, and those that rejected the consensus position. The vast majority of articles, 66 percent, did not take a position in the abstract on the "consensus position." But 33 percent did endorse the position, and with only about 1 percent either rejecting the position or reflecting uncertainty about it, Cook et al. could say that 97 percent of abstracts that actually took a position on anthropogenic warming said it was happening.

Of course, any such categorization exercise is highly subjective and categorizers may well disagree; indeed, 27 percent of the time, Cook's categorizers disagreed on which category to put an abstract. Moreover, when volunteers are used to do the categorization, as in Cook et al., the volunteers are not a random sample of informed readers of scientific journals but people who care about the project. Cook is a climate activist who runs a website, SkepticalScience.com, dedicated to buttressing the view that anthropogenic climate change will be catastrophic. The evidence suggests that Cook's survey project attracted like-minded volunteers. This evidence is the fact that Cook's volunteers categorized as "endorsing" the "consensus statement" abstracts of articles by many scientists whose work questions the foundations of that consensus. We know this because those scientists themselves said Cook had miscategorized their work.[2]

These attempts to categorize abstracts or entire scientific articles[3] as either supporting or rejecting a very general statement about anthropogenic climate change are so coarse – in terms of how they categorize articles – and so highly subjective as to be virtually useless to any person who wants to get a sense of what is found in the scientific literature. They are useful to climate activists, who use them to stifle critical thought by proclaiming that "97 percent of scientists agree," but the numbers they report are not very informative about anything. In this, they are completely unlike knowing that a majority of the unbiased, perfectly informed experts presumed by the Condorcet jury theorem agree.

There is another type of study that seeks to elicit scientists' opinions about climate change, a survey where scientists are directly asked their opinions. The problem with such surveys is that they are surveys. Whether a survey asking scientists what they think about climate change generates a potentially accurate – that is, valid and reliable – picture of scientific opinion depends on whether the survey was designed and administered to overcome psychological factors known to induce biased survey responses.

There are many such biases, but here are a few that likely arise in surveys of scientists' opinions about climate change:

- The first and most obvious reason why this is true is that unlike the decision makers in the world of the Condorcet jury theorem, respondents to a survey aren't jurors who have to vote on guilt or innocence and want to vote in accordance with what they know to believe to be true about world. Instead, they are people who actually chose to respond to a survey conducted by a particular known person or organization, in a particular way (online or phone, for example), and they are responding to particular questions phrased in a particular way by those conducting the survey. Survey results may depend on all of these things – who conducted the survey, who responded, which questions were included and how they were worded, and the medium in which the survey was administered.
- As for who responds to a survey, some biases in who responds to a survey can be measured and corrected for ahead of time. If, for example, it is known that men respond more than women to a survey attempting to get at what a population of men and women believe, then responses by men can be weighted down while those of women are weighted up. But if response rates are determined by things that can't be observed and measured before the survey – such as whether the person really cares about the issues the survey is asking about, or whether the person trusts the surveyor to keep results confidential – then bias cannot be corrected for ahead of time. Bias that is not corrected for destroys the validity of a survey – for example, the fact that lots of patients say they were satisfied with health care from a particular provider may vastly overestimate patient satisfaction if only those who were very satisfied respond to such a survey.[4] Similarly, if people who don't respond to a survey fail to respond because they disagree with or distrust the survey organization to keep results confidential, then an entire group of consumers, voters, or scientists with likely highly correlated opinions but otherwise unknown characteristics will be missing from the survey. And the severity of this problem may vary with the medium used to conduct the survey – people may be more willing to do an online survey, for example, than a phone survey.
- Even if there is no bias in who responds to a survey, there are lots of other things that can cause biased responses.[5] If respondents gain prior knowledge about the survey and its purposes prior to actually responding, this may bias their

responses. If, for example, it is known that a survey is being used to decide where to locate a hazardous waste disposal facility, then respondents may tailor their answers in ways they believe will lead to the facility being put as far away from their own homes as possible.

- Another bias is the social desirability bias. This bias – which may help explain why polls prior to the 2016 US presidential election were off in so many states by 5–6 percent (favoring Clinton over Trump) – occurs when people answer questions that trigger social norms in ways that are consistent with the norm rather than with what they really believe. If a survey, for example, asked the question "Do you think it is okay to occasionally get really drunk?" then the vast majority of people would likely answer "no," because that is the socially acceptable response, even if they believe otherwise.
- Another set of biases arise from the question format. In some cultural settings (not all) questions that are answered on a scale of responses in the form of numbers (say, 1 to 5) or statements (strongly agree to strongly disagree, for example) are known to elicit extreme responses rather than those in the middle. This tendency seems to more pronounced, the lower is the respondent's education level. The content of the question can exacerbate this problem. A question with responses on the strongly agree – strongly disagree scale that states "US imperialism is responsible for most of the problems in the developing world" is not likely to get many responses in the middle. Of course, there is the opposite problem, called neutral bias, where generally indifferent and hurried respondents simply mark down a middling choice on many questions in order to finish the survey quickly.
- A problem that survey designers have spent considerable effort to overcome is called acquiescence bias. Regardless of why it arises – out of a respondent's need to please the researcher or to find something in his or her own experience that is consistent with the question – acquiescence bias is the tendency for respondents to answer questions to agree with the survey. To overcome this problem, survey designers include related questions that would in a sense catch an acquiescing respondent. One could ask, for example, a yes-or-no question if getting 8 hours of sleep was important to the respondent, and then, to identify acquiescence, ask whether the respondent agreed or disagreed with the statement "I would sleep all day rather than miss a few hours of sleep." A respondent who somehow had inferred that the survey endorsed long hours of sleep might agree with the second; an honest response even from someone who felt 8 hours of sleep was important might well be to disagree with the second statement.

This is a very abbreviated and incomplete list of the hurdles that a survey designer has to deal with in creating a survey that elicits honest and unbiased responses from an unbiased and representative sample of respondents. It is complete enough, however, to provide a critical viewpoint on surveys of climate scientists used to support the proposition that there is a consensus among such scientists about climate change.

A survey that meets many of the criteria for survey validity was a December 2011 email survey of the roughly 7,000 members of the American Meteorological Society by Stenhouse et al. (2014, 1029–1040). They asked respondents to give their estimate of the proportion of scientists who believe that human-caused global warming was happening, and also asked respondents about the cause of global warming over the last 150 years. The response set for the latter question was: "mostly caused by human activity, mostly caused by natural events, more or less equally caused by human activity and natural events, I don't think we know enough to say yet to determine the degree of human versus natural causation even in general terms," or, finally, "I don't know." The survey was done online. The response rate of 26 percent was not high but about average for online surveys.

Stenhouse et al. found pronounced differences between respondents who self-identified as "climate scientists" and scientists who self-identified as doing meteorology and atmospheric science. There is only one US PhD program in "climate science," located at Penn State, home of Michael Mann, who as we have seen earlier brought a defamation action against media critics. Whereas 78 percent of self-described "climate scientists" publishing on climate saying that global warming has been happening over the last 150 years and is mostly human caused, only 61 percent of meteorologists and atmospheric scientists who publish mostly on climate agreed with this statement. An even smaller 57 percent of such meteorologists and atmospheric scientists who publish mostly on nonclimate topics agreed that mostly human-caused climate change has been occurring over the last 150 years. Strikingly, whereas only 7 percent of "climate scientists" publishing on climate thought the evidence about human versus natural causation insufficient to judge between the two or to say whether global warming was even happening, a full 22 percent of meteorologists and atmospheric scientists who publish mostly on climate thought the evidence was too thin judge between human and naturally caused warming (11 percent) or even to say whether warming had occurred over the last 150 years (11 percent).

Thus whereas one often hears it said that "97 percent of scientists agree" that human CO_2 emissions are causing climate change, what may well be the best survey yet actually found something very different: that fully 40 percent of meteorologists and atmospheric scientists who publish *mostly* on climate did not agree even with the statement that global warming has been happening over the last 150 years and is mostly human caused,

Notes

The title of this chapter borrows the title of Aaron Wildavsky (1997), a book that in many ways inspired the research project of which this book is but a part.

1. Here is one proof. Let p give the probability that each identical juror is correct about the state of the world (whether the defendant is guilty) and suppose we have N jurors. The majority vote decision rule is that if at least $M = N/2 + 1$ jurors vote to convict, then the defendant is convicted. Hence the probability that the defendant is convicted is given by

$$\sum_{i=M}^{N} \binom{N}{i} p^i (1-p)^{N-i} = 1 - \sum_{i=1}^{M} \binom{N}{j} p^i (1-p)^{N-i}$$

   We are interested in whether this probability increases or decreases with N as we vary p. To see this, take the logarithm of the term $p^i\ (1 - \ p)^{\ N-\ i}$, which is given by $i \log p + (N - i) \log (1 - p)$, and differentiating this with respect to p, we get $\frac{i}{p} - \left(\frac{N-i)}{1-p}\right)$. But $N - i > i$ in this range, and so if and only if $1 - p < p$, or $p >$ 1/2, does the expression $1 - \sum_{i=1}^{M} \binom{N}{j} p^i (1-p)^{N-i}$ increase in p. That is, if the probability of jurors getting the state of the world correct is better than a random flip of the coin, then the probability of a jury decision by majority vote being correct goes to 1 as the number of jurors increases.
2. 97% Study Falsely Classifies Scientists' Papers, according to the scientists that published them, PopularTechnology.net, available at www.populartechnology.net/2013/05/97-study-falsely-classifies-scientists.html.
3. For a survey of this line of work, plus the survey discussed next, see Tol (2016, 048001).
4. See, e.g., Mazor et al. (2002, 1403–1417).
5. For a lucid discussion of these in the marketing context, see Cameron Johnson, "Understanding the 6 Types of Response Bias (with Examples)," *Nextiva* (blog), August 30, 2018, available at www.nextiva.com/blog/response-bias.html.

11

"Born in Politics"

The Rise of the Climate Change Science Production and Assessment Complex

A very typical story leading to domestic environmental legislation in countries such as the United States is one in which people in a number of localities within the country begin to experience harm from a particular kind of pollution and then legislators from those places take up the cause and ask scientists to identify which pollutant or pollutants are causing that harm so that legislation can be passed to curb the harmful pollution.[1] As discussed earlier, precisely such a process led to the passage of the Clean Air Act of 1970. One might suppose that a similar pattern occurred on the international level with global warming: some countries might have been experiencing harmful warming, leading them to ask for international scientific cooperation to identify the cause of the warming. Such a pattern – a problem is identified, and scientists are asked to figure out what is causing it and what might be done to eliminate it – is what might be called the standard model of how science relates to policy.[2]

In the area of climate change, this standard patterned relationship of science and policy is almost the opposite of what actually occurred. During the 1970s and 1980s, without any great popular concern about particular harms from global warming in any country, environmentalists, activist scientists and international policy entrepreneurs at affiliated with the United Nations and other international organizations themselves called for international scientific cooperation in the study of climate change. The point of such cooperation was not to enlist scientists to explain ongoing weather-related problems, but for scientists to investigate the possible link between potentially harmful present and future climate change and fossil fuel energy.

Thus was the Intergovernmental Panel on Climate Change (IPCC) born. During precisely this same period in the United States, as 1970s fears about energy security triggered by Arab oil embargo and OPEC price increases faded in the face of rapidly increasing oil supplies and declining oil prices, government science agencies cast about for a new mission. They found such a mission under the rubric of global change. Under this umbrella a vast federal climate science bureaucracy, called the US Global Change Research Program (USFGCRP) arose. This program received

$50 billion in funding by 2014. This program did not attempt to fund broad research on the many pathways through which humans affect the climate and the many nonhuman factors causing climate change. Instead, like the IPCC, the USGCRP focused on the very narrow question of how human GHG emissions were causing potentially harmful climate change.

It is the IPCC and the USGCRP who produced the Assessment Reports of climate science relied upon by the EPA and the courts in fashioning and reviewing US climate policy during the Obama era. As I explain in some detail by focusing on the IPCC, the institutional structure by which the IPCC produces Assessment Reports generates "reports" that are not attempts to discuss and weigh scientific work pro and con various policy-relevant findings, but instead scientific advocacy documents that build a case for activist policy focused solely on reducing human GHG emissions.

I CLIMATE SCIENCE BEFORE GOVERNMENTS CARED

Both scientists and the general public were interested in climate change long before the creation of the international and national climate science assessment organizations whose synthesis reports have provided the basis not only for EPA's 2009 Endangerment Finding but also much of what has been reported about climate change by the media over the last two decades. According to historians, the belief that humans affect climate was set out as early as by Aristotle, who thought that the "vapors and exhalations of a country determined its climate" (Fleming 2005, 11). Later, Hume theorized that the "gradual conversion of shady forests to sunny croplands had warmed the European continent" (Fleming 2005, 16–18) and by the nineteenth century, observers such as Thomas Jefferson believed that civilization had caused temperatures to increase in both Europe and the United States.

It was not until late in the nineteenth century, however, that the study of climate began to be based on "actual measurements and meteorological records" rather than "ancient authorities or the memories of the elderly" (Fleming 2005, 50). Looking for empirical evidence about climate, these late nineteenth-century investigators confronted challenges that still remain in the empirical study of climate. The chief scientist of the Army Signal Office, Cleveland Abbe, was one such investigator. Writing in 1889, he explained how given the "want of reliability" in the historically distant instrumental observations not only of temperature and rainfall but also things such as the dates of first and last frosts, students of climate change had looked to the "periodic phenomena of animal and vegetable life, such as the dates of the flights of birds, the budding, blossoming and ripening of plants." Concluding that "the study of each and all of these phenomena has failed to establish that there has been any sensible changes in the climate at any point of the earth's surface during the past 2000 years, Abbe worked with more recent, instrumental data on climate variables" (Abbe 1889, 687).

However, as Abbe explained, these measurements were themselves beset by all kinds of errors. These included observer error, changes in the type of thermometers used, and changes in thermometer location and surroundings, such as new building or the encroachment of vegetation. Abbe was pessimistic about the chances of ever detecting a statistically significant change in the average. As he said, "what with changes due to instruments and their exposures, superadded to this irregular variability in temperatures, the indices of variability for all the temperature records known to meteorology are so large and the constant errors are so insidious, that there is scarcely a single station with respect to which we have data competent to decide the question as to whether the mean temperature for any month may have changed 0.2° centigrade or 0.5° Fahrenheit during the past century" (Abbe 1889, 683–684). Abbe – who defined climate in general terms as the "average about which the temporary conditions permanently oscillate" – despaired that even if these measurement challenges were overcome, "any satisfactory discussion of the question whether our climate has changed or not is rendered difficult . . . by the intrinsic variability of the climate itself, which is such that we can hardly determine what the climate is, as preliminary to the question of whether or not it has changed" (Abbe 1889, 687).

The nineteenth century was also the period during which discoveries in physics and physical chemistry initiated actual scientific inquiry – versus, say, Aristotle's speculations – about the basic forces determining the earth's climate. By the second half of the nineteenth century, scientists have invented an experimental apparatus (a ratio spectrophotometer) that could be used to explore the transmission of radiant heat through different media. Using such an apparatus,[3] in 1859 the British scientist John Tyndall reported the results of experiments showing that the elemental gases oxygen, nitrogen, and hydrogen absorbed very little radiant heat, but several of the compound gases – water vapor, carbon dioxide, and ozone – were powerful absorbers and reflectors of such heat. He focused especially on water vapor, reporting that it:

> acts more energetically upon the terrestrial rays than upon the solar rays; hence, its tendency is to preserve to the earth a portion of heat which would otherwise be radiated into space.
>
> . . . It is perfectly certain that more than ten percent of the terrestrial radiation from the soil of England is stopped within ten feet of the surface of the soil. This one fact is sufficient to show the immense influence which this newly-discovered property of aqueous vapors must exert on the phenomenon of meteorology. This aqueous vapor is a blanket more necessary to the vegetable life of England than clothing is to man. (Fleming 2005, 71, quoting Tyndall 1863, 204–205)

By the 1890s, scientists had made significant progress in inferring key relationships that would be important in understanding global climate and in beginning to make systematic measurements of aspects of climate. Stefan had discovered what we know today as Stefan–Boltzmann law, which says that the total heat radiation emitted by a body is proportional to its temperature taken to the fourth power; Langley had measured the transmission of heat through the atmosphere; Ångström had provided estimates of how water vapor and CO_2 absorbed light at different wavelengths, and Buchan had charts of mean monthly temperatures across the globe (Fleming 2005, 76).

Certainly most relevant to the contemporary question of how increases in CO_2 might affect future climate was the work of Svante Arrhenius, a Swedish electrochemist who won the Nobel Prize in Chemistry in 1903 for his discovery in the early 1880s of the mechanism of electrolytic dissociation. During the 1890s, he applied his work in physical chemistry to develop theories of what may be called the physics of the earth, the solar system, and the universe. In 1895, Arrhenius wrote a paper setting out what one would today call "back-of-the-envelope" calculations exploring whether the advance and retreat of the continental glaciers – the coming and going of ice ages – might be due to fluctuations in the concentration of carbon dioxide in the atmosphere. Arrhenius built on earlier work showing that the atmosphere absorbed radiation almost entirely in the invisible long wave bands. For this reason, he argued absorption by these gases must have a "comparatively small" influence on heat from the sun, "but must be of great importance on the transmission of rays from the earth" (Arrhenius 1896, 239). Using experiments and observations done by Langley and Ångström, Arrhenius came up with estimates for the fraction of longwave radiation emanating out from the earth absorbed by both CO_2 and water vapor. To the recently discovered Stefan–Boltzmann law – which says that the total heat radiated by a body is proportional to its temperature taken to the fourth power – Arrhenius added in a coefficient adjusting for earth's albedo – the reflection back of the sun's rays by the earth's surface. Arrhenius understood that albedo varies depending with the type of surface – snow, for example, has a higher albedo than a forest – and so he adjusted his albedo coefficient to the proportion of various surface types on earth. He also added another adjustment for the percentage of the earth's surface shielded by clouds.

Arrhenius used his mathematical model to estimate the variation of temperature that could occur due to a variation in the amount of carbon dioxide in the atmosphere. Using a recently created series of monthly estimates of temperature and humidity across the earth, he calculated how much mean temperatures at different latitudes would vary as the amount of carbon dioxide in the atmosphere ranged (as a proportion of the then-present level) over 0.67, 1.5, 2, and 2.5. This conceptual exercise led to several conclusions: (1) that the amount of temperature increase due to an increase in CO_2 would be higher at higher latitudes; that the increase would be (2) greater in the winter than in the summer, (3) bigger for land than for the oceans, and (4) bigger in the southern hemisphere and in higher latitudes where warming caused snow melt and therefore a decrease in surface albedo; and, finally, (5) that it would have a bigger effect on nighttime than daytime temperatures (Arrhenius 1896, 266). Arrhenius's model implied that the general relationship between temperature and atmospheric carbon dioxide was logarithmic (linear increases in carbon dioxide cause less than linear increases in temperature), and made the specific observation that to get a 3°–4°C increase in temperature, it would be necessary to have atmospheric carbon dioxide go up somewhere between 2 and 2.5 times.

Recall that Arrhenius's original goal had been to determine the plausibility that swings in atmospheric carbon dioxide had caused the great climatic variations due to the coming and going of the ice ages. On his model, for variation in CO_2 to account for the enormous variation in climate that occurred over millions of years on the earth – from 8° or 9°C warmer during the Tertiary period to 4°–5°C colder during the previous ice age – the level of CO_2 would have had to have been 2.5 to 3 times higher during the warmest periods in earth's history and about 0.5 lower than at the then-present level (Fleming 2015, 268). Arrhenius argued that work by his colleague Arvid Högbom on the geochemistry of carbon, which revealed an enormous amount of carbon dioxide in limestone, far greater than that in the atmosphere, was clearly consistent with periods in earth's history when the atmospheric levels of CO_2 had been much higher (Fleming 2015, 273). He thus argued that his theory was consistent with the evidence, and in fact explained evidence of long-term climatic fluctuation much better than did competing theories.

Arrhenius was a brilliant and highly creative scientist, but many of his theories did not fare well when later confronted with increasingly precise empirical observations.[4] Throughout the late nineteenth and early twentieth centuries, scientists developed all kinds of theories to explain the ice ages and long-term fluctuations in climate. As summarized by the climatologist C. E. P. Brooks in 1950 (446–475),[5] some such theories pointed to changes in solar radiation, to sunspots, or to changes in various aspects of the earth's orbit; others looked to changes in the circulation of the oceans, the relative proportions of the earth in land versus ocean, or the size and elevation of landmasses, while still others, such as Arrhenius, pointed to changes in atmospheric composition, caused sometimes by volcanic dust (Fleming 2015, 111). There were arguments in favor of each of these, and during the 1950s, a majority of climatologists believed that some combination of changes in solar activity and mountain building had caused the earth's major climatic changes (Fleming 2015, 111).

Variations in carbon dioxide were not viewed by most climatologists as likely responsible for major climate epochs. While some climatologists had long believed that CO_2 increases attendant upon the increased use of fossil fuels during industrialization had caused temperature to increase and would continue to cause future increases,[6] by the 1950s most climatologists disagreed. They doubted that CO_2 could have much independent effect, as CO_2 and water vapor absorbed infrared radiation in the same spectral regions and the current amount of atmospheric CO_2 was already accomplishing the maximum absorption by that particular gas, while water vapor was a more powerful absorber (Fleming 2015, 111–113). Even those, such as G. S. Callender, who thought that increases in atmospheric CO_2 caused by industrialization had warmed the planet thought this was a good thing, as not only would elevated CO_2 increase growing seasons and plant growth rates but "the return of the deadly glaciers should be delayed indefinitely."[7] By 1961, Callender had compiled an impressive time series of observed atmospheric CO_2, showing that the rise of CO_2 had corresponded closely to industrialization, going from about 290 ppm preindustrialization to about 330 ppm by the mid-1950s, and he concluded that this rise in CO_2 correlated with a rise in temperatures (Fleming 2015, 117–118).

By the early 1950s, there was significant scientific and public concern about rising temperatures. There were scientific studies reporting that average temperature in Iceland over the period 1926–1947 was over 1°C higher than the average over the period 1872–1925; that global temperatures too had increased since 1885 and that from 1890 to 1940, Artic sea ice thickness decreased by an average of 30 percent and the area covered by such ice by 15 percent (Fleming 2015, 118). A pioneer in infrared physics, Gilbert Plass argued in 1956 that "if at the end of this century, measurements show that the carbon dioxide content of the atmosphere has risen appreciably at the same time the temperature has continued to rise throughout the world, it will be firmly established that carbon dioxide is an important factor in climate change" (Fleming 2015, 122, quoting Plass 1956, 387). By 1958, the US Geological Survey reported that the Arctic ice pack was 40 percent thinner in 1958 than in 1944 and that sea level was rising at a rate of 2 feet per century, rather than the previous estimate of only half a foot per century (Fleming 2015, 132).

As for the popular press, in 1950 an article entitled "Is the World Getting Warmer?" appeared in the *Saturday Evening Post.* The article discussed not only recent unprecedented weather events – such as three January thaws in a row on the Penobscot River near Old Town, Maine – but quoted at length from Swedish climatologist Hans Ahlmann discussing the possibility of rising sea levels that could displace millions of people, retreats in glaciers and the Greenland ice cap, and changes in fisheries and agriculture.[8] In 1953, the cartoonist Virgil Partach published *Today's Revolution in Weather!*, an entire book filled with contemporary news items and cartoons on extreme weather and global warming (Fleming 2015, 119).

The very next year, however, *Fortune* magazine published an article entitled "Climate: The Heat May Be Off,"[9] and four years after that Betty Friedan published an article in *Harper's Magazine* popularizing a recent article published in the journal *Science* that set out a nightmarish scenario of a coming ice age caused, ironically enough, by global warming – induced changes in the Arctic.[10] By the mid-1970s, the journalist George Will reported that CIA documents showed that scientists were concerned that the "average temperature in the Northern Hemisphere, at least, may decline by 2° or 3° by the end of the century. If that climate change occurs, there will be megadeaths and social upheaval because grain production in high latitudes ... will decrease."[11] A *National Geographic* article one year later relayed that US National Science Foundation had reported that world temperatures had fallen for over 20 years, with the sharpest fall occurring during the preceding decade (Matthews 1976, 581). Buckminster Fuller prognosticated that the superpowers would soon be fighting for land near the equator in order to be able to survive the coming "big chill" (Fleming 2015, 134, citing Ponte 1976, 177–231).

II THE EVOLUTION OF NATIONAL AND INTERNATIONAL GOVERNMENT-FUNDED CLIMATE SCIENCE ADVOCACY

It was in the 1970s – a very cold decade of falling temperatures – that national governments and international organization began to fund climate science. This funding was actively pursued by government agencies seeking to retain and build their budgets, by activist scientists and environmentalists, and, perhaps most importantly, by international organizations within the United Nations. By 2014, the United States alone had spent $50 billion on federal climate science initiatives. This massive spending created a huge, federally funded climate science advocacy infrastructure that produced not only the lengthy climate science assessment reports relied upon by the EPA and US courts but also far more frequent public announcements that were intentionally designed to influence public opinion and political action.

A *Government-Directed Climate Research: The Early Years*

(a) The United States: The National Climate Program of 1978

In the United States, the federal government's interest in climate science began way back in 1975 with Democrat representative George Brown of California's introduction of legislation calling for a National Climate Program.[12] The 1970s was a cold decade, and it was concern over "severe climatic anomalies" such as drought in the African Sahel, floods, drought and an early frost in the US Midwest in 1974 and the coldest winter ever recorded in the United States in 1977 that led Congress to eventually pass the National Climate Program Act in 1978.[13] This law created the National Climate Program (NCP) in the Department of Commerce. Today, the NCP's board consists not only of the Climate Program director but also representatives from no fewer than 12 federal agencies or offices, the Departments of Agriculture, Commerce, Defense, Energy, Interior, State, and Transportation; the Environmental Protection Agency; the National Aeronautics and Space Administration; the Council on Environmental Quality; the National Science Foundation; and the Office of Science and Technology Policy. The NCP structure has thus ensured that a very large number of federal agencies are involved in and therefore potential direct beneficiaries of funding for climate research.

The NCP has a very broad mandate: it was to assess climate impacts on everything from agricultural production to human health and national security; conduct "basic and applied research" into the social, economic, and political implications of climate change; "develop methods for improving climate forecasts"; actively disseminate "information and assessments"; and finally, undertake including mechanisms for consultation with current and potential users; and, finally, undertake "measures for increasing international cooperation in climate research, monitoring, analysis and data dissemination."[14]

The NCP also empowered the State Department (and the Commerce Department) to "coordinate" US efforts in climate research with efforts by foreign governments and international organizations. Congress specifically instructed that the NCP to manage representation by the State and Commerce Departments at "climate-related international meetings and conferences" and itself to coordinate with climate programs of other nations and international agencies and organizations, including the World Meteorological Organization, the International Council of Scientific Unions, the United Nations Environmental Program, [and] the United Nations Educational, Scientific, and Cultural Organization."[15]

Under the 1978 NCP law, by 1983, the Program was to issue a "5 year plan." The 5-year plan was to include "mechanisms" for studies by universities and the private sector on the effects of climate on "agricultural production, water resources, energy needs, and other critical sectors of the economy," and for "advice to regional, State and local government agencies regarding climate-related issues."[16] In the meantime, the Program was authorized to make annual grants to States to fund "public or private educational institutions, ... State agencies, and ... other persons or institutions qualified to conduct climate-related studies or provide climate-related services."

The 1970s was a time when growing environmental concern coincided with worldwide panic over energy supply. The 1973–1974 oil embargo and subsequent quadrupling of oil prices have been discussed previously. After the embargo, OPEC was formed, and it succeeded in hiking oil prices just as steeply in 1978–1979. It was in 1977 that President Jimmy Carter gave his infamous speech to the nation setting out a goal of reducing US dependence on oil imports and declaring that the energy crisis was the moral equivalent of war (or "MEOW" for short). By the late 1970s, many people believed that developed countries had no choice but to end their use of fossil fuels for energy, and especially to wean themselves from oil.

According to Roger Pielke, Jr., early on NOAA, NASA, and NSF became the three major players in climate change science. Overall, because of focus on the energy crisis, the Department of Energy "was the most active agency in the climate change area in the late 1970s and early 1980s."

Even before the passage of the NCP, in 1977, the year of Carter's MEOW speech, the National Academy of Sciences (NAS) produced a report entitled *Energy and Climate* (National Research Council [NRC] 1977). That report contains 10 separate reports, organized by area of inquiry. The content of this 1977 report is interesting for more than just historical reasons. First of all, the 1977 NAS report clearly displays the unreliability of long-term projections of future energy use. For example, the chapter entitled "Projected World Energy Consumption" predicted that in 2025, US carbon dioxide emissions from energy (coal, oil and natural gas) would total 20,000 million metric tons, and that all of Communist Asia (which of course included China) would emit only 7,700 million tons (NRC 1977, 47).

This projection will prove to be fabulously wrong. As of 2012, US energy-related carbon dioxide emissions were only 5,290 million metric tons and falling at a rate of 3.8 percent,[17] while Chinese carbon dioxide emissions in 2011 were 8,715 million metric tons and growing at rate of 9 percent per year.[18] Even if the rate of decline in US CO_2 emissions and increase in Chinese emissions are both cut in half (to a 2 percent decline for the United States and 4 percent increase for China), projecting ahead from 2012 (or 2011 in the case of China), US carbon dioxide emissions in 2025 would be 4,063 million metric tons,[19] while Chinese carbon dioxide emissions in that year would be 15,066 million metric tons. In other words, based just on 2011 data, and making very conservative assumptions about the rate of increase in Chinese emissions and rate of decline in US emissions, when one compares the National Research Council's (NRC) 1977 projection to my simple but more recent projection, it turns out the NRC projections likely got things completely backward, with errors of 500 percent and 200 percent: the United States, projected to emit over 20,000 million metric tons in 2025, will be more like 4,000 million metric tons, while China, projected to emit at most 7,700 metric tons, will be over 15,000 million metric tons.

Another respect in which the 1977 NAS report is noteworthy is the cautious and careful tone of its scientific reports. In his chapter entitled "The Changing Climate," J. Murray Mitchell Jr. of NOAA made several observations which remain true, and important, today. Among his wisest comments are his remarks and inherently and unpredictably changeable nature of climate:

> the climate of the earth is now known beyond any doubt to have been in a more less continual state of flux. Changeability is evidently a characteristic of climate on all resolvable time scales of variation, from that of aeons down to those of millennia and centuries. The lesson of history seems to be that climatic variability must be recognized and dealt with as a fundamental quality of climate and that it would be potentially perilous for modern civilization to assume that the climate of future decades and centuries will be free of similar variability. (Mitchell 1977, 52)

Mitchell continued to explain how over the "several centuries," there have been "typical fluctuations of 30 year averages of climatic variables," with regional variations in temperature on the order of "1–2°C, and those of precipitation, of the order of 10–20 percent."

As for the earth's recent climate history, according to Mitchell, writing again in 1977:

> in the first half of the twentieth century, the world was enjoying a full recovery, at least temporarily, from the Little Ice Age. . . . At that time, a general warming of the earth occurred, which was most pronounced in the Atlantic sector of the sub-Arctic.

> A rapid worldwide retreat of mountain glaciers and a poleward extension of the ranges of many flora and fauna took place then. ... There is considerable evidence that, between the 1940's and about 1970, the climatic changes of the earlier part of this century had tended to undergo a reversal. Temperatures had mostly fallen, especially in the Arctic and Atlantic sub-Arctic, where sea ice has been increasing. The circulation of the northern hemisphere appears to have shifted in a manner suggestive of an increasing amplitude of the planetary waves and of greater extremes of weather conditions in many areas of the world. ... These events have culminated, at times in the last several years, in the emergence of anomalous conditions in the monsoon belt of the tropics and in widespread drought in the Sahel zone of Africa and in northwest India. ... To what extent these calamitous recent events are related to each other as manifestations of a globally coherent fluctuation of climate is not clear. In any event, *they dramatize the fact that climatic variability, whether globally coherent or not, is to be expected no less on time scales of months and years than on time scales of centuries and millennia. An evident faltering of these tendencies of climate, in just the last five or ten years, attests also to the ephemeral nature of all climatic "trends." Such is the nature of climate and climatic variations.* (Mitchell, in National Research Council (1977, 55)

Contributions to the 1977 "Energy and Climate" volume which discuss then state-of-the-art computer climate modeling reveal inherent uncertainties that weaken model confidence, things that as we shall see in the next part of this book, many climate scientists say are still true today. Charles Keeling and Robert Bacastow's contribution, entitled "Impact of Industrial Gases on Climate," discusses Manabe and Wetherald's pioneering 1975 three-dimensional computer climate model. Kelling and Bacastow point out the model's widely publicized prediction of a 2.5°C increase in temperature from a doubling of atmospheric CO_2. But they also point out its key limitations – including uncertainty about heat transport by oceans, the assumption that there would be no change, after a doubling of CO_2, in the distribution of low-, middle-, and high-latitude clouds; and, finally uncertainty over the capacity of carbonates in the oceans to remove carbon dioxide via dissolution. The Manabe and Wetherald computer model assumed that the oceans' capacity to remove carbon dioxide was low and rapidly diminishing was atmospheric CO_2 increased. But the Manabe and Wetherald model also implied that if the oceans were better at removing CO_2 (and the removal occurred in both shallow and deep water), then future temperature increases due to increased atmospheric CO_2 would be lower, even by 2500 (Keeling and Bacastow 1977, 72, 73, 81–82).

In his contribution, Joseph Smagorinsky (1977, 133) noted that over the six years prior to 1977, the problem of "developing a fundamental understanding of the mechanisms and dynamics of climate" had "received extraordinary attention," that was compiled in two major publications.[20]

Perhaps most interesting is Smagorinksy's discussion of the nature of the climate system and his remarks on the kind of "sensitivity experiment" that can actually be conducted with climate models. On the nature of the climate system:

> One is tempted to presume that climatic change is primarily the result of extraterrestrial influences. For example, the most spectacular of all the sensible climate changes is the seasonal cycle in response to solar radiation changes as an orbital consequence. Nevertheless, the complex earth-atmosphere-ocean-cryospheric system (the "climate as system"), because of its highly interactive nonlinearity, could conceivably be responsible for all past evidence of climatic change, including ice ages. This could be the result of positive and negative feedbacks with a variety of relaxation times. This would mean that for fixed external boundary conditions, a unique stable equilibrium does not exist. (Smagorinksy 1977, 135)

I include this quote from Smagorinsky not to indicate that he is correct – the evidence that ice ages were caused by wobbles in the earth's axis and/or orbital ellipse and not anything internal to the climate system itself is very strong – but to show that even in 1977, climate scientists understood that the complex feedback effects found in the earth's climate system could themselves generate climate cycles without any external "forcing" such as human GHG emissions. Smagorinksy was just as insightful and prescient on the use of computer climate models:

> In a sense, we use the results of comprehensive model simulations, where necessary, as a substitute for observation in gaining insight into dominant operative mechanisms. By this procedure, we can decide when and how we can simplify the models and still have meaningful and useful predictions. . . . In any case, simple models are didactically useful in isolating the nature of the interaction of particular sets of processes. However, *unless it can be satisfactorily shown that other candidate processes are negligible in the parameter range of interest, one may not extrapolate to quantitative or even qualitative predictions of the real complex geophysical medium* . . ., consistency of modeling precision may limit the admissible sophistication of the operative physical processes (e.g. in the radiation algorithms, ice dynamics, ocean coupling) below the threshold where meaningful sensitivity experiments can be performed. (Smagorinksy 1977, 138, emphasis added)

What Smagorinsky is saying in the above quote is crucial to understand and remember: even in today's age of supercomputers that were not available when Smagorinsky wrote, it is still true that computer models of climate are based on particular sets of equations that express things like how ice sheets change in response to changing surface temperatures, and how ocean temperatures are affected by a warming atmosphere. As scientists are still learning about the processes captured by such equations, those equations may be wrong, and if they are, then computer models may not be able to produce "meaningful" projections of how the earth's climate responds to forcings such as an increase in atmospheric CO_2 (climate "sensitivity").

A final and crucial aspect of the 1977 NRC *Energy and Climate* report is the tremendous gap between the sophistication and subtlety of its substantive chapters and the policy implications discussed in its "Overview and Recommendations" chapter. That chapter deals not with climate science but discusses a series of policy implications that are only loosely supported, if at all, by the climate science chapters. Among other things, the "Overview and Recommendations" states that

> if the potential for climate change discussed in this report is further substantiated, then it may be necessary to reverse the trend in the consumption of fossil fuels. . . . In the face of so much uncertainty regarding climate change, it might be argued that the wisest attitude would be laissez-faire. Unfortunately, it will take a millennium for the effects of a century of use of fossil fuels to dissipate. If the decision is postponed until the impact of man-made climate changes has been felt, then, for all practical purposes, the die will already have been cast. (3)
>
> . . . *The climatic effects of limiting carbon dioxide release may be the primary limiting factor on energy production for fossil fuels over the next few centuries.* The prospect of damaging climatic changes may thus be the stimulus for greater efforts at conservation and a more rapid transition to alternate energy sources than is justified by economic considerations alone.
>
> . . . The possibility of modification of the world's climate by carbon dioxide released in the production of energy from fossil fuels should be given prompt consideration by concerned national and international organizations and agencies. Two kinds of action are needed: organization of a comprehensive worldwide research program and new institutional arrangements.
>
> *Consideration should be given to the establishment at the national level of a mechanism to weave together the interests and capabilities of the scientific community and the various agencies of the federal government in dealing with climate-related problems.* Solutions to those problems will involve coordination of research in many scientific disciplines and are likely to require adjustments in national policy or the formulation of new legislation. Such a mechanism might embodied in a Climatic Council with the following functions: 1. To serve as the focal point within the United States for the development of a global research and action program.

Only after setting out these conclusions and recommendations did the "Overview and Recommendations" chapter then go on to summarize (7–27) the content of the substantive contributions. However, even that part of the Overview and Recommendations began with a discussion of the dire consequences of warming, including: how a warming of the top 1,000 meters of ocean water by 5°C would raise sea level by 1 m, due to the expansion of water volume; how annual snowfall in Antarctica might increase, resulting in a possible mass ice slide and the destruction of the West Antarctic ice cap, leading to an increase in sea level of 5 m within 300 years; how "large changes in climatic relationships within regions such as might be brought about by a doubling or quadrupling or atmospheric carbon dioxide would almost certainly exceed the adaptive capacity of presently grown crop varieties"; how the most serious effects of future climate changes could be in the arid and semiarid regions, where "the human disasters caused by drought in these regions are familiar and dramatic," and where "over shorter times, the effects [of a marked climate change] might be adverse, perhaps even catastrophic" (8–11). I shall briefly recall these 1977 prognostications later, for they are virtually identical to what the IPCC is saying as recently as 2018.

The tremendous difference between the substantive chapters and the "Overview and Recommendations" policy chapter of the 1977 NAS report may in part be due to the fact that the policy chapter was not written by a scientist. It was written by Roger Revelle, the chair of the "Panel on Energy and Climate." Although he successfully portrayed himself as the "granddaddy" of the theory of global warming,[21] Revelle had, by his own admission, no training in either physics or mathematics.[22] This lack of training did not stop Revelle from achieving enormous success as an academic and governmental administrator. As director of the Scripps Institute of Oceanography, Revelle succeeded in making that institution part of the then-new University of California at San Diego. He served as president of the first International Oceanographic Congress and as the science advisor to Secretary of the Interior Steward Udall during the Kennedy administration. And when he failed after that to realize his ambition of becoming chancellor of UCSD, Revelle switched fields entirely and by 1964 had become the founding Director of the Center for Population Studies at Harvard University (Fleming 2015, 124).

The National Academy of Science produced new assessments of climate modeling in 1979 and again in 1982. At least as early as 1983, the EPA was involved. In that year, EPA's Stephen Seidel, who was ultimately put in charge of EPA's Stratospheric Protection program to implement the Montreal Protocol on Substances that Deplete the Ozone Layer, coauthored a report by the Office of Policy and Resource Management entitled "Can We Delay a Greenhouse Warming? The Effectiveness and Feasibility of Options to Slow a Build-up of Carbon Dioxide in the Atmosphere" (Seidel and Keyes 1983). For its overview of the science on CO_2 and global warming, the report relied primarily (although not entirely) upon the NAS's 1979 and 1982 assessments (Charney 1982; Smagorinsky 1982). EPA endorsed the use of computer climate models for projected future warming, saying that "in the absence of unambiguous empirical evidence of the relationship between atmospheric CO_2 and temperature, climate models provide the next best tool for characterizing this relationship" (Seidel and Keyes 1983, 2–5). EPA then explained that computer models projected between 2°C and 4°C increase in temperature caused by a doubling of CO_2 relative to preindustrial levels, with the difference accounted for by different assumptions about changes in cloud height and heat transport by oceans and changes in sea ice (Seidel and Keyes 1983, 2–5). The report's analysis of "The Economic and Political Feasibility of Energy Policies" concludes "that only policies that ban coal, or coal and shale oil, would significantly delay a warming of 2 degrees centigrade or more. Furthermore, a ban on coal and shale oil would be effective in reducing the temperature rise in 2100" (Seidel and Keyes 1983, 5-1). Despite its effectiveness, the report concluded that given its estimates of asset losses and increases in the price of alternative fuels, a coal ban would be economically infeasible, and given that most of the world's coal was in only three countries – the United States, China, and the

USSR – a coal ban would likely be politically infeasible on an international level (Seidel and Keyes 1983, vii). Interestingly, the report at several points does worry about equity concerns from policies to reduced GHG emissions, noting in particular that the "consequences from [climate] changes will differ dramatically from country to country. In fact, some areas of the world are likely to experience more desirable temperatures and increased rainfall, and therefore would benefit from rising CO_2" (Seidel and Keyes 1983, 5–17).

EPA's 1983 "Can We Delay a Greenhouse Warming?" report proved to be a springboard to further congressional action. Among other people, the authors of this study acknowledged comments from John Hoffman, who was described as directing EPA's research program on greenhouse effects. Mr. Hoffman passed away in 2011, and in the following year, the Climate Institute posted a remembrance of Mr. Hoffman written by one of the Institute's co-founders, John Topping Jr. That remembrance is quite informative about the early history of EPA's involvement with greenhouse gas regulation and how EPA was instrumental in encouraging further congressional involvement. It is so informative that I quote it at length:

> In March 1983 a conference John and Jim Titus organized on sea level rise implications for the US placed the climate issue in the US news media with prominent coverage in the Christian Science Monitor. Can We Delay A Greenhouse Warming?, an analysis by John's team in the policy office, received front page coverage in the *New York Times* and sparked a flurry of media interest in the fall of 1983. Soon after that Joe Cannon, who had moved to head EPA's Office of Air and Radiation where I was his Chief of Staff, recruited John to spearhead a risk assessment of CFCs carried out so skillfully that it is likely to have cut a couple years off the time to negotiate a robust agreement to protect the stratospheric ozone layer.
>
> In July 1986, Joe Cannon and I, who had had our interest in climate change awakened by John before returning to private law practice, and seven colleagues joined to form the Climate Institute. In our first few weeks our fledgling group was approached by the Senate Appropriations Committee staff as Senator Patrick Leahy of Vermont was considering providing a significant boost in the EPA budget to support analytical work on climate and stratospheric ozone protection. We immediately contacted John Hoffman, who quietly assigned his trusted colleague, Steve Seidel, to develop a detailed budget justification. This was persuasive enough that Leahy won the support of Appropriations Subcommittee Chairman Jake Garn for a $6.5 million allocation to EPA for work on climate and stratospheric ozone, roughly a ten-fold increase from EPA's funding the previous year for these issues. This allocation was to provide the bulk of funding for EPA's analytical work on CFCs and halons that provided the intellectual rationale for the Montreal Protocol; it also provided the resources for two EPA reports whose studies provided an impetus for the formation of the IPCC and helped make the 1992 Framework Convention on Climate Change much more robust – *The Potential Effects Of Global Climate Change On The United States and Policy Options for Stabilizing Global Climate.*[23]

To summarize, according to Topping's firsthand account, in 1986, EPA got a 10-fold increase in its budget to work on climate and stratospheric ozone and climate, and with this funding it produced two reports providing an "impetus" for the creation of the IPCC and strongly influencing the sole international climate agreement that the United States has joined. Ronald Reagan, not Jimmy Carter, was the US president in 1986, and the energy crisis of the 1976–1980 years was by then a distant memory. Reagan was no fan of any kind of environmental regulation. He proposed eliminating both the Department of Energy and NOAA, and although these agencies managed to survive (and in the case of NOAA, actually get budget increases), the majority of the agencies involved in the NCP faced budgetary pressures during the 1980s.

The preferences of the Reagan administration, reelected by a huge margin in 1984, didn't stop EPA in 1986 from getting a 10-fold increase in its climate budget and from producing reports that strongly supported GHG emission reduction policies. EPA adapted by going straight to a Democrat-controlled Senate committee for funding. Other agencies involved in the US NCP also adapted to Reagan administration opposition. A NOAA administrator during this period commented later that the budgetary pressures inflicted by the Reagan administration "force[d] us to work closer and closer together." Global change emerged as the theme of such interagency cooperation. During the 1980s, NOAA developed a program called Climate and Global Change, NASA was promoting a "global habitability" program, and NSF had a program called Global Geosciences. By the late 1980s, global change had become "a large-scale program of research" created by a "well-defined community" that stretched across many federal agencies and offices.

B *Outside the United States: Climate Change Becomes the Greatest International Science Funding Opportunity Ever*

Internationally, in 1972, the World Meteorological Organization (WMO) – an organization comprising national meteorological agencies – held a symposium on Long-Term Climatic Fluctuations. The proceedings of that symposium, published in 1975,[24] contain work that is now viewed as pathbreaking in investigating methods to find evidence about long-term climate fluctuations. In an abstract, Shackleton explained that the analysis of oxygen isotopes found in deep sea sediments was informative about temperatures during the far distant past of 50 to 3 million years ago, but that over the last 2 million years, that form of analysis could reveal little about temperatures, although it did show that glaciations had been occurring throughout the 2 million years of the Pleistocene era, with glaciations occurring about each 100,000 years, with the last glacial episode beginning quickly, about 115,000 years ago. Other contributions in the 1975 Symposium volume are likewise concerned with explaining long-term climate fluctuations, for example discussing the possible use of pollen and tree rings as records of paleoclimate. Very few contributions to this 1972 WMO Symposium are interested in discovering trends in long-term climate data, and only one looked at the impact of anthropogenic aerosols on climate (Kellogg and Coakley XXXX, 323). While a number of papers discussed progress in building numerical models of climate (including, interestingly a paper by Stephen Schneider and Clifford Mass using an early general circulation model developed at National Center for Atmospheric Research to analyze the possible impact of volcanic dust and sunsports in influencing long-term climate trends), not a single contribution of roughly 30 looked specifically at the question of how changes in atmospheric CO_2 might impact climate.

Long-term climate fluctuations were also the focus of another early 1970s international conference. In 1974, in the aftermath of the Arab oil embargo and the overnight quadrupling of oil prices, the International Energy Agency created the Coal Working Group. Although it might seem now somewhat tangential to that group's purpose – to explore "means by which countries interested in minimizing their dependence on imported oil could cooperate" (Smith 1978) – in 1978 the Coal Working Group produced a report on possible causes of long-term fluctuations in climate, including variations in the earth's orbit, volcanic dust, solar flux variations, and continental drift. An entire chapter of this report was devoted to discussing the possible climatic impacts of increasing carbon dioxide in the atmosphere. That chapter reported that the most advanced computer model of that time (Manabe and Wetherald 1975, 3) generated a predicted a 1°C warming by 2020 (assuming a 1.5× preindustrial level of CO_2 by then) and a temperature increase of between 1 and 5 degrees centigrade if atmospheric CO_2 were to reach two times preindustrial levels (Smith 1978, 23–24). While not opining on their relative qualitative or quantitative importance, the report discussed most of the major feedbacks of CO_2-induced warming that might amplify or lessen the final amount of warming – including changes in cloud cover, temperature dependence of ocean uptake of CO_2, and possible changes in polar ice (Smith 1978, 26–27). The report briefly discussed possible impacts of warmer temperatures, notably pointing out that the then available studies[25] of the of the Altithermal – a period 4,000–8,000 years BP when temperatures were believed to be 2°–3°C warmer than today – indicated that "things were not necessarily worse at higher global temperatures. At that time, North Africa was generally more favorable for agriculture that it is now, Europe was wetter, Scandinavia dryer, and a belt of grass lands extended across North America" (Smith 1978, 28).

The year 1974 also marked the creation of the first climate change expert panel by the Executive Committee of the World Meteorological Organization (WMO). The WMO organization "recognized technological and political opportunities" and charged a panel to "consider the possibility of global warming in preparation for the 1975 WMO World Congress" (Boehmer-Christiansen 1994, 154). In 1975, the United Nations General Assembly added its voice to the call for the WMO to study climate change, formally asking that WMO panel of experts on climate change to "'prepare a definitive statement on the climate change issue and to develop plans for an integrated international effort to study climate changes and the implications for man's natural environment and for world food production" (Boehmer-Christiansen 1994, 154). By 1976, the Scientific Committee on Problems of the Environment of the International Council for Science (ICSU) reported that existing numerical models projected "alarming" increases in CO_2 over the next 200 years and an increase in temperatures of between 2° and 3°C and acidification of the oceans (Boehmer-Christiansen 1994, 154).

Three organizations took the lead in international climate change science and policy: ICSU, WMO, and UNEP. It is useful to review very briefly what these organizations are all about. WMO is perhaps the most purely scientific in focus, with its mission focused on such things as facilitating cooperation in establishing networks of meteorological observation stations and promoting the standardization and sharing of such observations. The members of WMO are national meteorological services, the director of each of which is a permanent representative to the WMO.[26]

The ICSU has evolved to have a much more mixed agenda of science *for* policy. The ICSU was until 1998 known as the International Council of Scientific Unions, and although its name has changed, it has retained a membership structure consisting of "national scientific bodies" and "international scientific unions" (e.g., the International Union of Pure and Applied Chemistry). Although the original mission for the ICSU was to "provide a forum for scientists from different countries to and disciplines to address issues of common concern," by 2005 the ICSU stated its mission as being to address "specific global issues through the development of Interdisciplinary Bodies and developed partnerships with other organizations, in particular various United Nations organizations."[27] After merging with the International Science Council in 2017, the ICSU has an even more overtly policy-driven mission, to "...support scientists to contribute solutions to complex and pressing matters of global public concern" and "... advise decision makers and practitioners on the use of science in achieving ambitious agendas such as the Sustainable Development Goals (SDGs) adopted by world leaders in 2015."[28]

UNEP (the United Nations Environment Program) is the most purely policy-oriented of the three organizations that moved to put climate change on the international agenda. Governed by a Board ("Bureau") consisting of United Nations ambassadors, [29] UNEP's mission is to assess global, regional and national environmental conditions, and to foster the development and growth of environmental regulation, both in the form of international agreements and at the national level.

Although the extent to which they officially focus on science versus policy applications of science varies – from a relatively pure focus on science at the WMO to a pure policy focus at UNEP – all three of these organizations have a clear and undeniable interest in identifying and publicizing global environmental problems that require both more scientific research and an international response policy response. The bigger and more widespread globally and the more harmful the potential environmental problem, the stronger the case that can be made to national governments for more funding for both scientific research and for international organizations that facilitate international treaty-making and national policy responses. Hence merely based on their basic missions and membership, one would expect that WMO, UNEP, and ICSU would actively seek to identify and publicize such potential international problems.

Just such an agenda seems to characterize early, pre-IPCC climate change institutional activism. By 1980, the WMO, ICSU and UNEP had cooperated to sponsor a conference of experts in Villach which concluded that that the probability of serious impacts was sufficiently great that international cooperation in research was warranted (Boehmer-Christiansen 1994, 155). As one commentator observes, by the early 1980s:

> The institutions of science, together with the UN agencies, were preparing to mobilize public opinion and policy. ... Too many research opportunities had attached themselves to climate change and world diplomacy was beginning to show an interest when Crispin Tickell (now Sir) realized its global policy potential and disseminated the idea among the diplomatic community. (Boehmer-Christiansen 1994, 155)

Of course, as noted, these three agencies differ in their concern with policy, and in particular one would predict rather less interest by the WMO in policy per se. With the mid-1980s effort to mobilize public opinion, institutional leadership clearly shifted from the WMO, which had several times failed to advocate a clear policy response, to the UNEP. Its leader Mustafa Tolba had already spoken, at First World Climate Congress in 1979, of an "uncontrolled experiment" and the UNEP began "using the climate change threat ... to advance its own more policy-oriented research agenda and to draw attention to global mutuality and therefore questions of development" (Boehmer-Christiansen 1994, 155).

Efforts by these international organizations were strongly supported by the German government. During the late 1970s, the German government-funded conferences and research that focused not on explaining long-term climate fluctuations but on identifying possible human contributions to climate change. In 1978, the Federal Republic of Germany, through its Department of Interior and Environmental Agency, sponsored an international conference entitled "Man's Impact on Climate." In 1980, two more conferences, on energy/climate interactions and climate/food interaction, were held were under the auspices of a German Interdisciplinary Governmental Research Program on Climatology. The 1980 Energy/Climate Interactions workshop (the "Munster workshop") was introduced as intended to "join the relevant multinational activities of the WMO and the Commission of the European Community, which is to give basis for political decisions to protect man and his environment from harmful effects" on the climate from energy use.[30]

The 1980 Munster workshop had several important features. First, as a clear antecedent to the structure of future IPCC assessment reports, the 1980 Munster workshop was organized by three working groups. Second, the conclusions reached by those working groups back in 1980 – a decade before the IPCC was even created – show how many policy-relevant conclusions about climate science haven't changed one iota in almost four decades.

For example, Working Group I of the 1980 Munster Conference projected that "if energy consumption follows current projections, it seems probable, based on present knowledge of the carbon cycle, that atmospheric CO_2 will reach twice the preindustrial level around 2050 [and] ... present estimates center around a global average value of 2–3 degrees C surface air temperature increase per doubling of atmospheric CO_2 concentration with a 3–4 fold temperature increase in northern polar regions." It cautioned, however, that "if the exploitation of fossil fuels is not restrained and no large storage of carbon in the biosphere occurs, the most likely global average temperature rise could be of the order of 4 to 6 degrees C."[31] The report highlighted that even though computer models of the general circulation of the earth's atmosphere and oceans were known "to contain systematic errors," they had a "particularly valuable future contribution to make to the estimation of likely impacts of an increase in CO_2 on the climate." More concretely, using historical and geological evidence on past climates, the Working Group report then hypothesized on what alternative future temperature increases might look like. The Group reported that based on evidence of the medieval warm period (AD 900–1050), an increase of even 1 could involve the "disappearance of sea ice in East Greenland, frequent warm and dry summers in central and western Europe, a 1–2 week lengthening of growing season in high latitudes, decreasing winter rainfall and increasing drought in subtropical areas, and decreased drought in the tropics."

As for a global temperature increase of 2°–2.5°C, the 1980 German energy/climate workshop Working Group said that as this would be "similar to the last interglacial (125,000 BP)" it expected that "arctic sea ice would be restricted to its core area, permafrost would retreat by 100 km, with a likely increase of 5–7 m in sea level, possibly caused by the collapse of the Western Antarctic ice sheet." As for a an even bigger 4°C temperature increase, the Working Group said that such a temperature increase was "similar to the early to mid-Pliocene (3–5 million years BP)," and although "most present day mountains, including the Alps and Tibetan highlands, had only begun their uplift and had reached only a 'small portion of their present height,'" back then, it still was able to say that it expected that "the Arctic Ocean would be ice-free and surrounded by boreal forests," with a "substantial northward shift in the northern subtropical arid zone, perhaps all the way to near Vienna." While temperature increase of 6°C was "believed to have characterized the northern hemisphere during the Oligocene/mid-Miocene (15–38 million years BP)," the 1980 Munster Working Group said that "too little is known about climate then to draw any lessons."[32]

Equally interesting, especially as a comparison point with IPCC reports to be discussed later, was the report of Working Group III, on "Objectives of a Climatic Impact Study Program." That report first clarified the set of questions that needed to be asked: "if there are so many uncertainties in our understanding of climatic impacts, can we make any useful predictions of their implications? Are there ways to build resilience to climatic changes, whether carbon-dioxide induced or natural? Will decision-makers be willing to rely on the results of this program? What incentives and disincentives exist for taking policy action on the carbon dioxide climate issue? What is the long-term purpose of the research effort?"[33]

The 1980 Munster conference Working Group III then recommended that rather than forecasts, a small number of "global climate scenarios" should be developed, including moderate average warming, extreme average warming, and moderate cooling, where for each scenario, mean values and their variability should be reported, by region and season, for climate variables including temperature, rainfall, and soil moisture, where the basis for the scenarios could be both coupled ocean-atmosphere general circulation models and observations of past climates (such as the Holocene Altithermal of 4,500–8,000 years BP, or the Eemian–Sangamon warm interglacial that occurred prior to the last ice age).[34]

It is no coincidence that the German government sponsored the 1980 Munster Workshop. By 1980, the oil price spikes of 1973–1974 had incentivized the exploration and development of vast new oil reserves, and with oil coming online from the North Sea and Mexico during the mid-1970s, it was clear to most observers that the world's oil was not going to run out anytime soon. In 1980, oil prices began a decline that lasted for decades, and although even as late as the mid-1980s some economists thought that oil prices would soon begin to increase once again,[35] by 1980 it was quite clear to most people that the world would not be forced off of fossil fuels by a lack of supply. As will be discussed in Part III, Germany has no domestic oil or natural gas supply and is exceptionally vulnerable to disruptions in international oil markets. The organizers of the 1980 Munster workshop were quite clear that the focus of the workshop was on how energy use, in particular fossil fuel energy, potentially contributed to climate change. As they said:

> In the decades ahead, decisions have to be made to reduce or avert the impacts of a climatic change before all the answer have been obtained. Although a climatic impact assessment program is faced with many uncertainties, it nevertheless has to be started now, because society cannot afford to wait until all variables are quantified to the satisfaction of all the parties involved. Additionally, as a precautionary measure, society should follow a low risk-climate-energy-land use policy which would ... promote the more efficient end use of energy, [and] Secure the

> expeditious introduction of energy sources that release little or no carbon dioxide to the atmosphere.[36]

Supported by such national level efforts, in 1985 a Second Joint UNEP/ICSU/ WMO meeting was held in Villach. Entitled the "International Assessment of the Role of Carbon Dioxide and Other Greenhouse Gases in Climate Variations and Associated Impacts," the 1985 Villach meeting had 89 participants, including scientists from 29 developed and developing countries and the three sponsoring organizations (Franz 1997, 11, quoting Cooper 1989, 180–181). According to one leading history of climate change policy, the scientists who attended this 1985 meeting were selected by the three sponsoring agencies, UNEP, ICSU and WMO, and if they came from UNEP or WMO, then they were likely "government scientists, or scientists on contract to government" (Franz 1997, 14).

According to this same history, the WMO was the "least activist of the three, urging a clear statement of current knowledge . . . and consequent effects for the use of policy makers and guidance for future research h to reduce uncertainties" (Franz 1997, 14). The more active sponsoring agencies, the UNEP and ICSU, directly and strongly called for policy recommendations; indeed, the participants were "urged to recommend the establishment of an international coordinating committee on greenhouse gases . . . to discuss in greater detail the options being placed before the world's leaders, encouraging a 'wider debate on such issues as the cost and benefits of a radical shift away from fossil fuel consumption'" (Franz 1997, 14).

Describing the 1985 Villach meeting, climate policy historian Sonja Boehmer-Christiansen (1994) says:

> several of the organizers of the Conference were deeply involved in energy policy and policy research and determined to initiate a dialogue with policy makers. In fact, the meeting can be seen as having been called by scientists from energy-poor, pro-nuclear European countries jointly with environmental activists from the USA and member of the UN scientific bureaucracies. (156)

It is hardly surprising that a meeting comprising environmental activists, government scientists from countries that out of necessity had already committed themselves to low carbon energy sources and United Nations bureaucrats would view scientific uncertainty as no obstacle to clear policy advice. According to one climate historian, this move – from uncertain science to clear policy advice – was strongly advocated by UNEP Director Mostafa Tolba:

> When participating experts concluded that climate change might be twice as urgent as originally thought because of the original warming influence of greenhouse gases other than carbon dioxide, it was Mostafa Tolba who encouraged them to, for the first time, collectively signal climate change as a policy concern and to "create a machinery to get the ball rolling" in the direction of coordinated international policy responses to climate change. (Andresen and Agrawala 2002, 43)

The importance of the 1985 Villach conference in setting a basic outline for the future IPCC process can hardly be overestimated. Within the United Nations, UNEP Director Mostafa Tolba

> had no doubts about the future course of action on climate change. Flush with the success of negotiating the Vienna Convention on Ozone, he felt that the time was ripe to repeat the "ozone" miracle for climate. Indeed, UNEP in its long range planning document of 1985 had called for a climate convention. In the wake of the 1985 Villach workshop, Tolba began active consultations for a possible convention with WMO and ICSU, UNEP's two long-standing collaborators on climate change. He also wrote to then US Secretary of State George Schultz urging the US to take appropriate actions. (Agrawala 1998, 609)

At the level of the UN General Assembly, the conclusions of the Villach report were "used to develop the agenda of climate change within the United Nations specialized agencies," in particular with the creation of the Advisory Group on Greenhouse Gases (AGGG) (Franz 1997, 22). The AGGG was "conceived as a small group of independent scientists who would advise the heads of UNEP, WMO and ICSU" (Boehmer-Christiansen 1994, 157). The AGGG was set up with great "hastiness ... in the euphoria following Villach 1985," and "one close observer compared the six AGGG members to a group of private consultants to the *heads* of WMO, UNEP and ICSU. In fact, there were no formal requirements for the group to report on its activities, or to seek direction from even the governing bodies of the three sponsoring organizations, let alone national governments" (Agrawala 1998, 613).

A perhaps even more significant outcome of the 1985 Villach conference was the production of a set of peer-reviewed scientific papers. Published in 1986 by WMO/ICSU/UNEP as the Scope 29 Report, this volume was so similar to subsequent IPCC Assessment reports in both "substantive and presentational ways," that "a senior British IPCC coordinator and scientist has called the [Scope 29 Report] the bible of the IPCC" (Boehmer-Christiansen 1994, 157).

III GOVERNMENT CLIMATE SCIENCE ADVOCACY COMES OF AGE: THE IPCC AND THE USGCRP

A *The Creation and Financing of the USGCRP*

During 1985–1986, the US Senate held its first hearings on climate change in over half a decade. In June 1986, NASA scientist Robert Watson told Congress that "I believe global warming is inevitable. It is only a question of the magnitude and the timing" (Pielke Jr. 2000, 17). The following year, Congress passed the Global Climate Protection Act of 1987.[37] This law did not authorize EPA or any other agency to impose limits on GHG emissions. But it did provide authority for EPA to develop a "coordinated national policy on global climate change" and for the State

Department to coordinate international diplomatic efforts to combat global warming.[38] Perhaps even more importantly, in Section 1102(1) of this law, Congress itself said that "the release of carbon dioxide, chlorofluorocarbons and other trace gases into the atmosphere – may be producing a long-term and substantial increase in the average temperature on earth." President Reagan opposed the law but signed it, keeping the coordination of research across federal agencies in a separate White House coordination committee (originally called the Committee on Earth Sciences or CES). Despite this effort at White House control, NASA, NOAA, and NSF, all of whom had developed global change programs, were actively involved in this White House committee and indeed lobbied to keep it going (see Pielke 2000, 19).

For most of the United States, summer 1988 was extremely hot and dry and in June, the biggest forest fire on record burned a substantial portion of Yellowstone National Park. It was during that summer that NASA scientist James Hansen testified before a Senate committee. Sitting in a hearing room staged to be stiflingly hot by turning off the air conditioning, Hansen told Congress:[39] 1) that global warming was occurring by too large an amount to be due to "chance fluctuation," and 2) it was already "large enough to affect the probability of extreme events," in particular increasing the probability of a "hot summer" in Washington D.C. by up to 70 percent by the 1990's. The next year, Hansen criticized the newly elected Bush administration for interfering with new testimony he was preparing to give to Congress. With global climate change now squarely in the media and political spotlight, by 1989, coordinated by the CES, the US Global Change Research Program–focused budget across all involved agencies was about $190 million (Pielke 2000, 20).

President George H. W. Bush came into office promising action on climate change, but as discussed in an earlier chapter, he did not support legislation imposing GHG emission limits. G. H. W. Bush did, however, sign a number of laws that funded climate research. Most importantly, the Climate Change Research Act of 1990[40] created the Global Change Research Program (USGCRP). The law's stated purpose (Section 101) was to "provide for development and coordination of a comprehensive and integrated United States Research program which will assist the Nation and the world to understand, assess, predict, and respond to human-induced and natural processes of global change." Bush also signed the Global Climate Change Prevention Act of 1990, which directed the Department of Agriculture to study the effects of climate change on forestry and agriculture).[41] A final law signed by G. H. W. Bush was the Energy Policy Act of 1992.[42] As discussed earlier, that law initiated federal subsidies for renewable electricity. It also ordered the Secretary of Energy to prepare an annual inventory of GHG emissions.

G. H. W. Bush was criticized for using scientific uncertainty to justify his administration's policy inaction on climate (Pielke Jr. 2000, 139). Paradoxically, however, G. H. W. Bush vastly increased funding for federal climate science advocacy that would increasingly be argued to lessen uncertainty about climate science. Even though the same allegedly obfuscatory interagency CES created during the Reagan years remained in charge of implementing the new Global Change Research Program, the budget for Global Change Research Program dwarfed previous federal spending on climate-related research. Across the many federal agencies involved, spending focused on the USGCRP (as opposed to merely related to it) increased from $134 million in 1989 to $1.4 billion in 1994, making it, according to one analyst, "one of the largest science programs ever conducted" (Pielke Jr. 1995, 39–77). Indeed, looking only at money that was actually focused on climate change research (vs. indirectly contributing to it), between 1989 and 2000, the USGCRP received over $16 billion in federal funding. Notably, although the Clinton administration may have failed in its effort to enact Kyoto-like GHG emission limits into domestic US law, it facilitated big increases in USGCRP funding, especially during its early years, and funding for the USGCRP stayed around $1.7 billion or more from 1994 until 2000 (Pielke Jr. 2000, 10).

The funding paid off. In June 2000, the US Global Change Research Program released the first national assessment of the possible effects of global warming on various regions in the United States.[43] The study found that if global temperatures continued to rise at current levels, the United States "may experience substantial consequences in coming decades, including lower crop production, increased erosion of coasts, extreme dry and wet conditions, and disproportionately hotter urban areas." The assessment was written by the so-called National Assessment Team, a committee of experts drawn primarily from USGCRP funded federal agencies. It received heavy press coverage,[44] with the *Washington Post* headlining the report as "Drastic Climate Changes Forecast; Global Warming Likely to Cause Droughts, Coastal Erosion in US."

Like his father, George W. Bush did not support laws or regulations imposing GHG emission limits. But also like his father, his administration supported increased government funding for climate science. As part of its US Climate Change Research Initiative, the G. W. Bush administration supplemented the USGCRP with a separate program, called the Climate Change Science Program (CCSP). The Climate Change Research Initiative had the stated goal of creating a "global community empowered with the science-based knowledge to manage the risks and opportunities of change in the climate and related environmental systems." It directed that climate change research focus on scientific information that could be developed within 2 to 5 years to assist in the evaluation of strategies to address global change risks.[45] The CCSP was eventually folded back in to the USGCRP by the Obama administration, but while in existence, it produced 21 synthesis and assessment products.[46] With funding provided under both the USGCRP and the CCSP, between 2000 and 2008, the G. W. Bush administration provided another $18.6 billion for climate science. By far the biggest recipient of this funding was NASA, which never received less than $1 billion per year. That National Science

Foundation and three other agencies – the Departments of Energy, Commerce, and Agriculture – each received at least $100 million per year in climate science funding.[47]

Under the 2009 stimulus bill discussed earlier in the context of federal subsidies for renewable energy, federal funding for the USGCRP jumped by around 33 percent. With NASA again getting the largest amount, between 2009 and 2014, the federal government authorized over $14 billion for the USGCRP.[48]

Thus in the 25 years between and 1989 and 2014, through the USGCRP and related programs, the US federal government provided almost $50 billion in funding for climate science.

B *The Creation of the IPCC*

The 1987 Bellagio and Villach AGGG meetings discussed earlier have been described as a "pathway of diffusion that was orchestrated directly by the scientists. The first meeting of the AGGG provided an opportunity for the activist scientists to begin an initiative to formulate links to policy" (Franz 1997, 24). The Bellagio meeting was, notably, attended by "a senior member of the German government and former minister responsible for energy policy, as well as a representative of the European Commission's Research Directorate" (Boehmer-Christiansen 1994, 158). The second AGGG workshop, held in Villach later in 1987 (with papers published in *Climatic Change* in 1989), "was notable for its focus on targets and timetables. Several participants noted that this shift was calculated to provide not only relevant policy information, but to derive yardsticks for government action. It represented an attempt to transform scientific facts into political facts" (Franz 1997, 26).

The 1987 AGGG conferences fed directly into the June 1988 Toronto Conference, which brought together 341 delegates, including 20 politicians and ambassadors, 118 legal advisors and senior government officials, 73 physical scientists, 50 industry representatives and energy specialists, 30 social scientists, and 50 environmental activists, with 15 agencies of 24 international organizations also represented (Franz 1997, 27). By the summer of 1988, the climate change issue had undergone an "identifiable leap to the public arena, the highest levels of national governments, and the international agenda beyond the United Nations." By the time of the conference, the serious heat wave discussed earlier had hit the United States and the media "had provided extensive coverage of the extreme weather and to its connections to climate change. . . . International media attention to the problem of climate change began a steep rise in 1987–1988, peaking in 1990" (Franz 1997, 27).

The conclusions of the Toronto conference were the epitome of alarmism. The conference statement began by declaring that "Humanity is conducting an unintended, uncontrolled, globally pervasive experiment whose ultimate consequences could be second only to a nuclear war. . . . It is imperative to act now," and predicted that "no country would benefit in toto from climate change" (Bodansky 1994, 49).

The conference report stridently recommended "immediate action . . . to counter the ongoing degradation of the atmosphere. . . . An Action Plan for the Protection of the Atmosphere needs to be developed, which includes an international framework convention" (Franz 1997, 28). However, as Franz observes, "the contribution of science to this outcome was minimal," with the conclusions of the Toronto conference failing to bear "any resemblance" to the bottom line conclusions of the AGGG Villach/Bellagio reports (Franz 1997, 28). The Toronto conference recommended a reduction of CO_2 emissions by 20 percent of 1988 levels by 2025.

According to one observer, the recommendations of the Toronto conference were drafted "drafted by a committee composed mostly of environmentalists and discussed in less than a day" (Bodansky 1994, 53). It remains unclear precisely where the 20 percent reduction target came from. Some individuals who participated in the 1988 Toronto conference opined when interviewed later that the 20 percent reduction resulted from NGO pressure; others said that the targeted 20 percent reduction relative to 1988 levels by 2005 came from the energy working group (Franz 1997, 29). Another explanation that has been advanced is that the 20 percent reduction target was simply "borrowed from other environmental agreements, most notably the ozone regime" (Andresen and Agrawala 2002, 44). Regardless of where it came from, a former State Department negotiator has commented that the target/timetable "captured and riveted the public's attention. It provided a simple litmus test of a country's environmental commitment. It required no painstaking feasibility analysis. It was political genius" (Reifsnyder 1992, 44).

Summarizing the end product of institutional climate change activism prior to the creation of the IPCC, Boehmer-Christiansen argues that "global warming rather than climate change rose to the top of the international political agenda toward the end of the 1980's after an unprecedented effort by an alliance of scientific research institutions and environmentalists predicting catastrophe" (Boehmer-Christiansen 1994, 192).

It was against this backdrop – the burgeoning success of a concerted effort by environmentalists, a relatively small group of scientists and key international organizations to put global warming on the agenda for international policy action – that the IPCC was created. Ironically, it was the United States, the developed country that over time has been perhaps the most reluctant to take costly steps to respond to global warming, that pushed for the creation of the IPCC.

The IPCC was created in 1988 by the World Meteorological Association and the United Nations Environment Program. According to Boehmer-Christiansen (1994, 189), the US State Department in particular was crucial in pushing for the creation of the IPCC, because it wanted to replace the AGGG with a body that gave governments more power to veto participants and influence it agenda, and through the WMO, the State Department felt it would be able to do this. As another historian comments:

> the trigger for the IPCC was the activism by Mostafa Tolba, the dissatisfaction in the US about the AGGG, and sharply differing views on climate change among various US government agencies and the White House administration . . . there were . . . strategic attempts both by WMO and the US to prevent Mostafa Tolba from "capturing" climate, the way he had, ozone. (Agrawala 1998, 612)

On this widely shared view of the origins of the IPCC, "the IPCC was the product of an intensely *political* process within the US and the UN system. The specific purpose for setting it up was also political: to engage governments worldwide in climate change decisionmaking" (Agrawala 1998, 617–618). According to Tolba's key advisor during the ozone negotiations, Peter Usher, "the ad-hoc," low key science-driven (if politically undemocratic) nature of the early ozone assessments which led to the Vienna convention could not be duplicated in climate change. This is because "while politics caught up with ozone, climate change was born in politics" (Agrawala 1998, 614).

The 1988 UN resolution on climate change[49] was itself ambiguous, calling for the IPCC both to provide "internationally coordinated assessments of the magnitude, timing and potential environmental and socio-economic impact of climate change and realistic response strategies" and "to initiate action leading as soon as possible to a comprehensive review and recommendations with respect to: . . . the identification and possible strengthening of relevant existing international legal instruments having a bearing on climate; [and] elements for inclusion in a possible future international convention on climate" (Bodansky 1994, 53). Given that its "informal mandate was 'in part to reassert governmental control and supervision over what was becoming an increasingly prominent political issue'" (Brunner 2001, 6, quoting O'Riordan and Jager 1996, 346), it is unsurprising, at least in retrospect, that "the IPCC was caught up in political divisions within and among the governments of the United States, European and other industrialized nations, and the less developed nations – divisions over energy, economic development, equity and other issues that had become entangled with global warming."[50]

If the motivation of the United States and other actors in pushing for the creation of the IPCC was somehow to reduce or neutralize the impact of climate change scientist advocates, then the United States and others were extremely naïve about the relationship between science and policy in the climate change area. As Boehmer-Christiansen (1994, 196–198) comments:

> Is a group of WMO/UNEP/ICSU science managers, or a self-selected group of research scientists dependent on lobbies and foundations for funding, the best body to assess the knowledge required for environmental policy? . . . Scientific knowledge can never be used without assessment and judgment. The important political question is whose assessment and whose judgment. . . .
>
> . . . Policy advice is not readily deduced from uncertain scientific knowledge, which typical of complex natural systems undergoing change. As such, facts as well as ignorance and the possibility of more knowledge becoming available in the

> future, turn into political tools which can be used by all the actors in the bargaining process. This tends to make scientific institutions major winners by giving the false impression that decisions can be left to future science. . . .
>
> By relying primarily on natural scientists and numerical modellers as representatives of relevant knowledge (or rather by allowing the global change research enterprise to capture the issue for itself), governments gained time and lost influence. The enlarged their freedom of action, but also made themselves hostages to future findings and existing uncertainties, thereby inviting the politicization of science itself. Governments, NGO's, the UN bureaucracy all used scientific advice less for the purpose of informing their own actions than for the promotion of their own agendas, justifying commitments in need of authoritative support.

Thus from its inception, the IPCC was a science advocacy organization, a group designed to assess climate science in a way that justified the policy outcomes preferred by the national and international actors responsible for its creation.

Notes

1. This is precisely what occurred with passage of the federal Clean Air Act in the United States. See Krier and Ursin (1978) (telling the story of how smog emerged as a problem in California and how auto emissions were identified as the cause, leading eventually to a push for federal auto emission standards), Christopher J. Bailey, Congress and Air Pollution (1998) (showing how the history of attempts to enact federal auto emission standards tracked the spread of smog as a local pollution problem across metropolitan areas of the United States).
2. See Pielke Jr. (2007, 2–7) (arguing that this traditional model casts the role of scientists in policy making as either that of "Pure Scientist" or "Science Arbiter," a role that risks scientists instead serving as "Stealth Issue Advocates").
3. A picture of which appears in Fleming (2005, 69).
4. As Fleming (2015, 76) quotes Arrhenius's grandson and biographer, "theoretical explanations of poorly known natural systems display a high mortality rate when confronted with accumulating evidence."
5. Brooks's summary is neatly displayed in table 9.1 of Fleming (2015, 109).
6. Among such proponents of the CO_2 efficacy view, Fleming (2015, 108, 111) cites Callender and Eckholm.
7. Quoted in Fleming (2015, 115).
8. Albert Abarbanel and Thorp McClusky, "Is the World Getting Warmer?," *Saturday Evening Post*, July 1, 1950, 22–23.
9. Francis Bello, "Climate: The Heat May Be Off," *Fortune*, August 1954, 108. Discussed at Fleming (2015, 131).

10. Betty Friedan, "The Coming Ice Age," 217 *Harper's Magazine* 39–45 (September 1958).
11. George F. Will, "A Change in the Weather," *Washington Post*, January 24, 1975. Quoted in Fleming (2015, 133).
12. My discussion here relies upon Pielke (2000, 10–14).
13. National Climate Program Act of 1978, P.L. 95–367, 92 Stat. 601 (1978) (as amended at 15 USC. §§2901–2908). See 15 USC. §2904(d) for the mission of the new office.
14. 15 USC. §2904(d).
15. 15 USC. §2904(f).
16. 15 USC. §2904(d)(7), (d)(9).
17. US Energy Information Administration, US Energy-Related Carbon Dioxide Emissions 2012, available at www.eia.gov/environment/emissions/carbon/.
18. See US Energy Information Administration, International Energy Statistics, available at https://www.eia.gov/international/data/world#/?.
19. Note that if this projection is even roughly correct, US carbon dioxide emissions will be lower in 2025 than at any point since at least 1970. See http://wattsupwiththat.com/2012/07/02/us-co2-emissions-may-drop-to-1990-levels-this-year/.
20. The first was a 1971 Stockholm conference published as W. H. Mattews, W. W. Kellogg, and G. D. Robinson, eds., *Inadvertent Climate Modification, Report of the Study of Man's Impact on Climate* (MIT Press, 1971), while the second publication was the 1975 GPS No. 16, *The Physical Basis of Climate and Climate Modeling, Report of the Study Conference on the Physical Basis of Climate and Climate Modeling* (WMO, 1975).
21. Successfully, in that this is how he was portrayed in obituaries; see Fleming (2015, 122n45, 46).
22. See Fleming (2015, 127), quoting Revelle as telling an interviewer after being awarded the National Medal of Science in 1990 that "I was never well-educated . . . geologists in those days didn't get much physics or mathematics."
23. John C. Topping, Jr., "Remembering John S. Hoffman: A Friend Who Made a Difference," available at www.climate.org/publications/Climate%20Alerts/2012-winter/john-s-hoffman.html.
24. WMO, Proceedings of the WMO/IMAP Symposium on Long-Term Climatic Fluctuations, WMO No. 421, Norwich, August 18–23, 1975.
25. Two in particular: Kellogg (1977, 49) and WMO, Report of the Scientific Workshop on Atmospheric Carbon Dioxide, WMO Report No. 474, 1977.
26. For the current mission statement of the WMO, see www.wmo.int/pages/about/mission_en.html.
27. See ICSU, Draft Strategic Plan for the International Council for Science 2006–2012, p. 9, available at www.iupesm.org/ICSU%20Strategic%20Plan.pdf.

28. International Science Council, ICSU-ISC merger, A Brief History, available at https://council.science/about-us/a-brief-history/icsu-issc-merger/.
29. For UNEP's mission statement and Bureau (board) composition, see www.unep.org.
30. Interactions of Energy and Climate (1980, vii).
31. Interactions of Energy and Climate (1980, xv).
32. Interactions of Energy and Climate (1980, xii–xiv).
33. Interactions of Energy and Climate (1980, xxvii).
34. Interactions of Energy and Climate (1980, xxxi).
35. See, e.g., Gately (1986, 237).
36. Interactions of Energy and Climate (1980, x).
37. P.L. 100–204.
38. 15 USC. §2901 et seq. at Sections 1103(b) and 1103(c).
39. Hansen's 1988 opening statement can be found at https://www.sealevel.info/1988_Hansen_Senate_Testimony.html.
40. Global Change Research Act of 1990, 15 USC. §§2921–2938, Public Law 101–606.
41. 7 USC. §6701.
42. 42 USC. §§13381–13388.
43. National Assessment Synthesis Team, US Global Change Research Program, *Climate Change Impacts on the United States: The Potential Consequences of Climate Variability and Change: Overview Report* (December 2000), available at www.gcrio.org/NationalAssessmentl or http://sedac.ciesin.columbia.edul NationalAssessment.
44. Curt Suplee, "Drastic Climate Changes Forecast; Global Warming Likely to Cause Droughts, Coastal Erosion in US, Report Says," *Washington Post*, June 12, 2000, A3; H. Josef Hebert, "Rising Temps Forecast Changes," Associated Press, June 6, 2000; "Forecast for 2100: Hotter," *USA Today*, June 13, 2000, 4A.
45. Transcript of June 11, 2001, Presidential Rose Garden speech, White House, https://georgewbush-whitehouse.archives.gov/news/releases/2001/06/20010611-2.html.
46. CCSP Information on Synthesis and Assessment Products web page, archived August 19, 2007, by the Wayback Machine.
47. Congressional Budget Office, Federal Climate Change Programs: Funding History and Policy Issues 8, March, 2010.
48. Jane A. Leggett et al., *Federal Climate Change Funding from FY2008 to FY 2014*, Congressional Research Service report R43227, September 13, 2013.
49. UN General Assembly Resolution 43/53.
50. According to Agrawala (1998), after the IPCC was established, it became "buffeted by political pressures" and "the authorizing agencies: WMO and UNEP played increasingly marginal roles in IPCC design. The United States,

though, still continued to wield considerable influence through its scientists and bureaucrats who were members of the Panel. Second, a new cast of influential individuals emerged led by the Chairman of the IPCC, Bert Bolin. Third, the IPCC was shaped considerably by exogenous pressures which included the demands from the bodies of the Framework Convention on Climate Change (FCCC) and increased scrutiny of the IPCC process by many oil exporting countries and special interest groups such as the US fossil fuel lobby."

12

Settling Science and Propagandizing for Action

The Structure, Process, and Products of the Climate Science Production Complex

As known not only by lawyers, judges, and regulators but also businesspeople, scientists and pretty much anybody who has ever had to make a decision on the basis of technical assessments of the relevant world, in any tough decision of this sort, there is conflicting evidence and opinion. Some things are known with certainty. We know for certain, for example, that the sun will rise in the east (or southeast, during the northern hemisphere winter). But most important decisions are taken under conditions of uncertainty. A farmer deciding when to plant his fields with corn should consider evidence about the likelihood of a late, crop-killing frost; in deciding how to design a new product for market, a prudent business will get evidence about likely consumer demand for alternative designs at varying prices; a court deciding whether or not the defendant committed a crime will hear not only the prosecution's evidence but also the defendant's. Even after hearing evidence on both sides, a decision maker will not be certain about the state of the world relevant to her decision. But at least she will be able to form an estimate of the chances that her decision is correct and will best serve her goals, whether those are maximizing profits from new product introduction, avoiding crop loss, or minimizing the chance of convicting the innocent.

In producing climate science assessments, the IPCC and other climate science assessment do not follow processes designed to ensure that conflicting scientific evidence and hypotheses are fully considered and discussed. Instead, the follow processes and produce reports that are very much like the legal briefs on one side of a court case, or the evidence and arguments presented by proponents of one among many alternative product designs.

This is not what the EPA or the courts said about the IPCC assessment process. According to the EPA's Endangerment Finding, IPCC assessment reports "undergo a rigorous and exacting standard of peer review by the expert community," indeed so rigorous that individual studies appearing in peer-reviewed journals "do not go through as many review stages, nor are they reviewed and commented on by as many scientists."[1] The DC Circuit in *Coalition for Responsible Regulation* endorsed IPCC assessment reports as "peer-reviewed assessments synthesiz[ing] thousands of individual studies on various aspects of greenhouse gases and climate." These statements suggest a process in which the IPCC exposes its Assessment Reports to review by scientists holding a wide range of disparate views, with a full opportunity to comment and disagree with reports, ending in the IPCC responding to such comments and criticism.

It is understandable that the DC Circuit would have held this view, for the IPCC itself went to great lengths to communicate to the public the rigor of the process by which its Assessment Reports are produced. In an interview in 2007, the year that the IPCC produced its Fourth assessment report, the then Chair of the IPCC, energy economist Rajendra Pachauri emphasized that "you know when we send out drafts or reviews, they go to everyone. They go to government and governments can pass them out to all kinds of people. And if there are governments who have a cozy relationship with the naysayers, then they would naturally send it to these people."[2] Thus the Chair of the IPCC went to some lengths to emphasize how the IPCC process "naturally" was open to dissenting scientific views. Looking more closely at what Pachauri actually said, however, it seems that dissenting views from such scientific "naysayers" would become part of the Assessment Report production process if governments gave the report to the naysayers. This should be surprising – why and how, one might ask, are governments involved in the production of scientific Assessment Reports?

I POLITICS ALL THE WAY DOWN: THE IPCC'S ASSESSMENT REPORT PRODUCTION PROCESS

The IPCC stands for Intergovernmental Panel on Climate Change, and the Panel itself is made up of officials, only some of whom are scientists, appointed by the governments who are signatories to the UN Framework Convention on Climate Change. The government appointees who compose the IPCC panel have ultimate control over the process by which Assessment Reports are created.[3] The panel sets guidelines for Assessment Report production and chooses the members of the Bureau, a group that directly supervises the Assessment Report production process. The actual Assessment Reports are produced by three working groups that produce three separate reports – the Physical Science Basis (Working Group – WG I), Impacts, Adaptation and Vulnerability (WGII), and Mitigation of Climate Change (WGIII). Well before these full reports are released to the public, a Summary for Policymakers is written for each working group report. While the first draft of each Summary for Policymakers is written by scientists who have written the full Working Group report, governments comment upon and revise that draft. Then, over several days, a plenary session of the entire IPCC panel of government representatives go through the summary line by line. During this review, although scientists responsible for the full Working Group reports and initial summary drafts are involved, governments may insist that portions of the summary be completely rewritten or deleted entirely. As one observer has described this process as resembling "a fox-trot performed by a drunken couple ...

the final negotiated statements from such sessions are often based on least common denominator conclusions written in carefully hedged language" with "frequent trade-offs between maintain scientific credibility and enhancing the policy specificity of their conclusions."[4]

The Panel thus itself has direct responsibility for the production of the final version of each Summary for Policymakers. It is the Bureau, appointed by the Panel, however, which works with governments to choose the scientists who write the WG reports – called coordinating lead authors, lead authors, and contributing authors – and to choose also the outside expert reviewers and internal review editors who review those reports. Government agencies get complete draft texts of each working group's Assessment Report, and those reports must get government approval before being finalized. Indirectly, it is governments, and not scientists, who choose the scientists who write and review IPCC Assessment Reports; directly, governments themselves go through Summaries for Policymakers on a line-by-line basis before they are finally produced and released to the public.

The Bureau comprises the IPCC chair, several IPCC vice chairs, and other IPCC leaders. The Bureau does not give notice of its choice of coordinating lead authors and lead authors for IPCC assessment reports. Although the IPCC says vaguely that the choice of coordinating lead authors and lead authors is based on "their publications and works," the Bureau does not make public the criteria by which these choices are made.[5]

By whatever system the authors of IPCC Assessment Reports may be chosen, the widespread faith in IPCC Assessment Reports flows primarily from the belief that reports are subject to rigorous peer review. Indeed, the IPCC itself says that "hundreds of scientists check[ing] into the soundness of drafts check the soundness of the scientific information contained in them." After such review, the IPCC says, "normally" two review editors then "make sure that all comments are taken into account."[6] The reality about such peer review may be much different, however, and even the best peer review is irrelevant if authors are free simply to ignore what peer reviewers say when they publish.

As for the type of peer review to which IPCC Assessment Reports are subjected, consider chapter 9 of the IPCC's 2007 Working Group I Assessment Report on the physical science of climate change. This is a very important and controversial chapter on the attribution of climate change to human GHG emissions. There were 56 contributing authors for this chapter and 62 reviewers. Seven of the reviewers were also authors, 3 of the reviewers were authors of other IPCC chapters, and 26 were authors or coauthors of papers discussed in that chapter, 10 of whom argued in favor of their own papers in their review comments. "Self-review" is not what is meant by peer review. Peer review means that an expert in the field other than the author reviews the author's work. If we remove "outside" reviewers of this attribution chapter who were self-reviewing their own work, there were only 30 truly independent outside reviewers of the 2007 attribution chapter. Of these, only four expressed general support for the chapter.[7]

Even generally negative outside reviews of a chapter, however, can be completely ignored by lead authors of such a chapter. Up until 2000, the IPCC gave the job of "evaluating and incorporating" outside peer reviewers' comments to chapter lead authors. This flips the peer review process on its head. Peer-reviewed journals have editors who send articles out for outside peer review, and the editors then determine whether in light of such outside reviews, the articles should be accepted, required to be revised, or simply rejected. Up until 2000, the IPCC gave a very limited editor's job to chapter authors, making authors responsible not for deciding whether to publish their chapter – that decision had already been made when the chapter was written – but whether to modify it in light of outside comments.

Since 2000, members of the Bureau who serve as Working Group co-chairs select two scientists who were not involved in the production of the WG's report to be "review editors." However, review editors may be members of the Bureau, and they may be nominated to be review editors by the very same lead authors whom they are supposed to review. Thus review editors are chosen by the people ultimately responsible for writing the Report that these editors review.

Finally, such review editors are not like journal editors who make the decision whether to accept or reject or revise an article. Their job is limited to ensuring that lead authors "take account" of critical outside reviews. Lead Authors are free to simply reject critical outside comments. Review Editors can only ensure that lead authors considered such comments; they cannot overrule the Lead Author's rejection decision.[8]

In the fall of 2009, thousands of emails were hacked from University of East Anglia's Climate Research Unit, an organization that produces one of the two or three most widely used data sets on historical surface temperatures around the globe, the HadCRUT data that I present at several points in chapters to come. The emails revealed leading establishment climate scientists continuously communicating with one another about how to make sure their work and opinions on climate science and policy would defeat the views of scientists whose work conflicts with the establishment view. This incident was dubbed "Climategate" by some in the media.

Concerned that Climategate had weakened public confidence, in 2010 the IPCC and the UN together enlisted an outside institution, the InterAcademy Council, to review the IPCC's processes and procedures. The InterAcademy Council criticized virtually the entire process by which the IPCC produces its Assessment Reports, ranging from the "lack of criteria" for selecting key participants in the assessment process, to failure to follow its own rules requiring that non-peer-reviewed source by clearly identified as such, to the practice of lead authors of simply ignoring alternative views when they disagreed with their own. The InterAgency Council suggested a solution might be found were Assessment Reports written under the guidance of review editors who were both truly independent – selected by somebody not involved in any way in writing the Assessment Report – and vested with the authority to require lead authors to actually respond to critical outside reviews.

The Council, however, concluded that there was no "scientific body [with] the recognized scientific legitimacy and capacity to carry out such a large task" as selecting review editors for IPCC Assessment Reports.[9] This dismal observation was inevitable. The IPCC Assessment Report process was designed so that governments could control and influence the scientific assessment process to produce reports consistent with the activist goals that gave birth to the IPCC in the first place. Selecting lead authors whose chapters accomplish this goal would be completely subverted were the lead authors subject to being overruled by "review editors" chosen by independent scientists rather than politicians.

II DELIBERATELY DISABLING INFORMED CRITICAL INQUIRY: THE IPCC SUMMARIES FOR POLICYMAKERS

The full IPCC Assessment Reports have increased in length from a few hundred pages each to well over a thousand pages for each Working Group.[10] The Summary for Policymakers for each Working Group's full Assessment Report appears months before the full report is available in any form to anybody. Summaries are much shorter and made widely available to the media, environmental interest groups, and politicians across the world. The summaries make various assertions about climate science that are backed up with citations to the full reports. If a curious reader wishes to read the portion of the full report that has been cited in support of a particular assertion in summary, however, she cannot do so. The reason is that the full report is not available and will not be available for several months.

If summaries were produced solely by the Lead Author scientists who write chapters in the full reports, this might be of little concern. One would expect that lead authors would be careful to ensure that their summaries matched quite closely what they actually say in the chapter they have produced. But this is not how the summaries are produced. Drafts of the summaries are written by lead authors and exposed to outside review. But every draft of each summary is reviewed by governments. Moreover, while all IPCC Working Group Reports must be formally endorsed by the IPCC Panel of government appointees, special rules apply to a Summary for Policymakers. The Panel may simply "accept" material in a full Report, where "acceptance" means that the Panel does not unanimously agree on every line or section but nevertheless unanimously agrees that the material "presents a comprehensive, objective and balanced assessment of the subject matter."[11] But for a Summary for Policymakers, the procedure is radically different. The full Panel of government, not scientific, officials goes over each and every line in summary and a summary is not released to the public until it is "approved" by the Panel. As the IPCC explains, "'approval" means that the material has been subjected to detailed line-by-line discussion and agreement." Hence whereas scientists produce each draft Summary for Policymakers, every final Summary for Policymakers has been produced and unanimously approved, on a line-by-line basis, by the politicians who compose the IPCC Panel.

The result of having governments write and unanimously approve Summary for Policymaker reports is that those reports not only systematically downplay scientific uncertainties revealed and discussed in a full Report but often simply misstate what the Report actually says. For example, in the 2013 Summary for Policymakers to the Working Group I report on climate science, the IPCC said that it had "medium" confidence that a pause in global warming that occurred between 1998 and 2011 was due in part to natural internal climate variability.[12] But the summary then goes on to say[13] that over the longer period 1951–2010, it was "likely" that natural internal climate variability had contributed only between −0.1 and 1°C – or precisely 0° on average – to global temperature change. As I discuss in more detail later, when one actually looks at the full Report that is supposedly being summarized in this passage, one finds that it saying that the climate models whose output is the basis for IPCC opinions about the role of internal variability actually have no ability to reproduce any of the long-term climatic cycles that generate internal variability. Thus the actual IPCC Report does not support a statement, with any degree of confidence, about the contribution of internal climate variability to 1951–2010 global temperature change.

Over the years, leading IPCC scientist activists have actually been quite open about why there is such a gulf between the typical Summary for Policymakers and the Report being summarized. The only Report that is issued simultaneously with its summary is what the IPCC calls a Synthesis Report. Issued in advance of any full Assessment Report and widely distributed to the media even before its official release, the 2007 Synthesis Report – intentionally released during the December 2007 Bali, Indonesia, climate change negotiations – was described by one IPCC scientist as intended to clarify "how we can take these findings and formulate a policy response that's quick enough and big enough?" Another, the famous environmental activist scientist Michael Oppenheimer, said the summary was designed to "light a fire under policy makers." Like the Synthesis Report, every Summary for Policymakers is a political, policy-oriented document that is released to the media and the public with the deliberate intention of disabling any actual intelligent, critical discussion.

III ADVOCACY BECOMES EXPLICIT: THE 2018 "SPECIAL REPORT"

In the fall of 2018, the IPCC issued a "Special Report" entitled "Global Warming of 1.5C." Notably, for the first time, an IPCC Report was subtitled in a way showing that its purpose was to marshal evidence supporting particular global warming policies: "An IPCC Special Report on the impacts of global warming of 1.5C above pre-industrial levels and related global greenhouse gas emission pathways, in the context of strengthening the global response to the threat of climate change, sustainable development, and efforts to eradicate poverty."[14] Thus the 2018 Special Report is not an update on climate science, but rather a report on "impacts . . . in the context of strengthening the response to the threat of climate change, sustainable development and efforts to eradicate poverty."

The main goal of the 2018 IPCC Report was to quantify the decrease in anthropogenic CO_2 emissions that will be necessary to limit future global temperature increase to 1.5°C. Thus the primary focus of the 2018 Report was on computer projections of how different level of atmospheric CO_2 translate into future temperatures. In order to make the case for potentially hugely costly emissions decreases, however, the 2018 IPCC Special Report did update that organization's assessment of the evidence about what has been happening with things such as sea level rise and extreme weather events. But perhaps its most famous contribution was not a summary of recent observations about climate, but rather a projection that major cuts in global CO_2 emissions would be required in the very near future, at least by 2030, for global warming to be kept at 2°C or less. I discuss the way that the IPCC came up with this projection in a later chapter. The point for present purposes is that the 2°C goal has nothing to do with science. It is the goal that was agreed upon in the Paris Climate Accord of 2015, and the governments which were parties to that agreement then commissioned the IPCC to do a report on what it would take to reach the agreed upon goal.

IV NO BETTER PROCESS: THE USGCRP NATIONAL CLIMATE ASSESSMENT REPORTS

Since the beginning of the USGCRP, IPCC Assessment Reports have provided the basis for National Climate Assessment done periodically by the USGCRP. The IPCC Assessment Reports are the primary basis for EPA regulation and for international climate negotiations and regulation outside the United States. Still, if somehow the USGCRP National Assessment were based on a process that is more akin to something like what the IPCC has touted its process to be – an objective, peer review exercise with thousands of scientists involved from across the world relatively insulated from political influence – then it might be that the National Climate Assessments are more credible than the IPCC's own Assessment Reports.

From the existing evidence, this seems clearly not to be the case. The process by which USGCRP assessments are produced seems if anything to be even more oriented to producing advocacy science than is the IPCC process. Michaels and Knappenburger (2015, 97–124) describe how the very first 2000 National Climate Assessment mentioned earlier based its projections of future temperatures on only two models, both of which had been shown to be worse at predicting 10 year moving average temperatures than a simple guess based on long-term average temperatures. According to Michaels and coauthors, the 2009 Assessment was even worse, completing neglecting to even mention peer-edited scientific literature that contradicted the 2009 Assessment conclusions findings. These omissions were especially glaring in the Assessment's complete failure to mention the fertilization effect – whereby enhanced atmospheric CO_2 increases primary plant production – an effect well established by pioneering figures in plant physiology. As another example of advocacy, as Michaels and Knappenburger explain, the 2014 Assessment flatly states the "changing patterns of precipitation are expected to emerge," but fails to explain that those patterns may not be statistically distinguishable from natural variation in precipitation for over 500 years.

The 2014 National Assessment was explicitly publicized as a "key deliverable of President Obama's Climate Action Plan." Thus the 2014 Assessment was viewed not as an objective assessment of the science, but as an element of a regulatory policy designed to end the coal industry. It is true that in adversary proceedings, each lawyer marshals the evidence that best supports her case, with no obligation to find and discuss evidence that supports the other side's position. But in an adversary proceeding, the opposing side has a chance to jump up and add the missing evidence. That the USGCRP employs such techniques, however, is inconsistent with its stated mission of assessing climate science rather than marshaling scientific evidence on one side of a policy debate.

Such science advocacy, rather than science assessment, is inherent in the structure of the USGCRP Assessment production complex. For the most recent, November 2018, USGCRP National Assessment of Climate Change Physical Science, the three coordinating lead authors were all federal government employees, two of the three review editors were government employees, and 19 of 29 lead authors were governmental employees. At least the majority of the remaining 10 lead authors had been heavy recipients of federal climate science funding. Within the ranks of scientists who play official roles in producing USGCRP assessments, I have unable to find a single scientist who is not either actually employed or funded by one of the many federal global climate change offices.

V THE CLIMATE SCIENCE PROPAGANDA MACHINE: NASA GISS'S "HOTTEST YEAR EVER" REPORTS

Beyond their production of Assessment Reports and summaries for policy makers, climate science assessment agencies have long been very active in producing short reports and announcements that are best described as propaganda. As defined by the Cambridge Dictionary, propaganda consists of "information., [and] ideas . . . often giving only one part of an argument, that are . . . spread with the intention of influencing people's opinions." The word *propaganda* originated as proper noun taken from the Latin term *congregatio de propaganda fide*, or "congregation for the propagation of the faith." The short-tenured Pope Gregory XV created this organization in 1622 to act as the missionary organization of the holy see. In its modern meaning, propaganda was most fully elucidated by Edward Bernays in his 1928 book *Propaganda*. Bernays had gotten his start as a member of the US Committee on Public Information that the great progressive Woodrow Wilson created to advertise and sell World War I to the skeptical American people as necessary to "Make the World Safe for Democracy." In *Propaganda*, Bernays set out his views on what he viewed as the tremendously exciting possibilities for government and businesses to use propaganda to manipulate the mass voting and consuming public.

At its core, propaganda conveys information in a way designed to influence the mass public to believe certain things that will lead them to take actions desired by the producers of propaganda. Some information conveyed in propaganda may be true but what defines propaganda is the speaker's goal of persuading the public to hold certain beliefs.

In the United States, the climate science propaganda campaign has been spearheaded by a federal government agency – NASA's Goddard Institute for Space Studies (GISS). As described earlier, during the early 1980s, NASA was one of three federal agencies at the core of the new federal Global Change Research Program. Before the late 1980s, however, NASA's main focus was on sending rockets and satellites into space. A search of the Nexis US newspaper database over the entire period 1975–1988 turns up lots of articles discussing the space shuttle and satellites but not a single story about anyone from NASA saying anything about global warming or rising temperatures. However, in 1985, NASA's space program suffered a major setback when the space shuttle Challenger blew apart shortly after its launch. The hot media topic in 1986 was whether, in the wake of the Challenger disaster, NASA could possibly recover and survive as an agency.

By 1988, with the Soviet bloc beginning to crumble and the end of the Cold War with the Soviet Union clearly in sight, NASA's mission and survival were even more in doubt. On August 15, 1988, in congressional testimony by James Hansen, the director of NASA's GISS, the agency found a future. After receiving his PhD in physics from the University of Iowa, Hansen spent his early career studying the planet Venus, which with an atmosphere composed mostly of CO_2 has in incredibly high surface temperature of 470°C (or 800°F). Hansen had been with NASA for his entire career when in 1981 he published an article entitled "Climate Impact of Increasing Atmospheric Carbon Dioxide." Using a simple single-dimensional model of the earth's energy balance of a sort I describe in a bit more detail later, Hansen et al. (1981, 966) said that anthropogenic CO_2 emissions had caused the growth of atmospheric CO_2 and that this increase accounted for about 75 percent of the warming of the earth's atmosphere since the 1880s. Hansen et al. (1981) predicted further that warming of an additional 2.5°C would occur over the next century (assuming slow energy growth and a mixture of nonfossil and fossil fuel use). Hansen et al. (1981, 996) contextualized this temperature increase by declaring that such temperatures would "would exceed the temperature during the altithermal (6000 years ago) and the previous (Eemian) interglacial period 125,000 years ago and would approach the warmth of the Mesozoic, the age of dinosaurs." The year that this article was published, Hansen became director of NASA's GISS.

The summer of 1988 was hot. In a catastrophe that ended the National Park Service's newfound enthusiasm for forest fires as an element of "natural" ecosystem management, 250 separate fires that began in the middle of June of that year eventually converged into seven major fires that by November had destroyed about 740,000 acres of Yellowstone National park. On June 23, 1988, just a week after the Yellowstone fires began and on a stiflingly hot day in Washington, DC, Hansen testified before the US Senate's Committee on Energy and Natural Resources. Sitting in a room in which the air conditioning had been deliberately turned off in order to dramatize the heat, Hansen declared[15] that 1988 was the hottest year on earth since temperature measurements had systematically been made in the late nineteenth century, that these high temperatures were caused by human GHG emissions, and that over the period 1988–1998, droughts and heat waves in the US Midwest and southeast would become more frequent than they had been over the period 1950–1980.

Hansen's June 1988 congressional testimony drew immediate national media coverage, with the *New York Times* headlining that "Global Warming Has Begun, Expert Tells Senate."[16] Dozens of other papers carried the story. As we shall see, it is now undisputed that Hansen was likely correct that human GHG emissions have contributed to warming since the late nineteenth century. But he was wrong about 1988 being the warmest year since temperature measurements had been taken. And he was very wrong about droughts and heatwaves becoming more common in the Midwest and Southeast. The one thing that we can say for certain about Hansen's 1988 testimony is that it made climate change a major and continuing news story, one fueled by a propaganda campaign by NASA's GISS that continues until this day.

A core feature of this campaign has been NASA GISS's practice of periodically announcing high temperature records. The practice began shortly after Hansen's 1988 congressional testimony, with a 1991 announcement that 1990 was the hottest year ever recorded.[17] A few years later, in 1996, Hansen reported that 1995 was the hottest year on record. Precisely the same news story carrying this announcement was reprinted at least 37 times.[18] As evidence that the campaign was succeeding, Hansen's 1999 announcement that 1998 was "by a wide margin" hotter even than 1995 was repeated verbatim in at least 43 US newspapers.[19]

During the twenty-first century, the GISS "hottest ever" propaganda effort has continued unabated:

- Unable to announce a new hottest temperature year for several years, in the fall of 2005, Hansen announced not a temperature but a climate model projection that 2005 would turn out to be the hottest year ever recorded and the hottest temperature for a million years, explaining further that if temperature rose only one more degree, the earth would be locked into a further 2°–3° rise, temperatures last seen "about three million years ago when sea levels were 80 feet (25 meters) higher than today";[20] a story[21] in which the *New York Times* reporter Andrew Revkin explained the significance of these projections was reprinted or discussed 105 times, and will still being mentioned occasionally in May 2007.
- Steve McIntyre, an independent investigator, pointed out that GISS temperature data for the United States for the year 2000 and following years were

erroneous. After GISS corrected the data, it turned out that in the United States, 1998 had been cooler than the year 1934. In statements reprinted in at least 30 newspapers, Gavin Schmidt, who was soon to replace Hansen as head of GISS, quickly went on the offensive to explain that for the world as a whole, 1998 was tied with 2005 as the hottest year ever, and "there is no question that the last five to 10 years have been the hottest period of the last century."[22]

- Even in the midst of the most serious economic downturn since the Great Depression, Hansen, and GISS were unable to report that the year 2007 was the hottest, but they were able to report that 2007 was the second hottest, trailing only 2005, and "as we predicted last year, 2007, was warmer than 2006, continuing the strong warming trend of the past 30 years that has been confidently attributed to the effect of increasing human-made greenhouse gases."[23]
- In late 2009, in an announcement discussed in at least 190 newspaper articles over the next two years and formally in a congressional hearing, NASA reported that the first decade of the twenty-first century had been the hottest in recorded history, with every year since 2001 being in the top 10 hottest years on record and 2009 the second hottest year ever.[24]
- Beginning in 2012 if not earlier, NASA GISS began to relax its standard for "hottest temperature" announcements, proclaiming in early 2012, for example, that the average global surface temperature for 2011 was the "ninth warmest in the modern meteorological record," with Hansen pointing out that "11 years of the new century were notably hotter than the middle and late 20th century";[25] the very next year, 2013, NASA GISS announced that 2012 was now the ninth warmest year on record, with the nine warmest years in the last 132 years all occurring since 2000;[26] in early 2014, NASA GISS reported that 2013 was the "seventh warmest year since 1880," and again stressed that 9 of the 10 warmest years since 1880 had occurred since 2000.[27]
- Sometime during the second decade of the twenty-first century, NASA GISS began to announce *monthly* temperature records, proclaiming in 2014, through its new director Gavin Schmidt, that May 2014 was the warmest May in recorded history,[28] and that August 2014 was the hottest August since records began.[29] Even more recently, GISS announced in 2019 not only that June 2019 was the warmest June in 140 years of global temperature records, but that 50 of the last 54 months at least tied for the top five warmest months, with 11 separate months over the June 2015 to August 2016 period setting warmest month ever records.[30] And in March 2020, during the onset of the Coronavirus pandemic, GISS proclaimed that globally, December 2019–February 2020 were the second warmest December–February period on record.[31]

As explained by the IPCC in its 2013 AR, climate is the "average weather" of a place, defined as the mean and variability in key weather variables such as temperature and precipitation, where "classically the period for averaging these variables is 30 years, as defined by the World Meteorological Organization"

(IPCC 2013, 126). As the IPCC continued to explain, "climate change" "refers to a change in the state of the climate that can be identified (e.g., by using statistical tests) by changes in the mean and/or variability of its properties *that persists for an extended period, typically decades or longer* [emphasis added]." Under Hansen and Schmidt's leadership, since 1990, GISS has not been reporting changes in 30 year average temperatures, as would be appropriate if it was reporting data relevant to climate change. GISS has instead been selectively reporting annual average surface temperatures anomalies that are high relative to longer-term historical averages. NASA GISS did not report temperatures for years where the annual average was lower than long-term annual averages. More recently, it has begun reporting even high monthly average temperatures. High, or low, monthly temperatures relative to a long-term average are not indicative of anything regarding climate change. What high monthly temperatures are relevant to is public perception, not science.

Perhaps even worse, a substantial body of work that I discuss below finds that the long-term average surface temperatures that GISS has used as a baseline for its "hottest temperature ever" reports may substantially overestimate warming. As I explain shortly, there are a number of problems with surface temperature measurements. Perhaps the most glaring is that weather stations in which temperature measurement instruments are housed have been contaminated by site changes such as the construction of nearby parking lots and buildings. These site changes are known to increase nighttime temperature readings, thus biasing upward the daily average temperatures that GISS reports.

The lower level of the earth's atmosphere, the troposphere, is the atmospheric level at which GHG-induced warming should be observed. Measurements of tropospheric temperatures from satellites and radiosonde balloons do not go back very far – only to around 1980 – but since the inception of the GISS propaganda campaign around 1990, GISS researchers were surely aware of active scientific disagreement over whether satellite data on tropospheric temperatures showed that surface temperature measurements overstated warming. And yet NASA GISS "hottest ever" reports were issued without any caveats regarding this crucial ongoing debate.[32]

It is no accident that GISS "hottest ever" reports have now collapsed into reports about particular months or groups of months. There is now a set of weather stations deemed by NOAA to be located in good sites, free of things like nearby buildings and parking lots that bias temperature readings upward (I discuss such problems with surface temperature measurements later in more detail). This set of stations is called the US Climate Reference Network, or USCRN. Figure 12.1 depicts the average temperature (measured as the departure from 1981 to 2010 average) in degrees Fahrenheit for the USCRN stations since 2005.[33] As one can see from Figure 12.1, even the very hot El Niño year of 2016–2017 did not exceed the average temperature in 2012. Overall, from Figure 12.1, one would eyeball flat or very slightly increasing annual average temperatures in this set of weather stations since 2005. (And this eyeball guess is borne out by a linear regression analysis,

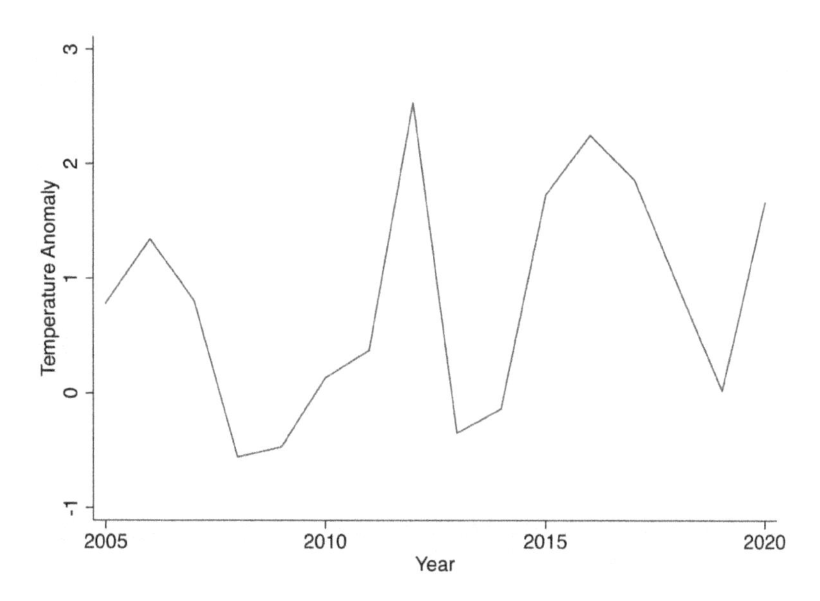

FIGURE 12.1 USCRN anomaly °F since 2005.

which shows no statistically significant linear time trend in US temperatures since 2005 and no significant linear relationship between U.S. temperatures and atmospheric CO2 over that period.) Notably absent from GISS temperature reports are those that would have reported, for example, that the average US temperature measured at high quality USCRN stations fell between 2005 and 2019.

A *Packaging Science to Support Precautionary Climate Policy: GISS Advocacy Science*

Reporting these facts would be rather mundane, and would hardly further the purpose of dramatizing the urgency of the climate change problem in way that mobilizes public opinion to support particular policies. That GISS leaders have indeed presented data about climate in way designed to mobilize support for particular climate change policies cannot be disputed – they have in fact explicitly and publicly stated that they are policy advocates and have advocated for particular policies. Here are just a few examples of such explicit policy advocacy by GISS leaders:

- Back in 2006, then – GISS Director Hansen argued in a lengthy New York Review of Books article[34] that if annual emissions of CO_2 and other human GHGs continued to increase at their then current rate for another 50 years, the earth's average temperature would go up by about 5°F relative to today, increasing global sea level by 80 feet. As he dramatized that prospect:

Eighty feet! In that case, the United States would lose most East Coast cities: Boston, New York, Philadelphia, Washington and Miami; indeed practically the entire state of Florida would be under water. Fifty million people in the US live below that sea level. Other places would fare far worse. China would have 250 million displaced persons. Bangladesh would produce 120 million refugees, practically the entire nation. India would lose the land of 150 million people.

In a somewhat calmer tone, the remainder of Hansen's 2006 article praised the three books under review and advocated curbing carbon dioxide emissions from cars and power plants. Hansen spent little time actually reviewing the three books. But he was notably unworried by the criticism that there was little data to support the estimate in Flannery, *The Weather Makers* that 60 percent of non-human species will become extinct if GHG emissions continue because "estimates are needed and Flannery is as qualified as anyone to make them." Hansen similarly praised Al Gore's book and movie *An Inconvenient Truth* as presenting a "coherent account of a complex topic . . . the story is scientifically accurate and yet should be understandable to the public."

Most of Hansen's 2006 book review was actually about policy. He praised the state of California and Europe for taking the lead in enacting policies to lower GHG emissions, but castigated most American politicians for failing to acknowledge the "heavy legal and moral responsibilities" that the United States has "for what is now happening," by favoring the "short term profits of energy companies and other special interests" over the interests of future generations. According to Hansen, by "refusing to participate in the Kyoto Protocol," the United States undermined the "attempt of the international community to slow down the emissions of developed countries" and eliminated the possibility of reducing the "growing emissions of India and China" through the Clean Development Mechanisms created by the Protocol. Hansen's policy forecast was dire indeed: according to him, the United States had "ten years to fundamentally alter the trajectory of greenhouse emissions," without which change "climate disasters will be unavoidable."

- Hansen's climate policy prescriptions while serving as director of NASA's GISS did not end with his 2006 essay. They continued and became increasingly draconian and dramatic. In 2007, testifying before the Iowa Utilities Board but not, according to Hansen as a government employee directing GISS, but "as a private citizen, a resident of Kintersville, Pa., on behalf of the planet, of life on Earth, including all species," he declared that "if we cannot stop the building of more coal-fired power plants those coal trains will be death trains – no less gruesome than if they were boxcars headed to crematoria, loaded with uncountable irreplaceable species."[35] The very next year, Hansen proclaimed that the CEO's of fossil fuel energy companies should be "tried for high crimes against humanity and nature,"[36] and in recent years (after his retirement from NASA) has actively participated in what he calls the climate change policy "war" by supporting litigation against such companies.[37]

- Hansen may be retired from NASA, but other high profile climate scientists engaged still in active research have been just as involved in policy disputes. In 2007, a British court ruled that Al Gore's film *An Inconvenient Truth*, so strongly endorsed in Hansen's book review, could be shown in schools but only if teachers alerted students to what the court found to be scientific errors in the film. As reported by the *Washington Post*, British High Court judge Burton said that there is "now common ground that it is not simply a science film – although it is clear that it is based substantially on scientific research and opinion – but that it is a political film," with errors that "arise in the context of alarmism and exaggeration in support of his political thesis."[38] Two of America's most prominent climate scientists, Gavin Schmidt and Michael Mann, immediately wrote an editorial – which the *Post* refused to publish – defending Gore's film. In the editorial – which became a post on Schmidt's blog "Real Climate" – they argued that the judge incorrectly held Gore's movie to the standard of a scientific paper and that a close reading of the actual film script showed that Gore did not say what the judge said he did while what Gore did say was perfectly consistent with established climate science.[39] Schmidt and Mann are two prominent and highly influential climate scientists – Gavin Schmidt took over as Director of NASS GISS when Hansen retired, and Mann has been for many years closely involved with the production of IPCC Assessment Reports that I described earlier. Thus in this blog post we see two very prominent climate scientists engaged in contesting a court ruling about a popular film by a politician. This seems like scientists wading directly into the policy and political waters.
- Even more recently, in accepting the Stephen Schneider award from the American Geophysical Union in 2013, Dr. Schmidt gave a talk entitled "What should a climate scientist advocate for? The Intersection of Expertise and Values in a Politicized World." In the talk,[40] Schmidt argues that "scientists who communicate widely cannot avoid advocacy," and that responsible advocacy consists of scientists making the connection between their values and policy choices explicit, and explicitly explaining that different values imply different policy choices. Fascinatingly, when Schmidt asked for an informal show of hands among those attending the lecture as to whether they would view being called an advocate as a positive or negative, to his confessed surprise, the vote was about 50–50.

We thus have a major lecture by a preeminent climate scientist at one of the climate science community's major annual conferences openly admitting that many decisions by climate scientists – including what scientific questions are important and worth working on – are strongly impacted by normative values. And, from Schmidt's reaction, we have about 50 percent of the scientist attending saying that such conflation of normative values and policy preferences in the evaluation of scientific projects is perfectly okay, and – at least from what one hears watching the video – none of the scientists in attendance stood up to dispute Schmidt's easy admission that advocacy cannot be avoided when scientists communicate with the public.

There can be little doubt that the scientists who have led NASA GISS for the last 40 years do not view the funding and production of climate science as an enterprise undertaken merely to advance human understanding of global climate, but rather as an activity designed to support precautionary climate policy. NASA GISS is not the only government science agency to have publicized statements about climate and weather as well as climate science that are at best misleading. In my discussion of climate science that begins in the next chapter, I point out other instances of climate science propaganda.

Notes

1. EPA Endangerment Finding, 74 Fed. Reg. 66510–66511.
2. As quoted in McKitrick, "Adversarial versus Consensus Processes for Assessing Scientific Evidence," in Johnston (2012, 59).
3. My discussion here is based on Johnston (2012, 17).
4. Agrawala (1998, 627).
5. McKitrick, "Adversarial versus Consensus Processes," in Johnston (2012, 61).
6. McKitrick, "Adversarial versus Consensus Processes," in Johnston (2012, 62).
7. McKitrick, "Adversarial versus Consensus Processes," in Johnston (2012, 63).
8. McKitrick, "Adversarial versus Consensus Processes," in Johnston (2012, 64).
9. This discussion of the Interagency Council draws upon Johnston (2012, 38–39).
10. The following section is drawn from Johnston (2012, 24–26).
11. IPCC, "About Preparing Reports," available at www.ipcc.ch/about/preparingre ports/.
12. IPCC, Summary for Policymakers, in *Climate Change 2013: The Physical Science Basis. Contribution of Working Group I to the Fifth Assessment Report of the Intergovernmental Panel on Climate Change* 15, Thomas F. Stocker et al., eds. (Cambridge University Press, 2013).
13. IPCC. Summary for Policymakers 2013, 17.
14. IPCC Global Warming of 1.5C (2018).
15. Greenhouse Effect and Global Climate Change, hearing before the Committee on Energy and Natural Resources, US Senate, 100th Cong., 2nd sess., on the Greenhouse Effect and Global Climate Change, Senate Hearing 100–461, Part 2, p. 43 (June 23, 1988).
16. Philip Shabecoff, "Global Warming Has Begun, Expert Tells Senate," *New York Times*, June 24, 1988, available at www.nytimes.com/1988/06/24/us/global-warming-has-begun-expert-tells-senate.html.

17. See Bob Davis, "Was 1990 Hotter than Other Years? It's a Heated Debate – NASA Internal Disagreement on Temperature Measure Has Political Implications," *Wall Street Journal*, January 8, 1991, B4.
18. Randolph E. Schmid, "NASA's Hansen Reports '95 Hottest Year," Associated Press, July 13, 1996.
19. The story's typical version is illustrated by Randolph E. Schmid, "1998 Was Hottest Year on Record," Associated Press, January 11, 1999.
20. Mike Swain, "Hottest for a Million Years; Global Warming Near a Crisis Point," *Daily Record*, September 27, 2006; a story in which the *New York Times* reporter Andrew Revkin explained the significance of these projections – Alex Chadwick, "Andrew Revkin Discusses NASA Data That 2005 Will Be the Hottest Year on Record," NPR, October 13, 2005 – was reprinted or discussed.
21. Alex Chadwick, "Andrew Revkin Discusses NASA Data That 2005 Will Be the Hottest Year on Record," NPR, October 13, 2005.
22. "Climate: 1934, Not 1998, the Hottest Year on Record, NASA Confirms," 10(9) *Greenwire*, August 15, 2007.
23. See Tom Spears, "NASA Data Shows Earth's Temperature Keeps Rising: 2007 Second Hottest Year on Record," *Edmonton Journal*, January 18, 2008, A5.
24. See Bradford DeLong, "Climate; NASA Data Spell Trouble," *Charleston Gazette* (West Virginia), April 25, 2010; John M. Broder, "Past Decade Was Warmest on Record, NASA Data Show," *International Herald Tribune*, January 23, 2020; "NASA: Last Decade Warmest on Record," UPI News Track, January 21, 2010; on the congressional hearing, see "Upcoming Select Committee Hearing: State of Climate Science," States News Service, November 24, 2009.
25. "2011 Was Ninth-Warmest Year since 1880," *Climate Spectator*, January 21, 2012.
26. "NASA Finds 2012 Sustained Long-Term Climate Warming Trend," NASA Documents and Publications, January 15, 2013.
27. David Millward, "NASA Confirms Global Warming Trend: Latest Data from NASA Show Long Term Rise in Global Temperatures Compared with the Middle of the Last Century," *Telegraph*, January 22, 2014.
28. Eric Hotlhaus Slate, "NASA: May 2014 Was the Hottest May on Record," *St. Paul Pioneer*, June 17, 2014.
29. Ellie Zolfagharifard, "August Was the Hottest on Record – and 2014 Could Be One of the Warmest Years since Climate Change Began, Say Experts," *Mail Online*, September 17, 2014.
30. Jonathan Erman, "We Just Experienced the Hottest June on Record and It's Part of a Larger, Troubling Trend," Weather Channel, June 18, 2019.
31. Doyle Rice, "What Winter? Earth Just Had Its Second Warmest December–February," *Visalia Time-Delta*, March 17, 2020.
32. See Davis, "Was 1990 Hotter than Other Years?"
33. The data are available at NOAA, National Temperature Index, www.ncdc.noaa.gov/temp-and-precip/national-temperature-index/time-series?data

sets%5B%5D=uscrn¶meter=anom-tavg&time_scale=12mo&begyear=1984&endyear=2018&month=12.

34. Jim Hansen, "The Threat to the Planet," *New York Review of Books*, July 13, 2006, available at www.nybooks.com/articles/2006/07/13/the-threat-to-the-planet/.
35. "NASA's Hansen Gets a New Gig," *Investor's Business Daily*, April 8, 2013, A18.
36. James Hansen, "Twenty Years Later: Tipping Points near on Global Warming," *Guardian*, June 23, 2008, www.theguardian.com/environment/2008/jun/23/climatechange.carbonemissions.
37. See Hansen's statement about the activities of his Climate Science Awareness and Solutions organization at www.columbia.edu/~jeh1/mailings/2015/20150626.LegalFront.pdf.
38. Mary Jordan, "U.K. Judge Rules Gore's Climate Film Has 9 Errors," *Washington Post*, October 12, 2007, available at www.washingtonpost.com/wp-dyn/content/article/2007/10/11/AR2007101102134_pf.html.
39. Gavin Schmidt and Michael Mann, "Convenient Untruths," October 15, 2007, available at www.realclimate.org/index.php/archives/2007/10/convenient-untruths/.
40. www.youtube.com/watch?v=CJC1phPS6IA.

13

Recent Observed Climate Change in Longer-Term Perspective

The EPA's Endangerment Finding relied entirely upon IPCC Assessment Reports (and, to a lesser extent, USGCRP Assessments) as supplying more than enough evidence that rising atmospheric CO_2 concentrations have caused changes in various measures of climate and that without steps to reduce anthropogenic CO_2, climate changes will get even worse in the future. Having already explained how both the IPCC and USGCRP have developed into science advocacy organizations, rather than assessment institutions, in this chapter I begin my brief critical analysis of the output produced by the IPCC. I focus on the IPCC because its reports are the primary basis for not only the Endangerment Finding but for precautionary US climate policy more generally.

This chapter begins by discussing observations of recent climate change. A precautionary policy response does not actually require any evidence that a feared risk of an irreversible harm is actually materializing. We have seen this with both the European beef ban and the Montreal Protocol's CFC ban. At the time the beef ban was implemented, there was no evidence that by eating hormone-grown beef, humans were exposed to any additional risk. And while there was evidence that CFC's were causing a depletion of stratospheric ozone when the CFC ban was adopted, the evidence regarding where and how this effect was occurring was thin. In the case of climate change, with a precautionary policy response entailing costs many orders of magnitude higher than either the beef or CFC ban, the IPCC and USGCRP have always begun by adducing evidence that anthropogenic climate change is already happening. I begin as well with observations of actual climate change, for by looking closely at the evidence adduced by the IPCC, we see two things: first, that temperatures have clearly risen during the industrial era, but, second, that the surface temperatures the IPCC and USGCRP leaders emphasizes are almost surely biased and overstate the extent of the warming.

I OBSERVATIONS OF RECENT CLIMATE

One can sort observations about past climate change into two categories. The first are annual measures of temperature and sea level. The second are measures of various kinds of extreme weather events.

A *The Surface Temperature Measurements Are Actually Adjusted Data, Not Observations, and Increases in Surface Temperature Are Much Bigger than Increases in Tropospheric and Sea Surface Temperatures*

According to the IPCC's 2013 AR5, it is "certain" that global average surface temperatures have increased since the late nineteenth century, with "each of the past three decades ... successively warmer at the Earth's surface than any [*sic*] the previous decades in the instrumental record, and the decade of the 2000's has been the warmest." Based on the surface data set with the longest record – that produced by the Hadley Center/Climate Research Unit (Had CRUT)– surface temperatures increased by 0.78°C between the average of the 1850–1900 period and the 2003–2012 period, and based on this and two other data sets, of the 0.85°C warming between 1880 and 2012, 0.72°C of this warming occurred between 1951 and 2012.[1] According to the IPCC, it is "unlikely" that these temperature increases reflect any increases caused by the urban heat island effect or land use change effects, as these have been corrected out.

As for US temperatures, according to the USGCRP's 2014 report,[2] there has been "significant warming over the US since the instrumental record began in 1895." The linear trend for the US over the period 1895 to 2012, according to the USGCRP, was between 1.3° and 1.9°F (0.7°–1°C) The USGCRP reports that the average temperature over the 2002–2012 period was 1.9°F (1°C) warmer than the average over the 1895–1905 period, and more generally, average temperature increased at a faster rate since about the mid-1940s.

The IPCC relies upon surface temperature data sets produced by NASA's Goddard Institute for Space Studies (GISS), NOAA's National Climate Data Center (NCDC), and the Hadley Center's Climate Research Unit, an organization jointly sponsored by the United Kingdom's Meteorology (Met) Office and the University of East Anglia. GISS temperature data go back to 1880, while the HadCRUT data set extends back the farthest, to 1850.[3] The data are published as monthly averages, which in turn are formed from daily averages. A daily average is computed as the midpoint between the nighttime minimum and daytime maximum temperature as measured at weather stations around the world. Weather stations are installations containing instruments for measuring weather variables including temperature, precipitation, wind, and barometric pressure.

GISS, NOAA and HadCRUT have not put together their long-term temperature measurements simply by computing average temperatures from the recorded maximum and minimum temperatures at these weather stations. Their measurements are much more convoluted than this.

First, as explained by the creators of these temperature data sets,[4] they do not simply record temperature. Global temperatures are always expressed as a deviation – called an "anomaly" – from the average temperature over a 30 year reference period. The 30 year reference period is used because the most common definition of a region's climate is the 30 year average of temperature and precipitation over different seasons of the year.[5] Anomalies, or deviations in monthly averages from the averages over the reference period partly because such differences arguably capture a change in climate (understood as a change in the average over a reference period of suitable length).

The other reason that anomalies are used is troublesome. According to HadCRUT, anomalies are used because "stations on land are at different elevations, and different countries measure average monthly temperatures using different methods and formulae. To avoid biases that could result from these problems, monthly average temperatures are reduced to anomalies."[6] What is being said here is that by looking at changes in temperature, place-based but time-invariant factors that affect temperature are being held constant. But even if a weather station's elevation and location stay the same, places change in lots of other ways. Suppose, for example, a weather station is in a place that underwent rapid urbanization prior the beginning of the reference period and that such urbanization itself increased average temperature there (something for which there is, as we will see, overwhelming evidence). Older temperatures at the station will be lower in part just because urbanization hadn't yet happened, thus creating an artificial increase when compared to later, post-urbanization temperatures.

As for the reference period over which the average is computed, scientific concern with measurement accuracy would indeed seem to recommend that the reference period is recent enough so that temperature measurements during the period are relatively reliable. But a concern with accuracy is clearly not the only thing determining reference period choice. As Hansen et al. explain, the GISS chose and has retained a 1951–1980 reference period in part because "many graphs have been published with that choice for climatology" and also because "*many of today's adults grew up during that period, so they can remember what climate was like then*" (Hansen et al. 2010). The selection of the 1951–1980 reference period seems to have little to do with science and lots to do with advocacy. After all, there is no scientific reason for caring whether lots of people can remember weather during the reference period. Moreover, as we will shortly see, the decades 1951–1980 were the coldest 30 year period in the United States for the entire twentieth century. Choosing the coldest three decades of the twentieth century as the reference period for calculating departures for the average ensures that there will be lots of positive departures. And the fact that lots of adults will remember back to that period means that many people will agree that temperatures are warmer now than they used to be. While such effects might be exactly what one would want if computing anomalies to persuade people that the world has gotten warmer, they would not seem relevant to the scientific goal of getting accurate temperature measures.[7]

I have not found anywhere where HadCRUT data set creators say that the temperature reference period is chosen partly because people can remember how cold it was back then. According to HadCRUT, anomalies are calculated relative to 1961–1990 because it is the period with the "best coverage." However, HadCRUT explains that "many stations do not have complete records for the 1961–90 period … [and so] several methods have been developed to estimate 1961–90 averages from neighboring records or using other sources of data." Incomplete or missing records for the reference period 1961–1990 is clearly a problem for very many stations. For example, based on the full set of US weather stations in the National Center for Environmental Information's (NCEI) Cooperative Observer Weather station network, the vast majority of weather stations in Phoenix, Arizona have been in existence only since 1998, and there is only one, the Phoenix Skyharbor Airport, that both has a reasonably long temperature record and is actually still reporting. If, according to hadCRUT, "many stations" do not even have measurements for the reference period, but estimates from other stations have to be used, the one must ask how the main virtue of computing anomalies – that time-invariant station characteristics are thereby controlled – can possibly be realized.

None of the GISS or HadCRUT explanations for the use of anomalies seems all that persuasive. The only thing that is certainly true of anomalies is that they make any given temperature change look a lot bigger than if one looked at an actual time series graph of temperatures over time. To see this, consider Figures 13.1 and 13.2, which plot NOAA average temperature and temperature anomalies (in degrees Fahrenheit) for the contiguous 48 US states.

The second figure, with the temperature anomaly, looks a lot scarier than the first figure, which shows average temperature. Both show an increase in average contiguous US temperatures since sometime in the late 1990s, but when we look at the first figure, we can see that average US annual temperature is still within, although close to the top, of the 50°–55°F range that it has been in since 1895. Average temperature reached 53.52°F by 2018, and it was even higher, almost 55°F, in 2016. But way back in the 1934, average temperature was 54.10°F. Indeed, one might well say that Figure 13.2 shows how US temperatures have only very recently reached the very high levels that they last reached between about 1920 and 1935.

The bottom figure is harder to contextualize, but it shows that the anomaly has recently reached relatively high levels, at the very top of the range. It is true that if I compressed the y-axis scale of the first temperature graph to run only from, say 50°–56°F, then it would like very much like the temperature anomaly graph. But compressing the temperature range in such a way would be essentially to focus only on variation around the average, which is what the anomaly graph does.

(a) The Many Adjustments That Go into Surface Temperature Measurements

The GISS and HadCRUT global temperature data sets are now based on thousands of weather stations, with global average temperature calculated from around 4,800 stations in the HadCRUT data set and over 7,000 used by GISS.[8] One should not be misled by these numbers into thinking that GISS and HadCRUT have huge data

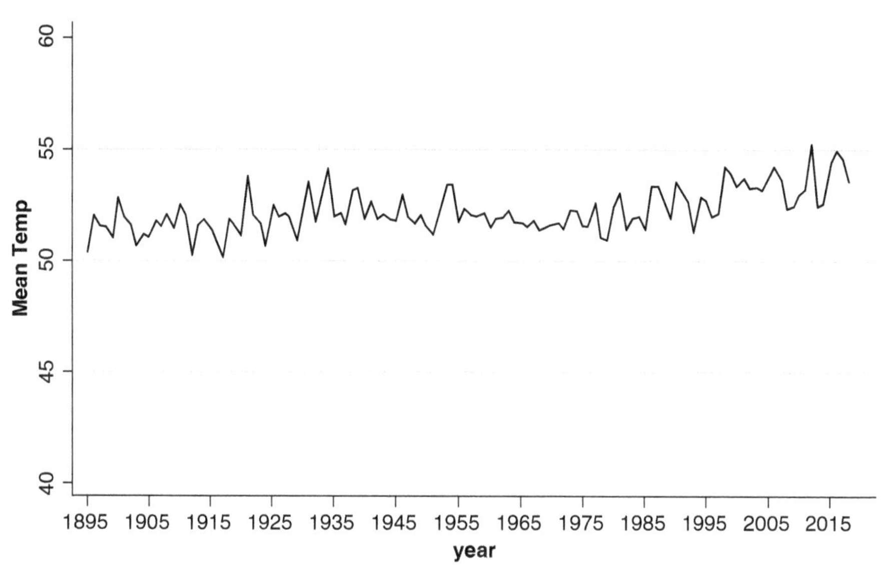

FIGURE 13.1 Average US temperatures (°F) since 1893.

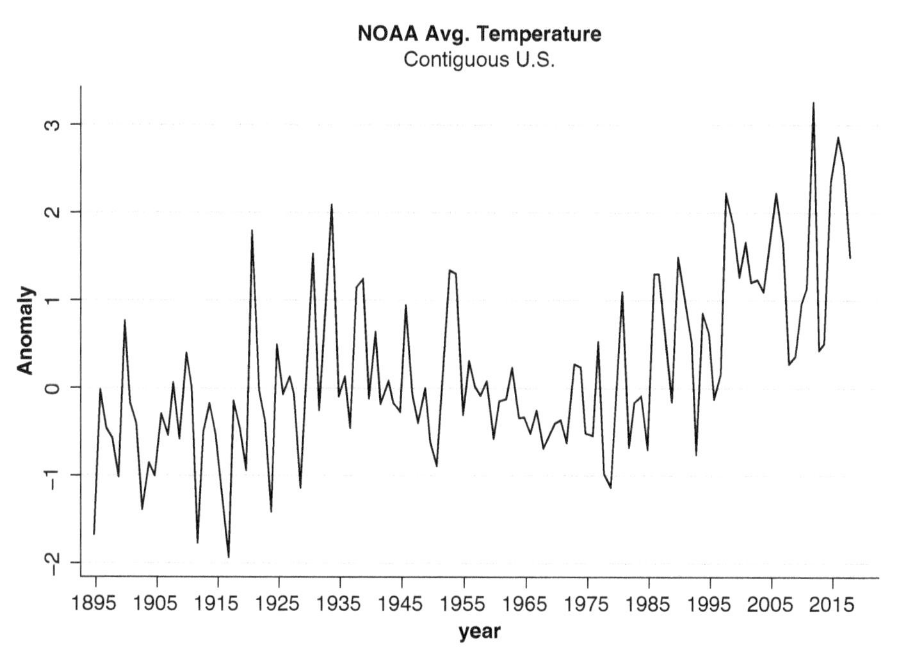

FIGURE 13.2 Average US temperature anomaly (°F) since 1893.

sets from which they compute temperature change since the nineteenth century. In the GISS weather station group, only 28 percent of the stations have temperature measurements going back 80 years, to the late 1930s, only about 56 percent even have measurements going back 40 years, to the 1970s and less than 30 percent are used for the most recent temperature measurements, since 2000. Moreover, in the GISS surface temperature weather station network, there are a grand total of roughly two dozen stations in the entirety of sub-Saharan Africa excluding South Africa, and less than 20 stations in the entire region of southeast Asia.[9] Weather stations in relatively urbanized areas of developed countries are strongly overrepresented in the global surface temperature data sets.

If one is trying to use measured temperature as an indicator of potential change in climate – which is the reason, after all, that the HadCRUT and GISS data sets were created – then one needs temperature measures which reflect only changes in weather, not other, extraneous factors. The most important such extraneous factors are changes in the instruments used to measure temperature, the 24 hour time period over which temperature is measured, and changes in the site where the weather station is located. The surface temperature measurements used by GISS and HadCRUT have been adjusted, or corrected, to offset any such extraneous factors. In the climate science business, such adjusted temperatures are called "homogenized" measures.

We can understand these adjustments by considering weather stations included in the US Historical Climatology Network (USHCN). In the words of a group of researchers heavily relied upon by the IPCC, the USHCN stations are a group of 1,218 US weather stations chosen from among thousands of so-called cooperative observers stations because they have "long, continuous temperature records, rural or small-town locations and other factors intended to produce as unbiased an estimate as possible of long-term climate changes" (Hausfather et al. 2016, 1695–1701). In other words, the USHCN are selected to be very high quality, long-term weather data sets. USHCN stations are included in both the HadCRUT and GISS time series. For example, since 2010, the HadCRUT data set has included 892 of the 1,218 stations included in the USHCN (Jones et al. 1994), and these stations make up about half of the roughly 1,600 US weather stations from which HadCRUT gets its long-term temperature measurements.

Up until the mid- to late 1980s, USHCN temperature readings were taken by liquid-in-glass (LIG) maximum and minimum thermometers housed in white, louvered wooden shelters called Stephenson Screens (or Cotton Region Shelters). Beginning in the mid-1980s, most weather stations in the USHCN switched to measuring temperatures with an electronic MMTS sensor housed in plastic bee-hive-shaped container. In the 1990s, new shelters were introduced as part of the Automated Surface Observing System.

For measuring temperature trends, the most important thing to know is that a group of researchers at the National Climate Data Center, Quayle et al. (1991, 1718–1723), found that for every season of the year, maximum temperatures were lower (by about 0.4°C on average) and minimum temperatures higher (by about 0.3°C on average) with MMTS sensors than with the old thermometers. During the 1990s, USHCN temperatures recorded with MMTS were revised as suggested by Quayle et al. (1991). As described by Menne et al. (2009), after 2009, temperatures in the HSHCN temperature data were revised generally (so that this data set is called the USHCN version 2; see Menne et al. 2009, 998). Under this method, the switch from LIG thermometers to MMTS sensors was estimated to decrease maximum temperature by 0.52°C and increase minimum temperatures by 0.37°C. The net effect of adjusting for the switch to MMTS sensors (by increasing maximum temperatures and decreasing minimum temperatures) has thus been to increase average temperature by about 0.075°C since the mid-1980s (see Menne et al. 2009, 998).

Another adjustment to USHCN temperatures has been made for a change in what is called the time of observation. The time of observation is the time of the day when a new maximum-minimum temperature measurement period begins (that is, the time when the thermometer is reset). In most US weather stations, from 1900 until 1959, maximum and minimum temperatures were recorded for the 24 hours ending between around 5:00 and 8:00 PM; since 1959, most (but by no means all) of the weather stations in the USHCN moved to 7:00 or 8:00 AM as the time of observation (DeGaetano 2000, 49–67). An evening time of observation can cause biased measurements of maximum temperatures. This happens when a warm day is followed by a cooler day, so that the maximum temperature recorded on or before the time of observation for the first day is likely very close to the maximum temperature recorded on or after the time of observation for the second day. Both maximums occur on the same 24 hour day but the one that occurs after the evening thermometer reset is recorded as being on the second day. Conversely, a time of observation of 7:00 or 8:00 AM will cause minimum temperature readings to be biased downward when a cold day is followed by a warmer day. On such days, minimum temperatures that occur on the first 24 hour day end up being recorded on two days because one occurs before and one after the time of observation.

To really correct for changes in the time of observation from evening to morning, one would need to know the actual hourly temperatures for every day of each year for each weather station. When researchers have actually compared hourly temperatures to those recorded using different time of observation values, they have found that compared to 7:00 AM observation time, average monthly temperatures based on a 5:00 PM observation are typically about 1.5°C warmer in the winter and 0.5°C warmer in the summer (DeGaetano 2000, 51). This is just as what one would predict if, as expected, early morning time of observation sometimes double counts cold day mornings and an evening time of observation sometimes double counts warmer day evenings.

The time of observation adjustments to temperature measurements in the USHCN are much more complicated than this. They are based on a very old paper, Karl et al. (1986, 145) that estimated time of observation bias for any station based on the variation in daily average temperature on different days of the year for a station at a given latitude. Adjustments to both daily maximum and daily minimum temperatures were generally small and negative, averaging less than −0.1°C until 1959.[10] After that date however, adjustments to both maximum and minimum temperatures have been steadily increasing, reaching over 0.2°C per year by 2009.

According to Menne et al. (2009), over the entire period 1895–2007, the time of observation adjustments increased the overall trend of maximum temperatures by 0.015°C per decade and of minimum temperatures by 0.022°C per decade (Menne et al. 2009, 996). Thus over the entire 11 decade period 1895–2007, such adjustments increased maximum temperature by 0.165°C and minimum temperature by 0.242°C. Since the adjustments were consistently negative up until at least 1960, this means that since 1960, adjustments have accounted for more than a 0.165°C increase in maximum temperatures and 0.242°C increase in minimum temperatures. Together, taking average temperature as the simple average of maximum and minimum temperatures, since 1960, the adjustments have increased average US temperatures used by the IPCC by about 0.20°C.

When the 0.075°C increase in post-1980s temperatures generated by the adjustment for the switch to MMTS sensors is added to the time of observation adjustment, we find that these two adjustments increased post-1980s temperatures by 0.275°C. To put this in context, recall that according to the 2014 National Climate Assessment, US average surface temperature increased between 0.7° and 1°C between 1895 and 2012, with most of the increase since the mid-1940s. Even assuming the utmost good faith on the part of people who have produced the adjusted USHCN temperatures, their adjustments account for between 27.5 and 39 percent of the reported 1895–2012 temperature increase.

From a policy point of view, this is a staggeringly high proportion of adjustments to total change. To see just how staggering, consider US economic growth. From the Great Recession up until the beginning years of the Trump administration, the TV news channels carried stories on whether the growth rate in the real (inflation adjusted) US economy was above or below 2 percent and when and whether it would exceed 3 percent. If adjustments in estimated US annual economic growth rates were as large as the adjustments to USHCN temperatures, the adjustment to the growth rate – at around 30 percent of the rate – would be so large as to account for most (between 0.6 and 0.9 percent) of the difference between a 2 and 3 percent growth rate.

For another perspective on the size of adjustments to just US temperatures that underlie the GISS and HadCRUT data sets, consider what that the Commerce Department's Bureau of Economic Analysis (BEA) has to say about the statistics that it generates on the performance of the US economy. According to the BEA, whatever revisions it makes to such statistics, they must be small enough so that "economic policy decisions should not need to be reconsidered in the light of revisions to GDP estimates, and policymakers should be able to rely on the early estimates as correctly indicating the state of the economy."[11] Such revisions must not "substantively change BEA's measures of long-term growth, the picture of business cycles, and trends in major components of GDP." US surface temperature measurement adjustments would fail this test: they significantly increase the rate of growth of temperatures, and such adjustments are highly policy relevant, because if they were removed, and reported temperature increases were much lower, then as we shall soon see, it might be impossible to say that late twentieth-century temperatures are higher than temperatures in the 1930s.

(b) Poor Weather Station Site Quality Leads to Warm Biased Daily Minimum (and So Average) Temperatures

Most people now know that because asphalt pavement holds heat, summertime nighttime minimum temperatures in city centers are almost always higher than in suburban or exurban areas outside such city centers. Unsurprising, under World Meteorological Organization Guidelines, weather stations that measure temperature are not supposed to be located near heat sources such as asphalt paved roads.

What is perhaps not so widely known is that even beyond things like asphalt pavement, surface structure around a weather station has a bigger impact on nighttime minimum temperatures than on daytime maximum temperatures. Weather station instruments are typically located about 1.5–2 m (5–7 feet) above the ground. According to meteorologists, during the daytime, when there is lots of vertical mixing of air, temperatures at even the relatively low 1.5–2 m height are representative of temperatures higher up in the troposphere and are thus a good proxy for the "content of a substantial mass of the lower atmosphere" (Christy et al. 2009, 3342). Thus the daily maximum temperature proxies the temperature of a large quantity of air.

This is not true of daily minimum temperatures, which typically occur during the nighttime. According to one group of meteorologists, Klotzbach et al. (2009, D21102), nighttime measurements are completely unreliable indicators of GHG-induced warming:

> Physically, the nighttime boundary layer is not a good place to detect the accumulation of heat … the stable boundary layer is so shallow in most cases that it represents an insignificant mass of the atmosphere. Additionally, as shown by [reference omitted], any positive forcing such as additional greenhouse gases destabilizes the boundary layer, increases its depth, and mixes warm air aloft to the surface. Thus, the warming is amplified at the surface but represents a redistribution of heat rather than accumulated heat from the additional forcing. Use of surface data in which minimum temperatures are included in the data set then leads to a direct warm bias if interpreted as a heat accumulation.

A minimum temperature measured at only 1.5–2 m above the ground represents the temperature of only a very shallow layer of air and anything that impacts mixing between very low and higher layers of air may have an enormous impact on nighttime temperatures as measured at that height.[12] Meteorologists say that anything that causes increased turbulence (and more mixing with higher layers) in this bottom nighttime layer of air will tend to increase minimum nighttime temperatures (Klotzbach et al. 2009). Among the things that could cause such increased turbulence are trees or buildings (by increasing surface roughness) (McNider et al. 1995, 1602), things leading to increased surface heat capacity, such as pavement,[13] and anything that causes enhanced downward longwave radiation and hence more downward nighttime mixing of warm air, such as increases in water vapor and various types of aerosol pollutants such as sulfur dioxide and oxides of nitrogen (Jacobsen 1997, 587).

Changes in the surface characteristics near weather stations are thus especially likely to bias upward measured changes in minimum temperatures. This matters enormously to the temperature changes reported by the IPCC and the USGCRP. The reason, as explained by Pielke et al. (2007) (a paper with 19 coauthors) is that

> one of the most significant features in the observed surface data set is the asymmetric warming between maximum and minimum temperatures. Minimum temperatures have risen about 50% faster than maximum temperatures in the observed surface data set since 1950 [Vose et al., 2005]. Thus this nocturnal warming is the largest component of the "global daily average" increasing temperature trends that are used as measures of global climate change and to which models have been compared.

In other words, the increase in minimum temperatures has accounted for most of the reported increase in surface temperatures. If the increase in minimum temperatures is due in part to changes in the characteristics of the land surface near weather stations, then those changes would need to be controlled for statistically in order to isolate the impact of actual changes in climate.

The World Meteorological Organization (WMO) classifies weather station sites according to their susceptibility to things that cause such biased measurements of temperature (and also precipitation). According to the WMO, the best, Class 1 site, is one that is flat, covered with "natural and low vegetation representative of the region," at least 100 meters away from heat sources and reflective surfaces such as buildings and concrete surfaces, and away from projected shade.[14] A Class 4 site – one subject to bias of up to 2°C – by contrast has up to 50 percent of artificial heat sources and reflective surfaces such as buildings, concrete, car parks within a 10 meter radius of the weather station unit. Class 5 sites have even more of such surfaces within 10 m of the measuring instrument. The WMO considers only Class 1 and 2 sites to be "acceptably representative" for temperature measurement.

Between about 2007 and 2012, the meteorologist Anthony Watts enlisted volunteers from across the country who went out and personally surveyed and photographed about 75 percent of all of the weather stations in the USHCN network that supply US surface temperature data sets used by the IPCC.[15] Watt's volunteers categorized the quality of different weather stations using the WMO criteria for station quality just discussed.[16] They found many very poorly sited weather stations. One such station, located in Roseburg, Oregon, is depicted below.[17] As one can see, the plastic "beehive" monitor is on a roof, next to an air conditioning unit, surrounded by buildings and other structures.

Shockingly, the detective work by Watts et al. determined that such poorly sited weather stations were far from the exception. Only 272 stations, or 35 percent of the total, were classified as being in the acceptable Class 1 or Class 2 quality categories. *In other words, 65 percent of the USHCN weather stations surveyed were subject to large temperature measurement biases due to poor site quality.*[18]

Now of course if over at entire time period, a particular station was on a roof next to an air conditioning unit, or surrounded by pavement in a parking lot, then there would be no change in site quality and so change in site quality could not contribute to and bias the measured change in temperature at the station. That is, the temperature measurement at the station might well be biased, but given a time-invariant bias, the change in temperature over a given time period would not be biased. Watt's volunteers reported on what stations looked like at a particular point in time, not the change in station site quality over any given period.

Watts et al. did, however, find strong evidence that deterioration in site quality over time caused an upward bias in measured temperatures. Such evidence is provided by their finding that the 1979–2008 trend in average temperatures for "compliant" (i.e., high site quality) rural stations without airports was 0.108°C/decade, *less than half as big* as the 0.0.228°C/decade trend measured by low quality, noncompliant rural stations. We can also compare the temperature trend at high quality rural station to the trend for the same period for the whole continental United States as reported in the NASA GISS measurements, which is one of the three data sets that the IPCC used for twentieth-century surface temperature trends. (The NASA GISS temperature data set does not extend as far back to the nineteenth century, and it is for this reason that I have primarily discussed the HadCRUT data set, which extends back to 1850.) The continental US temperature trend in the NASA GISS for the relevant period is 0.31°C/decade, *about three times as large* as what Watts et al. found for the high quality US rural station sites. As Watts et al. note, the GISS estimated trend is similar to the trend they found if one uses just the worst, noncompliant stations.

Prior to 2009, the USHCN surface temperature measurements relied upon by the IPCC and USGCRP did not attempt to take into account site quality or changes in site quality or location. Since 2009, the USHCN temperature measurements relied upon by the IPCC have been adjusted to take account of changes in weather station location and site characteristics. These adjustments are not based upon the kind of comparisons of temperature trends at well-sited versus poorly sited stations made by

FIGURE 13.3 Poorly sited weather station in USHCN.

Watts et al. Instead, the adjustments are made by statistical approaches designed to identify and correct for inhomogeneities in general – that is, any factors, observed or unobserved, that make measured temperatures at a station a biased representation of what was actually happening to surface temperatures over the time period.[19]

For temperature, statistical homogenization works by comparing the temperature time series at a particular weather station to other stations, either pairwise, or to a composite time series for the other stations (Acquaotta and Frattiani 2014). There are a variety of homogenization techniques,[20] but the idea behind all of them is identify – relative to some reference group of other stations – temperature measurements at a particular station that show an abrupt, discontinuous change or change in trend that is sustained over a period of years and statistically significant. When such a difference is detected, temperatures for the particular station are corrected to be more in line with temperatures at the reference group stations.

The particular homogenization procedure that has been applied to USHCN temperatures has had generally small impacts. Menne et al. (2009) report that the net effect of statistical homogenization adjustments was less than 0.1°C. This about the size of the 1979–2008 temperature increase found at high quality US stations by

Watts et al. and it is only half of the roughly 0.2°C bigger increase at poor quality US stations than at high quality US stations. In other words, statistical homogenization does not seem to come close to correcting for the enormous difference that Watts et al. found between temperature trends found at well-sited versus poorly sited US weather stations.

(c) Making the Hot 1930s Go Away: The Impact of Adjustments on GISS Measures of US Temperatures

To summarize the kind and magnitude of adjustments to temperature time series just discussed, we have:

- Whereas adjustments for changing time of observation (tobs) were consistently negative for both maximum and minimum temperatures up until about 1960, since that time such adjustments have accounted for more than a 0.165°C increase in maximum temperatures and a 0.242°C increase in minimum temperatures for a 0.2° adjustment up in average temperature. Again, this compares to a 0.7–1°C increase in average USHCN temperature for the entire 1895–2012 period.
- Statistical homogenization techniques have been used to make adjustments for changes in site characteristics, station location and the change in measuring instruments from LIG thermometers to MMTS sensors, and together those have increased average USHCN temperatures about 0.075°C since 1977.

With these adjustments included, one gets the most recent (as of May 2019) US average surface temperature time series produced by GISS.[21]

As GISS says in a footnote,[22] this graph depicts departures in average US continental surface temperatures relative to the 1951–1980 mean and because of corrections things such as changing time of observation, it shows a much bigger increase in temperatures than earlier GISS US surface temperature graphs. To see just how big an impact these adjustments have had on GISS temperatures, compare Figure 13.4 to Figure 13.5(a) (the left-hand graph in Figure 13.5). Figure 13.5 is a graph depicting US and global temperatures that GISS posted on its website back in 1999.[23] I have reproduced the 1999 GISS graph directly from the GISS website because apparently the GISS removed the 1999 data. So too has the GISS removed both the temperature data and the temperature graph that it put on its website in 2001. With the 2001 data and graph and 1999 data all removed from the GISS website, one is left with only the 1999 GISS graph.

Looking carefully at the graph (at the actual observations, the black squares, not the red smoothing line), one can see that before the various adjustments (the left-hand graph, Figure 13.5(a)), US average surface temperature anomaly in 1998 was a bit lower than −0.1°C. This is more than 1.5°C lower than the maximum anomaly that was reached in 1934. After the adjustments (Figure 13.4),[24] the US surface

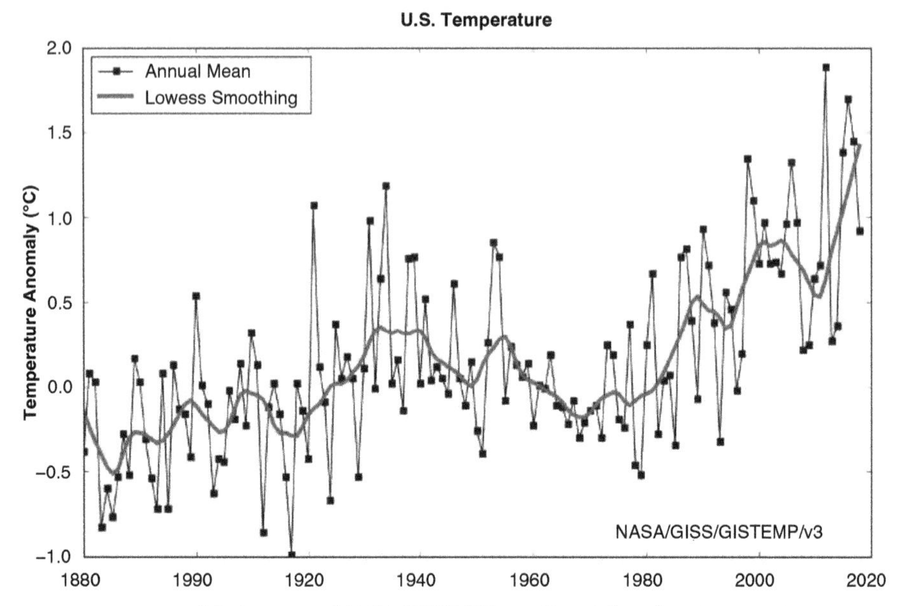

FIGURE 13.4 Vintage 2019 NASA GISS US continental surface temperatures.

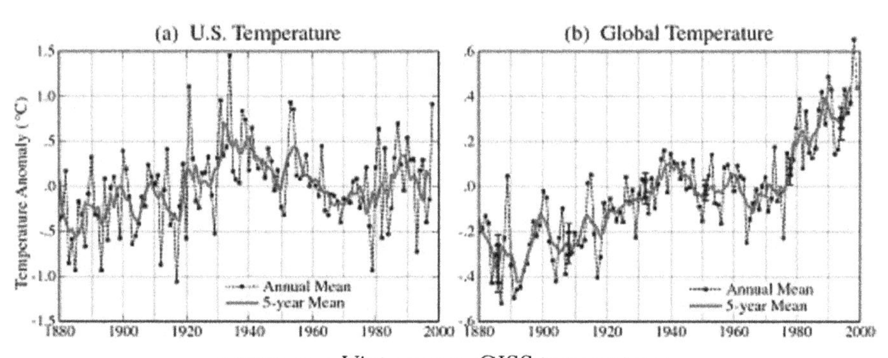

FIGURE 13.5 Vintage 1999 GISS temperatures.

temperature anomaly in 1998 was 1.35°C, exceeding even the 1934 anomaly, which had been revised down from 1.5°C in the 1999 figure below to only 1.22°C. In other words, *the adjustments cut the 1934 anomaly by about 20 percent while increasing the 1998 anomaly from about −.1°C to 1.35°C, a change from negative to positive with a magnitude (relative to the initial 1934 estimate) of over 1,400 percent.*

Once again comparing Figure 13.4 with Figure 13.5(a), one can see that the GISS adjustments kicked in to increase US temperatures beginning sometime in the early to mid-1980s. This is precisely the time when the large upward adjustments to temperatures for changing time of observation and measurement instrument began to be made. Together these two adjustments increased annual average temperatures by about 0.3°C. If we imagine shifting the red curve in in the most recent, vintage 2019 Figure 13.3 down by about this much, it is clear that while the curve would still show an increase in US surface temperatures without the adjustments, the increase would be on average about 40 percent smaller.

It is important to point out that the NOAA contiguous US average temperature and anomaly graphs that I presented earlier depict "homogenized," that is, adjusted temperatures. The increases in both the average temperature and average anomaly that one can see beginning in the mid-1990s in the those figures reflect the upward adjustments of about 0.275°C made to US temperatures.

The HadCRUT and GISS temperature data sets have been designed to test computer models of global climate change and therefore present an estimate of global average surface temperature. On the global level, the vintage 2019 GISS estimated global surface temperatures since 1880 look like Figure 13.6.[25]

The HadCRUT global surface temperature time series[26] goes back a bit further than does the GISS, but as can be seen in Figure 13.7, it displays a very similar temporal trend since 1880.

These measurements of global average temperatures are at least as subject to measurement errors and biases that have been "corrected" via various adjustments as are the US temperatures I have discussed above. Indeed, they may be even more so. For example, according to Christy et al. (2009, 3345), in East Africa, there are hardly any temperature measurements before 1905, and although there are a relatively large number of temperature observations after 1945, temperature measurements after

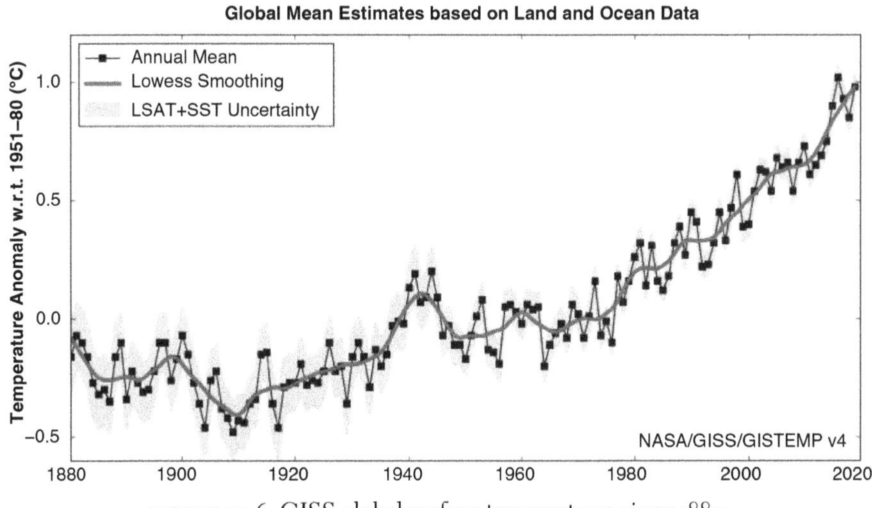

FIGURE 13.6 GISS global surface temperatures since 1880.

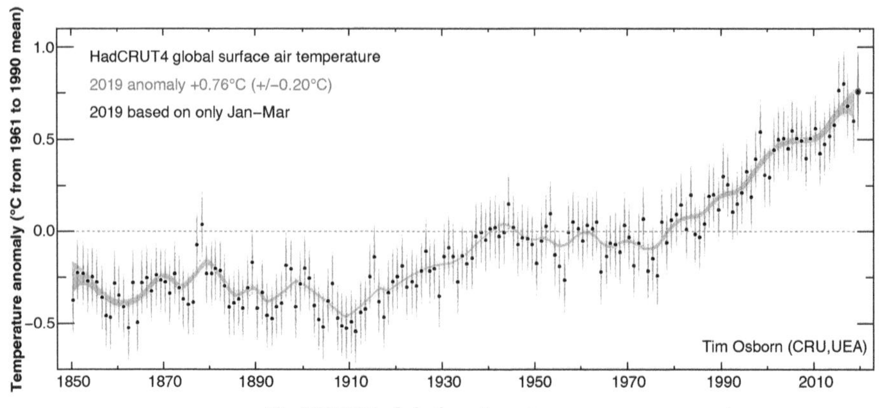

FIGURE 13.7 HadCRUT global surface temperature anomaly.

1978 are likely significantly impacted by the substantial population growth and urban migration that has taken place since then. Indeed, when Christy et al. (2009) looked at an expanded data set for East Africa, they found that just as for many other regions of the world, while minimum temperatures had increased, there has been no statistically significant increase in maximum temperatures, with the increase in minimums becoming especially pronounced since 1979. Such a divergence between the trend of minimum and maximum temperatures is precisely what one would predict is urbanization and land use conversion is driving temperature change.

(d) Tropospheric Temperature Trends

With all of the problems with surface temperature measurements discussed above, it is useful to look at an alternative temperature measurement, the temperature of the lower troposphere, the earth's atmosphere from the surface to about 5 miles (or 25,000 feet) up. As will be explained in a bit more detail later, on the most basic model of GHG-induced warming, it is the troposphere that should have warmed (with the upper level of the earth's atmosphere, the stratosphere, cooling). Since about 1978, tropospheric temperatures have been measured by satellite. The process of getting satellite measurements of temperature is more complex than simply getting readings from a sensor or thermometer,[27] there are multiple satellite measurements plus earlier measurements from radiosondes in balloons, and there is ongoing controversy over which measurements are the most accurate. For present purposes, however, what matters is that the tropospheric temperature trends measured by various instruments are quite close (within about 0.01°C per decade according to Christy and McNider 2017, 511–518), and none are subject to the various problems that beset surface temperature measurements.

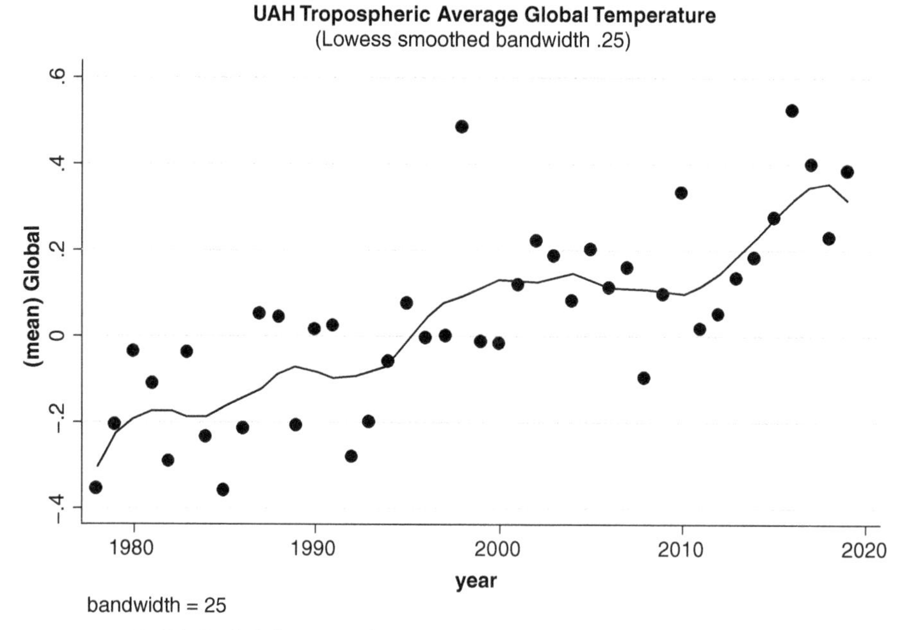

FIGURE 13.8 UAH global tropospheric temperature anomaly (relative to 1981–2010 average).

If we look at annual mean temperatures in the lower troposphere as measured by the University of Alabama Huntsville (UAH) satellites for the globe as a whole, we have Figure 13.8.[28]

One cannot directly compare the anomalies reported by these satellite measurements of tropospheric temperatures to the anomalies reported in the graphs giving the GISS global temperatures. The reason is that anomalies are departures from average measurements over a period and the UAH and GISS use different base periods for calculating these departures. Moreover, while one can compare changes, the change depends upon which particular years are selected for the comparison.

With these caveats, if we compared US temperatures in 1979 (the first year for which full year UAH satellite measurements became available) to US temperatures in 2018 (the last year for which I have GISS data), then we would find that the UAH tropospheric temperature (anomaly) increase of 0.44°C (from −0.21° to 0.23°C) is only 64 percent as big as the GISS (and NOAA) surface temperature increase of 0.69°C (from 0.16° to 0.85°C).

Rigorous published empirical studies have found that tropospheric temperatures are not rising as quickly as the surface temperatures reported by GISS and HadCRUT. When Klotzbach et al. (2009, D21102) compared surface temperature trends to tropospheric temperature trends as measured by two satellites between 1979 and 2009, they found that surface warming was actually greater than tropospheric warming, a finding that they interpreted as indicating that surface temperature measurements were biased upward.

More recently, for different combinations of two surface and two tropospheric temperature data sets, the best estimates of the ratio of tropospheric to surface warming trends over the period 1979–2014 found by Vogelsang and Nawaz (2017, 640–667) ranged from 0.64 to 1, a range whose lower bound is precisely what I just reported for the period 1979–2018.

In summary, there is clearly a big discrepancy between warming as measured in the troposphere and as indicated by adjusted surface temperature measurements. It is in this light that one should view the NASA GISS practice recounted in the previous chapter of continual "hottest ever" surface temperature public announcements. GISS is making announcements about surface temperature trends that it knows rely upon many adjustments and which are inconsistent with tropospheric temperature trends but without ever disclosing these important caveats. If people were informed both that the GISS surface temperature trends rely upon very large, albeit perhaps justified adjustments to actual temperature measurements and also that those trends are much bigger than satellites have recorded in the troposphere, the GISS "hottest ever" reports might have a very different impact on public opinion. Were GISS to practice full disclosure, it would also inform the public that evidence that surface temperatures are rising much faster than tropospheric temperatures surface temperatures is actually inconsistent with the hypothesis that human GHG emissions are responsible for all of the increase in temperature. As I discuss and explain in the next chapter, the only precisely testable implication of the GHG-induced warming theory is that tropospheric warming should be *bigger* than surface warming (by about 1.2 globally and 1.4 in the tropics). One would have thought that rather than repeatedly proclaiming a new "hottest temperature ever," an agency with the primary mission of informing the public would have reported evidence that surface temperature increases have been bigger than tropospheric temperature increases. Because such evidence suggests either surface temperature increases have been overestimated in the GISS and HadCRUT data sets and/or that surface temperature increases are being driven partly by increasing atmospheric GHGs but also by other forces, it would be highly relevant to the public policy debate.

(e) Sea Surface Temperature Measurements

The oceans make up about 70 percent of the earth's surface and the global surface temperature measurements presented by both HadCRUT and GISS look at both land and sea surface temperatures. For sea surface temperatures, both HadCRUT and GISS use measurements of ocean surface temperature taken from ships and buoys. Sea surface temperature measurements from ships go back to the early twentieth century. Prior to World War II, ships measured sea surface temperatures by throwing canvas or wooden buckets out into the sea and then measuring the temperature in those buckets. After that, ships measured sea water temperature at the engine's cooling system seawater intake. The people who put together sea surface temperature measurements believe that the bucket based measures were too cold and so these were adjusted upward (Vose et al. 2012, 1679). These adjustments were very big, having a "substantial impact when averaged over the entire ocean surface." Temperature measurements from drifting and moored buoys became available only in the 1970s (Smith and Reynolds 2004, 2466–2477).

Satellite measurements of sea surface temperatures became available in 1981. These have much more complete coverage of the world's oceans than either buoys or ships. By 2004, Smith and Reynolds (2004) put together a measure of global sea surface temperatures using such satellite data and making corrections for the amount of sea ice found at locations. As this data set "incorporate[d] satellite and in situ data," and had much lower error when compared to recent observations, Smith and Reynolds (2004) said that "we consider it to be a close approximation of the truth." Despite this, by 2010, "because the satellite SSTs were not found to add appreciable value to a monthly analysis on a 2° grid, and they actually introduced a small but abrupt cool bias at the global scale starting in 1985," they were no longer used to estimate global sea surface temperatures (Vose et al. 2012, 1680).

With the satellite SST measurements dropped, NOAA's most recent graph of SST's over time[29] (which NOAA calls the Extended Reconstructed Sea Surface Temperatures or ERSSTv.4, with SSTA giving the departure or anomaly from the 1970–2000 average) looks as in Figure 13.9.

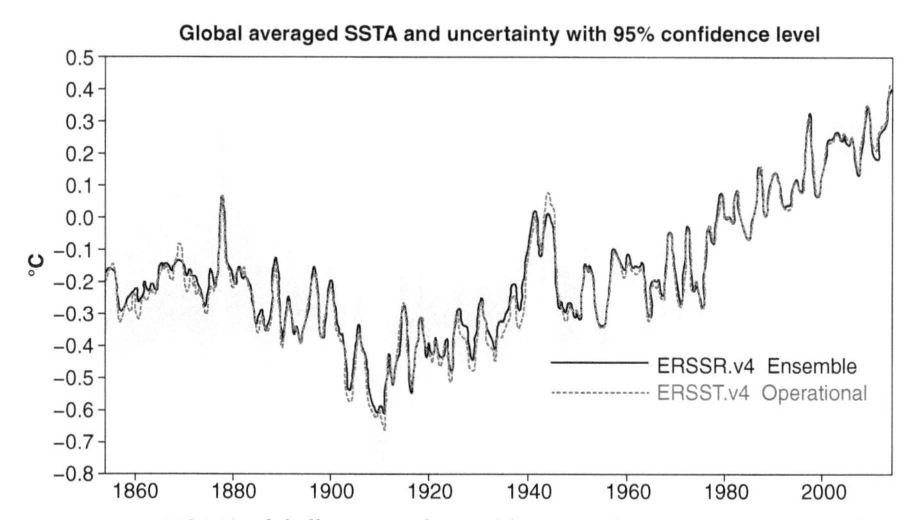

FIGURE 13.9 NOAA's globally averaged monthly sea surface temperature anomalies relative to 1970–2000 average.

Meteorologists believe that over 90 percent of the forcing (increased warming) from increased atmospheric concentration of GHG's since the 1960s has been felt in the upper 0–700 m of the world's oceans (Lyman and Johnson 2014, 1945; Ablain et al. 2017, 8). Like sea surface temperature measurements, measurement of the temperature of the global oceans below the surface was spotty and highly imperfect until very recently.[30] As described in one recent attempt to synthesize various estimates (Palmer et al. 2017, 910), ocean heat and temperature estimates (called Ocean reanalyses (ORAs)) "employ a variety of ocean general circulation models (OGCMs) and data assimilation schemes to synthesize a diverse network of available ocean observations in order to arrive at a dynamically consistent estimate of the historical ocean state." Thus ocean heat estimates are just that – the best estimates, not simple measurements.

With this caveat, the Japan Meteorological Agency has developed one such reanalysis. Figure 13.10[31] presents this reanalysis in the form of a time series for the heat content of the upper 700 and 2,000 m of the ocean (relative to 1955) for the period 1955–2019 (with the light (dark) blue area showing the annual mean global ocean heat content for the upper 700 m (700–2,000 m) and the dashed line giving the 95 percent confidence interval). Note that following convention, this time series expresses heat in zeta joules (joules, the standard heat measure, taken to the 10^{22} power).

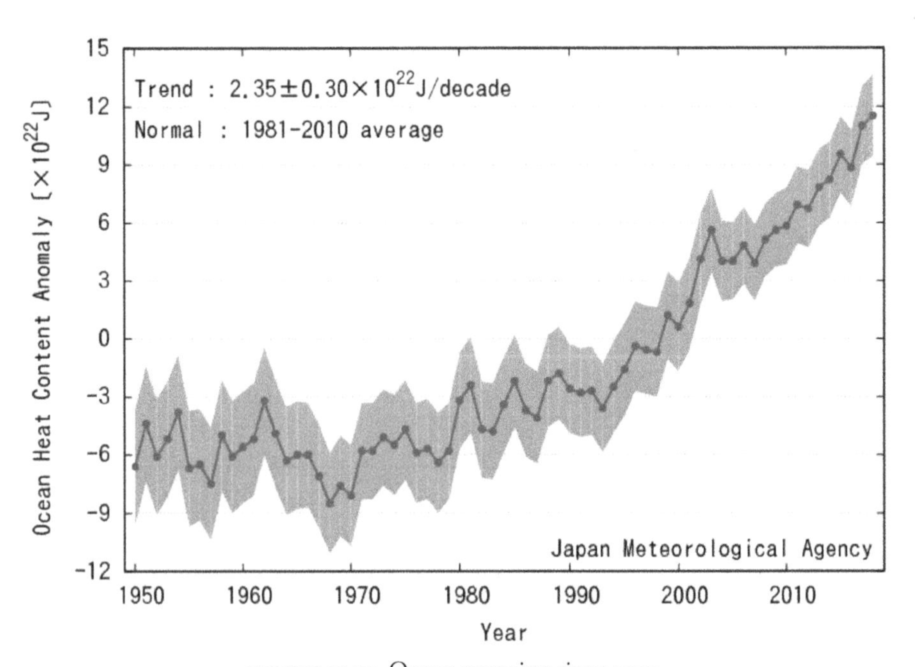

FIGURE 13.10 Ocean warming since 1955.

The Japanese data are consistent with other recent attempts to estimate ocean heat content (see Palmer et al. 2017, 909–930), and they show that the ocean has warmed considerably since the mid-1990s.[32] However, Figure 13.10 measures ocean heat in zeta joules. Joules are a measure of heat energy, and when this heat is translated into temperature (using the heat capacity of ocean water and the mass of the oceans), the Japan Meteorological Society reports that there has been a rise of 0.02 ± 0.001°C per decade in the globally averaged upper ocean (0–2000 m) temperature. This translates into about a 0.13°C increase in ocean temperatures over the period 1955–2019.

As was true when we compared the GISS global surface temperatures to satellite measurements of temperature in the lower troposphere, there is a discrepancy, and big one – of over 300 percent – between the JMA's estimate of about a 0.13°C increase in the temperature of the upper ocean since 1955 and NOAA's estimate of an increase in surface sea temperature of at least 0.6°C since 1951. Scientists agree that up to 90 percent of the GHG-induced warming has been felt in the upper 300 m of the ocean, but the JMA data above suggest that the ocean has warmed much less than the surface warming rate estimated by GISS and HadCRUT.

The bottom line: surface temperature measurements show a warming, but a much bigger warming than recorded for recent decades in the ocean and troposphere

Recall that the IPCC's 2013 AR gave precise numbers for twentieth-century global surface temperature increases and was certain that the increase in recent decades has been the biggest in over a century. But the increase in recent decades is an increase in adjusted temperatures, with the adjustments accounting for a large percentage of the post-1980s increase, and surface temperature increases reported by HadCRUT and GISS are much larger than the warming measured in the troposphere and the oceans. In light of all this, it is very difficult to see how the IPCC could express "certainty" regarding the magnitude of temperature change over the twentieth century, or even over more recent decades.

For meteorologists, that the surface temperature measures reported by GISS and HadCRUT are badly flawed and overestimate recent temperature increases has the direct lesson that temperature change can only reliably be gauged by looking at tropospheric and ocean temperature measures. But the general public never hears anything about tropospheric temperature measurements. Instead, as discussed in the previous chapter, the general public hears a never-ending stream of news stories on how surface temperatures are higher than ever. Were the IPCC the objective assessment body that it touts itself to be, the IPCC would not emphasize surface temperature trends as it does, and would surely not use those trends as reliable evidence of the magnitude of climate change.

II ARE RECENT AIR TEMPERATURES HISTORICALLY UNUSUAL? TEMPERATURES HAVE BEEN HIGH BEFORE AND WILL BE AGAIN

One thing that every scientist does seem to agree upon is that there have been cycles in global temperature, cycles that range in scale from interannual, to decadal, to multidecadal, centennial, millennial, and even longer. We can see this in Figure 13.11, which depicts HadCRUT global surface temperatures since 1850.

Using one particular smoothing algorithm (a loess smoothing the uses the nearest 9 percent of points for estimating the best-fit line at each point), Figure 13.11 depicts multidecadal cycles in temperature: an increase of about 0.5°C from 1859 to 1879, followed by a fall of about 0.45°C from 1879 to 1899, followed by an increase of 0.4°C from 1899 to 1939, a slight decline over the period 1939–1979, and then a long increase of about 0.7°C until today. Looking back at Figure 13.9 one sees similar multidecadal cycles in global sea surface temperatures.

Such multidecadal temperature cycles are also found in particular regions of the world. Looking back at Figure 13.4, we can see this for the United States.[33] Temperatures rose (as did anomalies or departures from any average) 1.65°C between 1895 and 1939, then fell by 1.8°C between 1939 and 1979, and have risen 1.45°C between 1939 and 2018.

The Arctic, an area often used to demonstrate the perils of climate change, also exhibits multidecadal temperature cycles. Figure 13.12, an average of temperatures

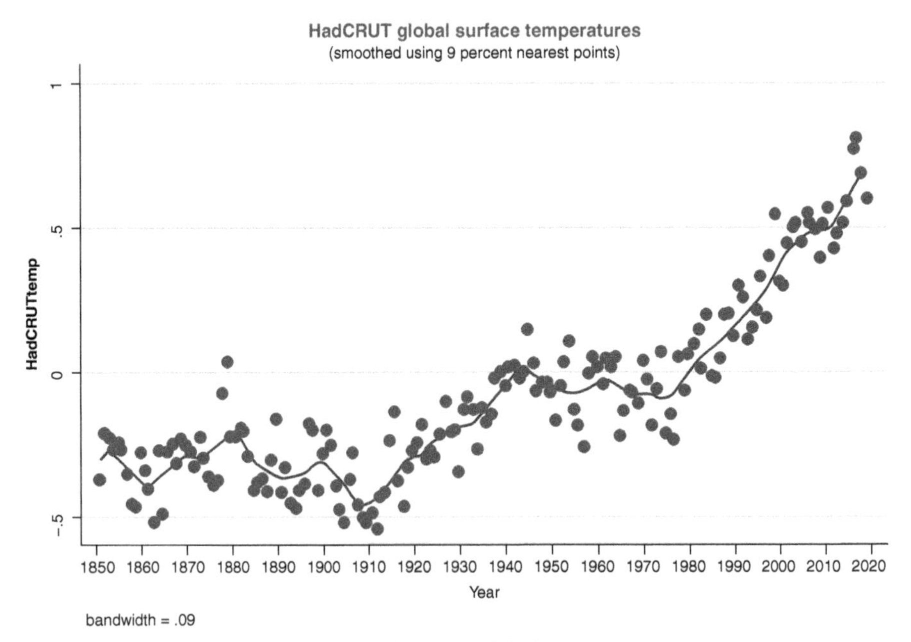

FIGURE 13.11 Cycles in HadCRUT global temperatures since 1850.

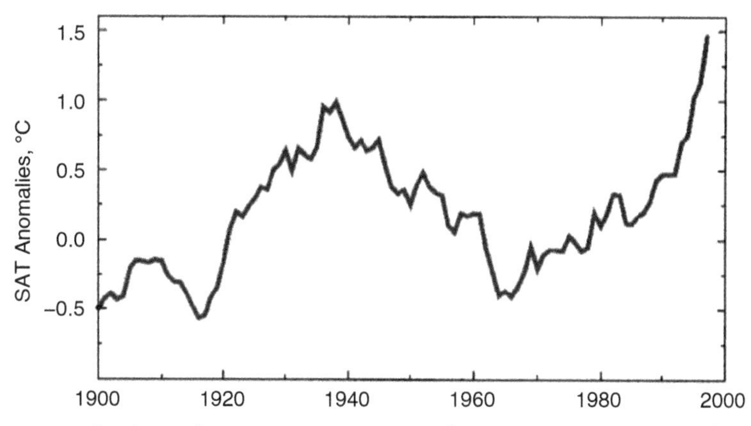

FIGURE 13.12 Arctic surface temperature anomalies since 1900. A reproduction of figure 1 from Bengtsson et al. (2004, 4046) © 2004 American Meteorological Society.

over the entire Arctic region, shows an increase of about 1.7°C between around 1920 and 1940, an almost equivalent fall in temperatures between then and the early 1960s, and an increase of almost 2°C between the early 1960s and the early 2000s.

Switching focus to a particular Arctic region, Figure 13.13 depicts very similar annual trends (with summer and the annual monthly maximum broken out as well) at two Greenland weather stations. As of 2005, at one station, Godhab, none of these temperatures – annual average, summer, or maximum monthly – had exceeded the levels they reached in the late 1930s.

Temperature cycles are also apparent on much longer time scales. Figure 13.14 below shows a number of different Northern Hemisphere temperature reconstructions covering the last 2000 years (the so-called Common Era, or CE). There are of course no actual instrumental measurements of temperature going back 2000 years. These are "reconstructions" based on various proxies for temperature, such as tree rings and ice core readings of various atomic isotopes whose concentration varies with temperature. But with this qualification, in Figure 13.14, one can clearly see long-term temperature cycles. Between 900 and 1100 or so, temperatures were as high as today, and for centuries. As one can also see, between about 1500 and 1800, temperatures were very low. This period, called the Little Ice Age, ended when temperatures began to increase in the late nineteenth century, a trend that has continued and accelerated in the twentieth century.

It is worth noting that back in 2001, in its third Assessment Report, the IPCC presented a very different picture of global temperatures over the last 1,000 years. Whereas Figure 13.14 shows that temperatures have only recently crept back up into the level they reached during the period AD 800–1100, the picture the IPCC reported as true back in its 2001 AR3, reprinted as Figure 13.15, is radically different.

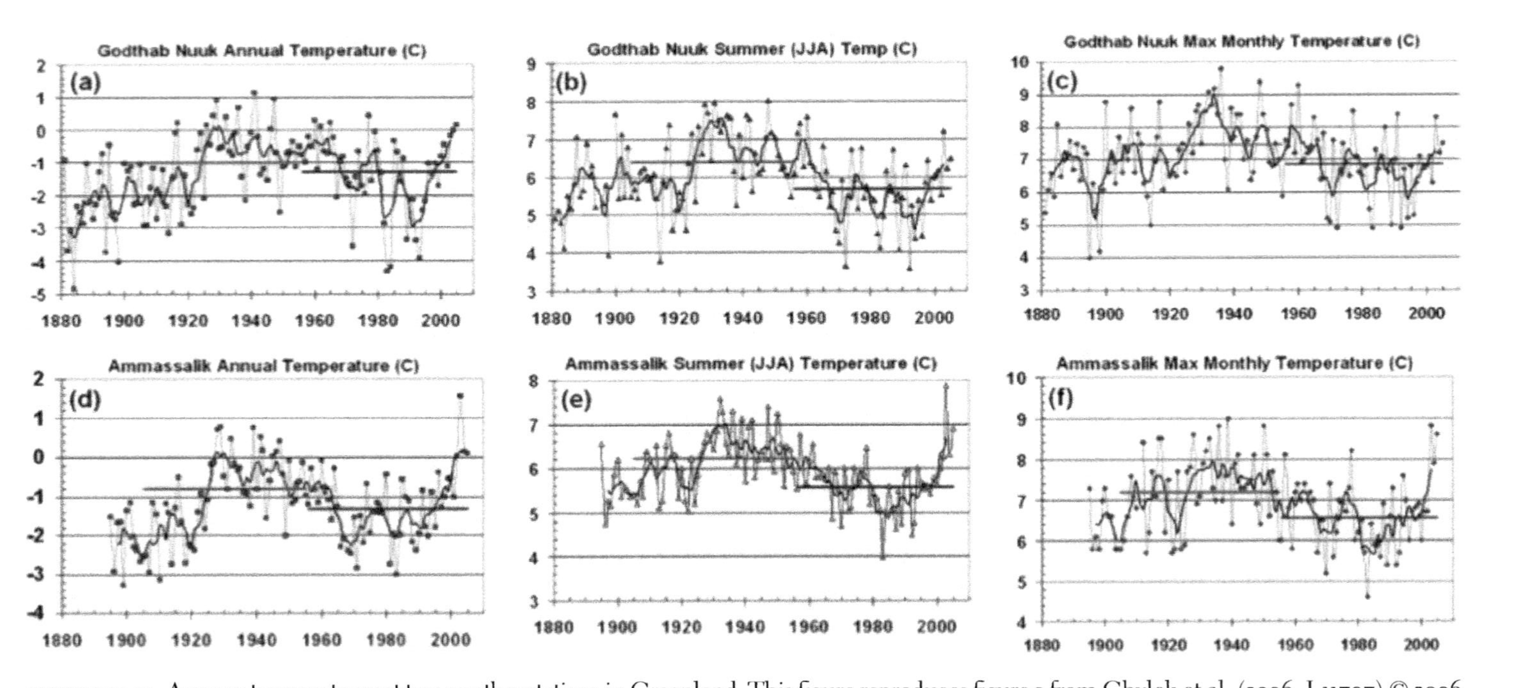

FIGURE 13.13 Average temperatures at two weather stations in Greenland. This figure reproduces figure 2 from Chylek et al. (2006, L11707) © 2006 American Meteorological Society.

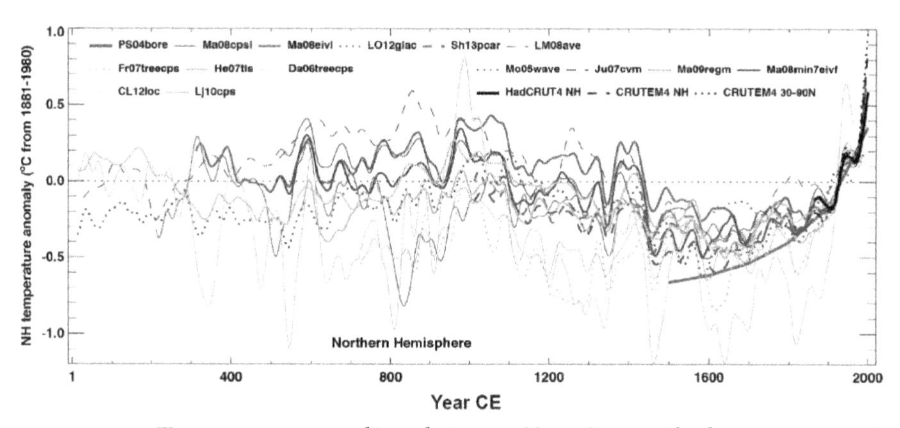

FIGURE 13.14 Temperature anomalies relative to 1881–1980 over the last 2,000 years. A reproduction of the figure provided by NOAA, National Centers for Environmental Information, Reconstructed-Northern-Hemisphere-annual-temperature-during-the-last-2000-years-v2.jpg, available at www.ncdc.noaa.gov/file/reconstructed-northern-hemisphere-annual-temperature-during-last-2000-years-v2jpg.

It shows that sometime in the early twentieth century, temperatures reached levels that were the highest in the last 1,000 years.

The IPCC's 2013 AR5 does not present this comparison of these two graphs. It does not tell the reader that what it trumpeted in 2001 as a remarkably important "fact" – that recent temperatures are the highest in the last 1,000 years – no longer seems to be a "fact" in that reconstructions now suggest that recent temperatures have returned to levels they started at 1,000 years ago.

If one compares the long-term, 2,000 year temperature graph in Figure 13.14 with any of the previous temperature time series figures – whether for the United States, the globe, land or sea surface or both, or even for the Artic or Greenland – one sees that at virtually any temporal scale – whether 2,000 years, 120 years, or even shorter periods of 10–50 years – average temperature is always changing. Such cycles are true of other aspects of climate, in particular annual rainfall. As I discuss very shortly, in some places, such as the western United States, drought and wet periods also cycle, at time scales ranging from a year or several years to decades and even centuries.

III LIKE SURFACE TEMPERATURE, SEA LEVEL MEASUREMENTS ARE HIGHLY UNCERTAIN AND VARIABLE AND REVEAL LONG-TERM CYCLES

As we have seen, prominent in GISS Director Hansen's advocacy for policies ending the use of fossil fuels for energy were highly dramatic projections of future sea level rise of up to 25 m by 2100. I discuss later the actual basis for projections of future sea

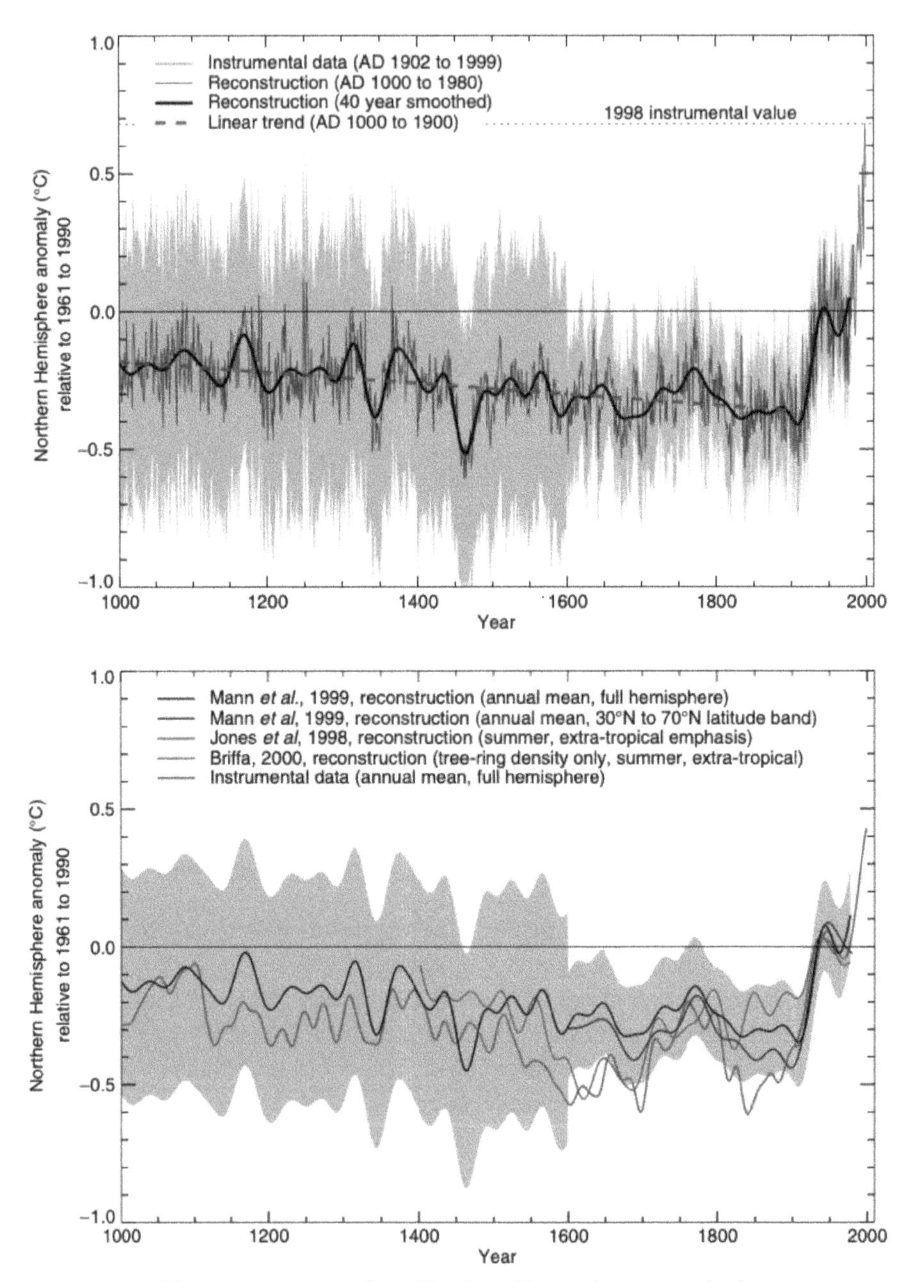

FIGURE 13.15 Temperature anomalies (Northern Hemisphere) over the last 1,000 years, as reported in the IPCC's 2001 Assessment Report but reported no more. *IPCC, Climate Change 2001: The Scientific Basis*, ed. J. T. Houghton et al. (Cambridge University Press, 2001), p. 134.

level rise. But the idea that sea level is already rising and causing harm has been prominent in climate policy debate. In *Massachusetts v. EPA*, states like Massachusetts only had a legal right to sue because Michael McCracken, the first head of the USGCRP, asserted in a sworn affidavit that their shores were soon to be engulfed by rising seas. This theme has been echoed in countless media stories dramatizing how climate change–induced sea level rise is already submerging US coastal communities and islands across the world. And as shall see, the harm from such alleged ongoing sea level rise is the basis for lawsuits by coastal cities seeking billions of dollar in damages from fossil fuel companies.

Back in 2013, in its AR5, the IPCC said it was "very likely" that over the period 1901–2010, sea level has risen at a rate 1.7 mm/year, accelerating to 3.2 mm/year between 1993 and 2010 (the era when satellite measurements of sea level became available), although "similarly high rates likely occurred between 1920 and 1950." In the fall of 2018, the IPCC put out a "Special Report" on 1.5°–2°C temperature increase. As I described earlier, this report did not purport to assess the post-2013 scientific literature, but was instead a very explicit policy advocacy document, marshaling evidence in favor of the 2015 Paris Climate Accord recommendation that nations adopt policies to keep the global temperature increase (relative to preindustrial levels) below 2°C. Like the 2013 AR, the 2018 Report reiterated that "sea level has been rising since the late 19th century from low rates of change that characterized the previous two millennia." However, it then says that "slowing in the reported rate over the last two decades may be attributable to instrumental drift in the observing satellite system ... and increased volcanic activity. Accounting for the former results in rates (1993 to mid-2014) between 2.6 and 2.9 mm/year."[34]

There is thus a not insignificant change between IPCC vintage 2013 and IPCC vintage 2018: whereas in 2013, the IPCC said with "very high confidence" that sea level had been rising at 3.2 mm/year over the 1993–2010 period of satellite measurements, its most recent view is that 1993 to 2014 sea level rise might be as low as 2.6 mm/year, about 20 percent lower. Perhaps even more importantly, the IPCC's most recent statement is that there is "instrumental drift in the observing satellite system and volcanic activity." It seems that now the IPCC isn't so sure at all about recent sea level trends.

To the layperson who has not been reading up on climate science, the IPCC's terse explanation of why it lowered estimated sea level rise is surely almost unintelligible. How do satellites measure sea level? What is satellite drift? How could "volcanic activity" impact sea level measurements? This section answers such questions.

When one takes a close, critical look at what the IPCC and the actual sea level experts have said, there seems reason to wonder whether anyone actually knows what is happening to sea level. In a pattern that is strikingly parallel to what one finds for surface temperature measurements, sea level measurements are themselves subject to many adjustments and corrections for all kinds of biases and errors. These biases and errors are known to be on the scale of tens of centimeters. Given this, it is unclear how the IPCC and USGCRP and other government – funded researchers can report that they are confident in distinguishing between sea level changes to a precision of half a millimeter – 0.05 cm. When a longer-term perspective is taken, one sees that there is no dispute that sea level was rising at rates much higher than today for thousands of years after the last glaciation, and abundant evidence that sea levels were higher during the medieval warm period of roughly 900–1200. The issue is entirely whether sea level rise is increasing from historically very low rates. Some experts, relied upon by the IPCC, believe that despite fuzzy measurements, this question can be answered quite definitively. Other experts, ignored by the IPCC, believe that it cannot currently be answered with any degree of precision.

A *Tide Gauge Sea Level Measurements*

There are two senses of sea level. Absolute sea level is the level of the sea relative to the Earth's center of mass. Relative sea level is sea level relative to the land surface at a particular point.[35] For more than 200 years, tide gauges have measured variations in sea level relative to a point of known elevation above sea level. Since 1992, absolute sea level measurements have also been made by satellite.[36]

Writing in 1991, Douglas observed that estimates for global sea level rise presented during the twentieth century ranged from 1 to 3 mm/year, with error bounds of 0.15 to 0.9 that almost were equal to the estimate, a "scatter of results" making "impossible a meaningful interpretation of the global balance of water in its various forms and locations" (Douglas 1991, 6981). Douglas's 1991 paper is the seminal paper estimating sea level change from tide gauge records. In so doing, he faced several challenges.

As recently as the late nineteenth century, there were relatively few tide gauges with sea level observation, and those were located mostly in Europe with a few along the US Atlantic and Pacific coasts.[37] The first problem confronting Douglas was thus which tide gauges to study. He chose tide gauges based on a number of criteria. Three of these were "length and completeness of record, [and] general agreement with other nearby stations over a common time interval." We have of course, seen such criteria before: they are exactly the same criteria used by HadCRUT and GISS to select weather stations for temperature measurements.

Using these selection criteria, Douglas excluded a number of tide gauges with very old records. For example, he excluded very long-term tide gauge records at Philadelphia and Boston because the estimated sea level trends at these two sites were "so far in value from neighboring sites" (Douglas 1991, 6985). After such exclusions, Douglas ended up studying only 21 tide gauge records across the entire globe. Based on these records, Douglas estimated that over the twentieth century,

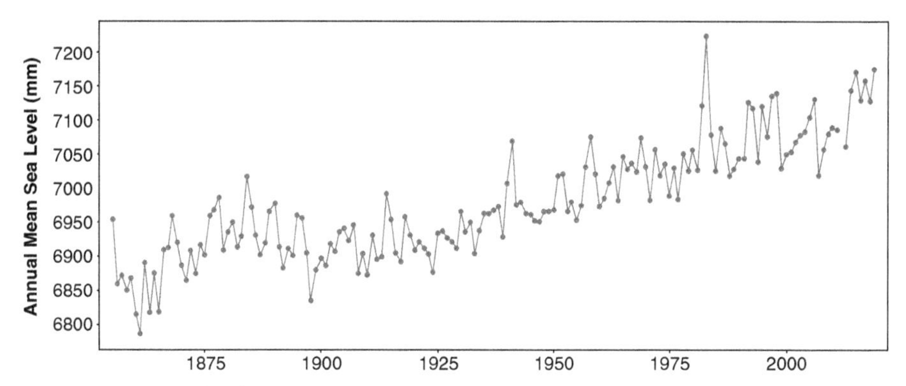

FIGURE 13.16 Sea level observations at San Francisco. Reproduces data presented by the Permanent Service for Mean Sea Level, San Francisco, available at www.psmsl.org/data/obtaining/stations/10.php.

global sea level had increased at a rate of around 1.7 or 1.8 mm/year.[38] Scientists who provide the sea level change estimates relied upon by the IPCC now routinely report as an established fact that since the beginning of the twentieth century, the global mean sea level has been rising at a mean rate of 1.7 ± 0.3 mm/year as recorded by in situ tide gauges (Albain et al. 2017).

The annual twentieth-century sea level increase of 1.7 mm is almost exactly the thickness of a US quarter (25 cent) coin. The annual 1.7 mm increase translates into 17 mm or 1.7 cm/decade and 170 mm or 17 cm/century. In inches, the estimated twentieth-century sea level rise is two-thirds of an inch per decade or 6 1/2 inches per century. Published roughly 30 years ago, Douglas's paper itself suggests that the 1.7 mm/year estimated twentieth-century sea level increase is a lot more complicated and uncertain than repeated assertions of 1.7 mm as a fact by the IPCC and others would imply. He identified three key problems that remain today.

B *Sea Level Cycles*

First, Douglas recognized that there are both short-term and longer-term cycles – periods of rise and fall – in sea level as measured at particular tide gauges. Such cycles mean that to detect a long-term trend apart from the cycles, especially the long-term cycles, some kind of smoothing has to be applied to the data. That the same problem arises for temperature measurements that I discussed earlier is no accident. Just as with temperature, to detect long-term sea level changes driven by things such as increasing atmospheric CO_2 concentration, one has to separate out cyclical changes.

Figure 13.16 shows such cyclical changes at the oldest US tide gauge, from San Francisco.[39] Tide gauge data at San Francisco begin in 1855, and Figure 13.16 depicts annual average tide gauge measured sea levels since that year. The figure depicts a long-term, 140 year increase of about 200 mm, or about 1.5 mm/year. But there have been long 25–30 year periods of generally falling sea level – for example, from about 1880 until 1910 – and periods of rising sea level – for example, from 1925 to 1955. The estimated 30 year trend at San Francisco in fact ranges from −2 to +5 mm/year, depending on which 30 years in the 140 year time series one considers.[40]

Because sea levels as measured by tide gauges are subject to known cycles of about 30 years in duration, any sea level measurement taken over a period of less than or equal to 30 years may simply be capturing a relatively short-term trend that will soon change. For example, if one were measuring sea level change in San Francisco over the period 1920–1950, one would have observed a rapid rise in sea level, but one that was temporary, and indeed has still not yet been seen recorded again at that location. For a tide gauge – based sea level trend to be reliable, the period over which it is measured must be longer than 30 years.

C *Tide Gauge Elevation Change and Regional Variation in Sea Level*

Relative sea level and sea level change varies enormously from place to place across the globe. This can be seen in Figure 13.17, which reproduces figures produced by the Permanent Service for Mean Sea Level, an international network of tide gauge stations. I have produced sea level graphs for three places: Kasko (or Kaskinen) Finland (Figure 13.17(a)), Galveston, Texas (Figure 13.17(b)), and Key West, Florida (Figure 13.17(c)). As one can see, sea level trends at these stations range from the negative trend of −6.37 mmm/year in Kasko to a positive +6.42 mm/year in Galveston.[41]

Tide gauges measure sea level relative to the height of the land where the tide gauge is located, and one of the most important reasons that sea level changes vary so much across stations – from +6.4 mm at Galveston to −6.4 mm at Kasko in Figure 13.17 – is long-term change in the elevation of the land where tide gauges are mounted.

Elevation at tide gauge locations changes for a number of reasons. One reason is that the earth is still rebounding from the last ice age. This rebounding has two effects on landmasses. For those high-latitude landmasses that were formerly completed covered by glaciers (sometimes called formerly glaciated high-latitude landmasses, or FGHLs), the land is still rising after having been freed from the burden glacial era ice. Other mid-latitude landmasses that were just outside the area of glaciation had been pushed up by the glaciers and as the glaciers receded, landmasses in these bulge areas have been falling. (Imagine pushing down on an inflatable raft at one end; the air pushes up the raft in front of the push and will come back down after one stops pushing.) If the land is rising where a tide gauge is housed, then solely due to this effect, the gauge will show that sea level is falling. If conversely, the land is subsiding, then solely due to this effect, the tide gauge will show that sea level is rising.

As Figure 13.17 suggests, at regional levels, sea level changes vary enormously across places, ranging from −1 to more than 10 mm/year over since 1993 (Esselborn et al. 2018). According to Houston and Dean (2012, 739–744), in the formerly glaciated high-latitude

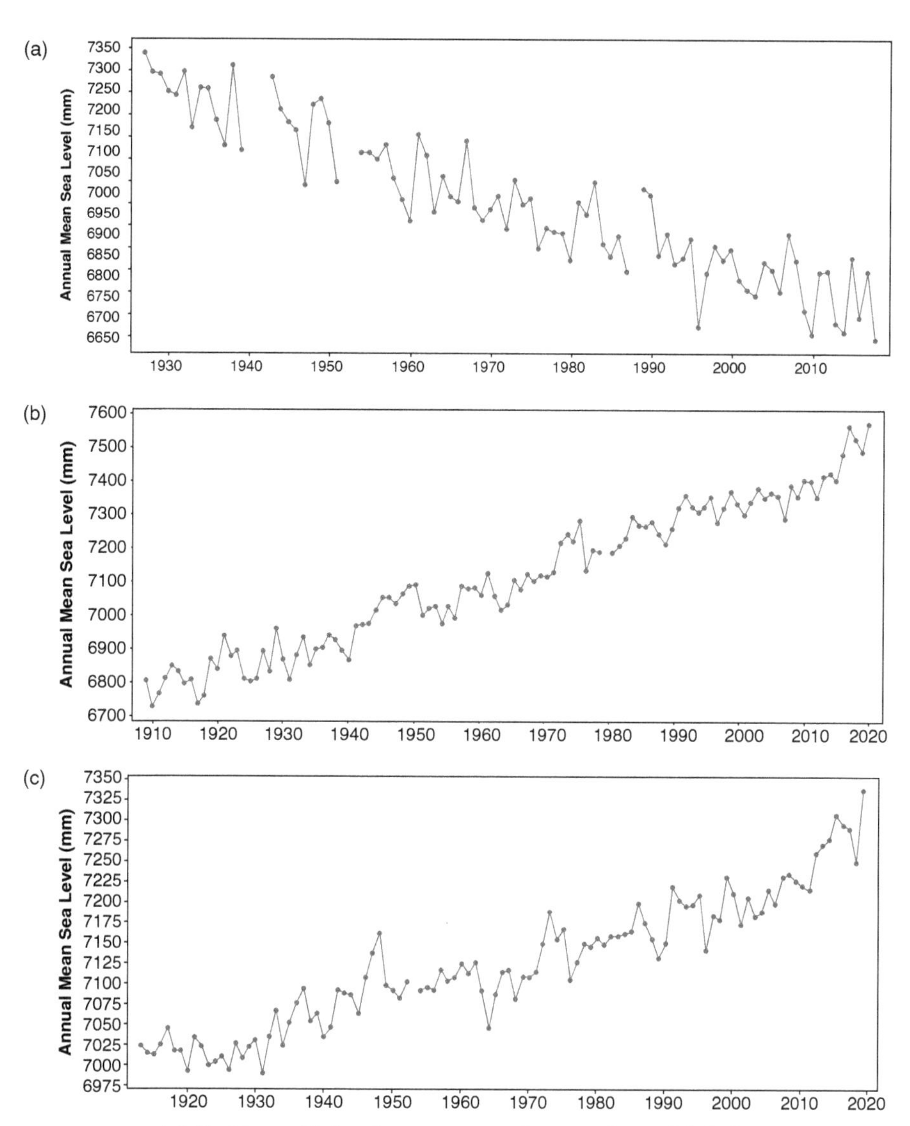

FIGURE 13.17 (a) Kaskinen, Finland, 1924–2019, −6.37 mm/year. (b) Galveston, Pier 21, Texas, USA, 1900–2016 (6.42 ± 1.8 mm/year). (c) Key West, Florida, USA, 1913–2018 (2.41 ± 0.13 mm/year).

(FGHL) areas, land is rising as fast as 10 mm/year; in the peripheral bulge areas (such as most of the US eastern seaboard), land is subsiding at a rate as high as 2–5 mm/year. Such changes are obviously huge relative to the 1.7 mm/year average change in sea level estimated by Douglas, and to have any validity at all, sea level estimates have to be corrected for such vertical land movements at tide gauge locations.

The corrections are based on models, not observations. Back in 1991, Douglas used a then-new theoretical model of postglacial rebound (called the ICE-3G model developed by Tushingham and Peltier 1991, 4497–4523) to correct for vertical land movement at tide gauge locations due to postglacial rebound (more precisely called glacial isostatic adjustment, or GIA). Such GIA models are still used to adjust tide gauge measurements of sea level change.

Now that GPS observational data on elevation changes is available, such data can be compared to the elevation changes predicted by GIA models. Such comparison tends to show that the model-based adjustments to tide gauge elevations may not be very accurate outside the FGHL areas. Studies that use actual GPS observations of vertical land movement have found that the GIA model corrections can be biased by as much as ±1 or 2 mm/year (King et al. 2012, L14604) and have little or no correlation with the corrections that GPS measurements would dictate (Houston and Dean 2012, 743). As the vast majority of tide gauges are outside FGHL areas, these errors in adjustment for GIA are likely to affect the vast majority of tide gauges.

Another important reason why tide gauge elevations change is that many tide gauges are located in areas that are still seismically active. As dramatized by several major earthquakes, San Francisco is a seismically active location. At short inter-annual scales, the tide gauge measurements for San Francisco depicted earlier reflect land elevation change due to seismic movements of the land.

A final reason for tide gauge elevation change is that coastal development and land use itself may cause land to subside. It is generally agreed that twentieth-century development along the US east and gulf coasts has caused land subsidence. Other things equal, when the land on which a tide gauge is located subsides, the gauge records a sea level increase.

Another famous region of substantial land subsidence is along the US Pacific Coast, where intensive oil drilling in southern California caused the California south coastal areas to subside. No one is still alive today who can remember the era, but as shown in Figure 13.18, which depicts oil drilling in Huntington Beach, California, circa mid-1920s, the scope and impact of 1920s oil drilling in southern California was enormous. It is not hard to see how the extraction of millions of barrels of oil from beach areas can cause such land areas to subside.

D *The Satellite Era*

With all of these issues with tide gauge measurements of sea level, one may breathe a sigh of relief to know that since 1992, sea level has been measured by altimeters in satellites. Here is the explanation of how such measurements work produced by Ablain et al. (2017), a group of IPCC-endorsed researchers:

> The concept of (nadir) satellite altimetry measurement is rather straightforward. The onboard radar altimeter transmits a short pulse of microwave radiation with

FIGURE 13.18 Huntington Beach, California, circa 1920s.

> known power toward the nadir. Part of the incident radiation reflects back to the altimeter. Measurement of the round-trip travel time provides the height of the satellite above the instantaneous sea surface (called altimeter range R). The quantity of interest in oceanography is the height of the instantaneous sea surface above a fixed reference surface (typically a conventional reference ellipsoid). This quantity (called SSH) is simply the difference between the height H of the satellite above the reference ellipsoid and the altimeter range R: SSH = H-R. H is computed through precise orbit determination, a long-tested approach in space geodesy, which combines accurate modelling of the dynamics of the satellite motion and tracking measurements. (Ablain et al. 2017, 7–31)

Based on this much of what Ablain et al. (2017) have to say, satellite measurements seem to be very precise and a big improvement over tide gauge measurements.

But this is not all they have to say. Ablain et al. (2017) continue:

> The range from the satellite to the sea, R, must be corrected for various components of the atmospheric refraction as well as for biases between the mean electromagnetic scattering surface and mean sea surface at the air–sea interface in the footprint of the radar. Other corrections due to a number of

geophysical effects must also be applied [and corrections for] drifts and bias from onboard instruments.

This is a bit cryptic, leaving unanswered what might be the causes of atmospheric refraction of the signal, electromagnetic scattering at the sea surface, and kind of "drift" and "bias" affect onboard instruments. Comprehensive answers are provided in an authoritative text, Stammer and Cazanave (2017),[42] whose editors are two of leading IPCC-endorsed scientists who work with satellite measurements of sea level. Below are just some of the many corrections that Stammer and Cazanave (2017) say need to be made to offset bias and error in satellite measurements of sea level:

- Atmospheric corrections have to be made because the speed of the radar signal is affected by the ionosphere and both the dry and wet troposphere. The first refers to electrons in the ionosphere, and this correction depends on the solar cycle (the number or sunspots) with an average value of 45 mm and a huge standard deviation of 35 mm. The dry tropospheric correction has an average value of 2,300 mm with a standard deviation of 30 mm. Water vapor in the atmosphere necessitates the wet tropospheric correction.
- The sea state or electromagnetic bias is related to wave height and has an average value of 100 mm. Sea state bias may arise from the nonlinearity of waves from peak to trough, and there is no theoretical method for estimating this, so an empirical method is employed.
- A barometric pressure correction must be made because high pressure depresses sea surface and low pressure elevates it, with a tiny 1 mb change in barometric pressure (standard air pressure in mb at sea level is 1,013) equal to a 1 cm – that is, 10 mm – change in sea surface height. The corrections made are said to be good in middle and high latitudes and bad in the tropics.
- Tides must be corrected for, and "in general" global tidal models are used to make predictions which are then subtracted from the observed signal.
- Satellite orbits are not perfect, but vary by about 3–5 cm, that is, 30–50 mm.

If one adds up the size of just these listed corrections (there are several more discussed by Stammer and Cazanave (2018)), they amount to at least 100 mm, or 10 cm. As Curry (2018) explains, when one reads the Products Handbook for the current satellite altimeter (called JASON), it turns out that errors in many of the steps in processing raw satellite data are measured in centimeters. The calibrations, or corrections, end being "far larger than the resulting changes in global mean sea level." Using satellite altimeters to measure changes in sea level on the order of a few millimeters seems a bit like using a telescope that can misjudge the diameter of moon craters by tens of meters to judge the size of boulders in the crater.

Perhaps even more noteworthy is the fact that old-fashioned tide gauge measurements are used to calibrate (that is, correct) and validate satellite altimeter sea level measures. Such calibrations have revealed that even the corrections themselves can introduce errors. Perhaps the most important correction is an instrument correction for what is called instrument "drift." Referred to in my quote from Ablain et al. (2017) but not included in the list drawn from Stammer and Cazanave (2018) that I presented, drift refers to drift in the "altimeter range owing to thermal or other changes in the internal hardware components of the system" (Beckley et al. 2017, 8372). Attempts to quantify the impact of satellite drift and drift corrections are ongoing. Several of these use tide gauge measurements to try to identify the size of the satellite altimeter error introduced by drift.[43] Indeed, Beckley et al. (2017, 8371) stress that "comparison of altimeter measurements against independent measurements of local sea level at tide gauges plays a critical role in establishing the validity of the altimetric time series." Inasmuch as highly imperfect tide gauge measures are used to correct and validate satellite altimeter sea level measurements, it seems quite wrong to think that satellite altimeter sea level measurements provide a degree of precision beyond tide gauges. Just as importantly, the 30–60 year cycles in sea level clearly revealed by tide gauge measurements must be removed to identify long-term trends in satellite measurements. That is, having satellite measurements does not somehow magically eliminate the problem of separating long-term trends from shorter-term cycles.

Writing back in 2007, Wunsch et al. (2007, 5905), a group of Harvard and MIT researchers specializing in quantitative ocean modeling, were not optimistic about getting precise measurements of long-term changes in sea level:

> At best, the determination and attribution of global-mean sea level change lies at the very edge of knowledge and technology. The most urgent job would appear to be the accurate determination of the smallest temperature and salinity changes that can be determined with statistical significance, given the realities of both the observation base and modeling approximations. Both systematic and random errors are of concern, the former particularly, because of the changes in technology and sampling methods over the many decades. … It remains possible that the database is insufficient to compute mean sea level trends with the accuracy necessary to discuss the impact of global warming – as disappointing as this conclusion may be. The priority has to be to make such calculations possible in the future.

Writing about 10 years later, Wunsch (2016, 27) was not noticeably more optimistic about the accuracy of sea level change measurements (or measurements of changes in other global ocean features, such as heat and salinity), saying that "apart from temperatures in the upper quarter of the ocean over the last ten years, available determinations of changes in heat content (mean temperature), freshwater content (salinity), or mean sea level are dependent on various untested statistical models. Many results are plausible and possibly even correct, but they are fragile because data are lacking to test the assumptions." Closing the sea level budget means identifying the portion of sea level change attributable to the various potential causes of such change, such as ocean thermal expansion, melting glaciers, Greenland and Antarctic ice sheets and water storage on land. Wunsch (2016) seems to have been most pessimistic about identifying

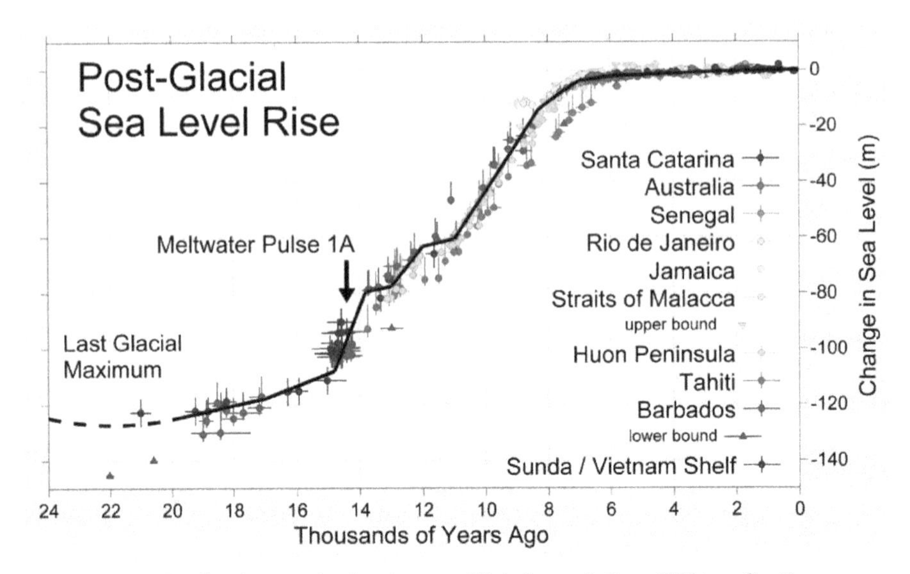

FIGURE 13.19 Sea level since the last ice age. This figure is from Wikimedia Commons, File: Post-Glacial Sea Leve.png, available at https://upload.wikimedia.org/wikipedia/commons/1/1d/Post-Glacial_Sea_Level.png, and reports measurements derived from a number of published papers, where the measurements, like tide gauge measurements, adjust for post-glacial rebound.

all the causes of sea level change, saying that "closing the budget of altimetric mean sea level incurs the same errors in the hydrography [as affect measures of salinity and heat] in addition to those implicit in the altimetric observations themselves." To be sure, sea level researchers to whom the IPCC has entrusted its assessments of sea level change, most prominently, perhaps, Cazanave, are much more sanguine about getting accurate sea level trend measures. But if the IPCC was assessing what top workers in the field think, rather than marshaling evidence to support decarbonization policies, they would surely have discussed at much greater length the kinds of problems with sea level trend measurements pointed to by Wunsch.

E *Present-Day Sea Level Change in Long-Term Historical Perspective*

Just as with temperatures, there have been attempts to reconstruct sea levels over longer periods of times past. As explained by Curry (2018), using proxy records – such as analysis of oxygen isotopes in fossilized ocean organisms found in once-submerged shorelines and fossil reefs – sea levels since the last glacial period ended about 20,000 years ago have been reconstructed. As shown by Figure 13.19 around the time that the Holocene warmth began to kick in (14,000 years ago), such reconstructions shows that sea level rose dramatically as the vast glaciers melted. This steep increase, of around 120 m, began to plateau around 7,000 years ago.

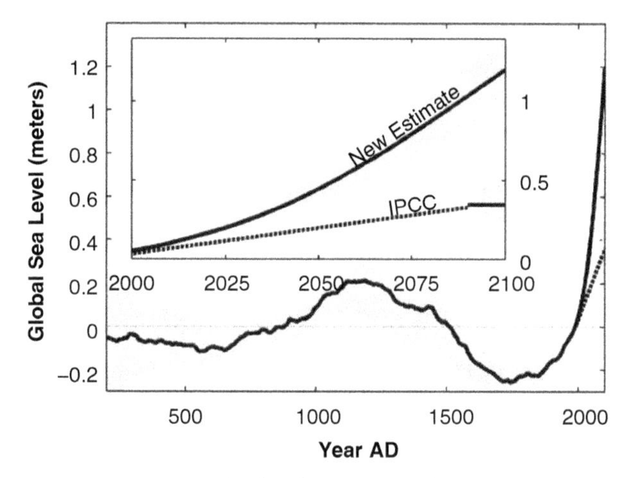

FIGURE 13.20 Sea level over the past 2,000 years.

Proxy reconstructions of sea level (measured in meters) over just the most recent 2,000+ years are displayed in Figure 13.20 (a reproduction of the presentation version of figure 7 of Grinsted et al. 2009). Reconstructions in Figure 13.20 end at 2,000; the lines after that show two projections (including the IPCC's) or the future (with the projections isolated in the separate box). The figure carries two important lessons. First, one can see very long cycles in sea level, with changes of tens of centimeters over periods of many centuries. In particular, on the reconstruction of Grinsted et al. (2009) depicted in Figure 13.20, sea level rose about 20 cm, or 200 mm, during the medieval warm period that lasted approximately from AD 800 to 1200. From 1200 to 1700, a period including the little ice age, sea level then fell by almost 40 cm, reaching a low around 1800 from which it has since been recovering.

The second important thing to see is that in this reconstruction, even allowing for uncertainty (the 95 percent confidence intervals are shaded in purple), sea levels in present times, circa the year 2000, are still almost 20 cm, or 200 mm, below the maximum levels they reached during the medieval warm period. These numbers provide some context within which to view the possible recent acceleration of sea level rise from 1.7 mm/year to perhaps around 3 mm/year.

III THINGS YOU'D NEVER LEARN FROM READING THE NEWSPAPER: EVIDENCE (SOMETIMES FROM THE IPCC ITSELF) THAT EXTREME CLIMATE EVENTS ARE NOT GETTING MORE EXTREME OR FREQUENT

At this point in this chapter, a skeptical reader might well say that even if temperature increases in the oceans and troposphere has been much less than at the surface – indicating a bias in surface temperature trends – and even if temperatures are at levels that have been seen previously, as during the Medieval Warm Period, and even if sea level increase is highly uncertain and not especially great by long-term historical standards, there still has been an increase in the severity and frequency of really bad climate events – hurricanes, heat waves and droughts, and extreme, flooding rainfall. It is these extreme events, it may be said, that cause most of the harm from climate change, and "we" "know" that these have been getting more frequent and more severe.

It turns out that for the most part, even the IPCC disagrees with this final statement, and when one adds to the IPCC's discussion and looks just a bit into the literature, it is hard to find much that does agree with the statement that extreme weather is becoming more frequent and more severe. Precisely the opposite is true in the popular media: with rare exceptions, with help from individual activist scientists, mainstream media broadcast a message completely at odds with what one finds in the literature and often also with what the IPCC itself say, claiming a connection to climate change for virtually every extreme weather episode.

A *Hurricanes*

In its 2013 AR4, the IPCC reported that even its 2007 AR said it that while it was "likely" that there had been increase in intense tropical cyclone activity in some regions of the world since 1970, "there was no clear trend in the annual numbers of tropical cyclones." As of its 2013 AR5, the IPCC concluded that "current data sets indicate no significant trends in global tropical cyclone frequency over the past century," and while increases in tropical cyclone frequency and "the frequency of very intense tropical cyclones have been identified in the North Atlantic," "argument reigns over the cause of the increase and on longer time scales the fidelity of these trends is debated." The IPCC's bottom line on what has been happening with hurricanes was that "no robust trends in annual numbers of tropical storms, hurricanes and major hurricane counts have been identified over the past 100 years in the North Atlantic basin."[44] On the other hand, the IPCC says it is "virtually certain" that there has been an "increase in the frequency and intensity of the strongest tropical cyclones" in the North Atlantic since the 1970s.

So, according to the IPCC, there is no general increase in hurricanes but there is a "virtually certain" increase in the most intense North Atlantic hurricanes. While the IPCC cited work by NOAA hurricane expert Christopher Landsea in its 2013 AR, it did go into any detail about Landsea's findings. If it had, it could have explained, as do Landsea et al. (2010) that a major problem in estimating long-term trends in hurricanes is that until the late twentieth century, hurricanes were not precisely captured by satellites. Satellites detect even relatively weak and short-lived hurricanes, and they detect them regardless of whether they ever make landfall anywhere. As explained by Landsea, since the advent of satellite measurements in the 1960s they have gotten finer and finer grained, able to capture smaller and shorter-lived

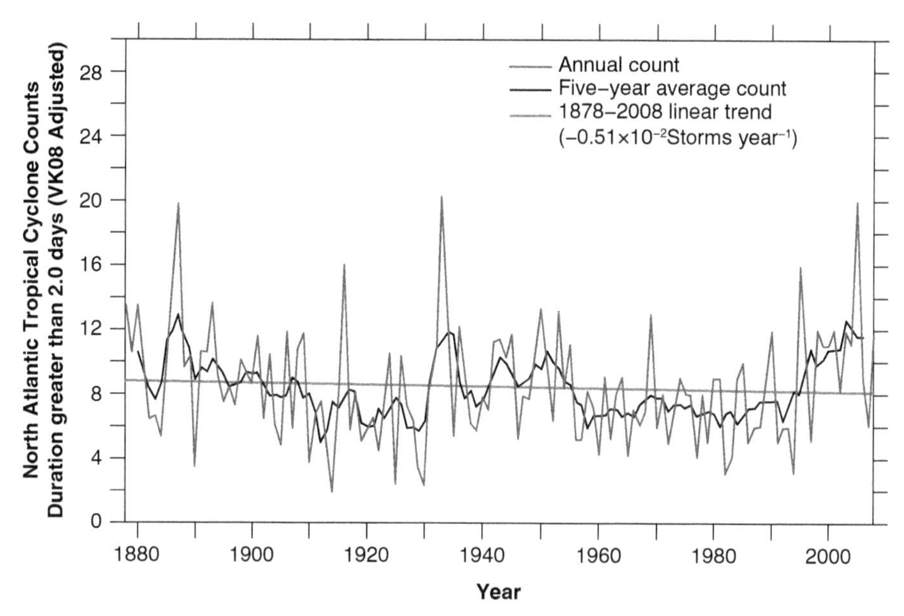

FIGURE 13.21 Annual number of medium- and long-duration North Atlantic hurricanes. Reproduces figure 5 from Landsea et al. (2010, 2514).

hurricanes. Prior to the satellite era, hurricane measurement was basically by happenstance.

Unlike instrumental surface temperature measurements, which have been recorded in the United States since around 1890, before satellites, hurricanes were observed only if they made landfall somewhere or were seen and recorded by ships. Until the opening of the Panama Canal in 1914, there was only one main shipping line from Europe to the US Mid-Atlantic, and one shipping line running south from Europe along the west coast of Africa. Moreover, according to Landsea, even after the Panama Canal opened, “there still remained about half of the tropical and subtropical Atlantic Ocean that had almost no ship traffic.” Landsea et al. (2010) estimated the number of medium to long-lived hurricanes that were likely missed during the presatellite era. When they added these to long-term hurricane records, and removed the very short-lived satellite era hurricane hurricanes (which they could not estimate for the presatellite period) they came up with Figure 13.21.

As one can see, in Figure 13.21 – which includes the intense 2005 hurricane season, the year of Hurricane Katrina – there is a long-term linear downward trend in the number of medium- and long-duration North Atlantic hurricanes. Clearly visible are cycles in hurricanes that seem to correspond roughly with the temperature cycles we have seen earlier. But there is no increase in the number of such storms.

As for the IPCC’s claim that it was “virtually certain” that there has been an increase in the most severe category 4 and 5 hurricanes in the North Atlantic,

Klotzbach and Landsea's (2015) update of the primary research upon which the IPCC's conclusion of "virtual certainty" was based is revealing. They too found that over the 1970–2004 period, there had indeed been a statistically significant positive trend in such storms in the Atlantic, northwest Pacific, south Indian, and South Pacific Oceans. However, when they updated the data, Klotzbach and Landsea (2015) found that trends over the period 1990– 2014 were not statistically significantly different than 0, either "for any basin individually, for either hemisphere or for the globe." They interpreted these results as providing "more evidence that the changes … that occurred in number and percentages of category 4–5 hurricanes globally during the 1970s and 1980s were likely primarily due to improved observational capabilities."

The mainstream media, with help from individual activist climate scientists, tell precisely the opposite story. For example, in 2019, Hurricane Dorian, a strong category 5 hurricane, stalled over the Bahamas, causing devastating damage. According to the *New York Times*,[45] climate change contributed to the storm's strength and the fact that it lasted so long. The *Times* did find and quote a scientist who specializes in the study of hurricanes, Landsea coauthor Gabriel Vecchi, who was said to have "cautioned against saying that every intense storm was made more powerful because of global warming, since 'there have been intense storms in the past.'" However the same article was able to quote Jennifer Francis, described as "a scientist with the Woods Hole Research Center" as saying that Dorian was "yet another example of the kind of slow-moving tropical systems that we expect to see more often as a response to climate change," and Andrew Dessler, who served as a science advisor to then Vice President Al Gore, stated that while "picking out trends" in hurricanes was difficult, there was "very strong consensus" that rainfall associated with hurricanes was increasing.

This is nothing new. Virtually every time a major hurricane makes landfall in the United States, activist climate scientists, many working for taxpayer-funded government climate science bodies, rush to attribute the worst of the storm to human GHG emissions. Back in 2017, when hurricane Harvey hit Texas with extremely heavy rainfall, many such scientists were critical of the media for not more clearly blaming anthropogenic climate change for Harvey's heavy rainfall. According to one media story,[46] Brock Long, the head of FEMA, said, "You could not dream this forecast up. Climate change is taking us to uncharted territory, fueling storms that were previously unimaginable. Warm water, humid air and rising seas conspired to make Harvey an uncommonly destructive storm." Unequivocally, activist scientist Michael Mann – whose published work is not primarily on hurricanes – said that climate change "worsened the impact of Hurricane Harvey." Finally, Kevin Trenberth of the taxpayer-funded National Center for Atmospheric Research – who has published work using climate models to try to predict ocean cycles – told the *Atlantic* magazine that "the human contribution can be up to 30 percent or so of the total rainfall coming out of the storm."

If one goes even further back, the same pattern of public advocacy is found. Back in 2006, GISS's Hansen went on the TV news show *60 minutes* to complain that NASA higher ups were stifling his advocacy efforts, and in particular were preventing GISS scientists from informing the public that climate change was responsible for hurricanes. Back then, MIT climate scientist Kerry Emmanuel had recently published a scientific paper predicting that the increase in potential energy caused by rising sea surface temperatures was causing a big increase in severe hurricanes. Emmanuel, like Hansen, went directly to the media to publicly criticize NOAA for failing to proclaim the truth according to his theory.[47] According to Emanuel as quoted then, his theory – that "Worsening storms are no coincidence. ... They are feeding off ever-warming ocean waters" was the truth – and in having the temerity to talk about "natural cycles" when there was "no evidence that is cyclic," NOAA "was telling the wrong story." Just by looking back at Figure 13.21, one can see that there are cycles in hurricane activity. As for Emmanuel's theory of a how the energy increase from rising sea surface temperatures would increase the frequency of intense hurricanes, as early Smith et al. (2008), that theory had been shown to suffer from a "fundamental problem" (in assuming gradient wind balance in the boundary layer, which Smith et al. (2008) say exists only because of gradient wind imbalance).

B *Heat Waves and Droughts*

(a) Heat Waves

Back in 2013, the IPCC said with "medium confidence" that it was "likely" "that heat wave frequency had increased" since 1951 "over large parts of Europe, Asia and Australia." With the "highest confidence," the IPCC opined that in Europe and North America, there "have likely been increases in either the frequency or intensity of heavy precipitation."[48] Heat waves are not measured in the ocean or the troposphere, but by surface temperatures. Given all of the problems with surface temperature measurements revealed by my earlier discussion, one would be cautious about any statements about heat waves captured in such surface temperature measurements. In this light, it is disturbing to find that the IPCC's 2018 Special Report on 1.5–2°C warming saying that "the quality of temperature measurements obtained through ground observational networks tends to be high compared to that of measurements for other climate variables."[49] It is not reassuring to be told that the likely biased surface temperature measurements are the best climate change measures.

Heat waves are defined as sustained, multiday periods of unusually high maximum temperatures. When one actually looks at data for the United States, it is very difficult to see that heat waves have become more frequent. If we look at the record of US heat waves as compiled by the US EPA, we have the following.

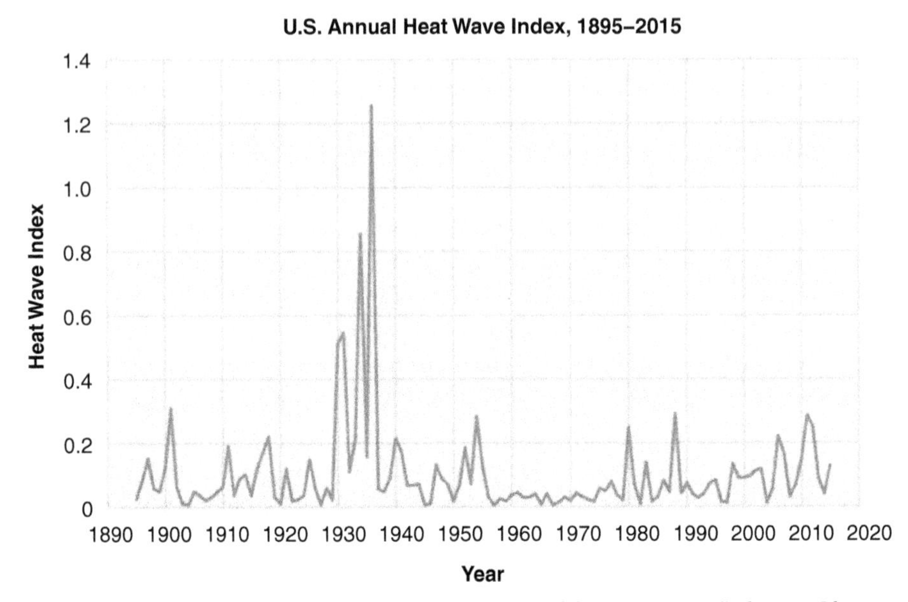

FIGURE 13.22 US annual heat wave index. Reproduced from US EPA, "Climate Change Indicators: High and Low Temperatures," available at www.epa.gov/climate-indicators/climate-change-indicators-high-and-low-temperatures.

As can be seen from Figure 13.22, at least in the United States the annual heat wave index reached levels during the early to mid-1930s that have never been approached since.

This is just for the United States. It is somewhat difficult to find similarly long-term and precisely defined heat wave data for other countries. For the United Kingdom, since at least 1911, newspapers have carried stories about heat waves.[50] But actual data on the number and length of UK heat waves has only been generated in the last 10 years or so, but the data from Sanderson et al. (2017, figure 2)[51] show that over the period 1961–2016, although there has been an increase in the length of the longest heat waves in many parts of that country, in most parts of the country the number of heat waves per decade has fallen.

And perhaps even more strikingly, Sanderson et al. (2017, figure 3) generated a record of heat waves for St. James Park in London. This is reproduced below as Figure 13.23. With heat waves identified as two or more consecutive days above the 93rd (red circles) or 95th (green triangles) percentile of annual average temperatures over the 1971–2000 base period, if we look just at the data, there are clearly cycles in the number of heat waves, with a large number of relatively long (more than 5 days) heat waves in the 1930s, with the number and duration falling by 1960 and then remaining roughly constant until rising in the 1980s. Perhaps most interestingly, the number of long heat waves – those above the horizontal dotted line, has been falling since 1975.

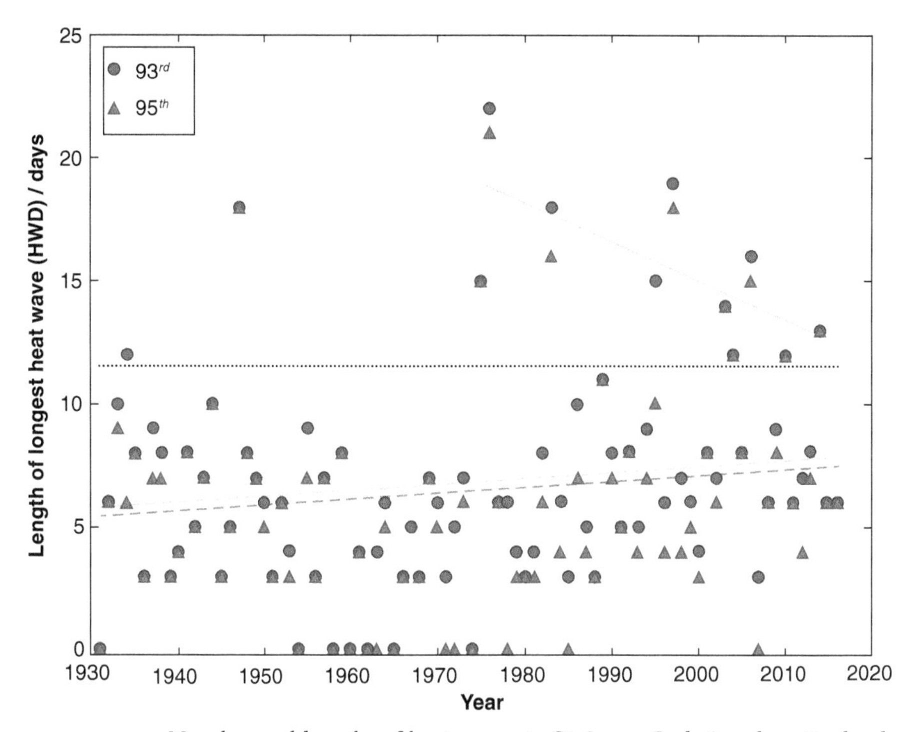

FIGURE 13.23 Number and lengths of heat waves in St. James Park, London, England. This is figure 3 from Sanderson et al. (2017).

(b) Drought

A very broad search for the word "drought" within 20 words of "climate change" on the Lexis/Nexis database of US newspapers turned up an astounding 13,830 newspaper articles (or blogs picked up by news services) between the years 1980 and 2019. As with other extreme weather event stories, the vast majority of such stories have appeared in recent years: between 1980 and the end of 2010, there were only 2771 such articles, meaning that over this four decade period, 11,059 articles, or 80 percent, have been published in the last decade of this almost four decade – long period. This suggests that perhaps the IPCC has become much certain that climate change is causing an increase in the severity or frequency of drought. In fact, precisely the opposite is true.

In its 2013 AR5, the IPCC said that due to "lack of direct observations, dependencies of inferred trends on index choice and geographical inconsistencies in the trends," there is "low confidence in a global scale observed trend in drought or dryness." In its 2018 Special Report, the IPCC summarized its earlier 2013 Report as having only low confidence in whether drought has been increasing or decreasing globally since 1950 but high confidence that drought has been increasing in some regions, such as the Mediterranean and West Africa, and decreasing in others, such as central North America and northwest Australia. The 2018 Report also noted that in AR5, the IPCC said there was only low confidence in scientific ability to attribute global changes in droughts to anthropogenic climate change and made no attempt to attribute regional changes in drought frequency to climate change.[52]

In recent decades, drought has been measured by what is called the Palmer Drought Severity Index (PDSI)), a measure developed in the 1960s to allocate disaster aid to farmers (Sheffield et al., 2012). It is simple to compute, and estimates soil moisture from a combination of surface temperature and a model that estimates soil moisture by balancing precipitation, evaporation, and runoff. The National Center for Atmospheric Research assures citizens that the "PDSI has been reasonably successful at quantifying long-term drought" and "can capture the basic effect of global warming on drought through changes in potential evapotranspiration." This is not what Sheffield et al. (2012) found. Using a model of actual evaporation based on physical principles, they found that the widely reported increase in global drought over the past 60 years based on the PDSI had overestimated drought trends. What they called their "more realistic calculations" showed that "there has been little increase in drought over the last 60 years."

When one looks at the long-term historical record of drought, it quickly becomes apparent that even if there were an actual increase in drought over the past 60 years, it would not be unusual. Figures reproduced from Cook et al. (2007) below show that over the last 1,200 years, in the United States, there have been cycles of extreme drought that last over periods ranging from half a decade to centuries. As shown by Figure 13.24, when the American west was first explored by Americans during the early nineteenth century, they encountered a region in the midst of a decades-long drought. The late nineteenth-century period of mass western settlement was, by contrast, a period of several episodes that were extremely and (as the settlers eventually found out) atypically wet.

As Figure 13.25 shows, going back as far as the thirteenth century, vast regions of the United States have endured periods of severe drought ranging from 5 to 20 years in length. As the reader may well expect by this point, like temperature, sea level change, hurricanes, and pretty much any other feature of climate, US drought has consistently cycled.

Such cycles are depicted by the final Figure 13.26. As one can see from this figure, for most of the twentieth century, when the western United States was settled and intensively developed, the region was unusually wet by long-term, multicentury standards. The twenty-first-century return to more arid

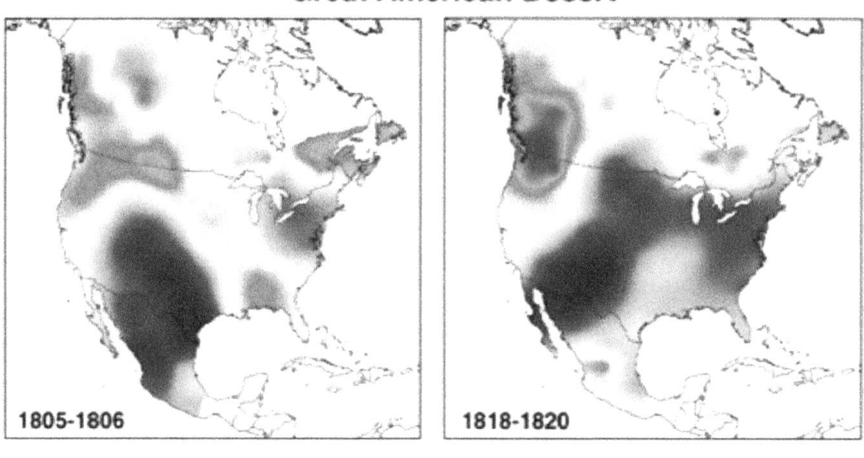

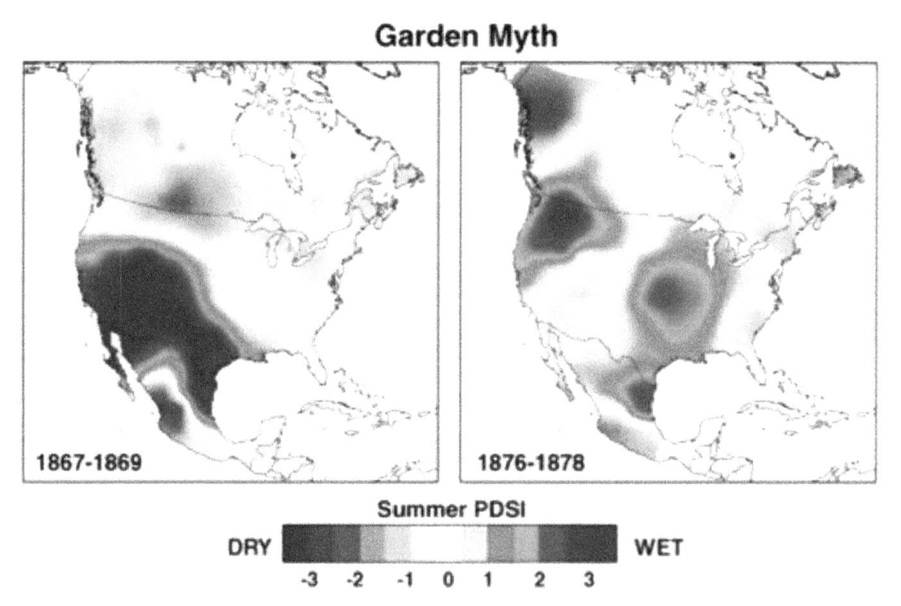

FIGURE 13.24 Very wet and very dry years in the nineteenth-century United States. A reproduction of figure 13 from Cook et al. (2007, 114).

conditions is not, in long-term perspective, unusual at all, but rather similar to many other cycles in western aridity that have occurred over the last 1,200 years.

In depicting periods of intense drought that have cycled throughout western US history, Cook et al. (2007) are far from alone. Some of these drought were severe and long-lasting. Meko et al. (2007), for example, identified the

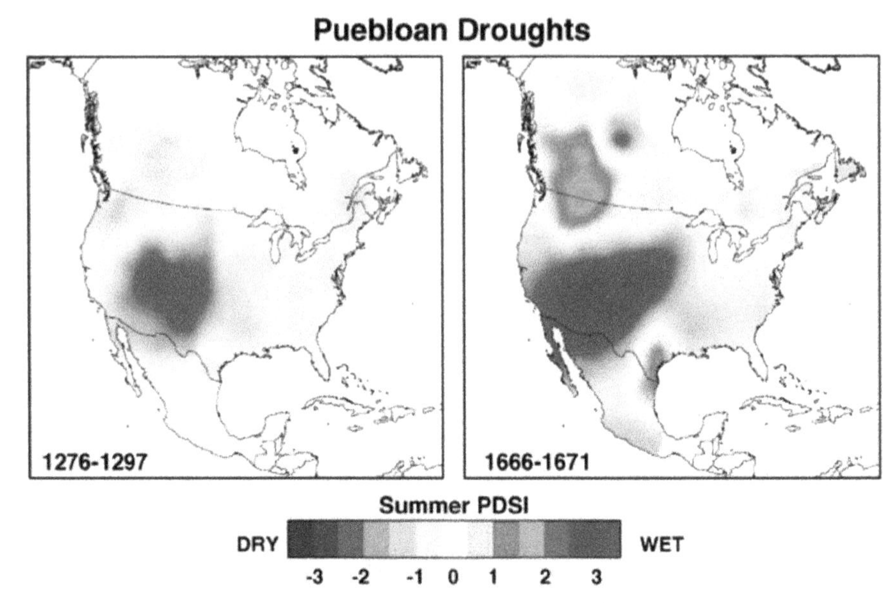

FIGURE 13.25 Multiyear and multidecadal western US droughts. A reproduction of figure 11 from Cook et al. (2007, 111).

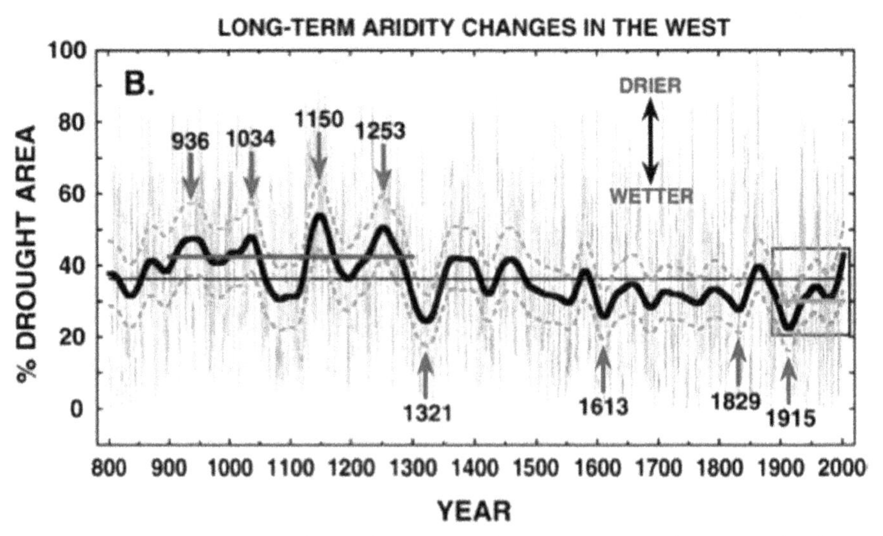

FIGURE 13.26 Centennial cycles in drought in the western United States. This figure reproduces figure 10 from Cook et al. (2007, 110).

Colorado Basin as suffering a 62 year drought in the mid-1110s that brought Colorado River flow levels roughly 20 percent below their twentieth-century levels. Century-long droughts for the Great Basin region of the western United

States have been identified from tree rings as ending 1,800, 1,200, 800, and 500 years before the present. While pollen records (see, e.g., Mensing et al. 2008), indicate that some of these may not have been severe, they provide confirming evidence for centuries-long droughts in this region during some periods (such as that extending between 180 and 800 years ago).

Notes

1. IPCC, WGII, AR5 p. 37.
2. US Global Change Research Program, Climate Change Impacts in the United States: The Third National Climate Assessment, 28 (2014), available at http://s3.amazonaws.com/nca2014/high/NCA3_Climate_Change_Impacts_in_the_United%20States_HighRes.pdf.
3. Climate Change 2007, the Physical Science Basis, 241–242.
4. See Ruedy et al. (2010, RG00034), Jones (1994, 1794), Jones et al. (1999, 173–199).
5. As Hansen et al. explain, "The United States National Weather Service uses a three-decade period to define 'normal' or average temperature."
6. HadCRUT Temperature, emphasis added.
7. The most recent version of HadCRUT, HadCRUTv4, uses a different reference period, 1961–1990, for the stated reason that this period has the largest number of reliable temperature measurements, and uses fewer stations, 4,800. See HadCRUT, Temperature, available at https://crudata.uea.ac.uk/cru/data/temperature/.
8. NASA, GISS, GISS Surface Temperature Analysis, available at https://data.giss.nasa.gov/gistemp/stdata/; HadCRUT, Temperature, available at https://crudata.uea.ac.uk/cru/data/temperature/.
9. Like GISS, however, there are very few HadCRUT weather stations from the interior of Africa and South America. See HadCRUT, Temperature.
10. Taken from Menne et al. (2009, 996).
11. Dennis J. Fixler, Ryan Greenaway-McGrevy, and Bruce T. Grimm, "The Revisions to GDP, GDI, and Their Major Components," US Bureau of Economic Analysis, August 2014, available at www.bea.gov/news/2016/gross-domestic-product-4th-quarter-and-annual-2015-third-estimate-corporate-profits-4th.
12. See Pielke et al. (2007, D24S08). See also Van de Wiel et al. (2002, 2567); Walters et al. (2007, L12709).
13. See generally X. Shi (2005, 1811). On asphalt pavement in particular, T. Asaeda, V. T. Ca, and A. Wake, "Heat Storage of Pavement and Its Effect on the Lower Atmosphere. Atmospheric Environment," CUTEST '92: conference on the urban thermal environmental studies in Tohwa, Fukuoka, 30 *Japan* 413–422 (1996), report that "at the maximum, asphalt pavement emitted an additional

150 W m-2 in infrared radiation and 200 W m-2 in sensible transport compared to a bare soil surface. Analyses based on a parallel layers model of the atmosphere indicated that most of the infrared radiation from the ground was absorbed within 200 m of the lower atmosphere, affecting air temperature near the ground."

14. WMO, ANNEX 1.B, Siting Classifications for Surface Observing Stations on Land, available at www.wmo.int/pages/prog/www/IMOP/SitingClassif/SitingClassif.html.
15. To be precise, Watts's volunteers surveyed 1,065 out of the 1,218 stations in the USHCNv.2 set of stations, categorizing 779 of these. For a more complete description of this project, see Watts et al. (2012).
16. For a discussion of Watt's station survey, see Fall et al. (2011, D14120).
17. www.surfacestations.org/images/Roseburg_OR_USHCN.jpg.
18. Watts et al. did not attempt to measure and account for the type of vegetation surrounding a station or for other factors. The direction of bias caused by such factors is unclear. For example, as noted by Watts et al., poorly sited stations surrounded by buildings may be in shade much of the day, introducing a cooling bias that might partially offset a warming bias caused by proximity to heat sinks and sources. Conversely, some of the most well sited rural sites may suffer from a warming bias due to dense ground vegetation.
19. A detailed and transparent discussion of homogenization techniques is provided by Acquaotta and Frattiani (2014).
20. As described in some detail by Acquaotta and Frattiani (2014, 28).
21. NASA GISS, GISS Surface Temperature Analysis (v.3), available at https://data.giss.nasa.gov/gistemp/graphs_v3/.
22. NASA GISS, GISS Surface Temperature Analysis (v.3), available at https://data.giss.nasa.gov/gistemp/graphs_v3/.
23. James Hansen, Reto Ruedy, Jay Glascoe, and Makiko Sato, "Whither US Climate?," NASA GISS (August 1999), available at www.giss.nasa.gov/research/briefs/hansen_07/.
24. With the actual data available at the GISS website.
25. NASA GISS, Surface Temperature Analysis (v. 4), available at https://data.giss.nasa.gov/gistemp/graphs_v4/.
26. HadCRUT4 Global Surface Temperature Graphs, available at https://crudata.uea.ac.uk/~timo/diag/tempdiag.htm.
27. As described by Roy Spencer, who is one of the researchers responsible for satellite measurements at the University of Alabama at Huntsville, satellites "measure the thermal microwave emission from atmospheric oxygen in the 50–60 GHz oxygen absorption complex, and the resulting calibrated brightness temperatures (Tb) are nearly equivalent to thermometric temperature, specifically a vertically weighted average of atmospheric temperature with the vertical weighting represented by weighting functions." See Roy Spencer, "Global

Warming," www.drroyspencer.com/2015/04/version-6-0-of-the-uah-temperature-dataset-released-new-lt-trend-0-11-cdecade/.

28. Data for Figure 13.8 are taken from University of Alabama at Huntsville, 29 (9) *Global Temperature Report*, December 2019, available at www.nsstc.uah.edu/climate/2019/December2019/GTR_201912Dec_1.pdf.
29. NOAA, NCEI, Extended Reconstructed Sea Surface Temperatures ERSSTv.4, available at www.ncdc.noaa.gov/data-access/marineocean-data/extended-reconstructed-sea-surface-temperature-ersst-v4.
30. According to Lyman and Johnson (2014), from the 1930s until about 1966, mechanical bathythermographs (MBTs) were used to measure the upper ocean temperature down to at most 300 m, at which time the expendable bathythermograph (XBT) began to replace the MBT for upper ocean thermal sampling. As they explain, "shallow XBTs (sampling as deep as 460 m) [were] dominant in the 1970s and 1980s, and deep XBTs (sampling as deep as 760m) dominant in the 1990s. Like MBTs, XBTs are not very accurate (±0.1 C for temperature)." Since 2000, ocean temperature has been measured by the Argo network of 3,800 floats that drift through the ocean at depths down to 2,000 m and then measure temperature and salinity at different depths as they periodically ascend to the surface to report. See Argo, available at www.argo.ucsd.edu/.
31. A reproduction of the "Global Ocean Heat Content" figure provided by the Japan Meteorological Agency at www.data.jma.go.jp/gmd/kaiyou/english/ohc/ohc_global_en.html.
32. Japan Meteorological Agency, Global Ocean Heat Content, www.data.jma.go.jp/gmd/kaiyou/english/ohc/ohc_global_en.html.
33. The US time series data since 1895 are available at NOAA, NCDC, Time Series, available at www.ncdc.noaa.gov/cag/national/time-series/110/tavg/12/12/1895–2019?base_prd=true&firstbaseyear=1901&lastbaseyear=2000.
34. IPCC 2018 Report, p. 206.
35. On relative versus absolute sea level, see Santmaria-Gomez et al. (2017, 24–32).
36. Judith Curry, *Sea Level and Climate Change* 12–13 (Special Report Climate Forecast Applications Network, November 25, 2018).
37. IPCC AR5, figure 3.A.4.
38. Note that while one could say that this was Douglas's estimated trend for the period 1880–1987, the longest period covered by any station's records, one could also say that was the estimate for 1933–1964, the 31 years for which all 21 stations included by Douglas actually had readings.
39. The San Francisco data are discussed in Smith (1980).
40. As pointed out by Douglas (1995, 1427).
41. Tide gauge sea level time series for these stations is provided at Permanent Service for Mean Sea Level, Obtaining Tide Gauge Data, www.psmsl.org/data/obtaining/; data for Kaskinen are provided by the Finnish Meteorological Institute and are available at www.psmsl.org/data/obtaining/stations/285.php;

data for Galveston Pier 21 are from NOAA and are available at www.psmsl.org/data/obtaining/stations/148.php; while data for Key West are from NOAA and are available at www.psmsl.org/data/obtaining/stations/188.php.

42. *Satellite Altimetry over Oceans and Land Surfaces (Earth Observation of Global Changes)*, ed. Detlef Stammer and Anny Cazenave (CRC Press, 2017);

    Detlef Stammer, Observing the Ocean using Satellite Altimeter Data, University.
43. In addition to Beckley et al. (2017), see Watson et al. (2015, 565–568).
44. IPCC, *Climate Change 2013: The Physical Science Basis, Contribution of Working Group I to the Fifth Assessment Report of the Intergovernmental Panel on Climate Change* 216, ed. Thomas F. Stocker et al. (Cambridge University Press, 2013).
45. John Schwartz, "How Has Climate Change Affected Hurricane Dorian?," *New York Times*, September 3, 2019.
46. "NBC, ABC Fail to Mention How Climate Change Worsened Impacts of Hurricane Harvey," *CleanTechnica*, September 15, 2017.
47. Peter Lord, "US Hiding Truth about Hurricanes, Scientists Say," *Providence Journal*, March 26, 2006, A-01.
48. IPCC AR5, p. 46.
49. IPCC 2018 Report, p. 189.
50. A rundown of newspapers stories since 1911 on British heat waves can be found at www.theguardian.com/theguardian/from-the-archive-blog/2014/jul/18/heat wave-weather-summer-temperatures.
51. Michael G. Sanderson et al., "Historical Trends and Variability in Heat Waves in the United Kingdom," 8 *Atmosphere* 191 (2017).
52. IPCC 2018 Report, p. 196.

14

Beyond CO_2

Causes of Regional Climate Change That the IPCC Has Ignored

In the Summary for Policymakers to its AR5, the IPCC makes a number of unqualified statements attributing observed climate change to human GHG emissions:

- The "best estimate" of the human-induced contribution to warming from 1951 to 2010 was similar to the entire observed warming, and human GHG emissions contributed a temperature increase in the range of 0.5°–1.3°C over this period, offset by between −0.6 and 0.1 from the effect of other anthropogenic emissions, most prominently aerosols, temperature over the period 1986 to 2008.
- Both natural forcings and internal variability of the climate system over this period likely net out to 0 (ranging only from −1.0° to 0.1°C); and with "high confidence" the IPCC says that "changes in total solar irradiance have not contributed to the increase in global mean surface temperatures over the period 1986 to 2008."

Thus the IPCC expresses "high confidence" that human GHG emissions are responsible for virtually all of the observed increase in global temperatures since 1951, and that neither natural internal climate variability nor external climate forcers such changes in solar radiation have contributed much of anything to the post-1950 increase in global temperatures.

In this chapter, I report on voluminous scientific work that directly contradicts the IPCC's assertion that the rise in atmospheric CO_2 has caused the entire rise in temperatures observed over both the entire industrial era and shorter periods of a few decades (which are called "multidecadal" periods in the climate literature). This literature points in particular at least three other major contributors to climate change in various regions of the world over these periods: conversion of undeveloped land to urban and suburban use, black carbon (soot) emissions, and long cycles in climate that are internal or inherent to the climate system because many of its components – in particular the oceans – are very slow moving and cycle at very long periods.

I TUNING, NOT EXPLANATION: HOW CLIMATE MODELS ATTRIBUTE POSTINDUSTRIAL TEMPERATURE INCREASE TO CO_2

As noted in my explanation of climate change survey results back in Chapter 10, there are very, very few propositions about human CO_2 emissions and climate change with which literally every scientist agrees. But there is one proposition that literally all scientists do seem to agree upon : that some increase in tropospheric and surface temperatures has been caused by the human-generated increase in atmospheric CO_2. To understand why this proposition is beyond dispute, we need to overview the basics of how atmospheric CO_2 warms the planet.

The sun emits radiation at a variety of wavelengths, with the complete spectrum running (in order of increasing wavelength) from ultraviolet (UV), to visible, and, finally, infrared (IR). About 96 percent of solar radiation is within the short wave UV and visible spectrum that runs from 300 to 3,000 nanometers (nm), with the maximum intensity of the solar spectrum found at the blue end of visible range (500 nm).

Not all of the primarily short wave solar radiation reaches the earth's surface. Some is absorbed and reflected by components of the earth's atmosphere. Moving from the surface up, the lower level of the atmosphere, the troposphere, is defined at that part of the atmosphere within which – due to decreasing air pressure and atmospheric mixing – temperature decreases with altitude. About 75 percent of all of the air in the atmosphere, and almost all of the water vapor is found in the troposphere. The tropopause is that level at which these forces have diminished to the point where temperature no longer changes as altitude increases. The tropopause is lowest at the poles, where it is about 7–10 km above the Earth's surface and highest (about 17–18 km) near the equator.

Above the troposphere is the stratosphere. It extends upward from the tropopause to about 50 km. It contains much of the ozone in the atmosphere. Ozone absorbs almost all of one type of harmful UV radiation (UV-B) (but almost none of another type (UV-A)). Due to the absorption of UV-B rays, within the stratosphere, temperature increases with height, and for the same reason, temperatures in the stratosphere are highest over the summer pole, and lowest over the winter pole. Above the stratosphere lies the mesosphere, another region where temperature decreases with altitude (reaching a low of about −90°C at the "mesopause") and above that, reaching to about 80 km above the earth's surface, is the thermosphere, a region in which temperatures increase with altitude because of the absorption UV and X-ray solar energy.

The layers from the stratosphere on up absorb and scatter a good portion of the sun's shortwave energy. More such shortwave energy is scattered by high clouds and aerosol particles in the troposphere, with the end result that about half of the total incoming solar radiation ends up reaching the earth's surface. There it is absorbed and reflected back, mostly as invisible infrared, longwave radiation.[1]

Within the troposphere, the earth's atmosphere is relatively opaque with respect to the longwave radiation upwelling from its surface. This means that at these levels, the atmosphere absorbs and reflects a good portion of the upwelling infrared radiation. The most powerful such agent is water vapor, but especially at higher levels of the troposphere, other gases, including carbon dioxide, also absorb and reflect longwave radiation.

Upwelling longwave radiation is greatest at the surface, diminishing with altitude (for an explanation, see Lindzen 2007). When the amount of CO_2 in the troposphere is increased, as humans have done, more of the upwelling longwave radiation is absorbed within the troposphere and radiated back to earth. In the short run – that is, nonequilibrium state – with less longwave energy reaching the stratosphere and mesosphere from below, these atmospheric levels should cool. With a cooler troposphere, less radiation would be escaping into space than is being taken in, a disequilibrium condition. In the new, higher-CO_2 world, equilibrium would be restored with higher surface and tropospheric temperatures.

As summarized by Goessling and Bathiany (2016), the basic prediction that increasing tropospheric CO_2 should have led to cooling in the middle atmosphere – the stratosphere and mesosphere – has been confirmed by satellite observations. Because other things have been happening the in the stratosphere, cooling at every region of the upper atmosphere cannot be unambiguously attributed to increased tropospheric CO_2. In particular, cooling in the lower stratosphere has been attributed to decreasing stratospheric ozone during the study period rather than increasing tropospheric CO_2 (Goessling and Bathiany 2016). But with a few exceptions, alternative explanations for surface temperature changes that I discuss below – such as the long-term, inherent variability of climate, and major transformations of global land use – do not apply to temperature change in the stratosphere and mesosphere. There, the impact of increased tropospheric CO_2 on the vertical transfer of energy can be better isolated from other possible contributors to climate change.

As we have seen, both surface and tropospheric temperatures have increased. Figure 14.1 shows US (14.1(a)) and global (14.1(b)) temperatures on the same panel as atmospheric CO_2 concentration.[2] Over the entire length of these time series, one sees a remarkable coincidence, with temperature seeming to follow atmospheric CO_2 concentration quite closely. But when one looks closely, one can also see periods when temperature trends were not following the CO_2 trend. Both globally and in the United States temperatures declined from about 1880 until 1910, and then rose steeply between around 1910–1950 before slowly declining until about 1980. It would seem that even if the long-term CO_2 trend is highly correlated with the long-term temperature trend, something else must be going on that might drives shorter-term climate cycles. It seems natural to ask whether if that something else, whatever it is, can drive short-term cycles, it cannot also it cannot also account for longer-term trends. In other words, to pinpoint increases in CO_2 as the key driver of long-term

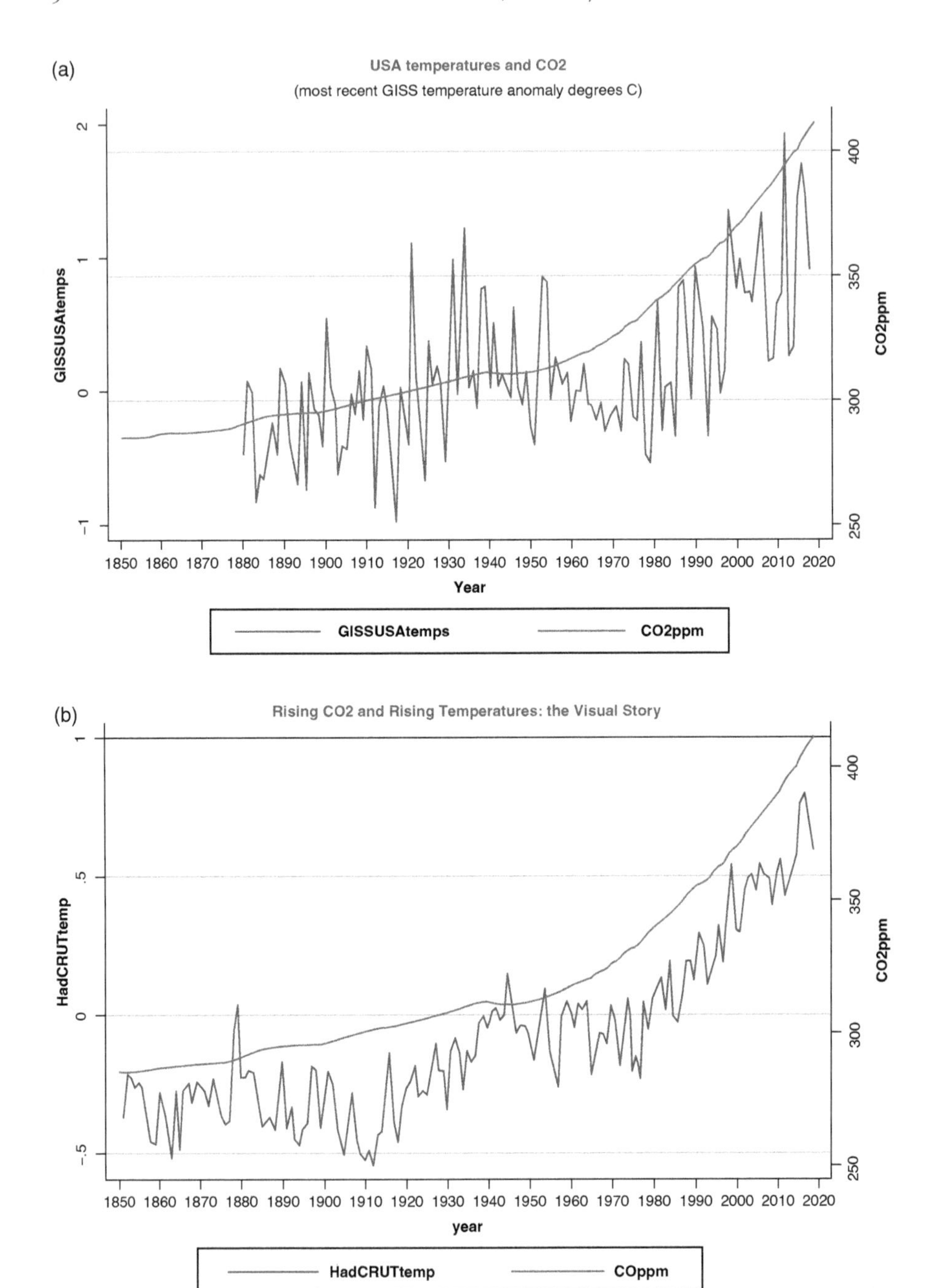

FIGURE 14.1 (a) US and (b) global surface temperature anomaly and atmospheric CO_2.

climate change, it would seem logically necessary that other potential causes be considered.

This is not the approach that has been taken by the IPCC and the USGCRP. That approach relies heavily on computer models of global climate. The most general computer climate models are actually called Coupled Ocean-Atmosphere General Circulation Models (or GCMs as I shall refer to them). What these models aim to do is to create a computer model of the general circulation of the earth's atmosphere and oceans. These models divide the entire globe into three-dimensional boxes, with the physical state of the atmosphere and oceans in each box represented by computer code with equations that are approximations of the physical laws governing such movements. As the earth's atmosphere and oceans are an interconnected system, the equations in each box connect to equations in other boxes. The models have hundreds of thousands of lines of code, much of which is now over 30 years old. The results they generate are obtained by plugging in alternative values for things, such as atmospheric CO_2 levels, that change the amount of radiation entering into radiative-sensitive approximating equations in the boxes, and then letting the equations iterate for hundreds or even thousands of time periods (typically years). Even with several supercomputers running full time, it takes days or even weeks to get the output from such runs (called simulations).

A *Simple Single-Dimensional Model of Climate Forcing*

For purposes of figuring out how CO_2 affects climate, however, all of the key features of these complex computer models can be seen in a relatively simple, single-dimensional model. Such a single-dimensional model is called a radiative balance model. The model is based on the basic physical fact – drawn from the first law of thermodynamics – that all energy must be accounted for somewhere. The energy that runs the earth's climate system comes (almost) entirely from the sun. Conservation of energy implies that the radiative energy entering the earth's atmosphere must be balanced by the energy leaving the atmosphere. It also implies that the increased longwave radiation generated by an increase in atmospheric CO_2 has to have an effect on temperature outside the troposphere, on the earth's land and ocean temperature. The relationship between increased radiative energy due to increasing CO_2 and temperature can be summarized in a single equation:[3]

$$\Delta T = S\Delta F_{2xCO_2} + f\Delta T - \Delta H.$$

Simplifying and rearranging, we have that

$$\Delta T = S\Delta F_{2xCO_2}/(1 - f) - \Delta H, \tag{1}$$

Where,

ΔT is the predicted change in surface temperature;
ΔF_{2xCO_2} is the total radiative forcing (energy increase) from a doubling of CO_2;

ΔH is the amount of heat from the CO_2 doubling that is taken up and stored in the oceans;
$f\Delta T$ is a feedback effect – additional temperature change induced by the initial CO_2 induced temperature change.

Equation (1) is a short but quite general bit of algebra. In it, we could generalize the forcing term ΔF to include forcings other than that from the increase in atmospheric CO_2. Forcing would include any external influence – external, that is, climate system itself – that can impact the amount of solar radiation that reaches the surface and/or the amount of longwave (or infrared) radiation that is absorbed in the atmosphere and/or emitted from the earth's surface. Climate forcings include both anthropogenic and natural influences.[4] The primary natural forcings are volcanic eruptions and solar variation. Anthropogenic forcings include not only the emissions of all the various greenhouse gases – including not only CO_2 but also methane (CH_4) and nitrous oxide (N_2O) and chlorofluorocarbons – but also changes in land use that alter the earth's surface albedo (or reflectivity). In addition to the warming, greenhouse gases, there is another kind of anthropogenic forcing that is crucial to climate models: the emission of aerosols, such as sulfur dioxide emissions from coal-burning industrial facilities. Greenhouse gases absorb longwave radiation and warm the earth. Other than black carbon – which as we will see shortly is a very strong warming agent – most aerosols, such as sulfur dioxide, cool the earth, both by directly reflecting solar radiation back to space before it has a chance to reach the earth's surface and by increasing the reflectivity of low-level clouds.[5]

As shown by the math in equation (1), the feedback effect $f\Delta T$ is crucial. The feedback effect f must be less than 1, for it were not, any positive forcing would cause the earth to warm uncontrollably. With $0 < f < 1$, we can see from equation (1) that the direct effect S of doubling CO_2 on temperature is smaller than the effect that takes account of feedbacks. In this case, the initial impact of doubling CO_2 is amplified by positive feedbacks. Conversely, were $f < 0$, the net feedback effect would be negative, so that the direct effect of doubling CO_2 would be reduced by feedback effects.

There are three main feedback effects from CO_2-induced warming. If a CO_2 increase warms temperatures and melts polar and glacial ice, then the albedo or reflectivity of polar and glacial areas of the earth is reduced. This means that more shortwave solar radiation is absorbed in such regions, which produces a temperature increase additional to the initial direct CO_2 induced temperature increase.

In addition to melting ice, another positive feedback effect is an increase in water vapor. A basic physical relation is that warmer air can hold more water. If CO_2 increases tropospheric air temperatures, then – provided that the nothing else changes in a new, high-CO_2 world that reduces evaporation of water from the lands and oceans – physics predicts that tropospheric water vapor content should increase. Because water vapor is the most powerful greenhouse gas, accounting for roughly two-thirds of all greenhouse warming, an increase in water vapor will amplify any warming generated by a CO_2 increase. The direction of the water vapor feedback is thus believed to be known, and for most regions of the world, measurements of atmospheric water vapor (or, more precisely precipitable water) taken since 1995 show that atmospheric water vapor has been rising along with tropospheric temperature (see Wang et al. 2016).

The final important feedback is the impact of CO_2 driven temperature change on clouds. As the discussion below will show, this feedback is a crucial way that climate models manage to reproduce industrial era temperatures, and I leave further discussion of the cloud feedback until that point in the book.

There are very few equations in the text of this book, and I've include equation (1) only because it really does summarize all the key variables that determine the impact of CO_2 on temperature. The crucial thing for the reader to understand is that potentially big temperature increases from an increase in CO_2 (high climate sensitivity ΔT) is *due entirely to such feedback effects*. From fundamental principles of physics, one can derive the basic, everything else constant, relationship between increases in CO_2 and increases in radiative (heat) energy. As shown by Figure 14.2,

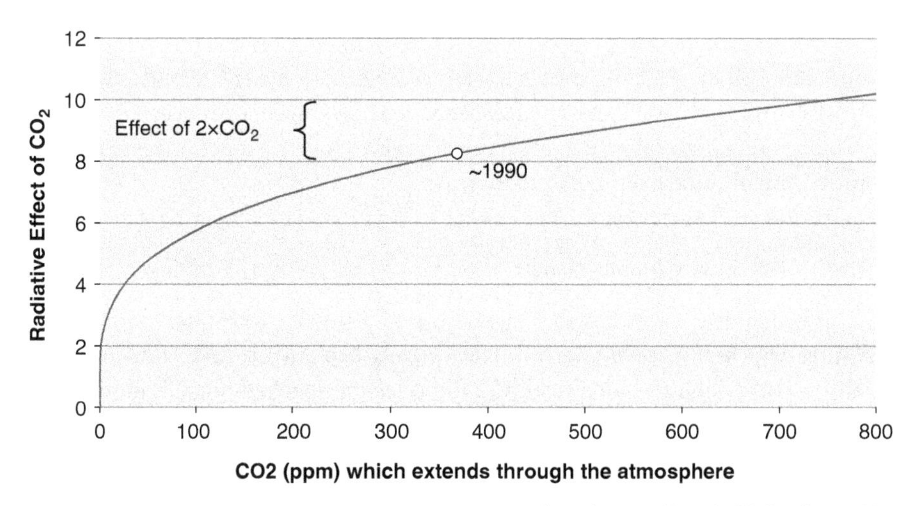

FIGURE 14.2 Logarithmic relationship between atmospheric CO_2 concentration and its radiative forcing. Taken from Roger A. Pielke, Sr., "The Radiative Forcing of CO_2 as a Function of Its Atmospheric Concentration," available at https://pielkeclimatesci.wordpress.com/2012/01/23/the-radiative-forcing-of-co2-as-a-function-of-its-atmospheric-concentration/. It was created by Joe Eastman while at Colorado State University and is a graphical depiction of the relationship $\Delta F = 1.73(CO_2)^{0.263}$ derived under the simplifying assumptions given in the text by Timothy M. Lenton, "Land and Ocean Carbon Cycle Feedback Effects on Global Warming in a Simple Earth System Model," 52 (5) *Tellus B: Chemical and Physical Meteorology* (2000), 1169.

that relationship is less than linear, or to be more precise, logarithmic. What this means is that if one holds everything else constant and just increases the CO_2 in the atmosphere – deriving what the IPCC calls "simplified radiative forcing" – then the additional radiative energy increases, but at a decreasing rate.

Since 1990, the IPCC Assessment Reports have used such a functional relationship for the simplified, all else constant, radiative forcing from increases in atmospheric CO_2 concentration.[6] Under this everything else constant, no feedback relationship, a doubling of CO_2 leads to a predicted temperature increase of only about 1.2°C.[7] (In terms of the notation of equation (1), $S\Delta F = 1.2°C$). As we can also see from Figure 14.2 in the range between the preindustrial atmospheric CO_2 level of 280 ppm and the current level of about 400 ppm, there relationship between further increases in CO_2 and increases in radiative forcing is slightly less than linear. Using the linear approximation, one would predict that if a 100 percent increase (doubling) of atmospheric CO_2 would directly induce a rise of 1.2°C in surface temperature, then the direct impact of the actual increase to date, 43 percent, ought to have been about 0.52°C.

This is just an approximation that could be made more precise using the actual function depicted in Figure 14.2. But what it shows is that without any kind of model, or even an equation like equation (1), from very basic known physical chemistry, one would predict about a 0.5°C increase in surface temperatures due the industrial era rise in atmospheric CO_2. As we have seen, according to the IPCC and USGRCP, and GISS and HadCRUT, the rise has been bigger, somewhere between 0.8° and 1° C. This is much bigger than the direct impact of CO_2 alone. Something else must be contributing to surface temperature increase.

B *How Climate Models "Explain" Industrial Era Warming*

The previous discussion has in fact uncovered a precise formulation of the key question of whether computer climate models explain the industrial era temperature rise as due to increased CO_2: the question is whether such models can find a combination of various feedbacks and forcings (remember, these include not just CO_2 but air pollutants like SO2 that increased greatly due to industrialization) that, together with the CO_2 change, replicate the temperature change. From the standpoint of being able to be confident about such climate model replications of recent (that is, industrial era) climate change, the best answer would be this: climate scientists have precise, empirically based estimates of all important feedback effects (and so know the term $f\Delta T$ in equation (1)) and also empirical observations of the change in not just CO_2 but all other important climate forcings (and so know the term ΔF in equation (1)), and when they plug these into the models and vary CO_2, the models spit out a temperature increase that is not statistically significantly different from that actually observed in GISS and HadCRUT data sets.

This is not at all the way climate models have been used to replicate industrial era temperature change. To understand climate model replication of industrial era temperatures, it is helpful to provide some perspective first on what a computer climate model does.

(a) Computer Climate Models: A Mixture of Known Physics and Parameterizations

The most general computer climate models are actually called Coupled Ocean-Atmosphere General Circulation Models (or GCMs, as I shall refer to them). What these models aim to do is to create a computer model of the general circulation of the earth's atmosphere and oceans.

As students learn in a basic high school earth science class, the movement of the earth's atmosphere is driven by two primary forces: the heating of the low latitudes relative to higher latitudes, and the rotation of the earth on its axis.[8] The relative heating of the tropics accounts for the Hadley circulation, a simple equator-to-pole circulation in which warm air rises in the tropics and flows toward the poles at relatively high altitudes, and is replaced (as the law of the conservation of mass requires) by cooler air flowing down from the polar regions at lower altitudes, where warmer air correspondingly descends.

To get a basic approximation of how the earth's atmosphere moves, one needs to take account of the acceleration due to the earth's spinning about on its axis. This account is provided by the Coriolis Force, the name given to the acceleration of air parcels due to the earth's rotation. Given the direction of the earth's rotation, and the Hadley cell movement of warm air out from the equator and toward the poles, the Coriolis force bends air parcels to the east (rightward relative to the direction of parcel motion in the northern hemisphere, leftward in the southern) in both hemispheres. Due to the Coriolis force, major global winds move from the west to the east (and because of the basic pressure gradient) along lines of constant pressure.

The earth's rotation is in fact so strong that a single equator-to-pole circulation cell – a single Hadley cell – is unstable The direct meridional circulation named after Hadley extends only to about 30° latitude in each hemisphere. At that latitude, in each hemisphere, the Hadley cell breaks apart into three cells: a tropical Hadley cell and, moving poleward a Ferrell cell, and, finally, a polar cell, each of which replicates the basic circular poleward flow of warm air toward cold (Taylor 2005, 50). The latter two are caused by large-scale eddy fluxes – cyclones and anticyclones (see Schneider 2006, 658). At least half of the total poleward heat transport in the atmosphere is accomplished by such eddies – mid-latitude storm systems and waves and other kinds of turbulence (Taylor 2005, 50). Outside the tropics, the transport of mass, energy, and momentum in the atmosphere are driven by these fundamentally turbulent eddies, rather than by the relatively simple Hadley circulation that is the dominant poleward force in the tropics (Caballero 2008, L18709).

As a consequence of the Hadley circulation, the surface pressure at 30° latitude (where air is subsiding) is generally greater than at the equator (where air is rising), and the tropical surface trade winds blow generally toward the equator from both hemispheres, meeting in the Intertropical Convergence Zone (ITCZ) where there is low surface pressure and large-scale upward motion with latent heat release (Hartman 1994, 155). In both hemispheres, the ITCZ moves with the seasons: the large area of convection centered over Indonesia moves southward, extending as far south as 30° S, during the southern hemisphere summer; in the Amazon, the heaviest rains fall during the early months of the year, and the lowest in August, when the ITCZ moves northward (Hartman 1994, 164). Moving longitudinally, regions within the moist ITCZ are not, of course, identical. In particular, the equatorial region surrounding Malaysia, Indonesia, and New Guinea – where there are few large land areas and shallow seas – is one of especially intense convection and precipitation, and the rising motion driving by latent heat release in this region generates a powerful circulation system of the tropical atmosphere characterized by east-west circulation cells along the equator with large regions of rising warm and moist air in the Indonesian, South American and African regions, and subsiding, dry air in between. The largest of these east-west equatorial circulation cells, known as the Walker Circulation, extends across the Pacific Ocean (Hartman 1994, 163).

Where air is subsiding along the belt between 10° and 40° latitude, rainfall is suppressed, and it is in this region where many of the world's great deserts are found. Moving further poleward, much seasonal climate is driven by the differential response of oceans and continents to seasonal variations in solar insolation: relative to the oceans, land surfaces warm up more rapidly in the summer and cool more rapidly in the winter. As cool air falls (increasing surface air pressure) and warm air rises (decreasing surface air pressure), the differential slow ocean and fast land response to changes in solar radiation give rise to a long-term predictable pattern where high pressure centers form over the oceans in summer and over the continents in winter (and vice versa for low pressure centers). The seasonal movement of maximum insolation across hemispheres likewise accounts for the monsoon, a seasonal change in wind direction that generates dramatic shifts in precipitation across many parts of Africa, Asia, and Australia. In the Asian monsoon, for example, heating of the Tibetan plateau in the summer generates persistent low pressure that sucks in warm, moist air from the ocean, generating large amounts of rainfall; in the winter, the pattern is reversed.

All in all, the general circulation of the earth's atmosphere is a complex nonlinear system. One can get an idea of this complexity just by watching a quickly flowing river. As it flows with gravity, the river is also flowing over rocks and boulders, downed trees, all located at various and changing depths and river bottom soil conditions. The river's flow has a pattern, but even just standing and watching, one can see the pattern change and shift, as eddies form, dissipate, and then redevelop.

Like a river flowing across boulders and downed trees over a streambed of varying geologic composition, the earth's atmospheric flow is not smooth and unbroken (laminar), but turbulent, with eddies (low pressure systems for example), forming and reforming, and different parts of the atmosphere moving in different directions at different speeds, all at the same time. But as just seen in my brief description, the circulation of the earth's atmosphere is much more complicated than a single turbulent flow. GCM's are trying to explain the whole set of complex circulation patterns – such as the Hadley Cell and extratropical eddies – that drive the earth's climate system.

These patterns result from the operation of basic physical laws, and these laws provide the basic building blocks for GCM's. As set out Wilkinson and Parkinson (2005), a leading text on three-dimensional climate modeling, atmospheric and ocean temperature flows in a climate model are set to conform to fundamental physical laws of conservation – of mass, energy, and momentum. To these they add – for the atmosphere – an equation relating the pressure, density and temperature and a moisture equation, and – for the oceans – a so-called equation of state relating pressure, temperature, density, and salinity (Washington and Parkinson 2005, 49). For the atmosphere, one ends up with a system of six equations in six unknowns, with several constants and friction and external temperature forcing to be specified (Washington and Parkinson 2005, 63).

In explaining how radiation from the sun is both absorbed and emitted as it travels through the atmosphere, given the chemical composition of the atmosphere, GCM models also rely on basic physical-chemical laws (Washington and Parkinson 2005, 76–91). These basic physical laws – confirmed in lab experiments – establish the warming and cooling properties of the three key atmospheric gases – ozone, or O_3, CO_2, and water vapor.[9] GCM models also rely on basic physical laws in modeling the ocean. For the ocean, the basic equation relates seawater density to temperature, salinity, and pressure. Ocean circulation patterns are driven in part by the horizontal Coriolis force, but such patterns also result from temperature and salinity differences in the ocean that vary across latitudes and by ocean depth (Washington and Parkinson 2005, 116–128).

The actual physical laws underlying climate models are expressed (for the most part) as continuous differential equations, for example, an equations like $\partial y/\partial t = t^3 - 2yt$. Such an equation states precisely, for continuous time, the change in the variable y over time t, expressed by $\partial y/\partial t$. One may remember such equations, either fondly, or with horror, from a high school or college class in differential equations. As explained by Essex and Tsonis (2018, 555–556), two leading mathematicians who study nonlinear systems, because computer models are not infinite, a computer climate model can at best approximate the physical differential equations upon which it is based. In computer climate model approximations, the actual equations are broken apart into discrete tiny linear segments within three-dimensional boxes. Given initial conditions within a grid box, the discrete approximations are used to predict the dynamics, or change. This process inherently involves error. Physical processes that operate at scales smaller than the size of each grid box cannot be captured and yet a fundamental thing about nonlinear differential equations is that over a long enough time period, tiny errors can propagate into massive changes in the final state of the physical system. If grid sizes are too small, however, even the fastest computer cannot find solutions in less than millions of years.

These are unavoidable limitations of computer modeling of complex nonlinear systems. In additional to such necessary discrete approximations of continuous physical laws, however, computer climate models include many parameterizations – or particular mathematical equations – that are not based on known physical laws. Such parameterizations reflect the fact that some very important climate processes are simply not understood and are being modeled with equations that seem to reflect what has been observed empirically while remaining consistent with known physical laws. As Hourdin et al. (2017), one of the leading climate modeling groups, explain:

> Parameterizations are often based on a mixed, physical, phenomenological and statistical view. For example, the cloud fraction needed to represent the mean effect of a field of clouds on radiation may be related to the resolved humidity and temperature through an empirical relationship. But the same cloud fraction can also be obtained from a more elaborate description of processes governing cloud formation and evolution. For instance, for an ensemble of cumulus clouds within a horizontal grid cell, clouds can be represented with a single-mean plume of warm and moist air rising from the surface [] or with an ensemble of such plumes []. Similar parameterizations are needed for many components not amenable to first-principle approaches at the grid scale of a global model, including boundary layers, surface hydrology, and ecosystem dynamics. Each parameterization, in turn, typically depends on one or more parameters whose numerical values are poorly constrained by first principles or observations at the grid scale of global models. Being approximate descriptions of unresolved processes, there exist different possibilities for the representation of many processes. (591)

What Hourdin et al. (2017) are saying, in the particular case of clouds, is that there is no known physical law (or set of laws), that explains how a field of clouds absorb and reflect radiation. Given this, a climate model might put in a relatively simple, empirically based equation in which the impact of clouds is a function of humidity and temperature. Or a climate model could choose a more complex relationship in which cloud impact is determined by an entire set of plumes of hot and moist air rising through lower level grid boxes from the surface.

Clouds, are one of the three most important climate feedback effects, with the other two being an increase in climate warming water vapor due to a CO_2-induced temperature increase and melting of ice caps and glaciers (which warms the planet by reducing the reflectivity of the earth). Unfortunately, there is great deal of uncertainty about how clouds would respond to initial CO_2-induced warming. Since at least the 1960s, scientists have known that clouds have two offsetting effects on the earth's surface temperature. By capturing and reflecting back longwave, infrared radiation emitted by the earth, high cirrus clouds heat the earth's surface; by reflecting back incoming shortwave solar radiation, low clouds of various types cool the earth's surface (Stephens 2005, 246). Both the negative or cooling impact of low clouds and the warming effect of high clouds are substantial. As one modeling group, Golaz et al. (2013) (the NOAA Geophysical Fluid Dynamics Laboratory or GFDL) puts the currently prevailing view, by reflecting shortwave radiation from the sun, clouds exert a cooling effect of about -47 W/m^2, but by reflecting longwave radiation back to earth, clouds have a warming effect of about 30 W/m^2. These are huge impacts: as the same group of GFDL researchers state, the net forcing due to the increase in atmospheric GHG concentration from preindustrial levels through 2012 was believed to be about 2.6 W/m^2 (Golaz et al. 2013, 2246–2251). In its 2007 AR, the IPCC recognized the potentially massive impact of clouds, pointing out that solely by altering the way that cloud radiative properties are parameterized, climate model predictions of sensitivity to CO_2 doubling range all the way from 1.9° to 5.4°C (IPCC 2007, 1113–1116).

Both warming or cooling from clouds are still viewed as possible. For example, Liu et al. (2017) find confirming evidence for the hypothesis of Lindzen et al. (2001) that surface warming in the tropics would increase convective precipitation there and reduce high cirrus cloud formation in the tropics, thus exerting a negative cloud feedback on warming. Without any clear empirical resolution, as Golaz et al. (2013, 2246) state, "Despite decades of efforts, clouds remain one of the largest sources of uncertainties in climate projections from general circulation models." With such uncertainty, there are a number of different cloud parameterizations in GCM models. One such formulation divides clouds into high-, mid-, and low-level clouds, with the fraction of each determined by maximum relative humidity at a given height. Another posits a nonlinear relationship between relative humidity and cloud formation, with few clouds produced as humidity increases from low levels even if cloud water exists, but a large amount of clouds produced as relative humidity increases from high levels.[10]

Clouds are not the only processes in climate models which are parameterized in a variety of different ways (Washington and Parkinson 2005, 119–121). There are no precise, known physical laws describing the complex ways in which the upper ocean waters mix vertically, or on how small ocean eddies (smaller than the box size used in the model) develop and evolve, or for wind stress at the top of the ocean. Sea ice is also important to climate model predictions, but texts depict a good deal of variation in how sea ice is modeled, and in particular for how sea ice thickness responds to temperature, and how sea ice moves. These are meant to capture key empirical observations and to be consistent with known physical laws, but as Washington and Parkinson explain, it is difficult to incorporate how sea ice thickness affects sea ice movement, and models often rely on simplifications – such as sea ice movement at speeds that are a constant fraction of wind speed with direction at a fixed angle relative to wind direction (Washington and Parkinson 2005, 128–146).

(b) "Tuning": How Computer Climate Models Reproduce Industrial Era Warming

Since climate models were first used, they have tended to generate temperature increases bigger than those actually observed. This has been acknowledged for some time (see Fyfe et al. 2013), even by the IPCC (see figure 9.8 and the discussion accompanying box 9.2. I in IPCC AR5 2013). and (implicitly, see figure 1a in Millar et al. 2017) by the model builders themselves. Despite this tendency to predict too great a temperature response to increasing CO_2, some of the models managed to replicate the observed industrial era temperature – CO_2 relationship.

How they managed to do this was not clear even to modelers themselves. After all, the computer models consist of thousands and thousands of lines computer code, much of it decades old. To figure out how the models work – that is, what it is that is allowing them to reproduce the temperature – CO_2 relationship – takes an enormous amount of work, much of which consists of changing one computer program subroutine – lines of code that make up a particular parameterization of a particular physical process, such as cloud formation – and then another, and seeing what happens to the output. But if this is what is being done, then in the traditional scientific sense of having set out a model which is then tested against observations, the models cannot really be said to be confirmed by past climate trends. Rather, the models are being chosen, or tuned, to replicate those trends.

That such tuning is indeed the method by which computer climate models reproduce industrial era warming is now explicitly acknowledged by climate modeling groups. Several recent review articles have appeared in which particular GCM modeling groups explain in some detail why and how GCM model tuning is done (Mauritsen et al. 2012, MA00A01; Hourdin et al. 2017, 589–602; Schmidt et al. 2017, 3207–3223). These not only provide a precise definition of tuning from the modelers themselves, but identify the cloud feedback effect as the key model feature being turned in the CMIP4 generation of models used for the IPCC's 2013 AR5.

As for what modelers are tuning to replicate, the answer supplied by 22 out of 23 modeling groups whose survey responses are reported in Schmidt et al. (2017) is that they adjust model parameters to achieve desired properties, and as for the "desired properties" to be achieved by tuning, the groups agreed on top-of-the-atmosphere radiation balance, and global mean surface temperature. As Hourdin et al. (2017, 592) explain the relationship between top-of-the-atmosphere balance and temperature in GCM models, "a dominant shared target for coupled climate models [is that] the climate system should reach a mean equilibrium temperature close to observations when energy received from the sun is close to its real value. This energy will be balanced by the energy lost to space by reflected sunlight and thermal infrared radiation." Schmidt et al. (2017, 3209) describe this goal – that the model generate a "near energy balance at the top of the atmosphere and surface in an initial state of a coupled model to prevent temperature drifts over time" – as being required for "useful numerical experiments to be performed in the first place." Of course, top-of-the-atmosphere radiative balance is a long-term, equilibrium condition, not something that should be observed during a period of ongoing changes in atmospheric forcing. As Schmidt et al. (2017, 3209) explain, tuning models to reproduce top-of-the-atmosphere radiative balance is "strictly speaking … not tuning to an observed quantity, but rather is a tuning to a situation that was approximately inferred to hold in the 'preindustrial' (PI) period … conditions around the mid-19th century around 1850."

Without such tuning, early climate models were failing to account for all of the energy coming in from the sun. This problem was fixed by choosing whatever model of the cloud feedback effect was necessary to reproduce radiative balance. As explained by Mauritsen et al. (2012):

> the need to tune models became apparent in the early days of climate modeling, when the top of the atmosphere (TOA) radiation imbalance was so large that models would quickly drift away from the observed state. Initially, a practice to input or extract heat and freshwater from the model, by applying flux-corrections, was invented to address this problem. … As models gradually improved to a point when flux corrections were no longer necessary, … this practice is now less accepted in the climate modeling community. Instead the radiation balance is controlled primarily by tuning cloud-related parameters at most climate modeling centers.

If the majority of models were spinning away from observed global temperature because of the top-of-the-atmosphere imbalance, and they were all tuned to instead achieve balance, then the fact that models manage to achieve balance at the top-of-the-atmosphere is hardly evidence of their reliability. As Mauritsen et al. (2012, MA00A01) observe, "evaluating models based on their ability to represent the TOA radiation balance usually reflects how closely the models were tuned to that particular target, rather than the models' intrinsic qualities."

(c) Tuning Aerosols and Clouds to Replicate Industrial Era Warming

It was only after the publication of the IPCC's 2007 AR4 that climate modelers themselves began to write explicitly about the model tuning problem. One of the earliest and most notable recognitions of the problem appeared in a short commentary by Schwartz et al. (2007, 24). A group of leading climate modelers, Schwartz et al. (2007) pointed out that because climate models differed hugely in their climate sensitivity (S in equation (1)), the past temperature record predicted by climate models "would be expected to be larger than that arising from the uncertainty in the forcing as it would also reflect uncertainties arising from the differences in the multiple climate models used." However, "contrary to such an expectation, the range in modeled global mean temperature change … is much smaller than that associated with the forcings, which is a factor of four." In other words, and in terms of equation (1), even though the models have widely varying climate sensitivities S, and little is known about the forcings ΔQ, the models are all pretty close in simulating past temperature changes, ΔT.

After the IPCC's AR4 appeared in 2007, modelers began to explore whether the mystery identified by Schwartz et al. (2007) was solved by model assumptions about aerosol forcing. Remember that aerosols, such as sulfur dioxide, scatter incoming solar radiation and so have a strong cooling impact. While scientists say that not only estimates of the historical levels of anthropogenic aerosols such as sulfur dioxide (Smith et al. 2011, 1101–1116) but also satellite estimates for the period 1980 until the present are highly uncertain (see, e.g., Chin et al. 2014, 3657–3690), atmospheric aerosols are, in principle at least, observable. As observed data, they should be entered into the forcing terms of climate models. After the IPCC's 2007 AR, however, modelers noticed that the set of models used for the 2007 AR (called the CMIP3 set of models) had a nearly threefold range in their assumed magnitude of aerosol forcing, and found that the range of aerosol cooling directly induced a similarly wide range in total anthropogenic forcing assumed by such models (Kiehl 2007, L22710). As a leading climate modeler explained (Kiehl 2007):

> in many models aerosol forcing is not applied as an external forcing, but is calculated as an integral component of the system. *Many current models predict aerosol concentrations interactively within the climate model and this concentration is then used to predict the direct and indirect forcing effects on the climate system.*[11]

In separate papers, Knutti (2008) and Kiehl (2007) found that even though aerosols are an external forcing imposed on the climate system, climate models were deriving aerosol concentrations "interactively … within the climate model" and thus were essentially calculating a value for the forcing, ΔF, that allows the model to predict late twentieth-century warming, given the model's presumed climate sensitivity S.

More precisely, Knutti (2008) found that "models with high sensitivity (strong feedbacks) avoid simulating too much warming by using a small net forcing (large negative aerosol forcing), and models with weak feedbacks can still simulate the observed warming with a larger forcing (weak aerosol forcing)" Kiehl (2007) found a "strong inverse correlation between total anthropogenic forcing used for the 20th century and the model's climate sensitivity … models with low climate sensitivity require a relatively higher total anthropogenic forcing than models with higher climate sensitivity [*sic*]." As Kiehl (2007) concluded, the reason why "models with such diverse climate sensitivity can all simulate the [late twentieth-century] anomaly in surface temperature" is because the model builders choose the "magnitude of applied anthropogenic total forcing" so as to "compensate" for the model's sensitivity parameter S. Even more starkly, Knutti (2008) concluded that such tuning would mean that "*current agreement between simulated and observed warming trends would be partly spurious, and indicate that we are missing something in the picture of causes and effects of large scale 20th century surface warming* [emphasis added]."

Some modeling groups appear to be very reluctant to admit that the aerosol has been tuned to replicate industrial era temperature increase. For example, Schmidt et al. (2017) merely remark that since the CMIP3 models were "not explicitly tuned to enforce the observed historical trend in temperature, the mechanisms that might explain" the observed negative relationship between model sensitivity and model aerosol forcing remain "unclear." Other groups are more explicit in stating that such tuning took place. Hourdin et al. (2017, 597) say that even though "modeling groups claim not to tune their models against twentieth century warming, … even for model developers, it is difficult to ensure that this is absolutely true in practice because of the complexity and historical dimension of model development."

According to both Hourdin et al. (2017) and Forster et al. (2013), the negative correlation between model sensitivity and aerosol forcing – evidence that models parameterize aerosols to offset too high sensitivity S – was much smaller in the CMIP5 models used for the IPCC's 2013 AR5 than in the CMIP3 models used in its 2007 AR4. Rotstayn et al. (2015) advance two hypotheses for why the correlation of aerosol cooling with temperature sensitivity S declined between the CMIP3 and CMIP5 generations of models: one is that "representations of aerosol-cloud interactions have become so complex that the emergent aerosol [effective radiative forcing] cannot be readily predicted or adjusted, and hence models must accept limitations in their historical simulations" of temperature. The other reason is that "standard aerosol emissions and concentrations were provided for CMIP5, but *they were not for CMIP3 and each group was free to select its own*; this may also have reduced the ability of the groups to tune." Rotstayn et al. (2015) continue to explain that once the CMIP5 modeling groups were actually trying to fit models of aerosol-cloud interactions to actual data on aerosols, the past temperatures predicted by 14 climate models was almost perfectly correlated with the size of the aerosol forcing generated by the model – all models generated negative aerosol forcings, and the more negative the forcing, the lower the temperatures simulated by the model. In other words, once modeling groups were constrained by actual aerosol observations and cloud-aerosol equations, they were no longer free to simply plug in aerosol forcing (cooling) numbers that allowed the model to reproduce industrial era temperatures. This meant that models were no longer all able to reproduce industrial era temperatures.

It cannot be overemphasized that aerosols are a climate forcing agent, just like atmospheric GHG concentration, and in principle, atmospheric aerosols should like GHGs be an *input* to computer climate models, which then simulate the impact of varying levels of aerosols. When the IPCC reports – as it has for over two decades – that the radiative forcing of doubled CO_2 is given by 3.7 W/m^2, it is reporting a basic physical fact about CO_2 that is derived from known laws of physics. This forcing is then put into climate models, which trace through the impact of such a forcing on global temperature and other climate variables. When, by contrast, the IPCC reported in its 2013 AR5 that the forcing from anthropogenic aerosols could be -1.9 W/m^2, it was reporting climate model *output*.

The recent reviews of climate model tuning by various modeling groups agree that models are now tuned primarily by choosing among parameterizations of clouds. They agree also that clouds are chosen for tuning because so little is still known about the cloud feedback effect that modelers face few theoretical or empirical constraints in how they model clouds. According to Hourdin et al. (2017, 593), as "many internal parameters are not directly observable … a common practice is to adjust the most uncertain parameters that significantly affect key climate metrics. … There is a fair consensus … that the most uncertain parameters that affect the atmospheric radiation are those entering into the parameterization of clouds and of the albedo of the Earth's surface." According to Mauritsen et al. (2012), "tuning cloud parameters partly masks the deficiencies in the simulated climate, as there is considerable uncertainty in the representation of cloud processes." Schmidt et al. (2017) openly state that sometimes models reproduce temperatures more accurately when they include cloud parameterizations that are not consistent either with known theory or observations. Schmidt et al. (2017) put forth as an example the fact that the twentieth-century temperature increase generated in the model of Golaz et al. (2013) "could be simulated more realistically (larger increase)" using values for the size of aerosol particles at which cloud droplets begin to precipitate that are "smaller than observed."

II THE CO_2-DRIVEN CLIMATE CHANGE HYPOTHESIS CANNOT EXPLAIN OTHER IMPORTANT OBSERVED TEMPERATURE CHANGES

A *Models Cannot Explain Why Temperatures Fell Even as CO_2 Rose during the Holocene*

If increasing atmospheric CO_2 as a powerful global warming force, and if this relationship holds for the industrial era, then it should hold for previous periods. In particular, over the course of the Holocene, generally taken to have begun about 11,300 years ago, rising CO_2 should correlate with rising temperatures.

The literature has thus far generally failed to find that rising CO_2 has led to rising temperatures over this longer period. Temperatures over the last 22,000 years are displayed in Figure 14.3.

Of course, the usual caveat applies to Figure 14.3: it displays temperatures reconstructed from ice cores (primarily), not observed temperatures. The temperature reconstructions come from two different research groups (Marcott et al. 2013, 1198–1201; Shakun et al. 2012, 49–54), and are shown in blue for the last 11,300 years and cyan (what I would call turquoise) before then. They show temperatures rising

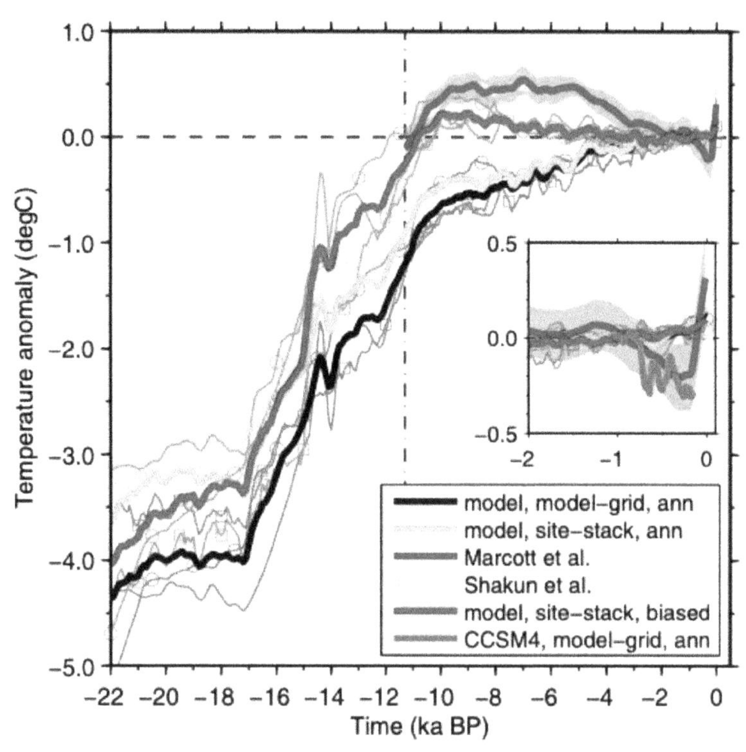

FIGURE 14.3 Global surface temperature over the last 22,000 years. Reproduces figure 1 from Liu et al. (2014, E3502).

about 3°–4°C as the last ice age ended between 17,000 and 10,000 years ago, followed by a clear cooling trend of about 0.5°C after what is called the Holocene Thermal Maximum (about 10,000–6,000 years ago), a cooling trend that ended in the Little Ice Age between about AD 1500 and 1800. As Liu et al. (2014) summarize, although Figure 14.3 displays just two temperature reconstructions, "numerous previous reconstructions have shown cooling trends in the Holocene."[12]

Liu et al. (2014) ran GCM temperature simulations with three climate models that were forced with realistic variations in solar insolation due to orbital fluctuations, atmospheric GHG, and continental ice sheet melt and associated meltwater changes. The results from those simulations are the yellow and black curves shown in Figure 14.3. As one can see, the models do a good job of simulating reconstructed temperatures until the about the beginning of the Holocene 10,000 years ago and – Liu et al. (2014) say because the models are forced with major aerosol cooling from volcanic eruptions and solar variation – they also do a pretty good job of catching the temperature fall during the little ice age (see the insert within the figure). But for most of the Holocene, when temperature were falling, the models simulate rising temperatures.

As one can see from Figure 14.4. all three climate models (whose simulated temperatures are in black and gray for the three models, respectively, in panels A–C) are being forced by atmospheric GHGs that as shown by the orange lines rise steadily over the last 11,300 years. The only other forcing that steadily increases during the last 11,300 years is the decrease in the ice sheets (the green ICE lines in Figure 14.4), a decrease that warms the earth by decreasing its albedo (reflectivity) and thereby increasing the amount of solar radiation absorbed at the surface.

Liu et al. (2014, E3503) view their results as raising a fundamental question: given that "Physically, either rising GHG's or retreating ice sheets will lead to a global warming. … What is the forcing mechanism to the coupled ocean-atmosphere system that can generate a global cooling in the Holocene?" Liu et al. (2014) rule out a number of potential explanations: wobbles in the earth's orbit are too weak over the period studied to account for such pronounced multimillennial cooling; cloud feedback is "highly uncertain" and "given different cloud parameterization schemes across models, it is not obvious why all of the models tend to exhibit a global warming trend bias"; polar ice cap and glacial meltwater mostly just alters the distribution of heat around the planet, not the global average; while volcanic aerosols are a powerful coolant within climate models, there is "no credible evidence," Liu et al. say, "of an intensification trend of volcanic activity in the Holocene."

Having ruled out all these possible explanations, Liu et al. (2014, E3504) are left with only one:

> the biases in current models, if they exist, are more likely to be related to their sensitivity to the orbital forcing and additional feedbacks in climate models. Whatever the biases, *the model biases have to exhibit a common warming bias across all of the current models with a total magnitude of at least ~1 °C*, such that removal of this model bias can generate a global cooling of ~1 °C, which overcomes the 0.5 °C warming by GHGs and ice sheets to leave a net cooling of 0.5 °C.[13]

Of course, if models have a 1°C warm bias then the bias in the models is as big as the industrial era temperature change that the models seek to replicate.

The inconsistency of rising CO_2 with earlier Holocene era cooling would strike at the core hypothesis that CO_2 change explains long-term climate change. Unsurprisingly, there is work that tends to restore faith in the models. But this work proceeds not by uncovering and fixing model biases, but by generating new temperature reconstructions. For example, Marsicek et al. (2018) argue that when a larger set of pollen-based temperature reconstructions are added to marine sediment reconstructions, Holocene temperatures do not begin to fall until about 6,000 years ago (vs. around 11,300 in earlier reconstructions). One must expect a response to Marsicek, but regardless of that response, there clearly is a serious and still open question about whether climate models fail to explain Holocene temperature trends because they generate too big a warming impact from CO_2.

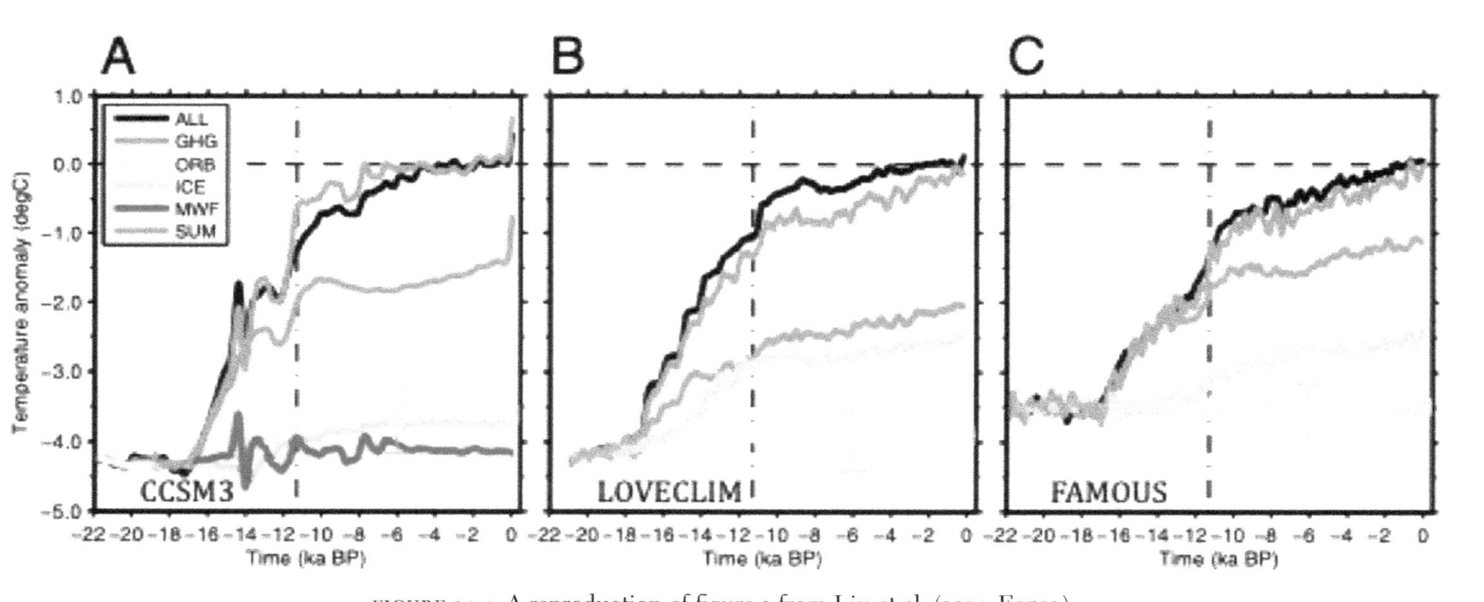

FIGURE 14.4 A reproduction of figure 2 from Liu et al. (2014, E3503).

B *Climate Models of CO_2-Driven Warming Have One Precise and Clearly Testable Prediction about Today's Climate, and It Seems to Be Disconfirmed by Observations*

The lapse rate is the rate at which a packet of air cools as it rises in the atmosphere. This cooling rate is determined by radiative processes (short wave radiation downward from the sun, longwave radiation upward from the earth's surface) and large-scale dynamical processes – such as weather systems in the mid-latitudes – and convection in the atmosphere.[14] In the tropics, the lapse rate closely follows the moist adiabatic lapse rate, which is the rate that a water-saturated air packet cools (due to reduced pressure) as it rises. The moist adiabatic lapse rate decreases with increasing surface temperature.[15] Hence, climate models that predict an increase in surface temperature also predict that, other things equal, the lapse rate will fall relative to the rate that prevails before GHG-induced surface warming (see Bengtsson and Hodges 2009). A falling lapse rate means that tropospheric temperatures will be warmer relative to surface temperatures after CO_2 forcing than before.

The tropical latitudes are relatively unaffected by weather systems (eddies) – cold fronts, high pressure systems, and the like – which are so important in determining US weather. In the tropics, there is only convection – rising warm moist air – and so the tropics provide the ideal place to test climate model predictions, in particular the prediction that any given surface warming will be amplified by a quantitatively predictable amount in the troposphere. For example, using arbitrary lapse rates for purposes of demonstration, if the prior lapse rate between the surface and a given level of the troposphere was 1/2, so that a 1° temperature increase at the surface would translate into a 1/2° warming at the given level of the troposphere, then if the lapse rate fell to 1/3, then a 1° increase in temperature at the surface would translate into a 2/3° increase in temperature at the given level of the tropical troposphere. Proportionately, the increase from 1/32 to 2/3 is 32 percent (or 0.32), meaning that the increase in GHG would cause the troposphere to warm at a rate equal to 1.32 times the surface warming rate. The GCM models used for the IPCC's 2007 AR4 actually predicated a slightly lower amplification, of 1.2 (see Santer et al., 2005).

In the chapter of its 2007 AR4 entitled "Understanding and Attributing Climate Change," the IPCC notes that in the tropics, "where most models have more warming aloft than at the surface … most observational estimates show more warming at the surface than in the troposphere" (IPCC 2017, 701). In other words, what the IPCC is saying rather obliquely here is that a crucial empirically testable proposition generated by climate models – that there should be more warming in the tropical troposphere than at the surface – has not been confirmed by the existing data.

Now there are two possibilities: either the data are bad, or something is wrong with the models. In its 2007 report, the IPCC is quite clear that the data, not the models, must be the problem. The IPCC explains that since on short-term time scales (monthly and annual), variations in tropical surface temperatures are indeed amplified in tropospheric observed temperature as the models predict, the fact that on longer time scales only one data set is consistent with the models' predictions means that the observational record must be afflicted by "inhomogeneities," that is, that there are errors in tropical tropospheric temperature observations (IPCC 2007, 701).[16] In the "Technical Summary" accompanying the full 2007 report, the IPCC said that there are likely errors in all of the existing measurements of tropospheric temperature trends, but stresses that many errors have been eliminated since the previous 2001 AR, leading to improved tropospheric temperature estimates and a "tropospheric temperature record … broadly consistent with surface temperature trends" (IPCC 2007, 36).

Around the same time that the IPCC's 2007 AR appeared, a number of articles were published in the top peer-edited geophysical journals in which climate scientists presented what they believed to be reliable tropospheric temperature data disconfirming the climate model prediction that warming will be amplified in the lower to mid-troposphere (Douglass et al. 2004, L13207). More such articles were published after the publication of the IPCC's AR4 in 2007.

- In 2008, Douglass et al. showed that certain satellite and balloon-based measurements of tropical surface and tropospheric temperature trends had measured tropospheric temperature trends that were more than two standard deviations away from those predicted by the mean linear trend estimate generated by climate models that predicted surface temperature trends well.
- In the very same issue of the very same journal, a group of authors lead by Benjamin Santer and constituting a virtual "who's who" of leading IPCC climate modelers published an article (Santer et al. 2008, 1703) in which they looked at completely different satellite and balloon-based temperature data and found that the linear trend in tropical tropospheric temperatures was well within two standard deviations from mean[17] trend estimates from a suite of no fewer than 49 individual climate models; however, Santer et al. inflated standard deviations in a way that is statistically questionable.[18]
- A third group of researchers (Bengstton et al. 2009), unrelated to the Douglass and Santer groups, examined yet a third, newer dataset on tropospheric temperature, and (employing a climate model that is calibrated on a 500 year dataset and which captures the periodic ENSO-induced cycles in tropical temperatures) found that the observations did not confirm the model's prediction of differential warming in the tropical troposphere (vs. tropical sea surface temperatures) (see Bengtsson and Hodges 2009).

In all of these attempts to statistically compare the topical tropospheric temperature trends predicted by GCM models with observed trends, the main challenge is to distinguish random cycles in temperature from longer-term trends. As remarked earlier, there are cycles in temperature, some lasting for a decade or so, some lasting up to 60 years. If one fits a straight line through data with such cycles, one cannot assume that the data are randomly scattered around the line the same way at each point in time. If temperature is way above the straight line trend one year, then it probably will be way above the next year and perhaps even the year after that – this is what cycles mean, after all. When one takes such a cyclic pattern into account – one in which the errors or deviations from the line are correlated with each other over time, and perhaps correlated over several periods in a row – then in fitting either a straight line or polynomial curve to the data, one should discount the data points that are caused by such correlated errors. That is, one should not be forcing (mathematically) the line to be close to such data points. Finally, one should not force cycles to last a certain period of time – by assuming, for example, that a deviation from trend one period only affects the expected deviation the next period – but instead let the data determine the period of time over which deviations from trend are correlated.

In a paper of very general usefulness not only for climate science but economics and other disciplines, Vogelsang and Frances (2005) discovered a way to test for compare trends while allowing for such data-revealed cycles (correlated error structures). Several papers have applied this approach:

- Using this approach where possible, McKitrick et al. (2010) found that over the period 1979–2009, GCM projected tropospheric temperature trends were between 200 and 400 percent bigger than the trend in actual observed temperatures.
- Extending the Vogelsang and Franses (2005) error estimation technique to allow for jumps in observed temperature data caused by things like volcanic eruptions (as set out in McKitrick and Vogelsang 2014), McKitrick and Christy (2018) found that the vast majority (82 out of 102) of models overestimated tropical temperature trends by as much as 100 percent when compared to observations (0.325°C per decade vs. 0.173°C per decade observed).
- As I noted in my discussion of the gap between tropospheric temperature increases and surface temperature change, Voegelsang and Nawaz (2017) found that the ratio of tropospheric to surface warming trends over the period 1979–2014 ranged from 0.64 to 1. This is far below the 1.2 predicted by GCM models; indeed, values above 1.1 could be statistically ruled out at the 95 percent confidence level for all comparisons.

It would seem at this point that the accumulating evidence disconfirming the GCM predictions of amplified warming in the tropical troposphere is becoming overwhelming. Of course, some of this work was not available at the time of the IPCC's 2013 AR. Still, what the IPCC had to say in its 2013AR4 is worth noting, because it is yet another example of what seems to be a general reaction of the IPCC to disconfirmation of its key claims. In the AR5, the IPCC said that whereas satellite observations of tropical troposphere temperature trends do not agree with models, radiosonde (balloon) measurements do, and since the two measures differ from one another, there is "low confidence in observations" and therefore also "low confidence" in the failure of climate models to correctly predict trends.[19] What we have here is the IPCC saying that it has "low confidence" in data disconfirming one of the few testable predictions of climate models. As we shall see just a bit later, this is very similar to what the IPCC says about the almost complete inability of climate models to explain long-term cycles in ocean circulation – the models may be poor, but so too are the data. When faced with data disconfirming climate model projections, the IPCC virtually always says the data are bad.

III ALTERNATIVE EXPLANATIONS FOR OBSERVED TEMPERATURE CHANGE THAT ARE IGNORED BY THE IPCC

A *Temperatures Have Been High Before and Will Be Again: Internal Variability as a Component of Climate Change over Multiple Time Scales*

Over virtually any time and geographic scale, the one clear thing about temperatures is that they cycle. We can see this by looking at Figure 14.5, the HadCRUT global temperature time series we saw earlier.

What may be called the IPCC approach – meaning not just its official reports but also the work of IPCC-endorsed scientists – to explaining climate cycles of virtually all durations is to try to find an external forcing that might account for the observed cycle. For the most recent, industrial era, climate models would predict a relatively smooth relationship between rising CO_2 and rising temperatures, not the choppy reality depicted by, Figure 14.5. To explain the choppiness, IPCC modelers look to other exogenous climate forcers, whether random external events such as volcano eruptions that inject solar-radiation-reflecting aerosol particles into the atmosphere, or well-known periodic fluctuations in total solar irradiance.

The intuition behind this approach is depicted by the graph in Figure 14.6. That graph was part of a tutorial on climate science requested by US District Court judge William Alsup in the 2018 public nuisance lawsuit *City of Oakland v. BP PLC*. The graph comes from a presentation by Oxford scientist Myles Allen, a Lead Author on IPCC Reports, who testified as an expert witness for the plaintiffs.[20]

Part of Allen's presentation consisted of a sequence of 15 graphs showing how the fit between the model temperature reproductions and actual temperature observations gets better and better by adding stronger and stronger long-term, anthropogenic CO_2 warming to the shorter 10–20 year fluctuations induced by volcanic and solar activity. I have just chosen the first and last of these graphs. These are not formal scientific demonstrations, but they display the basic IPCC model approach to explaining industrial era temperature change: find a CO_2 sensitivity that produces the best fit to temperature data when solar and volcanic forcing fluctuations are used to account for the shorter-term cycles. The top graph in Figure 14.6 shows the best fit without allowing for any contribution from anthropogenic CO_2 emissions (there is a typo in the graph heading, as the word "without" is omitted) and the bottom graph in

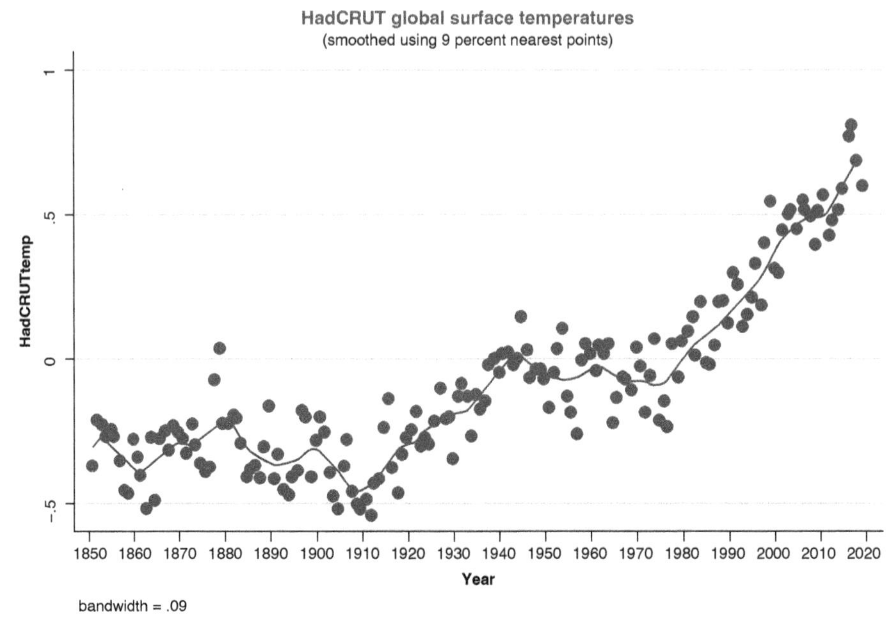

FIGURE 14.5 HadCRUT Post-Industrial Global Surface Temperature.

Figure 14.6 shows the remarkable fit when the appropriate, tuned amount of CO_2-induced warming is added.

As one can see from Figure 14.6, the modeled temperatures are not very close to observed temperatures in the top graph, which assumes no contribution from CO_2 to observed temperatures, but the modeled temperatures are very close when one models about a 0.7°C contribution from CO_2. If one looks a bit more closely, one can also see that the modeled relationship between volcanic and solar forcings, the blue line, changes dramatically as one attributes more and more of the warming to CO_2. But if one continues to look closely, when the model attributes basically the entire long-term temperature increase to CO_2, as in the bottom graph in Figure 14.6, the remarkable rise in temperature that occurred between about 1925–1945 is left unexplained. The best-fit, purple line that combines CO_2 with solar and volcanic contributions is below observed virtually the entire range of observed temperatures (the black line) over the entire 1925–1945 period (conversely, it matches quite closely the low temperatures of the 1960s, because solar/volcanic forcing accounts for these).

While heuristic, Figure 14.5 strongly suggests that something is missing from the way the IPCC explains industrial scale temperature change, that something other than changes in atmospheric CO_2 and other external forcings such as volcanic aerosols and solar variation must be contributing to climate change. A look back at the even longer-term, 2,000 year record displayed by Figure 13.14 provides further evidence for this hypothesis. While the reconstructions depicted there vary a good deal, virtually all of them show a pronounced warming, albeit with fluctuations, occurring between about AD 800 and 1100. This warming, commonly referred to as the medieval warm period, was followed by an even longer period, from roughly 1100 to 1800, of generally falling temperatures that is known today as the Little Ice Age. By today's standards, human CO_2 emissions before and during the medieval warm period were minimal. And while there were periods of intense volcanic activity at some points during the Little Ice Age, there was nothing like a 700 year period of continuing cooling volcanic aerosol injections. Without anything like the continuous industrial era CO_2 forcing, the earth's climate endured multicentury periods of rising and falling temperatures.

At virtually every time scale, the approach of the IPCC-endorsed climate modeling community to explaining cycles in temperature is to try to find some external forcing that might account for the temperature change. Hegerl et al. (2007) explained the warming from around 1918–1940 – which even has a standard name in the climate modeling world, the Early Twentieth Century Warming – as caused by increasing atmospheric GHGs and also decreased volcanic aerosol cooling. Further back in time, the so-called Little Ice Age from around 1400–1800 that we see in Figure 14.6 has been explained (see Miller et al. 2012; Lehner 2013) as due to a series of major, cooling volcanic eruptions together with a prolonged decrease in incoming solar radiation.

Recently, however, climate modelers that begin by trying to find a forcing that might explain a major temperature cycles often end up finding that at least some substantial fraction of a particular warming or cooling period might have been due not to any forcing, but to the natural (or internal variability) of the climate system. Crook and Forster (2011), for example, found that there was no forcing which allowed the then current set of climate models to replicate warming over the period 1918–1940, and Ring et al. (2012) argued that only strong internal climate variability could explain the hot temperatures of that period. Most recently, Hegerl et al. (2018) concluded that internal climate variability likely played a role in a number of anomalous twentieth-century climate episodes – including rapid Arctic warming in the 1920s and the US dust bowl of the 1930s, but also cold winters and hot summers in Europe in the 1940s.

Such internal climate variability has been described by Essex and Tsonis (2018, 558) as a system of "ultra-slow modes" in the climate system. In these modes, major ocean circulation systems synchronize, driving and sustaining persistent changes in regional and even global temperature, precipitation, and other climate variables. The climate system can get stuck for a very long time. And it gets stuck simply because the climate system is a complex, nonlinear system. No external force needs to act on the climate system to cause such cycling. Whether on the scale of several decades or even centuries, in the everyday sense, nothing "causes" such climate cycles. It is an inherent tendency of the highly nonlinear global climate system.

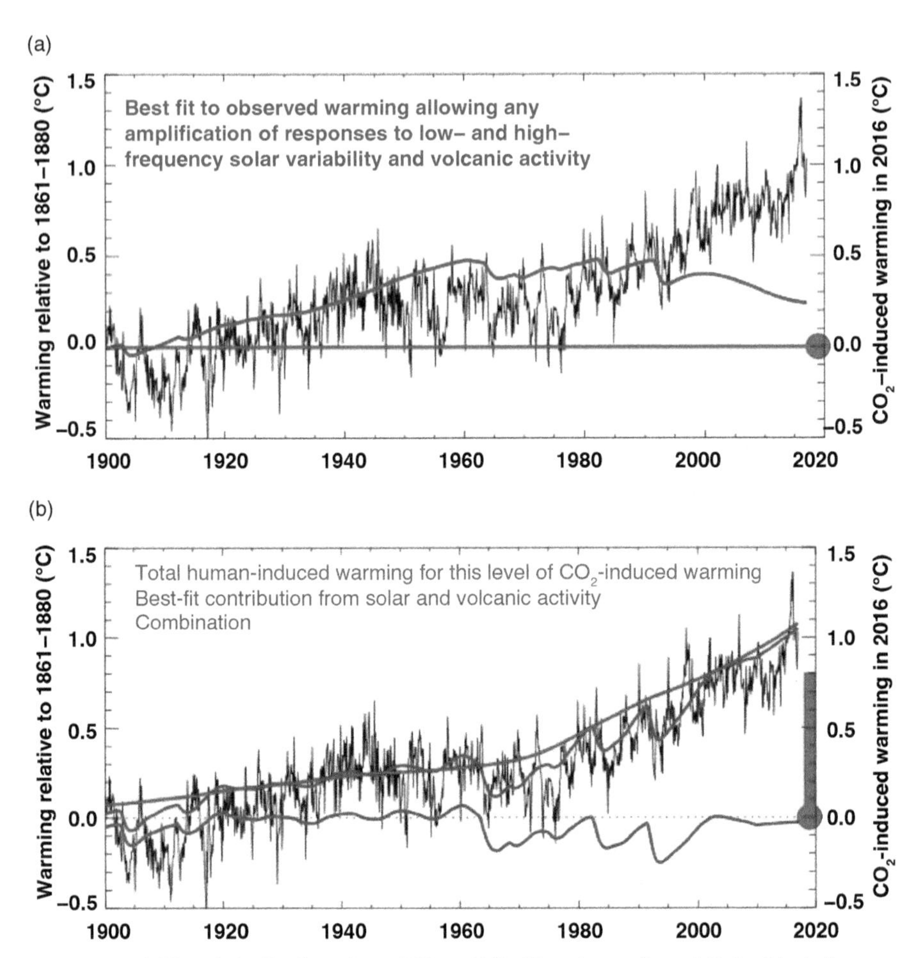

FIGURE 14.6 Heuristic Explanation of How CO2 Plus Aerosols and Solar Variation are Combined to Explain Long Term Secular Change and Short Term Cycles in Surface Temperature.

B *Climate Models Fail to Reproduce Major Ocean Circulation Patterns that Drive Internal Climate Cycles*

As of 2020, at least six such major ocean circulation systems have been identified. Several have only been discovered recently, and more may be identified in the future. One of the longest and best known such system is the El Niño–Southern Oscillation (ENSO). As the IPCC report explains, ENSO is a cycle of anomalous sea surface temperatures and winds in the tropical Pacific. In normal years, winds in the tropical Pacific blow from east to west, with warm water piling up in the western tropical Pacific that provides fuel for tropical monsoons, and cold water accumulating along the west coast of Central and South America. In an El Niño year, this pattern reverses, with westerly winds blowing across the Pacific, bringing unusually warm water to the west coast of the Americas and (often) drought to the Asian Pacific. El Niño has been described as the "dominant" mode of climate variability on seasonal to interannual time scales.[21] For example, as explained by Michaels and Knappenburger (2015) in 1997, an El Niño began with a wave of high sea surface temperatures spreading eastward to Peru. It was so strong that trade winds reversed direction (from northeasterly to southwesterly) and by 1998, global surface temperatures rose to their highest level in the 137 year modern history.

Climate scientists now have very good evidence that the El Niño–Southern Oscillation (ENSO) cycle can itself account for a great deal of the variation in both global and regional surface temperatures that has occurred since 1960. McLean et al. (2009, D14104) show that regardless of which lower tropospheric temperature measure is used, there is a distinct delayed relationship between the state of the ENSO cycle and tropospheric temperatures across the globe. McLean et al. find that the onset of an El Niño triggers an increase in global surface temperatures, while La Nina events are followed by falling average surface temperatures. Strikingly, they find that the global impact of El Niño events extends to the Arctic, correlating very strongly with periods of Arctic warming and decreases in sea ice extent. While the direction of causality is, according to McLean et al., "unclear," what is clear is that since the Great Pacific Climate Shift of 1976, the ENSO cycle has exhibited a pronounced bias toward warming El Niño events.

The head of the US National Climate Data Center at the time Thomas Karl – the same research administrator whose group put together the adjusted US temperatures that both the HadCRUT and GISS have relied upon) – declared that 1998 was the "change point," the beginning of dramatic global warming. Actually, 1998 turned out not to be the beginning of accelerated global warming, but the beginning of a 12 year "hiatus" from rising temperatures. The El Niño of 1998 was just a manifestation of short-term internal climate variability.

Much more important than El Niño in driving long-term climate cycles longer terms, ranging from a few decades to even centuries, are two systems in the Atlantic Ocean. The first, the Atlantic Multidecadal Oscillation (AMO) is a pattern of long-lived changes in sea surface temperature centered in the north Atlantic ocean. According to NOAA, it has alternating "cool and warm phases that may last for 20–40 years at a time and a difference of about 1°F between extremes." As NOAA says, these fluctuations "are natural and have been occurring for at least the last 1,000 years."[22] The AMO has a number of significant climate effects that include changes in ocean currents and subsurface temperatures, and it effects sea surface temperatures outside the North Atlantic (Gorssman and Klotzbach 2009, D24107). A substantial body of empirical work by climate scientists find that the multidecadal fluctuations of the AMO can have substantial impacts on temperature and precipitation in regions across the world.

For example, one (multiple regression) study finds that about 50 percent of the warming in the southwestern United States since 1975 is due to the Atlantic Multidecadal Oscillation (AMO) (Chylek et al. 2014, 119–129). Consistently, another found that ignoring the impact of the AMO caused the GHG-induced warming since 1950 to be overestimated by a factor of two – that is, 200 percent (Tung et al. 2013, 2058–2063).

A closely related Atlantic ocean system is the North Atlantic Oscillation (NAO). This involves a variation in the pressure gradient between the Icelandic (or subpolar) Low and the Azores (or subtropical) High. When the NAO index (the difference in pressure) is high, the subpolar low is especially low and the subtropical high is especially high. This big pressure difference generates a strong jet stream across the Atlantic, bringing storms and warm and moist air to northern Europe (but with typically higher air pressure in the eastern U.S., warmer temperatures and fewer storms to that region). During a negative NAO phase, both the subpolar low and subtropical high are weaker (the low is higher and the high is lower), and the lower pressure gradient means drier and colder northern European winters, with the eastern United States experiencing lower pressure and more winter storms (see Dahlman 2009). Over the period from the late 1960s to the mid-1990s, the NAO tended toward the positive phase. The NAO's impact is global. As Essex and Tsonis (2018) explain, through a variety of interactions with other systems, the NAO can strongly impact the northern Pacific.

The NAO is in turn heavily influenced by the Atlantic Meridional circulation. In this pattern, warm and salty water from the Gulf Stream flows into the North Atlantic current, substantially warming all of western Europe, especially coastal areas, as far north as Norway. Eventually, this salty water cools to the point where it sinks, causing downwelling just north of Iceland and in the Labrador sea southwest of Greenland. If for any reason this downwelling weakens, then the North Atlantic current slows down, leading to rapid decline in western European temperatures.

Recent work has found that both the AMO and the NAO by themselves drive both multidecadal and even multicentennial climate change. Wang et al. (2017) show that on multidecadal time scales, solar and volcanic forcings explain only a small amount (28 percent) of variation in the AMO, but that over the past 1,200 years, the AMO is strongly correlated with Northern Hemisphere temperature at both decadal and multidecadal time scales. Moffa-Sanchez and Hall (2017) similarly find that decreased downwelling of cold waters in the Labrador Sea, perhaps caused by NAO in the low index mode, might have enhanced the southward transport of polar waters, leading to the onset of the Little Ice Age.

Similar ocean current cycles are now known to exist in the Pacific. By the 1990s, climatologists had recognized distinct cycles in the northern Pacific ocean-atmosphere system, one occurring every 50 years or so (multidecadal) and another occurring at the frequency of about every one or two decades (decadal) (Minobe 1999, 855). According to Dong and Dai (2015, 2667–2681), scientists now recognize two separate multidecadal cycles in the Pacific, the Pacific Decadal Oscillation (PDO) in the North Pacific and the Interdecadal Pacific Oscillation (IPO) across the Pacific basin. There are a variety of competing explanations for these cycles,[23] but the main point for present purposes is that all the scientific work trying to explain these cycles presupposes that both the decadal and multidecadal cycles are not caused by anything external to the global climate system. Instead they are simply a manifestation of a natural oscillation in the ocean-atmosphere system.[24]

Another thing that climate scientists seem to be very certain about is that multidecadal cycles such as the IPO have major impacts temperature and precipitation in many regions of the world ranging from the southwestern United States to western Canada, Alaska, and eastern Australia and southern Africa.[25] As my earlier figures showing multidecadal cycles in temperature suggest, climate scientists say that major climatic regime shifts[26] have occurred in the 1920s, the 1940s, and the late 1970s.[27] It has been shown that these periods of very rapid and major climate regime shifts have been times when the decadal and multidecadal Pacific cycles synchronized and interacted.[28] Significant cooling was observed in regions of North America, Canada and Alaska observed in the 1940s, and significant warming observed over those places after the 1970s regime shift (Minobe 1999, 683).

(a) The IPCC Ignores Internal Climate Variability

In its first full-length AR, which appeared in 2001, the IPCC mentioned internal climate variability 12 times,[29] but only in dismissing such internal cycles as of any importance in explaining climate change. There was no discussion in 2001 of any attempt to use climate models to actually explain such internal variability.

If we skip ahead to the 2013 AR5, we find that in attributing recent climate change overwhelmingly to anthropogenic GHG emissions, the Summary for Policymakers in the IPCC's 2013 report barely mentions internal climate variability as a potential cause, stating only that such cycles likely contributed on net 0°C to industrial era warming.[30] On the other hand, According to the IPCC, "internal decadal variability" can cause 10–15 year hiatus periods in long-term temperature increases caused by things like increasing anthropogenic GHG emissions. As we can see from Figure 14.5, there was such a hiatus in HadCRUT temperatures over the period 1998–2011. Despite the fact that 111 out of 114 climate models used by the IPCC predicted temperatures that were higher than those observed over the 1998–2012 "hiatus" period – thus failing to predict anything like a hiatus – the IPCC still says that climate models can generate decade-long pauses in temperature increase even during a "prolonged phase of energy uptake by the climate system."[31] It concludes with "high confidence" that "most 15-year [temperature] trends in the near-term future will be larger than during 1998–2012."[32]

Given that 97 percent of climate models failed to predict the temperature increase slowdown that occurred between 1998 and 2012, it seems fair to ask how the IPCC can be highly confident in climate model predictions that temperature trends over 15 year periods in the near term will be larger than the temperature increase observed between 1998 and 2012, and virtually certain that internal climate variability has contributed exactly 0°C to temperature increases since 1951. For an answer, the IPCC Technical Summary refers the reader to the portion of its full AR that discusses the ability of climate models to explain decadal to multidecadal cycles in the earth's climate system. That discussion, however, shows precisely the opposite to what the IPCC says in its Technical Summary: climate models are unable to explain the earth's major ocean cycles that drive temperature cycles.

- As for cycles in the North Atlantic, the IPCC reports[33] that models do a very poor job:

> Models substantially overestimate persistence [of such cycles] on subseasonal and seasonal time scales, and have difficulty simulating the seasonal timescale. ... As described in the [2007] AR4, *climate models have generally been unable to simulate changes as strong as the observed NAO trend over the period 1965–1995 ... However, there are a few exceptions to this ... so it is unclear to what extent the underestimation of late 20th century trends reflects model shortcomings versus internal variability.*[34]

Remember that the IPCC Report says in its Summary for Policymakers that by using climate models, it is able to conclude that internal climate variability caused by cycles such as the NAO haven't contributed anything to recent warming. But in the quote above, the actual IPCC report says that the models fail to capture NAO cycles and it concludes with a nonsense sentence: as some models do better than others, it could be that some models have "shortcomings" or that there is apparently too much internal variability.

- As for the AMO – which as previously described here is an Atlantic cycle of much longer periods, indeed up to 70 years long according to the IPCC – the IPCC notes that the observed cycles are not "in phase" with those produced by computer climate models, which implies that the cycles do not result from increased atmospheric GHG. Hence the models do show a "key role for internal variability," but "the spatial patterns of variability related to the AMO" vary from model to model.[35]
- Turning next to the most famous ocean circulation pattern, ENSO, the IPCC first reports happily that the "representation of ENSO in climate models has steadily improved and now bears considerable similarity to observed ENSO properties," but then quickly admits that "simulations of both background climate ... and internal variability exhibit serious systematic errors ... many of which can be traced to the representation of deep convection, trade wind strength and cloud feedbacks, with little improvement" over two generations of climate models.[36]
- Turning finally to the PDO, a cycle recognized only in the 1990s, the IPCC says about half of the climate models simulate the spatial pattern and temporal frequency, but the models "strongly underestimate" the correlation between the PDO and sea surface temperature in the topical Indo-Pacific.[37]

I have seen nothing in the literature to contradict the IPCC's AR5 conclusions that it is "virtually certain that internal variability alone cannot account for the observed warming since 1951."[38] But this is a straw man. The question is not whether internal variability accounts for *all* recent temperature change, but rather *how much* of the recent warming is due to internal variability and how much is accounted for by the long-term increase in atmospheric GHG concentration. The report itself says that the models cannot explain any of the primary ocean circulation patterns that drive internal climate variability. According to the IPCC itself, the models are not in phase with the AMO, have "serious systematic errors" not only in accounting for ENSO but also in accounting for the equatorial climate background of ENSO, and "seriously" underestimate the impact of the PDO on sea surface temperatures. In light of how the models are doing, it seems more than possible that they might be underestimating internal variability by a factor of three, indeed, they could be underestimating it by a factor of 10. Regardless, the IPCC's conclusion set out in both the Summary for Policymakers that internal variability accounts for precisely 0° C of recent warming is completely unsupported by what the Report it is supposedly summarizing actually says.

(b) In Part because They Do Not Capture Internal Variability, Climate Models Cannot Reproduce or Predict Regional Climate

In its 2013 AR5, the IPCC (2013, 1222) explains that regional climates are determined both by what it calls "large-scale phenomena such as the El Niño–Southern Oscillation (ENSO) and other dominant modes of climate variability," by regional phenomena such as seasonal monsoons and by "local weather systems that control the net transport of heat, moisture and momentum into a region." As we have just seen, the IPCC reported that climate models are generally very poor at reproducing major ocean circulatory systems such as ENSO. As for cycles operating on even shorter time scales, models appear to be no better. The Madden–Julian Oscillation (MJO) – which as the IPCC describes (2013, 1237) is "the dominant mode of tropical intraseasonal (20 to 100 days) variability" – impacts tropical cyclone activity and causes "intraseasonal fluctuations" of the monsoons with implications for weather far outside the tropics. But as the IPCC concludes (2013, 1240), the computer climate models have "poor skill … in simulating MJO and the sensitivity of its change to SST [sea surface temperature] warming patterns that are themselves subject to large uncertainties in the projections."

As for explaining and projecting changes in monsoon systems themselves, models seem no better. The IPCC (2013, 1220) reached conclusions about changes in such systems with at most "medium" confidence and, just as often, "low confidence." Finally, for tropical cyclones, while the IPCC reports that models do generate some global predictions – such as the prediction that "based on process understanding and agreement in twenty-first-century projections, it is *likely* that the global frequency of occurrence of tropical cyclones will either decrease or remain essentially unchanged" – at the regional level, "the specific characteristics of the changes are not yet well quantified and there is *low confidence* in region-specific projections of frequency and intensity" (IPCC 2013 1220).

With such relatively poor ability to replicate many of the major forces shaping regional climate, it is unsurprising that general circulation climate models do not do a very good job of actually replicating observations of local and regional weather variables such as temperature and precipitation. Van Ulden and Van Oldenborgh (2005) found that "most" climate models could not accurately reproduce the North Atlantic Oscillation, with "bias patterns in sea level pressure fields simulated by global coupled models" at "very large scales of thousands of kilometers." For western Europe, the models generated much stronger wintertime westerlies (and hence warmer temperatures) than observed. Comparing observations versus model predictions at 55 weather stations across the world, Anagnostopoulos et al. (2010) found that while climate models could replicate seasonal (monthly) and latitudinal variation in temperature and precipitation, they did a very poor job of capturing annual variation in temperature and precipitation. Perhaps most disturbingly – given that climate is defined as the 30 year average of weather variables – Anagnostopoulos et al. (2010, 1102–1103) found that model predictions differed from "actual data in the change in the 30-year moving average temperature and precipitation through the 20th century, as well as in the maximum fluctuation of these variables across the entire period of study. ... In many cases, the model outputs show a temperature rise when the temperature actually falls." Thus it seems that climate models cannot reproduce even the *direction, let alone the magnitude* of local climate change.

To be sure, as explained by Pielke and Wilby (2011), regional climate models, downscaled from global climate models, are also used to derive regional climate projections. But this downscaling still suffers from the same errors in predicting important atmospheric and ocean regional circulations. Regional climate models have smaller grid boxes – higher resolution – then do global climate models, but the global models are still used to provide boundary conditions that constrain the behavior of regional models. As Pielke and Wilby (2012) explain, all of the problems with the global scale models – the inability to capture large-scale circulation patterns mentioned above, for example – plus the inherent error in using output at the relatively coarse global scale to constrain finer scale regional models mean that problems with global models propagate through to regional climate models. As Maraun (2016, 215) puts it, biases and uncertainties in global climate models are "inherited" by regional models. As Maraun (2016, 215) further explains:

> at regional scales, both global and regional climate models may mis-represent orography, feedbacks with the land surface, and sub-grid processes such that local surface climate is considerably biased. It is also not a priori clear whether sub-grid parameterizations, tuned to describe present climate, are valid under future climate conditions. For instance, there is evidence that the response of phenomena such as

summer convective precipitation is not plausibly captured by operational RCMs (regional climate models) at a resolution of 10 km and beyond. In other words, in several cases, simulated climate change trends might be implausible, and biases are expected to be time dependent.

With any kind of computer model (climate or economic), when biases are time dependent, statistical correction for model biases – using the statistical relationship between observed versus modeled past weather variables to change model output – cannot be relied upon to eliminate future bias.

C *Urbanization and Regional Land Use Change Cause Climate Change*

The importance of land use change to climate change at all scales – from the local to the global – is clearly and thoroughly explained in a recent study by Mahmood et al. (2014, 929–953). This study, coauthored by 19 scientists, discusses and cites more than 300 published papers finding the land use change has powerful and diverse impacts on climate. As Mahmood et al. summarize:

> LCC [land cover change] impacts on temperature depend on the type of conversion. In particular, urbanization leads to significant warming while agriculture often leads to cooling. Agriculture-related cooling is further magnified if irrigation is introduced. On the other hand, tropical deforestation may lead to net warming, while in the mid-latitudes it may lead to cooling. Globally, deforestation may result in cooling. Also, afforestation may lead to low-latitude cooling and high-latitude warming. (940)

There thus seems little doubt that regional land use change and development is an important cause of climate change. As for urbanization, as anybody living in a rapidly urbanizing place can tell you, such temperature changes are real. It really is a lot warmer at night in a downtown area than a lightly developed exurban area near the downtown. A weather station with a fixed location that was once farmland but is now paved over and surrounded by shopping malls and housing subdivisions and office complexes will record higher temperatures, especially at night, simply because of the change in land use. Higher temperature measurements at such a station do not reflect "bias," but an actual warming of the local climate.

A recent study (Gallo and Xian 2016, 77–83) using satellite imaging technology found that 87 percent of weather stations in the USHCN experienced such urbanizing changes in land surface (more precisely, an increase in impervious surface area) within 1,000 m (about 0.6 of a mile) of the station. In its most dramatic form – downtown areas of cities versus exurban areas – this is known as the urban heat island effect.

In a very large number of studies, the impact of urbanization and land use conversion is measured by comparing temperature trends at weather stations located within cities to those in nearby rural areas. Consistent with the sensitivity of minimum temperatures to land surface features, this literature finds huge differences between trends in minimum temperatures and much smaller differences in maximum temperature trends between cities and nearby rural areas.

- A study of Las Vegas found that between 1940 and 2009, the average minimum temperature at Las Vegas increased by 5.1°C, versus 1.1°C at the single rural Nevada station near Las Vegas that existed in 1940. Over the period since 1977, when more weather stations were put up in rural areas in the Las Vegas region, the minimum temperature in Las Vegas increased by 3.4°C, versus 0.6°C at an average of these more rural locations (Miller 2011, 30). These are enormous differences in trend, with minimum temperature increases in Las Vegas as much as 500–600 percent bigger than in the surrounding less developed region.
- Brazel et al. (2000) looked at how temperatures changed in urban versus rural sites in Baltimore and Phoenix over a period from around 1900 until the mid-1990s. They compared both maximum and minimum temperature trends for selected months in two rural locations 12–15 miles outside urban Baltimore and Phoenix to temperatures at various weather stations in those two cities. Even for the relatively slowly urbanizing Baltimore area, Brazel et al. found that urban minimum temperatures were increasing relative to rural minimums. A peak urban–rural difference of about 4°C was reached in the late 1960s. (After that time, population decline in Baltimore accelerated, and urbanization overtook their rural station in Woodstock, Maryland.) Phoenix underwent rapid post–World War II urbanization, and for Phoenix, the urban–rural minimum temperature difference steadily increased over the period since 1940, reaching between 4° and 6°C by 1995 (depending upon which urban Phoenix station is used).
- Fujibe's (2011) study of surface temperatures over the 1901–2008 period in Japan found that compared to surrounding nonurban sites (defined as places with population density less than 100 per square kilometer), temperature in the most densely populated locations (with density bigger than 3,000/km^2) increased by an additional 0.12°C per decade and that even small towns of between 100 and 300 persons per square kilometer increased an additional 0.03°–0.05°C per decade. Fujibe found that temperatures in Tokyo increased at a linear trend of 3°C per century, compared to 0.5°C per century at Hachijo Island located only 300 km south of Tokyo, and that the Tokyo urban heat island (with temperatures rising 1°C or more relative to rural areas) extended out about 100 km from the border of Tokyo, "covering dozens of cities and the surrounding rural areas."
- Kim and Kim (2011) found that over the 54 year period 1954–2008, urban warming accounted for 0.77°C of the average warming of the Korean peninsula of about 1.37°C, compared to greenhouse warming of 0.60°C. In multiple regression analysis, Kim and Kim found that whereas average population over

the period explained little of the temperature change (excerpt for the largest city, Seoul), population *growth* over the period explained a large part of the temperature change. Population growth in cities that rapidly industrialized beginning in the 1970s, such as Pohang, accounted for as much as about 1.2°C of warming.

- Summarizing over a dozen studies that have looked at homogenized temperature measures, Ren reports that over the period 1960–2000 (2004 for mainland China) urbanization-induced warming was 0.11°C per decade (or 0.44°C for the entire period) for North China and 0.08 per decade (or 0.32°C over the period) for mainland China (Ren 2015, 1–6).
- Mohan and Kandya (2015) found that even over the brief period 2001–2011, rapid urbanization in the Delhi, India, area drove up minimum temperatures, as whereas only 26.4 percent of the total area had a daily temperature range below 11°C in 2001, 65 percent of the Delhi area had such a narrow range by 2011.
- In two very general studies, McKitrick and Michaels and McKitrick and Neirenberg[39] found that socioeconomic variables capturing changes in economic development in an area were statistically significant in explaining *as much of half of observed temperature increases.*
- An equally general study by Kalnay and Cai (2003) estimated that in the United States, changes in land use such as urbanization and agriculture increased average surface temperatures by 0.27°C per century, more than twice as high as the figures used in IPCC-endorsed temperature datasets.

Work that actually compares temperature trends in urban versus rural weather stations thus finds that as population density increases and land use becomes more urban, so too does temperature. This work finds very large differences in temperature trends, with the difference between urban and rural minimum temperatures increasing over the period of a century by 300 percent (4°C) in Phoenix and average temperatures in Tokyo by 600 percent over a century, urban warming accounting for more than half of all warming in the second half of the twentieth century in Korea and 0.44°C for North China. All of these studies are consistent with the finding in work by McKitrick and colleagues that over half of observed warming can be explained by regional development and land surface change.

(a) Temperature Trends in Nonurbanizing Places: The Example of Iowa

With urbanization having such a huge impact in increasing surface temperatures, the obvious thing to do is to look at surface temperature trends at a large number of weather stations in nonurbanizing locations. To my knowledge, no one – including the producers of the HadCRUT and GISS data sets – has ever assembled temperature trends for a large number of nonurbanizing locations.

Iowa is a state that has a large number of such stations. During the second half of the twentieth century, the vast majority of towns in Iowa did not undergo development and urbanization, but the opposite, steadily losing population and deurbanizing. In addition, corn and soybeans have been the virtually exclusive crops grown in Iowa since at least World War II and they are grown without irrigation. (This matters because irrigation can markedly effect nighttime low temperatures.) Iowa is very important in the story of climate change policy, for 17 percent of all US corn is produced in Iowa,[40] and the remarkable increase in the productivity of Iowa corn farmers carries key lessons for climate change adaptation that I discuss in some detail later.

Since Iowa plays such a big part of the story I tell below of increasingly productive US agriculture, I have selected 14 Iowa weather stations in towns that span the state of Iowa (running from Rock Rapids, in the extreme northwest, down to Corning, in the southwest and Keosaqua in the southeast, up to Decorah, in the far northeast). The population in 11 of these 14 towns has steadily decreased since 2000.[41] Based on what is reported by NOAA's NCDC, these towns have also had a constant time of observation from at least 1948 until the mid-2000s.[42] Of my 14 stations, 11 are included in the network of stations used for the GISS US temperature measurements.[43] Only a few of my Iowa stations are included in the HadCRUT data set (most of the small-town Iowa stations included in HadCRUT station data set had both changing time of observation and instrument changes during the 1980s).[44]

Figure 14.7 depicts summertime average highs (14.7(a)) and lows (14.7(b)) since 1893 for my 14 Iowa weather stations. It must be cautioned that these are actual temperatures, not temperature deviations from an average over some period (that is, they are not anomalies). Note that the straight lines in this and subsequent Iowa figures cover gaps in temperature data from particular stations.

Just from casual observation of Figure 14.7 it seems apparent that even though my Iowa stations span the entire state, and therefore have summer temperatures that vary quite a bit for any given year, they move together very closely. It also seems clear that for the vast majority of stations, summer average high temperatures have never exceed the extremely high values that they reached during the mid-1930s. On the other hand, summer minimum temperatures do seem to have steadily increased since about 1980.

Next we can look at smoothed versions of these first two station-specific graphs. Such smoothed versions are displayed in Figures 14.8(a) and (b). I have used a smoothing algorithm that fits a linear regression model to each point, using the closest 9 percent of neighboring points. This is a shorter smoothing period than I previously used, and I have adopted the shorter period here because this is roughly the same smoothing approach taken in the most recent GISS temperature graphs presented above. With a shorter smoothing period, one gets a smoothed red line that picks up even relatively short-term (10 years or less) trends.

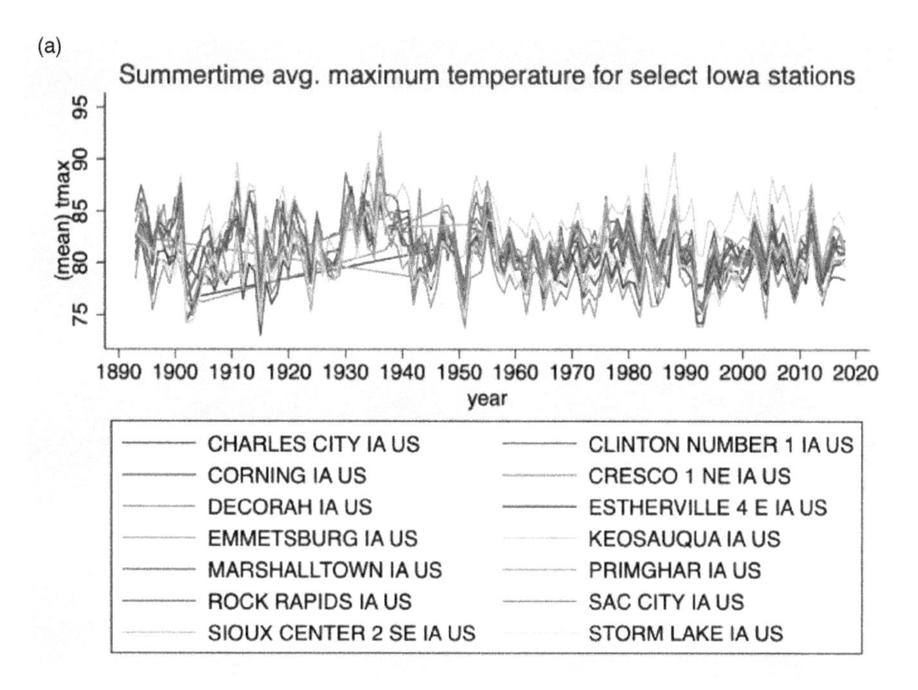

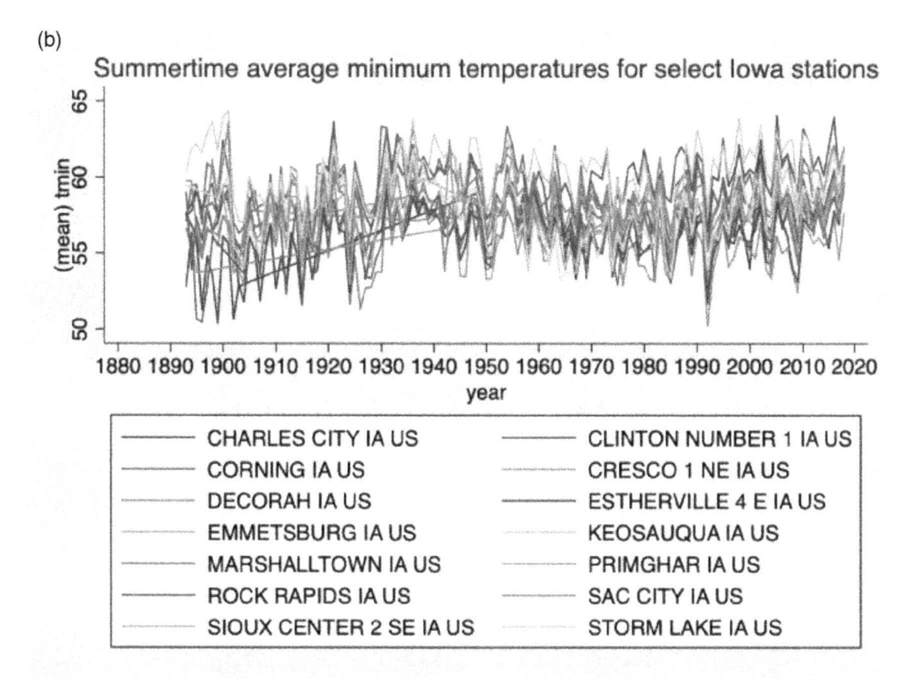

FIGURE 14.7 Average June–September (top) high temperatures and (bottom) low temperatures for selected Iowa stations, 1893–2018.

(a)

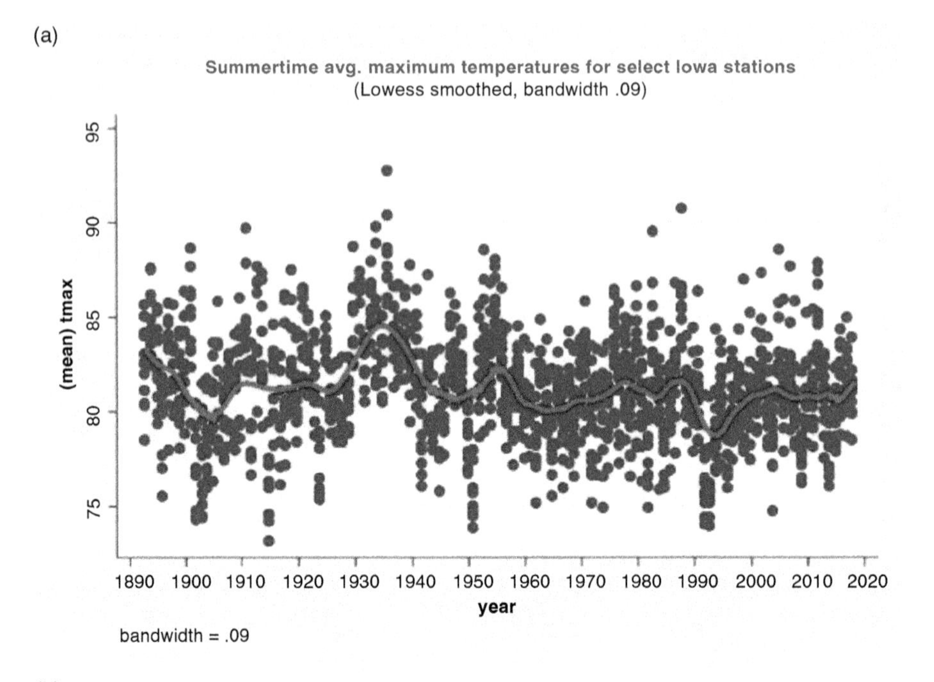

(b)

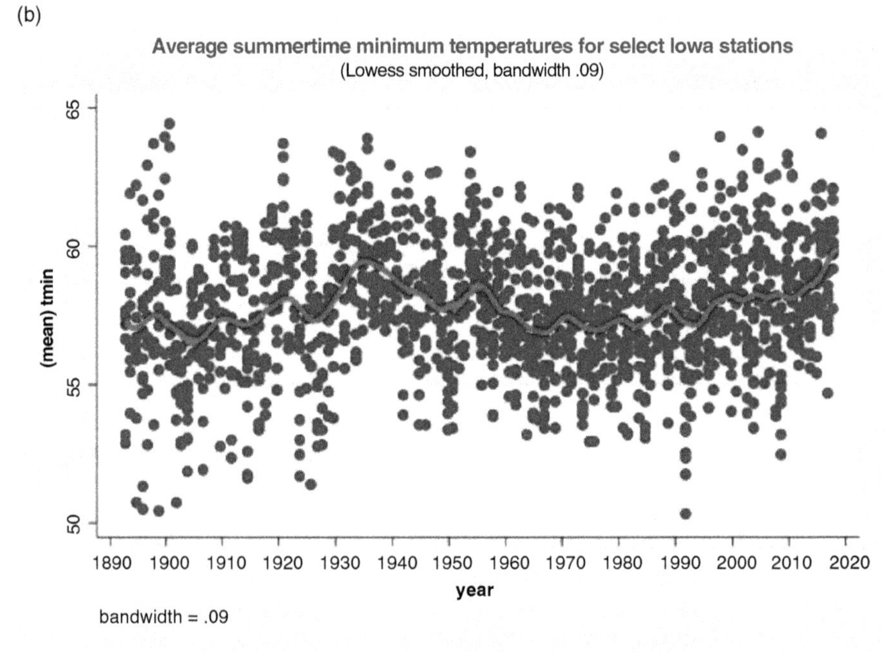

FIGURE 14.8 Loess smoothed summer average (a) maximum and (b) minimum temperatures for select Iowa stations.

Using this particular smoothing algorithm as a way to detect short and medium term (10–50 year) trends in the temperature data, we can see the incredible decade-long heat wave that spanned the late 1920s to late 1930s, the mid-1950s heat wave, and the roughly half-century period of stable or declining summer high temperatures that began in the late 1950s and continues today. As for summer minimum temperatures, we can see that the long increase in these that began around 1960 has finally brought summer lows above the very high levels they reached in the mid-1930s.

I chose my stations because they have had a long period of constant time of observation. Virtually all of them switched from LIG thermometers to MMTS sensors in the mid-1980s to mid-1990s, and I have not tried to correct for that. If we did make the standard corrections for this switch – slightly lowering minimum temperatures and increasing maximum temperatures by a bit more – average summer highs (Figure 14.8(a)) would show a slight increase since 1980 while the increase in average summer lows since 1980 would be smaller. Average summer highs, however, would still not approach the levels they reached in the 1930s.

Looking now at winter (December–March) average highs (Figure 14.9(a)) and lows (Figure 14.9(b)) for my Iowa stations (with winter 2019 included), we see a rather different pattern: essentially no trend in either highs or lows since 1893. Like virtually all smoothing algorithms, for most recent years, the smoothed red lines in Figure 14.9 overweight the last observation, the very cold winter of 2019. With this caveat, Figure 14.9 reveals trends that span decades (called multidecadal trends in the climate literature) – a steady increase in winter temperatures beginning in what seems to have been a very cold period ending about 1890 and lasting until the warm 1930s, a long decline from the 1930s until about 1980, and then a period of constant temperatures that may be ending in favor of declining temperatures. For the overall period 1893–2019, there appears to be no trend of any sort.

For my small, depopulating Iowa towns, we thus see essentially very little if any change in summertime or wintertime average highs and lows since 1893. Of course, my sample is small, only 14 towns. One would like to see temperature trends at hundreds of similarly rural, depopulating towns located in other regions in the United States and indeed across the world. As important as such evidence would be in distinguishing between land use change and atmospheric CO_2 change in causing rising surface temperatures, I am aware of no such study. The lack of any trend at my small, depopulating Iowa towns is important not only as a concrete illustration of temperature trends in depopulating places in one region of huge agricultural importance, but even more important in raising the question of why, with so much money devoted to climate change research, national and international databases of temperature trends at more such locations have not been produced.

At the national level, my Iowa stations are atypical. Since World War II, US population increases have been concentrated in suburban and (most recently) exurban areas. During both the 1960s and 1970s, the most rapidly growing counties had the highest rates of land conversion from rural to urban uses.[45] Back in 1994, US

(a)

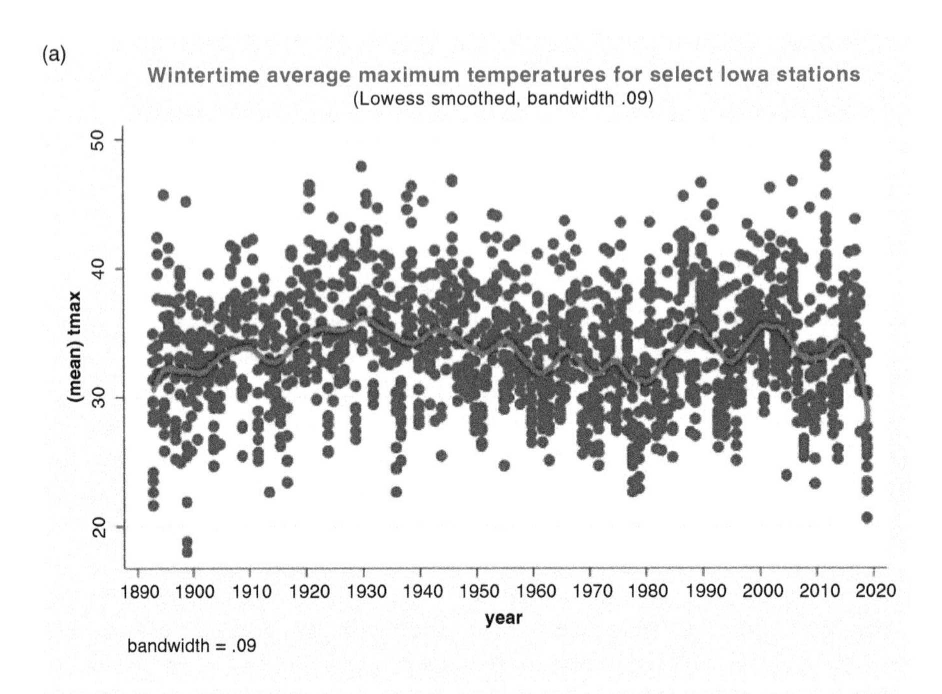

(b)

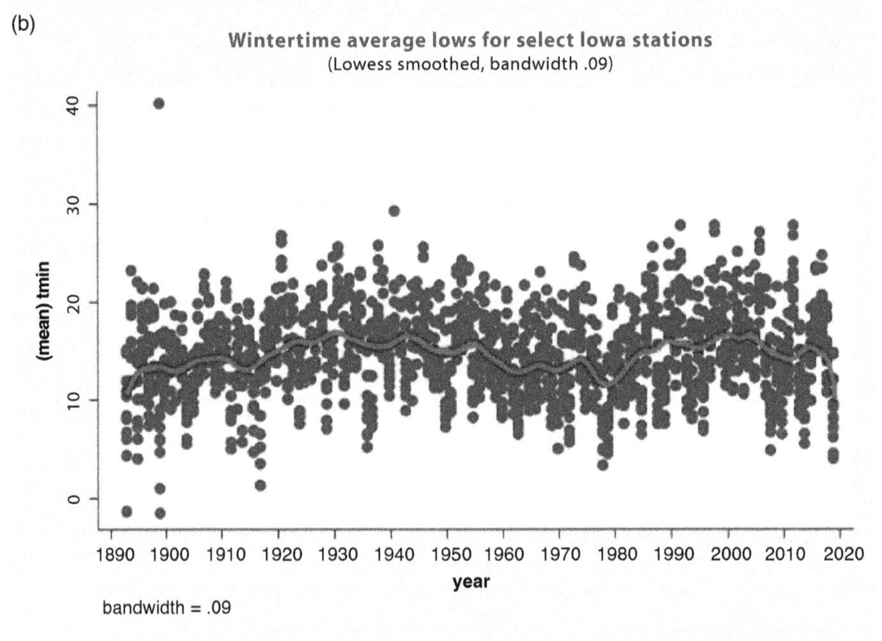

FIGURE 14.9 Loess smoothed winter average (a) maximum and (b) minimum temperatures for select Iowa stations.

Department of Agriculture researchers noted that there was still plenty of rural land in the United States and projected that if the 1960–1980 rate continued over the period 1980–2000, the US urban area would only reach 66 million acres by 2000. As can be seen from Figure 14.10, this projection was far too low.[46]

As can be seen from Figure 14.10, over the period 1982–2012, the amount of developed land in the United States increased by 58 percent, or almost 2 percent per year on average. As the figure shows, this rapid increase in the amount of developed land coincides very closely with the increase in US temperature anomaly reported by GISS.

Of course, Figure 14.10 does not prove that the increase in developed land has caused the increase in US temperature anomalies seen since 1982. After all, as we have seen previously, atmospheric CO_2 concentration also began to increase more rapidly in the 1970s. The point of Figure 14.10 is simply that there have been massive changes in land use since the 1970s, and a very large body of scientific work reports that such changes clearly impact regional and local surface temperatures.

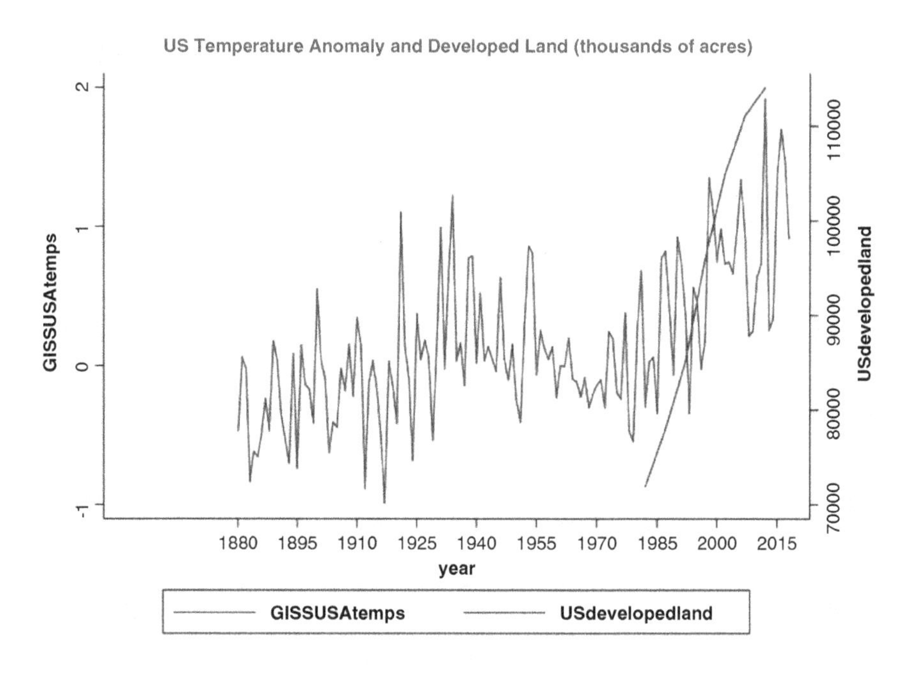

FIGURE 14.10 Increase in US developed land and US temperatures. Based on data summarized in USDA 2012 National Resources Inventory, 2015 Summary Report, available at www.nrcs.usda.gov/Internet/FSE_DOCUMENTS/nrcseprd396218.pdf.

(b) The IPCC Minimizes the Significance of Land Use Conversion and Urbanization for Climate Change

According to the IPCC's 2013 AR5,[47] along with problems with weather station sites, the effects of regional development in increasing temperatures have been corrected in various ways, and "despite the range of variations in approaches, the long-term variations and trends broadly agree among the various LSAT (land-surface air temperature) estimates, particularly after 1900." But the fact that corrected temperature time series tend to agree with one another says nothing about the reliability of how they incorporated the impact of regional development and land use change in altering global temperatures.

To be sure, in its AR5, the IPCC did mention some of the work finding that urbanization and economic development had contributed substantially to increasing (especially minimum) temperatures during the latter part of the twentieth century. For example, the IPCC AR5 cited the published work by McKitrick and Michaels (2007) and McKitrick and Neirenberg (2010)[48] that I summarized above. And the IPCC finds little or no work actually contradicting these findings. Instead, it looks completely away from actual empirical studies, and compares the results of statistical analysis of the relationship of temperature change and socioeconomic development trends to what models predict. This may seem shocking, so I quote:[49]

> A hypothesized residual warming artefact is … physically inconsistent with many other components of the global observing system according to a broad range of state-of-the-art data assimilation models. … Further [a 2010 study] estimate an absolute upper limit on urban influence globally of 0.02 C per decade, or about 15% of the total [surface temperature] trends, in 1951–2009.

To translate, the IPCC is saying that because computer models that explain various unspecified climate observations estimate that development and urbanization could not increase surface temperatures by more than 0.02°C per decade, empirical evidence that the increase is much bigger must be wrong. The IPCC concludes that "it is unlikely that any uncorrected urban heat island effects and [land use cover change] effects have raised the estimated centennial globally averaged [temperature] trends by more than 10% of the reported trend (high confidence, based on robust evidence and high agreement)."[50] This statement misstates the basis for the IPCC's conclusion. That conclusion is not based on "robust evidence," but on rejecting such evidence.

D *Soot Story: Policy Influences on the IPCC Reports about the Causes of Climate Change*

In a campaign designed to generate public support for regulations requiring a reduction in emissions of very small (less than 2.5 μm diameter) dust particles, the

EPA has for many years called such particles "soot." One can see the logic here, as when one hears the word "soot," one surely thinks of black, smoky emissions. But tiny dust particles are not "soot." Black carbon, or soot, is a black smoky emission, not tiny invisible dust particles. Atmospheric chemists define black carbon as an aggregate of small carbonaceous spheres formed during the burning of carbon-based fuels when oxygen levels are not high enough for complete combustion. It is insoluble, vaporizes only at extremely high temperatures, and has very low chemical reactivity in the atmosphere.

The atomic structure of most aerosols emitted from fossil fuel burning – such as sulfur dioxide and oxides of nitrogen – is such that they scatter sunlight and therefore have a cooling impact on climate. Unlike these, black carbon strongly absorbs light at all visible wavelengths. Indeed, as a recent assessment report states, "no other substance with such strong light absorption per unit mass is present in the atmosphere in significant quantities" (Bond et al. 2013, 5380). About 90 percent of black carbon emissions come from a small number of types of sources: diesel engines, which account for 70 percent of black carbon emissions in Europe, North America, and Latin America; residential solid fuels (biomass and coal), which account for 60–80 percent of African and Asian black carbon emissions; and residential coal burning in China, the former USSR, and some Eastern European countries. The remainder of black carbon emissions come from open burning of forests and grasslands. In its 2013 report, the IPCC estimated that in 2000, anthropogenic black carbon emissions totaled 4.8 Gt (gigatons), with 40 percent coming from China and India, 13 percent from the rest of Asia, 10 percent from Africa, and 8 percent each from Europe and North America.

The climate model simulations of industrial era warming that the IPCC relies upon do *not* include one very important aerosol, black carbon, or soot. As discussed above, black carbon is known to be a very strong warming force, second only to atmospheric GHGs. This is striking. Black carbon is known to have been responsible for a substantial portion of the twentieth-century warming in the Arctic, indeed some scientists have said as much as 80–90 percent of Arctic warming. One might well ask how it is that GCM models manage to simulate Arctic temperature increase without even including the aerosol that is known to have had such a huge warming impact there.

Way back in 2002, a *Science* magazine "Perspectives" article summarized the ongoing research into the warming impact of black carbon as suggesting that if black carbon was indeed an important contributor to atmospheric warming, then climate model simulations that somehow managed to reproduce twentieth-century temperature trends without even including black carbon might not be "meaningful" (Chameides and Bergin 2002, 2214). Since climate models omit black carbon, recent work showing black carbon to be a very strong agent of global warming adds weight to the belief that if climate models are explaining twentieth-century warming trends as due solely to increases in CO_2, then they must be vastly overestimating the sensitivity of the Arctic climate to increases in CO_2.

In its Summary for Policymakers and Technical Summary accompanying its 2007 AR, the IPCC had very little to say about black carbon, but what it did say was that although the deposition of black carbon (soot) on snow reduced surface albedo (reflectivity), such deposition was estimated to generate a global warming of only 0.1 W/m^2, a warming about which scientists had only a "low" level of understanding (IPCC 2007, 30). As the actual 2007 AR explained, in the atmosphere, "black carbon strongly absorbs solar radiation," meaning that black carbon in the atmosphere also causes warming. In 2007, in its AR4, the IPCC estimated the total warming effect of black carbon to be about 0.3 W/m^2 (IPCC 2007, 165). In the 2013 AR5, the IPCC increased this estimate to 0.4 W/m^2.[51]

These numbers constitute a very small amount of warming when compared with the 1.66 W/m^2 warming value given to CO_2 concentration increase (the actual increase to date, not a hypothetical doubling) by the IPCC in 2007 (Service 2008, 1745) and the higher value of 1.82 value assigned to CO_2 forcing by the IPCC in its 2013 AR.[52] According to the IPCC's 2013 AR5, black carbon accounts for a little more than tenth as much warming as does CO_2.

Beyond quantifying its warming at a very low level, the IPCC's 2013 assessment report says virtually nothing about black carbon. The 2013 IPCC Summary for Policymakers – which as I explained earlier is released months before the full assessment report to which it refers[53] – mentions black carbon only in stating that all atmospheric aerosols, including cloud adjustments, have a negative effect on warming, with only black carbon having a positive effect, but concluding with "high confidence that aerosols and their interactions with clouds have offset a substantial portion of global mean forcing from well-mixed greenhouse gases." The actual text of the 2013 climate science assessment says only that black carbon lasts only from a week to 10 days in the atmosphere[54] (and hence it is now typically referred to as a short-lived climate pollutant), and that black carbon is "more difficult to measure than scattering aerosols, but also induces a complicated cloud response."[55] This fleeting mention of black carbon is immediately followed by the IPCC reiterating that "the overall radiative effect from anthropogenic aerosols is to cool the planet."

(a) The Scientific Literature Shows, Contrary to the IPCC, That Black Carbon Causes Powerful, Regionally Concentrated Warming

If one relied just upon the Assessment Reports put out by the IPCC over the past 15 years, one would think that black carbon is insignificant in explaining recently observed climate changes. Yet there is abundant research, never discussed by the IPCC, to the contrary. As early as 2002, it was estimated that through a variety of mechanisms, black carbon "warmed the air 360,000–

840,000 times more effectively per unit of mass than did CO_2" (Jacobson 2002, 4410). In research that was published around the same time as the release of the 2007 AR, Flanner et al. estimated that in the Arctic, the warming impact of black carbon deposition on snow was a significantly more powerful global warming force than CO_2, indeed three times more powerful, and had resulted in an Arctic surface warming of between 0.5° and 1°C over the previous century (Flanner et al. 2007, D11202). By the summer of 2007, climate scientist Charles Zender was suggesting to *Scientific American* magazine that as much as 94 percent of warming in the Arctic over the last 100 years due to the deposition of black carbon on snow and ice in that region.[56]

About a year after the appearance of the IPCC's 2007 Assessment Report, a review article on black carbon was published in which the authors estimated that the warming from black carbon was 0.9 W/m^2 and noted that "similar conclusions regarding the large magnitude of [black carbon] forcing" had been "inferred" by four papers published over the period 1998 to 2003, papers whose own estimates ranged from 0.4 W/m^2 to 1.2 W/m^2 (Ramanathan and Carmichael 2008, 222). Work appearing since the 2007 Assessment Report goes in only one direction when it comes to black carbon: emissions of that pollutant are an even stronger driver of recent changes in Northern Hemisphere climate than was believed previously.

In work appearing in 2013, the very same year as the IPCC's AR5, no fewer than 31 climate scientists specializing in the study of atmospheric aerosols published a 172 page article in *Journal of Geophysical Research* assessing – on the basis not just of climate model simulations but also actual microphysical measurements and field observations – what is currently known about the climatic impact of black carbon (Bond et al. 2013, 5380). This 2013 black carbon (BC) assessment concluded that with a total climate forcing of 1.1 W/m^2, black carbon was the second most important warming agent (after CO_2).

The BC assessment did more than just produce a quantitative estimate of climate warming due to black carbon. It also summarized research showing that the effect of black carbon is not global, as is the effect of increasing GHG concentrations, but regionally concentrated. Unlike atmospheric CO_2, which is generally believed to exist in more or less uniform atmospheric concentration across the earth, BC is a short-lived atmospheric molecule and is concentrated in the mid- to high-latitude Northern Hemisphere. A lot is known about BC's warming effect, and with this understanding, the 2013 BC assessment was able to be pretty specific about where the effects of BC were being felt, pinpointing the Arctic:

> studies indicate that BC may be playing a significant role in two critical areas: *the unexpectedly rapid warming of the Arctic and the retreat of mountain glaciers, particular in areas such as the Himalaya which has high levels of pollution and*

> *where local populations rely heavily on a seasonally balanced hydrologic cycle with glacial melt as a water supply in summer. BC's is snow may have also contributed to the marked decline in Eurasian springtime snow cover since 1979, which has not been reproduced by models that only account for warming due to GHG's.*[57]

In light of the significance attached to Arctic warming and glacial melting as one of the sure signs of climate by the IPCC reports, the importance of the emphasized portion of the BC Assessment should not be missed: more than two dozen experts are saying that black carbon is significant in explaining both the "unexpectedly rapid" Arctic melting and rapid mountain glacier retreat. The BC report indeed explains how BC may be the missing factor which explains twentieth-century Arctic temperature anomalies:

> Notably, the early twentieth century peak in BC in the Greenland ice core (about 1890–1950) leads by about 20 years a period of strong positive regional surface air temperature anomalies from 1920 to 1965. ... This warming has generally been attributed to solar and natural variability. However, ... [in such models] only about half of the early twentieth century Arctic (60 degree to 90 degree N) temperature rise can be attributed to the combined effects of GHG's, natural forcings and tropospheric ozone. Natural variability is unable to account for the remainder in most models, implying that a portion of the warming should be interpreted as due to aerosol climate forcing.[58]

Scientists appear to have considerable knowledge not only of which regions of the world are most impacted by warming BC emissions, but also of where those emissions come from. surface-deposited BC in the Arctic comes from European emissions, and, more specifically, from biomass burning in Russia.[59] BC contributing to springtime melting in higher altitudes of Greenland is "most strongly influenced" by East Asian monsoons, which "loft pollutant to higher altitudes where they can transported long distances ... chemical analysis of surface snow samples from the Greenland plateau indicate that the BC is largely from biomass or biofuel burning sources in the spring and that fossil fuel sources dominate in the summer."[60] The source of BC in Himalayan snow varies a great deal across different locations; however, looking at sites on Mount Everest and across the Tibetan Plateau, one study found that BC in the atmosphere at all of these sites was from various regions of China, with site-specific contributions from India, Pakistan, and the Middle East. Another study, looking at the Himalayan and Tibetan Plateaus over the period 1996 to 2010, found that India, China, and other South Asian countries were the dominant contributors, with "significant contributions" also from Russia and the Middle East.[61] These BC depositions are important, as at least one model study found that BC in snow forcing over the Tibetan Plateau averaged 1.3 W/m^2 over the whole region and reached a maximum of 10–20 W/m^2 in the spring over snow-covered surfaces.[62] Thus even though the BC Assessment is at great pains to stress the difficulty of coming up with a "robust estimate of forcing by BC in snow in the Tibetan Plateau,"[63] the estimates that have been generated to date are very big indeed.

While much is known about where BC emissions come from and their regional impact, BC has not generally been incorporated into computer models of global climate. Unfortunately, as of 2013, by which time there had been literally thousands of published papers reporting the results of simulating computer climate models with varying GHG concentrations, there had been only one systematic study of the regional impact of BC aerosols from different regions.[64]

(b) The IPCC's 2013 Scientific Assessment Neglected Black Carbon Entirely for Policy, Not Scientific Reasons

Recall that in its 2013 assessment, the IPCC gave an estimate for black carbon forcing of only 0.4 W/m^2 a value that is about 66 percent smaller than what the experts on black carbon said in 2013. Had the IPCC gone with what the experts on black carbon said, 1.1 W/m^2, it would have been saying that black carbon's warming effect was almost two-thirds as big as the 1.8 W/m^2 that it attributed to carbon dioxide. Moreover, completely unmentioned by the IPCC's 2007 and 2013 reports was the enormous fraction of highly publicized arctic warming – as much as 94 percent over the last 100 years – that scientists who actually specialize in studying black carbon were willing to publicly attribute to black carbon. The IPCC's 2007 and 2013 reports seem to reflect a clear decision to virtually completely ignore a form of anthropogenic pollution – black carbon – that was not only a very substantial contributor to twentieth-century global warming, but an even more important – indeed the most important – factor in twentieth-century arctic warming. The only actual discussion of BC in the IPCC's AR5 is about one-third of a page. It does reference the 2013 BC Assessment, but emphasizes the "current challenges to understanding and quantifying the various effects" of BC.[65] The AR5 then simply states that several computer model studies have looked at the effects of BC (as well as organic carbon) from different regions, "however, examination of the results from these models reveals that *there is not a robust relation between the region of emission and the metric value – hence, regions that yield the highest metric value in one study do not, in general, do so in the other studies.*"[66] The reader should not expect to understand this "explanation." The reference to studies that fail to "robustly" tie regional BC emissions to various "metrics" is highly opaque and can only be understood if one first understands what the IPCC means by "metrics."

Climate metrics are not the same thing as a radiative forcing or feedback, or actually anything that I have yet discussed. Climate metrics are not a scientific concept at all. As the IPCC's 2013 report says, emission metrics are used to "quantify and communicate the relative and absolute contributions to climate change of emissions of different substances." Metrics add up the warming from an emission relative to CO_2, over a given period of time. As the IPCC's 2013 report admits, the choice of the time horizon over which to add up warming is "subjective and context dependent." It also explains that "near term climate forcers, such as black carbon, ... can have impacts comparable to that of CO_2 for short time horizons, ... but their impacts become progressively less for longer time horizons over emissions of CO_2 dominate." As further elaborated in the 2013 BC Assessment, the choice of time horizon is "essentially a value judgment, conceptually related to discounting future costs of the impacts of climate change,"[67] and the "relative importance of different emissions (i.e. the metric values) will depend on how far into the future that threshold is likely to be reached."[68]

The IPCC goes on to explain that metrics are not only based on "subjective" time horizons but are created entirely for policy purposes: "metrics do not define policies or goals, but facilitate analysis and implementation of multi-component policies, ... all choices of metric contain implicit value-related judgments such as type of effect considered and weighting of effects over time."[69] Thus climate "metrics" are measures of climate impacts of emissions of different types of chemicals that attempt to put the impacts on a common scale. "Metrics" are not something that climate scientists invented for the scientific purpose of furthering our understanding of the climate. Climate scientists produce metrics so that politicians negotiating international climate agreements have a currency to use in comparing and bargaining over different national proposal to contribute to the "war" on climate change. Both the effects and the time horizon over which such effects are measured by metrics are, as the IPCC frankly says, "subjective" and policy driven.

With this understanding of what the IPCC means by climate "metrics," one is now able to understand what the IPCC is saying when it dismisses any serious discussion of BC because "*there is not a robust relation between the region of emission and the metric value*." What the IPCC it is saying here is that climate models designed to deal with the impact of GHGs with centuries-long atmospheric half-lives can't generate metrics for BC. As a short-lived molecule in the atmosphere and because its effects are regionally concentrated, the metric value for BC's global impact will depend on region and timing of the emission. As the 2103 BC assessment explains quite precisely, the problem is that as "there have been no studies of the climate forcing due to emissions during different seasons, metric values cannot be differentiated as to when the emission takes place."[70] Moreover, both the indirect effect of black carbon in enhancing snow melt and reducing albedo and its direct short wave scattering effect of BC varies tremendously across different regions of the earth.[71] If one simply added the two effects, as climate metrics do, then the total of the two mechanisms would show little regional dependence.

Thus the IPCC completely fails to discuss the abundant evidence that BC emissions have been responsible for most Arctic warming observed during the twentieth century, and it does so because climate models cannot generate a quantitative value for BC emissions using metrics that are confessedly "subjective" and designed entirely for policy purposes. The use of a CO_2 equivalent metric will almost by definition attach little weight to reductions in the emissions of much shorter-lived molecules such as BC. It cannot be overemphasized that the use of a CO_2 equivalent metric has nothing to do with scientific inquiry into the causes of climate change. The metric reflects a *value judgment* as to how one weighs short-term versus long-term impacts, and its use will inevitably fail to "provide equivalence with respect to regional climate impacts or the temporal development of climate change. Although these latter impacts are the key end points of concern, they are farther down the causal chain and thus, more difficult to capture with simplified and policy-friendly metrics."[72] It is the use of "policy-friendly" metrics that precludes the IPCC from consideration of BC's highly significant role in influencing climate in the northern hemisphere.

When the IPCC AR5 justifies cutting the estimated warming impact of BC by 2/3 from the estimate given by scientists who actually are experts in the study of BC because there are no "robust" estimates of the climate "metric" for BC emissions from different regions, what it essentially is saying is that because BC is a short-lived, regionally concentrated agent of global warming, it will be discounted. But this has nothing to do with what scientists have said about the actual present-day impact of BC emissions on global climate. In fact precisely because BC is a short-lived atmospheric molecule, reducing BC emissions would likely have a very rapid effect on the climate in regions most impacted by BC emissions. In this light, the IPCC's decision to essentially neglect BC in its scientific assessment seems clearly to be driven by a belief that to divert attention to short-lived climate forcers like BC would reduce the apparent significant of CO_2 and other long-lived climate forcers. That is, that the case for reducing CO_2 emissions to avert potential long-term, far distant climate impacts would be weakened if people understood that reducing BC emissions would likely have an immediate impact in slowing warming in certain regions. This is quite obviously not a scientific question pertaining to the impact of emissions of different gases on global climate, but a policy decision.

Notes

1. This paragraph is based on NASA, Earth's Energy Balance, available at https://earthobservatory.nasa.gov/features/SORCE/sorce_02.php; and Kipp and Zonin, "Solar Radiation," available at www.kippzonen.com/Knowledge-Center/Theoretical-info/Solar-Radiation.
2. CO_2 data up to 2011 from https://data.giss.nasa.gov/modelforce/ghgases/Fig1A.ext.txt, after 2011 from Scripps CO_2 Program available at http://scrippsco2.ucsd.edu/data/atmospheric_co2/.

3. This formulation is a modified version of that found in Kiehl (2007, L22710). For a different formulation with the same qualitative meaning, see Hourdin et al. (2017, 597).
4. For a summary of the various forcings that depicts also the degree of uncertainty regarding their magnitude, see IPCC, *Climate Change 2007: The Physical Science Basis*, p. 4.
5. See Schwartz (2007, 23). Note that the indirect effect of aerosols on cloud reflectivity is more properly considered a feedback, and therefore captured in the climate sensitivity parameter, than an external forcing. See the discussion in Knutti (2008, L18704).
6. Thomas F. Stocker and Dahe Qin, *Climate Change 2013: The Physical Science Basis, Working Group I, 5th Assessment Report of the IPCC* (hereafter referred to as WGI AR5), 676 (2013). As they explain, "using the formula from table 3 of Myhre et al. (25 Geophysical Research Letters 2715 (1998)) … the CO_2 RF from 1750 to 2011 is 1.82 W/m^2." Turning to Myhre (1998), one indeed finds numerical estimates of the forcing given in table 3, but it turns out the forcing estimates are derived by using updated parameters but the same functional form as the IPCC used in 1990. The functional form for "simplified radiative forcing," or ΔF, from CO_2 is then given by

$$\Delta F = \ln (C/C_o).$$

   Thus we see that in AR5, the IPCC is still assuming this basic logarithmic relationship, which was assumed by the IPCC as early as 1990, the only difference being that WGI AR5 uses computer general circulation models, to be discussed later, to update the parameter from report to report.
7. Roe and Baker (2007, 630); IPCC, *Climate Change 2007: The Physical Science Basis*, p. 631.
8. This sentence, and much of what is contained in this and the next paragraph, is a summary and paraphrasing of Frederick (2008, 116–147).
9. Washington and Parkinson (2005, 88), but one may consult any climate science textbook for these facts about absorbtivity of O_3, CO_2, and H_2O.
10. On the variety of cloud parameterizations, see Washington and Parkinson (2005, 97–109).
11. Emphasis added.
12. It should be noted that Liu et al. thoroughly discuss how potential uncertainty in their temperature reconstructions might affect the trend they depict and catalog the large number of reconstructions that also show Holocene cooling trends.
13. Emphasis added.
14. See National Academy of Sciences, *Understanding Climate Change Feedbacks* 24 (2003).
15. National Academy of Sciences, *Understanding Climate Change Feedbacks* 24 (2003). This is because, unlike the dry adiabatic lapse rate, the moist adiabatic

lapse rate is affected by the moisture content of the air, with the release of latent heat decreasing the lapse rate. When tropical surface temperature increases, as predicted by climate models, surface air packets hold more moisture and so the moist adiabatic lapse rate near the surface falls, whereas the higher one goes in the troposphere, the colder and drier the air, and so the less affected is the lapse rate by increasing surface temperatures, the higher one goes in the troposphere. For a clear online explanation, see Jeff Haby, "Why the MALR Is Not a Constant," available at www.theweatherprediction.com/habyhints/161. Note that as a consequence of these basic facts, the change in the tropical moist adiabatic lapse rate predicted by climate models is a direct consequence of what they predict about changes in water vapor at low levels of the troposphere.

16. More detailed discussion and analysis of problems with atmospheric temperature data, and the conclusion that "it is uncertain whether tropospheric warming has exceeded that at the surface because the spread of trends among tropospheric data sets encompasses the surface warming trend," appears in the "Observations: Surface and Atmospheric Climate Change" chapter in *Climate Change 2007*, p. 271.
17. The mean for each model is used because the models are subject to large number of simulations, or runs, each generating a different temperature trend because each model includes noise term plus nonlinearities.
18. Inflated by decreasing the number of sample periods used to calculate the sample variance, a method employed by the authors to account for the autocorrelation in the error terms of the estimates due to regular – but assumed random – shifts in climate induced by ENSO cycles.
19. IPCC AR5, pp. 772–773.
20. Allen (2018); City of Oakland v. BP PLC, No. 3:17-cv-06012-WHA, Exhibit 5, Document 157–5 (N.D. Cal. March 23, 2018).
21. IPCC AR5, p. 803; Zhou and Tung (2013).
22. See NOAA, "Frequently Asked Questions about the AMO," available at www.aoml.noaa.gov/phod/amo_faq.php.
23. One may compare a summary of competing theories outlined about two decades ago by Luo and Yamagata (2001, 22212) with a more recent summary, Liu (2012, 1963–1995).
24. Indeed, the most recent view seems to be that the PDO connects with the ENSO found in the tropical Pacific (Newman et al. 2016, 4399–4427). On the intrinsic nature of the Decadal Pacific Oscillation, see Giese et al. (2002, 1–3); on the intrinsic nature of the 50–70 year oscillation, see Minobe (1999, 686).
25. See, e.g., Dong and Dai (2015, 2668), Bratcher and Giese (2002, 24–3), and Holland et al., (2007, 177) (noting that ice core records show "atmospheric teleconnections, on these [decadal] time scales, between the eastern tropical Pacific and Greenland").

26. According to Minobe (1999, 683), "a climatic regime shift is defined as a transition from one climatic state to another within a period substantially shorter than the lengths of the individual epochs of climate states").
27. See Minobe (1999, 683). See also Chao et al. (2000, 2261), Deser et al. (2004, 109).
28. Minobe (1997, 855857); Luo and Yamagata (2001, 22,226) ("the present analysis suggests that the 1976–77 climate regime shift is due to combined effects of the 1976–1977 ENSO event, positive phase of the ENSO-like decadal variability from 1976 to the early 1980's, and a positive interdecadal ENSO-like phase since the early 1980's").
29. IPCC, *Climate Change 2001: Synthesis Report* (Cambridge University Press, 2001), pp. pages 62, 71, 161,165, 169, 207, 208, 210, 211,229, 380, 387.
30. IPCC AR5, p. 17.
31. IPCC AR5, p. 61.
32. IPCC AR5, p. 63.
33. IPCC AR5, p. 801.
34. Emphasis added.
35. IPCC AR5, p. 801.
36. IPCC AR5, pp. 803–804.
37. IPCC AR5, p. 806.
38. IPCC AR5, p. 869.
39. Such as McKitrick and Michaels (2007) and McKitrick and Neirenberg (2010, 149–175).
40. As of 2018. See US Department of Agriculture National Agricultural Statistics Service, Iowa Ag News – 2018 Crop Production, available at www.nass.usda.gov/Statistics_by_State/Iowa/Publications/Crop_Report/2019/IA-Crop-Production-Annual-01-19.pdf.
41. Population has increased only in Storm Lake and Sioux Center, which have both become major meat packing centers, and in Marshalltown there has been an increase relative to 2000 but a fall relative to 2010, with Marshalltown population still below the level it reached in 1980. City of Marshalltown, "A Profile of Marshalltown," available at www.marshalltown-ia.gov/DocumentCenter/View/306/Chapter-1–Profile-PDF.
42. Ten of my Iowa stations had a constant time of observation until today, two switching from evening to morning but not until the mid-2000s, leaving only two the made the typical evening to morning switch in time of observation in the mid-1980s to mid-1990s. One of my stations, Emmetsburg, made the typical switch from evening (6:00 PM) to morning (7:00 AM), but this was not done until 2005. Charles City switched from 5:00 PM to 10:00 PM in 2006. Sometime in the 1980s or 1990s, Clinton No. 1 switched from 5:00 or 10:00 PM to 7:00 or 8:00 AM. Storm Lake has a very old and long documentation record, with time of observation recorded as 7:00 AM until 1929, then 7:00 PM or 5:00 PM from

1941 to 1961, 8:00 PM from 1961 to 1988, 6:00 AM from 1988 to 1996, 8:00 and 8:00 AM from 1996 until the present.

43. The full list of GISS stations is available at https://data.giss.nasa.gov/gistemp/station_data_v4_globe/v4.temperature.inv.txt.
44. By my count, the small-town Iowa stations in the HadCRUT data set are limited to Albia 3NNE, Belle Plaine, Clarinda, Clinton No. 1, Estherville 4E, Forest City 2NNE, Le Mars, Rock Rapids and Waterloo. Clinton No. 1, which I kept in my data set, was once in a lightly wooded area. It is now surrounded by a housing neighborhood and asphalt roads and parking lots. Forest City 2NNE is in an almost ideal site location; however, some of the other Iowa stations used by HadCRUT seem problematic: there is no online information about the equipment, location or general history of the Le Mars station, and measurements at Waterloo ended in 1950.
45. Marlow Vesterby, Ralph E. Heimlich, and Kenneth S. Krupa, "Urbanization of Rural Land in the United States," Resources and Technology Division, Economic Research Service, US Department of Agriculture, Agricultural Economic Report No. 673, March 1994, available at https://naldc.nal.usda.gov/download/CAT10662990/PDF.
46. At Section 3–1, the report explains that "the NRI developed land category includes (a) large tracts of urban and built-up land; (b) small tracts of built-up land of less than 10 acres; and (c) land outside of these built-up areas that is in a rural transportation corridor (roads, railroads, and associated rights-of-way)."

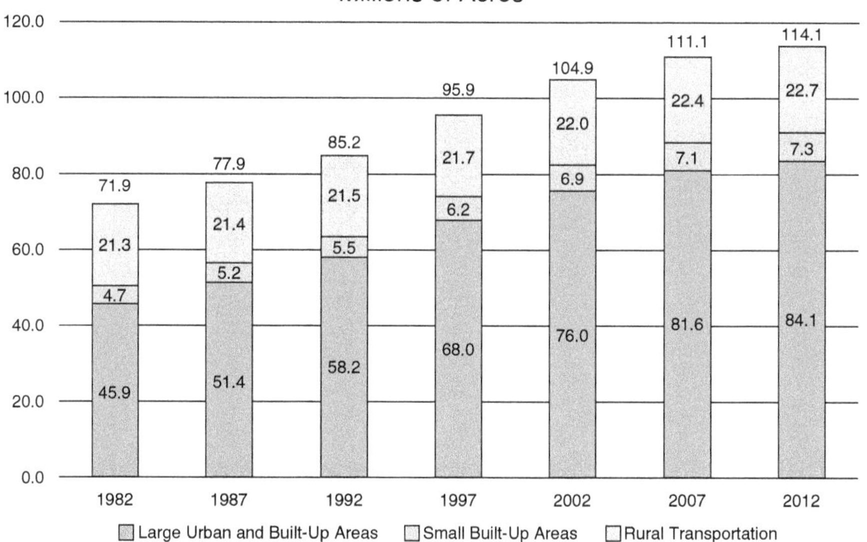

Increase in US developed land

47. IPCC, AR5, p. 187.
48. Such as McKitrick and Michaels (2007) and Mckitrick and Neirenberg (2010, 149–175).
49. IPCC AR5, p. 189.
50. IPCC AR5, p. 189.
51. IPCC AR5, p. 574.
52. I focus on CO_2 because as the IPCC pointed out in its AR5, while the forcing from all GHGs – including gases such as methane – was estimated at 2.83W/m^2, "nearly all of the increase" in GHG warming since 2005 is due to increasing atmospheric concentration of CO_2. IPCC AR5, p. 53.
53. Thomas Stocker et al., eds., *Climate Change 2013: The Physical Science Basis*, pp. 13–14.
54. IPCC AR5, p. 597.
55. IPCC AR5, p. 623.
56. See David Biello, "Impure as the Driven Snow: Smut Is a Bigger Problem than Greenhouse Gases in Polar Meltdown," *Scientific American*, June 8, 2007.
57. BC Assessment, p. 5467, emphasis added.
58. BS Assessment, p. 5475.
59. The BC Assessment, p. 5476, states that "biomass burning appears to be the source of high-concentration plumes observed in the Arctic in recent years, with Russian biomass burning playing a particular prominent role during the measurements of the International Polar Year 2007–2008. … Chemical analysis of snow samples from 36 sites across the Arctic … also indicates that the majority (in most cases, greater than 75%) of the BC in snow surface is associated with biomass or biofuel burning."
60. BC Assessment, p. 5476.
61. BC Assessment, p. 5476.
62. BC Assessment, p. 5480. Other studies, using snow BC concentrations based on measured values, come up with average BC in snow forcings of 4–16 W/m^2. BC Assessment, p. 5481.
63. BC Assessment, p. 5481.
64. That study was Shindell and Faluvegi (2009, 294).
65. IPCC AR5, p. 718.
66. IPCC AR5, p. 718 (emphasis added).
67. BC Assessment, p. 5514.
68. BC Assessment, p. 5515.
69. IPCC AR5, p. 58.
70. BC Assessment, p. 5514.
71. The two studies that have been done on the direct effect and snow albedo effect for regional emissions find regional variability of 30–40 percent for the direct

effect (which is biggest at lower latitudes with more solar radiation) and even larger variation regionally for the snow albedo effect, which ranges from 0 in the tropics to as much as 30–60 percent of the direct effect for emissions from Russia and the former USSR. BC Assessment, p. 5514.

72. BC Assessment, p. 5512.

15

Projecting Future Climate from Computer Models and Far, Far Distant Earth History

IPCC projections about future climate are based primarily on the computer models of the earth's coupled oceanic and atmospheric circulation system that I discussed earlier in Chapter 14. As we have seen, these models manage to reproduce industrial era temperature change only by tuning the way they parameterize – numerically approximate – certain crucial but poorly understood physical processes, in particular how clouds respond to a CO_2-induced warming. The models' one clear testable prediction about the present-day impact of rising CO_2 – that tropical tropospheric temperatures should be rising more than surface temperatures – has not been consistently confirmed. And over the course of most of our present climate era, the Holocene, work is conflicting on whether temperature has been rising along with CO_2.

For all these reasons, relying on what the very same models project about future temperatures would seem ill-advised. It would be one thing if computer climate models amounted to a modeled theory that has been tested against the evidence and proven itself able to explain such evidence. But that is most decidedly not the case with computer climate models. Instead, the models themselves tend to be taken as evidence. This conflates theory with observation in a way that completely flips the scientific method on its head.

Computer climate model simulations of past climate are, however, often claimed to be supported by paleoclimatic data – reconstructions of what the earth's climate looked like in the near and far distant past, meaning millions and even hundreds of millions of years ago. Such paleoclimatic reconstructions are built by taking ice cores from the polar regions and sediment cores from the oceans (and elsewhere) using carbon and other forms of dating to assign ages to different levels of the core, and then using the relative proportion of different isotopes of oxygen (and, more recently, other elements) as a proxy for surface temperature with atmospheric carbon dioxide similarly inferred indirectly from levels of carbon in cores.

In this chapter, I begin with a recent example drawn from journalism to make a simple but important point: computer model projections of future climate are not the same thing as observational evidence. Models are refined, parameterized theories, not evidence.

Next I explain the IPCC's most recent, 2018, model-based projection about what must be done to keep global surface temperature from rising above 2°C. This projection uses models to generate a CO_2-temperature relationship, and then plugs in what the IPCC calls a Representative [CO_2] Concentration Pathway (RCP) – an assumption about future economic growth and CO_2 emissions. The ICPP's highly publicized 2018 projection that unless the United States and other developed countries drastically reduce CO_2 emissions by 2030, a global temperature increase of 2°C is unavoidable is the basis for an entire political program in the United States, called the "Green New Deal." But the IPCC's recommendation actually says "if CO_2 emissions are not drastically reduced soon, the rapid increase in CO_2 emissions (RCP pathway) that we otherwise assume will occur will lead to a 2°C temperature increase." The problem with this projection is that rapid CO_2 increase RCP assumed by the IPCC is completely at odds with both the observed change in global CO_2 emissions and most reasonable assumptions about future economic growth and CO_2 emissions.

The IPCC's 2018 projection, like all its previous future climate projections, is based mainly on computer climate model projections. As I explain in this chapter, very important recent theoretical work shows the uncertainty over climate feedbacks, which as we have seen in the case of clouds is absolutely necessary for models to be able to reproduce twentieth-century warming, has been shown to mathematically imply that climate models will always attach positive probability to very scary big climate sensitivity. Such sensitivity is not due to anything, except the mathematical structure of a basic single-dimensional radiative forcing climate model. Moreover, under varying assumptions about how much heat is taken up the ocean, this theoretical work shows that high future climate sensitivity would evolve to high levels only over a period of centuries.

From the time of Arrhenius until very recently, projections of future CO_2-induced temperature increase were based entirely on models of varying dimensions. Recently, as measurements of CO_2 and temperature and other climate forcers such as aerosols have become available, estimates of climate sensitivity based on the CO_2-temperature relationship observed in the industrial period have become available. For the most part, these suggest climate sensitivity is much lower than the upper found of 4.5°C estimated first by Arrhenius and in climate models by the IPCC in AR's through its AR5.

I conclude by very briefly discussing paleoclimatic evidence about the CO_2-climate relationship believed to have existed over the past hundreds of millions of years. This does not show anything like a clear causal relationship between CO_2 and global temperature. Recent news stories indicate that the IPCC's Sixth Assessment Report, due in 2021, will attach greater weight to such paleoclimatic evidence. From such accounts, this is apparently due to the fact that the most recent computer climate models are deviating further and further from evidence about past climate, making them even more unreliable guides for policy.

I PROJECTIONS ARE NOT EVIDENCE

The distinction between observations of the natural world and projections about how various human activities may affect that world would seem to be fundamental to any rational policy. Purely as a matter of logic, a question of the form "were there more wildfires last year compared to the long-term average number of wildfires?" cannot be answered by the response "our computer model projects more such wildfires in the future if atmospheric CO_2 continues to increase." That is obviously not an answer to the question about whether the number of wildfires were historically unusual.

Activist climate scientists do not give such an obviously irrelevant answer. Instead they say that climate models can explain some recently observed unwelcome trends in various climate variables as due to increased atmospheric CO_2 concentration. For example, in 2018, Benjamin Cook, a scientist at NASA GISS wrote a long blog post for the website CarbonBrief.org, in which he explained that climate models showed that decreases in rainfall and increases in temperature due to anthropogenic CO_2 emissions had "played a role" in recent droughts.[1] Cook then went on quite quickly to explain that "with climate change already having an impact on droughts, we can reasonably expect this impact to increase as the climate warms further." Entirely missing from Cook's blog post is any discussion of whether recent droughts are historically unusual. This is odd, for the work discussed earlier in Chapter 13 shows that long periods of drought lasting many decades are not at all unusual in the American west. But rather than putting recent droughts in long-term perspective, Cook talks entirely about what climate models can explain and what they can predict.

Given that even GISS scientists seem to be conflating observations with model simulation so directly, it is hardly surprising that journalists do the same thing. For example, the fall of 2018 brought very late and very intense Santa Ana winds to California, and these winds helped ignite and strengthen some very severe wildfires. Janin Guzman-Morales, then a postdoctoral researcher at the Scripps Institution of Oceanography at the University of California, San Diego had recently published a paper using climate models to try to project whether increases in atmospheric CO_2 would cause such late season intense Santa Ana winds to become more frequent in the future. Such work, like the work discussed by Cook, uses computer models of global climate but then "downscales" these models to generate projections about future climate at the regional level. No model can possibly reliably simulate regional climate unless it can reliably capture the changes in ocean circulation patterns – such as the AMO and PDO discussed earlier – that drive regional climate. As computer climate models cannot do this, it is generally recognized, including by the IPCC, that computer climate models are not reliable in simulating or projecting regional climate. Without any recognition of this problem or perhaps even any awareness of it, both the *New York Times* and *Los Angeles Times* had stories devoted entirely to just-published climate model projections by Guzman-Morales.

Those stories had diametrically opposing headline interpretations of her work: the *New York Times* article[2] saw the paper as showing that "coupled with changes in patterns of precipitation that are also expected to occur as the climate warms, it may mean that California's wildfire season will shift from fall into winter, with longer and more intense fires later in the year." The *Los Angeles Times* story,[3] by contrast, understood Guzman-Morales's paper as showing that "Santa Ana winds – which routinely whip up walls of flame through brush-covered hillsides – are likely to be tempered in coming decades," becoming "about 18% less frequent toward the end of the century if climate change continues unabated." Rather than gathering and reporting facts about Santa Ana winds and California wildfires, in these stories, journalists – who typically have never taken a math or science class in college – are offering interpretations a of a recently published study using a computer climate model.

When model projections, not observations, become the focus of such stories, facts tend to be forgotten. Neither of the newspaper articles reporting on the Santa Ana work of Guzman-Morales actually quote or take anything directly from her dissertation or published articles. Had either journalist actually looked Guzman-Morales's published work,[4] they would found that the actual historical reconstruction of Santa Ana wind reconstruction is that depicted in Figure 15.1.

In this figure, only for the land area extent of the most extreme Santa Ana events (the bottom panel) is there a statistically significant linear trend in the frequency or duration or extent of Santa Ana events since 1948–1949. Looking at the top panel, one sees that the large number of extreme Santa Ana events seen in the late 2000s was matched by an equal number of such extreme events from (roughly) the late 1960's to late 1970's.

II THE IPCC'S 2018 SPECIAL REPORT: CLIMATE SCARE STORIES DRIVEN BY UNREALISTIC ECONOMIC PROJECTIONS AND CONFLATED POLICY GOALS

In several respects, the IPCC's 2018 "Special Report" (SR) is quite different than its previous Assessment Reports (ARs). First, the 2018 SR does not make long-term projections of how rising CO_2 will impact temperatures and other temperature-related aspects of climate. Instead, it is makes very short-term projections about levels of CO_2 that will generate 1.5°–2.0°C temperature increases relative to preindustrial levels and then – its primary objective – discusses all the very bad consequences of even these temperature increases.

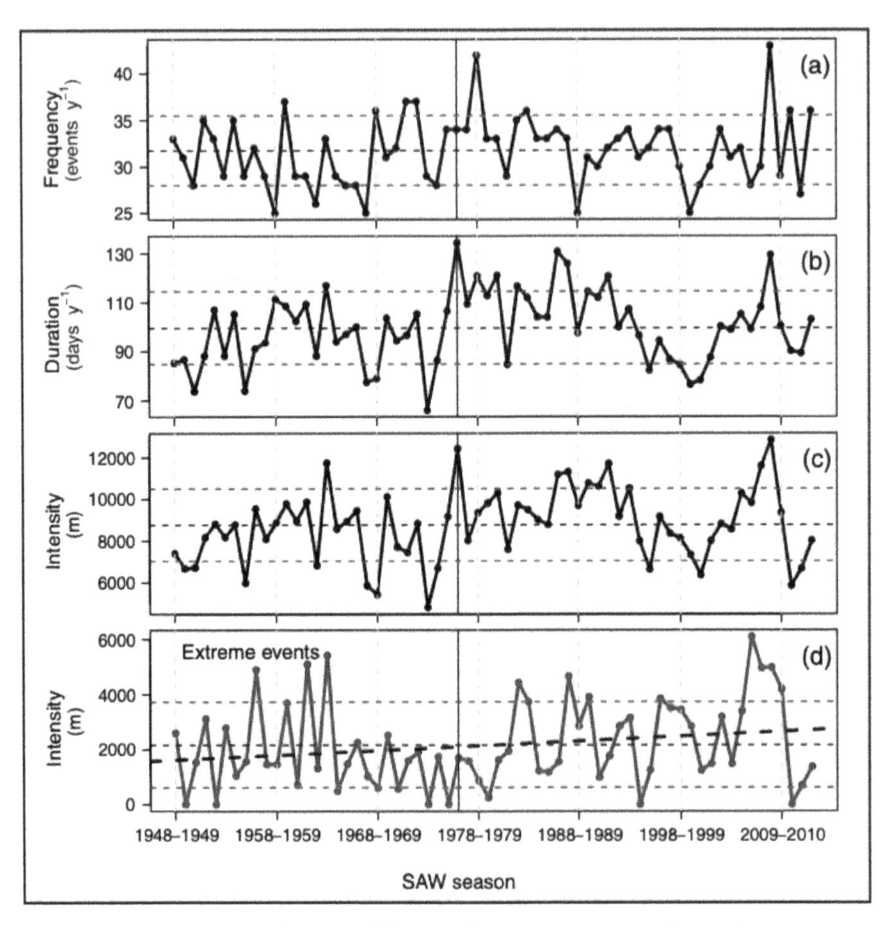

FIGURE 15.1 A reproduction of figure 4 from Guzman-Morales et al. (2016).

The second big difference between the 2018 SR and previous IPCC Assessment Reports is that the 2018 SR is not an assessment of climate science. As the Summary for Policymakers of the 2018 SR describes the SR's origins,[5] "as part of the decision to adopt the Paris Agreement, the IPCC was invited to produce, in 2018, a Special Report on global warming of 1.5°C above preindustrial levels and related global greenhouse gas emission pathways. The IPCC accepted the invitation, adding that the Special Report would look at these issues in the context of strengthening the global response to the threat of climate change, sustainable development, and efforts to eradicate poverty." Thus, the 2018 SR is explicitly and openly an advocacy document – the IPCC is looking at global warming of 1.5°C above preindustrial levels, but in the context of a "strengthened" response to the threat of climate change, "sustainable development and efforts to eradicate poverty." The 2018 SR is thus puts the 1.5°C warming entirely in the policy context of meeting "sustainable development" and "efforts to eradicate poverty."

Indeed, before the 2018 SR even discusses the science, it emphasizes[6] that "ethical considerations, and the principle of equity in particular, are central to this report, recognizing that many of the impacts of warming up to and beyond 1.5°C, and some potential impacts of mitigation actions required to limit warming to 1.5°C, fall disproportionately on the poor and vulnerable (*high confidence*)." The 2018 Report clearly views whatever may be the scientific case for reducing emissions as inseparable from various policy prescriptions:

> ambitious mitigation actions are indispensable to limit warming to 1.5°C while achieving sustainable development and poverty eradication (*high confidence*). Ill-designed responses, however, could pose challenges especially – but not exclusively – for countries and regions contending with poverty and those requiring significant transformation of their energy systems. This report focuses on "climate-resilient development pathways," which aim to meet the goals of sustainable development, including climate adaptation and mitigation, poverty eradication and reducing inequalities. ... Significant uncertainty remains as to which pathways are more consistent with the principle of equity.

With the science taking what is clearly a back seat to policy in the 2018 SR, that Report's discussion of climate science is extremely abbreviated relative to a full assessment report. Its certainly most highly publicized scientific message, however, can be seen in Figure 15.2, which reproduces figure 2.3 of the 2018 AR.[7] The figure shows the relationship between temperature change and anthropogenic CO_2 emissions since the preindustrial year 1876. The thin blue line shows actual cumulative emissions and temperature change with the point marked 2010 showing the average global 2006–2015 temperature compared to 1850–1900 and the point marked 2017 showing the 2017 versus 1850–1900 temperature change and cumulative CO_2 emissions as of 2017. The black line shows what models simulate for the past temperature–emissions relationship, and the red line is the average GCM model prediction for the future under what is called the RCP 8.5 emissions scenario (I will explain what this is shortly). The light red shaded area is the spread in actual model predictions and the purple area is the somewhat smaller range used in the 2018 SR. The graph depicts cumulative emissions, rather than atmospheric CO_2 concentration, because the point of the 2018 SR is to quantify how much additional CO_2 emissions are consistent with limiting the temperature increase to 1.5°C. Computer climate models are used for this projection, because cumulative CO_2 emissions are assumed by the models to translate directly (and linearly) into atmospheric CO_2 concentrations.

There are two things one sees straightaway in Figure 15.2. First, as of 2010 (the 2006–2020 average), according to the 2018 SR, temperature change relative to the preindustrial level was already 0.87°C, so we have only 0.63°C remaining temperature increase before we go over 1.5°C. According to the mean RCP8.5 model (the red

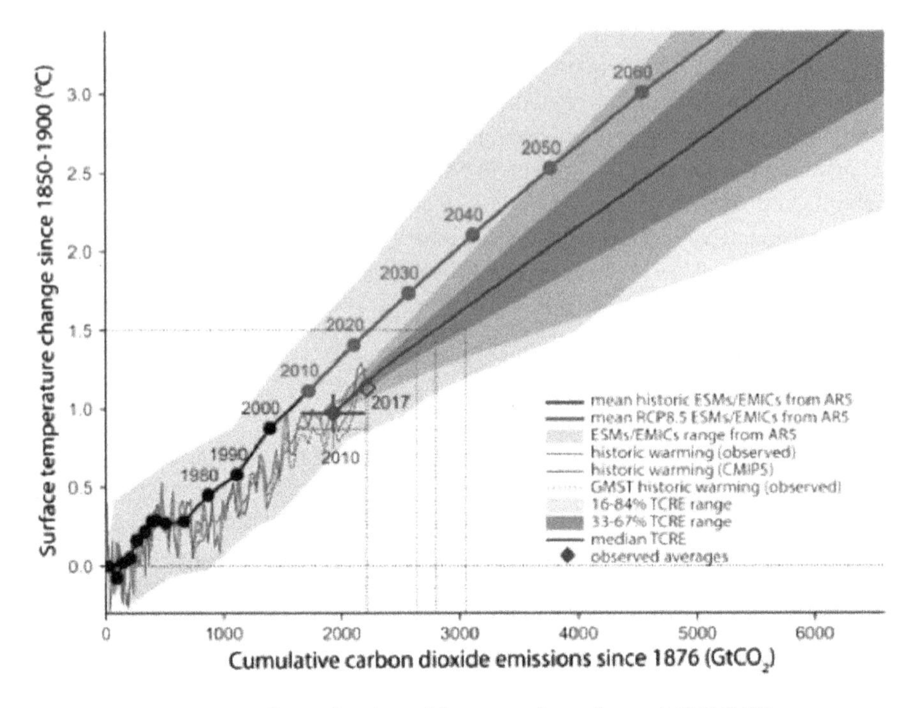

FIGURE 15.2 Reproduction of figure 2.3 from the 2018 IPCC SR.

line) the allowable increase in CO_2 from the 2010 level consistent with not going above 1.5°C is far less than 100 Gtc, a tiny fraction of the increase up to 2010. The other thing one sees, however, is that the very erratic blue line – erratic because it gives the actual observations of emissions increase and temperature change – is far below the mean model simulation (the black, past simulation, and red, future simulation, line). Even from Figure 15.2, the models seem to be off, and perhaps by an increasing amount. On the other hand, the 2018 SR is discounting the models' projections, looking not at the red line, the mean model projection, but the lower (observation constrained, as the 2018 SR says) purple cone.

The red line and purple and red cones, however, are both projections of future temperature change under what is called the RCP8.5 pathway. As explained earlier, RCP stands for Representative Concentration Pathway, and such pathways are future scenarios of CO_2 emissions and economic and population growth that are plugged into GCM models and computer models of climate and the economy. The RPC 8.5 pathway is the most extreme such future scenario. It assumes that atmospheric CO_2 concentration will reach about 1370 ppm by 2100, with a forcing of 8.5 W/m^2. This is *more than three times the present atmospheric CO_2 concentration and over twice the radiative forcing that has occurred since preindustrial times.*

Even more importantly, one gets these enormous values in the RCP 8.5 future because it is one that assumes rapidly growing economies that are not only highly energy intensive but also highly and steadily reliant on fossil fuels, especially coal (Van Vuuren et al. 2011, 5–31). Thus what Figure 15.2 and the IPCC's 2018 SR is actually reporting is emission reductions that will be necessary in a world with highly energy intensive and coal-reliant economies that are rapidly growing. In terms of Figure 15.2, the reason why the blue line – actual observations – in Figure 15.2 is so far below the red line and the various colored cones is because the red line and the cones are projections of the coal-based, energy intensive rapid growth future.

The problem with this scenario is that it is completely at odds with reality. As we have seen, the United States has very rapidly moved from getting most of its electricity from coal-fired plants to getting only about 20 percent. This is just as true of other developed countries. Germany, which I discuss in more detail later, is in the process of completely closing all of its coal-burning electricity generating plants.

Figure 15.3 shows total CO_2 emissions from the major emitting countries and regions (such as the EU and central Europe). As one can see in Figure 15.3, assuming

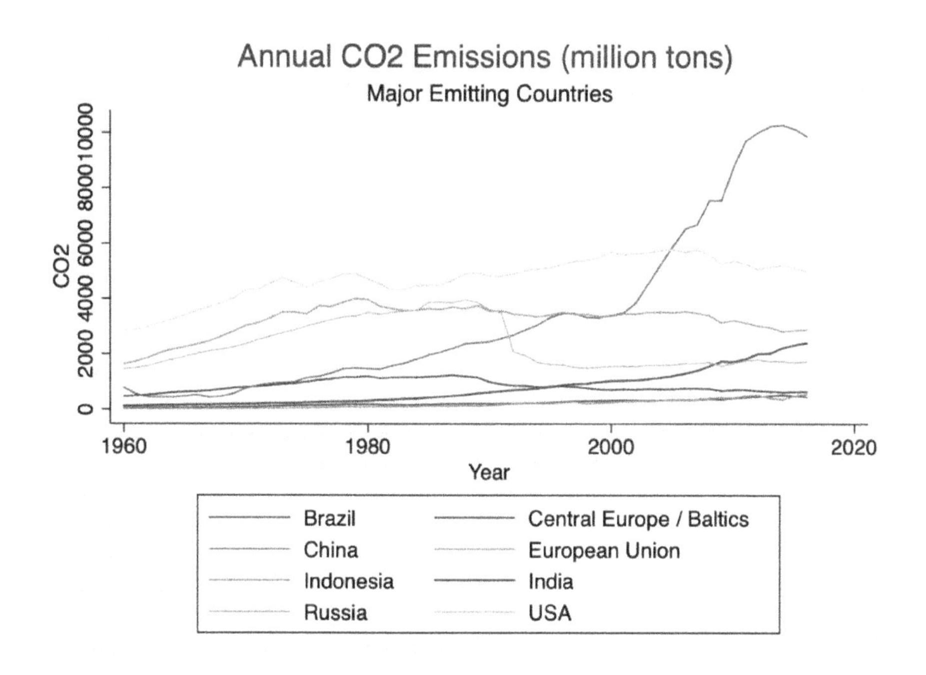

FIGURE 15.3 CO_2 emissions for major CO_2-emitting countries. Displays data on CO_2 emissions by country that are generated by the Carbon Dioxide Information Analysis Center, Environmental Sciences Division, Oak Ridge National Laboratory and which are available on the World Bank website at https://data.worldbank.org/indicator/EN.ATM.CO2E.KT.

that the Chinese emission slowdown is at least partly a Communist party fabrication – something strongly indicated by the continuing and even accelerating Chinese reliance on coal-fired electricity that I discuss later – only India and China have been rapidly increasing their CO_2 emissions. For the world to be on the RCP 8.5 path, not only would India and China need to massively increase their CO_2 emissions, but other developing countries such as Indonesia and Brazil would need to do so as well. This would only happen if world GDP was rapidly growing. But the worldwide economic growth rate has long been slowing, not increasing. Indeed, since 1960, the long-term, linear trend in the growth rate of world GDP has been negative.[8] For some years, the world economy has been becoming less global, not more so, and this trend has only been reinforced by the retreat within national borders spurred by the 2020 COVID-19 pandemic. It is much less likely that the worldwide growth rate will rise above 3 percent than that it will fall below 2 percent. As of 2020, it is clear that RCP 8.5 is not merely unrealistic but impossible.

The other thing to realize about figure 2.3 from the IPCC's 2018 Special Report (my Figure 15.2) is that the policy advice given in that Report regarding how much CO_2 emissions must be limited to stay below 1.5°C is *entirely based on GCM model projections*. Given my earlier discussion of what seem to be severe limitations of GCM models in actually explaining anything about past climate without simply "tuning" unknown parameters to replicate data and the failure to simulate interdecadal climate variation or to generate any testable hypothesis that has been consistently confirmed, one must wonder whether the emissions limitation advice in the 2018 SR actually has a sound scientific basis. Beyond this, the 2018 SR's brief discussion of climate science seems to leave out a good deal of what I will discuss immediately below:

- Regarding aerosol forcing, the 2018 SR says[9] that "a multimodel analysis … and a study based on observational constraints … largely support the AR5 best estimate and uncertainty range of aerosol forcing." This is flatly inconsistent with the body of recent work discussed in the very next section showing that aerosol forcing is almost surely smaller (less negative) than the AR5 assumed. Moreover, that recent work is not even mentioned in the 2018 SR.
- According to the 2018 SR,[10] "a revised interpretation of historical estimates and other lines of evidence based on analysis of climate models with the best representation of today's climate … suggest that the lower bound of ECS could be revised upwards, which would decrease the chances of limiting warming below 1.5°C in assessed pathways … such a reassessment has been challenged (Lewis and Curry, 2018), albeit from a single line of evidence." As we will see momentarily, Lewis and Curry (2018) is not the only recent empirical (or empirically constrained model) study showing that the lower bound on climate sensitivity may be well below 1.5. Many if not most of the recent studies estimate a decreased lower bound. Here again, the 2018 SR misstates what is in the literature and omits any discussion of conflicting work.

- The only feedbacks discussed in the 2018 SR[11] are the potential release of methane and CO_2 from melting permafrost or wetlands. This is a feedback that GCM modeling groups do not even mention when discussing GCM models. On the other hand, in the 2018 SR there is no mention anywhere of the understanding – fully disclosed by the recent review articles by GCM modeling groups discussed earlier – that cloud feedback is both uncertain and tuned to allow GCM models to reproduce twentieth-century warming.

These are glaring discrepancies, so glaring that they make the 2018 SR's discussion of the models it relies upon highly misleading.

III UNCERTAIN FEEDBACKS AND UNCERTAIN CLIMATE SENSITIVITY: THE MATH AND THE EVIDENCE

As I discussed above, according to very recent articles by climate modeling groups, those models are tuned now not by assuming things about aerosol forcing – apparently this is now somewhat constrained by observations and also too difficult to figure out how to do given the increased complexity of the models – but by assuming things about the highly uncertain impact of clouds. Unlike CO_2 or aerosols, clouds are not an external shock or climate forcing. They are internal to the climate system. Along with changes in atmospheric water vapor and changes in the earth's surface albedo due to potential loss of sea ice, clouds are one of the three key responses to the initial temperature change induced by a CO_2 increase. As such, they are called feedback effects, things that are driven by the initial temperature increase caused by an increase in atmospheric CO_2 and which then amplify or cut that temperature change.

Recall from the previous chapter that feedbacks account *entirely* for climate sensitivity (temperature change due to a CO_2 doubling) greater than 1.2°C. For this reason, uncertainty over the feedback S means uncertainty over future temperate change from a doubling of CO_2. According to the IPCC's 2013 AR5, this number – the temperature change predicted by GCM models after the climate system returns to equilibrium following a doubling of atmospheric CO_2 (also called equilibrium climate sensitivity, or ECS) – was "likely" between 1.5°C and 4.5°C and "very unlikely" to be less than 1°C or greater than 6°C.

What is most remarkable about this estimated range for ECS is that it the upper bound, about 4°C, is precisely the same that Arrhenius came up with through back-of-the-envelope calculations over 100 years ago. Moreover, although the last 30 years have seen a huge increase in computing power, in climate observations, and in the number of climate modelers, climate model predictions have changed hardly at all. In the 1970s, the predicted equilibrium global mean temperature increase resulting from a doubling of atmospheric CO_2 relative to preindustrial levels was between 1.6° and 4.5°C; in the 2007 IPCC Assessment Report, the predicted range of likely temperature increase is now between 2° and 4.5°C.[12] As Schwartz et al. (2001, 432) summarized the relatively lack of scientific progress on this issue, "despite extensive research neither the best estimate nor the estimated range for Earth's climate sensitivity has changed markedly in the last 39 years."

A *How Uncertainty about Feedbacks Generates Even Worse Uncertainty about Climate Sensitivity*

Perhaps even more importantly, it has recently been shown that models will always attach some positive probability to very high possible temperature increases because "the sum of the underlying climate feedbacks is substantially positive."[13] That is, climate model predictions will always be very uncertain, and skewed toward high temperature increases, and "foreseeable improvements in the understanding of physical processes, and in the estimation of their effects from observations, will not yield large reductions in the envelope of climate sensitivity" (Roe and Baker 2007, 631). Even if we significantly improve our understanding of the various climate feedback processes – narrowing our uncertainty regarding their individual impacts – this will have "little effect" in making more certain the predicted sensitivity of climate to CO_2 doubling: the models will still say that potentially very high temperature increases are possible (in the sense of occurring with positive probability) (Roe and Baker 2007, 632).

These results are elegantly derived by Roe and Baker (2007). As it rests on basic physical principles and also can be solved analytically (that is, without using a computer to generate numerical approximations), their equation has much to recommend it to economists in particular (who, unlike physicists, generally eschew numerical methods). The crucial result in Roe and Baker (2007) is that even a small amount of symmetric (bell-shaped) uncertainty regarding the size of feedback effects will generate a probability distribution over climate sensitivity that, over time, attaches a relatively high positive probability to very big temperature increases, those bigger than 5°C. That is, the distribution of climate sensitivity, S, is eventually skewed to the right, with a "fat tail" of relatively high probability attaching to really high climate sensitivity (big temperature increases).

Roe and Baker (2007) is a mathematical explanation of why virtually all computer climate models generate such a "fat tail" distribution. These computer model distributions are depicted in Figure 15.4, a reproduction of figure 2(a) from Calel et al. (2015, 134).[14] In the figure, each colored line gives the temperature projection generated by a particular climate models. As can be seen from Figure 15.4, the "fat tail" distribution of climate sensitivity means a skewed (as opposed to symmetric) distribution, with relatively great weight attached to really big temperature increases exceeding even 6°C.

In the very same issue of *Science* magazine in which Roe and Baker's article appeared was included a response by leading climate modelers Myles Allen and

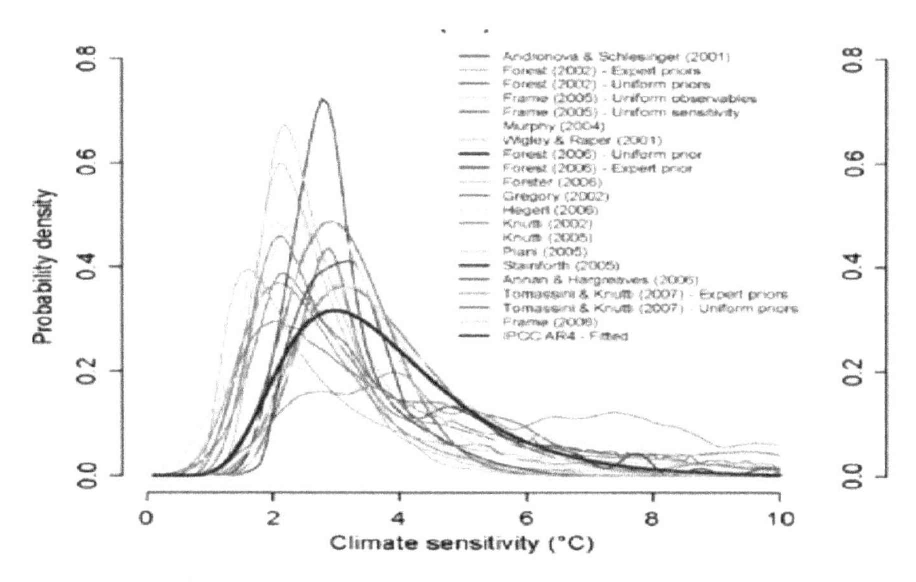

FIGURE 15.4 Climate models and the "fat tail" distribution of very high climate sensitivities.

David Frame. Allen, discussed at several points in this book, is an activist climate scientist who has participated in strategy sessions organizing climate litigation and has been an expert witness for the plaintiffs in such litigation. Notably, he served as a contributing author and as review editor on the two key chapters of the IPCC's 2007 AR dealing with the modeled attribution of ongoing climate change and with future projections (Allen and Frame 2007, 582). Allen and Frame's response did not fundamentally challenge the mathematical points that Roe and Baker are making: those points follow quite directly from the basic mathematical structure of the climate prediction problem, and are not controversial.

Rather than challenging Roe and Baker's scientific point – a point about the basic statistical structure of climate models – Allen and Frame instead argue that Roe and Baker's point is really not very important, because the goal of "avoiding dangerous anthropogenic interference in the climate system" does not mean that we have to be able to "specify today a stabilization concentration of carbon dioxide … for which the risk of dangerous warming is acceptably low" (Allen and Frame 2007, 583). What Allen and Frame argue is that if in the future, people use a rough rule of thumb and continuously toughen CO_2 reduction targets if warming is greater than models predicted, then they will never actually observe the very large temperature increases. As they put it, "if [climate sensitivity S] turns out to be toward the upper end of the current uncertainty range, we may never find out what it is … but provided our descendants have the sense to adapt their policies to the emerging climate change signal, they probably won't care." Hence Allen and Frame say that it is time to "call off the quest" for what has previously been considered the "holy grail" of climate research, "an upper bound on climate sensitivity" (Allen and Frame 2007, 583).

The obvious question raised by Roe and Baker (2007) is whether the positive likelihood of very high temperature increases from CO_2 doubling that they show is a necessary consequence of the models' assumption of strong positive feedbacks would be present even if there were important negative feedbacks. Baker and Roe (2009)[15] answered this question. The first thing shown by Baker and Roe (2009) is that – as one would have expected intuitively – the addition of an important negative feedback causes the probability of large temperature increases due to CO_2 forcing to fall, with probability concentrating instead around more moderate temperature increases. As a corollary, when there is a negative feedback, reducing uncertainty in positive atmospheric feedbacks does have a "significant" impact in reducing uncertainty about the ultimate (or equilibrium) temperature increase (Baker and Roe 2009, 4583).

Baker and Roe (2009) also show that when there is a negative feedback that dissipates only very slowly, then even for a known forcing (e.g., CO_2 increase) there is enormous uncertainty over how long it will take for large temperature increases to be realized. Sequestration of heat by the deep ocean is precisely such a slowly evolving process. When Baker and Bauman (2012)[16] used a simple but empirically validated (and IPCC endorsed) model of heat sequestration by the deep ocean, to a very high degree of confidence (two standard deviations), they found that temperature increases (climate sensitivity) above 4°C would occur only after about 450 years from the present. This is depicted in Figure 15.5 (which reproduces figure 3 (a) of Roe and Bauman (2013, 652)).

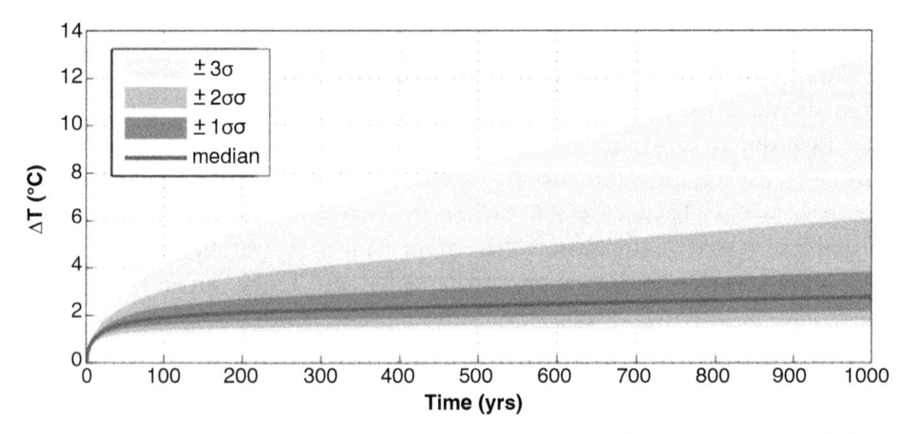

FIGURE 15.5 Evolution of the probability density function of climate sensitivity with deep ocean sequestration.

In Figure 15.5, temperature increases above 3°C can be realized in less than 200 years from the present only for extremely high positive climate feedbacks – so high as not only to be very unlikely (three standard deviations) but also to imply that the earth's climate system is unstable and will careen into unceasing warming.

As Roe and Bauman (2013) summarize, "even in the absurd limit of an infinite climate sensitivity, the amount of warming that can occur is limited by the rate at which the system can accumulate energy. ... Therefore, from the standpoint of the formal statistical definition – that the tail declines as a power in the limit of $T \rightarrow \infty$ – there is no fat tail to the climate response at finite time." In other words, even a positive probability of very high temperature increases from CO_2 doubling – not such increases themselves – cannot arise for many centuries.

B *New Estimates of Relatively Low Climate Sensitivity*

For decades, models were the only source of estimates for climate sensitivity. With steady increases in the amount and reliability of historical data on the climate system, however, it has recently become possible to generate actual empirical estimates of climate sensitivity. Such estimates are statistical, and involve gathering data on all the forcings that might be expected to influence global average surface temperature as well as on temperature itself. After removing the known impact on temperature of the measured forcings, and taking account of the amount of heat sequestered by the ocean, one can isolate the impact of a particular forcing, such as increases in atmospheric CO_2, on observed temperatures.

Following Allen and Frame's advice, climate scientists say they have indeed "called off the quest to find the upper bound of ECS" (Skeie et al. 2014, 140). Rather than trying to put a mathematical upper limit on ECS, scientists have been looking at the actual data to estimate both ECS and a shorter-term measure, called the transient climate response (TCR). The TCR is defined at the temperature response at the time of CO_2 doubling after a period of sustained increases in atmospheric CO_2.[17]

Such approaches are sometimes called empirical energy budget studies. The reason they are called energy budget studies is that they are based on a fundamental physics, the law of conservation of energy. This law requires that $\Delta TOA = \Delta F - \Delta t$, where ΔTOA is the change in the top-of-the-atmosphere (TOA) radiative imbalance, ΔF is the total forcing, and ΔT, the change in temperature. In words, radiative forcing can't be lost and must translate into temperature change and a change in the energy balance at the top of the atmosphere.[18] Such studies allow for internal variability (as a random error term, typically), and also control for forcings such as volcanic aerosols.

There are now a large number of published studies that take such an approach.[19] These studies generally find that climate sensitivity is much lower than predicted by climate models:

- By comparing data from an 1859–1882 base period with data from 1995 to 2011 (as well as 1930–1950 and 1987–2011), Lewis and Curry (2015)[20] estimated both equilibrium climate sensitivity (ECS) and transient climate response (TCR). Lewis and Curry controlled for variability in global temperatures that arise from internal oscillations such as El Niño–Southern Oscillation (ENSO) and the Atlantic Multidecadal Oscillation (AMO) and external factors such as solar variation. With these variables controlled, they estimated climate sensitivity (and transient climate response) under a variety of assumptions regarding the magnitude of the impact of cooling aerosols (such as sulfur dioxide). They estimated an equilibrium climate sensitivity of between 1 and 4.5°C and transient climate response of between 0.9 and 2.5°C. For virtually all assumptions about aerosol forcing, they get a best estimate of about 1.6°C for equilibrium climate sensitivity and about 1.3 for transient climate response. These estimates are lower than the IPCC's estimated range of between 1.5° and 4.5°C, and remained lower even when Lewis and Curry looked at final periods ending in 2000–2003 (thus removing the years 2003–2011 when it is acknowledged that there was very little warming).
- In a very recent paper taking a similar approach but using a more recent 2007–2016 period to compare to a 1869–1882 base, Lewis and Curry (2018) estimated a much lower range for ECS, of between 1.05° and 2.45°C and TCR of 0.9°–1.7°C).
- A number of papers have plugged actual observations of TOA energy balance, forcing and temperature into simplified computer climate models (that is, models that do not attempt to replicate atmospheric and ocean circulation). ECS estimates from papers since 2012 taking this approach are as follows:

  1. Aldrin et al. (2012) estimate an ECS of 1.2°–3.5°C (with a mean of 2.0°C);
  2. Bodman et al. (2013) estimate an ECS of 1.5°–5.2°C (with a mean of 3.2°C);
  3. Skie et al. (2014) estimate an ECS of 0.9°–3.2°C (with a mean of 1.8°C); and, finally,
  4. Johansson et al. (2015) estimate an ECS of 1.9°–3.3°C with a mean of 2.6°C).

As pointed out above, empirically estimating climate sensitivity and transient climate response is a relatively new enterprise. It is possible that future estimated sensitivity will increase or decrease relative to current estimates. However, thus far there is a consistent pattern: the old estimate of ECS between 1.5° and 4.5°C is coming down, especially on the upper limit, with all empirical estimates (save Bodman 2013) now putting an upper bound on ECS of 3.5°C or less.

IV PALEOCLIMATE: FUZZY LESSONS ABOUT CO_2 AND CLIMATE FROM FAR, FAR DISTANT EARTH HISTORY

Suppose one grants that there are many problems with GCM models – among other things, the models' inability to explain even twentieth-century warming without fixing the value of certain key unknown parameters involving aerosols (a key forcing agent) and cloud feedback effect, their inability to explain observations of long-term decline, not increase, in Holocene temperatures despite rising CO_2, the disconfirmation of the one real-time testable hypothesis generated by GCM's of amplified warming in the tropical troposphere, and, finally, empirical estimates of sensitivity that cut the upper limit almost in half. One might argue that regardless of the problems with GCM climate models, there is even better evidence of how rising CO_2 will lead to rising temperatures: earth history going back many millions of years that shows how changes in atmospheric CO_2 have changed global climate.

As I shall recount shortly, activist climate scientists such as James Hansen have repeatedly broadcast statements of the form "the last time global CO_2 was this high, many millions of years ago, sea level were [many, many] meters higher." As pretty much anyone who follows the news knows, leftist politicians sing the same doleful song. These dire warnings are ostensibly backed up by findings from what is called paleoclimate – efforts by paleontologists to reconstruct global climate over the past thousands, millions, and even hundreds of millions years.

When one actually looks at what is in the paleoclimatology literature, however, one looks in vain for any scientist unambiguously announcing evidence of a causal connection in which increases in atmospheric CO_2 then leading to increasing global temperatures. Instead, one sees scientific understanding that is still evolving but inherently limited by the difficulty of getting any precise temporal resolution of how changes in CO_2 related to climate change millions of years ago. As it stands now, the literature is best described as finding that CO_2 releases from the Southern Ocean in particular may have amplified temperature changes brought about by much more fundamental forces, such as change in earth's orbit, with no systematic relation between atmospheric CO_2 and global temperature over the far distant past.

A CO_2 *and Climate Change during the Last Glaciation and Immediate Deglaciation Periods, 115,000–22,000 Years Ago*

I have already discussed the divergence between what climate models say should have happened during the Holocene (the last 11,000 years or so) and what did happen. Because CO_2 was rising during the Holocene, climate models predict that temperatures should have risen. Instead, the majority of temperature reconstructions indicate that they fell until the twentieth century.

On the other hand, looking back at the figures in Chapter 13, we can see that during the initial period of deglaciation following the last ice age – roughly 22,000 to

11,000 years ago – both temperature and CO_2 rose quickly. This is just a rough impression. The real question is whether the rise in CO_2 occurred before or after the change in temperature. If the CO_2 increase occurred after, then temperature change is driving CO_2 change; if before, then it might be that CO_2 increase drove temperature increase.

A look at the literature shows that whether or not this question can even be answered and the answer itself depends on which ancient temperature reconstructions one looks at. Over 10 years ago, Stott et al. (2007) sampled sediment core data at a very fine, centimeter level scale that had built up over the eons at a location where sediments contain evidence on the temperature of both western tropical Pacific surface water and deep Pacific water the time of the last glacial transition (the end of the last ice age). This method allowed the researchers to overcome the shortcoming in previous research that there was no way to date temperature and CO_2 changes.[21]

By independently measuring data on southern ocean (that is, Antarctic) temperature and tropical sea surface temperature, Stott et al. found that

> nearly all of the warming in glacial/interglacial deep-water warming occurred before 17,500 years ago, and therefore before both the onset of deglacial warming in tropical Pacific surface waters and the increase in CO_2 concentrations … together that the onset of deglacial warming throughout the Southern Hemisphere occurred long before deglacial warming began in the tropical surface ocean … [and this means] that the mechanism responsible for initiating the deglacial events does not lie directly within the tropics itself, nor can these events be explained by CO_2 forcing alone. Both CO_2 and the tropical SST's did not begin to change until well after 18 kyB.P., approximately 1000 years after the benthic $\delta^{18}O$ record indicates that the Southern Ocean was warming. (Stott et al. 2007, 438)

Stott et al. "suggest that the trigger for the initial deglacial warming around Antarctica was the change in solar insolation over the Southern Ocean during the austral spring that influenced the retreat of the sea ice," that in turn led to decreased stratification of the Southern Ocean, promoting "enhanced ventilation of the deep sea and the subsequent rise in atmospheric CO_2."

This view is supported by the WAIS Divide Project Members (2013), who find that local summertime orbital forcing in the Antarctic between 22,000 and 18,000 years ago warmed the West Antarctic, causing a sea ice decline that extended to the South Atlantic. This group concludes that "the increased wind stress in the Southern Ocean drove upwelling, venting of CO_2 from the deep ocean, and warming in both West Antarctica and East Antarctica" (443). On this story, increasing CO_2 was a consequence of increased insolation in the Antarctic region.

To be sure, work by Marcott et al. (2014) and Perrenin et al. (2013), both published right around when the IPCC's AR5 came out, shows that the timing of CO_2 increases and temperature increases during the early period of the last deglaciation (22,000 to about 15,000 years ago) coincides much more closely. Of course, that work looks at different evidence of past temperature and CO_2 than did Stott et al. (2007). It also dismisses Greenland and Arctic ice cores more generally as evidence of past atmospheric CO_2 on the ground that Greenland ice cores contain too many "impurities," and instead looks at what are said to be much more precise and uncontaminated ice cores from Antarctica.

The findings by Stott et al. (2007), Marcott et al. (2014), and Perrenin et al. (2013) are not necessarily inconsistent, in that other work presents evidence that orbital driven warming of the Southern Ocean led to a venting of CO_2 from that ocean and eventually higher atmospheric CO_2 and warmer atmospheric temperatures (Lourantou et al. 2010, GB2015).[22] However, there seems to be a clear consensus now that the driving force ending the last glaciation was a change in the earth's orbit that increased insolation in Antarctica. While the warming of the Southern Ocean vented CO_2 and atmospheric CO_2 may well have amplified warming during the initial interglacial period (Timmerman et al. 2009, 1626), according to the leading paleoclimatology text (Cronin 2010, 199), both Greenland and Antarctica ice core records agree on the "temporal relationship between CO_2 and temperature for the interval between 10 and 15 [thousand years ago]. CO_2 concentrations definitely lagged temperature by about 600–1000 years."

All of this work shows a rise of CO_2 from about 180 ppm 22,000 years ago to 270 ppm, just below preindustrial levels, by the beginning of the Holocene 11,000 years ago (see Cronin 1999, 202). When we go back further, to the last glacial period that lasted between about 115,000 and 22,000 years ago, the most striking climatological features are the so-called Dansgaard–Oeschger events. Discovered in Greenland ice cores only quite recently,[23] these are abrupt changes in oxygen isotope measures of temperature. The top orange line in Figure 15.6 (which reproduces figure 1 from Ahn and Brook 2008, 84) shows Greenland ice core temperature reconstructions from 10,000 years ago (the leftmost point) to 90,000 years ago (the rightmost point). The numbers denote D-O events. The Antarctic ice core temperatures in the next line are marked climate changes named after a different scientist (Heinrich). The bottom two lines show reconstructions of atmospheric CO_2 and methane (CH_4) over the same period.

As one can see from the numbered D-O events in Figure 15.6, such events involved "rapid, decadal scale transitions" from cold to warm periods, followed by very slow centuries to millennia long transitions back to colder conditions (Boers et al. 2018, E11005–E11014). As one can also see, while abrupt increases in atmospheric CO_2 preceded rapid temperature increases during D-O events 19, 20, and 21, this is not a consistent pattern. During very abrupt warming periods between 30,000 and 45,000 years ago, CO_2 was steadily falling. Ahn and Brook (2008) found a correlation between increases in CO_2 and warming periods, but also found that unlike the large increases in methane that immediately preceded temperature increases (see the bottom CH_4 line in Figure 15.6), "CO_2 does not lead temperature, [and] CO_2

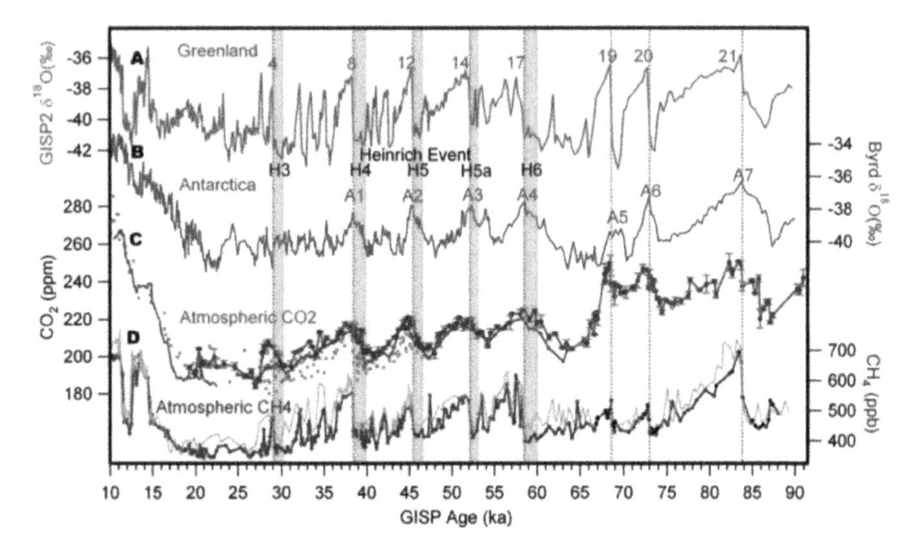

FIGURE 15.6 CO_2 during D-O cycles.

variations were not a direct trigger for the climate changes that occurred during the last glacial period."

Beginning over 30 years ago, scientists explained the abrupt temperature increases during D-O events not as due to increases in CO_2, but due to a strengthening of the Atlantic Meridional Circulation which transports warm water northward to Europe at the surface and then returns them southward in the deep ocean (Boers et al. 2018). These shifts in the meridional circulation were supposedly caused by huge pulses of glacier meltwater accompanying warming in North America. However, as Boers et al. (2018) summarize, not only is there disagreement over whether the data actually support such shifts in the meridional circulation, but large-scale reorganizations of ocean circulation take place very slowly, much too slowly to cause decadal CO cycles.

Boers et al. (2018) provide evidence for an alternative hypothesis, that the destabilization and eventual collapse of various Greenland ice shelves (some no longer existent) are the trigger for DO events. Regardless of how this theory holds up, while climate scientists go so far as to say that "oceanic uptake and release of CO_2 might play a role in millennial" DO climate events (Cronin 2010, 179), this is about as far as they go.

B CO_2 *and Climate over the Last 800,000 Years*

Glacial and relatively warm interglacial periods have cycled periodically over the last 800,000 years. Scientists believe that these have been driven by variations in the earth's orbit (Past Interglacials Working Group of PAGES 2016, 162–219). There are three such variations, and two have a large impact on the insolation reaching the earth: precession, which describes 11,000 year cycles in the time of the year when the earth is closest to the sun, has a huge impact of up to 40 W/m² (more than 10 times the impact of increased atmospheric CO_2 to date) in the lower, tropical latitudes. Obliquity, the tilt of the earth toward the sun relative to the plane of its elliptical orbit, varies on 41,000 year cycles between 22.05° and 24.5°. This wobble causes a net change of 17 W/m² in the solar radiation at the top of the atmosphere in high latitudes (poleward of 65°) (Cronin 2010, 114–117).

As can be seen in the top panel of Figure 15.7, big swings in solar insolation (the black line) accompany big swings in temperature and CO_2 over the nine generally recognized glacial terminations that have taken place over the last 800,000 years. It is generally agreed (Past Interglacials Working Group 2016, 193–194) that the two key amplifiers of changes in insolation that are internal to the climate system are atmospheric CO_2 concentration and land albedo (which changes significantly as ice sheets grow and retract).

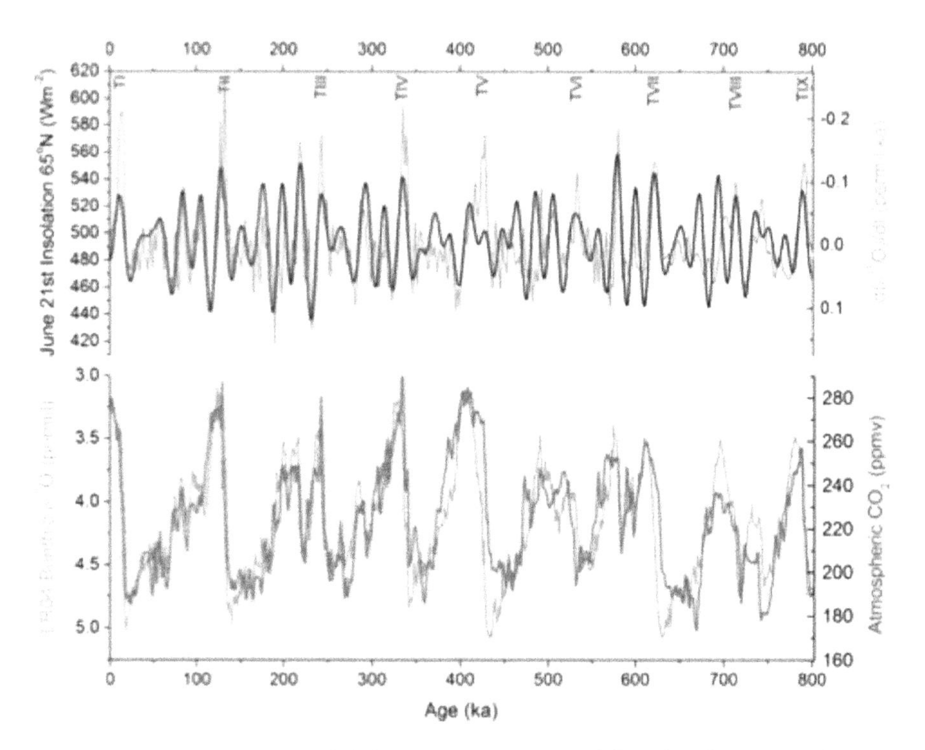

FIGURE 15.7 Temperatures and CO_2 over 800,000 years of glacial cycles. A reproduction of figure 13 from Past Interglacials Working Group of PAGES (2015, 194).

As one can see from Figure 15.7, rises of up to 80 ppm of atmospheric CO_2 were typical of glacial terminations of the last 800,000 years. There seems to be general agreement that the deep ocean is both where CO_2 is sequestered during glacial periods and where it is released during interglacials, and that the Southern Ocean is "most likely" the place where ocean-atmosphere CO_2 exchange took place. However, as the Past Interglacials Working Group (2016, 194) states, "no quantitative physical explanation has yet been advanced for the different CO_2 levels and trends that were experienced during each interglacial of the last 800,000 years. … The exact mechanism linking insolation forcing and deglacial CO_2 rise remains unclear."

C *Global Climate over the Cenozoic Era, the Last 65 Million Years*

To get information about climate even beyond the last million years or so, scientists cannot rely on ice cores. Instead, according to the leading paleoclimatology text, they rely (primarily but not entirely) on the study of isotopes of oxygen and carbon in the calcium carbonate shells of an ancient single-celled plankton (foraminifera) and other animals found in ocean floor sediments (Cronin 2010, 82). These reveal a progressive cooling of planet earth over the last 65 million years, with notable interruptions of the cooling during what is called the Paleocene–Eocene Thermal Maximum about 55 million years ago and the Pliocene Thermal Optimum about 4.5 to 3 million years ago.

During the Cenozoic, the Himalaya and Rocky Mountains were formed by uplift; and the Tasmanian Gateway between Australia and Antarctica and the Drake Passage between South America and Antarctica were also created by tectonic forces, effectively isolating Antarctica from the oceanic heat flow from low to high latitudes in the southern hemisphere. Scientists disagree about the direction of causation, disagreeing for example, about whether the uplift of mountain ranges caused Cenozoic cooling or whether Cenozoic climate somehow caused continental uplift (Cronin 2010, 90–98).

According to Cronin,[24] "the most important feature of the Cenozoic paleoclimate record is the existence of extreme climate states, primarily periods of global warmth, low pole-to-equator thermal gradients, ice-free polar regions, and elevated CO_2 concentrations." The most intense such period was the so-called Paleocene–Eocene Thermal Maximum (or PETM). Scientists think that around 55 million years ago, sea surface temperatures increased as much as 8°–9°C in only 6,000 years, somewhere between 2,000 and 4,500 gigatons (Gt) of carbon was released into the atmosphere with atmospheric concentrations reaching between 600 and 2,800 ppm, and major changes in ocean circulation patterns, temperature, and chemistry.

There are scientists who think that the PETM was caused by an increase in atmospheric GHGs, especially methane. However, even those scientists who believe that the increase in atmospheric GHGs played a role in the PETM have noted that the rise in CO_2 "did not coincide with, nor was of sufficient magnitude to produce, the mean warming of 5–10C" (Cronin 2010, 104). Indeed, scientists do not know what caused the PETM CO_2 increase – the oxidation of 5,000 Gtc of organic carbon.

Another period of extreme temperatures during the Cenozoic period occurred during the middle Pliocene epoch, about 4.5 to 3 million years ago. Also called the mid-Pliocene Thermal Optimum (MPTO),[25] this was a 500,000 year period of relatively little climate variability. In some respects – continental topography, ocean basin configuration, and ocean circulation patterns and even atmospheric CO_2 – the MPTO is said by scientists to be similar to the present. It was, apparently, warmer, with high-latitude sea surface temperatures at much as 8°–10°C warmer and sea level 15–25 m above present.

According again to Cronin (2010), there are a variety of explanations for the MPTO. Enhanced North Atlantic circulation and a stronger Gulf Stream "might explain elevated temperatures in the polar and subpolar North Atlantic and Arctic Oceans" and "produce many observed high latitude paleoceanographic patterns." Other researchers have hypothesized that the "emergence of the [Central American Isthmus, or CAI, now known as the Panamanian Isthmus] shoaled the straits connecting the Pacific and the Caribbean to less than 100 m water depth and altered surface salinity on both sides of the Isthmus. CAI shoaling at 4.7 and 4.2 million years ago would initially lead to mid-Pliocene warmth, especially in high northern-latitude regions, because of increased heat and perhaps salt transport." Cronin summarizes that research showing "intra-Caribbean and Pacific-Caribbean salinity variability at orbital and longer timescales during the closure … supports the CAI-ocean climate mechanism to explain long term Pliocene trends."

As for the role of atmospheric GHG concentration in explaining the MPTO warmth, "Methane concentrations for the MPTO are not available," but CO_2 reconstructions for the period "range from about 340–370 ppm … about 10–30% higher than typical late Pleistocene interglacial concentrations (280–330 ppm)." This, however, is a reconstruction solely from European fossil leaf stomatal records. Interestingly, as of 2010, a new hypothesis was that the MPTO represented a "semi-permanent El Niño climate state," with the idea being that "the absence of cool SST's in the eastern tropical Pacific can induce warming in extratropical regions through changes in tropical evaporation-precipitation and atmospheric feedbacks." This idea is said to be supported by various lines of evidence, including ancient tropical SST reconstructions. Still, Cronin concludes by saying that "modestly higher atmospheric CO_2 concentration" is a "potential" explanation for the MPTO.

D *Climate Change from 65 Million to 3.8 Billion Years Ago*

Paleogeographic maps display a very different earth in the far, far distant past (what Cronin 2010, 57, calls "deep time.") At the beginning of the Cenozoic epoch 65 million years ago, the earth looked somewhat like it does today, but only somewhat, as present-day continents were split and only partially formed, with present-day Europe and Africa, for example, under the oceans. If we go even further back in time, say 130 million years ago to the Mesozoic epoch, the continents had just begun developing, emerging from the single supercontinent known as Pangea that is believed to have existed around 260 million years ago.

According to Cronin (2010, 67), "one major issue of deep time paleoclimatology is whether atmospheric CO_2 concentrations directly control or amplify large-scale climatic fluctuations over millions of years." The reconstructions of both ancient CO_2 and temperature levels provided by Rothman (2002) seem to show pretty clearly that at very long time scales, changes in atmospheric CO_2 concentration does not correlate very closely to temperature change. One can see this in Figure 15.8.

In this figure, the gray bars at the top correspond to cool climate periods and the white spaces in between are warm periods. As one can see from the figure, at this time scale, there is no clear correlation between changes in CO_2 and the onset of long warm or cool periods. For example, the CO_2 fall between 450 and 400 million years ago preceded a warm period, and the CO_2 increase around 190 million years ago preceded a very long cool period. What is most clear from Figure 15.8 is that the earth was until very recently in a long cool period with falling CO_2.

With the present continental configuration of the earth not even existent until the last 65 million years, Figure 15.8 is obviously depicting CO_2 and temperature for a very different planet earth. The problem of explaining how the influence of atmospheric CO_2 in a world with, for example, a single supercontinent, might differ from its influence in today's world cannot be answered simply by running simulations

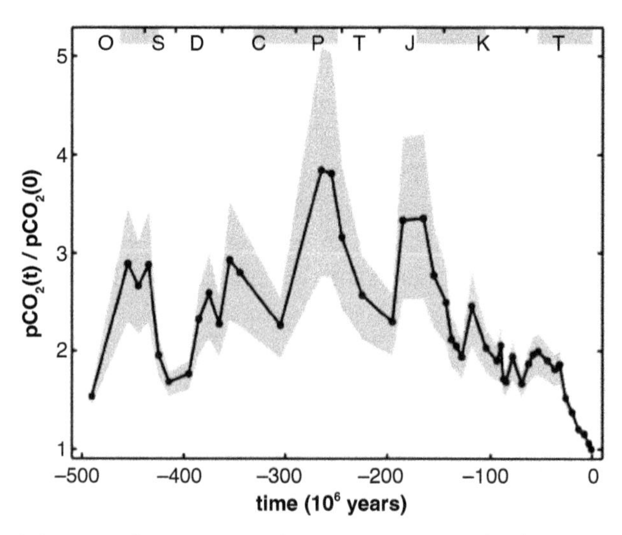

FIGURE 15.8 CO_2 (partial pressure) and temperature over the last 500 million years. A reproduction of Rothman (2002, figure 4).

with climate models. It is far from clear how models that cannot explain twentieth-century temperature change without a variety of "tunings" could be used to simulate climate in that world with a single supercontinent that existed 260 million years ago to today's world.

V FUTURE IPCC AR'S MAY RELY LESS AND LESS ON GCM MODEL PROJECTIONS

One of the scientific journals that has published many important climate science papers is *Science*. That journal is a general scientific journal, not one that is focused on climate or even geophysics more broadly. Each issue contains peer-reviewed original scientific work, but each issue begins with a news and editorial section. According to a very recent *Science* news story by Voosen,[26] GCM modelers now say that with their recent refinements – such as much finer grid boxes over which approximations are calculated – the GCM models are now potentially able to actually reproduce ocean eddies and therefore interannual oscillations such as ENSO. On the other hand, the models are now generating ECS – the equilibrium temperature increase after a doubling of CO_2 – around 5°C. This is far from what has been observed and the opposite of the decreasing upper bound found in the empirical studies I have discussed above.

It is also far from what is believed to have been true during far distant climate periods. The Eocene describes the period that lasted from 56 to about 34 million years ago. It is believed to have been a warm and rainy period (it can be seen as a white gap in Figure 15.8). One of the climate models in the large set of such models that are being used to generate the climate projections for the forthcoming 2021 IPCC Assessment Report is called the Community Earth System Model version 2 (or CESM2 for short). When Zhu et al. (2020) compared what this model simulated for the Eocene with the proxy reconstructions of climate for that era, they found that the model simulated temperatures that were 5.5°C greater than the upper limit of proxy temperature reconstructions. The model's simulated average land temperature of 55°C (or 131°F) was, according to Zhu et al. (2020, 378), "much higher than the temperature tolerance of plant photosynthesis and is inconsistent with fossil evidence of a Neocene tropical rainforest."

According to one modeling group (at the National Center for Atmospheric Research or NCAR), the problem seems to be, as it has been for decades, aerosols and clouds and the interaction between them. When the NCAR model was fed actual updated data on aerosols the model fail to replicate twentieth-century warming – it predicted very little – but when that problem was fixed, the model apparently generated a big decrease in low level, radiation reflecting clouds, causing a big warming feedback.

With the GCM models possibly getting worse, not better, at replicating past climate, one should not be surprised to hear that the IPCC seems prepared to reduce its reliance on GCM models in its next Assessment Report. According to the *Science* news article by Voosen:

> In assessing how fast climate may change, the next IPCC report probably won't lean as heavily on models as past reports did, says Thorsten Mauritsen, a climate scientist at Stockholm University and an IPCC author. It will look to other evidence as well, in particular a large study in preparation that will use ancient climates and observations of recent climate change to constrain sensitivity. IPCC is also not likely to give projections from all the models equal weight, Fyfe (a GCM modeler with the Canadian Center for Climate Modelling and Analysis) adds, instead weighing results by each model's credibility.

If by credibility Fyfe means ability to reproduce the past relationship between temperature and CO_2 without relying on tuning of uncertain feedback parameters, and the ability to generate testable predictions that have not been disconfirmed, then at least from my review, is not clear which GCM models would have nonzero weight.

Notes

1. The entire text of Cook's May 22, 2018, post is available at www.skepticalscience.com.
2. Henry Fountain, "How Climate Change Could Shift California's Santa Ana Winds, Fueling Fires," *New York Times*, October 28, 2019.
3. Joshua Emerson Smith, "Climate Change Should Tamp Down California's Wildfire-Fanning Santa Ana Winds, Study Finds," *LA Times*, January 31, 2019, available at www.latimes.com/science/sciencenow/la-me-ln-climate-change-santa-ana-winds-20190131-story.html.
4. Morales (2018), available at https://escholarship.org/uc/item/6hm499nj.
5. IPCC, Summary for Policymakers of IPCC Special Report on Global Warming of 1.5°C approved by governments, available at www.ipcc.ch/2018/10/08/summary-for-policymakers-of-ipcc-special-report-on-global-warming-of-1–5c-approved-by-governments/.
6. IPCC 2018 SR, p. 51.
7. Found at p. 105 of the IPCC Special Report.
8. World Bank, GDP Annual Growth Rate, available at https://data.worldbank.org/indicator/NY.GDP.MKTP.KD.ZG.
9. IPCC 2018 SR, p. 102.
10. IPCC 2018 SR, p. 103.
11. IPCC 2018 SR, p. 107.
12. See both Allen and Frame (2007, 582) and Roe and Baker (2007, 629).
13. For a very clear derivation of this result, see Roe (2007, 15–18).

14. Calel et al. take the model climate sensitivities from Meinshausen et al. (2009, 1158), a synthesis article written by a group of past and present lead authors of IPCC Assessment Reports.
15. The particular negative feedback that they consider – uptake of heat by the deep ocean – is often modeled not as a feedback per se but as a linear dampening effect.
16. Taken from Roe and Bauman (2013).
17. The TCR is defined by Lewis and Curry (2015, 1009) as the "extent of global warming at the time of the CO_2 doubling following a linear increase in CO_2 forcing over a period of 70 years." Alternatively, Skeie et al. (2014, 140) define the TCR as "the global mean temperature change at the time of CO_2 doubling under a scenario of a 1% per year increase in CO_2." The same somewhat more precise definition is used by Lewis and Curry (2018, 6054).
18. As shown by Lewis and Curry (2018, 6053), if we substitute for ΔT from the equation in the text into the definition of the feedback $\alpha = \Delta R/\Delta T$, then we get $\alpha = (\Delta F - \Delta N)/\Delta T$, where there are now estimates for all the variables on the right-hand side.
19. For a good survey, see Curry (2018, 6055); Lewis and Crok (2014, 13).
20. Lewis and Curry (2015, 1017).
21. Paraphrasing, roughly and summarily, the argument at Stott et al. (2007, 438).
22. Saikku et al. confirms a similar pattern for Antarctica, in which atmospheric and deep-water temperatures "begin warming and reach peak values in advance of rising CO_2." Like Ahn and Brook, Saikku et al. hypothesize that changes in wind strength and sea ice extent in the Southern Ocean may have accounted for the increased release of CO_2 from the oceans to the atmosphere.
23. On D-O cycles, see generally Cronin (2010).
24. This quote and the following discussion come from and are based upon Cronin (2010, 101–105).
25. This discussion of the MPTO summarizes Cronin (2010, 107–110).
26. Paul Voosen, "New Climate Models Predict a Warming Surge," *Science Magazine*, April 16, 2019, available at www.sciencemag.org/news/2019/04/new-climate-models-predict-warming-surge.

16

The Precautionary Social Cost of Carbon

There are, generally speaking, two types of harm from climate change: harm to human health, economic prosperity and welfare, and harm to nonhuman species and ecosystems. In this chapter, I discuss how the human cost of climate change has been estimated for US regulatory purposes. This estimate is called the social cost of carbon (SCC). It is the most rigorous monetized measure of the harm to human economies from climate change. Harm to humans is not the only potential harm from changing climate, but as the quantification of such avoided harm was the primary benefit advanced to justify Obama-era climate change regulations, I focus here solely on the SCC.

The social cost of carbon (SCC) is a dollar estimate of the global marginal harm caused by an additional ton of carbon dioxide (CO_2) emitted into the atmosphere. Or, as explained by the federal Interagency Working Group that the Obama administration put together to produce SCC estimates, the SCC is "an estimate of the monetized damages associated with an incremental increase in carbon emissions in a given year." A more precise definition, given by the economist William Nordhaus, a developer of one of the models that has been used to come up with a number for the SCC, is that the SCC "is the change in the discounted value of the utility of consumption per unit or additional emissions, denominated in terms of current consumption" (Nordhaus 2014, 273). By the same token, the marginal benefit of a reduction in CO_2 emissions is given by the SCC thereby avoided.

As a measure of the marginal benefit of reducing human CO_2 emissions, the SCC has played an important role in both US climate regulation and in the more general formulation of climate policy. As the Obama administration SCC Working Group explained, "the purpose of the SCC estimates … is to allow agencies to incorporate the social benefits of reducing carbon dioxide (CO_2) emissions into cost-benefit analyses of regulatory actions that have small or "marginal" impacts on cumulative global emissions."[1] As a quantitative measure of the benefits of CO_2 emission reduction, the SCC was crucial in allowing the Obama-era EPA to claim that its regulations were cost-benefit justified, thereby clearing the path to their approval within the Executive Branch and finalization as legally binding.

It is true that although courts have sometimes held that some federal statutes do require federal agencies to consider the climate change impact of regulatory decisions,[2] a strictly quantitative estimate of the benefits of cutting GHG emissions such as that provided by the SCC is required neither by the CAA nor any other federal statute. But such a quantitative estimate is required as part of the regulatory impact analysis (RIA) mandated by Executive Order 12866 (and subsequent revisions thereto). Thus within the regulatory process, the most important role played by the SCC is in allowing EPA to present an RIA of GHG emission reduction regulations that satisfies the cost-benefit requirement of Executive Order 12866.

As a quantification of the benefits of cutting GHG emissions, SCC estimates also allow regulators to argue that various GHG emission regulations under the CAA are not only justified by the precautionary benefits of regulation but also by scientifically derived numbers. Often, without including the SCC as a measure of the harm from climate change avoided by regulations mandating GHG emission reductions, such reductions would not look good on cost-benefit grounds. As Greenstone and colleagues (2011) point out, EPA estimated that the upfront technology costs of its GHG tailpipe emission regulation for light duty gasoline powered cars and trucks (which required increases in average miles per gallon fuel efficiency) was $350 billion. Without taking the SCC into account, the various benefits of the regulation – such as impact on energy security, and on local air pollutants, noise, and congestion – was only $280 billion. Once the EPA added in a measure of the SCC (using the central value from a survey of SCC estimates to be discussed further below) as a quantified benefit of the rule in reducing damages from climate change, however, what would have been a negative net benefit of $70 billion from the rule became a positive net benefit of $100 billion.

During the Obama administration, an Interagency Working Group (IWG) developed and then in 2013 raised its estimate of the SCC, raising its SCC estimate for the year 2020 from $7, $26, or $42 per ton of CO_2 emitted to $12, $43, or $65 per ton (under three interest rate assumptions of 5 percent, 3 percent, and 2.5 percent, respectively).[3] These raises correspond (for the respective interest rate assumptions) to 85, 65, and 55 percent increases in the estimated SCC. They occurred because the three IAMs used by the Interagency Working Group had been updated in various ways, many of which were (as I explain below) completely arbitrary and had no basis in either economics or the physical science of climate change but were made instead solely for computational reasons. After these increases in the estimated SCC, the Obama-era EPA was able to claim that the Clean Power Plan would generate over $10 billion in benefits (using a 3 percent discount rate) just by 2025.[4] This is remarkable, because as we have seen in the previous chapter, climate models do not project very much change in temperature to occur in the relatively few years that remain before 2025. Compared to what EPA said were only $1 billion in compliance costs by that year, its SCC estimate allowed EPA to find that not even including reduced air pollution, the net benefits – benefits minus costs – of its CPP were around $18 billion.

More generally, as a dollar figure estimated by economists, the SCC is enormously helpful to advocates of precautionary policies, for it allows them to actually quantify the harm averted by such policies. In theory, one could come up with an SCC estimate which itself does not incorporate precautionary assumptions. As I shall explain in this chapter, however, SCC calculations used to justify Obama-era federal climate change regulation in fact rest upon assumptions that are highly precautionary. SCC estimates are generated by computer models of how present-day CO_2 emissions affect future economic performance. As they attempt to assess how the physical impact of CO_2 emissions on climate impacts future economic performance, these are called Integrated Assessment Models. The most important thing to know about the SCC estimates generated by such IAMs is that they assume that even developed economies have very little ability to adapt to changing climate. In Part III, I show that this assumption is not supported by US economic history.

The IAMs also simply assume a particular relationship between average temperature and economic performance. This is important to understand: the IAMs that generate SCC estimates in no way try to explain or model how changes in global surface temperature affect economic performance. Instead, they informally get the relationship between economy-wide (or macroeconomic) performance and climate – as captured by temperature – from empirical studies of the impact of changing climate on various economic sectors, such agriculture, and other measures of human well-being, such as civil war and malaria. Hence IAM estimates of the SCC are only as good as the underlying studies of climate and economic performance in particular industries and regions upon which they rely.

With rare exceptions, the studies used in IAMs focus narrowly on climate, identifying a statistical relationship between climate and economic performance in a particular economic sector, or on a particular social bad, such as civil war, without even attempting to control for other important known determinants of the impact of rising temperature on the sector or measure being studied. For this reason, I call such empirical papers "climate and …" studies. Other, broader studies have shown that when the full range of factors affecting the human outcome are included in empirical analyses – whether household size in malaria studies, measures of political exclusion in civil war studies, or agricultural disaster payments and subsidized insurance indemnity payments – climate is discovered to be of much less significance than "climate and …" studies find. My overall conclusion is that the majority of the simple "climate and …" empirical studies upon which IAMs rely to get their climate damage functions tend to overestimate the likely harm from future temperature increases, in many cases by substantial amounts.

Finally, SCC estimates use worst case scenarios for how increases in atmospheric CO_2 impact future temperature and climate risk. Modelers don't say that they are assuming worst case scenarios involving very high climate sensitivity – big temperature increases due to increased atmospheric CO_2. But the accumulating work in climate science reviewed in Chapter 15 shows this to be effectively what the IAMs are doing. Recall that the theoretical work surveyed shows that large and potentially severely harmful increases in temperature do not begin to occur with positive probability for centuries, well beyond the 70 to 100 year time frame that IAMs model. And recent empirical work derives estimates for climate sensitivity – the size of possible future temperature increases due to increases in atmospheric CO_2 – much lower than IAMs assume. As (most) IAMs used for estimating the SCC presume that climate damages increase, the bigger is the future temperature increase, overestimating the probability of big future temperature increases adds to the overestimation bias likely in IAM-based SCC estimates.

I THE SOCIAL COST OF CARBON FROM INTEGRATED ASSESSMENT MODELS

The SCC is hardly an intuitive concept. It might seem that a single additional ton of CO_2 in the atmosphere cannot by itself cause any additional harm from climate change. After all, it is generally acknowledged that the atmosphere contains about 720 billion tons of CO_2, and it is estimated that humans have emitted between 910 and 1,400 Gt (thousand billion tons) since the industrial revolution.[5] As the discrepancy between postindustrial human emissions and the amount actually in the atmosphere indicates, less than half of the CO_2 that humans emit ends up in the atmosphere. Most of the CO_2 emitted is absorbed by the oceans and the biosphere (a process called the carbon cycle). Still, with humans emitting more than 40 billion tons of CO_2 per year,[6] to be able to put a dollar value on the harm caused by one additional ton emitted, economists would have to have identified the precise functional relationship between atmospheric CO_2 and harm.

By "functional relationship," I mean something like the algebraic equation (1):

$$\text{GDP}\$ = b_1 CO_2 + b_2 X_2 + b_3 X_3 + \cdots b_n X_n. \quad (1)$$

Where GDP$ is gross domestic product for a country over a fixed period of time, CO_2 gives CO_2 emissions over the same period of time and the X_i are all the other variables believed to potentially determine (or explain) GDP for a period. The b_i are numbers that give the change in GDP for a marginal (say one unit) change in an X_i variable.

The stock and trade of empirical economics is to look to the data to statistically estimate relationships like equation (1). Economists would estimate equation (1) by using actual observations on GDP and CO_2 and all the other X_i variables. Such a model explains observed GDP for each period based on observed values for all the X_i explanatory variables. The b_i coefficients are calculated and they are set at values that minimize the distance (measured in various ways) between the GDP predicted using those coefficients and the GDP actually observed. The idea is to let the data dictate the weights, the b_is that produce a line that best fits the data.

The relationships estimated in this way can be much more complex than equation (1). They don't need to be linear, and one does not need to force a particular relationship on the data at all, and one can include past observations of all the variables as potential explanatory variables. A moment's reflection, however, is enough to realize that estimates of how present period CO_2 emissions impact GDP and other economic measures of human welfare cannot be generated by statistically estimating something like equation (1), no matter how much complexity is added to it. The reason is that present-day CO_2 emissions have no direct present-day impact on GDP or any other measure of human welfare. The most fundamental feature of the climate change problem is that present-day GHG emissions build up in the atmosphere, where they have a very long lifetime, affecting centuries-distant climate.

This is a crucial point in understanding not only SCC estimates but climate policy issues in general. While it may seem obvious to some readers, my own teaching experience suggests that lots of people do not understand it and so it is important to pause for a moment to clarify how the difference between the mechanism by which CO_2 emissions have an impact and the mechanisms at work with ordinary air pollution.

Emissions of traditional air pollutants like sulfur dioxide and carbon monoxide have immediate impacts on air quality that affects human health, economic performance, and ecosystem health. However, if we shut down all emissions of traditional air pollutants completely, air quality would improve very quickly. For example, sulfur dioxide is emitted by power plants and other industrial facilities that burn coal or other fossil fuels. Because sulfur dioxide only stays in the troposphere for a few days,[7] if we shut down all plants that emit it, then after a few days the atmosphere would be free of sulfur dioxide. By contrast, outside extreme cases – melting dry ice in a small closed room – present-day carbon dioxide emissions have no impact on present-day air quality. Yet unlike pollutants such as sulfur dioxide, which are gone from the atmosphere within days, CO_2 stays in the atmosphere a very long time. At the very least – given the present rate at which CO_2 is taken out of the atmosphere by the oceans and biosphere – it would take 50 to 100 years for the 100 parts per million (ppm) of excess CO_2 in the atmosphere to be removed (Archer et al. 2009, 117–134). Present-day CO_2 emissions change the atmospheric concentration of CO_2 for a long time, and this persistent change in atmospheric CO_2 concentration changes temperatures for many years. Thus the impact of present-day CO_2 emissions on human well-being and economic performance occurs in the future, through the impact of present-day CO_2 emissions on atmospheric CO_2 concentration and future climate.

For this reason, the functional relationship between CO_2 emissions and economic performance is that economic performance (and human well-being more generally) today is affected by past CO_2 emissions, as those past emissions have increased atmospheric CO_2 concentrations which in turn have affected climate. More specifically, CO_2 emissions in any prior year have increased atmospheric CO_2 not only in the present year, but for many prior years, affecting both climate and potentially economic performance for many prior years. Past CO_2 emissions thereby affect current economic performance by their impact on the whole time path of both climate and the economy up until the present.

But of course many other things have affected past economic performance and also climate. So to isolate the future impact of present-day CO_2 emissions is an extremely difficult task. One has to somehow not only identify how present climate affects present economic performance but also how past climate has impacted past economic performance, and how such past economic performance has influenced present-day economic performance, and to separate the influence of past CO_2 emissions on climate and economic performance from other things that may have impacted both. Such influences stretch back potentially decades, or even longer.

Unsurprisingly, it turns out that it is actually impossible to write down and solve an equation expressing how past CO_2 emissions have affected present-day economic performance. What it *is* possible to do is to write down a set of equations that express (1) how the present level of CO_2 emissions control determines CO_2 emissions for present period GDP, (2) how present period CO_2 emissions changes atmospheric CO_2 concentration for future periods, (3) how temperature in a given period depends upon atmospheric CO_2 concentration in the present period (this is called climate sensitivity), and (4) how present period GDP depends upon present period temperature. With these four equations in hand, computers can then be used to crank out how different levels of CO_2 emissions (and expenditures to reduce CO_2 emissions) in the present and future periods affect future period temperatures and GDP.[8]

Because these equations mix science with economics, models that incorporate them are called Integrated Assessment Models (IAMs). As pointed out by Yale economist William Nordhaus, the creator of the oldest IAM, three IAMs are the basis for "virtually all" SCC estimates (Nordhaus 2014, 291). Indeed, as Li and Nordhaus report (as cited in Nordhaus 2014), of 27 studies producing independent estimates of the SCC over the period 1980 to 2012, 19 were different versions of three different IAMs, while the 8 others were reduced form versions based on one of the 3. The Obama administration Interagency Working Group (IWG) relied on three such IAM models in getting the SCC estimate that it used to justify its GHG regulations.[9] As all three IAMs are structurally similar, in the analysis below I use the equations in the DICE model.[10]

Both the economic and the physical science relationships expressed in the equations are enormous simplifications of very complex relationships. They have to be simple in order to be computable. But the simplifications encompass countless assumptions. For example, the equation giving the cost of reducing CO_2 emissions in each period actually is shorthand for a very, very complex and uncertain relationship. It has to assume a whole bunch of things about which technological approach is the cheapest way to reduce CO_2 emissions in any given period and how expenditures translate into emission reductions. Even more uncertain is the physical science equation stating how future atmospheric CO_2 concentration translates into future temperature. This is called climate sensitivity, and as we have seen, estimates of climate sensitivity are still highly uncertain. As explained, recent work suggests that sensitivity may be less than the IPCC and others have assumed, but the main point is that the output of an IAM computer run depends crucially on assumptions about the functional relationship between future atmospheric concentration and future temperature.

In fact, IAM output is best understood as the predicted future economic consequences of alternative paths of CO_2 emissions under a whole range of assumptions about both physical and economic relationships. To be more concrete, IAMs generate results of the following type: "If we assume that future atmospheric concentration generates a certain probability distribution of future temperatures, and that future temperature affects future GDP in a known way, then given any time path of CO_2 emissions (and so also atmospheric CO_2 concentration levels) here is the dollar impact on future GDP of alternative time paths of CO_2 emissions." The best thing about this kind of output from a model is that it doesn't restrict analysis to a particular set of assumptions about either physical or economic relationships. One can run the model under alternative assumptions about how atmospheric CO_2 concentration affects future temperatures and about how future temperatures affect GDP. One can also run the model under different assumptions about how the cost of reducing CO_2 emissions changes over time and alternative paths of CO_2 emission reduction – for example, with some paths calling for large immediate reductions, when the cost is quite high, versus other paths that call for delaying most of the CO_2 reduction until a later time, when the cost of CO_2 emission reductions will, it is assumed, be lower due to technological progress. One can see how both the cost of reducing CO_2 emissions and the benefits – in terms of reduce future economic harm – vary with the time path of CO_2 emission reduction.

Of course, the dollar figures for costs and benefits that one is comparing in such an exercise depends upon how one treats future costs and benefits. More concretely, the issue is how one compares present-day dollar costs of CO_2 emission reduction with benefits – reduced economic harm – that may occur far in the future, 50, 100, or even 200 years from now. Economists generally think that future costs and benefits should be discounted back to present-day value terms. I explain below the various and often conflicting considerations that come to play in justifying such discounting. But for present purposes, the thing to see is that if one uses a high discount rate, of say 10 percent, then any benefit that takes the form of protecting future GDP from harm due to rising temperatures even in the medium distant future will be discounted to a very small sum. For example, suppose our climate damage function says that by spending $1 today on CO_2 emission reduction we could save $100 in harm to GDP due to climate change that would occur 50 years from now. Using a 10 percent discount rate, the \$100 in harm has a present value of about 80 cents (depending upon assumptions about compounding). This is less than the \$1 cost of averting it, and thus the discounted dollar benefit would be less than the cost of CO_2 emission reduction.

As this example shows, whenever most of the benefits from CO_2 reduction accrue in the distant to far distant future, discounting can make the SCC of CO_2 – which after all gives the benefit of reducing CO_2 emissions – smaller than the cost of CO_2 emission reduction. As the rate used to discount future benefits in IAM calculations can radically impact the policy implications of the SCC calculated with IAMs, I explain below how the discount rate is determined by economists. Still, what matters for present purposes is that one can run the IAM computer models for various assumptions about the discount rate, and for each assumption get a different value for the present value of the harm to GDP that is caused by one ton of CO_2 – the SCC.

Precisely the same thing is true for the underlying assumptions that IAMs make about how atmospheric CO_2 concentration determines temperatures and how temperatures in turn affect GDP. The SCC estimated by IAM models – which gives the monetized benefit of reducing CO_2 emissions today – depends entirely upon the functional relationships that IAMs plug in for how CO_2 emissions today affect future temperature, how future temperature affects future GDP, and how changes in potentially far distant GDP are converted into present value. Thus the SCC estimates generated by IAMs depend entirely upon assumptions about three things: (1) the rate at which future harm is discounted into present value, (2) how temperature change causes economic harm, and (3) how CO_2 emissions cause future temperature change. I explain each of these in turn.

A *The Discount Rate in IAMs*

The most highly publicized controversy over how the SCC is calculated has to do with the discount rate r (with $0 < r < 1$) that is used to convert future harm into present value terms. Such a discount rate works by converting some amount of future damage D that occurs, say, T periods from the present into an amount $D/(1 + r)^T$ (in the discrete time case) or $e^{-rT}D$ (where e is the exponential function, used in the case of continuous time). For any $r > 0$, such discounted future damage is less than undiscounted damage. If we value the benefit from present-day CO_2 emission reductions as a reduction future discounted damage from higher temperatures, then the benefit is less than if we valued it by the reduction in undiscounted future damage.

In the context of everyday money management, where the "discount rate" is understood as the market rate of interest, most people are used to using discount rates. Consider a person setting a goal of having available \$1,000 for consumption to occur when she retires 10 years from now. Our retiree wants to know the amount by which she needs to reduce present consumption – in other words, the amount she needs to save and invest – in order to have $1,000 to spend on goods and services in 10 years. If we let S denote the present amount saved, and assume that it is invested to earn a rate of r compounded annually, then to have available $1,000 in 10 years, S must be such that $S(1 + r)^{10} = 1{,}000$. Rewriting this expression, we have that $S = 1{,}000/(1 + r)^{10}$ If we solved this equation with a 5 percent interest rate r, then we would find that S = $615. If we had a longer investment horizon, needing the $1,000 in only, say, 20 years, then the required investment amount would be lower, only $377.

In finance, the amount S_T is called the present value of $1,000 to be received T periods in the future. If we simply rewrite our equation for S with an arbitrary number of T periods ahead in the future, and an arbitrary amount of consumption of C dollars, then the present value of such consumption $S = C/(1 + r)^T$. Obviously, the bigger is r, the discount rate, and the bigger is T, the time until future consumption, the smaller is the present value of the future consumption. When we remember that the present value of future consumption is the amount of present consumption we need to sacrifice in order to save for a fixed amount of future consumption, this equation makes perfect sense. It says that the higher is the return on saving and investing (the interest rate) and the longer the period of saving until consumption occurs, the less one needs to save today.

To translate this idea of present values to the world of estimating the SCC, remember that the SCC gives the future consumption (through lowered national income) that is lost due to warmer temperatures caused by the accumulation of CO_2 in the atmosphere. The SCC is designed to answer is whether the cost of reducing present consumption and investing in CO_2 emission reduction is worth the future benefit of averted damages (lost consumption) from warmer temperatures. The CO_2 emission reduction may be thought of as an investment which pays off in a future reduction of D$ in damages. Thought of as an investment that pays off *D*$ at some time T periods in the future, it is natural to say that the present value of such an investment is given by $D/(1 + r)^T$. This the amount that we would need to save and invest at the interest rate r in order to get the benefit of *D*$ at T periods in the future. Alternatively, we may think of this as the market value of an investment that would generate the market rate of return and pay off *D*$ in T periods. The actual cost of this investment is the cost of present-day CO_2 emission reduction. If present-day CO_2 emission reduction costs more than the market price of an investment paying off *D*$ T periods in the future – the averted climate damage – then it would be rejected as an investment and would not be cost-benefit justified.

This approach to discounting is called the opportunity cost of capital (or social opportunity cost of capital) approach.[11] Even on its own terms it is not free from complexity. I have referred to the market rate of return r, but there are different rates of return. The pretax rate of return to invested capital is a natural metric for evaluating investments. It was estimated at 8.5 percent in the United States over the period 1959–1996. The actual rate of return on savings, however, is posttax, which (when all taxes, corporate, property, and personal income) are accounted for is much lower, around 3.5 percent.

For purposes of calculating the SCC, the use of some such market interest rate as the discount factor is justified by the idea that the opportunity cost to the 100 year distant generation of a dollar spent reducing GHG emissions today is precisely the amount of human and physical capital that that generation would otherwise have available to it were the money saved and invested today. But the social cost of capital approach to discounting is not the only approach. An alternative approach derives what is called the social rate of time preference. This rate, also called the social discount rate, accounts for both the higher value of present versus postponed consumption, possible growth in per capita consumption, and possible change in the marginal utility from consumption as the level of consumption increases.

The social discount rate approach has solid foundations in the economic theory of individual behavior,[12] but empirical estimates of its component parts vary wildly. As Burgess and Zerbe (2013, 392–394) catalog, studies measuring time preference come up with estimates ranging from negative 6 percent all the way to infinity, with a median value of 24 percent and an interquartile range of 8–158 percent. As for growth in per capita consumption, some economists think that per capita consumption will increase by as much as 1.9 percent per year, while others opine that it will be zero., Economists' estimates of the final factor determining the social discount rate, the marginal utility of consumption (more precisely, its elasticity), vary almost as much.

There is an even more fundamental disagreement among economists about the discount rate. As explained by MIT economist Robert Pindyck in an insightful critique of IAMs, there is no general agreement over whether the discount rate should be based on how much people *should*, as an ethical matter, discount the consumption of future generations or instead on the basis of current rates of return to capital investments that people *actually require* before investing (Pindyck 2013, 863–865). For example, for the ethical reason that the interests of (more technically, consumption by) future generation should count just as much as the present generation's, the well-known Stern Report set an extremely low (0.1) rate of pure time preference, which together with an assumption of a low (elasticity) of the marginal utility of consumption (of 1) and a low growth rate in consumption (of 1.3) led to an overall discount rate of future climate damages of 1.4 (see Burgess and Zerbe, 2013, 392–394). Such a rate compares to discount rates based on the opportunity cost of capital that are typically in the range of 3–5 percent.

While IAMs can calculate a SCC for any given discount rate, for purposes of calculating the SCC, the Interagency Working Group used the market rate approach under a variety of rates.[13] For present purposes, the key thing to see is that a low discount rate amounts to dramatically inflating the future damages from climate change that might be averted by present-day expenditures on CO_2 emission reduction. Yet economists not only do not agree on what the value of the discount rate should be, they do not even agree on how the discount rate used in IAMs should be calculated. Because SCC estimates derived from IAMs may vary by orders of magnitude depending upon the interest rate chosen for discounting the future damage from climate change, the assumption of a sufficiently low discount rate can justify virtually any decarbonization policy, no matter its present-day cost.

B *Climate Damage Function in IAMs*

One might well suppose that economists have formulated and then empirically tested models of how individuals and firms react to changing climate, not only to possible temperature change but also to the one aspect of climate change which is known with virtual certainty – an increase in atmospheric CO_2. If empirically verified, such models would then provide a relationship between climate variables and economic performance that could be plugged into AIM computer models.

This is not how IAMs work. In DICE, the most widely used IAM, rising average temperature is simply assumed to lower output (and consumption), and damage from rising temperatures is assumed to increase with the change in temperature. To be more precise mathematically, in DICE, the damage from average global temperature change ΔT, given by $D(\Delta T)$ is assumed to be given by a function of the form:

$$D(\Delta T, t) = a_1 \Delta T_t + a_2 \Delta T_t^2, \qquad (2)$$

where a_1 and a_2 are positive time-invariant constants. Assuming that one has accurately measured the globally averaged temperature change, ΔT_t, in this function the damages from climate change are entirely dependent upon the magnitude of the coefficients a_1 and a_2, and as these are positive, equation (2) assumes that damages from climate change increase with rising average temperatures.

That temperature increase should cause damage to human economies is far from intuitive. After all, on very long time scales, human civilization advanced only *because* temperatures increased with the advent of our Holocene era about 12,000 years ago. On a somewhat shorter time scale, the so-called Little Ice Age that lasted from around 1300 until the beginning of the Industrial Age around 1850 was both very cold and very damaging to humans. During the Little Ice Age, glaciers overwhelmed European towns and villages, and cold temperature along with widespread and recurrent drought led to crop failures causing famines and horrible disease outbreaks, with what one historian[14] calls "catastrophic" episodes occurring in the 1310s, 1430s, 1690s, 1740s, and 1810s.

As shown by Figures 16.1 and 16.2, the twentieth century's post–World War II period of rapid economic growth also happened to the period when global temperatures increased. From the figures, it is clear that when temperatures were relatively low, so too was real GDP per capita in developed countries. As temperatures increased relative to the 1951–1980 norm beginning in the late 1940s, so too did developed country real GDP per capita. The basic time series relationship between temperature and real GDP per capita depicted in Figures 16.1 and 16.2 suggests if anything that increasing average surface temperatures increase real GDP per capita, rather than the opposite.

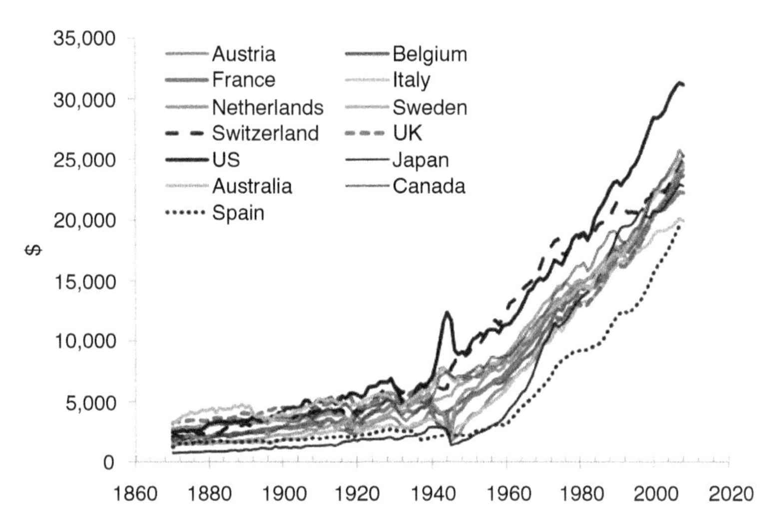

FIGURE 16.1 Real GDP per capita in 13 developed countries, 1870–2011. A reproduction of figure 2 from Kitov and Kitov (2012), available at http://arxiv.org/ftp/arxiv/papers/1205/1205.5671.pdf.

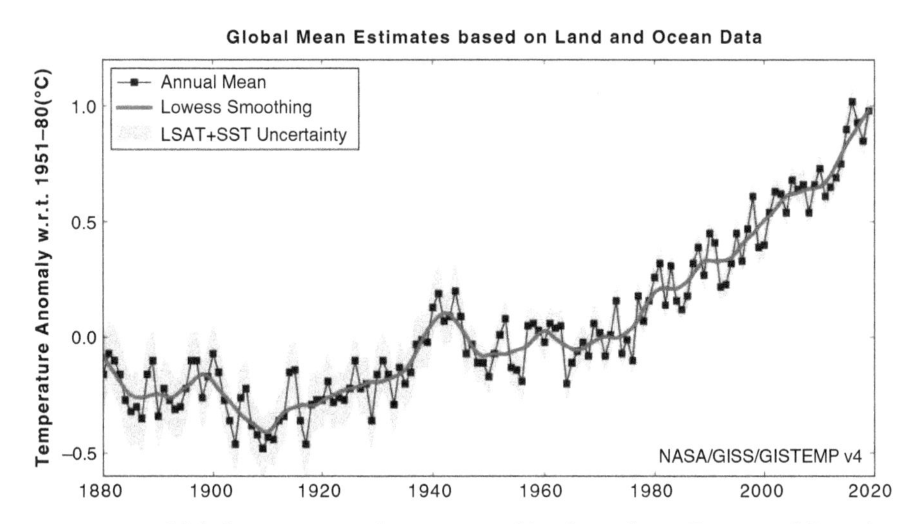

FIGURE 16.2 Global temperature change since 1880. Reproduces Figure 13.6 from this book.

Of course, this comparison is much too simplistic. The question of interest is how increasing average surface temperature would impact real GDP per capita, holding all else constant. The comparison does not hold all else constant. All sorts of important changes occurred in developed countries after the late 1940s. These changes included many – such as remarkable increases in productivity and the pace of technological innovation – that are known to have boosted per capita GDP. Such changes must be statistically controlled if one is to isolate the impact of average surface temperature on real GDP per capita.

The most rigorous economic derivation of an equation like equation (2) would have indeed built up to such an empirical estimation. It perhaps would have begun from a formal, mathematical model of how production and consumption decisions are affected by temperature (working from the primitives of production and utility functions), and then aggregated the model across economic sectors and countries to derive an empirically testable relationship between economic output, temperature, and a long list of other variables affecting production and consumption decisions.

In no version of DICE has equation (2) been derived in this way. And indeed, as commented by MIT economist Robert Pindyck (2013, 868), to get the key coefficients (or parameters) a_1 and a_2 in the climate damage function given by equation (2), "theory can't help us, nor is data available that could be used to estimate or even roughly calibrate the parameters. As a result, the choice for these parameters is essentially guesswork." Even more strongly, Pindyck continues, from an economic point of view, "the damage functions used in most IAM's are completely made up, with no theoretical or empirical foundation."

While it is true that the DICE damage function was not itself derived empirically, it was loosely based on estimates of damages from climate change for particular economic sectors and regions of the world generated by other economists.[15] Up until 2013, Nordhaus and colleagues looked at the existing empirical studies of how temperature affected different economic sectors and chose the estimated impacts from those studies that they subjectively believed to be the best. Such subjective choices fully reflected a precautionary approach. For example, the particular study that Nordhaus et al. primarily relied upon for estimating the impact of rising temperature on agriculture was chosen because it included several regions, and was based both on "detailed agronomic data as well as equilibrium modeling of land use and economic impacts" (Nordhaus and Boyer 2000, 74). Whatever its merits, that study excluded CO_2 fertilization effects as "too speculative" (Nordhaus and Boyer 2000, 75). As I explain in more detail in Part III, increasing atmospheric CO_2 vastly boosts plant productivity. Thus by relying on a study that assumes away such effects, Nordhaus et al. likely biased upward their estimate of the net harm to agriculture from rising temperatures.[16]

For economic sectors other than agriculture, Nordhaus et al. often made major adjustments to previously estimated impacts. With few if any exceptions, these adjustments increase estimated harm from climate change. For example, studies had been done of the economic impact of sea level rise, but as these failed to include the impact of storms, undeveloped land, and the cost of resettlement, Nordhaus et al. made upward adjustments to numerical estimates of the impact of sea level rise, noting. After noting that sea level rise might double the economic cost of coastal storms to the United States, Nordhaus and Boyer stated that it was "reasonable" to adjust upward published estimates of the impact of sea level rise of at most 0.0019 percent of income to a value of 0.1 percent (a 100-fold increase) (Nordhaus and Boyer 2000, 77).

For most other categories of potential economic harm, Nordhaus and Boyer did not even rely upon numerical estimates from previous studies. With no systematic studies of the long run impact of changing climate on health, they estimated health impact by using a single 1996 study on the years of life lost due to climate-related diseases including malaria, various tropical diseases, dengue fever, and pollution. They simply assumed that that one-half of the years that the study estimated were lost over the period 1990–2020 would be lost due to a 2.5°C warming, and "judgmentally" adjusted the years lost for each subregion (Nordhaus and Boyer 2000, 81–82). As for the impact of climate change on both human settlements – by which they mean cities and towns, especially those exposed to rising sea level – and natural ecosystems, "given the lack of any comprehensive estimates," Nordhaus and Boyer simply assumed that every subregion of the world had willingness to pay to avoid climate "disruption" associated with a 2.5°C temperature increase of 1 percent of the capital value of climate sensitive human settlements and natural ecosystems (with the dollar value of such climate sensitive systems assumed to vary between 5 and 25 percent of subregional output) (Nordhaus and Boyer 2000, 86).

As for potentially catastrophic impacts of climate change – such as "wholesale reorganizations of North Atlantic and even global climate systems" which, they say, "climate research" has shown to have occurred in the past over periods "as short as a decade" (Nordhaus and Boyer 2000, 87) – there were no studies at all for Nordhaus and Boyer to look to for impact estimates. Instead, they asked a group of unidentified experts of undisclosed size to attach a probability to a permanent loss of 25 percent or more of global income caused by global warming of different magnitudes. The experts on average thought that the probability of such catastrophic harm was only 0.5 percent for a 3°C warming and 3.4 percent for a 6°C warming (both occurring in 2090). However, in light of what they called "growing" scientific concerns about catastrophic warming, Nordhaus and Boyer doubled these survey estimates (Nordhaus and Boyer 2000, 88). Nordhaus and Boyer then used these probabilities in to derive estimates of the willingness of risk averse people to pay to avoid harm from catastrophic climate change of between 0.45 and 1.9 percent of income for a 2.5°C warming and between 2.5 and 10.8 percent of income for a 6°C warming (Nordhaus and Boyer 2000, 89).

These estimates of the cost of catastrophic harm from climate change (or in their terms, willingness to pay to avoid such harm) are a very big fraction of total harm estimated in the DICE model, making up by the 2007 version "approximately half" the estimated damages from a 6°C climate change (Nordhaus and Boyer 2000, 144). With these "recalibrated" costs of catastrophic damages, plus changes to the estimated harm in regions with big predicted temperature increases, the 2007 version of the DICE model increased estimated climate damages relative to the 2000 version of that model.

Crucially, while DICE tries to capture every conceivable harm from climate change, it simply assumes away economic adaptation to changing climate. As I explain in considerable detail in Part III, adaptation to climate is not only one of the most basic facts of human existence, but abundantly evidenced by both economic history and recent econometric work. Assuming that people cannot cut the damage from changing climate by adapting to altered climate is thus a completely unrealistic assumption. And yet because it amounts to calculating the worst case scenario, it is also a completely precautionary assumption.

We can see the impact of the DICE model's assumption of no adaptation on its estimated SCC by comparing the DICE climate damage function to the damage function in two other IAMs used by the Obama administration IWG to derive SCC estimates. These other two IAMs are called FUND and PAGE. As explained by the Obama administration IWG,[17] FUND allows for explicit harm-reducing adaptation to sea level rise, and also assumes that increasing wealth reduces the harm to the energy sector and human health. Like FUND, PAGE explicitly allows for adaptation, and differentiates between adaptation in developed versus undeveloped countries, assuming – more or less arbitrarily – that developed countries can eliminate 90 percent of the adverse impacts from temperature increases above 2°C but undeveloped countries can eliminate only 50 percent of adverse impacts, which occur for any positive temperature increase.

These are not the only differences between DICE and the other two models (for example, in FUND, for low temperature increases, the agriculture and forestry sectors of the economy actually benefit from CO_2 fertilization and temperature change), but by allowing adaptation, PAGE and FUND generate a climate damage function that is always less than the DICE climate damage function. We can see this in Figure 16.3. As shown by the figure, not only are climate change damages always less in PAGE and FUND than in DICE, but because FUND allows for increased output from agriculture and forestry due to elevated CO_2 at low temperature increases, FUND estimates *net global benefits – not harm* – from temperature change less than or equal to 3°C. Neither PAGE nor DICE portray possible benefits from CO_2-driven temperature increase. But this reflects an assumption, not actual knowledge of whether there could be such benefits from small CO_2-driven temperature increases. DICE and PAGE *do not mathematically permit* the possibility that small temperature increases could actually generate benefits rather than damage.[18]

IAMs are subject to continual revision, and the damage functions shown by Figure 16.4 – used in the 2010 Obama administration IWG on the SCC – have

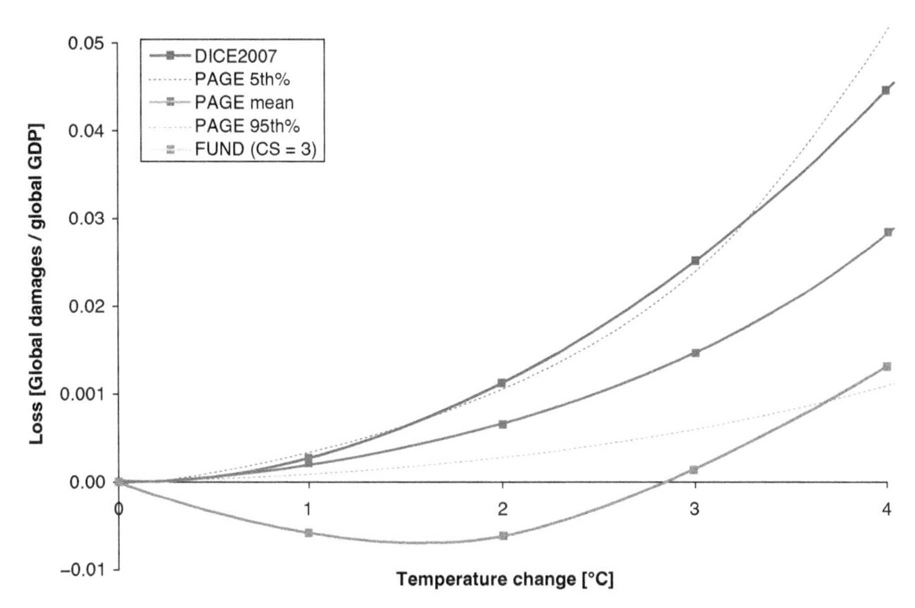

FIGURE 16.3 SCC in DICE, FUND, and PAGE (consumption loss as a fraction of global GDP in 2100 due to temperature increases up to 4°C). From Interagency Working Group, TSD on the SCC, p. 10.

since been revised. However, as described by the Interagency Working Group in 2013,[19] all three of these IAMs were revised in ways that increased estimated climate damages. The increased damage estimates arise for different reasons in different IAMs. The DICE 2010 version gets higher damages because it assumes that sea levels continue rising long after temperatures stop rising, and damages from sea level rise are (like damages generally) assumed to take a quadratic (increasing) functional form and to be permanent.[20] The PAGE model was revised to explicitly include sea level rise, but also lowered the threshold value for and probability of catastrophic damages – a change increasing estimated damages – and perhaps most importantly greatly reduced its assumed effectiveness of adaptation, from eliminating 50–90 percent of economic sector damages from low levels of warming (1–2°C) down to eliminating only 15–30 percent of such damages. Moreover, the new version of PAGE assumes that nothing can be done to adapt to sea level rises greater than 0.25 m (about 10 inches).[21]

As my discussion in Part III details, revisions to IAMs to effectively assume that despite rising income and wealth, countries cannot adapt to rising sea level is inconsistent both with empirical climate damage studies looking at the impact of adaptation and a vast amount of work in economic history. Recent work suggests to the contrary that with proper policies in place to incentivize private responses to changing climate, adaptation may be very effective. This makes it highly implausible that damages from sea level rise could persist forever (the DICE revised assumption). In general, the revisions to IAMs that the Interagency Working Group used in deriving its drastically higher 2013 SCC estimates make IAMs even more arbitrary and more at odds with actual economic evidence.

An even more recent revision of DICE moves that IAM even further away from any connection to actual empirical evidence about the impact of climate change on different economic sectors. The damage function in DICE 2013 is not derived by looking through category-specific studies and choosing what Nordhaus and colleagues consider the best category-specific climate impact estimate (and then aggregating across categories). Instead, the data used by Nordhaus and Sztorc for the 2013 version of DICE were estimates of the impact of global temperature change on global GDP generated by 13 previous papers that themselves had been surveyed in a 2009 paper by Richard Tol. As explained in more detail by Howard and Sterner (2014), this methodology is extraordinarily problematic on a variety of grounds. The key point to grasp, however, is this: estimating the average damage function estimated by previous studies cannot improve upon study estimates unless the studies have strong economic foundations, and yet *none* of the 13 study estimates used by Nordhaus and Sztorc pass this test. Of the 13 studies that generate the data points for the Tol and Nordhaus and Sztorc damage functions, one 1994 study by Nordhaus was simply a report of what a small number of experts thought that the climate damage function might look like, while five others were precisely the same kinds of studies that previous versions of DICE had been based on (studies taking what Tol calls the "enumerative" approach), while the final group of seven studies were simply cross-sectional regressions of various economic measures (prices, expenditures, income, consumption, or even happiness) against temperature. By concealing details of the underlying studies, the Nordhaus/Sztorc study of studies (called meta-analysis), doesn't fix anything. It merely compounds the problems with using such studies to estimate the climate damage function. It is to those problems that I now turn.

II LIMITATIONS AND PROBLEMS WITH "WEATHER AND ..." EMPIRICISM

As discussed, the climate damage function in IAMs is derived in an ad hoc manner from empirical studies of the impact of various climate variables – in particular temperature and rainfall – on the performance of different economic sectors, and on human health indicators of one sort or another. These empirical studies have the virtue of at least looking at actual data – on what has actually occurred – but they nonetheless suffer from serious limitations. Without exception, they look at weather – over days or at most seasons – and not climate, the working definition of which is the 30 year average of weather. They do not provide reliable evidence of the impact of future climate change. Even worse, they tend to overestimate the impact of climate on human health and welfare. In this section, I explain why this is so.

A *Even the Best Empirical Studies Look at the Impact of Weather, Not Changing Climate*

As I will discuss in Part III, there is abundant evidence from both economic history and recent empirical work that given the right incentives and institutions, people all over the world are extremely successful in adapting to diverse climates. The fundamental problem with empirical studies of climate and various aspects of economic performance – such as labor productivity, or the performance of particular industrial sectors, or even economies as a whole – is that they have not actually looked at climate, but rather variations in weather – variations in things like daily, monthly, or annual temperature or precipitation. For very basic economic reasons, looking at the impact of things like unusually hot days says nothing about the potential future impact of a milder warmer climate.

To make this point concrete, I consider the climate economic impact that has been the most rigorously studied empirically: the impact of changing weather on agriculture. Early studies of the impact of changing climate on agricultural tended to view the relevant variable of interest as being yield per acre – a physical measure of agricultural productivity. Such studies first looked to agronomic studies to get the empirical relationship between a climate variable – say average temperature during the growing season – and productivity, then plugged in possible future changes in average temperatures that were deemed likely by climate models (such as 2.5°C), and got an estimated change in agricultural output. This output was then sometimes multiplied by prices to get an estimate of the economic impact of climate change on agriculture.[22]

Economists objected to this approach on the ground that one cannot simply assume a fixed relationship between climate and productivity, because farmers choose crops and crop growing practices to optimally adapt to the climate of different regions. If farmers do so adapt, then at any given point in time, when one looks cross-sectionally at, say, corn yields per acre as a function of average temperature across corn growing regions of the United States, then one will be observing yields given the equilibrium, income-maximizing choices of farmers regarding crop types and growing practices. Studies that took this approach (sometimes called the Ricardian approach), generally found much lower and even positive impacts from rising temperature on agriculture than had agronomy-based studies.[23]

An important advance in the estimation of the impact of climate on agricultural yields occurred with empirical work by Schlenker and colleagues showing that increasing temperatures would likely be more harmful to dryland or nonirrigated agriculture and than irrigated agriculture (Schlenker et al. 2005, 395). Another important advance was the discovery by Schlenker that the number of days during the growing season of extreme heat – days when maximum temperatures exceed 29°–32°C (or 87°–89°F) – sharply depress yields for corn, soybeans, and cotton (Schlenker and Roberts 2009, 15594).The finding that the number of days of extreme heat depresses yields has been replicated, not just by Schlenker and colleagues but by other researchers working with different data sets (Roberts and Schlenker 2012, 271). The deleterious impact of extreme heat on agricultural yields has been demonstrated in models of considerably specificity. Schlenker and Roberts (2009), for example, used a panel data set of county-level crop yields and daily temperatures for all US counties east of the boundary between the irrigated west and the dryland east (100° longitude) for the time period 1950–2005. Lambert (2014) used a panel data set of 331 Kansas farms for the period 1993–2011 that included not only farm-specific data on yields and temperature but also agricultural inputs, where the latter included hired labor, crop inputs such as seed, fertilizer, and herbicides and insecticides.

These studies shed light on the effect of extreme temperatures, *given* the baseline or average climate conditions prevailing over the study period. Indeed, temperatures are extreme only relative to the average temperature at a particular time and place. A July with high temperatures in the 90s would be extremely cool for most of Texas, for example. To provide an economic analysis of the impact of climate on agriculture, it is absolutely crucial to distinguish extreme daily (or even seasonal) temperature and the average temperatures at a particular time and place. The reason is that as I show in great detail in Part III, farmers adapt everything they do – from seed choice, to time of planting, to fertilization and harvesting – to the climate (and soils) where their farms are located. From the short run point of view of annual farm production decisions, things like climate and soil are taken as fixed inputs. Farmers choose their other, variables inputs to maximize expected production given expected weather – climate – and soil type. Only when farmers become reasonably confident (I specify what this might mean in Part III), that growing season temperatures have changed will they consider altering things such as the type of corn they plant.[24] To give a concrete example, suppose that in a future warmer climate, northern regions in the United States would become more similar to today's southern US regions, with a longer growing season and likely more episodes of extremely high temperatures and perhaps also more episodes of drought. Were this to occur, one would expect that northern US farmers would adapt to both a more southern climate and/or drought, significantly ameliorating the impact of such climate changes on agricultural output.

I describe such adaptations in considerable detail in Part III. What matters for present purposes is that statistical "climate and agriculture" studies that look at temperatures extremes cannot possibly capture the impact of such extremes in a hypothetical future climate where both the average temperature is higher and what are now extreme temperatures have become much less extreme relative to the norm to which farmers have adapted.

(a) The Omitted Variables Problem in "Weather and …" Studies: If You Look Only for the Effects of Weather While Ignoring Other Explanations for a Social or Economic Problem, You're Sure to Overestimate Weather's Impact

While they cannot capture possible future long-term adaptation to changing climate, empirical studies of the impact of climate on agriculture have at least developed to the point where the studies do attempt (in various ways) to control for the range of variables that determine the relationship between short-term variations in weather (in particular hot days during the growing season) and agricultural output. Such controls are often absent even from highly publicized and influential studies of the impact of climate on damages in other areas of concern. Without controlling for all variables that will importantly influence the observed relationship between climate variables and the dependent variable of interest, such empirical studies are almost certain to mis-estimate the impact of climate.

(1) WEATHER AND DISEASE. One prominent example of this problem is the relation between climate and climate-related diseases. Among the most highly publicized such diseases is malaria. One can find published studies that posit a simple relationship between average temperature, precipitation and malaria, and which find the if temperatures increase due to climate change, then malaria incidence will increase. To take just on such relatively recent study, Béguin et al. (2011, 1209) estimate a logistic regression model of the form:

$$\text{Malaria\_presence} \cong \text{T\_min} + \text{pr\_max} + \sqrt{(GDPpc)}, \tag{3}$$

where T_min is the mean temperature of the coldest month in a country, pr_max the mean precipitation of the wettest month (over the entire study period 1961–1990) and GDPpc per capita GDP. Béguin and colleagues estimated the relationship (3) for the period 1961–1990 and then plugged in possible future values under climate change for T_min, pr_max and future GDPpc. When they did so, the found that all three variables had an impact on future malaria presence, but that unless future GDP per capita rises significantly, as many as 5 billion people would be put at risk of contracting malaria due to warming temperatures and increased precipitation due to climate change.

But of course climate change models generally predict climate changes out at a minimum of 100–200 years. What is really relevant to predicting the impact of climate change on the incidence of malaria is not a highly simplified regression like (3) that estimates a highly simplified short-term relationship but a study of how malaria incidence has changed with long-term climate change.

Fortunately, there is such a study. Gething et al. (2010, 342) compared a fine-grained global map of the proportion of individuals with malaria parasites in their peripheral blood (the parasite rate) in 1900 with a similarly fine-grained map for

2007. The period between 1900 and 2007 was undeniably one of increasing average global surface temperature. However, as Gething et al. show, the period 1900–2007 was also a time when the global malaria rate fell dramatically. Malaria's geographical range shrank almost by half (with the range of endemic/stable malaria falling from 58 percent of the world's land surface in 1900 to 30 percent by 2007) to become a disease largely restricted to the tropics. Additionally, in two-thirds of this smaller range, malaria endemicity fell.

Gething and colleagues provide a cogent explanation of how and why one can get a very misleading picture of climate change and malaria from studies (such as Béguin et al.) that extrapolate the current spatial distribution of surface temperatures and malaria to predict future changes in malaria under scenarios of rising global temperatures. As Gething et al. explain, such an extrapolation is valid only if (1) all other factors remain constant or have a negligible effect and (2) the link between climate and global malaria distribution is "effectively immutable."

Gething et al.'s evidence shows that neither assumption is likely to be true. It indicates first what they call "a decoupling of the geographical climate-malaria relationship over the twentieth century … indicating that non-climatic factors have profoundly confounded this relationship over time" (Gething et al. 2010, 343). As they explain, even granting that there is a link between temperature and malaria epidemiology (arising from the known biological effects of temperature on different life stage of both the mosquito that carries the malaria parasite and the parasite):

> empirical predictions are only credible if the role and relative influence of non-climatic factors is considered. A simple interpretation of the observed global recession in malaria since 1900 is that *non-climatic factors, primarily direct disease control and the indirect effects of a century of urbanization and economic development, although spatially and temporally variable, have exerted a substantially greater influence on the geographic extent and intensity of malaria worldwide during the twentieth century than have climatic factors*. (Gething et al. 2010, 343, emphasis added)

As I read this, given the predominance of nonclimatic factors in reducing the global incidence of malaria over the last century, a simplistic empirical relationship such as (3) cannot provide any useful evidence on the likely impact of long-term climate on malaria. Instead, it can only mislead the policy choice by vastly overestimating the importance of climate.

Indeed, studies that focus on explaining malaria incidence today – after a century of success in curbing the range and prevalence of malaria – find that climate variables are not only of lesser importance than other factors, but that climate is relatively insignificant. A potentially important factor in eradicating malaria is the use of the insecticide DDT. Limitations on the use of DDT have become something of a poster child for the negative consequences of focusing too much on potential harm to nonhuman species and too little on harm to humans (see, e.g., Spencer 2010). But as the only countries that use DDT to control malaria are those with a malaria problem, to actually statistically identify the causal impact of DDT use on malaria requires using a measure of DDT which effectively controls for the endogeneity of DDT use – the fact use is driven by malaria incidence.

In a study that carefully does this, and looks cross-sectionally at malaria incidence in 220 countries in 2000 as a function of a long list of economic, socioeconomic, geographic, and climate variables, Huldén et al. (2013) find that while increases in national per capita income do have a large impact in reducing malaria rates, the biggest decrease in malaria rates came from reducing the average size of the household below a four person threshold. However, for an income increase to generate the same decrease in malaria frequency generated by a reduction below the four person household size threshold (when evaluated at sample mean values), income would have to increase by over $12,000, almost double the average income for the countries studied. Other factors that were statistically found to reduce malaria frequencies were urbanization, the fraction of the population of Muslim religious affiliation, and mean annual temperature. Most strikingly, when other variables such as income and latitude were controlled, an *increase in mean annual temperature actually decreased malaria frequency*, while DDT use had a positive impact in reducing malaria only when household size was not included as an explanatory variable. Huldén and colleagues speculate that the statistically significant impact of both small household size and Muslim affiliation comes about because both generate sleeping arrangements in which relatively few people share a room for sleeping, and distributing people across more rooms during the nighttime makes it more difficult for mosquitoes to transmit the parasite to new household members.

(II) WEATHER AND CIVIL WAR. The relationship between climate and disease is only one of many such "climate and ..." relationships that have been empirically estimated using techniques that have much too narrow and short-term a focus to really be credible indicators of how climate change may impact the category or sector being studied. The same problems characterize studies of climate and civil wars. A widely cited study by Burke and colleagues estimates a positive relationship between rising temperatures and the incidence of civil war (Burke et al. 2009, 20670). In subsequent work with the same data set, however, Buhaug (2010, 16477) found that the result depended entirely on using country dummy variables (country fixed effects) as a proxy for societal explanations for civil war and a time trend variable that was the same for all countries. When Buhaug dropped the country fixed effects and time variables from regressions, temperature was no longer statistically significant; even when the country fixed effects and time variable was included, temperature explained less than 1 percent of the variance in civil war incidence.

Buhaug then looked at a much larger set of civil wars – including armed intrastate conflicts with fewer than 1,000 deaths per year – and included not just average temperature but also temperature shocks (measured as deviations from annual means). He looked a much larger set of potential explanatory variables, and found that civil war risk increased as national GDP per capita declined, as the share of the population excluded from political influence increased, and that baseline risk of civil war in sub-Saharan Africa jumped with the collapse of the cold war system. These results were consistent with what political scientists had already discovered about the determinants of civil war in sub-Saharan Africa, but would be missed in an study that focused too narrowly on climate alone.

The debate did not end there. Burke and colleagues responded to the Buhaug critique by arguing that for "econometric" reasons, country fixed effects and a time trend had to be included as explanatory variables in regressions attempting to estimate the relationship between climate and civil war (Burke et al. 2010, E185). This is more or less a truism as a general statistical matter: if one wants to identify the impact of temperature on civil war, then one has to control for other, unobserved variables that may impact civil war. However, by including a dummy, 0–1 variable for each country in a regression, one effectively isolates the impact of temperature on civil war within a country. Yet as explained in a rebuttal by Buhaug (2010), political scientists do not think that country identity per se has any impact on civil war. Rather, they believe that certain key features of political institutions – in particular, the extent to which minority groups are excluded from the government – are what matter.

A country variable does not measure these, but instead is a more or less random noise variable. Too see why, suppose that there were 10 countries in a sample such as that studied by Burke et al. Suppose that over the study period, in five of the countries at various times institutional changes occurred that greatly increased the strength of civil society institutions while giving minority ethnic groups a role in government for the first time. Political scientists have identified such changes are significant in lowering the odds or frequency of civil war. Now suppose that only a country variable is included as an explanatory variable in statistical (panel data) analysis. With respect to the real explanatory variable – institutional change – country is completely random.

Moreover, by including a time variable, Burke et al. identify the impact of temperature on civil war within a country after subtracting for the time trend of civil war in that country over the study period. But as pointed out by Buhaug, one of the most basic facts about African civil war is that although surface temperatures in Africa have increased over the last 30 years, the frequency of civil war has declined (with an even stronger negative trend in fatalities). This is due to changes over time in many political and civil institutions in Africa over this period, changes that because they occurred at different times in different places cannot possibly be captured by a simple time variable that applies in the same way to all places in the study.

Burke et al. argued that proper econometric methods required that their analysis include country fixed effects and time variables. To the contrary, what Burke et al. did was to add two variables – time and country identity – that are so coarse as to be more or less random variables with respect to the actual determinants of civil war. In a sense, temperature had to be statistically significant in the regressions run by Burke et al., because they did not include any other variables that could explain civil war at a sufficiently localized level. Burke et al. found that when added to a statistical model that does include such variables, temperature was not statistically significant. As Buhaug points out, temperature adds very little to explaining civil war outbreak (explaining only about 0.002 out of a total explained variance of 0.657), and temperature completely loses statistical significance when more recent years are added to the sample period studied.

(III) WEATHER AND WILDLAND FIRE. One of the most widely cited papers ever published on the harmful impacts of climate change is a simple univariate regression by Westlering et al. (2006) showing a positive and statistically significant relationship between average summer temperatures and the number of large (500 hectare (ha) or bigger) wildfires in the western United States over the period 1970–2003. Westerling et al. did not attempt to control for any other factor that might explain an increase in the number of such large wildfires.

There are, however, a number of things other than summertime temperatures that might explain an increase in the number (as well as duration) of large western US wildfires over the 1970–2003 period. One of these is fire suppression policy – how quickly, if at all, fires are put out. Other than in California, large wildland fires in the western United States occur in the National Forests and National Parks. After the high temperatures and severe droughts of the 1930s led to massive and widespread wildfires, the US Forest Service (USFS) adopted its famous "10 am policy." Under this policy, the USFS aimed to put out all reported wildfires, even those that ignited in remote, backcountry areas. By the 1970s, however, the new discipline of forest ecology maintained that fires were part of the native ecology in western forests. Under the philosophy of natural fire use, "natural lightning-set fires" had to be tolerated and "surrogate, prescribed fires" sometimes deliberately set by forest managers.[25] By 1974, all major US national parks had prescribed (deliberately set) fire programs, and lightning-caused fires were allowed to burn within more than 3 million acres of designated fire zones within national parks. By 1978, both the USFS and US Park Service had officially adopted prescribed natural fire policies that gave preference to the policy of allowing fires to burn within natural barriers rather than trying to put them out with aggressive firefighting.

By 1988, the natural fire policy had become well established throughout the western United States. During the hot and droughty summer of 1988, more than 50 fires struck Yellowstone National Park, and under the natural fire policy then in place, most were at first allowed to burn naturally. They burned out of control, however, eventually provoking the Park Service to step in with old style, aggressive firefighting. Before the fires ended, almost 1.4 million acres of Yellowstone National Park had burned. Although the natural fire policy was suspended in the aftermath of the Yellowstone conflagration, by the mid-1990s it was resumed on a more limited basis.

The period 1970–2007 studied by Westerling et al. was thus a period during which the official policy of the federal agencies in charge of managing western wildland fires changed dramatically from putting such fires out as soon as possible to allowing them to burn. One would suspect that such a policy change might well have increased both the number of large (bigger than 400 ha) fires and also their size and duration. Figure 16.4 shows that even after controlling for the effect of higher summertime temperatures (Figure 16.4(b)), the number of large western wildfires did indeed begin to increase right around 1978, the year when both the Forest and Park Service adopted the natural fire policy for all of the lands in their jurisdiction. Johnston and Klick (2012) also found that when a fire policy variable – the percentage of fires fought aggressively (according to the 10 am policy) – was included in statistical analysis, the estimated impact of higher summertime temperature on the number of fires changed compared with analysis that did not include the policy variable.

Such a result is especially notable in that the natural fire policy might have been expected to have impacted the size and duration but not the number of large western wildfires. That its inclusion altered the estimated effect of summertime weather on the number of large western wildland fires is evidence that the role played by summertime weather was likely overestimated by Westerling et al. This is not to deny that hotter and dryer summers are positively correlated with more large western

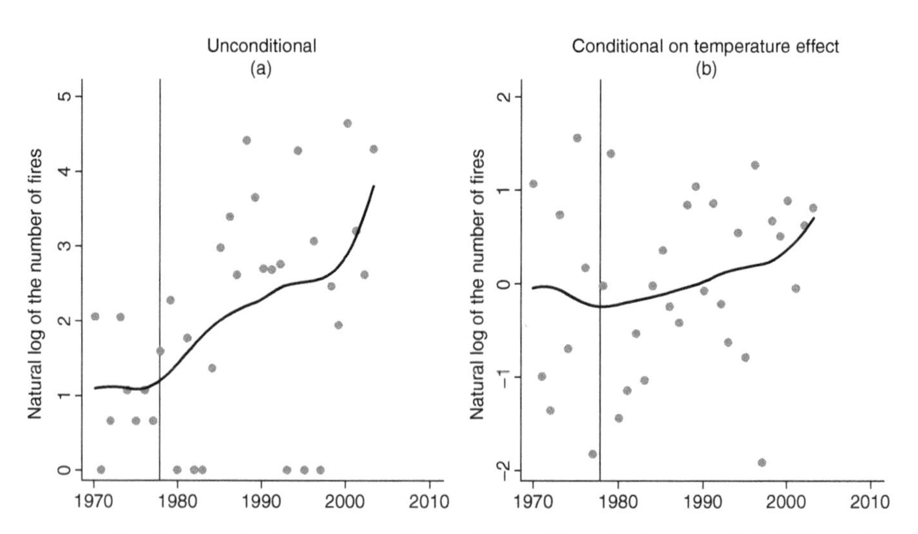

FIGURE 16.4 Increase in the number of large wildland fires during period of wildland fire use. Reproduced from figure 9.5 of Klick and Johnston (2012, 171).

wildfires. But estimates such as those produced by Westerling et al. provide the building blocks for SCC dollar figures produced by IAM computer models, and if estimates such as those produced by Westerling et al. are biased upward due to the failure to control for all relevant explanatory variables, then so too will SCC estimates be biased upward.

In many of the most recent and highly publicized wildfires in California, fire suppression policy is not the most important variable that must be considered in order to isolate the impact of weather on fire. In California, the Forest Service did not aggressively move to the natural fire policy (Stephens and Ruth 2005, 532–542). Instead, the California Department of Forestry and Fire Protection has long had in place an "initial attack" approach that – like the old "10 am" rule – tries to limit the extent of the area burned in wildfires. According to Stephens (2005, 218) that approach long succeeded in preventing the burned area in California from increasing despite an increase in the relative number of fires.

California has seen a dramatic increase not in the size but in the number of wildfires. The evidence is clear that the increase in the number of fires in California has been due primarily to an expansion of housing development into fire-prone areas. Looking at the periods 1960–1980 and 1980–2000, Syphard et al. (2007) found that the number of California fires was highest in areas where low density housing development had extended into places where wildland vegetation was still prevalent and made up more than half of the area (such areas are called intermix wildland-urban interface (WUI)). In California, fire danger is highest where such low density housing development has pushed into the chaparral shrublands; indeed, Syphard et al. (2007) found that putting housing in a landscape dominated by chaparral shrublands not only increased the number of fires, but also increased the area burned.

These finding are paralleled for the United States as a whole. Theobald and Romme (2007, 340–354) found that over the period 1970–2000, the amount of development in the WUI in the United States increased by 52 percent, with about two-thirds of the WUI by 2000 found in areas either where fire risk is naturally high due to vegetation type or has been made high by decades of fire suppression under policies such as the Forest Service's 10:00 AM rule. The trend of expanding low density housing into risky, fire-prone landscapes has accelerated. Studying the more recent period 1990–2010, Radeloff et al. (2018) found that the area of especially risky intermix WUI increased by 27 percent, with 4.78 million more houses in the intermix WUI in the United States in 2010 than in 1990. The expansion of development into such risky areas has had a clear impact on the number fires. Across all regions of the United States, Nagy et al. (2018) found that humans ignited four times as many large wildfires as did lightning (about 143,000 vs. 33,000), with the west coast of the United States in particular "dominated" by human-ignited fires.

Fire season weather is understood to play a common sense role in increasing the number or size of fires, with hot and droughty summers known to increase the number of lightning-ignited, western US wildfires. Over the 1992–2012 period, however, 84 percent of the wildfires documented by the US federal government were started by people (Balch et al. 2017). Human-ignited wildfires occur in the fall, winter and spring seasons that used to be relatively free of fire, indeed, Balch et al. (2017) find that over 1992–2012, fully 78 percent of human-started fires occurred in these seasons, when such fires added 840,000 wildfires, a 3,500 percent increase above the number of lightning-started fires. Simply put, pushing low density housing into risky, fire-prone areas increases the number of fires.

On the other hand, Syphard et al. (2017) found that the effect of humans on fire is more complex than merely increasing the number of fires. Once housing and population density get sufficiently high, landscape fragmentation may actually reduce the spread of fires even though such development lengthens and alters the seasonal timing of the fire season. Such complex effects likely explain Syphard et al.'s (2017, 13753–13754) most striking finding, which is that the "overall amount of fire in a region was not significantly related to the importance of climate." As they conclude, while climate change, bringing hotter and dryer fire season weather "may indeed be a concern for those areas with strong fire–climate relationships," "in some areas, anthropogenic factors diminish the influence of climate on fire activity." As for the length of the fire season, Balch et al. (2017, 2950) conclude that whereas "climate change has extended the fire season" in parts of the United States by "a couple of weeks," an increase in the number of fires started by humans "increased the length of the fire season by more than three months." This recent work shows that any study of how summertime weather effects the number or size of fires that fails to properly statistically control for human land development and other activities increasing the number of fires cannot possibly yield reliable estimates.

Despite this, the climate risk funding machine continues to support studies that make no serious attempt control for nonclimate variables. For example, Abatzoglou and Williams (2016) look at the impact of anthropogenic climate change on western US wildfires. But as they blithely admit, they treat the impact of climate change on fire as "independent from the effects of fire management (e.g. suppression and wildland fire use policies), ignitions, land cover, … and vegetation changes." By omitting so many clearly important additional explanatory variables, they have almost surely misestimated the size and statistical significance of the impact of climate change. Rather than cautioning the reader to this, Abatzoglou and Williams simply state (Abatzoglou and Williams 2016, 11773) that such "confounding influences … contribute uncertainty to our empirical attribution of regional burned area to [anthropogenic climate change]." As with all "weather and …" studies, this is a vast understatement: omitting explanatory variables means that estimated effects of variables that are included are incorrect, and may well lack statistical significance.

(IV) THE MOST IMPORTANT OMITTED VARIABLE FROM "WEATHER AND …" STUDIES: POLICY. The importance of government policy in determining the economic impact of weather extends far beyond the wildland fire context studied by Johnston and Klick (2012). Whatever the weather event – ranging from tornados and hurricanes to heat waves and droughts – government policy is a crucial determinant of the economic impact of the event. Policies regarding climate change are discussed in Part III of this book. For present purposes – understanding the precautionary bias built into statistical "weather and ..." studies – it is important to understand that the omission of policy variables from such study is very general and indeed the rule rather than the exception.

For a particularly important example, consider again statistical studies of weather and agriculture. By practicing conservation tillage practices that leave more crop residue on the field after harvest, farmers of water-sensitive crops such as corn and soybeans can realize both short- and medium-term private benefits in the form, respectively, of improved soil moisture and reduced topsoil runoff (Schoengold et al. 2014, 898). During precisely the period of late twentieth-century warming in surface temperatures, roughly 1980 to 2010, however, the US Congress greatly increased both the coverage of federal crop insurance and also ad hoc disaster payments, with major expansions in crop insurance subsidies in 1980, 1994, and 2000. As summarized by Schoengold and colleagues, a substantial body of research has shown that even as it incentivizes farmers to plant more acres, crop insurance may by a substitute for costly risk-reducing cropping rotations by farmers (Schoengold et al. 2014, 900). In their own work, which carefully controlled for this endogeneity – the fact that the size of crop insurance payments may not only influence farmer practices but themselves be determined in part by those practices – Schoengold and colleagues find that over the period 1990–2004, when insurance and disaster payments are included as explanatory variables, the number of recent drought years actually *decreased* the use of no till and other conservation tillage practices. Moreover, for conservation tillage practices that are cheaper than no till, a $10 increase in disaster (insurance) payments was associated with a 5 (7) percent reduction in the use of conservation tillage (Schoengold et al. 2014, 914).

While the work by Schoengold and colleagues looked at episodes of drought, when Schlenker has extended his own work on the impact of extreme temperature on corn and soybean yield to control for the fraction of the crop that was federally insured, he found results that are consistent with those obtained by Schoengold and colleagues. Annan and Schlenker found that the sensitivity of corn yield to extreme heat was 67 percent larger for insured corn than uninsured corn and 43 percent larger for insured soybeans versus uninsured soybeans (Annan and Schlenker 2014). There thus is accumulating evidence that just as economic theory would predict, ad hoc disaster and crop insurance that insulate farmers from damage that occurs during drought and episodes of extreme heat severely reduce farmers' incentives to adopt practices that may reduce such harm.

In light of this evidence of a strong effect of ad hoc disaster payments and crop insurance indemnity in increasing harm to crop yield from drought and extreme heat, that ad hoc crop insurance and insurance payments have dramatically increased over precisely the period of late twentieth-century warming (1980–2000 in particular) means that any empirical analysis of the relationship between climate and crop yields that failed to control for such payments would have been fundamentally misspecified. Such specification error generates systematically biased estimates of the impact of the included variable, weather. More general work on trends in agricultural yields suggests that the failure to control for ad hoc disaster and crop indemnity payments is just the tip of the iceberg when it comes to the misspecification of models attempting to estimate the impact of climate on agriculture. The steady expansion in corn yields due to the introduction of new hybrids that occurred over the 1953–2000 period has stagnated or (in some regions) reversed (Gaffney et al. 2015, 1608). In explaining the relative stagnation in yields, Gaffney and colleagues point to both policy problems – inconsistent global regulations and lack of protection for intellectual property rights – and also the lack of infrastructure and markets in regions where large productivity gains are possible. Any estimate of the impact of climate on agriculture that fails to control for such important determinants of incentives to introduce and use new hybrids is misspecified and will generate biased estimates.

III FREEZING SCIENCE: SCC ESTIMATES ARE BASED ON OUTDATED PROJECTED FUTURE TEMPERATURE INCREASES THAT ARE TOO HIGH AND THEREFORE LEAD TO OVERESTIMATES OF THE SCC

Getting climate damage functions such as those depicted in Figure 7.3 is only the first step in the calculating a SCC estimate. Those functions plot climate damage as a function of future temperature increase. To calculate the damage from any particular increment of CO_2 – the SCC – one needs to know how increases in atmospheric CO_2 translate into future temperature increases. As explained in Chapter 15 this relationship – called *climate sensitivity* – is standardly expressed as by the increase in global average surface temperature caused by a doubling of CO_2 relative to its preindustrial baseline of about 280 ppm. Climate sensitivity is rarely expressed as a single number, but rather as a range, such as temperature increases of between 1.5 and 4.5°C as a result of a doubling of atmospheric CO_2. A range is given because there is uncertainty over the sensitivity of the climate to changes in atmospheric CO_2.

For many years, the hope was that climate models could reliably quantify and narrow the range of climate sensitivity. As also explained in Chapter 15 this now seems unlikely. Uncertainty of climate sensitivity seems unavoidable, and such uncertainty translates directly into uncertainty about the SCC. Moreover, the most recent work shows that climate sensitivity over the time period used to calculate the SCC is likely much lower than IAM models have assumed. Thus the SCC estimates used by the Obama-era IWG are likely much too high.

In building IAMs, economists have, naturally enough, used the distribution of climate sensitivities currently available from climate models (as summarized in IPCC Assessment Reports). The Interagency Working Group used the same set of climate sensitivities when it did its own run of IAMs to generate a SCC (but fitting different probability distributions, including that generated by Roe and Baker (2007) so as to incorporate uncertainty about sensitivity into its SCC estimates). The equilibrium climate sensitivities used by the Interagency Working Group are depicted in Figure 16.5. In the figure, each colored line gives the projected probability density of different temperatures generated by a particular climate model. Note that all the major computer climate models used by the IPCC were also used by the Interagency Working Group.

As one can see from Figure 16.5 the Obama administration IWG used climate sensitivity probability density functions that attach significant probability to temperature increases above even 5°C. Indeed, even that Group's preferred "calibrated Roe and Baker" function attaches a probability in excess of 10 percent to temperature increases of almost 5°C.

Such probability density functions are said to have "fat tails," because relative to the standard normal distribution, there is much more probability weight attached to the extreme high values. If we look back at equation (1), we see that the damage from climate change assumed in IAM models such as DICE increases very steeply as temperature increases. When "fat tail" climate sensitivities such as those depicted by

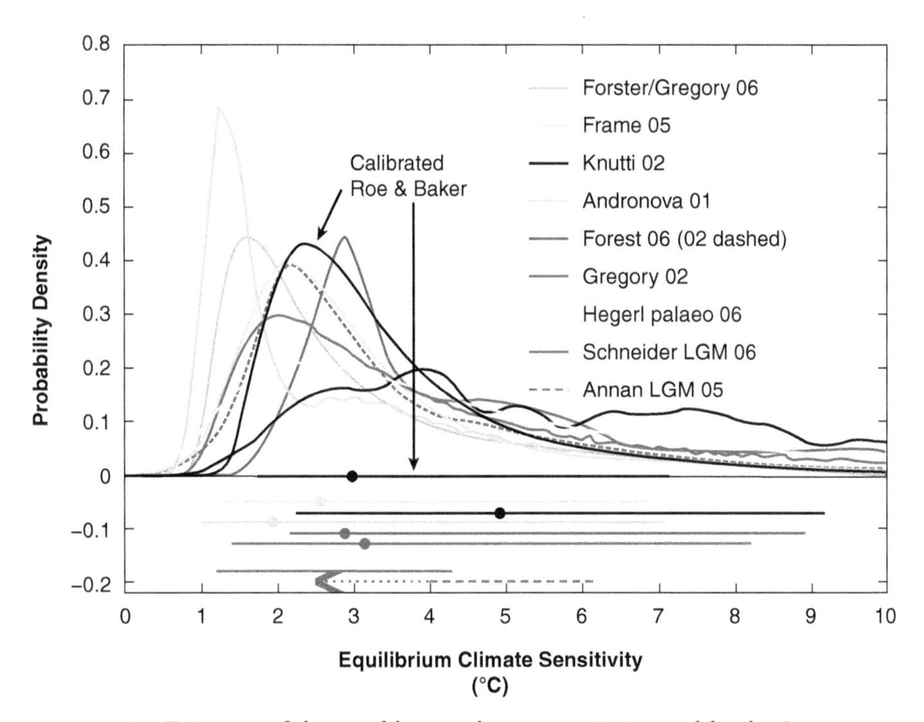

FIGURE 16.5 Estimates of the equilibrium climate sensitivity used by the Interagency Working Group in calculating the SCC. Reproduces figure 2 from the Interagency Working Group (2010, 14).

Figure 16.5 are assumed to hold, IAM projections of the damage from climate change based on equation (1) simply have to be big.

A *Misspecified Climate Sensitivity in SCC Calculations, I: Misunderstanding the Time Path of Temperature Change*

The Roe and Baker (2007) climate sensitivity function was taken by many economists[26] as the standard for calculating the SCC. However, as I explained in the previous chapter, Roe and colleagues have published articles correcting what they view as the misuse of climate sensitivity distributions in calculating the SCC. The problem with the use by economists – including not only the Interagency Working Group but also IAM builders – of equilibrium climate sensitivity estimates is that economists have failed to take into account more recent work showing that climate sensitivity is likely to evolve to high levels only very slowly over time.

As we've seen, such very slow evolution of the global surface temperature response to increases in atmospheric CO_2 occurs because the deep ocean sequesters vast amounts of heat. To recall, Baker and Roe (2009) found that when an empirically validated model of ocean heat sequestration was added to a climate sensitivity model, the model simulated that earth surface temperature increases above 4°C would occur only after about 450 years from the present.

Although unrecognized by IAM models and the SCC Working Group, the slow evolution of potentially great climate sensitivity is enormously significant for the estimation of possible climate-related damages. Roe and Bauman (2013) explain how misunderstanding of this important scientific relationship affects damages calculated in IAMs:

> Even in the absurd limit of an infinite climate sensitivity, the amount of warming that can occur is limited by the rate at which the system can accumulate energy. … Therefore, from the standpoint of the formal statistical definition – that the tail declines as a power in the limit of $T \to \infty$ – *there is no fat tail to the climate response at finite time.* This is not an esoteric point: simple analytical damage functions can be highly sensitive to the integration limits.
>
> … Recent economic analyses have explored how uncertainty in the physical climate predictions affect policy guidance. Because such analyses invariably include discounting, the results can depend dramatically on how quickly the uncertainty grows into the future: the possibility of large, relatively short-term damages matters more than if those same damages occur in several centuries. Proper representation of [physical factors that matter to when damages occur] tends to reduce the rate at which uncertainty grows with time, and our example calculations with a simple economic model suggest that the impact on economic analyses is significant. In one example of an application of such analyses, *none of the three IAMs used in a recent interagency report on the social cost of carbon (Interagency Working Group 2010) represent any of these three physical effects.*[27]

The Interagency Working Group's SCC estimates are based on its understanding that "equilibrium climate sensitivity includes the response of the climate system to increased greenhouse gas concentrations over the short to medium term (up to 100–200 years), but it does not include long-term feedback effects."[28] If one pays attention to the findings in Baker and Roe (2009) and Roe and Bauman (2013), this is a serious misunderstanding of how scientists have derived climate sensitivity probability distributions. Those distributions evolve over very long time frames, with virtually no likelihood that temperature increases above 3°C could be realized over the next 200 years. Were climate damage functions $D(t)$ used in IAMs such as DICE to generate SCC estimates of the sort the Interagency Working Group relied upon to take account of the analysis in Roe and Bauman (2013) they would attach essentially zero probability to very large and harmful temperature increases until reaching a point at least 200 years from now. As for the largest temperature increases, say above 6°C, these would never occur with positive probability. For any positive discount rate, updating the SCC estimates to take account of what Roe and Bauman discuss above would substantially lower the estimated SCC.

B *Misspecified Climate Sensitivity in SCC Calculations, II: New, Empirically Based Estimates of Climate Sensitivity Indicate Lower Temperature Increases and a Much Lower SCC*

Since in IAM models, damage from climate change increases more than linearly with rising temperatures, with really big damages flowing from the highest temperature increases, it must be that if IAMs were run using the more recent, empirical estimates of climate sensitivity that I reviewed in the previous chapter, damages from higher temperatures, and hence the SCC, would be lower than the dollar figures used by the Obama-era IWG.

Two recent studies, by Dayaratna et al. (2017) and Dayaratna et al. (2020) have performed just such IAM runs. These confirm that the SCC is much, much lower when one uses the most recent, empirically based estimates of climate sensitivity. Dayaratna et al. (2017) used the climate sensitivity estimates provided by Lewis and Curry (2015) in the FUND and DICE models. As previously discussed, the Lewis and Curry (2015) best estimate for climate sensitivity was 1.6°C (and about 1.3°C for transient climate response), much lower than the older, model-based estimates used by the Obama-era IWG but in agreement with virtually all of the newer, empirical estimates. With these newer, lower climate sensitivity estimates, Dayaratna et al. (2017) found that the DICE model estimated SCC for the year 2020 fell from the $37.79 Obama-era IWG estimate to $19.66. In the FUND model, which as explained earlier allows for the possibility of increased agricultural and forest productivity due to CO_2 fertilization, the SCC fell even more, by 83 percent (from $19.33 to $3.33).

Most recently, Dayaratna et al. (2020) ran the FUND model with even more recent estimates of climate sensitivity, from Lewis and Curry (2018) and Christy and

McNider (2017). To recall, the FUND IAM model, developed by Tol, allows for both adaptation to climate change and for a potentially negative SCC – that is, that climate change is actually beneficial, not harmful. Figure 16.6 shows how much recent, empirically estimated temperature distributions differ from the Roe–Baker (2007) distribution used by the Obama-era IWG. As one can see, the new distributions are centered at an equilibrium temperature increase less than 2°C, and attach barely any positive probability to temperature increases above 3°C.

Dayaratna et al. (2020) used the FUND model because it is the only IAM that allows for CO_2 fertilization effects. I discuss such fertilization effects in more detail in my analysis of human adaptation to climate in the next chapter. As I explain there, while it is true that not all plants get the same boost in growth rates from higher-CO_2 environments (even corn and soybeans, for example, have very different responses), the vast majority of plants grow faster in high-CO_2 environments. Even with no CO_2 fertilization effect at all, when using the temperature distribution estimated by Lewis and Curry (2018), Dayaratna et al. (2020, table 2) found a SCC of only \$1.61 in 2020. This compares to an SCC of \$19.33 using the Roe–Baker (2007) distribution. When they allowed for fertilization effects of either a 15 or 30 percent boost in agricultural and forest productivity, Dayaratna (2020, table 2) found a negative SCC of, respectively −\$0.82 and −\$2.74 in 2020. A negative SCC means that there is *not net harm but a net economic benefit* from a higher-CO_2 world, even allowing for possible damage from higher temperatures in some economic sectors.

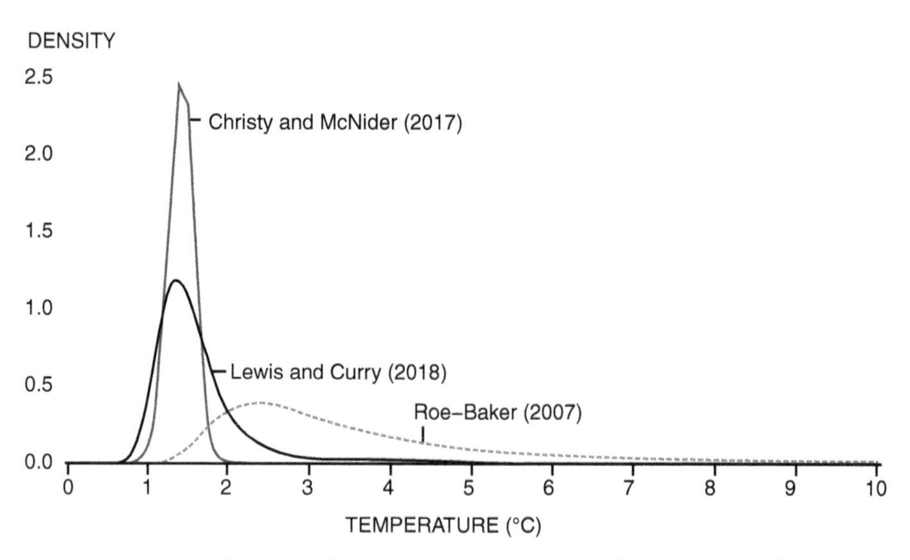

FIGURE 16.6 Reproduction of figure 2 from Dayaratna et al. (2020). Reproduced with permission granted by the terms of the Creative Commons Attribution License 4.0 that governs Springer Open Access publications.

Notes

1. Interagency Working Group on Social Cost of Carbon, US Government, Technical Support Document: Social Cost of Carbon for Regulatory Impact Analysis under Executive Order 12866, p. 1 (February 2010), available at www.epa .gov/otaq/climate/regulations/scc-tsd.pdf.
2. See, e.g., *Center for Biological Diversity v. National Highway Traffic Safety Administration*, 538 F.3d 1172 (9th Cir. 2008).
3. Interagency Working Group on the Social Cost of Carbon, YSD: Technical Update of the Social Cost of Carbon for Regulatory Impact Analysis under Executive Order 12866, p. 2 (2013).
4. See EPA, RIA for the Final Clean Power Plan, table ES-9.
5. These figures are a bit dated, but close enough for present purposes, and are taken from two activist websites, respectively, Carbon Brief, www.carbonbrief .org/doha-infographic-gets-the-numbers-wrong-underestimates-human-emis sions, December 7, 2012, and the climate scientist activist blog *Skeptical Science*, How Do Human CO_2 Emissions Compare to Natural CO_2 Emissions, available at https://skepticalscience.com/human-co2-smaller-than-natural-emissions.htm.
6. Michon Scott Rebecca Lindsey, "Which Emits More Carbon Dioxide: Volcanoes or Human Activities?," NOAA Climate.gov, available at www.climate.gov/news-features/climate-qa/which-emits-more-carbon-dioxide-volcanoes-or-human-activities, June 15, 2016.
7. SACS, "Sulfur Dioxide in the Atmosphere," available at http://sacs.aeronomie .be/so2-atmos.php.
8. A similar summary description of how IAM models work is provided by Greenstone et al. (2011, 4), available at www.nber.org/papers/w16913, who explain as follows: "The three IAM's translate emissions into changes in atmospheric greenhouse gas concentrations, atmospheric concentrations into changes intemperature, and changes in temperature into economic damages. The emissions projections used in the models are based on specified socio-economic (GDP and population) pathways. These emissions are translated into concentrations using the carbon cycle built into each model, and concentrations are translated into warming based on each model's simplified representation of the climate and a key parameter, climate sensitivity. Finally, transforming the stream of economic damages over time into a single value requires judgments about how to discount them."
9. See Interagency Working Group on the SCC (2010) and also Interagency Working Group on the SCC, US Government, Technical Support Document: Technical Update of the Social Cost of Carbon for Regulatory Impact Analysis under Executive Order 12866 (May 2013).

10. As it actually allows for potential adaptation and the possibility that small temperature increases might actually generate benefits, I also discuss below the FUND model, which is described by its developer, Richard Tol, in "Estimates of the Damage Costs of Climate Change: Part I: Benchmark Estimates," 21 Env'l & Res. Econ. 47 (2002), and "Estimates of the Damage Costs of Climate Change II: Dynamic Estimates," 21 Env'l & Res. Econ. 135 (2002).
11. This definition and the subsequent discussion are drawn from Burgess and Zerbe (2011).
12. See the derivation in Moore et al. (2012, 1–16).
13. Interagency Working Group TSD on the SCC 18–19.
14. White (2017, 76), and on the Little Ice Age more generally, 70–87.
15. As the derivation of climate change damages did not change in DICE until DICE 2013-R, this discussion is based on the explanation of how climate change damages were derived in the DICE 2000 model, which itself was a globally aggregated version of a model called RICE 1999. The explanation of how region- and sector-specific impacts were estimated in that model that my discussion is based upon can be found in Nordhaus and Boyer (2000, 69–98).
16. For regions not included in the preferred study, Nordhaus et al. used estimates of the impact of climate on agriculture derived from cross-sectional studies of climate and agriculture. Nordhaus and Boyer (2000, 75).
17. Interagency Working Group, TSD on the Social Cost of Carbon, pp. 7–8.
18. It is for this reason, a mathematical assumption, that PAGE damages are always bigger than FUND damages. Marten (2011, 2011–18), available at http://dx.doi.org/10.5018/economics-ejournal.ja.2011-18.
19. See Interagency Working Group on the SCC, Technical Update of the SCC.
20. Interagency Working Group, 2013 Update on the SCC, p. 7.
21. Interagency Working Group, 2013 Update on the SCC, p. 11.
22. An explication and defense of this approach is provided by Darwin (1999, 371).
23. For an illustration of a study illustrating the then state of the art, see Mendelsohn et al. (1994, 753).
24. For another discussion of this important point, see Kolstad and Moore (2019).
25. Johnston and Klick, "Fire Suppression Policy, Weather, and Western Wildland Fire Trends: An Empirical Analysis," in Bradshaw and Lueck (2012, 158–177).
26. Economists using the Roe and Baker (2007) analytics include not just the IAM model builders and Interagency Working Group but also Weitzman (2009, 1) and Pindyck (2011, 258).
27. Emphasis added.
28. Interagency Working Group TSD on the SCC, p. 12.

PART III

Toward Rational Climate Policy

17

Adapt and Prosper

The US Experience

As long as our species has been on planet Earth, humans have had to adapt to their external physical environment. During the cold upper Paleolithic era – which runs from about 40,000–10,000 years ago – Neanderthals died out, and most remaining homo sapiens were hunter-gatherers. They lived in widely dispersed bands that followed herds of animals such as reindeer. Such hunter-gatherer Paleolithic life was precarious, subject to cycles in the population of prey animals. Still, even during these cold and grim Paleolithic times, recent research has found evidence that in favorable locations, some human groups adopted agriculture and expanded rapidly after the Last Glacial Maximum (about 25,000 years ago) or perhaps even earlier, 60,000–80,000 years ago.[1] Moreover, even during this, the stone age, humans colonized new territories, such as Australia and the Americas, and by the end of the Paleolithic had domesticated dogs.

After surviving several cold snaps during the early Holocene, humans responded to the much more hospitable warmer and wetter Holocene climate by cultivating wheat, barley, and other crops and domesticating sheep and goats. By 8000 BC or so, such agriculture had spread from the fertile crescent area of the Middle East to encompass much of Euro-Asia. Around the same time, maize, squash, and beans were cultivated in central and South America. Global human population is generally thought to have increased tenfold between the end of the Paleolithic and 8000 BC.

No one argues against the proposition that the human transition from the primitive stone age of Paleolithic hunter-gatherer bands to the rapid development of the Holocene was not due at least in part to a warmer and wetter climate. But of course the Holocene climate itself did not do anything. It was human adaptation to the Holocene climate that led to rapid increases in human population and technological and cultural development. Humans have always adapted to their climate. I shall argue in this chapter that while technological progress has made such adaptation more and more successful, it is not technology, but institutions and in particular the legal, social and political institutions of a place that are the primary determinants of the ability of a country to adapt to environmental change. As adaptation to climate change determines the economic impact of such a change, and as legal, social, political and economic institutions determine the pace and success of adaptation, one cannot predict the economic impact of changing climate unless one can predict institutional change.

As explained in the previous chapter, for US federal regulatory purposes, the dollar estimates for the economic benefits from present-day GHG emission reductions are captured by the so-called social cost of carbon (SCC). As explained in that chapter, the SCC used to justify Obama-era GHG emission regulations under the CAA was generated by computer models of climate and the macroeconomy that assume that people have either no or at most very limited ability to adapt to climate change.

More specifically, the DICE computer model of the economic impact of climate change completely assumes away adaptation. Like DICE, a second model used for Obama-era SCC estimates (called FUND) derives the regional economic impact of climate change on by adding up the impact in different sectors of economic activity, such as agriculture and forestry. Unlike DICE, the FUND model actually does allow for benefits from rising temperatures and from CO_2 fertilization (at least for lower temperature increases) and FUND does allow for explicit harm-reducing adaptation to sea level rise. The third computer model used to derive the Obama-era SCC is called PAGE. That model explicitly allows for adaptation, and it differentiates between adaptation in developed versus undeveloped countries. The PAGE model once assumed – more or less arbitrarily – that developed countries can eliminate 50–90 percent of the adverse impacts from temperature increases above 2° C but that at any temperature increase, however small, undeveloped countries can eliminate only 50 percent of adverse impacts via adaptation. The Obama administration used a revised version of PAGE that for unspecified reasons greatly reduced its assumed effectiveness of adaptation. That version of PAGE assumed that developed economies could eliminate only 15–30 percent of economic sector damages from small (1°–2°C) temperature increases. This is a drastic reduction from the 50–90 percent of economic sector damages that the model previously assumed could be reduced by adaptation. Moreover, the version of PAGE used to compute Obama-era SCC estimates assumed that nothing can be done to adapt to sea level rises greater than 0.25 m (about 10 inches).[2]

These computer models rest solely upon assumptions about the human ability to adapt to changing climate. They do not even attempt to model the role of institutions in determining incentives to adapt to changing climate. They not do themselves derive estimates of the human ability to adapt to climate, nor do they incorporate systematically the existing evidence about the human ability to adapt to climate. This is not because such evidence isn't available. Scholars in disciplines ranging from geography to economic history have provided voluminous evidence not only of the human ability to adapt to climate, but about the institutional determinants of such adaptation.

In this chapter, I review and attempt to add to that evidence by looking at adaptation in corn production in the United States and in the eventual universal American adoption of air conditioning. In the next chapter, I consider the remarkable case of agricultural adaptation in the African Sahel, one of the more precarious environments for agriculture on earth. This evidence confirms that fundamental insight of Nobel Prize winner Friedrich Hayek (1945, 524–525) that as "the economic problem of society is mainly one of rapid adaptation to changes in the particular circumstances of time and place, ... the ultimate decisions must be left to the people who are familiar with these circumstances, who know directly the relevant changes and of the resource immediately available to meet them." As will be seen from the discussion below, the evolving empirical evidence on the likely harm to various economic and noneconomic aspects of human well-being do not support a general assumption that people cannot effectively adapt to things such as rising temperatures and sea level. To the contrary, the evidence shows that policies that protect private property rights will incentivize private responses to changing climate. Conversely, policies that either centralize the control of resources and/or redistribute the costs of failure to adapt will cut incentives to adapt.

I ADAPTATION IN US AGRICULTURE: THE PAST, PRESENT, AND FUTURE OF CORN

A *Recent Empiricism*

For economists attempting to get dollar estimates of the economic impact of climate change, agriculture has been perhaps the most-studied part of the economy. After all, weather has always been and still is a primary determinant of annual crop yield (production per acre), and for many decades, agencies like the Department of Agriculture have collected data on agricultural output. Early studies of the impact of changing climate on agricultural tended to view the relevant variable of interest as being yield per acre – a physical measure of agricultural productivity. Such studies first looked to agronomic studies to get the empirical relationship between a climate variable – say, average temperature during the growing season – and productivity, then plugged in possible future changes in average temperatures that were deemed likely by climate models (such as 2.5°C), and got an estimated change in agricultural output. This output was then sometimes multiplied by prices to get an estimate of the economic impact of climate change on agriculture.[3]

Economists objected to this approach on the ground that one cannot simply assume a fixed relationship between climate and productivity, because farmers choose crops and crop growing practices to optimally adapt to the climate of different regions. If farmers do so adapt, then at any given point in time, when one looks at a given point in time at, say, corn yields per acre as a function of average temperature across corn growing regions of the United States, then one will be observing yields given the equilibrium, income-maximizing choices of farmers regarding crop types and growing practices. Studies that took this approach (sometimes called the Ricardian approach), generally found much lower and even positive impacts from rising temperature on agriculture than had agronomy-based studies.[4]

As discussed in the previous chapter, important advance in the estimation of the impact of climate on agricultural yields occurred with empirical work by Schlenker et al. (2005, 395) showing that increasing temperatures would likely be more harmful to dryland or nonirrigated agriculture than to irrigated agriculture. Another important advance was the discovery by Schlenker that the number of days during the growing season of extreme heat – days when maximum temperatures exceed 29°–32° C (or 87°–90°F) – sharply depress yields for corn, soybeans, and cotton.[5] The finding that the number of days of extreme heat depresses yields has been replicated, not just by Schlenker and colleagues but by other researchers working with different data sets (Roberts and Schlenker 2012, 271; Lambert 2014, 439).

The deleterious impact of extreme heat on agricultural yields has been demonstrated in models of considerably specificity. Schlenker and Roberts (2009), for example, used a panel data set of county-level crop yields and daily temperatures for all US counties east of the boundary between the irrigated west and the dryland east (100° longitude) for the time period 1950–2005. Lambert (2014, 445–446) used a panel data set of 331 Kansas farms for the period 1993–2011 that included not only farm-specific data on yields and temperature but also agricultural inputs, where the latter included hired labor, crop inputs such as seed, fertilizer, and herbicides and insecticides. These estimates of the effect of extreme temperature have thus attempted to control for factors other than episodes of extreme temperature that might affect agricultural yield.[6]

When Roberts and Schlenker (2012, 279) allowed their empirically estimated relationship between extreme temperature and yield to vary over time, they found that the heat tolerance for corn in the northern states in their sample and soybeans in the southern states had actually decreased over time. As measured by the slope of the regression line with corn yield and number of days with a maximum temperature above 29°C (84°F), Roberts and Schlenker (2011, 241) observe that up until 1960, US corn yields were becoming less sensitive to the number of extreme heat days, but since 1960, the slope has become a more negative, so that extreme heat has become "most damaging in recent years when corn varieties were optimized for maximum average yields." Roberts and Schlenker (2012, 280) take this as evidence that farmers in their sample have failed to successfully adapt to warming temperatures. They go on to suggest that the option of responding to changing climate by developed new varieties of crops that are more drought resistant may be limited, as most increases in corn heat tolerance are achieved at the cost of reduced yield.

This quite recent and carefully rigorous econometric work raises a serious question about the ability of US corn farmers to adapt to changing climate. American farmers have been growing corn since first colonizing the continent, and it is to the history of corn in America that I turn first in search of an answer.

B *Corn in America: A Long History of Continuing Adaptation*

As historians have clearly documented, it took Europeans "generations" to understand that even though American colonies were mostly found within what Europeans regarded as temperate or even warm Mediterranean latitudes, colonial climate was decidedly not Mediterranean, with hot summers and exceptionally cold winters (White 2015, 556). As explained by economic historians Olmstead and Rhode (2008), when the colonists came to America, they thought that

> climate is constant in any latitude around the globe. Newfoundland, which is south of London, was expected to have a moderate climate, and Virginia was expected to be like southern Spain. It required decades of harsh empirical evidence before settlers gave up their dreams of growing oranges and olive trees in Virginia. Biological learning was a slow and costly process. (Olmstead and Rhode 2008, 68–69, quoting Kupperman 1982, 1262–1289)

As American schoolchildren still learn today, what allowed the early American colonists to survive was that Indians shared both corn seed and their knowledge of how to grow corn. Early American colonies were "dependent on maize for their staple diet," and only slowly began to experiment with wheat and other types of grain brought from England (Kupperman 1982, 1285).

For at least 2,000 years, humans have been growing corn, and adapting distinct species of corn adapted to particular locales. Such localized adaptation is necessary because corn, like wheat, exhibits what is now called photoperiodism, sensitivity of plant development and yield to the relative length of dark and light periods. Whereas wheat is a long-day plant, with flowering occurring only after the length of the day increases above a certain minimum, corn is a short day plant, flowering only after the number of hours of daylight falls below a certain maximum. For short day plants such as corn, growing plants outside their latitude of adaptation causes the plants to mature too early or too late and can dramatically lower yield (Olmstead and Rhode 2008, 69).

As the American frontier moved westward and settlers crossed the Appalachians during the nineteenth century, American farmers at first simply continued their old farming practices, using the same corn varieties they had used before migrating. Although scientific understanding of photoperiodism wasn't established until the next century (Olmstead and Rhode 2008, 69), farmers had adopted practices, such as "planting by the moon," that reflected their knowledge that the number of hours of sunlight was important. Nineteenth-century immigrant farmers in the Old

Northwest discovered very quickly that if they went too far north or south from their original latitudes, they had poor corn yields. When word of mouth brought this information back home, it encouraged future migrants to move west along the same latitude. Farmers acquired place-specific skills, learning how to plow, plant, and cultivate and harvest particular crops under particular weather conditions. Farmers seeking to maximize the return on their existing investments in human capital sought places where the soil, climate, and terrain were similar. Economists have confirmed empirically this latitudinal stratification pattern of crop specialization along east-west lines between the Appalachians and the Great Plains as of 1850 (Steckel 1983, 23–24).

While this stratification was true for many major crops, such as cotton, tobacco, and grains, corn was even more highly localized. According to an early corn breeder, while "a variety of wheat may dominate in several states, a variety of corn is more likely to be adapted to a group of counties" (Steckel 1983, 72–73). By planting several different varieties of corn in their fields, farmers continually experimented in an attempt to find the best corn variety for a particular location. Thousands of such cross breeds were created by farmers seeking to maximize yield. To do so, they had to find the right corn variety for a given latitude. This is strikingly confirmed by empirical work by the economist Richard Steckel (1983, 22), who statistically explored the yield achieved when seeds from 80 different locations were grown over an almost 100 year period at the agricultural experiment station at the University of Illinois in Champaign. Steckel found that while the longitude of the seed's origin had little impact on yield, latitude had a huge impact, with seeds adapted 250 miles north (south) generating only 72 (62) percent of the yield at Champaign of the seeds adapted to Champaign (Olmstead and Rhode 2008, 73).

As settlement pushed westward and corn growing extended into the Great Plains and arid west, farmers encountered a radically different climate. Taking averages over a 100 year period, a farmer moving from Ohio to Kansas would enjoy 15 more frost free days but face average temperatures 9° higher with 38 percent less rainfall; moving to North Dakota from Ohio, a farmer would face an even more radically different climate, one with 56 percent less rain, much colder average low temperatures, and only 120 frost free days (Olmstead and Rhode 2008, 26). As settlement spread into such very different climates, corn farmers continually adapted. They mixed breeds from the east, such as Dents, with local Indian corns, and eventually, as latitude and altitude of settlement increased and rainfall decreased, corn varieties from the Ree and Mandaan Indians provided the base (Olmstead and Rhode 2008, 75). As farmers continued to experiment with corn breeding, by 1883, there were "numberless" varieties of corn, with at least 150–200 varieties actually cultivated, with 507 separate strains listed in 1899.

With the discovery of new, early ripening corn varieties and improved cultivation practices, between 1869 and 1929, the frontier where corn production overtakes wheat moved from a line just sought of the forty-third parallel between longitudes

87°–95° to a line near the Canadian border for these latitudes and remained north of the forth-third parallel all the way to the hundredth meridian (Olmstead and Rhode 2008, 84–85). Thus an area including most of Minnesota, South Dakota, and Nebraska moved from wheat to corn production over this period. According to economic historians Olmstead and Rhode, the shift to corn in these states increased agricultural productivity. This was not because corn yield was so high there – indeed "the movement of Dents to the more northern and arid lands had the effect of reducing national corn yields" – but because of the impact of "adding corn, a relatively safe crop, to the portfolio of choices available to farmers and of increasing the number of different crops that could be inserted into a farm's rotation" (Olmstead and Rhode 2008, 86).

By the end of the nineteenth century, there were 189 distinct corn varieties grown in the United States with different types adapted to different maturities (23°–42°N latitude), adapted soil types, specific plant and ear types, and specific kernel types and colors (Hallauer 2011, 199). As observed, however, by agronomist Arnel Hallaur, "the development of distinctive cultivars did not contribute to greater grain productivity." Even with localized adaptation in seeds and cultivation practices, moving the location of corn production into regions with more difficult climates during the late nineteenth and early twentieth centuries ensured that national corn yield did not go up.

One can clearly see this in Figures 17.1(a) and (b). Among agronomists, Figure 17.1 (a) is famously called the corn yield "hockey stick." Figure 17.1(a) is called the hockey stick because beginning in the late 1930s, corn yield began and long and continuing increase. From Figure 17.1(b), one can see that although yields fall drastically during years of severe drought in the Corn Belt – the most recent of which was 2012 – there has been no long-term increase in the number of such drought years. The lowest yield year, not closely approached even in 2012, remains 1901.

As one can also see from Figure 17.1(a), since the late nineteenth century, corn yields in the United States have increased by about 700 percent. Four factors drove this remarkable sustained increase in corn yield: a change in the location of corn production to places with better weather, the creation and widespread adoption of hybrid corn, and, synergistically, the mechanization of corn planting and harvesting and the application of nitrogen fertilizer.

To understand the impact of growing season weather on corn yield, it is necessary to review how corn grows. Corn has three stages of growth: (1) vegetative (when the plant is growing and setting its leaf index area), (2) reproductive (when corn ears are formed and silks emerge from the end of corn ears), and (3) ear forming (or grain filling) (Hicks and Thompson 2004; see also Butler and Huybers 2015). Corn is very sensitive to both extreme heat and drought during the six weeks before and three weeks after silking, which occurs around mid-July in the American Midwest (Kaufmann and Snell 1997, 181), extending into early August in more northerly regions of corn production (Thompson 1963, 21). During this period, high

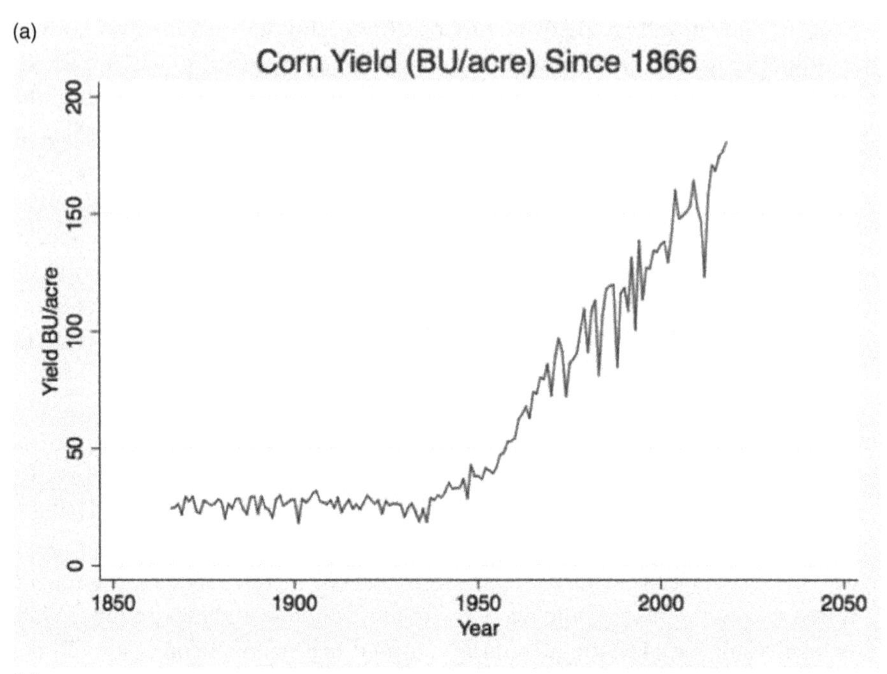

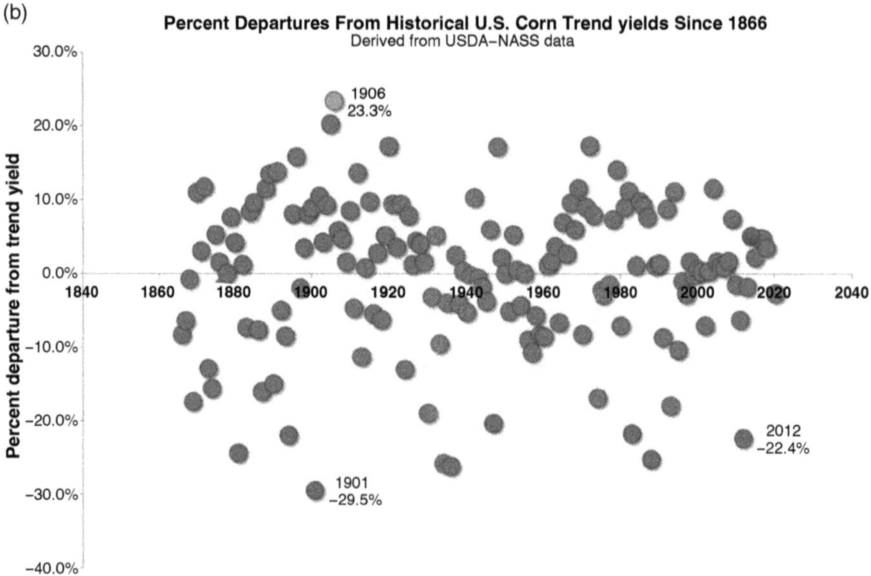

FIGURE 17.1 (a) (top) US corn yield (by year). Figure 17.1(b) (bottom) reproduces figure 2 from R. L. (Bob) Nielsen, "Historical Corn Grain Yields for the US," Corny News Network, updated April 2020, available at www.kingcorn.org/news/timeless/YieldTrends.html.

temperatures and lack of rain damage silks and reduce kernel fertilization (Butler and Huybers 2015). High temperatures are even more damaging when they occur during the final, ear forming stage, when they reduce kernel mass (Thompson 1963, 25; see also Hicks and Thompson 2004). Summarizing, as has long been known (Thompson 1963, 17), the worst kind of summer for corn is one with a dry July and hot August.[7]

These are biological facts about how variations in rainfall and heat during the growing season affect corn yield. Based on these facts, Beddow (2012) constructed a bioeconomic weather index of the suitability of a location for corn production using county-level information on temperature and precipitation over the growing season.[8] During the long period between 1879 and 2007, national corn acreage increased from 62 million to 86 million bushels, but this net national gain concealed big regional shifts, with the Southeast and Appalachian regions losing 12 million acres of corn production over this period while the Northern Plains, Lake States, and Corn Belt states gained about 37 million acres (Beddow and Pardey 2015, 225). Beddow et al.[9] found that over the period 1889–2007, Beddow's bioeconomic index was almost always higher for the area where corn was actually grown than where it had been grown in 1909 (Beddow 2012, 107–108). Controlling for technological change by anchoring relocation effects (on either the base year or current year), Beddow and Pardey (2015, 242) that between 16 and 21 of the increase in corn yield since the 1909 and 2007 was due to relocation of production.

By 1954, when a severe drought hit the plains states and southern portions of the Corn Belt, the impact on national corn yield was relatively minor, the reason being, according to the 1954 USDA Agricultural Census, "favorable weather conditions in most parts of the important corn producing States, the use of fertilizer and hybrid seed, and the improvement in tillage" (Beddow and Pardey 2015, 14–15). As this quote indicates, movement in the location of corn production was not the only long-term adaptation that increased US corn yields. There is no dispute that the increase in yields from the 1930s to 1960 was due to in large part to the adoption of double-cross hybrid corn.

As explained by Sutch (2011, 206–208), until 1918, American farmers planted corn that was the product of natural cross-pollination. Pollen produced by the tassels of one ear of corn blow in the wind and reach the cornsilks of nearby plants, where they grow down, fertilize the egg, and start the growth of a seed. The development of locally adapted corn varieties during the nineteenth and early twentieth centuries was done mainly by farmers themselves, who saved and replanted seeds from the best ears of corn. This process, called open pollination, constituted a form of natural hybridization.

In 1918, it was discovered that by breeding two pure inbred lines of corn (homozygous strains), the resulting "double-cross" hybrid seed was highly productive and relatively cheap to produce. Corn yield tests in Iowa over the period 1926–1933 showed that the double-cross hybrids had a yield advantage of 7–9 percent over the older open pollinated varieties. Over the course of the 1920s, Henry Agard Wallace, Franklin Roosevelt's first Secretary of Agriculture, founded the still extant Hi-Bred

Seed Company and relentlessly produced and promoted the "astonishing" new double-cross hybrid corn seed. Widespread adoption of double-cross hybrid corn did not begin, however, until the mid-1930s.

Nationally, the impact of hybrid corn was massive. Between 1930 and 1965, corn production increased by over 2.3 billion bushels while there was a reduction of 30 million acres in land from which corn was harvested (Kloppenburg 1988, 91). In a series of 1950s papers still famous in the economic literature on innovation, Chicago economist Zvi Griliches tried to explain what he regarded as the puzzling delay in farmers' adoption of double-cross hybrid corn. By about 1940, the double-cross hybrid made up over 90 percent of corn acreage in Iowa, but it did not reach the same level of use in Kentucky until the 1950s. Griliches observed a logistic pattern in the rate of hybrid seed adoption in different states over time (with the adoption rate slow at first and then increasing before flattening out). He thought that the puzzle was to explain why double-cross hybrid corn hadn't been adopted even more quickly. On Griliches's theory, the seed industry expanded across states according to the likely profitability of the new hybrid in different regions, and farmers adopted the new seeds more quickly where their expected return was highest (Griliches 1957, 501–522).

More recently, Richard Sutch has shown that far from such a smooth and predictable adoption path, the adoption of double-cross hybrid corn by farmers was marked by a discrete jump in adoption rates after the severe droughts of 1934 and 1936. In Iowa, where in typical years about 90 percent of the corn crop planted was harvested, less than 70 percent of that planted was harvested in 1934 and 1936; in Kansas, where at least 70 percent of the corn planted was typically harvested, less than 30 percent was harvested in 1934 and 1936 (Sutch 2011, 197–198). What became apparent during the drought years was that the "*relative* yield of hybrid corn was greatest when the *absolute* yields were generally depressed." As the president of a leading seed company commented afterward, "yield differences became plainly evident in 1936, which was also a severe drought year in Iowa. . . . Yields of hybrids under these conditions in many areas of the state were approximately double the yields of other corn grown on the farm." Seed companies not only advertised and promoted the new hybrids but also lowered prices and effectively subsidized adoption by giving away free seeds, sometimes for years, so that reluctant farmers could experiment and see the performance of hybrid seed with their own eyes (Sutch 2011). The adoption rate of hybrid corn exploded. Sales in 1937 of Wallace's Pioneer Hi-Bred Seed company's hybrid seed were almost triple those of 1933 (Sutch 2011).

After the mass, drought-induced switch to double hybrid corn, hybrid seed corn sales increased from essentially zero in 1934 to over $70 million in 1944 (Kloppenburg 1988, 93–94), achieving market dominance that Sutch terms "self-sustaining and irreversible." Certainly one thing contributing to the long-term dominance of hybrid seed was the massive increase in seed company profits generated by widespread adoption. These profits were a source of funding for continuing research that eventually ensured that hybrid seed was superior in a wide variety of weather conditions (Sutch 2011). Indeed, yields of hybrids in agricultural trials from the 1930s to the 2000s increased linearly at a rate of 77 kg/ha/year (Grassini et al. 2015, 29).

But financing alone seems inadequate to explain the long-term success of hybrid corn. Property rights too were crucial. Whereas farmers can save and successfully replant seed from open pollinated corn, seed from double-cross hybrid generates a very low yield when replanted. In addition, the process by which double-cross hybrids is produced is too complex to be used by the average farmer. With farmers unable to replant hybrid corn seed and economically incapable of creating such seed themselves, property rights over the unique inbred lines from which double crosses are produced means the producer effectively also owns the double-cross hybrid (Kloppenbrug 1988, 99). These three factors together meant that once farmers switched to hybrid corn, they lost the ability to produce their own seed. To plant hybrid corn, farmers needed to buy hybrid seed from the seed companies. According to a 1919 text on corn breeding, this revolutionized agricultural incentives, as "for the first time in agricultural history . . . a seedsman is enabled to gain the full benefit from a desirable origination of his own" (East and Jones 1919, 224, quoted in Kloppenburg 1988, 99). In urging corn seed developers to adopt double-cross hybrids, it was argued that by so doing "the originator of valuable strains of corn [gets] the same commercial right that an inventor receives from a patented article" (Kloppenburg 1988, 103).

Either by establishing their own preferential access to seed stock developed by experiment stations and colleges, or by rebranding and treating as trade secrets seed stock that was actually publicly developed, the large seed companies (such as Pioneer, DeKalb, and Funk Seed), managed to preserve the economic rents from hybrid seed development. Between 1940 and 1950, the fraction of corn acres planted with double-cross hybrid grew from 15 to 80 percent and seed company revenues tripled (Kloppenburg 1988, 106–107). During the 1950s and 1960s, seed companies selectively adopted new inbred seed stocks developed by agricultural experiment stations and land grant universities, and by 1970, the farmer had virtually disappeared "as an autonomous producer in the seed-corn business." By 1980, the hybrid seed business was dominated by eight companies with 72 percent of the seed corn market, a dominance that had "less to do with economies of scale or production considerations than with access to research" (Kloppenburg 1988, 110).

The dominance of hybrid corn had a synergistic impact in changing how corn is planted, stimulating the use of nitrogen fertilizer and increasing the mechanization of corn harvest and planting. Open pollinated corn was genetically diverse, with plants bearing different numbers of ears at different stalk locations and ripening at different rates, and most open pollinated corn plants were afflicted by lodging (falling over). For these reasons, mechanical harvesters had trouble with open pollinated corn, missing lodged plants, failing to strip ears located at different levels on different plants, and destroying overripe crops. Hybrids, by contrast, are uniform and resist lodging and can be bred with stiffer stalks and multiple ears so as to conform to the needs of the mechanical harvesters. A related trait reduced hybrid corn's need for sunlight, and together with reduced risk of lodging, this allowed greatly increased planting density. Such increased density required heavy use of nitrogen fertilizer, but such fertilizer had a greater impact on hybrid corn and indeed was necessary to fully realize its potential for increasing yield (Sutch 2011).

The historical facts clearly depict the production synergies between hybrid corn, mechanization, and nitrogen fertilization. The percentage of corn harvested by machine increased from 15 to 70 percent between 1935 and 1945 (Kloppenbrug 1988, 117). The new inbred populations developed during the 1950s and 1960s were especially designed to generate hybrids that could be planted closer and heavily fertilized with nitrogen fertilizer, and between 1950 and 1980, the amount of nitrogen fertilizer increased by 1,700 percent. With closer planting, hybrid seed sales increased 60 percent, even though the number of acres planted with corn increased only 2 percent. Close planting also increased the risk of disease and insect infestation, thus stimulating the demand for herbicide and insecticide sales, and as corn production volume increased and prices fell, large feedlot operations became economic, increasing the supply and lowering the price for pork, beef, and poultry (Kloppenbrug 1988, 119).

Figure 17.2 graphically shows how the adoption of hybrid corn stimulated further technological change in corn production. Between the 1930s and roughly 1960, the

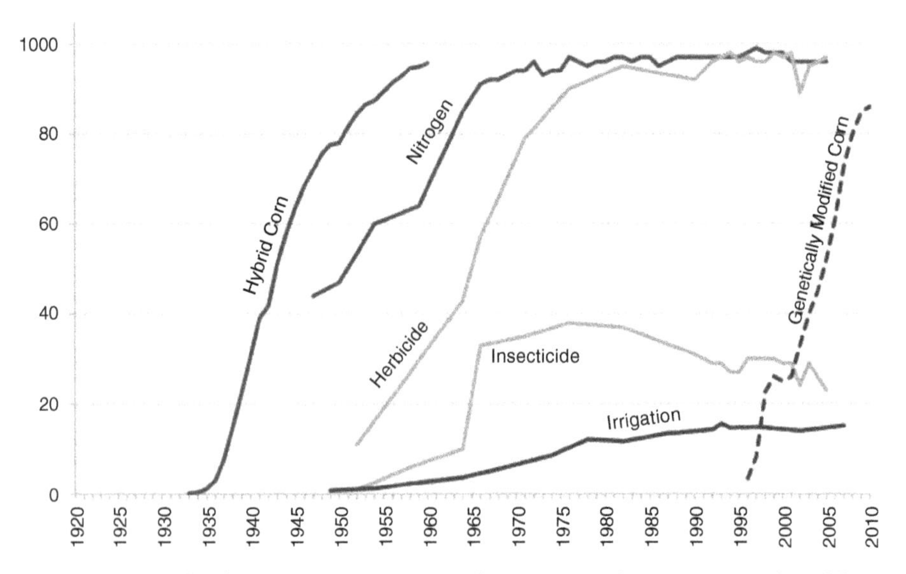

FIGURE 17.2 Technology adoption in corn production since the 1930s. Reproduced from figure 6 of Beddow and Pardey (2015, 243).

use of hybrid corn and nitrogen fertilization of close-planted crops became virtually universal among US corn farmers.

Looking again at Figure 17.2, one might infer that with virtually 100 percent adoption of hybrid corn, close planting/fertilization and herbicide use and "little" potential for further adaptation by relocation, Roberts and Schlenker may be correct in suggesting that US corn producers have only limited potential for future adaptation to extreme heat.

There are several reasons for thinking such suggestion will almost surely turn out to be wrong. The first reason for optimism comes from the history I have just recounted. To summarize what is known about corn adaptation: by switching to hybrid corn during the drought, yield was doubled relative to earlier varieties and in the worst drought years – 1934 and 1954 – the movement in the location of production made production about 20 percent less sensitive to drought.[10] Over about a 50 year period in the twentieth century, by adopting hybrid corn while increasing mechanization and nitrogen fertilization, farmers steadily increased yield (Beddow and Pardey 2015, 240, figure 5, middle panel). The history of US corn production shows that extreme weather itself may provide the impetus to widespread adaptation, which itself then generates synergies – close planting, mechanization, and nitrogen fertilization. To be more concrete, before the catastrophic droughts of 1934–1936, no one predicted that the droughts themselves would actually spur the widespread, wildfire-quick adoption of hybrid seed, which in turn vastly increased the economic return to mechanization, close planting, and nitrogen fertilization – a chain of events that led eventually to about a 700 percent increase in yield.

A second reason to be more optimistic than Roberts and Schlenker is a bit technical but important to understand. Like virtually all econometric work on climate and agriculture, Roberts and Schlenker's statistical estimation technique doesn't include variables measuring innovation in corn seed type, or the degree and type of mechanization, or fertilization, or planting practices. Instead these estimations include typically only a time variable (and/or a variable that is a function of time). If one is just interested in projecting future productivity growth due to technical change that follows existing time trends, then this approach may be useful.[11] But if one is interested in predicting what might generate entirely new technological adaptations in response to alternative future weather and climate scenarios, these sorts of statistical estimation techniques are worse than useless. They generate numbers for things like the change in yield under warmer temperature conditions, but those numbers are based on past trends, and provide no insight into what determined those trends and therefore no insight into whether those trends really will continue.

For example, the history just discussed shows that one of the most important adaptations in US corn production has been a shift in where corn is grown. When the location of production changes, studies that attempt to measure the impact of global climate change are likely to "misattribute impacts to global climate change" that are actually due to location change. As explained by Beddow and Pardey (2015, 244), "movement in the footprint of US corn production since 1839, ... has decreased the average temperature under which corn is grown ... with both direct effects on the growing environment and indirect effects insofar as the climate affects the suitability of the growing environment to the various pests and diseases that hinder production." If one used an estimated negative relationship between high temperatures and corn yield to get a quantitative estimate for the impact of future high temperatures on US corn yield, that estimate would almost surely be too negative, because the location of corn production within the US likely will change in response to a change in the climate.

Perhaps the most important policy lesson about agricultural adaptation from the history of corn production in the United States is the crucial role played by technical knowledge and the incentives for the production and application of such knowledge created by property rights. Even before the widespread adoption of hybrid corn in the mid-1930s, farmers themselves constantly experimented with new open pollinated varieties as they pushed corn production further and further west. Corn farmers moving from Ohio to Kansas faced radical climate change – a 38 percent decrease in rainfall and 9°F, or 5°C increase in summertime temperatures – changes far greater than those projected to result from even a doubling of atmospheric GHGs. And yet without any form of government assistance, they adapted to the new climate and became profitable. The introduction of hybrid corn generated even greater gains in productivity and adaptability, and while it is true that eventually the land grant universities played an important role in developing new seed stock, from the 1930s until today, a key factor driving continuing innovation in hybrid corn were the de facto property rights that seed companies had in such corn. Excludability and appropriability created the incentives and economic profits that led to a half-century of steadily rising corn yields.

C *Are Corn Farmers Adapting, and Will they Adapt in the Future?*

(a) The Weather Has Been Great for Corn, but Insignificant Compared to Technological Change

As suggested by Figure 17.1(b), aside from the extremely unusual drought year of 2012, since 1980, US corn yield has been increasing at an increasing rate. There are several factors that explain this accelerating increase in yield. First, the weather in the US Corn Belt has been fabulous for corn growing. This is not new: as we saw with my small-town Iowa weather stations discussed earlier in Chapter 14, over the entire latter half of the twentieth century in Iowa there was little if any change in average temperature. Growing degree days are a measure (in temperature units) of the presence of favorable weather for plant growth during the growing season. The hottest days, often called killing degree days, actually reduce growth. A decline in average high temperatures on really hot days reduces killing degree days.

Figures 17.3(a) and (b) display this decline for one weather station, located in Tipton, Iowa, a small-town in east-central Iowa that is included in the weather stations used to construct the Had CRUT long-term temperature data series. Figure 17.3(a) shows the annual average maximum temperature on days when the maximum temperature was 90°F or above. Just eyeballing the figure, one can see that over the 1893–2010 period, there was no increase in the average maximum temperature on very hot days in Tipton. Figure 17.3(b) goes beyond eyeballing by displaying the polynomial equation that best fits the raw Tipton data. As one can see, since the late nineteenth century, there has been a long-term trend toward lower maximum temperatures on very hot (tmax > 90°F) days in Tipton.

Tipton is typical not only of Iowa weather during the twentieth century, but of midwestern US weather more generally. Butler et al. demonstrate that over the period 1981–2017, for every corn growth phase, the number of growing degree days for corn in the US Midwest increased while the number of extremely hot killing degree days have decreased (Butler et al. 2018). These findings carry an important lesson about interpreting findings, such as those of Roberts and Schlenker, indicating that US corn farmers don't seem to be adapting to episodes of extreme heat: because very hot days have been getting cooler, there hasn't been a trend toward extreme heat to which farmers might have adapted. To the contrary, farmers should rationally have adapted to an environment in which very hot days have become less severe.

Ironically, such rational adaptation to favorable weather may have increased susceptibility to drought. The rate of nitrogen fertilization in the US Corn Belt almost doubled from 1960 to 1975 (Grassini et al. 2015, 27, figure 2). The use of nitrogen fertilizer (N) makes possible increased corn planting density, and corn planting density has increased at a rate of 400 plants per acre, almost tripling since the 1960s.[12] The other major change in US corn has been an almost fourfold increase in the irrigated maize area in the western Corn Belt, from 0.9 million hectares (Mha) in 1970 to 3.2 Mha in 2010. Irrigation in this region "amplified the benefits of N fertilizer and higher plant densities" (Grassini et al. 2015, 31). Research indicates that narrow row high plant density planting may generate reduced yields in low yield hot and dry years.[13] Thus since the 1960s, US corn has been planted in a way that increases average yields while potentially increasing susceptibility to drought. In an era of less extreme heat on hot days, such a practice has been just what one would predict.

Another long-term trend has helped increase US corn yields. Earlier planting extends the growing season and total absorbed solar radiation, thus increasing yield. According to a 2010 article by Iowa State agronomists, the average corn planting date in Iowa was earlier in 2010 than it had been in 1980, but that date had been constant (at about April 15) since 1990.[14] This trend toward earlier corn planting seems to have occurred across the US Corn Belt. Indeed, one recent study finds that in 6 of the 12 northern and western Corn Belt states, 19–53 percent of the state level 1979–2005

(a)

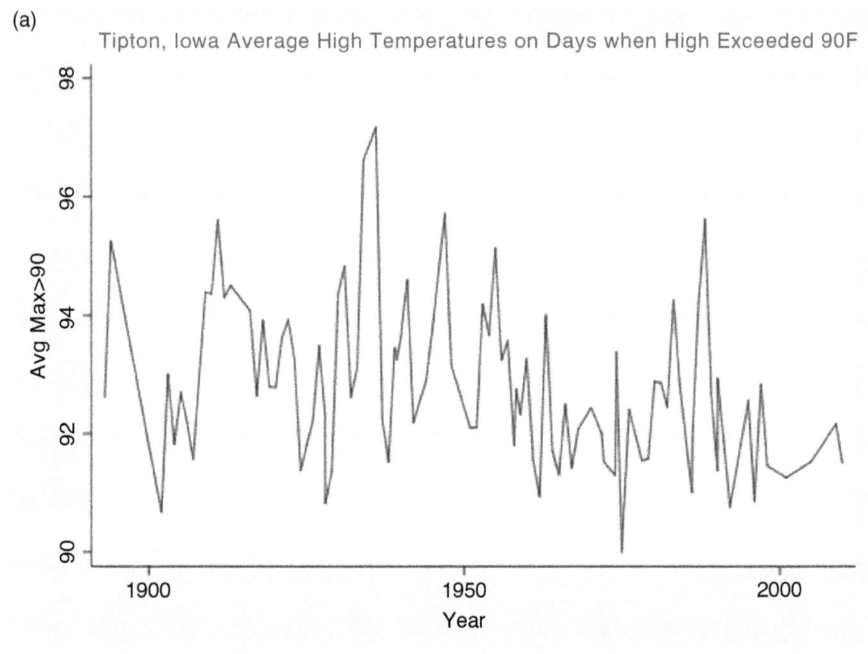

(b)

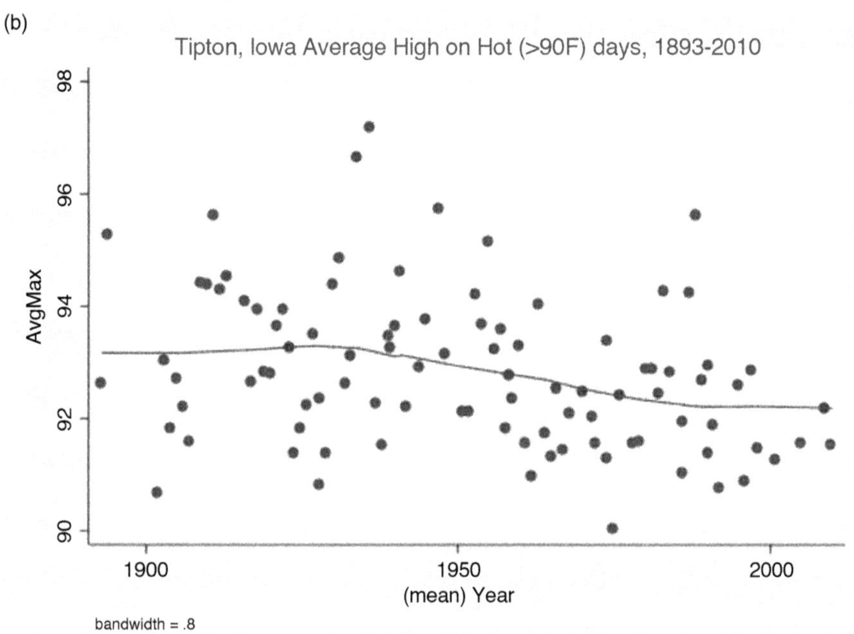

FIGURE 17.3 (a) Average hot (>90°F) day maximum temperatures, Tipton, Iowa, 1893–2010. (b) Tipton, Iowa, average hot day maximum temperatures, LOESS weighted regression.

yield increase was due to earlier sowing (Grassini et al. 2015, 31). Agronomists have explained that "earlier planting dates contribute to higher realized yields through the capture of a greater proportion of the growing season, the ability to use longer season hybrids, and the increased probability that physiological maturity will occur before a killing frost" (Abendroth et al. 2017).

Butler et al. (2018) find that this movement toward earlier planting dates was almost as important in increasing corn yields over their 1981–2017 study period as was a moderation in extreme heat. To be more precise, given the observed growing season weather and the estimated weather-yield relationship, Butler et al. (2018) found that yields were higher assuming planting occurred when it did during the early planting dates that prevailed during 2008–2017 than they were under the assumption that planting occurred when it did over the 1981–1990 According to Butler et al. (2018), this suggests that earlier planting dates have increased yields under the current climate.

Agronomists do not, however, ascribe the long-term trend toward earlier planting in the US Corn Belt primarily to climate but instead to a variety of other factors. First, a "primary" reason for earlier planting was an increase in the amount of land managed per producer. Even with increases in planting speed, corn planting takes on average six to eight weeks. With farmers planting more acres knowing that the yield penalty for planting too late is bigger than the penalty for planting too early, farmers have to begin planting earlier if they want to plant most of their crop during the optimal planting period for their region of the state.[15]

Even more important drivers of earlier corn planting are a group of factors that may be called technological change. Agronomists detail that "technological advancements include the increased early-season stress tolerance of hybrids, use of improved seed treatments, increased herbicide use, reduction in tillage operations, larger equipment, tile drainage, and mechanical improvements in planters that distribute seed more uniformly in suboptimal conditions."[16] I am aware of no study that analyzes the statistical relationship between corn planting dates in the US Corn Belt and average springtime weather while controlling for the full range of other factors – including at least farm size, cost, and availability of cold-tolerant hybrids, seed treatments, herbicide use, tillage practices, and mechanical planter type – that affect a farmer's expected net return from earlier planting.

Even without such rigorous statistical evidence, there is other evidence that warmer springtime weather is only a minor factor in incentivizing farmers to plant corn earlier. While it is universally agreed that yields are higher when planting is finished early – by early May, for example, in Indiana – planting date accounts for a small portion of variation in yields – about 10 percent in Indiana. Some years when corn was planted late in Indiana due to cold, wet springs, such as 2009, had yields above the trend average, while years with early plantings, such as the 2012 drought year, had yields far, far below the trend average (for 2012, 38 percent below the trend yield).[17] Moreover, if we look across locations of varying temperature at a given point in time, early planting seems clearly not to be an adaptation to warmer springtime weather. In Iowa, the world's corn capital, the optimal planting date is earlier in the northeastern part of the state – which borders Minnesota and Wisconsin – than it is in the southern part – which borders Missouri.

This is shown by Figure 17.4.[18] Northeastern Iowa is significantly colder than southern Iowa. For example, the northeastern Iowa city of Decorah, has an average high temperature in April of only 57°F; Clarinda, a similarly small town in far southwestern Iowa has an average April high of 63°F, about 3.4°C warmer. Agronomists think that in northeastern Iowa, the optimal planting date is early because of the "limited growing season length and the need to maximize photosynthetic capacity." That the optimal planting date is latest in the warmer southwestern and southeastern regions of Iowa is, they say, "possibly related to summer rainfall patterns and the impact of warmer temperatures during the grain-fill period favoring certain planting dates based on the crop's reproductive development" (Abendroth et al. 2017). Whatever may explain the relationship between yield and planting date across different regions of Iowa, it is clearly not the case that the optimal planting date in northeastern Iowa is earlier than in southwestern Iowa because April is warmer in northeastern Iowa than in the southwest. In fact, the optimal planting date is earlier in a region that is 3.5°C colder.

In summary, recent decades have witnessed continuing increases in US corn yields. Good weather – lower average temperatures on very hot days, and increases in summer rainfall – is one reason for increases in yields. But weather is relatively insignificant when compared to other factors. These other factors – such as the development of hybrid corn seed that can tolerate early-season cold, reduction in tillage, and increased use of herbicides and larger and better planting equipment – represent technological change in US corn production.

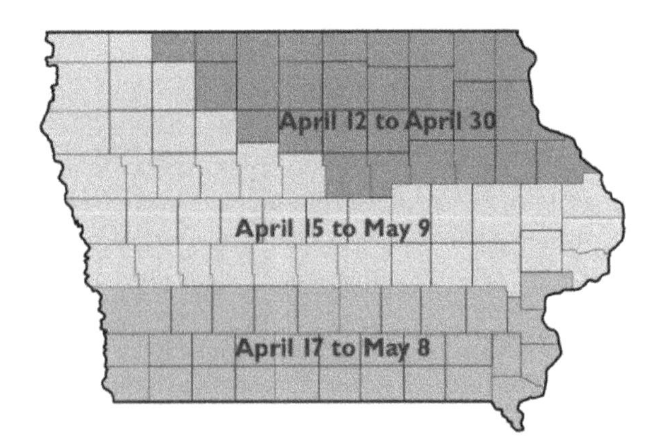

FIGURE 17.4 Optimal corn planting dates in Iowa. From Nick Upah, "2018 Corn Planting Considerations," Iowa State University Integrated Crop Management, April 17, 2018, available at https://crops.extension.iastate.edu/blog/nick-upah-mark-licht/2018-corn-planting-considerations.

(b) Due to Continuing Adaptation, Whatever May Be the Future Weather, Corn Yields Will Almost Surely Increase

As remarkable as it may seem given the history of steady increases in US corn yield, both the spread of existing technologies and likely future technological change promise to increase corn yields even further and make such yield growth more resilient to variation in climate. The first such technology is irrigation. A clear lesson of US corn production history is that years of extreme drought are very bad for corn.

This is illustrated in Figure 17.1(b). As one can see by looking back at Figure 17.1 (b), the really big downward departures from long-term trend expected corn yields occur during years of extreme drought such as 1901, 1934, 1936, 1953, 1988, and 2012. The worst such year was 1901. In July of that year, in Iowa, Illinois and Indiana (the heart of the Corn Belt) there was virtually no rain and incredibly high temperatures: Evansville, Indiana, for example, recorded only 18 inches of rain in July, and with a rainfall shortage of 20 inches or more, 1901 remains the driest year ever recorded in Illinois and Missouri.[19]

Irrigation is the most direct way to deal with extreme heat and drought. Irrigation has been shown to significantly reduce the sensitivity of corn yields to extreme heat (Butler and Huybers 2013, 68). In terms of quantitative impact, one recent study[20] found that over the 1981–2012 period, irrigation eliminated about two-thirds of the negative impact of episodes of extreme heat for corn and soybeans.

For US corn (and even more, soybean) production, the adaptive capacity from widespread irrigation remains just that – as yet unrealized potential adaptation. One can see this by comparing the top and bottom panels in Figure 17.5. The top panel shows harvested maize and soybean area and the bottom panel shows irrigated area (with one dot representing 810 ha in both panels). Comparing the top and bottom corn panels in Figure 17.6, one sees that the vast majority of acres in the US Corn Belt – including virtually all of Illinois and Iowa – are rain fed (shaded in light green), with no irrigation at all. Whatever may be the present-day impact of heat and drought in the Corn Belt, that impact would be far less in a world with widespread irrigation.

And irrigation is not the only possible adaptation. Looking at corn yields for the period 1981–2012 in eastern (nonirrigated) states in a data set allowing them to identify daily temperatures during different periods of the corn crop life cycle, Butler and Huybens found that whereas an increase in extreme high temperature, killing degree days reduced the periods of both early and late grain filling in northern states, increase in such days actually increased the grain filling period in southern states. These scholars (Butler and Huybers 2015, 5–6) suggest that the resilience of southern corn to high temperatures may be because corn hybrids in the southern states have been modified to alter "the duration of grain filling in response to higher temperature." The answer to the question put by these authors – if such a corn type "reduces corn yield losses, then why has it not been introduced into Northern

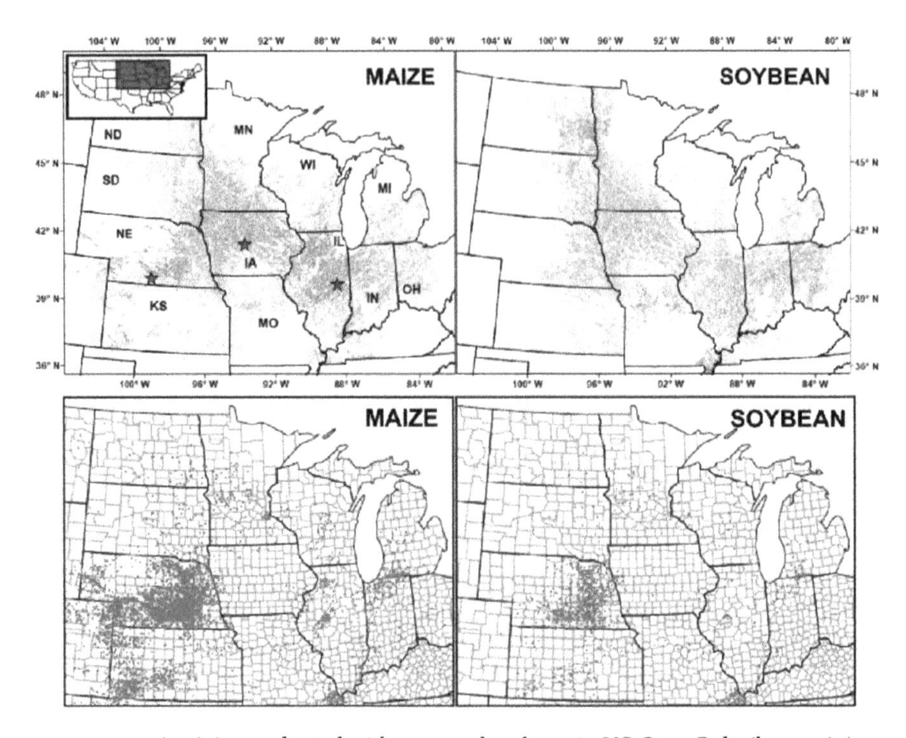

FIGURE 17.5 (top) Acres planted with corn and soybean in US Corn Belt. (bottom) Acres irrigated. From Grassini et al. (2015, 17).

States?" (Butler and Huybers 2015, 5–6) – would seem to be that the climate has not yet changed sufficiently in northern states to warrant whatever trade-off is incurred when switching to the southern corn. More precisely, as Butler and Huybens speculate, southern methods of growing corn – planting about a month earlier and using tropical or temperate-tropical varieties – may only be "physiologically feasible" under "warmer conditions, possibly because of a longer growing season." In other words, it may be feasible for corn farmers in the north to employ corn types and planting schedules only when the northern states' climate – meaning average temperatures and the length of the growing season – more closely resembles that of the southern states.

If Corn Belt climate were to become much hotter – rather than cooler, as has been the case for decades – it seems almost certain that farmers will be able to choose from a range of drought- and heat-tolerant corn varieties. Plant geneticists are now actively working to discover the genetic traits that make corn drought-tolerant. Such research is very new. As the authors of a recent review article put it, the maize genome is "large and complex … more than 85% of which consists of repetitive sequences" (Xiao et al. 2017, 359). As they go on to explain, "in the last decade, the explosive development of next-generation sequencing (NGS) technologies, and the release of the maize B73 reference genome [in 2009], have largely promoted maize genetic research into the genomics era" (Xiao et al. 2017, 360). In less than 10 years, there have been several detailed studies of one particularly important trait for adaptation of maize to climate change, drought tolerance.

Plant geneticists describe drought tolerance as "a particularly complex quantitative trait controlled by many loci with small effects" (Xiao et al. 2017, 364). That complexity is now being unraveled[21] – for example, one group of researchers (Zhang et al. 2016, 1449–1463) identified 23 genetic loci likely associated with drought tolerance and found a set of 10 metabolite-associated loci, the favorable alleles of which were significantly enriched in corn hybrids with high drought tolerance. The advances are already being translated into new commercial varieties. One group of agronomists have recently reported (Gaffney et al. 2015, 1608) that on-farm testing over the 2011–2013 period has confirmed that a recent hybrid, produced by DuPont, offers stable yields under drought with no yield penalty in normal years. As for corn varieties, they explain how seed companies are employing a variety of strategies for increasing crop tolerance to drought, with transgenic "drought-tolerant" hybrids becoming commercially available in 2013 for the first time, and one seed company claiming yield gains of from 12 to 55 percent under drought for transgenic drought-tolerant versus nontransgenic isogenic lines, and another claiming yield gains of 9 percent under drought and 2 percent under normal conditions for nontransgenic drought-tolerant versus conventional hybrids (Grassini et al. 2015, 37). There is every reason to expect the future commercial availability of variety of drought-tolerant, high-yield corn varieties.

In addition to irrigation in the US Corn Belt and the genetic modification of corn, precision agriculture techniques may revolutionize how farmers adapt to changing weather and climate. Precision farming, is "a management system that is information and technology based, is site specific and uses one or more of the following sources of data: soils, crops, nutrients, pests, moisture, or yield, for optimum profitability, sustainability and protection of the environment" (quoted by Finch and Lane 2014). Rather than the traditional assumption that soil, nutrient, moisture, weed, insect and growth conditions are uniform on a farm, precision farming recognizes the reality "spatial and temporal variability of soil and crop factors between and within fields." Using local wireless networks in combination with GPS and other remote data, over the last decade or so researchers have developed and tested irrigation systems that deliver water to particular parts of fields based on readings from water stress indicators distributed within fields (Wang and Li 2013, 171–199). Remote-sensing techniques have been used to fine-tune the application of nitrogen fertilizer allowing a whole range of new practices that have generated reductions in nitrogen fertilizer application compared to traditional approaches of up to 50 percent and reducing leaching losses by 47 percent (Delgado et al. 2010, 117–171).

In the United States, the US Department of Agriculture's has installed a national network of 400 Soil Climate Analysis Network, or SCAN sites. These provide hourly data on soil moisture and temperature as well as air temperature, solar radiation, relative humidity, wind speed, wind direction, and precipitation. The sites are located near irrigated agricultural areas on what are believed to be benchmark soils. According to one Utah farmer who agreed to install a SCAN tower, "The SCAN data has helped me determine the optimum time to water and as a result, last year I had the best corn crop I've ever had on this farm."[22] More generally, it is expected that precision farming will increase profitability by increasing crop yields.[23]

(c) Today's Climate May Not Be the Best: Even If Adaptation Is Costly, Farmers May Be Better Off in a New, High-CO_2 World

It may be said that even if ongoing technological change will enable future farmers to efficiently adapt to changes in climate, they will still be worse off than if climate remained unchanged. Putting aside the absurdity of supposing that climate would not change were it not for human GHG emissions, the notion that farmers must be worse off after climate change than in the status quo climate assumes that the current climate is the best for crop growing.

There is virtually no evidence to support this view. To the contrary, there are literally thousands of scientific papers demonstrating that current atmospheric CO_2 levels are too low to optimize plant productivity and that yields from a wide variety of important crops will be higher in a higher-CO_2 world.

This follows from the most fundamental facts about plant growth through photosynthesis. As the Ontario Ministry of Agriculture explains on its website, "Photosynthesis is a chemical process that uses light energy to convert CO_2 and water into sugars in green plants. The difference between the rate of photosynthesis and the rate of respiration is the basis for dry-matter accumulation (growth) in the plant."[24] As that website goes on to explain, "the concentration of CO_2 outside the leaf strongly influences the rate of CO_2 uptake by the plant. The higher the CO_2 concentration outside the leaf, the greater the uptake of CO_2 by the plant." For most plants, increasing the ambient CO_2 level to 1,000 ppm will increase the photosynthesis by about 50 percent over ambient CO_2 levels.

This relationship between ambient CO_2 concentration and the rate of plant photosynthesis (relative to a baseline of 340 ppm) is depicted in Figure 17.6. As one can see from the figure, increases in the rate of plant photosynthesis from increasing ambient CO_2 increases are quite large until they begin to tail off at around 900 ppm. Greenhouse growers know this, and they also know the other thing that Figure 17.6 shows, which is that the photosynthesis rate declines faster and faster if ambient CO_2 falls below about 300. For this reason, greenhouse growers try to keep the ambient CO_2 level at 1,000 ppm. The current ambient CO_2 level, around 410 ppm as of 2018, is far below the optimal level for plant growth.

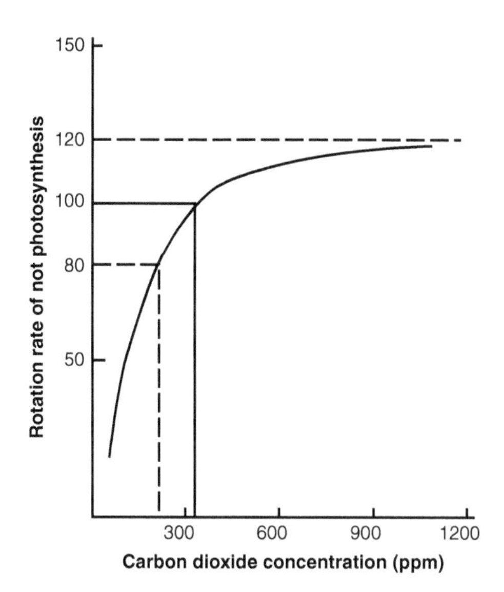

FIGURE 17.6 Ambient CO_2 and rate of photosynthesis. A reproduction of figure 1 in Blom et al. (2009).

To be sure, not all crops are grown in greenhouses and not all crops respond the same way to increases in ambient CO_2. Globally, however, there is abundant and uncontradicted empirical evidence that increasing atmospheric CO_2 over the twentieth century has stimulated plant growth. One study finds that over the course of the twentieth century, there was about a 30 percent increase in gross primary production – the amount of CO_2 that is taken up by plants through photosynthesis (Campbell et al. 2017, 84–87). Other studies directly identify the increase in atmospheric CO_2 as the most important factor in stimulating this twentieth-century plant growth (Li et al. 2017, 250; Nemani et al. 2003, 1560–1563).

Of course, what matters for agriculture is how increasing atmospheric CO_2 impacts the growth of important crops. Throughout the US farm belt, corn and soybeans are the most important commercial crops. In 2017, for example, 95 percent of all acres planted commercially in Iowa and Illinois were planted with corn and soybean;[25] in Nebraska in that same year, 78 percent of acres were planted with corn and soybean.[26] Soybeans are in a group of plants called C3 plants that rely upon an enzyme called Rubisco to convert CO_2 into sugars. Conversion by Rubisco at current atmospheric CO_2 levels is not maximized, and so for C3 plants like soybeans, increases in atmospheric CO_2 will increase plant photosynthesis and growth rates. Corn, by contrast, is a C4 plant, and such plants rely upon a more complex process for CO_2 conversion, one in which CO_2 is taken up and then concentrated in cells containing Rubisco (Ainsworth and Gillespie 2010). Because of the different pathways for CO_2 uptake and conversion, increasing CO_2 has a much bigger impact in stimulating C3 plant growth than C4 plant growth. One review article finds a doubling in atmospheric CO_2 will generate about a 30 percent increase in growth of C3 plants like soybeans but less than 10 percent growth increase for C4 plants like corn (Hatfield et al. 2011, 353); another finds that under conditions of ample nitrogen and water, elevated CO_2 may have little impact on C4 crops like corn (Kimball 2016, 40).

Increases in CO_2 have a limited effect on growth of C4 plants like corn because increases in CO_2 do not speed up the rate of photosynthesis in such plants. Increased ambient CO_2, however, effects not just the rate of photosynthesis but also how plants are affected by drought. As schoolchildren learn, tiny pores (called stomata) in plant leaves open and close to allow CO_2 to diffuse into the leaf. When these pores open, water vapor escapes from the plant. Because the pores do not need to open as far to capture CO_2 when ambient CO_2 increases, less water vapor is lost from plants under conditions of such elevated CO_2.[27] Experiments have shown that doubling CO_2 reduces water vapor loss through plant pores (so-called stomatal conductance) by about 40 percent for both C3 plants like soybeans and C4 plants like corn (Hatfield et al. 2011, 353–354). In experiments involving increases of 200 ppm in ambient CO_2, increases in grain yield of about 30 percent have been found for C4 plants under conditions of limited water availability (Kimball 2016, 40). In other words, in an enhanced CO_2 environment, plants such as corn better conserve water, and this enables them and grow longer during dry periods after irrigation or rainfall (Kimball 2016, 40). While it is true that this positive effect of enhanced CO_2 in reducing plant water vapor loss becomes tiny when temperatures are extremely high – with daily maximums above 40°C (104°F) – the positive effect of CO_2 is pronounced even for daily highs of 28°F (or 84°F) – temperatures that economists categorize as high temperatures where yields begin to fall.

It must be stressed that the effects of CO_2 in stimulating the growth of both C3 plants such as soybeans and (under low water conditions) C4 plants such as corn are not based on a theory or a computer model or even on experiments in greenhouses but on observations from experiments with elevated CO_2 levels over actual open field crops (so-called free-air CO_2 enrichment, or FACE). These experimental results show how agricultural productivity could well be higher in a future, higher-CO_2 world. This is most clearly the case for C3 crops like soybeans, but the FACE experiments also show how farmers could be better off after costly adaptation to provide irrigation for a C4 crop such as corn in a new, higher-CO_2 world than under present-day conditions. To be more concrete, suppose – as has been true in Iowa and most of the traditional midwestern corn and soybean belt – that under present climate conditions, the cost of installing an irrigation system is too high relative to the expected increase in yield it generates for the irrigation cost to be economically justified. Suppose, however, that in a new climate, the irrigation system would be much more productive in increasing yield and total revenue. If this is so, then not only may farmers rationally invest in irrigation in a new climate when such investment is not rational in the status quo climate, but they may have higher net revenues after such a costly investment in the new climate than net revenues in the present climate without such an investment.

This claim can be proven with a little algebra (which I will quickly supplement with a numerical example for those readers who are algebra averse). Suppose that there are two annual growing season weather states: one with adequate rainfall, and one with drought. Annual net revenue in the drought state of the world is given by L_i and is less than annual net revenue in the adequate rainfall state of the world, given by H_i. Present-day conditions are indicated by $i = 0$ and future high-CO_2 conditions by $i = 1$. The annualized cost of irrigation (amortized capital cost plus operating costs) is given by S. Irrigation does not affect crop production and revenue in the adequate rainfall state of the world but increases net revenue in the drought state, from L_0 to L_0' under present conditions and from L_1 to L_1' in future high-CO_2 conditions. Denote the probability of drought (adequate rain) by p $(1 - p)$ under present-day conditions and the forecast probabilities for the future high-CO_2 world to be q $(1 - q)$.

The farmer's expected net revenue today and in the future is given by the summation over all weather states of the probability of a weather state multiplied by the net revenue in that weather state. For those readers unacquainted with expected value terminology, one may think of the expected revenue as the farmer's average revenue over a period of years. So, using a simple example for illustration, if the probability of drought and adequate rain are 0.1 and 0.9, then we are saying that out of every 10 years, only 1 year will be a drought year. If the farmer's net revenue in a drought year is \$100 and \$500 in an adequate rainfall year, then over a 10 year period, the farmer's average net revenue will be \$460. This is the expected net revenue.

With this notation, the farmer's expected net revenues in the present-day and future high-CO_2 worlds as a function of whether the farmer invests in irrigation are depicted in Table 17.1.

As is true today in Iowa, Illinois, and Indiana, consider the case where it is not economic to invest in irrigation in the present climate regime. In terms of the Table 17.1 algebra, this means that

$$p(L_0' - L_0) < S, \qquad (1)$$

TABLE 17.1 *Expected net revenue with and without irrigation in the present and future high-CO_2 worlds*

	No irrigation	With irrigation
Present day	$pL_0 + (1 - p)H_0$	$pL_0' + (1 - p)H_0 - S$
Future high CO_2	$qL_1 + (1 - q)H_1$	$qL_1' + (1 - q)H_1 - S$

that is, whatever net gain may be generated in the current world from investing in water storage and irrigation is not worth its cost. On the story we are investigating with this algebra, in the new climate regime, it would be economic to invest in the storage and irrigation adaptation. Algebraically, this means that

$$q\ (L_1' - L_1) > S. \qquad (2)$$

Suppose now the grim case supposed by some recent climate assessments, one in which drought becomes more likely in the future high-CO_2 world. This means that $p < q$. Now recall the FACE evidence just discussed. This evidence shows that irrigation is likely to be much more effective in boosting net productivity and revenue in the future high-CO_2 world than in the present CO_2 world. In terms of the notation used in (1) and (2), this means that $L_0' - L_0 < L_1' - L_1$. Hence for two reasons – a higher probability of drought and increased impact of irrigation given drought – the farmer will invest in irrigation in the future world when she would not do so in today's world.

The real question, however, is whether the farmer could actually be better off after a costly adaptation – irrigation – in the future high-CO_2 world than she is in today's world, where she does not rationally make such a costly investment. To see that this is indeed not only possible but perhaps even likely, I make two assumptions that capture the empirical evidence about a C4 crop such as corn discussed above. First, I assume that the installation of irrigation does not affect output and net revenue in the adequate rainfall state of the world, and also that in the future high-CO_2 world, output and net revenue in the adequate water state is equal to its level in the current CO_2 environment. Second, to capture the evidence about how high-CO_2 affects corn growth under conditions of drought, I assume that in the drought state of the world, irrigation is more productive in increasing net revenue in the high-CO_2 world than in the current CO_2 environment. Using the notation displayed in Table 17.1, I am assuming that $H_0 = H_1$ and that $L_0' < L_1'$.

Certainly for corn, the assumption that irrigation increases yield much more under drought conditions than conditions of adequate rainfall seems to be clearly borne out by the evidence. This is clearly depicted by Figure 17.7. To interpret Figure 17.7, note that Kukal and Irmak (2019) use the term *irrigation-limited yield gap* for the yield increase due to irrigation (the ratio of irrigated vs. rain-fed crop yield) in a particular county. There are a number of things that one can see from the figure. For example, in some relatively arid US states, in particular Idaho, irrigation has boosted yields of multiple crops (in Idaho, alfalfa and both spring and winter wheat) by between 200 and 400 percent. Most importantly for present purposes, for corn, irrigation is much more effective in increasing yields in dry regions than in relatively wet regions. In Figure 17.7, irrigated corn field yields in

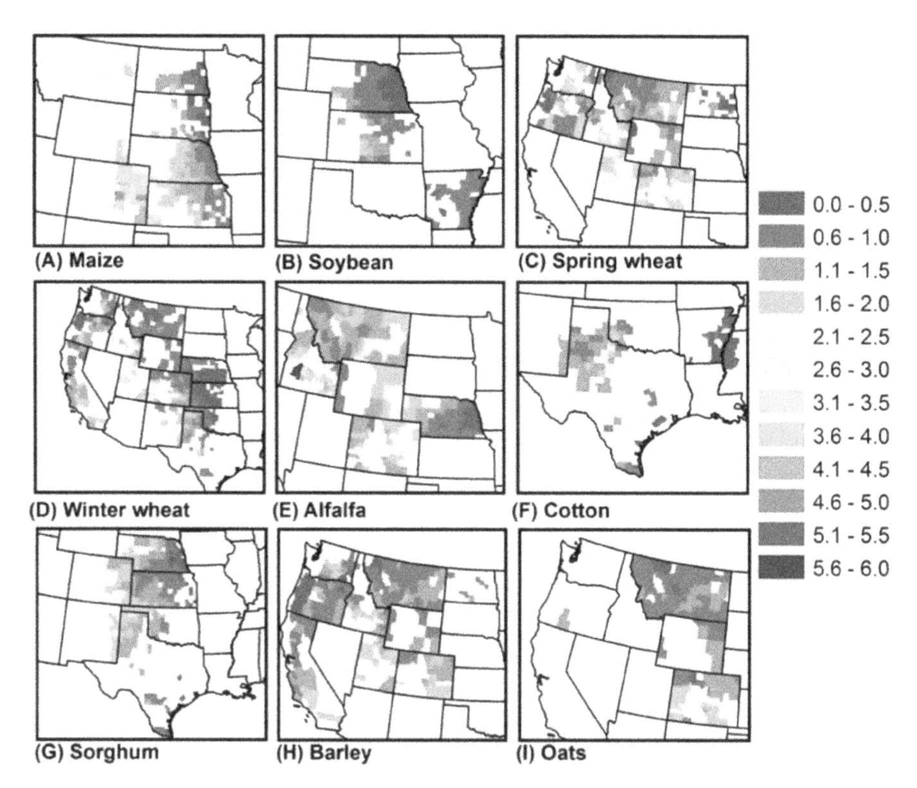

FIGURE 17.7 Post-1950 county-specific irrigated crop yield relative to rain-fed crop yield. Reproduces figure 3 from Kukal and Imak (2019, 6). This figure is reproduced under the standard Creative Commons 3.0 license under which Kukal and Irmak (2019) was published.

eastern Nebraska are not much higher and in some cases are actually even lower than in nonirrigated fields, whereas in western Nebraska, irrigated field corn yields are 200 to 300 percent the yields of rain-fed fields (Kukal and Imak (2019) find that nationally, at 1.7 times the rain-fed yield, corn irrigation generates the biggest yield increase of any crop).

The evidence thus supports two factors that would potentially make a corn farmer better off in a future high-CO_2 world that is most drought-prone: a drought-dependent positive CO_2 fertilization effect and a much greater increase in yield from irrigation under drought conditions.

To capture these effects with the algebra, from the payoffs displayed in Table 17.1, we see that the farmer is better off in the future high-CO_2 world with costly irrigation than in the present-day world without such an investment provided that

$$qL_1' + (1-q)\,H_1 - S > pL_0 + (1-p)\,H_0,$$

rewriting under the assumption that $H_0 = H_1$, whenever

$$qL_1' - pL_0 > S + (q - p)H_0. \tag{3}$$

In words, equation (3) says that the farmer has higher expected profits in the future CO_2 world with costly irrigation than in the present world without it whenever the increase in expected drought state yield with irrigation in the high-CO_2 state of the world is big relative to drought state yield in the present state of the world and this difference is bigger than the sum of the irrigation cost and the expected lost yield due to a lower probability of adequate rainfall in the high-CO_2 state of the world.

To make some comparisons, I now write drought net revenue in the future high-CO_2 world with irrigation in terms of the increase relative to drought net revenue without irrigation in the current state of the world, that is, let $L_1 = kL_0$ with $k > 1$ expressing the empirical evidence that higher CO_2 will boost output in the drought state for corn. The experimental evidence discussed earlier shows that that if we were comparing irrigated corn crops in the current ambient CO_2 world with those same crops in an irrigated future high-CO_2 (meaning a doubled CO_2 concentration) world, then $k = 1.3$ would be about correct. In (4), however, we are comparing drought output in a high-CO_2 world with irrigation to drought state output in the current CO_2 world without irrigation, that is, what is relevant is not L_1 drought state yield in a future high-CO_2 world, but drought state yield in such a world with irrigation. Using the evidence from Figure 17.7 and being conservative, relative to nonirrigated high-CO_2 world drought state yield L_1, irrigated high-CO_2 drought state yield L_1' is likely equal to at least $2L_1$ which taking account of CO_2 fertilization is equal to $2(1.3)L_0 = 2.6\ L_0 = L_1'$.
Substituting this value for L_1' inequality (3) becomes

$$[(2.6)q - p]L_0 > S + (q - p)\ H_0. \tag{4}$$

A widely cited tree ring study[28] of Iowa's climate over the period 1640–1982 has estimated that over the period 1877–1982 severe or worse drought occurred in Iowa with a about a 0.12 probability. As discussed earlier, climate models do a very poor job of replicating past climate on regional or smaller levels, and this is true when it comes to drought probabilities; indeed, a highly publicized recent model simulation of future climate predicts a severe water stress probability for Iowa of only 0.08, much lower than the 0.12 estimate for the last century or so obtained from actual tree ring observations.[29] Still, this same model gives an upper bound probability of drought in a future higher-CO_2 world for the Corn Belt of 0.3. Using the 0.3 value for q, and the historically based value of $p = 0.12$, inequality (4) becomes

$$0.78L_0 > S + 0.18\ H_0. \tag{5}$$

If we express the irrigation cost S as a fraction of present world adequate rainfall output αH_0, then a sufficient condition for (5) to hold is that

$$\frac{L_0}{H_0} > \frac{\alpha + 0.18}{0.78} \tag{6}$$

If $\alpha = S = 0$, then (6) holds provided only that $L_0/H_0 > 0.23$, meaning that present-day drought state yield must be at least 23 percent of present-day adequate rainfall state yield. As S, the cost of irrigation, increases, inequality (6) becomes harder to fulfill, and indeed if $S > 0.6H_0$, the condition cannot hold. Still, provided that the cost of irrigation is not too high, under reasonable assumptions about the probability of present and future drought and the increase in yield generated by irrigation in a high-CO_2 world, we have that it is possible for farmers to be better off after investing in costly irrigation in a future high-CO_2 world than they are without such an investment in the lower-CO_2 but less drought-prone present world.

The requirements for a corn farmer to be better off in a future high-CO_2 world with costly irrigation than in the present world without such an investment can be put dollar terms. According to the Irrigation Association, as of 2012, a center pivot irrigation system capable of irrigating a quarter section (with 125 acres of the 160 irrigated), cost about $72,000, with an expected lifetime of 25 years and roughly $10,000 per year in variable costs.[30] Assuming for simplicity straight line depreciation (with about $3,000 per year amortized) and an interest rate of 5 percent (with an annual interest cost of $3,600) Such a system would pay for itself if it increased revenue from corn production by at least $16,600 per year. With the exception of the drought year of 2012, corn yield per acres in high productivity cropland in places like Illinois has run around 200 bushels per acre or 25,000 bushels per 125 acres.[31] Since 2009, corn prices have fluctuated widely, but $4.00 per bushel, for gross revenue of $100,000 per 125 acres, is a rough average. Using these numbers, in a new, higher-CO_2 but much more drought-prone world, irrigation would have to increase yields by about 17 percent to be worthwhile and to make the farmer better off than without such irrigation today. But we have just calculated that the combined effect of CO_2 fertilization under drought conditions and the yield increase due to irrigation in such a world would increase yields by about 260 percent. This is an order of magnitude larger than the yield increase necessary to make a farmer better off than today.

It should be stressed that in using corn as an example, I have used the *only* crop for which large yield increases in a doubled CO_2 world occur only under conditions of low water availability. For virtually every other food crop, yields increase in the higher-CO_2 world under both low and ample water conditions. For example, wheat, rice, and soybean yields increase on average about 20 percent or more under both low and ample water conditions (Kimball 2016, 39). The typical farmer in the US Corn Belt plants corn and soybeans, with corn and wheat more common in the western Corn Belt. With either crop mix, the existing experimental evidence implies that farmers will likely be better off in a future high-CO_2 world with irrigation than they are in today's lower-CO_2 world without irrigation.

D *The Time Path of Agricultural Adaptation*

As shown by the history of how American farmers adapted corn varieties to the new climate conditions they found as corn farming moved westward, adaptation is not an instantaneous process. It took years of learning and experimentation for farmers to find new seed varieties and planting methods suited to new locations. The mid-twentieth-century adoption of hybrid corn was initiated by the doubling in yields that were achieved during drought years during the 1930s and fueled by the continuing investments made by seed companies. There were strong incentives for such investments, because as holders of property rights in seed stock, the seed companies capitalized a substantial portion of the benefits from hybrid seed adoption. However, as full realization of the yield gains from hybrid corn depended on investing also in mechanized planting and harvesting and nitrogen fertilization, switching to hybrid corn involved large sunk cost investments that many farmers were initially reluctant to make.

Future adaptations by corn producers will also take some time to occur. As one group of agronomists note, "if there is a steep learning curve, producer adoption of a new management practice will be cautiously measured. As a result, agronomic yield improvement still tends to be gradual – not immediate" (Grassini et al. 2015, 28). There seems little doubt that many unrealized savings still exist, with one paper finding that 50 percent of irrigated maize fields in central Nebraska get more irrigation than necessary to maximize yields and 30 percent of current water use for corn irrigation could be saved with little yield penalty just by "replacing existing surface irrigation systems by center pivot and by adjusting irrigation management according to real-time crop water requirements" (Grassini et al. 2015, 38). In Nebraska, there is large variation in irrigation practices across fields, and variations in farmer risk aversion explain as much variation in irrigation practices as does variation in crop and soil conditions (Grassini et al. 2015, 34).

Precision agriculture will almost surely allow farmers to realize increased efficiencies. For example, studies indicate that only 40 percent of nitrogen (N) fertilizer applied in the Corn Belt is absorbed, but "data from well-managed crops" show that this could be increased to 64 percent by applying the nitrogen during the season instead of presowing with split applications, and by adopting "within-field site-specific N management and adjustment of N-fertilizer recommendations according to residual soil N." Likewise, 30 percent less irrigation water could be used "by optimizing irrigation scheduling based on crop phenology and soil water status," and by "replacing existing surface irrigation systems by center pivot and by adjusting irrigation management according to real-time crop water requirements" (Grassini et al. 2015, 38; see also Grassini et al. 2011, 133–141). Precision agriculture technologies – including global positioning system (GPS) soil mapping, yield mapping (Ymap), equipment autoguidance systems (GSYS), and variable-rate input application (VRT)) – are a way for farmers to fine-tune the timing, amount, and location of both irrigation and N fertilization.

(a) Uncertainty over Future Climate Means It Is Economically Optimal to Delay Adaptive Investments

However, smart agriculture technologies are expensive. For example, GPS systems that are accurate to within inches cost between $15,000 and $20,000 in 2010. Moreover, there appear to be strong complementarities in these technologies, with for example, the savings through a better use of inputs and optimal application of seed and fertilizer from adopting variable-rate input application (VRT) fully achievable only if the farmer has invested in getting a GPS-based soil properties map (Schimmelpfennig and Ebel 2016, 107–108). Given the sunk costs of adopting new technologies and the need for site-specific information to fully realize their value, farmers seem to be adopting the PA technologies sequentially. Smart agriculture technology adoption rates have been increasing, but as recently as 2000, none of the technologies enjoyed majority adoption (Schimmelpfennig and Ebel 2016, 98, figure 1).

There are many reasons that farmers delay investments in new, adaptive technologies. Such delay is not inconsistent, however, with rational, profit-maximizing behavior. To the contrary, in recent decades, economists have come to realize that when the return from an investment is uncertain and investment involves large costs that are sunk in that they cannot be easily undone and redeployed elsewhere, it is typically rational to delay investment.[32] We can see why by again using some algebra. (Readers averse to algebra can skip this derivation and proceed to the numerical example (9) and intuition following the derivation of the formula.)

Imagine a farmer considering an investment of S in an irrigation system with a lifetime of N years. Suppose that beginning next year, there are two possible future worlds: a drought-ridden world in which drought is very likely and the irrigation system generates an average increase in net revenue of D, and a wet world in which drought is not likely in which irrigation generates an average increase in net revenue of only W. All of the evidence shows that irrigation produces a bigger increase in net revenue in drought years than wet years. In my notation, this means that W < D. Suppose that all that is known now is that the probability of a drought-ridden world is p while the probability of a wetter world is (1-p). However, if the farmer waits one year, then she will learn with certainty whether the world is drought ridden or wet. Assume that the farmer discounts future net revenues at an interest rate of r with $0 < r < 1$. To simplify notation, let $\delta = 1/(1 + r)$.

If the farmer invests today, then her expected net return from the irrigation investment is given by

$$\sum_{t=0}^{N} \delta^t [pD + (1-p)W] - S. \tag{7}$$

If the farmer waits to invest until the next period, she will learn whether the state of the world is drought ridden or wet. This gives her the option of investing only if the state of the world is the drought-ridden state, where the irrigation system generates a higher increase in net profits (of D instead of W). If the farmer waits one period and invests only if the drought-ridden world is realized, then her expected net return from the irrigation investment is given by

$$p\left[-\delta S + \sum_{t=1}^{N} \delta^t D\right] = p\left[-\delta S + \sum_{t=0}^{N} \delta^t D - D\right]. \tag{8}$$

After rewriting (7) and (8) using some basic facts about the sums of finite series, we have that the farmer's expected net return from waiting and investing in irrigation only if the drought-ridden world eventuates (expression (8)) is bigger than the farmer's expected net return from investing in irrigation now (expression (7)) if and only if

$$pD > (1-p)\left[\frac{W(1-\delta^N)}{(1-\delta)}\right] - (1-p\delta)S. \tag{9}$$

From inequality (9), it is clear that waiting to invest in irrigation will surely be best if the increased net revenue with irrigation is much higher in a drought-ridden world than in a wet world and the sunk cost of irrigation is not too high.

As promised, for those averse to algebra, we can write down inequality (9) with numbers instead of symbols. To do so, assume that the interest rate $r = 0.1$, which means that $\delta = (1 - r) = 0.9$. Now assume that in the current period, the drought-ridden world probability p is only 0.2, while a wet world has a probability of $1 - p = 0.8$. This means that the irrigation investment is unlikely to pay out, indeed, the odds that it pays out are 4/1. Suppose (to make calculations easier), that irrigation generates a per period payout of \$100 if the world turns out to be drought ridden. The work applied earlier suggests that the lifetime of a center pivot irrigation system is about 25 years. If we set $N = 25$ in inequality (9) along with the other numbers just given for δ, p, and W, then inequality (9) becomes

$$80 > 7.4W - 0.92\,S. \tag{10}$$

Recall that W is the increase in net revenue in a future wet world from irrigation. Historically, this has been 0, in which case (10) is sure to hold, making waiting optimal. Even if W, the increase in net revenue in a future wet world was 50, half of the increase in a drought-ridden world, inequality (10) would still hold provided that the sunk cost of irrigation was less than about bigger than about $315, a value that at only about three times the annual increase in drought state revenue it generates is an order of magnitude smaller than the actual sunk cost of irrigation. Under reasonable assumptions, waiting to invest in irrigation until the next period is almost surely the farmer's profit-maximizing strategy.

The reader may well object that I have made a number of simplifying and unrealistic assumptions. This is true. Perhaps most importantly, I assumed that in the next period, the farmer learns with certainty whether the world is wet or drought ridden, and I assume that this would be a new permanent state of the world. It may be more realistic to think that it will take the farmer some time to learn whether the climate in which she farms has indeed changed, and that such learning never ends with perfect knowledge of whether the world is "wet" or "drought ridden" but instead just with new beliefs about the probability that the world is in one of these two climate states.

Under these more realistic assumptions, not only is the farmer likely better off delaying irreversible adaptive investments, but she is likely better off with a longer delay. As confirmed by highly sophisticated recent empirical work (Kala 2017), farmers learn about changing weather patterns, but how they adjust their beliefs depends in part on what they have observed, with farmers experiencing big recent changes in weather patterns tending to attach greater weight to recent years and less weight to more distant years (compared with farmers who have observed more stable patterns). Moreover, even in developing countries, farmers' planting decisions respond more to weather forecasts that have a record of accuracy than to those that have a poor track record (Kala 2017). The simple model I have presented allows farmers to learn about the climate state only between the initial and following periods. When, more realistically, farmers rationally anticipate future learning, they expect learning to repeat between periods in a recursive fashion. This increases their incentive to wait until they get better information about the climate state before making an irreversible investment. Uncertainty over whether a change in climate state is actually permanent provides yet another reason to wait longer: an irreversible investment in irrigation is less likely to be optimally triggered by years of drought when the farmer believes that years of drought may suddenly be followed by years of abundant rainfall.

It must be stressed that the economic logic of waiting to make an irreversible investment under conditions of uncertainty does not hinge on investors being averse to risk. The basic economic definition of being risk averse is that a risk averse person acts as if a potential gain (loss) is worth less (more) than its expected value. If we take a situation where there is a 0.5 probability of gaining $100, the risk neutral person would evaluate this risky prospect as worth its expected value of $50 (0.5 multiplied by $100). A risk averse person, by contrast, would value this risky prospect as worth less than $50.

As in this example, a risk averse person values the gain realized from an irreversible investment when the state of the world turns out to be favorable for it at less than its expected value. Correspondingly, such a person values the potential loss from the irreversible investment when the state is unfavorable for it at even more than its expected value. With gains valued less and losses valued more, a risk averse person has an additional reason to wait to make an irreversible investment until uncertainty is resolved.

(b) Agricultural Subsidies Weaken Incentives to Adapt to Changing Climate

There is a final and crucial factor that influences incentives for and the speed of agricultural adaptation by farmers: policy. In the United States, since the passage of the Federal Crop Insurance Act of 1980, the federal government has subsidized crop insurance purchased by farmers. Under this subsidy, the federal government pays a portion of crop insurance purchased by farmers. The subsidy was initially only 30 percent of the premium, but since 1994, Congress has steadily increased the subsidy.[33] By the time of the drought year of 2012, an Illinois corn farmer could buy insurance guaranteeing her 85 percent of the revenue she was projected to earn based on historical data while paying only about 50 percent of the actual premium cost of moving to such a noncontingent 85 percent revenue guarantee.[34] With the federal government – meaning US taxpayers – picking up such a large fraction of the premium for crop insurance, US farmers generally and corn and soybean farmers in particular have virtually all signed up for subsidized crop insurance. Indeed, since about 2007, over 90 percent of the land planted with corn and soybeans in Iowa has been covered by federally subsidized crop insurance, and as of 2014, over 93 percent of such land was covered by federally subsidized insurance.[35]

Subsidized insurance promising farmers virtually no loss during drought years when yields are low dramatically lowers and may completely eliminate a farmer's incentive to adapt to higher frequency drought. It is important to understand how the subsidy, and not crop insurance itself, mutes adaptive incentives. If a farmer buys crop insurance at an actuarially fair rate, then she pays a premium roughly equal to the expected revenue loss indemnification – the probability of a revenue shortfall multiplied by the average amount of the shortfall. If a farmer invests in an adaptation such as irrigation that lessens her revenue loss in drought years, then she will be rewarded with lower crop insurance premiums. When as much as 50 percent of her crop insurance premium is paid for by the government, however, the farmer only gets 50 percent of the benefit of investing to reduce the revenue shortfall in bad years. From society's point of view, farmers who get only a fraction of the benefit from costly adaptive investments have too weak an incentive to make such investments.

The prediction that crop insurance subsidies weaken farmers' incentives to invest in adaptation is confirmed by the existing empirical evidence. Looking at US corn and soybean production over the period 1981–2013, Annan and Schlenker found that corn yields on farms with federally subsidized crop insurance insured farms are 67 percent more sensitive to yield-lowering extreme heat than corn yields on farms that do not have such insurance (and insured soybean yields 43 percent more sensitive to extreme heat than yields on uninsured farms) (Annan and Schlenker 2015, 264). This is precisely what one would predict. With up to 50 percent of crop insurance premiums paid for by the federal government, farmers not only load up on such insurance, insuring up to 85 percent of any revenue shortfall. In addition, because of the subsidy, the farmer gets only 50 percent of any benefit from adaptive investments that lower the amount of revenue shortfalls. For this reason, farmers invest too little in adaptation and suffer larger losses in bad years.

II BEYOND AGRICULTURE: AIR CONDITIONING AND THE LESSENED SIGNIFICANCE OF HEAT FOR HUMAN HEALTH AND PRODUCTIVITY

A *Air Conditioning and Productivity*

The first application of air conditioning in the United States was industrial, where humidity in particular was damaging to many production processes, and beginning in the 1910s, air conditioning was custom-designed for particular factories. With textile mills, Carrier Engineering Corporation, the great American air conditioning pioneer, matched the capacity of installed air conditioning not just to the square footage of a mill, but to the activities within the mill (Cooper 1998, 30–35). Patents for regain and dew point controls were important for early air conditioning pioneers, but so too was specialized engineering knowledge about how to match equipment to the heat load, and all such engineering knowledge, even knowledge of how horsepower translated into Btu, was treated as a trade secret with no disclosure of design methods (Cooper 1998, 36–37). A former Carrier Engineering Corp. employee recalled how "up to about 1925 Carrier people had, to all practical purposes, a monopoly on the brains and know-how of air conditioning. Consequently its policy was to educate its own people but at the same time to take extreme measures to prevent this knowledge and practical experience from getting into the hands of outsiders – especially competitors but including consulting engineers and contractors in pretty much the same class" (Cooper 1998, 39–40). Air conditioning did not necessarily replace the need for high skill labor in industries such as macaroni production and tobacco and leather drying, but in industries from rayon, film to chocolate, air conditioning improved productivity by providing cleaner ventilated air that was also at the proper humidity (Cooper 1998, 53–58).

Air conditioning's movement out of factories was led by the installation of air conditioning in movie theaters. In the midst of the Great Depression, air conditioned theaters provided a respite, and by 1938, 15,000 out of 16,300 theaters nationally were equipped with air conditioning. To cool large theaters without driving up the humidity required the invention of bypass systems (Cooper 1998, 81–109). It was during the 1920s and 1930s that companies including not only Carrier and other early industrial air conditioning firms but also refrigerator companies such as GE and Frigidaire began to develop small comfort air conditioning systems suitable for residential use (Cooper 1998, 114–130). In 1935, GE estimated that the residential air conditioning market could someday be worth $5 billion, and by 1936, the large companies had written a new product standard code; still, by 1938, only 0.25 percent of 22 million homes with electricity had air conditioning, and surveys showed that most people had no interest in air conditioning (Cooper 1998, 130). It was only after World War II that people began to adopt residential air conditioning, with room air conditioning sales growing from only 143,000 in 1945 to 1.3 million in 1956, and standardized floor plans spurring the installation of central air conditioning during the 1950s (Cooper 1998, 140–157). Still, as late as the 1960 census, only 1/8 of US housing units had air conditioning. The movement to make residential air conditioning standard was led by southwestern cities, with 25 percent of Phoenix houses air conditioned as early as 1960, and 42 percent in Austin and Dallas, Texas, by 1970. By 1969, 39 percent of peak load electricity demand was due to air conditioning. Early air conditioning was expensive, and it was adopted primarily by higher socioeconomic groups; during a 1966 heat wave in St. Louis with six consecutive days above 100°F, 70 poor residents died, and at a time when the national air conditioning adoption rate was 12 percent, less than 4 percent of black households had air conditioning (Cooper 1998, 166–172).

In the early 1950s, few office buildings had air conditioning; when heat waves hit, it was "routine practice" in northern cities such as New York and Detroit to simply close the office early, and as late as 1952, even Houston had only 196 office air conditioning units and 11 office buildings with central air conditioning (Cooper 1998, 159). Ad hoc tests of federal employees in 1946, however, had revealed productivity increases of up to 24 percent when offices were air conditioned, and by the mid-1950s, 88 percent of 376 companies surveyed said air conditioning was important for "office efficiency" while Philadelphia Electric Company called air conditioning an "accepted requirement" in new office buildings (Cooper 1998, 160). In 1955, the General Services Administration dictated that all new federal office buildings would be "block style" with air conditioning, requiring that air conditioning be operated even in northern states during sustained periods when effective outside temperatures were above 80° (Cooper 1998, 161–162).

The impact of air conditioning in increasing worker productivity is demonstrated not only by the historical data discussed above but also by dozens of studies done since the early 1970s that have explored the impact of temperature on office worker productivity. Surveying this work, Seppänen et al. (2006)[36] found a consistent inverted U-shaped relationship between office temperature and worker productivity. Figure 17.8 depicts the relationship between temperature and office worker productivity estimated (in a meta-regression) from the dozens of studies surveyed by Seppanen et al. As one can see from the figure, maximum performance occurs for office temperatures in the range of 21.5°–23°C (69°–73°F), and performance falls off

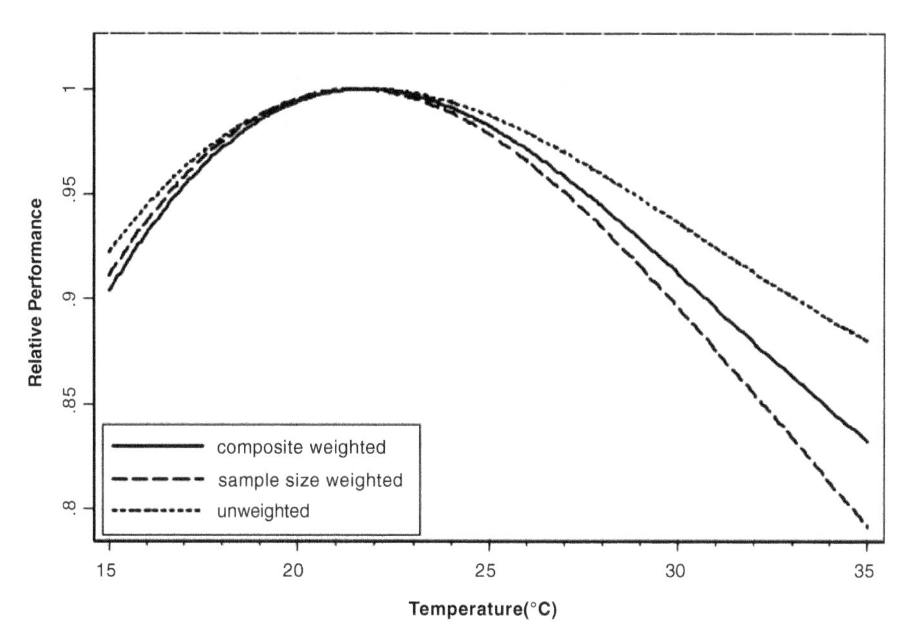

FIGURE 17.8 Normalized performance versus temperature (with maximum performance normalized to 1).

steeply in both directions, with[37] about a 10 percent loss in performance for both very cool, 15°C (59°F) and very warm 30°C (86°F) ambient office temperatures. Other studies have made the case for firms to incur the upfront costs of air conditioning by pointing out that the increased productivity due to an improved indoor climate likely ranges from 10 to 100 times operational and maintenance costs.[38]

These general historical findings regarding the impact of air conditioning in increasing productivity have been buttressed by recent work looking at how excessively hot days affect labor productivity in different regions of the United States. To be sure, work by Graf Zivin and Neidell found that in the very short run, workers may reduce hours worked on very hot days (Zivin et al. 2014, 1–26). Moreover, Park (2017) has found even more recently that across the entire United States, an additional day with a maximum temperature above 90°F (a hot day) causes a 0.03 percent decline in payroll and an even larger decline in payrolls in industries such as construction, where workers are exposed to the weather. Park's most dramatic finding, however, was that in the hottest quintile of US cities – including places such as Houston and Orlando – the impact of an additional hot day was not only tiny, lowering payroll by 0.13 of 1 percent, or about 1/1,000th, but 63 percent smaller than the impact of a hot day in very cool cities such as Seattle or San Francisco. Across all US counties, Park found that the negative impact of very hot days on labor payroll is smaller, the higher is air conditioning usage.

B *Air Conditioning and Health*

Residential air conditioning use in the United States has continued to grow, as in 2011 the Energy Information Agency reported that between 1993 and 2009, the proportion of occupied US housing units increased from 68 percent to 87 percent.[39] Since 2013, over 91 percent of new homes built in the United States have central air conditioning.[40] It is no coincidence that over this period, despite warmer conditions in most US metropolitan areas, there has been a "clear decrease" in human vulnerability to heat waves since 1975 (Sheridan and Dixon 2017, 70). Early work by Davis et al. (2003, 1712–1718) looking at data through 1998 has been confirmed by more recent studies looking at data through the mid-2000s. One study found that between 1975–1983 and 2002–2010, excess mortality due to heat waves in the United States has fallen somewhere between 10 and 20 percent (with the size of the fall dependent on how one defines a heat wave) (Sheridan and Dixon 2017, 61–73, figure 2); another study found that between 1987 and 2005 there was an even larger decrease in expected deaths due to heat waves in the United States from about 5 in 100 to 2 in 100, a relative fall of 60 percent (Bobb et al. 2014, 813). Similar declines in mortality due to heat waves have been found for countries ranging from Australia to Italy (Hondula et al. 2015, 146).

When it comes to average daily temperature and mortality, research has consistently found a U-shaped relationship, with mortality increasing on very cold and very hot days.[41] However, even controlling for per capita income, Barreca et al. (2016, 105–159) find a very large decline (of up to 85 percent for days with an average temperature above 90°F) in excess mortality in the United States due to high temperatures since 1960. This is shown in Figure 17.9. The left-hand graph in Figure 17.9 gives the relationship between average daily temperature and mortality estimated by Barreca et al. for the period 1931–1959 while the right hand graph gives the same estimated relationship for the period 1960–2004. As can be seen, while there is some decrease in mortality since 1960 for cold days below 30°F, this decrease pales before the large decrease in mortality for days with average temperatures above 80°F. More precisely, Barreca et al. (2016, 133) estimate that the impact of one additional day with a mean temperature above 90°F increased the monthly mortality rate by 2.16 percent over the period 1931–1959 but only by 0.34 percent over the period 1960–2004, a decline of more than 80 percent in mortality on extremely hot days.

A number of factors have contributed to the decline in heat-related mortality, including better health care, greater awareness of the risks of high heat, and air conditioned climate control in both home and work environments (see Sheridan and Dixon 2017, 61). There is, for example evidence that the excessive heat warnings that the National Weather Service and local cities began to issue around 1995 have had a statistically significant impact in lowering excess

TABLE 17.2(A) *Absolute changes in regional AC and central AC usage, 1970–2004*

Region	Fraction of homes with AC (central AC), 1970	Change in AC (central AC) fraction 1970–1980	Change in AC (central AC) fraction 1980–1990	Change in AC (central AC) fraction, 1990–2004	Fraction of homes with AC (central AC), 2004
South	70 (34)%	20 (34)%	6 (16)%	6 (12)%	97 (88)%
Northeast	28 (2)%	18 (4)%	10 (6)%	25 (12)%	76 (24)%
Central	38 (12)%	22 (19)%	10 (15)%	18 (21)%	90 (67)%

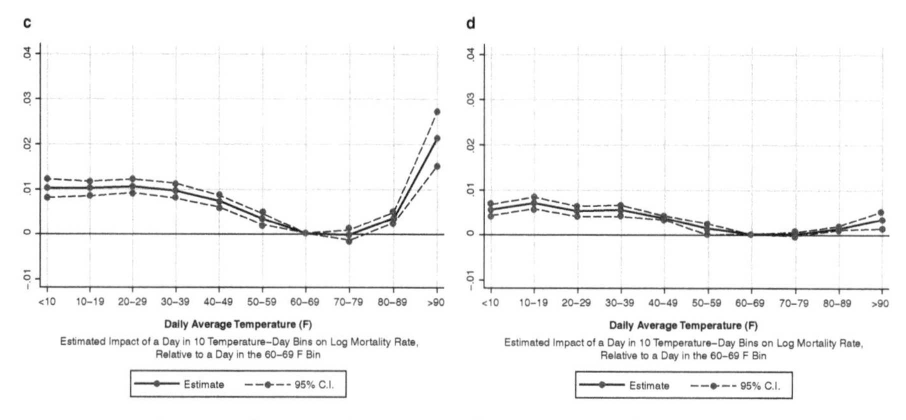

FIGURE 17.9 Impact of air conditioning in lowering mortality in the late twentieth century. Reprints figures 2c and 2d from Barreca et al. (2016, 129).

mortality during heat waves (Kalkstein et al. 2011, 1113–1119). As for air conditioning, Tables 17.2(a) and (b) strongly suggest that it has had a major impact in lowering excess mortality on hot summer days. The decline in excess mortality on hot days between 1975 and 2004 has been greatest in the two regions where the percentage of air conditioned homes increased the most. Indeed, in relative terms, the Northeast and Central cities, respectively, had an 81 and 62 percent decrease in excess morality on oppressively hot summer days over a period during which air conditioning (central AC) rates increased (respectively) by 380 (1,400) percent and 240 (558) percent. In the South, by contrast, where the relative increase in air conditioning (central AC) was much lower, at 39 (159) percent, there was if anything a slight increase in mortality on oppressively hot days.

Looking at the data on a city-by-city rather than regional basis, as does Table 17.3, we see a similar pattern. All of the cities with an increase in excess mortality over the

TABLE 17.2(B) *Absolute change in excess deaths on oppressive heat days, 1975–2004*

Region	Excess deaths on oppressive heat days, 1975[a]	Change in excess deaths on oppressive heat days, 1975–1980	Change in excess deaths on oppressive heat days, 1980–1990	Change in excess deaths on oppressive heat days, 1990–2004	Excess deaths on oppressive heat days, 2004
South	0.4	0.1	−0.1[b]	0.5	0.7
Northeast	2.7	−1	−1.4	0.1	0.5
Central	1.6	−0.6	−1	−0.6	0.6

[a] Includes all of the cities for which Sheridan et al. (2009) calculated mean anomalous mortality due to oppressive heat days over the May to August period, except those that either do not appear at all in the AHS or which were not included over the entire 1970–2004 period. Also, because the excess deaths reported by Sheridan et al. for Atlanta for the years 1975–1978 are orders of magnitude larger than any other report, I omit Atlanta from the South for the period 1975–1980. Also, Sheridan et al.'s excess deaths number for the Northeast does not include data from Hartford, whereas the Census AC numbers do.

[b] Neither Dallas nor Houston has a recorded value for years including 1990, so for these two cities, the excess mortality value for 1991 is used.

TABLE 17.3 *Air conditioning increase and the decline in excess mortality on oppressively hot days, 1975–2004*

City	Change in percentage of homes with AC (central AC), 1970–2004	Change in excess mortality during oppressive May–August days, 1975–2004[a]
Baltimore	55% (61%)	−1.1
Boston	61% (25%)	−1.3
New York	47% (12%)	−2.8
Buffalo	38% (22%)	−2.5
Philadelphia	42% (40%)	−1.3
Kansas City	27% (64%)	.3
Cleveland	50% (45%)	−2.1
Pittsburgh	70% (48%)	−4.7
Detroit	56% (56%)	−.7
Minneapolis	52% (64%)	−1.2
Chicago	49% (49%)	−1.3
St. Louis	38% (59%)	−1.9
Dallas	19% (50%)	−.2
Houston	22% (52%)	.4
New Orleans	27% (50%)	−.3
Miami	28% (71%)	.2
Phoenix	22% (35%)	1.3
Atlanta[b]	46% (68%)	−7
Denver[c]	48% (42%)	−.4
Seattle-Everett	7% (NA)	−1.1

TABLE 17.3 *(continued)*

Portland	34% (25%)	−3.7
San Diego	33% (31%)	−.3
Los Angeles	30% (31%)	−.8

[a] Data on the change in excessive heat mortality come from table 4 of Sheridan et al. (2009).

[b] For Atlanta and Denver, the mortality rates reported by Sheridan et al. (2009) for 1975–1977 were so high and low, respectively, 11 and −4, that for 1975 mortality, I used an average of their reported mortality over the period 1975–1978.

[c] Owing to the suspicion that the reported −4.0 value for Denver for 1975–1977 is erroneous, the average of 1975–1979 is used for Denver.

1975–2004 period had an (absolute) increase in air conditioning over the period of less than 30 percent.

This data is merely suggestive of the enormous impact of air conditioning in lowering mortality due to heat. It is true that there is one study, by Bobb et al. (2014, 812), which found that the annual rate of change in the prevalence of central air conditioning in US cities was not statistically significantly related to the mortality decline from above average heat over the period 1987–2005. However, while the Bobb study looked at 105 US "cities," air conditioning data – which they took from the Census Bureau's American Housing Survey (AHS) of metropolitan statistical areas – did not even exist for 26 of their 105 cities for the time period studied. Moreover, the Census Bureau does not do annual Housing Surveys but instead conducts the surveys at multiyear intervals that vary across cities.[42] Thus although Bobb et al. purport to include a variable called the annual rate of change in air conditioning use, such a variable cannot be constructed accurately from AHS data. With their air conditioning variable suffering from what is likely severe measurement error, it is unsurprising that it did not turn out to be statistically significant.

A contrary finding about air conditioning has been presented by Barreca et al. (2016, 140). Despite dealing with the same sort of coarse data on air conditioning at the state level as exists at the level of the metropolitan statistical area,[43] remarkably, Berreca et al. estimate that 86 percent of the decline in mortality on days with an average temperature above 90°F between the period 1931–1959 (when there was no residential air conditioning) and 1960–2004 was due to the adoption of air conditioning. They also found that the impact of air conditioning was greatest for infants and the elderly, with cardiovascular death rates among the elderly falling the most, and also greater for blacks than whites. Barreca et al. (2016) found that an increase in AC coverage in a state from 0 to 59 percent (the average share across states over the period 1960–2004) would lower mortality on days with an average temperature over 90°F by about 1 percent.

City	Percentage of homes with A/C (central A/C), 1970	(Absolute) percent increase in fraction of homes with A/C (central A/C), 1970 to ca. 1980	Percent increase in fraction of homes with A/C (central A/c), ca. 1980 to ca. 1990	Percent increase in fraction of homes with A/C (central A/C), ca. 1990 to ca. 1995	Percent increase in fraction of homes with A/C (central A/C), ca. 1995 to ca. 2004	Final 2007 fraction with A/C (central A/c)
Baltimore	43% (14%)	(1979) 24% (20%)	(1991) 11% (20%)	(1998) 6% (10%)	(2007) 7% (11%)	98% (75%)
Boston	23% (2%)	(1981) 26% (4%)	(1993) 8% (6%)	(1998) 8% (5%)	(2007) 19% (10%)	84% (27%)
New York	37% (4%)	(1980) 12% (2%)	(1991) 14% (4%)	(1999)12% (2%)	(2003) 9% (4%)	84% (16%)
Buffalo	13% (2%)	(1979) 10% (4%)	1988) 4% (3%)	(1994) 8% (6%)	(2002) 16% (9%)	51% (24%)
Philadelphia	52% (8%)	(1982) 15% (14%)	(1989) 10% (10%)	(1999) 15% (13%)	(2003) 2% (3%)	94% (48%)
Providence	15% (1%)	(1980) 22% (2%)	(1992) 10% (6%)	(1998) 9% (3%); as of 1998, some AC 56% (central 12%)	NA[b]	NA
Hartford	33% (3%)	(1979) 22% (4%)	(1991) 12% (10%)	(1996) 1% (2%)	(2004) 16% (8%)	84% (27%)
Kansas City	57% (22%)	(1982) 25% (31%)	(1990) 4% (13%)	(1995) 8% (9%)	(2002) 4% (11%)	98% (86%)
Cleveland	28% (6%)	(1979) 19% (12%)	(1990) 13% (16%)	(1996) 7% (5%)	(2004) 11% (12%)	78% (51%)
Pittsburgh	20% (5%)	(1981) 20% (11%)	(1990) 14% (12%)	(1995) 14% (9%)	(2003) 24% (16%)	90% (53%)
Cincinnati	35% (9%)	(1982) 35% (28%)	(1990) 13% (14%)	(1998) 6% (13%); as of 1998, 89% (64%)	NA[b]	NA
Atlanta	51% (24%)	(1982) 28% (36%)	(1991) 10% (15%)	(1996) 5% (8%)	(2004) 3% (9%)	97% (92%)
Detroit	26% (6%)	(1981) 24% (17%)	(1993) 14% (16%)	(1999) 18% (17%)	(2003) 0% (5%)	82% (61%)
Minneapolis	43% (7%)	(1981) 23% (19%)	(1989) 12% (16%)	(1998) 9% (14%)	(2007) 8% (15%)	95% (71%)
Chicago	44% (11%)	(1979) 20% (17%)	(1991) 11% (14%)	(1999) 13% (13%)	(2003) 5% (5%)	93% (60%)
St. Louis	59% (27%)	(1980) 26% (28%)	(1991) 5% (16%)	(1996) 4% (6%)	(2004) 3% (8%)	97% (85%)
Dallas	80% (42%)	(1981) 12% (28%)	(1989) 3% (12%)	(1994) 3% (5%)	(2002) 1% (5%)	99% (92%)
Denver	18% (7%)	(1979) 15% (8%)	(1990) 7% (7%)	(1995) 0% (3%)	(2004) 24% (24%)	66% (49%)

Houston	76% (37%)	(1979) 14% (29%)	(1991) 3% (14%)	(1998) 4% (5%)	(2007) 1% (4%)	98% (89%)
New Orleans	69% (26%)	(1982) 20% (25%)	(1990) 6% (13%)	(1995) −1% (3%)	(2004) 2% (9%)	96% (76%)
Tampa	NA	(1985) 91% (68%)	(1989) 2% (7%)	(1998) 4% (−3%)	(2007) −1% (19%)	96% (91%)
Miami	71% (18%)	(1979) 17% (26%)	(1990) 0% (28%)	(1995) 8% (4%)	(2007) 3% (13%)	99% (89%)
Phoenix	72% (57%)	(1981) 6% (18%)	(1989) 12% (11%)	(1994) −1% (0%)	(2002) 5% (6%)	94% (92%)
Salt Lake City	30% (13%)	(1980) 0% (8%)	(1992) 11% (5%)	(1998) 16% (11%); as of 1998, some AC 57% (central 37%)	NA[b]	NA
Seattle-Everett	4%	0%			11%	15%
Portland	9% (3%)	(1980) 9% (4%)	(1990) 10% (5%)	(1995) 16% (22%)	9% (10%)	43% (28%)
San Francisco	7% (3%)	(1982) 7% (6%)	(1989) 7% (6%)	(1995) 12% (5%)[a]	NA[b]	NA
San Diego	12% (4%)	(1982) 14% (8%)	(1991) 11% (12%)	(1994) 2% (3%)	(2002) 6% (8%)	45% (35%)
Los Angeles	27% (7%)	(1980) 13% (10%)	(1989) 11% (11%)	(1995) 2% (4%)	(2003) 4% (6%)	57% (38%)

[a] Oakland and other areas dropped; just San Francisco city.
[b] Discontinued in 1998.

Notes

1. For evidence of very early surges in some human populations, see Aiméa et al. (2013). Evidence that humans adopted agriculture in areas that warmed quickly after the Last Glacial Maximum is provided by Zheng et al. (2012).
2. Interagency Working Group, 2013 Update on the SCC, p. 11.
3. An explication and defense of this approach is provided by Darwin (1999, 371).
4. For an illustration of a study illustrating the then state of the art, see Mendelsohn et al. (1994, 753).
5. Schlenker and Roberts (2009, 15,594).
6. The basic relationship estimated by Roberts and Schlenker (2012, 274) takes the form

$$Y_{it} = \alpha_i + \beta_1 h_{it} + \beta_2 m_{it} + \beta_3 p_{it}^2 + t_s + t_s^2 + \varepsilon_{it},$$

where y_{it} is the relevant crop yield in county i in year t, α_i is a county fixed effect, m_{it} gives the number of moderate temperature degree days (degree days with the temperature between 10°C and the extreme temperature threshold for the particular crop, which is between 29° and 32°C depending on the crop), h_{it} gives the number of extreme heat days, p_{it} is the precipitation, and t_s and t_s^2 are state-specific time trends in yield.
7. Beddow (2012), looking at data for the period 1879–2007 across eight states (Ohio, Indiana, Illinois, Iowa, Nebraska, Kansas, Missouri, and Kentucky), found that June precipitation is only weakly correlated with corn yield and August precipitation is negatively correlated, with only July precipitation strongly positively correlated with corn yield. Across the Corn Belt, the higher July temperature is, the higher is the optimal amount of rainfall for corn production. Most damaging for corn yields are Julys with dry weather and high temperatures.
8. Both temperature and precipitation determine the bioeconomic index, because as pointed out by Thompson (1963, 20–27), as high temperatures historically have accompanied low rainfall, if one looks just at July temperature, one would find a nonlinear relationship (with yields first increasing and then decreasing with increasing temperature) between temperature and corn yield that would essentially proxy the relationship between July rainfall and corn yield.
9. Beddow et al. (2014), draft.
10. Production indexed to the location of current year's production was about 20 percent higher than production indexed to the 1909 location of production.
11. Beddow et al. (2014), draft.
12. Fred Below and Brad Bernhard, "Managing for Higher Corn Planting Densities," *Climate Fieldview*, April 19, 2018, available at https://climate.com/blog/managing-for-higher-corn-planting-densities.

13. University of Wisconsin Ag Extension Service, "Corn Row Width and Plant Density, Then and Now," available at http://corn.agronomy.wisc.edu/Extension/PowerPoints/2003_WFAPMC_RS.pdf.
14. Lori Abendroth and Roger Elmore, "Planting Date Trends," Iowa State University Extension and Outreach (text updated March 8, 2010), available at https://crops.extension.iastate.edu/corn/production/management/planting/earl ier.html.
15. Abendroth et al. (2017); see also Abendroth and Elmore (2010).
16. Abendroth et al. (2017); see also Abendroth and Elmore (2010).
17. R. L. (Bob) Nielsen, "The Planting Date Conundrum for Corn," Corny News Network, April 2, 2018, available at www.agry.purdue.edu/ext/corn/news/time less/pltdatecornyld.html.
18. Source for the figure and following discussion is Nick Upah, "2018 Corn Planting Considerations," Iowa State University Integrated Crop Management, April 17, 2018, available at https://crops.extension.iastate.edu/blog/nick-upah-mark-licht/2018-corn-planting-considerations. Abendroth et al. (2017) estimate that the optimum planting windows to achieve 98–100 percent yield are April 12–30 for north central and northeast Iowa, April 15–May 9 for northwest and central Iowa, and April 17–May 8 for southwest and southeast Iowa.
19. 44News WeatherBlog, "Remembering the Brutal 1901 Summer," August 8, 2017, available at http://44news.wevv.com/39355-2/.
20. Zhang et al. (2015, 331) (for corn, 183 fields studied were located in Colorado, Kansas, Nebraska, North Dakota, and South Dakota; for soybeans, 121 fields were studied from Arkansas, Kansas, and Nebraska; and for wheat, 101 fields were studied from Colorado, Kansas, Nebraska, New Mexico, and Oklahoma).
21. In addition to the study discussed in the text, see Wang al. (2016, 1233–1241) (identifying a particular genetic variation that improved drought tolerance, with the genetic loci of this variation a potential target for both genetic engineering and selection for drought tolerance) and Mao et al. (2015, 8326) (who found that increasing the expression of a particular gene in transgenic maize enhanced "drought tolerance at the seedling stage, improves water-use efficiency and induces upregulation of drought-responsive genes under water stress").
22. "Precise Soil, Climate, and Weather Data Help Dairy Optimize Water Use," available at https://toolkit.climate.gov/case-studies/precise-soil-climate-and-weather-data-help-dairy-optimize-water-use.
23. Geoffrey Ling and Blake Bextine, "Precision Farming Increases Crop Yields," *Scientific American*, June 26, 2017, www.scientificamerican.com/article/preci sion-farming/.
24. T. J. Blom et al., "Carbon Dioxide in Greenhouses," Ontario Ministry of Agriculture, Food and Rural Affairs (December 2002; revised August 2009), available at www.omafra.gov.on.ca/english/crops/facts/00-077.htm.

25. USDA, "2017 State Agricultural Overview, Iowa," available at www.nass.usda.gov/Quick_Stats/Ag_Overview/stateOverview.php?state=IOWA; for Illinois, USDA, "2017 State Agricultural Overview, Illinois," available at www.nass.usda.gov/Quick_Stats/Ag_Overview/stateOverview.php?state=ILLINOIS.
26. USDA, "2017 State Agricultural Overview, Nebraska," available at www.nass.usda.gov/Quick_Stats/Ag_Overview/stateOverview.php?state=NEBRASKA.
27. This description is taken from Ainsworth and Gillespie (2010), but the impact of increasing CO_2 in inducing "partial stomatal closure" is well known and is discussed, for example, in Hatfield et al. (2011, 353).
28. Cleaveland and Duvick (1992, 2611).
29. Kent et al. (2017, 054012).
30. Irrigation Association, "Comparison of SDI and Center Pivot Sprinkler Economics," Proceedings of the 2012 Irrigation Association Technical Conference, Orlando, Florida, November 2–6, available at www.irrigation.org/IA/FileUploads/IA/Resources/TechnicalPapers/2012/ComparisonOfSDIAndCenterPivotSprinklerEconomics.pdf.
31. Gary Schnitkey, "Corn and Soybean Revenue Projections for 2016 and 2017," Weekly Farm Economics, farmdoc daily (6):145 (University of Illinois Department of Agricultural and Consumer Economics, August 2, 2016), available at https://farmdocdaily.illinois.edu/2016/08/corn-soybean-revenue-projections-2016–2017.html.
32. The pathbreaking work on optimal investment delay includes MacDonald and Siegel (1986, 707–728) and Pindyck (1991, 1110–1148).
33. Alejandro Plastina and Chad Hart, "Crop Insurance in Iowa," CARD Agricultural Policy Review, Iowa State University, Fall 2014, available at www.card.iastate.edu/ag_policy_review/article/?a=26.
34. Environmental Working Group, "Taxpayers, Crop Insurance and the Drought of 2012," pp. 7–10 (see figure 4 especially) (April 2013).
35. Plastina and Hart, "Crop Insurance in Iowa."
36. See also the earlier paper Olli Seppänen, William J. Fish, and David Faulkner, "Control of Temperature for Health and Productivity in Offices," LBNL-55448, June 2004, available at https://escholarship.org/uc/item/39s1m92c.
37. Looking at the sample size weighted meta-regressions (the dashed line) in the figure.
38. See the discussion in Kosonen and Tan (2004, 987–993).
39. US Energy Information Administration, Residential Energy Consumption Survey 2009, available at www.eia.gov/consumption/residential/reports/2009/air-conditioning.php.
40. US Census, Presence of Air Conditioning in Homes Completed, available at www.census.gov/construction/chars/pdf/aircond.pdf.
41. For a summary of findings, see Deschenes (2014, 606–619).

42. For example, there is an AHS available for Atlanta for the years 1975, 1978, 1982, 1987, 1991, 1996, and 2004 and for New York for the years 1976, 1980, 1983, 1987, 1991, 1995, 1999, and 2003. Census Bureau AHS Surveys prior to 2014 are available at www.census.gov/prod/www/construction_housing.html. Strikingly, some time around 2011, the Census Bureau apparently discontinued the practice of producing a survey of housing characteristics for each MSA. MSA-specific housing survey reports for 2007 are available only for seven cities (Baltimore, Boston, Houston, Miami, Minneapolis, Tampa, and Washington, DC). See www2.census.gov/programs-surveys/ahs/2007/.
43. Barreca et al. used measures of state level air conditioning usage for the years 1960, 1980, and 1990 and then assumed that air conditioning ownership rates increased at the same rate between 1980 and 2004 as they increased over the period 1970 and 1980. This is likely relatively accurate on the national level, as the 76 percent air conditioning rate they interpolate for 2004 is just about equal to the actual rate for the metropolitan areas that generate my data in Table 17.3 and the appendix. As I note in the text, however, Barreca et al.'s interpolated 2004 air conditioning rate is likely not accurate at the regional or metropolitan statistical area level.

18

The Surprising Sahel

The Crucial Role of Property Rights and Decentralized Institutions in Creating Incentives for Adaptation

The African Sahel, shown in Figure 18.1, is a vast dryland area lying between the Sahara desert to the north and more humid savannah to the south. The timing and amount of annual rainfall in the Sahel fluctuates wildly from year to year, with the amount varying between 150 and 600 mm (or about 6 and 24 inches per year; in some years, Sahelian rainfall is similar to what the US desert city of Tucson, Arizona averages, while in other years it is several inches more than San Francisco usually receives).[1] Sahelian rainfall comes only during the 3–5 month period in the summer and early fall, when the intertropical convergence zone is at its northernmost, bringing a low-level southwesterly flow of monsoonal winds that interact with low-level northeasterly winds (Landsea and Gray 1992, 435). As shown by Figure 18.1, the Sahel cuts across a number of African countries and as that same figure suggests, the Sahel includes a variety of different climate and vegetation regimes. It is said by experts[2] to be similar in many respects to the drylands of India and those found in northeast Brazil. The Sahelian landscape comprises domesticated parklands mixing stands of trees with crops. These parklands are believed to have existed for more than 1,000 years.[3]

Despite the ancient pedigree of the man-made Sahelian parklands, the general view of the Sahel taken by foreign aid and development organizations for at least the last 80 years is that of a region in perpetual crisis. On this view, the endemic instability and violence of the Sahel are due ultimately to human-induced climate change, with the Sahel being overtaken by the Sahara desert encroaching from the north. This trend, called the "desertification" of the Sahel, has been ascribed to the primitive and destructive agricultural practices of the people of the Sahel.

The idea that Sahelian agricultural practices are degrading the Sahel is generally taken to have originated with a 1935 paper by E. P. Stebbing (1935) entitled "The Encroaching Sahara: The Threat to West African Colonies." According to Stebbing, Sahelian people would cut and burn forest, spread the ashes over the area as fertilizer, plant seed after the rains came, and then harvest when the crop was ripe, with no weeding at any point. When the weeds got too bad, Sahelian farmers just

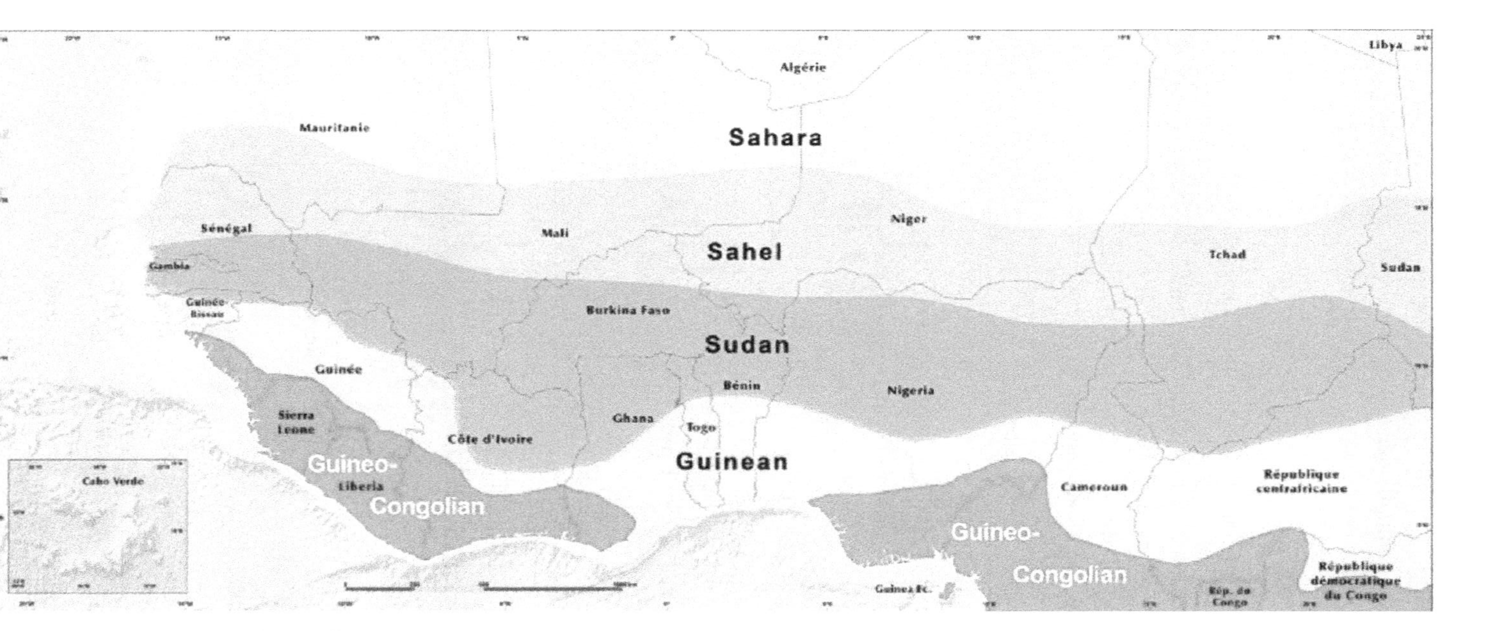

FIGURE 18.1 African Sahel rainfall and vegetation zones. Reproduces the figure found at US Geological Service, West Africa: Land Use and Land Cover Dynamics, available at https://eros.usgs.gov/westafrica/node/147.

moved on and cut more forest. According to Stebbing, it was obvious that land "treated in this fashion would gradually degenerate," and with an increasing population, "land hunger, and bush hunger" leading to inevitable and recurrent intertribal violence (Stebbing 1935, 507).

I A HISTORY OF DROUGHT AND ADAPTATION

Despite this early condemnation of Sahelian farming practices, for many years, the Sahel displayed not only recurrent drought, but also resiliency in the face of such drought. As Figure 18.2 shows, in the central and eastern Sahel, there were repeated periods of severe drought during the first several decades of the twentieth century.

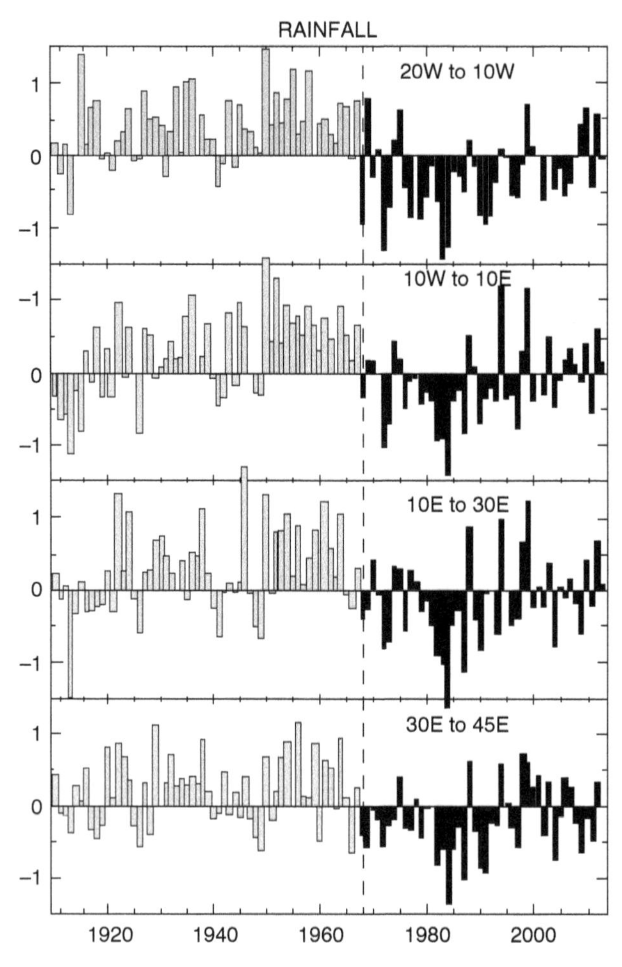

FIGURE 18.2 Rainfall departures for the African Sahel since 1910 (by longitude, from (top) west to (bottom) east). From Nicholson et al. (2018, 118).

These droughts did not have the catastrophic consequences of the 1972–1973 drought and the explanation has little to do with climate change and much to do with customs and institutions. Traditionally, both sedentary farmers and nomadic pastoralists inhabited the Sahel.[4] Nomads moved their herds of cattle along north-south routes, moving northward to the edge of the Sahara with the grass as the rainy season progressed and then back south into the savannah farmlands when the rainy season ended. They brought desert goods such as salt and dates with them when they returned south, and their cattle fed on farm field stubble, providing those fields with valuable fertilizer in the form of manure. While in the savannah, pastoralists bought feed such as millet for their cattle and also invested in stock breeding, helped finance agricultural production, and even bought land themselves. The routes taken by pastoralists were determined by the location of wells. These wells were owned by a particular clan, whose leaders regulated the use of the wells, even contracting with other clans for reciprocal well use rights. Cattle, by contrast, were privately owned. With pastures subject to communal ownership, overgrazing was controlled implicitly by the limited amount of time that could be spent at a well.

Sedentary farmers in the Sahel typically held landholding rights that were derived by inheritance. Such landholders held rights to the trees in their agricultural fields, with exclusive tree planting and cutting rights. Small plots were planted with long rotations that facilitated the regrowth of trees. While the landowner could permit others to prune their trees or gather tree products such as fodder for cattle, clan authorities used ceremonies to regulate to protect such highly valuable species.

A *Institutional Destruction due to French Colonization Set the Stage for Catastrophe*

The traditional Sahelian system, although not perfect, has been said to have been "relatively efficient and [to have] insulated its people from natural catastrophes" (Brough and Kimenyi 1998, 169). After several years of low rainfall, catastrophic drought struck the Sahel during the years of 1972–1974. "Unprecedented" media attention to the Sahel Drought presented pictures to the world of empty granaries and starving people eating the leaves of trees and herbs and selling livestock and whatever they could just to get the money to buy cheap ground cassava. Whole villages were empty as families departed en masse to towns and cities to beg (Mortimore and Adams 2001, 49).

As Figure 18.2 shows, the 1950s and 1960s were very wet decades in the Sahel. During this period, there was little international concern about desertification ion the Sahel (Kaptue et al. 2015, 12133–12138). The return of drought to the Sahel in the 1970s brought the Sahel back to the attention of the international development community and provided all the proof necessary that local agricultural practices in the Sahel were indeed causing desertification. Herds were too big for the carrying capacity of the Sahelian rangelands; crop producing systems had "collapsed"; inherently inadequate crop and livestock systems not only caused desertification and the drought but caused Sahelians to panic during the drought, cutting down even more trees and selling anything they could and finally migrating, but all for naught, as they eventually starved (Mortimore and Adams 2001, 50). On this story,[5] people of the Sahel are too poor and incompetent and do not possess the knowledge to pursue the correct high tech, top-down engineering adaptations necessary for the region as a whole (Mortimore 2010, 135). Without such adaptation, the region is one beset by constant violence, as tribes and other groups fight over limited agricultural production (Reich 2014).

If the indigenous or local agro-forestry practices of Sahelian people were really this dysfunctional, one would expect that by 2015, the Sahel would have completely collapsed and entirely emptied of people swarming to the cities. In fact, precisely the opposite has occurred. First, in what has been called a "most puzzling aspect," it seems that the Sahelian droughts were never as disastrous as claimed, as the drought was not "signaled clearly" in the economic performance of the region (Batterbury and Warren 2001, 2). Second, since the 1980s, the Sahel has become greener. A variety of different measurement methodologies – from satellite remote sensing to on-the-ground surveys – have revealed the greening of the Sahel. One recent study (Hänke et al. 2016, 117) finds that the loss of tree cover that occurred between 1968 and 1984 has completely reversed, with tree cover back to its 1968 levels by 2006; another study found a greening trend at 84 percent of 260 watersheds in four Sahel regions (of Senegal, Mali, and Niger), with the strongest reforestation trends in the drier, more northerly Sahelian watersheds (in Senegal and eastern Mali) (Kaptué et al. 2015).

As Figure 18.2 shows, over the last three decades, rainfall has returned to normal levels in the Sahel. And some have argued that it is this increase in rainfall that is responsible for the regreening of the Sahel (see, e.g., Brandt et al. 2015, 1610). However, there is abundant evidence that the harm suffered by people in the Sahel during the 1970s–1980s drought had more to do with institutions and incentives than with weather.

By the early twentieth century, the French had acquired vast colonial territory in West Africa including present-day Senegal, Mali, Burkina Faso, Benin, Guinea, Ivory Coast, and Niger. To acquire this territory, the French had to defeat the nomadic pastoralists. When they did this, the French eliminated clan ownership of wells. In so doing, the French eliminated the institutional means of controlling overgrazing. Unlike the British, who kept traditional political institutions in place in their colonial holdings, the French imposed a highly centralized system of direct rule in their colonies. By establishing military control, the French prevented clans from retaliating when they encroached on other clans' regions. The centralized administrative borders established by the French restricted traditional north-south nomadic routes. These changes significantly intensified land use.

The objective of this system was to make French holdings a source of net economic gain to France. In West Africa, the French focused in particular on increasing the production of groundnuts and cotton (Crowder 1990, 77). However, the steps that the French took to try to realize this goal proved to be disastrous. During the 1930s, the French passed administrative edicts nationalizing all forests, requiring permits for wood cutting, and declaring all lands not occupied for 10 years to be state property. With permitting more the exception than the rule, these edicts effectively destroyed customary rule and practices that had limited tree cutting and the use of the commons. Deforestation ensued as people collected wood – the primary energy source in sub-Saharan Africa – from what was now an open access resource. As was said of one district in Niger: "the inability to effectively exclude animals and humans from any but garden-sized plots during the dry season means that no one has any incentive to improve the quality of the woodstock grown on his own fields" (Brough and Kimenyi 1998, 172). When the region began to show signs of decline, the French response was to dig new wells and provide veterinary and health services. With the wells and common lands managed as open access resources, increased livestock populations just meant even more overgrazing near the new wells.

After achieving independence during the post–World War II period, the new African states retained the French system of nationalized ground cover and forests. In Niger, the Forest Code of 1974 gave the government exclusive rights to classified forests and required permits for a number of forest uses, strictly prohibiting any unauthorized cutting or pruning of many of the most valuable "protected" tree species. State interference in Niger extended to prohibiting – at the risk of fine or imprisonment – people from pruning tree on their own land. Elsewhere in the Sahel, permits to cut or prune trees were formally required, but often these requirements were either ignored or national forestry officials were simply bribed. Farmers had no incentive to invest in on-farm trees, and the degradation of the forest resources in the southern Sahel pushed Nomads further south. As they pursued their traditional slash and burn methods, farmers were in turn pushed into farming more marginal lands, some of which had traditionally been fallowed for up to 20 years. In Niger, the state agricultural service exacerbated the problems by advising farmers to use row planting methods that were incompatible with leaving trees in fields. As farmers cleared more new fields, cutting brushlands to meet the demand for food and fuelwood, erosion ensued, reducing soil fertility and yields. This pushed farmers into even more marginal lands.

By the late 1960s, both the farmers and nomads were extremely vulnerable to the periodic droughts which impact the Sahel. A drought in 1968–1969 devastated both nomads and farmers, with mass starvation of both animals and humans. The response of both international aid organizations and national governments again exacerbated the harm from the drought. Thousands of $200,000 wells were dug, but just as with French well-digging, these just increased herd sizes and the overgrazing problem on what had become an unmanaged commons. In Niger, supported by international aid, the government began a massively expensive ($1000/ha) program to reforest the country with exotic fuelwood species such as eucalyptus. This was accomplished by literally taking land from farmers and herders. Of the 60 million trees planted in the 1970s and early 1980s, less than half survived (Stickler 2002).

B *Property Rights and the Recovery of the Sahel*

Paradoxically, the economic impact of the 1970s droughts created the basis for Sahelian recovery. When government budgets eventually declined in Niger, there were not enough government foresters to enforce the laws, and farmers began to regard the trees as their own property.[6] Farmers took advantage of new techniques for managing trees, soil, and water and began to improve on-farm productivity. Under initiatives such as the farmer-managed-natural-regeneration project in southern Niger, farmers began again to manage naturally occurring on-farm trees that produce fodder for animals, fertilizer for soil and reduce wind and water erosion. As forestry expert Mahamane Larwanou described the change, "the farmers can sell the branches for money. They can feed the pods as fodder to their animals. They can sell or eat the leave. They can sell or eat the fruits. Trees are so valuable to farmers, so they protect them."[7] Even though the farmers were not given back their formal property rights in trees, tree cutting fines were suspended, and finally, in 1993, a new framework ordinance defining Guiding Principles for a new Rural Code for land and resource policy in rural Niger was passed.

Under the 1993 Rural Code Principles, local rights to protect, manage and benefit from on-farm trees were recognized, and customary rights to access and use natural resource were legally protected. By 2004, a new Forest Code formally recognized customary rights to collect firewood and edible and medicinal plants and to remove timber for tools from forest reserves. According to Stickler (2012, 5), "although the revised Forest Code did not go so far as to devolve freehold rights to trees to local individuals and farmers, campaigns to disseminate these reforms changed public perceptions about tree ownership that encouraged farmers to manage on-farm trees." As van Haren et al. (2019, 217–218) further explain, it was only through a variety of "informal initiatives" summarized by the term Farmer Managed Natural Regeneration that communities in Niger put a stop to uncontrolled tree cutting and livestock grazing and successfully regenerated on-farm trees. The trees are crucial to diversification of income sources. A *New York Times* journalist reported that by 2007, one farmer with 20 baobab trees in his fields in the Zinder region of Niger was able to get about $300 a year in additional income by selling leaves and fruit from his baobab trees. He used this money used to buy a "motorized pump to draw well water to irrigate cabbage and lettuce fields."

The restoration of traditional property regimes has been one important institutional change that has created incentives for the regreening of the Sahel. Farmers have responded to increased variability in rainfall since the late 1990s by expanding the genetic range of staple crops, retaining even rare varieties and adopting new crop varieties of key crops such as pearl millet and cowpea. Perhaps reflecting the social status that "innovative farming practice" confers on individual farmers (Mortimore and Adams 2001, 51), seed varieties developed at research stations, "diffuse[] rapidly through farmer-to-farmer exchange, without any government or project promotion" (Mortimore 2010, 137). Individual farmers "manage their own genetic pools by selecting and storing the best seed from each year's crop," maintaining a level of genetic diversity that is high compared to commercially produced seed in temperate countries and which provides a buffer against disease, pest, and climate hazards in the Sahel (Mortimore and Adams 2001, 53).

Although Sahelians have cleared natural vegetation for farmland over the past several decades, they have continued to manage farmlands as conservatories for economically important trees (Mortimore and Adams 2001, 53; Mortimore 2010, 139). Trees such as fruit trees have been planted, with 3 million ha of improved tree management in Niger and "dozens" of useful tree species conserved in northeastern (dryland) Nigeria (Mortimore and Adams 2001, 53; Mortimore 2010, 139). These trees have been said to provide foods, fodder, and medicinal and construction materials that together provide a buffer in times of drought and crop shortage (Mortimore and Adams 2001, 53). More systematic empirical evidence of Sahelian adaptation is provided by Hänke et al. (2016), who found that the tree species with the largest increase in density since 1984 have been drought-tolerant species found more in the northern Sahel. They take this as evidence of human adaptation, as without human intervention, less drought-tolerant species should have flourished in the wetter post-1980s Sahel climate. Further evidence for the key role played by human adaptation in Sahelian regreening found is provided by Hänke et al.'s (2016, 117) finding that the most dramatic tree density increase in the Sahel since the 1980s was for an exotic species, the Neem tree, whose numbers have increased significantly close to settlements. This parallels, they say, findings from other researchers looking at tree return in Burkina Faso, Niger, and Senegal, where the fastest increase has been found for exotic tree species (Kaptué et al. 2015).

In the Sahel, livestock are kept by farmers (either livestock producers with farms or farmers with livestock), versus nomadic pastoralists (Mortimore and Adams 2001, 54). Since the drought, in places like northern Nigeria, Sahelians have switched from cattle to "small ruminants, . . . as they are less costly, more hardy, easier to feed and reproduce faster than cattle" (Mortimore and Adams 2001, 54). During farming season, labor spent on tending such animals in dryland, Sahelian systems is low, as a "few small children can safely take the animals to graze on common pastures where an extensive, low density farming system is in operation, while everyone else works the farms" (Mortimore and Adams 2001, 54). Accusations that Sahelian pastoralists were responsible for land degradation have proven false in the light of new science on the capacity of grasslands to regenerate and new understanding of herd mobility on "patchy" landscapes. To be sure, there seems clear evidence that Sahelian pastoralists are facing challenges, but these challenges have less to do with drought and climate than with "inappropriate water point development, and the lack of commonly agreed or legal security over the rangeland commons" (Batterbury and Warren 2001, 4). All in all, even though rural populations in the Sahel have continued to increase at rates of 2–3 percent per year (Mortimore 2010, 138), "indigenous technical change" – adaptations including "indigenous forms of soil and water conservation, exploitation of wetter sites, cautious expansion and retraction of cultivated area, and maintenance of distinct seed stocks suited to variable conditions" – has been "adequate" to meet new challenges "even, perhaps specially, in areas of high population density" (Batterbury and Warren 2001, 4).

What has been called (Mortimore 2010, 138) "historic and fundamental transformation" of the Sahel since the 1980s has proven false the belief that Sahelians are too poor to successfully adapt: "some 25 years after the Sahel drought seemed to question the very survival of human communities, the farming systems persisted, village populations were stable or increasing, farming and livestock production were integrating and intensifying, and livelihoods were diversifying" (Mortimore 2010, 136). The "revolution" in the Sahel has been due not to massive aid from international development organizations, but "indigenous technical change."

It seems clear that in accomplishing such change, the incentives created by individual property rights and markets have at times supplanted traditional ownership systems. When migration to urban centers cut the growing season labor force, "labor markets emerged and labor-saving investment increased. There was more hiring of labor, plough teams and carts. As farm sized declined, and became more valuable, land markets and rental increased, although innovative resource tenure contracts ('derived rights') are widely preferred to outright sales." At the same time, "agricultural service markets (new seeds, herbicides, pesticides, and chemical fertilizers) began to appear," and there have been "reductions in the cost of acquiring knowledge" through innovations like cell phone and motorcycle passenger ride rentals" (Mortimore 2010, 139). As farm expansion cut the informal grazing rights of pastoralists, there have been a number of changes. One has been a "major revaluing of crop residues, which are conserved, sold, and bought in many areas." With the increasing value of cattle as investments, there has been a "decline in customary herding contracts between farmers and herdsmen" in favor of "cash herding contracts with city dwelling owners" (Mortimore 2010, 140). Sahelian farmers and herders also have turned to "urban informal sector" employment not as a replacement for farming or herding but as additional income sources that diversify Sahelian incomes. Even as traditional institutions are under new pressures, it remains true that "Sahelian societies ... are enjoying better access to education, information, personal freedom ... and ease of travel" (Mortimore 2010, 140).

Sahelians have always faced a difficult and changeable climate. As put by one long time student of the Sahel, through their traditional, customary mix of individual and shared property rights, Sahelians have pursued not just productivity enhancement, but risk avoidance through diverse and flexible agricultural responses to drought.[8] The French colonial experience in the Sahel shows the disastrous consequences of neglecting such traditional adaptations and simply trying to centrally impose agricultural systems designed to maximize "productivity at all costs." If scholars are correct that the potential for "indigenous intensification" in the Sahel depends on "rainfall and soil nutrients,"[9] then the logical policy response is not to supplant local institutions but to supplement them by providing "simple but reliable information on the onset and overall adequacy of the rains."[10]

Notes

1. See USGS, West Africa: Land Use and Land Cover.
2. Such as Mortimore (2010, 134).
3. See Hänke et al. (2016, 118), citing, among others, Maranz and Weisman (2003, 1505).
4. The discussion that follows in this paragraph is taken from Brough and Kimenyi (1998, 163) and Stickler (2002).
5. Accepted lock, stock, and barrel by the IPCC in 2007 (Boko et al., 2007). As discussed below, however, the IPCC's 2014 has a more nuanced discussion of Sahelian adaptation. *Climate Change 2014: Impacts, Adaptation and Vulnerability* 1226 ("overall adaptive capacity is considered low in Africa because of economic, demographic, health, education, infrastructure, governance, and natural factors") (2013).
6. Stickler (2002, 3) and Lydia Polgreen, "In Niger, Trees and Crops Turn Back the Desert," *New York Times*, February 11, 2007.
7. As quoted in Polgreen, "In Niger, Trees and Crops Turn Back the Desert."
8. Mortimore (2010, 140).
9. Mortimore and Adams (2001, 54–55).
10. Mortimore (2010, 140).

19

Selected Policy Implications

In this concluding chapter, I set out what may called the bottom line conclusions that I believe follow from the explanation and analysis provided by previous chapters of this book. These conclusions consist of recommendations for institutional responses to three fundamental problems of climate change: how to facilitate efficient adaptation to changing climate; how to curb present-day CO_2 emissions while minimizing the present-day environmental harms and the unfair, regressive costs imposed on today's poor; and, finally, what to do about the climate science advocacy industry that has produced some very interesting science, but also succeeded in moralizing scientific disagreement in a counterproductive and indeed dangerous way. My proposals follow logically from the analysis in previous chapters. I make no claim that and frankly know of no method for determining whether any of my proposals are politically feasible.

I ELIMINATE POLICIES AND PROGRAMS THAT HARM PRIVATE INCENTIVES TO ADAPT TO CHANGING CLIMATE AND PROTECT PROPERTY RIGHTS THAT CREATE SUCH INCENTIVES

If global human CO_2 emissions were immediately and permanently dropped to 0, global temperature would likely immediately increase by another 0.2°C, and then would stay elevated relative to preindustrial levels for many centuries. This is demonstrated by Armour and Roe (2011). The reason for the immediate increase in temperature is that completely eliminating CO_2 emissions would also mean huge drops in emission of aerosols and ozone that have a net cooling impact in the troposphere. Whereas atmospheric aerosols and tropospheric ozone would immediately fall to preindustrial levels, CO_2 would not. According to Armour and Roe (2011), because of its very long atmospheric half-life, it would take 170 years for CO_2 to fall to 40 percent of its peak value, at which level it would remain for many centuries.

Thus even the most aggressive CO_2 emission reduction policy possible would still imply centuries of higher global temperatures due to increased atmospheric CO_2. Perhaps the most robust and enduring lesson from the massive amount of climate change research over the past several decades, however, is that over periods ranging from decades to centuries, climate changes for reasons that have nothing to do with CO_2. Such inevitable climate change implies that human adaptation to changing climate is also inevitable.

The previous two chapters have revealed the key institutional determinants of the ability of an economy to adapt to changing climate. Because climate is an input to all economic productive and consumptive behavior, people implicitly adapt their choices to a given climate, no matter what the government's policy might be. This is a crucial point to understand. Government policies can inform and lower the cost of such adaptation, improving incentives for adaptation, or they can blunt and even reverse incentives to adapt. But if the state does not intervene, economic actors have a clear incentive to a given climate and to invest in gaining information about and adapting to climate change.

This strong incentive is present in both developed and developing economies. Hybrid corn was developed because there were strong property rights that guaranteed profits to its developers. Farmers adopted such corn because it greatly increased yields and provided enhanced resiliency against interannual swings in growing season weather. Air conditioning was developed and produced to satisfy a market demand for more pleasant and more productive indoor environments on hot days. Once traditional institutions were restored to the African Sahel, what had been becoming a desert became green again, as farmers and pastoralists regained incentives to manage their lands for the long term.

As with any choice, errors in climate change adaptation are possible. In a generic sense, a false positive arises when an economic actor overadapts. Such a false positive arises when the actor makes choices, such as investments, that are based on evidence that that climate will change in some way but in fact the change does not occur, or it occurs much later or on a smaller scale than believed. A false negative is most naturally understood as a failure to adapt based on evidence indicating that climate change will be smaller, or later, but this evidence turns out to be wrong. This sounds all very future-oriented, but the evidence may go to whether climate is already changing. In that case, a false positive, a false decision to invest in adaptation, is one that may be understood as an error in interpreting the evidence – the climate is not changing at all, or in a slower or smaller way than necessary to economically justify the adaptation. And the inverse is true for a false negative.

In a competitive economy that is completely free from government intervention, economic actors have no choice but to consider and adapt to climate and to forecasted climate change. If an Iowa farmer of the future correctly forecasts that the climate there is getting warmer and dryer and invests in irrigation, then that farmer will flourish and survive in the new climate. Her neighbor who interprets the evidence incorrectly – as failing to disconfirm the hypothesis of no change, meaning she assumes no climate change – and fails to invest in irrigation will certainly be less profitable and may well fail. The successful farmer can buy her neighbor's land and thereby increase the scope and profitability of her operations. In this way, farmers who correctly interpret evidence regarding climate change will be more profitable than those who make incorrect interpretations, thus rewarding investment and skill in interpreting and acting on evidence regarding climate change.

On this argument, the government's role in facilitating private adaptation to climate change should be primarily to avoid creating perverse incentives for people not to adapt. By and large, by subsidizing and insuring maladaptive behaviors, the US government has followed precisely the opposite path. As discussed in Chapter 16, in the case of agriculture, the US systems of agricultural subsidies and ad hoc disaster relief has cut the incentive for farmers to adapt to changing climate. More generally, the United States has developed a natural disaster relief program that has two central features: generous federal sharing of ex post disaster losses, together with federally funded development in disaster prone areas (Johnston 2012, 231–242).

The system of federal disaster relief, with payments and Federal Emergency Management Agency expenditures triggered by presidential disaster declarations, is highly political. Disaster declarations are higher in election years, and congressional districts and states of political importance or with politically powerful congressional representatives get more disaster dollars. (See the discussion of relevant work in Johnston 2012, 233.)

These ad hoc payments are not the only federal compensation to disaster victims. In a study of hurricanes, relatively localized but very costly disasters, Deryugina (2017, 195) found that when other, general federal social insurance programs such as unemployment insurance and Medicaid and Medicare are taken into account, the combined effect of disaster and nondisaster transfer to hurricane victims made up "a large share of estimated damage and wage losses in most cases." Being close to fully compensated against disaster losses reduces the incentive to choose costly behaviors to avoid such losses.

The market provides a tool for people to use to compensate them in the event of disaster losses, insurance. But here too the US government has intervened in a way that blurs and even eliminates entirely the signal the market prices would send. In the absence of government subsidies, if someone chooses to insure a home in an area that is known to suffer a higher probability of harm-causing natural disasters such as hurricanes or floods, that person will have to pay a much higher premium than if they located in a safer area. In the United States, 90 percent of natural disasters are flood related. Since 2000, through the National Flood Insurance Program (NFIP), the federal government has subsidized flood insurance premiums. Such subsidies reduce or eliminate entirely the higher premium that deters people from locating homes in flood-prone areas.

Over time, the bad, harm-increasing incentives created by the NFIP have been recognized and coastal and other flood-prone communities are supposed to generate hazard maps that allow premiums to be adjusted based on risk. This has been a slow process. The most basic fact about the NFIP is that the vast majority of NFIP subsidized insurance policies cover property that is located in the riskiest places, with one 2010 study finding that 70 percent of NFIP policies held in just five states, the coastal states of Florida, Texas, Louisiana, California, and New Jersey.

Optimal adaptation to climate change risks cannot occur if the government continues to cut the cost of failing to adapt by subsidizing insurance and almost fully compensating any uninsured losses that remain. These government policies are in a sense the zenith of precautionary policy irrationality – as a response to highly publicized, scary events such as landfalling hurricanes, they actually increase both the probability and magnitude of harm from such events. Moreover, like other precautionary policies, they do not help the poor. Instead, as shown by Ben-Shahar and Logue (2016), in addition to leading to more development in risky coastal areas, federal subsidies are regressive, in that they redistribute income to affluent homeowners who inhabit such coastal communities.

II RATIONAL VERSUS PRECAUTIONARY APPROACHES TO US CO_2 EMISSION REDUCTION

Private incentives to take steps to reduce CO_2 or other GHG emissions are very different than private incentives to adapt to changing climate. Economic actors who make the correct choices with respect to climate adaptation likely enjoy both lower costs and higher revenues than competitors who make the wrong choices. It would seem that by contrast, other things equal, an economic actor, say a private firm, that chooses to reduce CO_2 emission will generally sacrifice profits in so doing – either by decreasing revenues or increasing costs. Such a sacrifice would be made in the face of three harsh realities: first, as we know from the earlier discussion, climate has and will continue to change at various time scales regardless of what happens to human CO_2 emissions; second, there is generally no individual or firm whose CO_2 emissions are significant enough to make any difference to the rate of change of atmospheric CO_2 emissions; third, even if there were some individual actor whose activities alone were so massive in scope that the actor could reduce her climate impact by changing her activities, such changes entail private costs, and a private economic actor will have no incentive to incur such costs unless she is either somehow rewarded for doing so or sanctioned for failing to do so.

Economists call this problem one involving a divergence between private and social costs. Emitting CO_2 involves future social costs, whereas reduces such emissions involves private costs. This understanding of the problem leads directly to the common policy recommendation that the government must somehow intervene to force private firms to internalize the social cost of carbon and make costly investments that they would otherwise not make.

Remarkably, in recent years in the US electricity sector, this divergence between the private and social costs of CO_2 emissions has substantially lessened. What has been good for the electricity industry and American households has been good for the rate of atmospheric CO_2 increase. That force for good is called natural gas.

A *The Good News: The Rise of Natural Gas and the Decline of CO_2 Emissions from the US Electricity Sector*

As we have seen in earlier chapters, between 2005 and 2019, the congeries of federal and state renewable energy policies in the United States almost doubled renewable electricity's share of total US electricity generation, from 9 to 17 percent. If we recall further, as a share of total power generation, natural gas increased even more, doubling its share over this period to provide 38 percent of US electricity by 2019. The biggest loser has been coal, with its share cut by more than half, from 50 to 23 percent. Much differently, over the entire 2005–2016 period, nuclear has provided about 20 percent of US electric power.

The other important fact, that I did not mention earlier, is that US electricity production peaked in 2007. Since that time, it has remained roughly stable. US electric power generation has been growing very slowly since the Great Recession of 2007–2009, growing only about 3 percent over that period, or at an average of 0.2 percent per year.

Because generating electricity by burning fossil fuels emits CO_2, the US electricity generation switch from coal to natural gas and renewables has led to reductions in US electric power sector CO_2 emissions. This was partly because renewable power generation per se does not omit CO_2, and also because CO_2 emissions from natural gas are lower than from coal.

To isolate the impact of just the switch from coal to natural gas, one needs to compute the CO_2 emissions from getting electricity from coal versus natural gas. There are two steps in doing this. First, one needs to compute the amount of the fossil fuel that it takes to generate a certain amount of energy. Second, one needs to compute the amount of CO_2 generated by burning this amount of fossil fuel.

When one works through these computations (as I do in the appendix to this chapter), one finds that in terms of CO_2 emissions per Btu generated, burning natural gas generates only 58 percent of the CO_2 emissions as does anthracite coal. When we add in the efficiency advantage of natural gas, it turns out that natural gas generates somewhere around 43 percent of the CO_2 emission as does coal. In other words, switching from coal to natural gas for a given volume of electricity production can generate around a 60 percent reduction in CO_2 emissions.

For the period 2000–2016, when we combine the decreased GHG emissions from the switch away from coal and toward natural gas and renewables – a switch that should produce about a 24 percent decrease in electric power sector GHG emissions – together with the increase of about 20 percent in electricity generation – we get a substantial reduction in US electricity sector GHG emissions. As shown in the EPA figure reproduced as Figure 19.1, according to the EPA, at 1,700 million metric

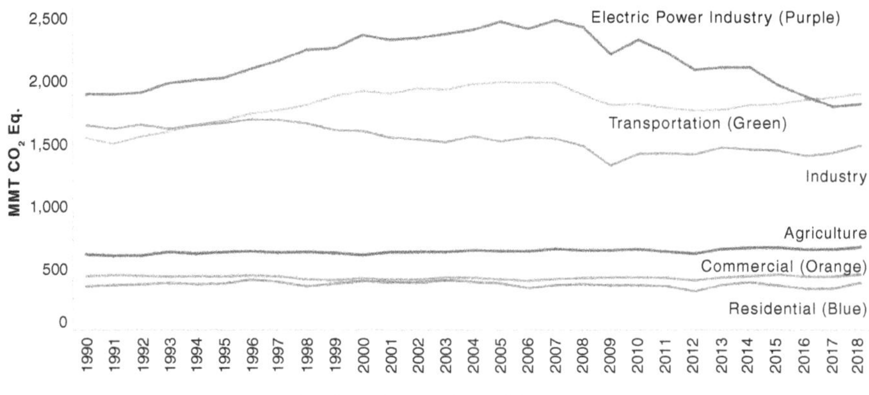

FIGURE 19.1 GHG emissions from US sectors since 1990.

tons (MMT), US electricity sector CO_2 emissions from fossil fuels in 2018 were actually slightly lower than the 1,800 MMT of such emissions in the year 1990.[1]

After increasing between 1990 and 2005, total US GHG emissions fell have fallen from 7,392 MMT in 2005 to 6,677 MMT in 2018 (about 9 percent).[2] Total US GHG emissions in 2018 are, according to EPA, only 3.7 percent higher than 1990 US GHG emissions. As in most other developed countries, other than electricity, transportation, and industry are the most important sources of GHG emissions. As we can see from Figure 19.1, GHG emissions in the big three emission sectors – industry, transportation, and electricity – fell sharply during the Great Recession of 2007–2009. Since then, GHG emissions from transportation and industry have returned roughly to 2008 levels, with only electricity sector emissions showing a sustained decline.

As this discussion shows, in a very real sense, the rise of natural gas and renewables in the US electricity sector has been responsible for a stabilization of US GHG emissions, a stabilization that is especially remarkable in light of IPCC projections of not that long ago. In 2007, for example, in its Fourth Assessment Report, the IPCC reported that in the absence of new policies to reduce GHG emissions, global CO_2 emissions from energy use would increase between 40 and 110 percent over the period 2000–2030. At least in the US electricity sector, precisely the opposite has been happening: by 2016, or about half way to 2030, US CO_2 emissions had *fallen* by several hundred million tons. Something very radical would have to happen for this trend to reverse.

To be sure, the congeries of federal and state renewables subsidies and mandates discussed earlier has roughly doubled the share of renewables since 2005. However, between 2005 and 2019, when US electricity generation from coal fell by 1,047 million GWh, renewable power generation increased by only 362 GWh. Electricity generation did not shift primarily from coal to renewables, but from coal to natural gas, generation from which increased by 821 million GWh.

There seems little doubt that as discussed earlier, this shift of electricity production from coal to natural gas was driven by the coincidence of a big and sustained fall in the price of natural gas along with coal cost increases caused by the Obama-era regulatory war on coal. The story told in that chapter is clear: many of the biggest utilities closed coal-fired power plants and switched some of them over to natural gas and at the same time invested billions of dollars in constructing massive new natural gas–fired plants. That story is buttressed by more rigorous econometric work showing clearly that electricity generators are highly responsive to changes in fuel prices, switching from high price to lower priced fuels (see Gao et al. 2013; Hartley et al. 2014). When producers saw what they perceived to be a likely long run fall in the cost of natural gas and rise in the cost of coal, they switched to natural gas in droves.

I am unaware of any rigorous economic study estimating just how big a shift from coal to natural gas would have occurred if the huge fall in natural gas prices had not been accompanied by the Obama-era war on coal. Recalling Figure 6.2, however, we have seen that the shift from coal to natural gas began back in 2008–2009, when natural gas prices fell sharply. At this time, while an increase in regulatory costs for the coal-burning power industry were certainly foreseeable, those costs had not yet been imposed. This strongly suggests that the drop in natural gas prices alone drove at least some of the switch away from coal. Such a switch, as we have seen, dramatically lowered CO_2 emissions by the electric power industry. Most importantly, for present purposes, it was a good news switch, one consistent with the profit maximization motive of power producers, because it both lowered their costs and lowered their CO_2 emissions.

B *The Bad News: Renewable Power Subsidies and Mandates Are Killing Nuclear; the Long-Term Solution to Reducing CO_2 Emissions While Protecting the Present-Day Environment*

A change in relative prices, however, is only one reason why natural gas usage has risen so spectacularly. The other reason, revealed by Chapter 7, is that as the fraction of power supplied by intermittent wind and solar power increases, so too does the need for dispatchable power. For this reason, an increase in renewable generation has two countervailing effects. On the one hand, renewable power displaces some highly efficient, low-cost power production by combined cycle natural gas – generally, solar during the day, and wind at night. On the other hand, renewable power increases the demand for easily dispatchable power – typically provided by gas turbines – that is needed during the evening and morning hours when neither solar nor wind is typically available.

We can see this in California. The increase in solar power generation in California between 2010 and 2017 was a spectacular 2,200 percent, from 90 GWh to 21,895 GWh.[3] This massive increase in solar power was paralleled by a 14,000 GWh decline in nuclear power output (from 32,000 GWh to 18,000 GWh) and an overall decline in natural gas power generation, from about 110,000 GWh to 90,000 GWh. On a proportional basis, solar obviously did not have nearly as big an impact on natural gas as it did on nuclear. Hydropower, which is easily dispatchable (within limits) also increased in California during the period of explosive growth in solar, from 34,000 to 43,000 GWh. In light of the more detailed analysis discussed in Chapter 7, these facts tell a story in which the rapid increase in solar power generation in California displaced nuclear and highly efficient combined cycle natural gas as baseload and daytime power suppliers, but the increased demand for readily dispatchable power caused by the rapid increase in solar power in California was met by both natural gas turbines and hydropower.

The key point here is that an increase in solar and wind power generates an increased demand for readily dispatchable power from natural gas turbines while severely reducing demand for baseload and daytime power supplied by nuclear plants and combined cycle natural gas. From the point of view of policy analysis, subsidizing wind and solar increases the demand for relatively costly but easily dispatchable gas turbine generated electricity but severely reduces demand for the power that nuclear plants supply. Whereas solar and wind are production substitutes for efficient combined cycle natural gas – fired plants and nuclear plants, they are compliments in production to high cost but dispatchable gas turbine – generated power.

In this light, the attack by many traditional environmental groups on natural gas is both unnecessary and perverse. It is unnecessary because subsidies for solar themselves significantly cut the demand for natural gas. It is perverse because solar and wind penetration cannot be increased, at least while preserving a reliable supply of electricity 24 hours a day, 365 days a year, without natural gas – supplied dispatchable power.

Despite the fact that natural gas is complimentary to increased penetration of solar and wind, environmental groups have been waging a litigation war against natural gas, using litigation under traditional environmental laws to delay and drive up the cost of new natural gas pipeline projects. For pipeline opponents, the easiest law to invoke to drive up the cost, delay and thereby potentially kill pipeline projects is the very same National Environmental Policy Act, or NEPA, that I discussed earlier. In the earlier discussion, I explained how the Obama administration had de facto waived NEPA's requirements for wind and solar projects. For natural gas, there was no such relaxation of NEPA.

Recall that the NEPA process involves an initial assessment as to whether a project involving a federal action has a significant environmental impact. If the assessment is that there is no such impact, then the process ends, but if there is a significant impact, then the responsible federal agency must prepare a full Environmental Impact Assessment, a document that typically runs to thousands of pages and takes years and millions of dollars to produce. Environmental groups have sued all kinds of federal agencies to stop natural gas production and distribution. In the 1980s, they sued Reagan administration federal land management agencies to stop them from leasing federal lands for natural gas exploration and drilling, and during the 1990s they sued a variety of permitting authorities to stop them from allowing natural gas storage facilities to be built. Since the beginning of the twenty-first century, they have sued FERC to stop that agency from granting certificates of convenience and necessity that the Natural Gas Act requires before FERC approves a new pipeline.

The environmental impacts alleged by plaintiffs in such suits are sometimes absurdly trivial. In *Delaware Riverkeeper v. FERC*,[4] for example, the plaintiffs argued that FERC needed to do a full EIS because a pipeline upgrade project would involve clearing 265 acres of forest and impact 50 acres of wetlands. To put this in context, with increasingly large blades, wind farms generally require around 200 acres per MW of installed power.[5] Thus even a tiny wind farm capable of producing only 10 MW of power would require about seven times as much land as was impacted by the pipeline upgrade project at issue in the *Delaware Riverkeeper v. FERC*.

In some NEPA suits against pipeline projects, the primary alleged environmental harm from the new pipeline is indirect – the CO_2 emissions from using the natural gas to produce power.[6] In light of the discussion in this book, one's first thought about such allegations should be that while burning natural gas generates CO_2, burning natural gas instead of coal is a big win for CO_2 emissions, and even a bigger win when the natural gas is burned to compliment zero CO_2 emitting renewable power. This implies that pipelines that allow natural gas to replace coal actually reduce GHG emissions.

In NEPA litigation, it doesn't matter whether natural gas pipelines have a net CO_2 lowering impact. NEPA does not say anything about how any given assessed environmental impact must affect the agency's decision. It just says that the agency must fully analyze the impact and see if it could be lessened somehow. And the permitting agencies don't develop pipeline projects. Private investor owned companies do. As Epstein (2018) has argued, NEPA allows virtually any person to challenge a project on any imaginable ground. NEPA suits cause so much delay, additional cost and, most importantly, uncertainty, that the calculus of investor owned Boards of Directors – whose fiduciary obligations run only to their shareholders – often eventually dictates that projects be cancelled or sold.

Killing natural gas projects that hold the promise of lowering the cost of providing dispatchable power that is necessary to assuring reliable electric supply in grids with high penetrations of renewable power would seem to be completely inconsistent with the goal of achieving a high fraction of power production from renewables. We have seen this with New York and New England, where preventing new natural gas pipeline has not only drastically increased the cost of electricity but jeopardized the reliability of electricity supply.

Some climate policy advocates, however, respond that there is a much more environmentally friendly type of dispatchable power, hydropower. As explained earlier, environmentalists have traditionally understood and still today understand that the preservation of undammed rivers and streams provides a wide range of benefits to people and to river ecosystems. Yet Jacobsen et al. (2015a) believe that existing dams can be made more efficient in producing power, as by modifying spillways and feedstocks. However, such construction projects themselves can have big adverse environmental impacts. Moreover, such modifications mean that existing old dams that might well be removed to provide a wide range of recreational and environmental benefits will not be removed but will be repurposed as tools to lower CO_2 emissions. Retention of such dams is itself a serious environmental harm.

C *It's Time to Get Past the Precautionary Panic over Clean and Efficient Nuclear Power, Eliminate Renewables Subsidies, and Move on to the CO_2-Free Future*

Even retaining and expanding electricity output from dams might be worth considering were there no other alternative for long-term CO_2 reduction than to couple the continuing build out of massive land guzzling, waste generating, bird killing wind and solar farms with expansion of inefficient gas turbine capacity. But there is an alternative, one that was rapidly returning to prominence before the post-2005 explosion of renewables subsidies and mandates. This alternative is nuclear power.

(a) Precautionary Opposition to Nuclear Power

Nuclear power plants are powered by nuclear fission reactors. The fuel for this fission process is uranium, processed and enriched to increase the proportion of unstable Uranium 235. The waste material from a nuclear reactor is mostly inert uranium-238 but also small amounts of radioactive plutonium-235. According to Mahaffey (2009, 308), all of the debris left over from the uranium-235 fission process is only about 3 percent of the mass of the spent fuel. It is a mix of radioactive isotopes of various elements, with half-lives that range from several months (as for iodine-131) to 30 years (as for strontium-90).

Not much such waste is produced. As Mahaffey (2009, 308) describes it, if all the electricity consumed by an person used in her entire lifetime were produced by nuclear power, the lifetime waste would fit in a coke can and weigh about 2 pounds. If that electricity had been produced by combusting coal, the waste would compose a "small mountain." Nuclear waste can be reprocessed and broken down into its radioactive and nonradioactive components with a mass only a tiny fraction of the beginning mass of the waste. Many countries in the world, including France and the United Kingdom, routinely reprocess nuclear fuel, and in 1976, in Barnwell, South Carolina, a state-of-the-art, privately owned reprocessing plant had been built and actually tested. The plant was able to extract valuable radioactive isotopes used by industry and in medicine in the treatment and cure of cancer, while encasing nonusable waste in insoluble borosilicate glass. The very next year, citing the risk of terrorism attack – only one of which has ever happened, at the French Superphoenix plutonium breeder reactor, where it was quickly and easily repulsed – President Jimmy Carter prevented the Nuclear Regulatory Commission from licensing the Barnwell plant. Not only did that decision mean the immediate loss of a $500 million investment; it made the United States completely dependent on other countries, including Canada, for the radioactive isotopes imported to the United States for use in cancer treatment and industry.

With no nuclear reprocessing facility, the US nuclear industry handles spent fuel by putting it first into steel lined 40 foot deep storage pools. After three years of storage in such pools, the waste is sealed inside steel-reinforced concrete containers. At a cost of about $1 billion per year as of 2007 (Cravens 2007, 295), storage takes place at about 100 nuclear plant sites across the country.[7]

Such on-site storage is not supposed to permanent. The Department of Energy thought it had located a permanent underground storage site in Yucca Mountain, Nevada. The ideal geologic conditions for underground nuclear storage are found at desert sites that were deep ocean bottoms millions of years ago but are now made up of layers of heavy clay, or salt beds that have been undisturbed by seismic activity for millions and millions of years.[8] Yucca Mountain is far from such a site. It is in an area of known seismic and volcanic activity. Yucca Mountain was chosen not because it is ideal from a geologic point of view, but because it is federally owned land that lies wholly within the Nevada Test Site, an area already contaminated by years of nuclear bomb tests. It was available, not ideal.

Even with its less than optimal geology, scientists say that there only three ways that radiation (more precisely radionuclides) could escape from Yucca Mountain – a volcanic eruption under the mountain, water flowing through the underground storage site, or, corrosion of the canisters containing the waste. There was no empirical evidence that a volcano had ever erupted under Yucca Mountain, and the 230 square mile project area is below sea level, in the Death Valley hydrologic basin, so that groundwater cannot flow out of Yucca Mountain, only in. Moreover, with about a thousand feet of rock between the repository and the water table, and with all nuclear waste contained in thick, corrosion proof steel alloy canisters shielded even from dripping water, the chance of water corroding the canisters to the point where radionuclides could leak out was viewed as very unlikely.

But not zero. The entire Yucca Mountain risk assessment process involved a layering of worst case, rather than realistic, scenarios (what Cravens 2007, 318, calls "conservative" assumptions) that made quantification of the risk that radionuclides could somehow escape the project area "impossible." Such worst case thinking is the precautionary principle at work – "continue looking for a problem, even if it means going to radical extremes." As Cravens (2007, 318) summarizes this process:

> Suppose that after thousands of years, the waste package [the deep underground tunnels in which cannisters are stored] finally is breached ... the dripping must then go for perhaps thousands of years more, this time through the pinhole, until the water fills what is in fact a container about eighteen feet long and seven feet in diameter. The water then must dissolve the Ziracloy cladding of the uranium pellets, then dissolve their radionuclides (most will be insoluble), and, after perhaps another thousand years, eat through the bottom of the double-shelled, film-sealed container. Possibly after thousands of years more, the contaminated liquid – maybe in droplets – has to make its way down through a thousand-foot-thick stone formation into the zone of rock and soil saturated with groundwater. This process, also highly unlikely, could takes still more centuries, and meanwhile many of the radionuclides would sorb along the way with clay or rock. Water in the saturated zone would dilute the concentration of radionuclides that happened to travel that far.

If an individual person based any decision of hers on such a layering of highly unlikely but not quite theoretically impossible worst case scenarios, we would say that she is completely irrational, and likely suffering from a mental illness. With scientists saying that it was "extremely unlikely" that radionuclides would escape from Yucca Mountain even for 100,000 years, and the worst case scenario – that all waste would have somehow escaped and been carried out of the Yucca Mountain repository – not possible until *a million years in the future*, one would suppose that this chain of reasoning could not possibly have guided US policy.

But it did. By the time EPA had to set standards for the safety of Yucca Mountain, many residents of the State of Nevada, and their powerful US Senator Harry Reid, had decided that they did not want nuclear waste to be stored in their state. Under such intense political pressure, in 2001, EPA set standards for waste disposal at the site by calculating risks over a 10,000 year horizon.[9] EPA's 10,000 year standard for the maximum allowable individual exposure to radiation from Yucca Mountain was 15 mrem/year (millirems per year). Natural background radiation exposure in Nevada is typically 350 mrem/year, but is as high as 600 millirem in some areas of the state. People living in Denver, Colorado, are naturally exposed to 700 mrem/year (Cravens 2007, 321–322). There is absolutely no evidence of any additional risk occurring at the levels of radiation to which people in Nevada and Denver are exposed. Nuclear scientist and former Georgia Tech professor James Mahaffey commented in 2009 that the Yucca Mountain nuclear repository "had been rendered safe as a sandbox by careful engineering," so safe that "Standing over a portal at Yucca, I would get more radiation exposure by eating a banana than I would from radiation leaking from the buried waste." (This is because, as he explains (Mahaffey 2009, 320), bananas contain potassium-40, a beta ray emitter, so that eating one banana delivers a radiation dose of 0.01 mrem.)

EPA's decision to set the standard for Yucca Mountain at less than 5 percent of the background level in Nevada was not based on any evidence. It was based on EPA's assumption that there is a linear dose-response relationship for radiation and harmful human effects. Because huge doses are known to be harmful, the linear dose-response assumption implies mathematically that there is a positive risk of harm, no matter how small the dose. This is an assumption, not an empirical finding. EPA maintains this assumption in all of its risk regulation decisions. It is not based on scientific evidence but rather on EPA's normative decision that as environmental statutes are generally precautionary, it should base risk standards on the worst case, linear dose-response relationship even for things like radiation, for which the evidence clearly shows that the assumption is wrong.

EPA was not precautionary enough for the DC Circuit Court of Appeals. In *Nuclear Energy Institute v. EPA*,[10] the state of Nevada and environmental groups led by the National Resources Defense Council challenged EPA's 10,000 year horizon as inconsistent with guidance from a National Academy of Sciences panel that positive risks might still exist after 10,000 years. As just discussed, this is literally true – it is impossible to say that there is a zero risk of radionuclides escaping from Yucca Mountain, even 1 million years from now. The court agreed, saying that as there was evidence that it was possible that "at least some potentially important exposures might not occur until after several hundred thousand years," EPA had to set standards for the full 1 million year period during which Yucca Mountain's geologic stability could be estimated.

EPA responded to this court decision in 2008 by promulgating[11] a new Yucca Mountain standard that kept the same 15 mrem/year maximum for the first 10,000 years but added a 100 mrem/year standard that would apply between the years 10,000 and 1 million. Despite the finalization of these standards, the Yucca Mountain repository has never become operational. Instead, nuclear waste is still stored in casks above ground, mostly at nuclear plant sites. The Department of Energy, with the legal responsibility to the nuclear industry to provide such a storage site, has paid out (as of 2019) $7.4 billion in legal settlement fees, and it is estimated that it will need to pay out another $28 to $50 billion in the future.[12]

(b) Renewable Power Subsidies Are Killing Nuclear Power and Need to Be Ended

Nuclear power plants generate precisely zero CO_2 emissions and no emissions of air pollutants. As explained by the EIA,[13] nuclear power plants operate at higher capacity factors than any other electricity generating technology, averaging 90 percent. Nuclear provided electricity is the opposite of electricity from wind and solar – always available, every day of every year (except for occasional shutdowns to replace fuel). With such high capacity factors, nuclear plants are ideal providers of baseload power. According to the US Department of Energy,[14] unlike wind and solar farms, nuclear plants need very little land, with a typical 1,000 MW nuclear plant taking up about a square mile, a tiny fraction of the amount of land that is required for solar or wind farms with comparable generation capacity.

Ironically, it was public concern over CO_2 emissions and climate change that in the early 2000s brought the nuclear power industry back from the grave. To add even more irony, nuclear power was put in the grave by coal. Recall that during the energy crisis years of the 1970s, Congress did everything it could to encourage coal-fired electricity generation. Back then, coal was valued because it was a low cost energy source that abundantly available in the United States and did not need to be imported. As explained by Mahaffey (2009, 312–321), by the 1970s, nuclear power plant technology had advanced so that such plants were safe and efficient, with little environmental impact. But in the high interest rate, intense regulatory environment of the late 1970s, nuclear lost out to cheap and seemingly safe coal. When the accident at Three Mile Island occurred in 1979, nuclear power disappeared from future US energy plans.

Concern over CO_2 emissions and climate change brought nuclear power back. The Energy Policy Act of 2005 provided loan guarantees for advanced nuclear power plant designs, a nuclear energy production tax credit, and even cost overrun guarantees for as many as six nuclear plants. By November 2008, construction permits had been sought for 12 of the newest model nuclear reactor. Between 2008 and around 2013, nuclear generating capacity in the United States surged, and it seemed that nuclear power had a bright future.

Renewable subsidies have ended this future. By 2015, nuclear power plants were being closed many years before their productive lifetimes had ended. In 2018, FirstEnergy and Exelon announced that they would be closing four nuclear plants in Ohio and Pennsylvania that together had generated more electric power than all the solar and wind power generation not just in those two states but in the entire PJM regional network of which they are a part. The closure was estimated to entail a $1.5 billion increase in electricity rates for customers in that region, the loss of 3,000 power plant jobs (not to mention thousands of jobs lost as a follow on consequence in local economies), and an increase of 21 million tons of CO_2 annually.[15] By 2019, plans were announced to close another dozen or so nuclear plants tin New England and California. The two Diablo Canyon plants that PG&E is closing in California alone produce 18 million MWh/year, 39 percent more power than all the power produced by wind in California.[16]

The stated reason for these nuclear power plant closures is typically that the power they sell is slightly more expensive to produce than power from natural gas – fired power plants. And it is indeed true that where nuclear power plants are closing, the power they used to produce is being replaced by power from natural gas–fired plants. But the reason that nuclear plants are closing (and the reason for the price difference with natural gas) is because, as explained back in Chapter 7, renewable power subsidies that have expanded the share of electricity provided by renewables have drastically cut the demand for the baseload power that nuclear plants are built to supply. Solar farms provide zero marginal cost power during the day, and wind farms (typically) provide zero marginal cost power at night. The high demand early morning and evening periods when intermittent solar and wind are not available, plus other, less predictable periods of low solar and wind production, are made up by easily dispatchable natural gas. There is less and less load left to be supplied by nuclear power. What is happening is that renewable subsidies are killing nuclear power.

Whether or not they realize it, states that are mandating big increases in renewable power, with the goal of someday being 100 percent renewable, are actually moving to a system with a big (but far less than 100 percent) share of expensive, intermittent renewable power and the remainder of their power supplied by natural gas. It is precisely to such a system that the Germans have moved. The German experience carries a lesson about the dangers involved in the new renewables-natural gas hybrid power systems.

Between 1992 and 2006, the majority of Germany's electricity was produced by nuclear power. However, in response to the tsunami-induced Fukushima nuclear disaster in Japan in 2011, Chancellor Merkel immediately ordered the closure of eight nuclear plants, with the remaining nine German nuclear plants to be limited in operation and offline by 2022. This abrupt and dramatic reaction to a distant nuclear accident was approved by 80 percent of the German parliament, with the Left Party objecting only because the nuclear guillotine didn't fall faster and wasn't included in the German constitution. As of 2020, Germany has closed all of its nuclear plants and is in the process of closing all of its coal-fired power plants. It is covering the North Sea with huge wind farms, power from which is supposed to be delivered throughout the country along a huge new north-south transmission line.

The transmission line construction has encountered increasing opposition from people who live near its route. Overall, however, despite a doubling of electricity prices since 2005, as of 2017, up to 70 percent of Germans polled still believed that the expansion of renewable energy is "very important," and only 17 percent said that they thought the cost to German consumers was too high.[17] Given such strong public support for renewable power, it is unsurprising that the German government has become even more ambitious, aiming to get 65 percent of German electricity from renewables by 2030.[18] The problem is that having closed all of its nuclear plants and coal-fired plants, it is far from clear how Germany can ensure power system reliability while basically doubling the share of its power provided by (primarily) wind. The Germans have found only one answer: easily dispatchable natural gas. But Germany also has a nationwide ban on fracking for natural gas. Without any domestic supply of natural gas, the only way for Germany to reliably run its new, high renewables electricity system is with imported natural gas, of which it is indeed the world's largest importer.[19] In 2017, Germany got 40 percent of its natural gas from Russia through the Nordstream I pipeline under the Baltic. With the Nordstream II pipeline having recently become operational, Russia will likely be supplying an even larger share of Germany's natural gas.[20]

With public opposition mounting to the huge network of new high voltage transmission lines that Germany calls its energy "superhighway" from North Sea wind farms, it is unclear precisely how large will be the ultimate share of wind power supplied by Germany. The one thing that is certain is that whatever fraction of German electricity does not come from wind will come from Russian natural gas. It is hard to see how any country that relies upon Russia for its natural gas supply and natural gas for its crucial dispatchable electric power can say that it has a reliable electric power system.

In their opposition to domestic natural gas, a number of US states with ambitious renewable power goals such New York and the New England states and California seem to be emulating the German model. These states are closing nuclear power plants even as they oppose new natural gas pipelines. While they needn't import natural gas from Russia, as must Germany, these states have intentionally or unintentionally tied their future to natural gas even while making it as expensive as possible. Choosing a power system based on renewables and natural gas involves the whole range of environmental harms from renewables that I have discussed in previous chapters. To be sure, CO_2 emissions from burning natural gas are, as we have seen, far less than from burning coal. Still, if a hybrid natural gas – renewables based economy grows, with natural gas providing a bigger and bigger share of its electric power – likely to exceed 50 percent under realistic assumptions about renewable power – such an economy's CO_2 emissions must also grow.

When one compares a nuclear energy – based electric power system, the choice seems obvious. Nuclear power has some present-day environmental costs (e.g., entrainment of aquatic organisms in the cooling water intake process), but these are far less than those of an electric power system reliant upon vast wind and solar farms. And unlike nuclear power, which generates zero CO_2 emissions, the evolving hybrid natural gas – renewables systems will have substantial and, if their economies actually grow, rising CO_2 emissions.

The superiority of nuclear has been increasingly recognized not only by environmentalists but also some of the famous climate scientist advocates whose work I have discussed at several points in this book. Arguing in the *Wall Street Journal*,[21] former GISS head James Hansen and environmentalist Michael Shellenberger recognize that nuclear power plants are being prematurely closed and replaced by natural gas – fired power. Their solution to this problem, however, misunderstands its cause. Hansen and Shellenberger argue that states that are already subsidizing solar and wind power should begin to subsidize nuclear power. If there is one clear lesson that emerges from the history of state and federal energy subsidies set out in this book, it is that such subsidies almost always have unintended, environmentally harmful consequences. The most direct route to an environmental future that both protects the present-day environment and greatly cuts CO_2 emissions is simply to eliminate renewable power subsidies and mandates. Free from such government interference, nuclear power will be the market winner.

III THE MORALIZATION OF SCIENCE MUST END: IT'S TIME TO SHUT DOWN THE CLIMATE–SCIENCE–INDUSTRIAL COMPLEX

The fundamental paradox raised by American climate change policy is how a policy supposedly based in science has become so completely political. As we have seen most dramatically in my discussion of the 2012 workshop on how to pursue litigation against fossil fuel producers, much climate change science has long been advocacy science, science produced and presented so as to support certain policy responses rather than to explain currently unexplained natural phenomena. To be sure, in the peer-reviewed literature, one can still find many examples of papers that do try to explore climate science puzzles that seem interesting solely on scientific grounds, regardless of their potential policy implications. But while produced and published, such papers are given very little if any attention by the official, government-funded climate science institutions such as the IPCC and the USGCRP. To the extent that the assessment reports produced by such organizations even mention work that tends to undercut the official or establishment story about climate change, the work is quickly dismissed without any serious or sustained substantive discussion. During the decades of its existence, IPCC reports have never reported a scientific finding that has actually marked a major advance in knowledge tending to seriously weaken any of the major claims underlying precautionary climate policy.

This discussion in fact contains two separate points. First, the precautionary principle itself says that provided that there is any evidence that serious and irreversible harm could result from continuing increases in atmospheric CO_2 concentration due to human CO_2 emissions, precautionary climate regulation is justified. The principle does not say anything about how such regulation is to be fine-tuned, based on changes in scientific understanding about things such as the multiple causes of climate change over varying time scales, or about how human adaptation lessens the harm from climate change. Instead, under the precautionary principle as long as there is some kind of scientific opinion suggesting a risk of serious or irreversible damage, for regulatory purposes, climate science is "settled." For the science to become "unsettled" to the point where it eliminates the case for precautionary regulation, new scientific work faces an insuperable burden of proof, in that it would have to somehow establish to a certainty there is no risk of future serious and irreversible harm from rising atmospheric CO_2.

It is in this precise sense that regulatory climate science is "settled." This is a crucial point to understand for it is a feature of regulatory science under the precautionary principle that clearly and sharply distinguishes it from science itself. Every science is built upon certain core laws that are taken to be true. One of the core laws underlying climate science is the first law of thermodynamics (also known as the law of conservation of energy). That law holds that within a given physical system, energy can be transformed from one form to another, but can neither be created nor destroyed. These core laws are indeed "settled," in that they are taken to be true. But while founded on core laws, scientific advancement means that understanding at the frontier of science is always changing. As described by Kuhn in *The Structure of Scientific Revolutions* (a book famous in many fields), science advances when more and more evidence is accumulated that fails to confirm or outright contradicts existing models of the world, and eventually – despite fierce efforts to defend the existing construct by those who have spent their lives building it – new models that better explain the observations become the new dominant paradigm. As the theoretical physicist Steven Koonin (who served as Assistant Secretary for Science in the Obama administration's Department of Energy) has stressed,[22] from the point of view of scientific practice, science is never "settled." If it were, scientific understanding would not progress.

From the very different point of view of providing a justification for precautionary regulation, by contrast, science is settled as soon as there is some evidence that the activity poses a risk of serious and irreversible harm. As discussed, in the case of potentially harmful climate change caused by human CO_2 emissions, such evidence has existed for decades. For advocates of precautionary climate change regulation, the threshold level of scientific evidence of risk that justifies precautionary regulation of human CO_2 emissions has long since been met.

This raises the question of why some $50 billion and counting has been spent on the climate science production and publications efforts of the IPCC and the USGCRP and the dozens of federal agencies and subagencies, such as the National Science Foundation, that have been funding climate science for the last 30 years. If the scientific case for decarbonization of the US economy has clearly been made out, why, one might ask, is more science being funded. The answer, quite simply, is that until what is viewed *politically* as an adequate response to the climate change risk has been taken, there will be a demand to produce more and more science.

This is the key to the climate change paradox: government-funded climate science is not being produced to illuminate fundamental unanswered scientific questions. It is being produced to justify precautionary policies. If the United States has not yet pursued policies deemed to be adequate precautionary responses to climate change risk, then more science needs to be produced. In other words, whatever precautionary policies have been adopted need to defended with more scientific evidence of risk, and new and even tougher policies can only be adopted by new science showing that risks are even bigger than first feared.

In this way, climate science has become inseparably linked to precautionary climate policies. Many people who expect to benefit from or already have benefited from such policies understand this link. They know, at least as a general matter, that the bigger is the potential risk from future climate change established by climate science, the more will present-day governments be willing to spend in climate policies, meaning, ultimately, the bigger is the private benefit that they stand to realize. Scientific work that tends to weaken or even complicate an understanding of climate change as due solely to anthropogenic CO_2 emissions directly threatens the very real and concrete economic benefits that subsidies and mandates confer, for example, on renewable power producers. As we saw in Chapter 8, during the Obama administration, billions and billions of dollars were conferred on particular firms and particular renewable energy projects. Scientific work that might be viewed as weakening the justification for such expenditures is not merely a matter of science. It threatens the livelihoods and, in some cases (see, for example, Tesla) the vast personal fortunes built on such subsidies. Viewed in this light, several things become explicable that otherwise are not. The IPCC and USGRCP emerge as the institutions responsible for coordinating climate science advocacy, the body of scientific work that supports the whole panoply of precautionary climate policies. It is inconceivable that an IPCC or USGCRP Assessment Report would every say that the case for dangerous human-caused climate change seems weaker than before. It is inconceivable that either institution would say that much more funding needs to be devoted to studies of how land use conversion has increased surface temperatures, or that conclusions about climate change in the Arctic cannot be confidently drawn unless and until black carbon emissions from China, India, and Russia are significantly reduced. Their institutional mission is to compile scientific reports that support radical decarbonization of western, developed economies.

Supported by the media in propagandizing the message of ever worsening climate change risks, the international climate science production complex has successfully settled the science. Paradoxically, "settling" the science means that the physical science of climate is now irrelevant to many people. Social psychologists studying individual attitudes have consistently found that personal ideology determines views about climate change. One formal statistical meta-analysis of studies on the determinants of climate change risk perceptions and concern, Hornsey et al. (2016, 4) summarize their findings as follows:

> many intuitively appealing variables (such as education, sex, subjective knowledge, and experience of extreme weather events) were overshadowed in predictive power by values, ideologies, worldviews and political orientation.

Thus it seems that not science, but "values, ideologies, worldviews and political orientation" best explain climate change risk perceptions.

What social psychologists mean when they refer to things like "worldviews" can be seen in another, highly publicized study, Kahan et al. (2012). This paper reports on survey tests of what the authors call "two competing accounts of public opinion on climate change." On what they called the "science comprehension thesis (SCT)," members of the public "fail to take climate change as seriously a scientists believe they should" because they do not know what scientists know or think the way scientists think. On the cultural cognition thesis, nonscientists fit their interpretations of scientific evidence to their one of two "competing cultural philosophies": a "hierarchical, individualistic" worldview that "ties authority to conspicuous social rankings and eschews collective interference with the decisions of individuals possessing such authority" and leads to skepticism about environmental risks, versus the "egalitarian, communitarian" worldview, favoring "less regimented forms of social organization and greater attention to individual needs," leading to moral suspicion of industry and commerce.

Kahn et al. (2012) tested several hypotheses about a person's degree of concern with climate change. They rejected the hypothesis that concern with climate change was positively correlated with numeracy/scientific literacy because in a simple linear regression of concern with climate change on their numeracy/scientific literacy variable, they found that the relationship was negative – more numerate and scientifically literate people had less concern over climate change. In a regression of concern about nuclear risks with the degree of scientific literacy, Kahan et al. (2012) again found that the relationship was negative – that people who were more numerate or scientifically literature had less concern with nuclear risk.

This result suggests that the climate science production complex propaganda has been effective in persuading only relatively innumerate people that they should be very concerned about climate change. But Kahan et al. (2012) also measured something that they called "cultural worldviews," with only two such worldviews allowed: "individual-communitarianism" and ""hierarchy-egalitarianism." Their test subject were put into one or the other category depending on how they answered six very general "agree-disagree" type questions such as the "the government interferes too much in our everyday lives," or "sometimes government needs to make laws that keep people from hurting themselves." One can quibble with these questions as the basis for categorizing a person as a communitarian – the latter question, for example, has nothing to do with communitarianism but rather paternalism. But given their categorization of respondents' worldviews, Kahan et al. (2012) included worldview along with scientific literacy and numeracy (and variable interacting the two) in a multiple regression analysis of individual concern about climate change.

What they found was that when worldview was included as an explanatory variable, it swamped scientific literacy and numeracy. The more individualistic and hierarchical a person, the less concerned they seem to be with climate change. Moreover, for people holding the individualistic, hierarchical worldview, increasing scientific literacy and numeracy decreased their concern with climate change, whereas such concern increased for more scientifically literate and numerate people holding the communitarian-egalitarian worldview. For nuclear risks, by contrast, concern fell strongly with scientific literacy and numeracy, regardless of whether worldview was also included as an explanatory variable.

Kahan et al. (2012) interpreted their findings as showing that "the contribution that culture makes to disagreement grows as science literacy and numeracy increase." They reach this conclusion primarily on the basis of statistical results that as scientific literacy and numeracy go up, perceived climate change risk stays roughly constant (increasing very, very slightly), for egalitarian communitarian types and down, much more rapidly (but still slowly compared to nuclear risk perception) for hierarchical individualists.

When I look at the results of Kahan et al. (2012) – meaning I look at the very same figures – I see that scientific literacy has very little impact on climate change risk perceptions of egalitarian communitarians but a much bigger impact on the risk perceptions of what they call hierarchical individualists. Kahan et al. (2012) did not do this,[23] but my bet would be if one tested the hypothesis of whether the scientific literacy/numeracy variable has a bigger impact on perceived climate risk among hierarchical individualists versus egalitarian communitarians, the answer would be yes at a high level of statistical significance.

Such a result could be interpreted a number of ways (this is generally true in social psychology, where hypotheses are not generated in precisely testable mathematical form). My own interpretation would not be that of Kahan et al. (2012) – which is that the hierarchical individualist worldview is so strong that such people ignore the scientific conclusions publicized by the IPCC climate science production complex. My interpretation of the results in Kahan et al. (2012) is that as scientific literacy and numeracy increases among those holding the communitarian-egalitarian worldview, so too does the likelihood that they work in the climate science field or have directly or indirectly benefited, or supported, or perhaps even been involved in the design and promulgation of precautionary climate policies. Precautionary climate policy is, after all, ostensibly science-based. Some fluency with the science would seem necessary to be part of the precautionary science policy community. This is likely not true of those who hold the individualist hierarchical view. It seems reasonable to think that such people are less likely to be involved in or benefiting from the government-funded climate science or precautionary policy complex. They are probably more likely on average to be on the other side of the fence, even working for fossil fuel companies. The main thing is that their scientific literacy/numeracy is likely to be unrelated to whether they are or are not part of the climate change science production, precautionary policy complex simply because so few are part of that complex. Hence for individualist/hierarchical types, the degree of their knowledge likely controls their views.

More recent work finds that while the vast majority of the public does agree that "climate change is real," there continues to "sharp division" about its causes and whether anything should be done. This division has increasingly finds that climate change has become a highly moralized issue involving group identity. Bliuc et al. (2015, 226) explore the hypothesis that "contrasting opinions of believers and skeptics about the causes of climate change provide the basis for social identities that inform what they, and other people, should do about climate change ... people come to see climate change beliefs and skepticism *not just as an opinion on an issue, but as an aspect of self that defines who they are, what they stand for, and who they stand with* [emphasis added]." This model comes out of a different branch of social psychology, one that seeks to explore the psychological and structural predictors of collective action. Bliuc et al. found that climate change believers are "more invested in their group identity than skeptics, as they were higher on opinion-based group identification, group efficacy beliefs, and especially anger towards the opposing group and commitment to socio-political action." Such findings suggest that by producing settled science, climate science institutions have provided a basis for the formation of politically significant groups who view those who do not share their views about the science as objects of opprobrium and political enemies.

The social psychological literature on the determinants of concern about climate change has continued to grow. Its consistent finding, however, is that climate change has long ceased being about the science. Rather, there are those who believe in precautionary policies, and that they should be even stronger, and those who are not so sure. For believers, those who question the scientific basis for radical decarbonization are demonized with a by-now official vocabulary of epithets. Like those who deny the reality of the past historical fact of the Nazi holocaust that took the lives of at least 6 million Jews and many million central and eastern European gentiles, people who question virtually any aspect of IPCC-endorsed climate science are called "deniers." Such conflation of denial of the historical facts about the holocaust with skepticism about computer model projections of future climate[24] is almost unspeakably dangerous. By confusing known reality with a computer-modeled future, it moves policy into a realm where no evidence can ever suffice to refute the justification for precautionary policies. However costly they may be, such policies can always be justified by future projections that can never be proven false.

The moralization of scientific disagreement is a hallmark of totalitarian societies. Infamously, the brilliant Russian biologist Nikolai Vavilov was imprisoned, tortured and ultimately murdered by the Soviet chief state scientist Trofim Lysenko[25] for disagreeing with Lysenko's completely false views about evolution and plant breeding, views that while completely false, were part of the justification for Stalin's deliberate murder by starvation of millions of Ukrainian people. The moralization of scientific disagreement, the branding as "deniers" of those who dispute the science advocacy produced by government-funded climate science organizations, can only end when such funding ends. With the rise of advocacy climate science production funded by multibillionaires such Michael Bloomberg, it is unclear why the US taxpayer should continue to fund public climate science advocacy institutions such as the IPCC and USGCRP. Public funding may be justified for research on fundamental and unanswered climate science questions – pertaining, for example, to the mathematical structure and behavior of the global climate system as distinct from weather. And public funding may be justified for balanced assessment of the costs and benefits of alternative climate policies. But it is not justified for one-sided, biased advocacy climate science produced not to help choose policy, but to justify an already predetermined policy response.

APPENDIX

Electricity from fossil fuels comes about by converting heat energy from burning the fuel into electric energy. To figure out CO_2 emission for different fossil fuel power sources, one needs first to compute how many million Btu (energy as heat) from the source are required to produce a billion kilowatt hours of power (energy as electricity). This depends upon the operating heat rate of the power source. Heat rate expresses the efficiency of a plant – how much of the energy source is needed, in terms of standard heat energy units, to produce electricity, measured in standard electricity energy units. Depending upon things such as plant efficiency and the impact of conventional air pollution controls, heat rates vary across different thermal plants.

Table 19.1 gives the average operating heat rates for the main US energy sources since 2007.[26] As one can see from the table, over the 2007–2017 period, the efficiency of conventional sources of electricity increased only for natural gas. By 2017, natural gas was about 25 percent more efficient than coal. There are two basic reasons[27] why natural gas is more efficient than coal. First, electric power from coal comes about only by burning massive amounts of coal to generate heat to create steam to drive turbines; natural gas is directly burned in turbines generating heat, some of which, like coal, is diverted to power steam turbines but some of which, unlike coal, generates electricity directly by powering the turbine. Second, part of the energy created when coal is burned is used to drive catalytic reactors, precipitators, and scrubbers that reduce air pollutants in a coal plant's exhaust. None of these pollutants result from burning natural gas.

Natural gas is not only more efficient than coal, but cleaner in terms of CO_2 emissions. Per Btu of energy, the following pounds of CO_2 are emitted for different fuels (Table 19.2).[28]

TABLE 19.1 *Average operating heat rate for selected electric power sources, 2007–2017 (Btu per KWh)*

Year	Coal	Petroleum	Natural gas	Nuclear
2007	10,375	10,794	8,403	10,489
2008	10,378	11,015	8,305	10,452
2009	10,414	10,923	8,160	10,459
2010	10,415	10,984	8,185	10,452
2011	10,444	10,829	8,152	10,464
2012	10,498	10,991	8,039	10,479
2013	10,459	10,713	7,948	10,449
2014	10,428	10,814	7,907	10,459
2015	10,495	10,687	7,878	10,458
2016	10,493	10,811	7,870	10,459
2017	10,465	10,834	7,812	10,455

TABLE 19.2 *Emissions by fuel type (pounds of CO_2 per Btu)*

Fuel type	Emissions
Coal (anthracite)	0.00023
Coal (bituminous)	0.00021
Coal (lignite)	0.00022
Coal (subbituminous)	0.00021
Diesel fuel and heating oil	0.00016
Gasoline (without ethanol)	0.00016
Propane	0.00014
Natural gas	0.00012

In the United States, 90 percent of the coal produced and used has been bituminous or subbituminous, with dirty and low energy lignite coal making up only 9 percent of production. Using this figure for the type of coal burning, one obtains the CO_2 emission figures given in the text.

Notes

1. EPA, Inventory of Greenhouse Gas Emissions and Sinks: 1990–2018, table 2-2, pp. 2–6, EPA 430-R-20-002, available at www.epa.gov/sites/production/files/2020–04/documents/us-ghg-inventory-2020-main-text.pdf.
2. These numbers, plus Figure 19.1, are from EPA, Inventory of US Greenhouse Gas Emissions and Sinks: 1990–2018, p. ES–25, chapter 2, "Trends in Greenhouse Emissions," available at www.epa.gov/sites/production/files/2018–01/documents/2018_chapter_2_trends_in_greenhouse_gas_emissions.pdf.
3. California Energy Commission, California Electrical Energy Generation, June 2020, available at www.energy.ca.gov/data-reports/energy-almanac/california-electricity-data/california-electrical-energy-generation.
4. 753 F.3d 1304 (D.C. Cir. 2014).
5. See *JHU Gazette*, "New Study Yields Better Spacing for Large Wind Farms," January 18, 2011, available at https://gazette.jhu.edu/2011/01/18/new-study-yields-better-turbine-spacing-for-large-wind-farms/.
6. See, e.g., *Allegheny Defense Project v. FERC*, 932 F.3d 940 (DC Cir. 2019).
7. This paragraph is drawn from US Department of Energy, Office of Nuclear Energy, *The Ultimate Fast Facts Guide to Nuclear Energy*.
8. This paragraph is drawn from Cravens (2007, 294–324).
9. Such standards were issued as 40 CFR Part 197.
10. 373 F.3d 1251 (D.C. Cir. 2004).
11. EPA, Public Health and Environmental Radiation Protection standards for Yucca Mountain, Nevada, 73 Fed. Reg 61255–61289, October 15, 2008.

12. Katie Tubb, "Making Nuclear Waste Disposal a Question of 'How,' Not 'Where,'" *Washington Times*, March 13, 2019, available at www.washingtontimes.com/news/2019/may/13/yucca-mountain-approach-nuclear-waste-results-poli/.
13. EIA, "Most US Nuclear Plants Were Built between 1970 and 1990," April 27, 2017, available at www.eia.gov/todayinenergy/detail.php?id=30972.
14. US Department of Energy, *The Ultimate Facts Guide to Nuclear Energy*.
15. See *World Nuclear News*, "Report Highlights Impact of US Nuclear Plant Closures," April 17, 2018, avaliable at www.world-nuclear-news.org/EE-Report-highlights-impact-of-US-nuclear-plant-closures-1704185.html.
16. See James Conca, "US CO_2 Emissions Rise as Nuclear Power Plants Close," *Forbes*, January 16, 2019, available at www.forbes.com/sites/jamesconca/2019/01/16/u-s-co2-emissions-rise-as-nuclear-power-plants-close/#503269770347.
17. Sören Amelang, Benjamin Wehrmann, and Julian Wettengel, "Polls Reveal Citizens' Support for Energiewende," *Clean Energy Wire*, November 15, 2018, available at www.cleanenergywire.org/factsheets/polls-reveal-citizens-support-energiewende.
18. Clean Energy Wire, "German Grid Agency Unveils Grid Expansion Scenario for a 65 Percent-Renewable Power Supply in 2030," June 18, 2018, available at www.cleanenergywire.org/news/record-14-bln-euros-stabilise-power-grid-renewables-goal-peril/german-grid-agency-unveils-grid-expansion-scenario-65-percent-renewable-power-supply-2030.
19. Julian Wettengel, "The Role of Gas in Germany's Energy Transition: Industry Bets on Gas as Last Trump Card in Energiewende," *Clean Energy Wire*, June 25, 2018, available at www.cleanenergywire.org/dossiers/role-gas-germanys-energy-transition.
20. See Institute for Energy Research, "Germany's Dependence on Fossil Fuels and Russian Gas," August 21, 2018, available at www.instituteforenergyresearch.org/international-issues/germanys-dependence-on-fossil-fuels-and-russian-gas/.
21. James Hansen and Michael Shellenberger, "The Climate Needs Nuclear Power," *Wall Street Journal*, April 4, 2019, available at www.wsj.com/articles/the-climate-needs-nuclear-power-11554420097.
22. Steven Koonin, "A Red Team Exercise Would Stengthen Climate Science," *Wall Street Journal*, April 20, 2017; Bliuc et al. (2015).
23. Among their communitarian/egalitarians, Kahan et al.'s (2012) score for perceived climate risk (a score they created for the experiment) rises from a tiny bit below 0.75 for the least numerate to only slightly above 0.75 (maybe 0.78) for the most numerate/scientifically literate. By comparison, while the least scientifically literature/numerate hierarchical individualists in Kahan et al.'s categorization had a score of about −0.62, the most sic/num hierarchical individualists have a score of about −0.85. These numbers are never presented by Kahan et al., and these differences in slope are not tested statistically.

24. Something that social psychological experiments have shown to be true of climate change believers.
25. See Peter Pringle, *The Murder of Nikolai Vavilov: The Story of Stalin's Persecution of One of the Great Scientists of the Twentieth Century* (Simon and Schuster, 2008).
26. EIA, available at www.eia.gov/electricity/annual/html/epa_08_01.html.
27. For an excellent explanation of these and other differences, see Daniel Frazier et al., "Coal versus Natural Gas Energy Production," Texas A&M Chemistry, available at www.chem.tamu.edu/rgroup/djd/chem483/Projects/Coal%20v.%20Natural%20Gas.pdf.
28. EIA, available at www.eia.gov/tools/faqs/faq.php?id=73&t=11, gives pound of CO_2 per million Btu. The numbers in the table round these to report per pound figures to five decimal places.

References

Abendroth, Lori & Elmore, Roger (2010). Planting Date Trends, Iowa State University Extension and Outreach (text updated March 8, 2010), available at https://crops.extension.iastate.edu/corn/production/management/planting/earlier.html.

Abendroth, Lori J., Woli, Krishna P., Myers, Anthony J. W. & Elmore, Roger W. (2017). Yield-Based Corn Planting Date Recommendation Windows for Iowa, 3 *Crop Forage Turfgrass Management*, DOI 10.2134/cftm2017.02.0015.

Acquaotta, Fiorella & Frattiani, Simona (2014). The Importance of the Quality and Reliability of the Historical Time Series for the Study of Climate Change, 14(10) *Revista Brasileira de Climatologia* 20–38.

Abarbanel, Albert & McClusky, Thorp (1950, July 1). Is the World Getting Warmer?, *Saturday Evening Post*, 22–23.

Abatzoglou, John T. & Williams, A. Park (2016). Impact of Anthropogenic Climate Change on Wildfire across Western US Forests, 113 (42) *Proceedings of the National Academy of Sciences* 11,770–11,775.

Abbe, Cleveland (1889). Is Our Climate Changing?, 6 *Forum* 679.

Abendroth, Lori J., Woli, Krishna P., Myers, Anthony J. W. & Elmore, Roger W. (2017). Yield-Based Corn Planting Date Recommendation Windows for Iowa, 3 *Crop Forage Turfgrass Management* 1, DOI 10.2134/cftm2017.02.0015.

Ablain, M., Legeais, J. F., Prandi, P., Marcos, M., Fengolio-Marc, L., Dieng, H. B., Benveniste, J. & Cazenave, A. (2017). Satellite Altimetry-Based Sea Level at Global and Regional Scales, 38 *Surveys of Geophysics* 7–31.

Adler, Jonathan H. (2007). Massachusetts v. EPA Heats up Climate Policy No Less than Administrative Law: A Comment on Professors Watts and Wildermuth, 102 *Northwest Law Review Colloquy* 32–43.

Aimé, Carla, Laval, Guillaume, Patin, Etienne, Verdu, Paul, Ségurel, Laure, Chaix, Raphaëlle, Hegay, Tatyana, Quintana-Murci, Lluis, Heyer, Evelyne & Austerlitz, Frédéric (2017). Human Genetic Data Reveal Contrasting Demographic Patterns between Sedentary and Nomadic Populations That Predate the Emergence of Farming, 30(12) *Molecular Biology and Evolution* 2629–2644.

Anagnostopoulos, G. G., Koutsoyiannis, D., Christofides, A., Efstratiadis A. & Mamassis, N. (2010) A Comparison of Local and Aggregated Climate Model Outputs with Observed Data, 55 (7) *Hydrological Science Journal* 1094–1110, DOI 10.1080/02626667.2010.513518.

Agrawala, Shardul (1998). Context and Early Origins of the IPCC, 39 *Climate Change* 605–620.

Agrawala, Shardul (1998). Structural and Process History of the Intergovernmental Panel of Climatic Change, 39 *Climate Change* 621–642.
Ahn, Jinhho & Brook, Edward J. (2008). Atmospheric CO_2 and Climate on Millennial Time Scales during the Last Glacial Period, 322 *Science* 83–85.
Aldrin, Magne, Holden, Marit, Guttorp, Peter, Skeie, Ragnhild Bieltvedt, Myhre, Gunnar & Berntsen, Terje Koren (2012). Bayesian Estimation of Climate Sensitivity Based on a Simple Climate Model Fitted to Observations of Hemispheric Temperatures and Global Ocean Heat Content, 23 *Environmetrics* 253–271.
Aldy, Joseph E. (2012, January). A Preliminary Review of the American Recovery and Reinvestment Act's Clean Energy Package 12, Resources for the Future Discussion Paper 12–03, DOI 10.2139/ssrn.1986948.
Allen, Myles (2018, March 23). Understanding How Carbon Dioxide Emissions from Human Activity Contribute to Global Climate Change, City of Oakland v. BP PLC, No. 3:17-cv-06012-WHA, Exhibit 5, Document 157–5 (N.D. Cal.).
Allen, Myles (2003). Liability for Climate Change, 421 *Nature* 891–892.
Allen, Myles & Frame, David (2007). Call off the Quest, 318 *Science* 582–583, DOI 10.1126/science.1149988.
Allen, Myles, Pall, Pardeep, Stone, Daithi, Stott, Peter, Frame, David, Min, Seung-Ki, Nozawa, Toru & Yukimoto, Seiji (2007). Scientific Challenges in the Attribution of harm to Human Influence on Climate, 155 (6) *University of Pennsylvania Law Review* 1353–1400.
Amelang, Sören & Wettengel, Julian (2018, November 15). Polls Reveal Citizens' Support for Energiewende, Clean Energy Wire.
American Rivers, Friends of the Earth & Trout Unlimited (1999). Dam Removal Success Stories xiii, Final Report.
Anderson, G. Brooke & Bell, Michelle L. (2012). Lights Out: Impact of the August 2003 Power Outage on Mortality in New York, NY, 23 (2) *Epidemiology* 189–193.
Anderson, Patrick L. & Geckil, Ilhan K. (2003, August). Northeast Blackout Likely to Reduce US Earnings by $64 billion, AEG Working Paper 2003–2.
Anderson, Soren & Newell, Richard (2004). Prospects for Carbon Capture and Storage Technologies, 29 *Annual Review of Environment and Resources*. 109–142, DOI 0.1146/annurev.energy.29.082703.145619.
Andrade, Juan & Baldick, Ross (2016). Estimation of Transmission Costs for New Generation 5–6, White Paper UTEI/2016-09-1.
Andresen, Steinar & Agrawala, Shardul (2002). Leaders, Pushers, and Laggards in the Marking of the Climate Regime, 12 *Global Climatic Change* 41–51, DOI 10.1016/S0959-3780(01)00023-1.
Annan, Francis & Schlenker, Wolfram (2014, December). Federal Crop Insurance and the Disincentives to Adapt to Extreme Heat, Working Paper, Columbia University.
Annan, Francis & Schlenker, Wolfram (2015). Federal Crop Insurance and the Disincentive to Adapt to Extreme Heat, 105 (5) *American Economics Review Papers & Proceedings* 262–266, DOI 10.1257/aer.p20151031.
Applegate, John S. (2000). The Precautionary Preference: An American Perspective on the Precautionary Principle, 6 (3) *Human & Ecological Risk Assessment* 413–443, DOI 10.1080/10807030091124554.
Archer, David, Eby, Michael, Brovkin, Victor, et al. (2009). Atmospheric Lifetime of Fossil Fuel Carbon Dioxide, 37 *Annual Review of Earth and Planetary Sciences* 117–134, DOI 10.1146/annurev.earth.031208.100206.
Armour, K. C. & Roe, G. H. (2011). Climate Commitment in an Uncertain World, 38 *Geophysical Research Letters* L01707, DOI 10.1029/2010GL045850.

Arnett, Edward B., Baerwald, Erin F., Mathews, Fiona, Rodrigues, Luisa, Rodríguez-Durán, Armando, Rydell, Jens, Villegas-Patraca, Rafael & Voigt, Christian C. (2016). Impacts of Wind Energy Development on Bats: A Global Perspective. In *Bats in the Anthropocene: Conservation of Bats in a Changing World*, 295–323 (Voigt, C. C. & Kingston, T., eds.; Berlin: Springer).

Arrhenius, Svante (1896, April). On the Influence of Carbonic Acid in the Air upon the Temperature of the Ground, 5 (41) *Philosophical Magazine and Journal of Science Series* 237–276.

Takashi, Asaeda, Ca, Vu Thanh & Wake, Akio (1996). Heat Storage of Pavement and Its Effect on the Lower Atmosphere. 30(3) *Atmospheric Environment* 413–427, CUTEST '92: Conference on the Urban Thermal Environmental Studies in Tohwa, Fukuoka, 30 JAPAN (07/09/1992), DOI 10.1016/1352-2310(94)00140-5.

Bailey, Christopher J. (1998). *Congress and Air Pollution* (Manchester, UK: Manchester University Press).

Baker, Marcia B. & Roe, Gerald H. (2009). The Shape of Things to Come: Why Is Climate Change So Predictable?, 22 (17) *Journal of Climate* 4574–4589, DOI 10.1175/2009JCLI2647.1.

Balch, Jennifer K., Bradley, Bethany A., Abatzoglou, John T., Nagy, R. Chelsea, Fusco, Emily J. & Mahood, Adam L. (2017). Human-Started Wildfires Expand the Fire Niche across the United States, 114 (11) *Proceedings of the National Academy of Sciences* 2946–2951, DOI 10.1073/pnas.1617394114.

Barclay, R. M., Baerwald, E. F. & Gruver, J. C. (2007). Variation in Bat and Bird Fatalities at Wind Energy Facilities: Assessing the Effects of Rotor Size and Tower Height, 85 (3) *Canadian Journal of Zoology* 381–387, DOI 10.1139/Z07-011.

Barreca, Alan, Clay, Karen, Deschenes, Olivier, Greenstone, Michael & Shapiro, Joseph S. (2016). Adapting to Climate Change: The Remarkable Decline in the US Temperature-Mortality Relationship over the Twentieth Century, 124 (1) *Journal of Political Economy* 105–159.

Barringer, Felicity (2008, February 27). Flooded Village Files Suit, Citing Corporate Link to Climate Change, *New York Times*.

Barton, Charmian (1998). The Status of the Precautionary Principle in Australia: Its Emergence in Legislation and as a Common Law Doctrine, 22 *Harvard Environmental Law Review* 509–558.

Batterbury, Simon & Warren, Andrew (2001). The African Sahel 25 Years after the Great Drought: Assessing Progress and Moving towards New Agendas and Approaches, 11 (1) *Global Environmental Change* 1–8, DOI 10.1016/S0959-3780(00)00040-6.

Beckley, B. D., Callahan, P. S., Hancock, D. W., III, Mitchum, G. T. & Ray, R. D. (2017). On the "Cal-Mode" Correction to TOPEX Satellite Alimetry and Its Effect on the Global Mean Sea Level Time Series, 122 (11) *Journal of Geophysical Research: Oceans* 8371–8384, DOI 10.1002/2017JC013090.

Beddow, Jason M. (2012). A Bio-Economic Assessment of the Spatial Dynamics of US Corn Production and Yields. (Doctoral Dissertation, University of Minnesota).

Beddow, Jason M. (2014, June). Reassessing the Effects of Weather on Agricultural Production 17, Draft Paper.

Beddow, Jason M. & Pardey, Philip G. (2015). Moving Matters: The Effect of Location on Crop Production, 75 (1) *Journal of Economics History* 219–249, DOI 10.1017/S002205071500008X.

Béguin, Andreas, Hales, Simon, Rocklöv, Joacim, Åström, Christofer, Louis, Valérie R. & Sauerborn, Ranier (2011). The Opposing Effects of Climate Change and Socio-Economic Development on the Global Distribution of Malaria, 21 (4) *Global Environmental Change* 1209–1214, DOI 10.1016/j.gloenvcha.2011.06.001.

Bello, Francis (1954, August). Climate the Heat May Be Off, Fortune, 108.

Ben-Shahar, Omri & Logue, Kyle D. (2016). The Perverse Effects of Subsidized Weather Insurance, 68 *Stanford Law Review* 571–626.
Bengtsson, Lennart & Hodges, Kevin I. (2009). On the Evaluation of Temperature Trends in the Tropical Troposphere, 36 *Climate Dynamics* 419–430, DOI 10.1007/s00382-009-0680-y.
Bengtsson, Lennart, Semenov, Vladimir A. & Johannessen, Ola M. (2004). The Early Twentieth-Century Warming in the Arctic – A Possible Mechanism, 17 (20) *Journal of Climate* 4045–4057, DOI 10.1175/1520-0442(2004)017<4045:TETWIT>2.0.CO;2.
Benson, Sally & Majumdar, Arun (2016, July 12). *On the Path to Deep Decarbonization: Avoiding the Solar Wall*, Stanford University.
Biello, David (2007, June 8). *Impure as the Driven Snow: Smut Is a Bigger Problem than Greenhouse Gases in Polar Meltdown*, Scientific American.
Binder, Sarah (2014). The Dysfunctional Congress, 18 *Annual Review of Political Science* 85–101, DOI 10.1146/annurev-polisci-110813–032156.
Bliuc, Ana-Maria, McGarty, Craig, Thomas, Emma F., Lala, Girish, Berndsen, Mariette & Misajon, RoseAnne (2015, March). Public Division about Climate Change Rooted in Conflicting Socio-political Identities, 5 *Nature Climate Change* 226–229, DOI 10.1038/nclimate2507.
Blom, T. J., Straver, W. A., Ingratta, F. J., Khosla, Shalin & Brown, Wayne (2002, December, revised 2009, August) Carbon Dioxide in Greenhouses, Ontario Ministry of Agriculture, Food and Rural Affairs, available at http://www.omafra.gov.on.ca/english/crops/facts/00–077.htm.
Blunt, Katherine & Gold, Russell (2019, July 15). PG&E Makes Thousands of Repairs after Inspections. *Wall Street Journal*.
Blunt, Katherine & Gold, Russell (2019, July 11). PG&E Knew Aging Grid Was Fire Risk. *Wall Street Journal*.
Bobb, Jennifer F., Peng, Roger D., Bell, Michelle L. & Dominici, Francesca (2014). Heat-Related Mortality and Adaptation to Heat in the United States, 122(8) *Environmental Health Perspectives* 811–816, DOI 10.1289/ehp.1307392.
Bodansky, D. M. (1994). Prologue to the Climate Change Convention, in Negotiating Climate Change: The Inside Story of the Rio Convention 45–74, DOI 10.1017/CBO9780511558917.003.
Bodman, Roger W., Rayner, Peter J. & Karoly, David J. (2013). Uncertainty in Temperature Projections Reduced Using Carbon Cycle and Climate Observations, 3 *Nature Climate Change* 725–729, DOI 10.1038/NCLIMATE1903.
Boehmer-Christiansen, Sonja (1994). *The Precautionary Principle in Germany – Enabling Government, in Interpreting the Precautionary Principle* (O'Riordan, Tim & Cameron, James, eds.; New York: Routledge).
Boehmer-Christiansen, Sonja (1994). Global Climate Protection Policy: The Limits of Scientific Advice: Part I, 4 (2) *Global Environmental Change* 140–159, DOI 10.1016/0959-3780(94)90049-3.
Boehmer-Christiansen, Sonja (1994). Global Climate Protection Policy: The Limits of Scientific Advice: Part 2, 4 (3) *Global Environmental Change* 185–200, DOI 10.1016/0959-3780(94)90002-7.
Boers, Niklas, Ghil, Michael & Rousseau, Denis-Didier (2018). Ocean Circulation, Ice Shelf, and Sea Ice Interactions Explain Dansgaard–Oeschger Cycles, 115 (47) *Proceedings of the National Academy of Sciences* E11005-E11014, DOI 10.1073/pnas.1802573115.
Boko, M. (2007). Africa, in *Climate Change: Impacts, Adaptation and Vulnerability Contribution of Working Group 2 to the Fourth Assessment Report of the Intergovernmental Panel on Climate*

Change 433–469 (Martin Parry, Osvaldo Canziani, Jean Palutikof, Paul van der Linden & Claire Hanson, eds., Cambridge: Cambridge University Press).

Bond, T. C., Doherty, S. J., Fahey, D. W., et al. (2013). Bounding the Role of Black Carbon in the Climate System: A Scientific Assessment, 118 (11) *Journal of Geophysical Research Atmospheres* 5380–5552, DOI 10.1002/jgrd.50171.

Brandt, Martin, Mbow, Cheikh, Diouf, Abdoul A., Verger, Aleixandre & Fensholt, Rasmus (2015). Ground- and Satellite-Based Evidence of the Biophysical Mechanisms behind the Greening Sahel, 21 (4) *Global Change Biology* 1610–20, DOI 10.1111/gcb.12807.

Bratcher, Amy J. & Giese, Benjamin S. (2002). Tropical Pacific Decadal Variability and Global Warming, 29 *Geophysical Research Letters* 1–4, DOI 10.1029/2002GL015191.

Brazel, Anthony, Selover, Nancy, Vose, Russell & Heisler, Gordon (2000). The Tale of Two Climates – Baltimore and Phoenix Urban LTER Sites, 15 *Climate Research* 123–135, DOI 10.3354/cr015123.

Brennen, Timothy J., Palmer, Karen L., Kopp, Raymond J., Krupnick, Alan J., Stagliano, Vito & Burtraw, Dallas (1996). *A Shock to the System: Restructuring America's Electricity Industry* 23–35 (Washington, DC: RFF Press)

Brickley, Peg (2019, June 10). PG&E Can Pull out of Green Power Deals, Wall Street Journal.

Brooks, C. E. P. (1950). Selective Annotated Bibliography on Climatic Changes, 1 *Meteorological Abstracts and Bibliography*, No. 1, 446–475.

Brough, Wayne T. & Kimenyi, Mwangi S. (1998). Property Rights and the Economic Development of the Sahel 163–179, in *The Revolution in Development Economics* (James A. Dorn & Steve H. Henke, eds., Cato Institute).

Brunner, Ronald (2001). Science and the Climate Change Regime, 34 (1) *Policy Sciences* 1–33, DOI 10.1023/A:1010393101905.

Buhaug, Halvard (2010). Climate Not to Blame for African Civil Wars, 107 (38) *Proceedings of the National Academy of Sciences* 16,477–16,482, DOI 10.1073/pnas.1005739107.

Buhaug, Halvard (2010). Reply to Burke et al.: Bias and Climate War Research, 107 (51) *Proceedings of the National Academy of Sciences* E186-E187, DOI 10.1073/pnas.1015796108.

Burgess, David F. & Zerbe, Richard O. (2011). Appropriate Discounting for Benefit-Cost Analysis, 2 (2) *Journal of Benefit-Cost Analysis* 1–20, DOI 10.2202/2152-2812.1065.

Burgess, David F. & Zerbe, Richard O. (2013). The Most Appropriate Discount Rate, 4 (3) *Journal of Benefit-Cost Analysis* 391–400, DOI 10.2202/2152-2812.1065.

Burke, Marshall B., Miguel, Edward, Satyanath, Shanker, Dykema, John A. & Lobell, David B. (2009). Warming Increases the Risk of Civil War in Africa, 106 (49) *Proceedings of the National Academy of Sciences* 20,670–20,674, DOI 10.1073/pnas.0907998106.

Burke, Marshall B., Miguel, Edward, Satyanath, Shanker, Dykema, John A. & Lobell, David B. (2010). Climate Robustly Linked to African Civil War, 107 (51) *Proceedings of the National Academy of Sciences* E185, DOI 10.1073/pnas.1014879107.

Butler, Ethan E. & Huybers, Peter (2013). Adaptation of US Maize to Temperature Variations, 3 *Nature Climate Change* 68–72, DOI 10.1038/NCLIMATE1585.

Butler, Ethan E. & Huybers, Peter (2015). Variations in the Sensitivity of US Maize Yield to Extreme Temperatures by Region and Growth Phase, 10 *Environmental Research Letters* 034009, DOI 10.1088/1748-9326/10/3/034009.

Butler, Ethan E., Mueller, Nathaniel D. & Huybers, Peter (2018). Peculiarly Pleasant Weather for US Maize, 115 (47) *Proceedings of the National Academy of Sciences* 11935–11940, DOI 10.1073/pnas.1808035115.

Caballero, Rodrigo (2008). Hadley Cell Bias in the Climate Models Linked to Tropical Eddy Stress, 35 (18) *Geophysical Research Letters* L18709, DOI 10.1029/2008GL035084.

Caldecott, Ben, Kruitwagen, Lucas & Kok, Irem (2016, May). Carbon Capture and Storage in the Thermal Value Chain, in COP21 and the Implications for Energy, 105 *Oxford Energy Forum* 50–55.
Calel, Raphael, Stainforth, David A. & Dietz, Simon (2015). Tall Tales and Fat Tails: The Science and Economics of Extreme Warming, 132 *Climatic Change* 127–141, DOI 10.1007/s10584-013-0911-4.
Campbell, J. E., Barry, J. A., Seibt, U., et al. (2017). Large Historical Growth in Global Terrestrial Gross Primary Production, 544 *Nature* 84–87, DOI 10.1038/nature22030.
Canis, Bill & Yacobucci, Brent D. (2015, January 15). The Advanced Technology Vehicles Manufacturing (ATVM) Loan Program: Status and Issues, CRS Report R42064.
Catalano, Ralph, Goldman-Mellor, Sidra, Saxton, Katherine, Margerison-Zilko, Claire, Subbaraman, Meenakshi, LeWinn, Kaja & Anderson, Elizabeth (2011). The Health Effects of Economic Decline, 32 *Annual Review of Public Health* 431–450, DOI 10.1146/annurev-publhealth-031210-101146.
Carothers, Leslie (2015). Upholding EPA Regelation of Greenhouse Gases: The Precautionary Principle Redux, 41 *Ecology Law Quarterly* 683–750.
Chao, Yi, Ghil, Michael & McWilliams, James C. (2000). Pacific Interdecadal Variability in this Century's Sea Surface Temperatures, 27 (15) *Geophysical Research Letters* 2261–2264, DOI 10.1029/1999GL011324.
Chameides, William L. & Bergin, Michael (2002). Soot Takes Center Stage, 297 (5590) *Science* 2214–2215, DOI 10.1126/science.1076866.
Charney, Jule (1982). Carbon Dioxide and Climate: A Scientific Assessment, National Academy of Science.
Chen, Wei, Guodong, Li, Pei, Allen, et al. (2018). A Manganese-Hydrogen Battery with Potential for Grid-Scale Energy Storage, 3 *Nature Energy* 428–435, DOI 10.1038/s41560-018-0147-7.
Chin, Mian, Diehl, T., Tan, Q., et al. (2014). Multi-decadal Aerosol Variations from 1980 to 2009: A Perspective from Observations and a Global Model, 14 *Atmospheric Chemistry and Physics* 3657–3690, DOI 10.5194/acp-14-3657-2014.
Christiansen, Thomas K., Hounisen, Jens P., Clausager, Ib & Petersen, Ib K. (2004). *Visual and Radar Observations of Birds in Relation to Collision Risk at the Horns Rey Offshore Wind Farm, Denmark*,Environmental Research Institute.
Christy, John R., Norris, William B. & McNider, Richard T. (2009). Surface Temperature Variations in East Africa and Possible Causes, 22(12) *Journal of Climate* 3342–3356, DOI 10.1175/2008JCLI2726.1.
Christy, John R. & McNider, Richard T. (2017). Satellite Bulk Tropospheric Temperatures as a Metric for Climate Sensitivity, 53 (4) *Asia-Pacific Journal of Atmospheric Sciences* 511–518, DOI 10.1007/s13143-017-0070-z.
Chylek, Petr, Dubey, M. K. & Lesins, G. (2006). Greenland Warming of 1920–1930 and 1995–2005, 33 (11) *Geophysical Research Letters* L11707, DOI 10.1029/2006GL026510.
Chylek, Petr, Dubey, Manvendra K., Lesins, Glen, Li, Jiangnan & Hengartner, Nicolas (2014). Imprint of the Atlantic Multi-decadal Oscillation and Pacific Decadal Oscillation on Southwestern US Climate: Past, Present and Future, 43 *Climate Dynamics* 119–129, DOI 10.1007/s00382-013-1933-3.
Clack, Christopher T. M., Qvist, Staffan A., Apt, Jay, et al. (2017). Evaluation of a Proposal for Reliable Low-Cost Grid Power with 100% Wind, Water and Solar, 114 (26) *Proceedings of the National Academy of Sciences* 6722–6727, DOI 10.1073/pnas.1610381114.
Cleaveland, N. K. & Duvick, D. N. (1992). Iowa Climate Reconstructed from Tree Rings, 1640–1982, 28 (10) *Water Resources Research* 2607–2615, DOI 10.1029/92WR01562.

Climate Accountability Institute and Union of Concerned Scientists (2012, October). Establishing Accountability for Climate Change Damages: Lessons from Tobacco Control, Report.

Cole, D. H. (1986). Reviving the Federal Power Act's Comprehensive Plan Requirement: A History of Neglect and Prospects for the Future, 16 *Environmental Law* 639.

Conca, James (2019, January 16). US CO_2 Emissions Rise as Nuclear Power Plants Close, Forbes.

Cook, Edward R., Seager, Richard, Cane, Mark A. & Stahle, David W. (2007). North American Drought: Reconstructions, Causes, and Consequences, 81 (1–2) *Earth-Science Reviews* 93–134, DOI 10.1016/j.earscirev.2006.12.002.

Cook, John, Nuccitelli, Dana, Green, Sarah A., Richardson, Markm Winkler, Bärbel, Painting, Rob, Way, Robert, Jacobs, Peter & Skuce, Andrew. (2013). Quantifying the Consensus on Anthropogenic Global Warming in the Scientific Literature, 8 *Environmental Research Letters* 024024, DOI 10.1088/1748-9326/8/2/024024.

Cooper, Gail (1998). *Air Conditioning America* 30–35 (Baltimore, MD: Johns Hopkins University Press).

Cooper, Richard N., Eichengreen, Barry, Holtham, Gerald, Putnam, Robert D. & Henning, C. Randall (1989). *Can Nations Agree? Issues in International Cooperation* 180–181 (Brookings Institution Press).

Corwin, Jane L. & Miles, William T. (1978, July). Impact Assessment of the 1977 New York Blackout 14, SCI Final Report, tSC1 Project 5236–100, Department of Energy.

Cox, Craig (2013, April). Taxpayers, Crop Insurance and the Drought of 2012, Environmental Working Group.

Cragg, Michael I., Zhou, Yuyu, Gurney, Kevin & Kahn, Matthew E. (2012). Carbon Geography: The Political Economy of Congressional Support for Legislation Intended to Mitigate Greenhouse Gas Production, 51 (2) *Econics Inquiry* 1640–1650.

Cramton, Peter, Ockenfels, Axel & Stoft, Steven (2013). Capacity Market Fundamentals, 2 (2) *Economics of Energy & Environmental Policy* 27–46, DOI 10.5547/2160-5890.2.2.2.

Cravens, Gwyneth (2007). *Power to Save the World: The Truth about Nuclear Power* (New York, Vintage Books).

Cronin, Thomas M. (1999). *Principles of Paleoclimatology* (New York: Columbia University Press).

Cronin, Thomas M. (2010). *Paleoclimatology* 199 (New York: Columbia University Press)

Crook, Julia A. & Forster, Piers M. (2011). A Balance between Radiative Forcing and Climate Feedback in the Modeled 20th Century Temperature Response, 116 *Journal of Geophysical Research* D17108, DOI 10.1029/2011JD015924.

Crowder, Michael (1990). *History of French West Africa until Independence, in Africa South of the Sahara* 77 (London, Europa Publications).

Curry, Judith (2018, Nov. 25). Sea Level and Climate Change 12–13, Special Report Climate Forecast Applications Network.

Curtis, E. Mark (2014, December). Who Loses under Power Plant Cap-and-Trade Program?, NBER Working Paper No. 208–8, available at https://www.nber.org/papers/w20808.

Dahlman, LuAnn (2009). Climate Variability: North Atlantic Oscillation. Climate.gov, August 30, available at https://www.climate.gov/news-features/understanding-climate/climate-variability-north-atlantic-oscillation.

Dai, Kaoshan, Bergot, Anthony, Lian, Chao, Xiang, Wei-Ning & Huang, Zhenhua (2015). Environmental Issues Associated with Wind Energy – A Review. 75 *Renewable Energy* 911–921.

Danelski, David (2017, January 23). *Ivanpah Solar Plant, Built to Limit Greenhouse Gases, Is Burning More Natural Gas*, The Press-Enterprise.

Darwin, Roy (1999). A FARMer's View of the Ricardian Approach to Measuring Agricultural Effects of Climate Change, 41 *Climatic Change* 371–411.

David, R. E., Knappenberger, Paul C., Michaels, Patrick J. & Novicoff, Wendy M. (2003). Changing Heat-Related Mortality in the United States, 111 *Environmental Health Perspectives* 1712–1718, DOI 10.1289/ehp.6336.

Davis, Lucas & Knittel, Christopher R. (2019). Are Fuel Economy Standards Regressive?, 6(sl) *Association of Environmental and Resource Economists* S97–S131.

Davis, R. E., Knappenberger, P. C., Michaels, P. J. & Novicoff, W. M. (2003). Changing Heat-Related Mortality in the United States, 111 *Environmental Health Perspectives* 1712–1718, DOI 10.1289/ehp.6336.

Davis, Steven J. & Von Wachter, Till M. (2011). Recessions and the Cost of Job Loss, 2 *Brookings Papers on Economic Activity* 1–55, DOI 10.1353/eca.2011.0016.

Dayaratna, Kevin, McKitrick, Ross & Kreutzer, David (2017). Empirically Constrained Climate Sensitivity and the Social Cost of Carbon, 8(2) *Climate Change Economics* 1–12.

Dayaratna, Kevin, McKitrick, Ross & Michaels, Patrick J. (2020). Climate Sensitivity, Agricultural Productivity and the Social Cost of Carbon, 22 *Environmental Economics and Policy Studies* 433–448, DOI 10.1007/s10018-020-00263-w.

De Rugy, Veronique (2012, July 18). A Guarantee of Failure: Government Lending under Section 1705, Testimony to the House Oversight Committee.

DeBare, Ilana (2008, August 15). *PG&E Plans Big Investment in Solar Power Plants*, San Francisco Chronicle.

DeGaetano, Arthur (2000). A Serially Complete Simulated Observation Time Metadata file for US Daily Historical Climatology Network Stations, 81 (1), *Bulletin of the American Meteorological Society* 49–67, DOI 10.1175/1520-0477(2000)081<0049:ASCSOT>2.3.CO;2.

Delgado, J. A., Gross, C. M., Lal, H., Cover, H., Gagliardi, P., McKinney, S. P., Hesketh, E. & Shaffer, M. J. (2010). A New GIS Nitrogen Trading Tool Concept for Conservation and Reduction of Reactive Nitrogen Losses to the Environment, 105 *Advances in Agronomy* 117–171, DOI 10.1016/S0065-2113(10)05004-2.

Department of Energy (2019) 2018 Wind Technologies Market Report 25, Office of Energy Efficiency and Renewable Energy.

Deryugina, Tatyana (2017). The Fiscal Cost of Hurricanes: Disaster Air versus Social Insurance, 9 (3) *American Economic Journal: Economic Policy*, 168–198, DOI 10.1257/pol.20140296.

Deschenes, Olivier (2014). Climate Change, Human Health, and Adaptation: A Review of the Literature, 46 *Energy Economics* 606–619, DOI 10.1016/j.eneco.2013.10.013.

Deser, Clara, Phillips, Adam S. & Hurrell, James W. (2004). Pacific Interdecadal Climate Variability: Linkages between the Tropics and the North Pacific during Boreal Winter since 1900, 17 (16) *Journal of Climate* 3109–3124, DOI 10.1175/1520-0442(2004)017<3109: PICVLB>2.0.CO;2.

Dong, Bo & Dai, Aiguo (2015). The Influence of the Interdecadal Pacific Oscillation on Temperature and Precipitation over the Globe, 45 *Climate Dynamics* 2667–2681, DOI 10.1007/s00382-015-2500-x.

Dooley, David, Fielding, Jonathan & Levi, Lennart (1996). Health and Unemployment, 17 *Annual Review of Public Health* 449–465, DOI 10.1146/annurev.pu.17.050196.002313.

Douglas, Bruce C. (1991). Global Sea Level Rise, 96 (C4) *Journal of Geophysical Research* 6981–6992, DOI 10.1029/91JC00064.

Douglas, Bruce C. (1995). Global Sea Level Change: Determination and Interpretation, 33 (S2) *Reviews of Geophysics*, Supplement, 1425–1432, 1427, DOI 10.1029/95RG00355.

Douglas, David H., Pearson, Benjamin D. & Singer, S. Fred (2004). Altitude Dependence of Atmospheric Temperature Trends: Climate Models versus Observation, 31 *Geophysical Research Letters* L13208, DOI 10.1029/2004020103.

Douglas, David H., Christ, John R., Pearson, Benjamin D. & Singer, S. Fred (2008). A Comparison of Tropical Temperature Trends with Model Predictions, 28 (13) *International Journal of Climatology* 1693–1701, DOI 10.1002/joc.1651.
Dowd, Philp (2016, April). A Solar Power Plant vs. a Natural Gas Power Plant: Capital Cost – Apples to Apples, Watts up with That.
Drabick, James R. (2005). 'Private' Public Nuisance and Climate Change: Working within, and around, the Special Injury Rule, 16 *Fordham Environmental Law Review* 503–541.
Drax (2018, June 8). The Great Balancing Act: What It Takes to Keep the Power Grid Stable.
East, Edward M. & Jones, Donald F. (1919). *Inbreeding and Outbreeding: Their Genetic and Sociological Significance* 224 (Philadelphia, Lippincott).
Egenter, Sven (2019, June). Renewables Hit Record in Germany in H1 2019, Outlook Uncertain, Clean Energy Wire.
Ela, Erik, Milligan, Michael & Kirby, Brendan (2011, August). Operating Reserves and Variable Generation, NREL, Technical Report 5, NREL/TP-5500–51978.
Electricity Consumers Council (2004, February). *The Economic Impacts of the August 2003* Blackout.
Eliason, M. & Storrie, D. (2009). Does Job Loss Shorten Life? 44 *Journal of Human Resources* 277–302, DOI 10.3368/jhr.44.2.277.
Epstein, Richard A. (2018). The Many Sins of NEPA, 6 *Texas A&M Law Review* 1–28, DOI 10.37419/LR.V6.I1.1.
Esselborn, Saskia, Rudenko, Sergei & Schöne, Tilo (2018). Orbit-Related Sea Level Errors for TOPEX Altimetry at Seasonal to Decadal Timescales, 14 *Ocean Sciences* 205–223, DOI 10.5194/os-14-205-2018.
Essex, Christopher & Tsonis, Anastasoios A. (2018). Model Falsifiability and Climate Slow Modes, 502 *Physica* A 554–562, DOI 10.1016/j.physa.2018.02.090.
Eubanks, William S., II (2015). Subverting Congress' Intent: The Recent Misapplication of Section 10 of the Endangered Species Act and Its Consequent Impacts on Sensitive Wildlife and Habitat, 42 (2) *Boston College Environmental Affairs Law Review* 259–303.
Fall, Souleymane, Watts, Anthony, Nielsen-Gammon, John, Jones, Evan, Niyogi, Dev, Christy, John R. & Pielke, Roger A., Sr. (2011). Analysis of the Impacts of Station Exposure on the US Historical Climatology Network Temperatures and Temperature Trends, 116 (D14) *Journal of Geophysical Research* D14120, DOI 10.1029/2010JD015146.
Farber, Daniel A. (2015). Coping with Uncertainty: Cost-Benefit Analysis, the Precautionary Principle, and Climate Change, 90 *Washington Law Review* 1659–1725.
Farber, Henry (2004). Job Loss in the United States, 1981–2001, 23 *Research in Labor Economics* 69–117, DOI 10.1016/S0147-9121(04)23003-5.
Fell, Harrison & Kaffine, Daniel T. (2018). The Fall of Coal: Joint Impact of Fuel Prices and Renewables on Generation and Emissions, 10 (2) *American Economic Journal: Economic Policy* 90–116, DOI 10.1257/pol.20150321.
FERC Office of Hydropower Licensing (1987). PURPA Benefits at New Dams and Diversions, Final Staff Report Evaluating Environmental and Economic Effects 1–2, Docket No. EL87-9.
Ferris, Ann E. & McGartland, Al (2013). A Research Agenda for Improving the Treatment of Employment Impacts in Regulatory Impact Analysis, in *Does Regulation Kill Jobs?* 170–189 (Philadelphia: University of Pennsylvania Press).
Finch, H. J. S., Samuel, A. M. & Lane, G. P. F. (2014). *Precision Farming, in Lockhart & Wiseman's Crop Husbandry Including Grasslands* (Woodhead Publishing, 9th Ed).
Fixler, Dennis J., Greenaway-McGrevy, Ryan & Grimm, Bruce T. (2014, August). The Revisions to GDP, GDI, and Their Major Components, US Bureau of Economic

Analysis, available at https://www.bea.gov/news/2016/grosscomestic-product-4th-quarter-and-annual-2015-third-estimate-corporate-profits-4th.
Flanner, Mark G., Zender, Charlses S., Randerson, James T. & Rasch, Phillip J. (2007). Present-Day Climate Forcing and Response from Black Carbon in Snow, 112 *Journal of Geophysical Research* D11202, DOI 10.1029/2006JD008003.
Fleming, James Rodger (2005). *Historical Perspectives on Climate Change* 11 (New York: Oxford University Press, 5th Ed).
Flynn, Damian, Rather, Zakir, Årdal, Atle Rygg, et al. (2017). Technical Impacts of High Penetration Levels of Wind Power on Power System Stability, 6 (2) *WIREs Energy and Environment* 216, DOI 10.1002/wene.216.
Forster, Piers M., Andrews, Timothy, Good, Peter, Gregory, Jonathan M., Jackson, Lawrence S. & Zelinka, Mark (2013). Evaluating Adjusted Forcing and Model Spread for Historical and Future Scenarios in the CMIP5 Generation of Climate Models, 118 (3) *Journal of Geophysical Research Atmospheres* 1139–1150, DOI 10.1002/jgrd.50174.
Fountain, Henry (2019, October 28). *How Climate Change Could Shift California's Santa Ana Winds, Fueling Fires*, The New York Times.
Franz, Wendy E. (1997, September). The Development of an Agenda for Climate Change: Connecting Science to Policy 11 (International Institute for Applied Systems Analysis, Interim Report IR-97–034).
Frederick, John E. (2008). *Principles of Atmospheric Science* 116–147 (Sudbury, MA, Jones and Bartlett Publishers).
Freeman, Jody (2011). The Obama Administration's National Auto Policy: Lessons from the "Car Deal," 35 *Harvard Environmental Law Journal* 344–385.
Freeman, Jody & Vermeule, Adrian (2007). Massachusetts v. EPA: From Politics to Expertise, 2007 *Supreme Court Review* 51–111, DOI 10.1086/655170.
Freeman, Jody & Spence, David B. (2014). Old Statues, New Problems, 163 (1) *University of Pennsylvania Law Review* 1–68.
Frick, W. F., Baerwald, E. F., Pollock, J. F., Barclay, R. M. R., Szymanski, J. A., Weller, T. J., Russell, A. L., Loeb, S. C., Medelin, R. A. & McGuire, L. P. (2017). Fatalities at Wind Turbines May Threaten Population Viability of a Migratory Bat, 209 *Biological Conservation* 172–177.
Friedan, Betty (1958, September). The Coming Ice Age, 217 *Harper's Magazine* 39–45.
"*Fuel Use Act Repealed*" (1988) in CQ Almanac 1987, 323–24, Washington, DC: Congressional Quarterly (43rd ed.)
Fujibe, Fumiaki (2011). Review: Urban Warming in Japanese Cities and Its Relation to Climate Change Monitoring, 31 (2) *International Journal of Climatology* 162–173, DOI 10.1002/joc.2142.
Fyfe, John C., Gillett, Nathan P. & Zwiers, Francis W. (2013). Overestimated Global Warming over the Past 20 Years, 3 *Nature Climate Change* 767–769, DOI 10.1038/nclimate1972.
Gaffney, Jeff, Schussler, Jeff, Loffler, Carlos, et al. (2015). Industry-Scale Evaluation of Maize Hybrids Selected for Increased Yield in Drought-Stress Conditions of the US Corn Belt, 55 *Crop Science* 1608, DOI 10.2135/cropsci2014.09.0654.
Gallo, Kevin & Xian, George (2016). Changes in satellite-derived impervious surface area at US historical climatology network stations, 120 *ISPRS Journal of Photogrammetry and Remote Sensing* 77–83, DOI 10.1016/j.isprsjprs.2016.08.006.
Gao, Jing, Nelson, Robert & Zhang, Lei. (2013). Substitution in the Electric Power Industry: An Interregional Comparison in the Eastern US, 40 *Energy Economics* 316–325, DOI 10.1016/j.eneco.2013.07.011.
Gately, Dermot (1986). Lessons from the 1986 Oil Price Collapse, 2 *Brookings Papers on Economic Activity* 237–284.

Gerster, Andreas (2016). Negative Price Spikes at Power Markets: The Role of Energy Policy, 50 *Journal of Regulatory Economics* 271–289, DOI 10.1007/s11149-016-9311-9.
Gething, Peter W., Smith, David L., Patil, Anand P., Tatem, Andrew J., Snow, Robert W. & Hay, Simon I. (2010). Climate Change and the Global Malaria Recession, 465 *Nature* 342–345.
Gibson, Katherine E. B., Yang, Haishun S., Franz, Trenton, et al. (2018). Assessing Explanatory Factors for Variation in On-Farm Irrigation in US Maize-Soybean Systems, 197 *Agricultural Water Management* 34–40, DOI 10.1016/j.agwat.2017.11.008.
Giese, Benjamin S., Urizar, S. Cristina & Fučkar, Neven S. (2002). Southern Hemisphere Origin of the 1976 Climate Shift, 29 (2) *Geophysical Research Letters* 1–3, DOI 10.1029/2001GL013268.
Gimeno-Gutiérrez, Marcos & Lacal-Arántegui, Roberto (2013). *Assessment of the European Potential for Pumped Hydropower Energy Storage*. Tech Rep JRC.
Glantz, Barnoya J. (2005). Cardiovascular Effects of Secondhand Smoke: Nearly as Large as Smoking, 111 (20) *Circulation* 2684–2698, DOI 10.1161/CIRCULATIONAHA.104.492215.
Goessling, Helge F. & Bathiany, Sebastian (2016). Why CO_2 Cools the Middle Atmosphere – A Consolidating Model Perspective, 7 *Earth System Dynamics* 697–715, DOI 10.5194/esd-2016–8.
Golaz, Jean Christophe, Horowitz, Larry W. & Levy, Hiram, II (2013). Cloud Tuning in a Coupled Climate Model: Impact on 20th Century Warming, 40 (10) *Geophysical Research Letters* 2246–2251, DOI 10.1002/grl.50232.
Gonzales, Richard (2019, October 18). California Can Expect Blackouts for a Decade, Says PG&E CEO, NPR.
Gordon, Richard L. (1979). The Powerplant and Industrial Fuel Use Act of 1978 – An Economic Analysis, 19 (4) *Natural Resources Journal* 871–884.
Gorssman, Iris & Klotzbach, Philip J. (2009). A Review of North Atlantic Modes of Natural Variability and Their Driving Mechanisms, 114 *Journal of Geophysical Research* D24107, DOI 10.1029/2009JD012728.
Gowrisankaran, Gautam, Reynolds, Stanley S. & Samano, Mario (2016). Intermittency and the Value of Renewable Energy, 124 (4) *Journal of Political Economy* 1187–1234, DOI 10.1086/686733.
Grassini, Patricio, Yang, Haishun, Irmak, Suat, Thorburn, John, Burr, Charles & Cassman, Kenneth G. (2011). High-Yield Irrigated Maize in the Western US Corn Belt: II. Irrigation Management and Crop Water Productivity, 120 *Field Crops Research* 133–141, DOI 10.1016/j.fcr.2010.09.013.
Grassini, Patricio, Specht, James E., Tollenaar, Matthijs, Ciampitti, Ignacio & Cassman, Kevin G. (2015). High-Yield Maize-Soybean Cropping Systems in the US Corn Belt, in *Crop Physiology: Applications for Genetic Improvement and Agronomy* 17–41 (Victor O. Sadras & Daniel E. Calderini, eds., New York: Academic Press, 2nd ed.).
Greenstone, Michael (2002). The Impacts of Environmental Regulations on Industrial Activity: Evidence from the 1970 and 1977 Clean Air Act Amendments and the Census of Manufactures, 110 (6) *Journal of Political Economy* 1175–1219, DOI 10.1086/342808.
Greenstone, Michael & North, Ishan (2019, May). Do Renewable Portfolio Standards Deliver?, University of Chicago Energy Policy Institute, Working Paper No. 2019–62.
Greenstone, Michael, Kopits, Elizabeth & Wolverton, Ann (2011, April). Estimating the Social Cost of Carbon for Use in US Federal Rulemakings: A Summary and Interpretation, Working Paper 11-04, MIT Economics Department.
Griliches, Zvi (1957). Hybrid Corn: An Exploration in the Economics of Technological Change, 25(4) *Econometrica* 501–522, DOI 10.2307/1905380.

Grinsted, Aslak, Moore, John C. & Jevrejeva, Svetlana (2009). Reconstructing Sea Level from Paleo and Projected Temperatures, 200 to 2100AD, 34 *Climate Dynamics* 461–472, DOI 10.1007/s00382-008-0507-2.

Grossman, David A. (2003). Warming Up to a Not-So-Radical Idea: Tort-Based Climate Change Litigation, 28 *Columbia Journal of Environmental Law* 1.

Guzman-Morales, Janin, Gershunov, Alexander, Theiss, Jurgen, Li, Haiqin & Cayan, Daniel (2016). Santa Ana Winds of Southern California: Their Climatology, Extremes, and Behavior Spanning Six and a Half Decades, 43 *Geophysical Research Letters* 2827–2834, DOI 10.1002/2016GL067887.

Hallauer, Arnel R. (2011). Evolution of Plant Breeding Crop Breeding and Applied Biotechnology, 11 *Brazilian Society of Plant Breeding* 197–206.

Hamdy, M. K. & Noyes, O. R. (1975). Formation of Methyl Mercury by Bacteria, 30 (3) *Applied Microbiology* 424–432.

Hänke, Hendrick, Börjeson, Lowe, Hylander, Kristoffer & Enfors-Kautsky, Elin (2016). Drought Tolerant Species Dominate as Rainfall and Tree Cover Returns in the West African Sahel, 59 *Land Use Policy* 111–120.

Hansen, J., Johnson, D., Lacis, A., Lebedeff, S., Lee, P., Rind, D. & Russell, G. (1981). Climate Impact of Increasing Atmospheric Carbon Dioxide, 213 (4511) *Science* 957–966.

Hansen, J., Ruedy, R., Sato M. & Lo, K. (2010). Global Surface Temperature Change, 48 *Review of Geophysics* RG4004, DOI 10.1029/2010RG00034.

Hansen, James & Shellenberger, Michael (2019, April 4). The climate needs nuclear power, Wall Street Journal.

Harper, Benjamin P. (2006). Climate Change Litigation: The Federal Common Law of Interstate Nuisance and Federalism Concerns, 40 *Georgia Law Review* 661.

Hartly, Peter R., Medlock, Kenneth B., III & Rosthal, Jennifer (2014). Electricity Sector Demand for Natural Gas in the United States, Rice University Economics Department, Working Paper No. 14–026.

Hartly, Peter R., Medlock, Kenneth B., III & Jankovska, Olivera (2019). Electricity Reform and Retail Pricing in Texas, 80 *Energy Economics* 1–11.

Hartman, Dennis L. (1994). *Global Physical Climatology* (Elsevier Science, 2nd ed.).

Hatfield, J. L., Boote, K. J., Kimball, B. A., Ziska, L. H., Izaurralde, R. C., Ort, D., Thomson, A. M. & Wolfe, D. (2011). Climate Impacts on Agriculture: Implications for Corn Production, 103 (2) *Agronomy Journal* 351, DOI 10.2134/agronj2010.0303.

Hausfather, Zeke, Cowtan, Kevin, Menne, Matthew J. & Williams, Claude N., Jr. (2016). Evaluating the Impact of US Historical Climatology Network Homogenization Using the US Climate Reference Network, 43 (4) *Geophysical Research Letters* 1695–1701, DOI 10.1002/2015GL067640.

Hayek, F. A. (1945). The Use of Knowledge in Society, 35 (4) *American Economics Review* 519–530.

Heede, Richard (2014, January). Tracing Anthropogenic Carbon Dioxide and Methane Emissions to Fossil Fuel and Cement Producers, 1854–2010, 122 *Climatic Change* 229–241, DOI 10.1007/s10584-013-0986-y.

Heide, Dominik, Von Bremen, Lueder, Greiner, Martin, Hoffman, Clemens, Speckmann, Markus & Bofinger, Stefan (2010). Seasonal Optimal Mix of Wind and Solar Power in a Future, Highly Renewable, 35 (11) *European Renewable Energy* 2483–2489, DOI 10.1016/j.renene.2010.03.012.

Heinzerling, Lisa (2008). Climate Change and the Supreme Court, 38 *Environmental Lawyer* 1–18.

Heinzerling, Lisa (2008). Climate Change, Human Health, and the Post-Cautionary Principle, 96 *Georgetown Law Journal* 445.

Hegerl, Gabriele C., Crowley, Thomas J. & Pollack, Henry N., et al. (2007). Detection of Human Influence on a New, Validated 1500-Year Temperature Reconstruction, 20 *Journal of Climate* 650–666, DOI 10.7916/D8FN1GQ6.

Hernandez, Kristian (2018, October 8). *An Uncertain Future for America's Wind Energy Capital*, Public Integrity.

Hicks, D. R. & Thompson, P. R. (2004). *Corn Management, in Corn: Origin, History, Technology and Production* (C.W. Smith, Javier Betrán & Edward C.A. Runge, eds., Hoboken, NJ: John Wiley and Sons).

Hiltzik, Michael (2017, November 21). *A Stanford Professor Didn't Just Debate His Scientific Critics – He Sued Them for $10 Million*, Los Angeles Times.

History (2003, August). Blackout Hits Northeast United States.

Holland, Christina L., Scott, Robert B., Soon-Il, An & Taylor, Frederick W. (2007). Propagating Decadal Sea Surface Temperature Signal Identified in Modern Proxy Records of the Tropical Pacific, 28 *Climate Dynamics* 163–179, DOI 10.1007/s00382-006-0174-0.

Holt, Mark & Glover, Carol (2006, March 8). Energy Policy Act of 2005: Summary and Analysis of Enacted Provisions, CRS Report for Congress.

Hondula, David M., Balling, Robert C., Jr., Vanos, Jennifer K. & Georgescu, Matei (2015). Rising Temperatures, Human Health, and the Role of Adaptation, 1 *Current Climate Change Reports* 144–154, DOI 10.1007/s40641-015-0016-4.

Hongoltz-Hetling, Matt (2020, June 22). US Demand for Clean Energy Destroying Canada's Environment, Indigenous Peoples Say, The Guardian.

Hornsey, Matthew J., Harris, Emily A., Bain, Paul G. & Fielding, Kelly S. (2016, February 22). Meta-analyses of the Determinants and Outcomes of Belief in Climate Change, 6 *Nature Climate Change* 622–626.

Hourdin, Frederic, Mauritsen, Thorsten, Gettelman, Andrew, et al. (2017). The Art and Science of Climate Model Tuning, 98 (3) *Bulletin of the American Meteorological Society* 589–602, DOI 10.1175/BAMS-D-15-00135.1.

Houston, James R. & Dean, Robert G. (2012). Comparisons at Tide-Gauge Locations of Glacial Isotstatic Adjustment Predictions with Global Positioning System Measurements, 28 (4) *Journal of Coastal Research* 739–744, DOI 10.2112/JCOASTRES-D-11-00227.1.

Howard, Peter H. & Sterner, Thomas (2014). Loaded DICE: Refining the Meta-analysis Approach to Calibrating Climate Damage Functions, 2014 Annual Meeting, July 27–29,2014, Minneapolis, MN 169952, Agricultural and Applied Economics Association, DOI 10.22004/ag.econ.169952.

Hu, Aixue, Levis, Samuel, Meehl, Gerald A., et al. (2016). Impact of Solar Panels on Global Climate, 6 *Nature Climate Change* 290–294.

Huldén, Lena, McKitrick, Ross & Huldén, Larry (2013). Average Household Size and the Eradication of Malaria, 177 (3) *Journal of the Royal Statistical Society Series* A, DOI 10.1111/rssa 12036.

Institute for Energy Research (2019, November 1). The Cost of Decommissioning Wind Turbines Is Huge.

Institute for Energy Research (2018, August 21) Germany's Dependence on Fossil Fuels and Russian Gas.

Interagency Working Group on the Social Cost of Carbon, US Government (2010). Technical Support Document: Social Cost of Carbon for Regulatory Impact Analysis Under Executive Order 12866, available at https://www.epa.gov/sites/production/files/2016-12/documents/scc_tsd_2010.pdf.

IPCC Climate Change (2013). Climate Change 2014: Impacts, Adaptation and Vulnerability, Contribution of Working Group II to the Fifth Assessment Report of the Intergovernmental Panel on Climate Change (V.R. Barros et al. eds., Cambridge and New York: Cambridge University Press).

IPCC Climate Change (2013). The Physical Science Basis, Contribution of Working Group I to the Fifth Assessment Report of the Intergovernmental Panel on Climate Change 216 (Thomas F. Stocker et al. eds., Cambridge and New York: Cambridge University Press).

IPCC Climate Change (2007). Climate Change 2007: Impacts, Adaptation and Vulnerability, Contribution of Working Group II to the Fourth Assessment Report of the Intergovernmental Panel on Climate Change (M.L. Perry et al. eds., Cambridge: Cambridge University Press).

IPCC Climate Change (2007). The Physical Science Basis, Contribution of Working Group I to the Fourth Assessment Report of the Intergovernmental Panel on Climate Change (S. Solomon et al. eds., Cambridge and New York: Cambridge University Press).

IPCC Climate Change (2001). *The Scientific Bases* 134 (J.T. Houghton et. al, ed.: New York: Cambridge University Press).

Istvan, Rud (2019). Grid Scale Battery Storage, Watts up with That.

Jacobs, J. Roger (2014). The precautionary Principle as a Provisional Instrument in Environmental Policy: The Montreal Protocol Case Study, 37 *Environmental Science and Policy* 161–171, DOI 10.1016/j.envsci.2013.09.007.

Jacobson, Mark (2013). Evaluating US Fuel Economy Standards in a Model with Producer and Household Heterogeneity, 5 (2) *American Economic Journal: Economic Policy* 148–187, DOI 10.1257/pol.5.2.148.

Jacobson, Mark (2011). Fuel Economy, Car Class Mix and Safety, 101 (3) *American Economic Review Papers & Proceedings* 105–109, DOI 10.1257/aer.101.3.105.

Jacobson, Mark (2002). Control of Fossil-Fuel Particulate Black Carbon and Organic Matter, Possibly the Most Effective Method of Slowing Global Warming, 107 *Journal of Geophysical Research* D19, 4410, DOI 10.1029/2001JD001376.

Jacobson, Mark (1997). Development and Applications of a New Air Pollution Modeling System – Part III. Aerosol-Phase Simulations, 31 (4) *Atmospheric Environment* 587–608, DOI 10.1016/S1352-2310(96)00201-4.

Jacobson, Mark, Delucchi, Mark A., Cameron, Mary A. & Frew, Bethany A. (2015). Low-Cost Solution to the Grid Reliability Problem with 100% Penetration of Intermittent Wind, Water, and Solar for All Purposes, 112 (4) *Proceedings of the National Academy of Sciences* 15060–15065, DOI 10.1073/pnas.1510028112.

Jacobson, Mark, Delucchi, Mark A., Bazouin, Guillaume, et al. (2015). 100% Clean and Renewable Wind, Water, and Sunlight (WWS) All-Sector Energy Roadmaps for the 50 United States, 7 *Energy & Environmental Science* 2093–2117, DOI 10.1039/C5EE01283J.

Jarrell, Gregg A. (1978). The Demand for State Regulation of the Electric Utility Industry, 21 (2) *Journal of Law and Economics* 269–295.

Jones, P. D. (1994). Hemispheric Surface Air Temperature Variations: A Reanalysis and Update to 1993, 7 (11) *Journal of Climate* 1794–1802, DOI 10.1175/1520-0442(1994)007<1794:HSATVA>2.0.CO;2.

Jones, P. D., New, M., Parker, D. E., Martin, S. & Rigor, I. G. (1999). Surface Air Temperature and Its Changes over the Past 150 Years, 37 (2) *Review of Geophysics* 173–199, DOI 10.1029/1999RG900002.

Johansson, Daniel J. A., O'Neill, Brian C., Tebaldi, Claudia & Häggström, Olle (2015). Equilibrium Climate Sensitivity in Light of Observations over the Warming Hiatus, 5 *Nature Climate Change* 449–453, DOI 10.1038/NCLIMATE2573.

Johnson, Cameron (2018, August). Understanding the 6 Types of Response Bias (With Examples), Nextiva blog at https://www.nextiva.com/blog/response-bias.html.
Johnston, Jason Scott (2014). A Positive Political Economic Theory of Environmental Federalization, 64 (4) *Case Western Reserve Law Review* 1549–1617.
Johnston, Jason Scott (2012). Disasters and Decentralization, 37 *The Geneva Papers on Risk and Insurance* 228–256.
Johnston, Jason Scott (1998). The Cost of Cartelization: The IPCC Process and the Crisis of Credibility in Climate Science, in *Institutions and Incentives in Regulatory Science* (Lanham, MD, Lexington Books).
Johnston, Jason Scott & Klick, Jonathan (2012). Fire Suppression Policy, Weather, and Western Wildland Fire Trends: An Empirical Analysis, in *Wildfire Policy: Law and Economics Perspectives* 158–177 (Karen M. Bradshaw & Dean Lueck eds., Washington, D.C.: RFF Press).
Joskow, Paul L. (2011). Comparing the Costs of Intermittent and Dispatchable Electricity Generating Technologies, 100 (3) *American Economic Review: Papers and Proceedings* 238–241, DOI 10.1257/aer.101.3.238.
Joskow, Paul L. (2008). Capacity Payments in Imperfect Electricity Markets: Need and Design, 16 (3) *Utilities Policy* 159–170, DOI 10.1016/j.jup.2007.10.003.
Joskow, Paul L. & Tirole, Jean (2005). Merchant Transmission Investment, 53 (2) *Journal of Industrial Economics* 233–264.
Kahan, Dan (2012, August 16). Why We Are Poles Apart on Climate Change, 488 *Nature* 255, DOI 10.1038/488255a.
Kahan, Dan M., Peters, Ellen, Wittlin, Maggie, Slovic, Paul, Ouellette, Lisa Larrimore, Braman, Donald & Mandel, Gregory (2012). The Polarizing Impact of Science Literacy and Numeracy on Perceived Climate Change Risks, 2 *Nature Climate Change* 732–735.
Kala, Manrata (2017, December). Learning, Adaptation, and Climate Uncertainty: Evidence from Indian Agriculture, MIT Center for Energy and Environmental Policy Research, CEEPR Working Paper 2017–023.
Kalil, Ariel & Wrightman, Patrick (2011). Parental Job Loss and Children's Educational Attainment in Black and Middle-Class Families, 92 (1) *Social Science Quarterly* 57–78, DOI 10.1111/j.1540-6237.2011.00757.x.
Kalkstein, Laurence S., Greene, Scott, Mills, David M. & Samenow, Jason (2011). An Evaluation of Progress in Reducing Heat-Related Human Mortality in Major US Cities, 56 *Natural Hazards* 113–129, DOI 10.1007/s11069-010-9552-3.
Kalnay, Eugenia & Cai, Ming (2003). Impact of Urbanization and Land-Use Change on Climate, 423 *Nature* 528–531, DOI 10.1038/nature01675.
Kaptué, Amerl T., Prihodko, Lara & Hanan, Niall P., et al. (2015). On Regreening and Degradation in Sahelian Watersheds, 112 (39) *Proceedings of the National Academy of Sciences* 12133–12138, DOI 10.1073/pnas.1509645112.
Karl, Thomas R., Williams, Claude N., Jr., Young, Pamela J. & Wendland, Wayne M. (1986). A Model to Estimate the Time of Observation Bias Associated with Monthly Mean Maximum, Minimum and Mean Temperatures for the United States, 25 *Journal of Climate and Applied Meteorology* 145–160, DOI 10.1175/1520-0450(1986)025<0145:AMTETT>2.0.CO;2.
Kaufmann, Robert K. & Snell, Seth E. (1997). A Biophysical Model of Corn Yield: Integrating Climate and Social Determinants, 79 (1) *American Journal of Agricultural Economics* 178–190, DOI 10.2307/1243952.
Keall, Michael D. & Newstead, Stuart (2008). Are SUVs Dangerous Vehicles? 40 (3) *Accident Analysis and Prevention* 954–963, DOI 10.1016/j.aap.2007.11.001.

Keeling, Charles D. & Bacastow, Robert B. (1977). Impact of Industrial Gases on Climate, 72–73 *Energy and Climate* 81–82.
Kellogg, W. W. (1977). Effects of Human Activities on Global Climate, Geneva, WMO Technical Report Note No. 156, P. 49.
Kellogg, W. W., Coakley, J. A. & Grams, G. W. (1975). Effect of Anthropogenic Aerosols on the Global Climate, in *Proc. WMO/IMAP Symposium on Long-Term Climatic Fluctuations* 323–330.
Kennedy, Brian (2016, February 25). *Public Support for Environmental Regulations Varies by State*, Pew Research Center FactTank.
Kent, Chris, Pope, Edward, Thompson, Vikki, Kirsty, Lewis, Scaife, Adam A. & Dunstone, Nick (2017). Using Climate Model Simulations to Assess the Current Climate Risk to Maize Production, 12 *Environmental Research Letters* 054012.
Kiehl, Jeffrey T. (2007). Twentieth Century Climate Model Response and Climate Sensitivity, 34 *Geophysical Research Letters* L22710, DOI 10.1029/2007GL031383.
Kim, Maeang-Ki & Kim, Seonae (2011). Quantitative Estimates of Warming by Urbanization in South Korea over the Past 55 Years (1954–2008), 45 *Atmospheric Environment* 5778–5783, DOI 10.1016/j.atmosenv.2011.07.028.
Kimball, Bruce A. (2016). Crop Responses to Elevated CO_2 and Interactions with H_2O, N and Temperature, 31 *Current Opinion in Plant Biology* 36–43, DOI 10.1016/j.pbi.2016.03.006.
King, Matt A., Keshin, Maxim, Whitehouse, Pippa L., Thomas, Ian D., Milne, Glenn & Riva, Riccardo E. M. (2012). Regional Biases in Absolute Sea-Level Estimates from Tide Gauge Data due to Residual Unmodeled Vertical Land Movement, 39 *Geophysical Research Letters* L14604, DOI 10.1029/2012GL052348.
Kirschen, S. & Strbac, Goran (2019). *Fundamentals of Power System Economics* 155–167 (Hoboken, NJ, Wiley Publishing, 2nd ed.).
Kitoy, Ivan & Kitov, Oleg (2012). Real GDP Per Capita since 1870.
Klier, Thomas & Linn, Joshua (2010). Corporate Average Fuel Economy Standards and the Market for New Vehicles, 3 (1) *Annual Review of Resource Economics* 445–462, DOI 10.1146/annurev-resource-083110–120023.
Klier, Thomas & Linn, Joshua (2012). New-Vehicle Characteristics and the Cost of the Corporate Average Fuel Economy Standard, 43 (1) *RAND Journal of Economics* 186–213, DOI 10.1111/j.1756-2171.2012.00162.x.
Kloppenburg, J. Ralph (1988). *First the Seed: The Political Economy of Plant Biotechnology, 1492–2000* (Cambridge: Cambridge University Press).
Klotzbach, Philip J. & Landsea, Christopher W. (2015). Extremely Intense Hurricanes: Revisiting Webster et al. [2005] after 10 Years, 28 *Journal of Climate* 7621–7629, DOI 10.1175/JCLI-D-15-0188.1.
Klotzbach, Philip J., Pielke, Roger A., Sr., Pielke,Roger A., Jr., Christy, John R. & McNider, Richard T. (2009). An Alternative Explanation for Differential Temperature Trends at the Surface and in the Lower Troposphere, 114 *Journal of Geophysical Research* D21102, DOI 10.1029/2009JD011841.
Knutti, Reto (2008). Why Are Climate Models Reproducing the Observed Global Surface Warming So Well? 35 *Geophysical Research Letters* L18704, DOI 10.1029/2008GL034932.
Kober, Amy S. (2019, June 27). Twenty Years of Dam Removal Successes – and What's Up Next: The lesson from the Kennebec after Twenty Years? Dam Removal Works., American Rivers.
Kolstad, Charles D. & Moore, Frances C. (2019, February). Estimating the Economic Impacts of Climate Change Using Weather Observations, NBER Working Paper No. 25537.
Kontokosta, Constantine E., Reina, Vincent J. & Bonczak, Bartosz (2020). Energy Cost Burdens for Low-Income and Minority Households, 86 (1) *Journal of the American Planning Association* 89–105, DOI 10.1080/01944363.2019.1647446.

Koonin, Steven (2017, April 20). A Red Team Exercise Would Strengthen Climate Science, Wall Street Journal.
Kosonen, R. & Tan, F. (2004). Assessment of Productivity Loss in Air-Conditioned Buildings Using PMV Index, 36 *Energy and Buildings* 987–993, DOI 10.1016/j.enbuild.2004.06.021.
Kramer, Bruce M. (1978). The 1977 Clean Air Act Amendments: A Tactical Retreat from the Technology-Forcing Strategy?, 15 *Urban Law Annual* 103–157.
Krekel, Christian & Zerrahn, Alexander (2017). Does the Presence of Wind Turbines Have Negative Externalities for People in Their Surroundings? Evidence from Well-Being Data, 82 *Journal of Environmental Economics & Management* 221–238, DOI 10.1016/j.jeem.2016.11.009.
Krier, James E. & Ursin, Edmund (1978). *Pollution and Policy: A Case Essay on California and Federal Experience with Motor Vehicle Air Pollution, 1940–1975* (Berkeley, CA: University of California Press).
Kroposki, Benjamin (2017). Integrating High Levels of Variable Renewable Energy into Electric Power Systems, 5 (6) *Journal of Modern Power Systems and Clean Energy* 831–837, DOI 10.1007/s40565-017-0339-3.
Kukal, Meetpal S. & Irmak, Suat (2019). Irrigation-Limited Yield Gaps: Trends and Variability in the United States Post-1950, 1 *Environmental Research Communications* 061005, DOI 10.1088/2515-7620/ab2aee.
Kupperman, Karen Ordahl (1982). The Puzzle of the American Climate in the Early Colonial Period, 87 (5) *American Historical Review* 1262–1289.
Kysar, Douglas A. (2011). What Climate Change Can Do about Tort Law, 41 (1) *Environmental Law* 1–71.
Kysar, Douglas A. (2004). Climate Change, Cultural Transformation, and Comprehensive Rationality, 31 *Boston College Environmental Affairs Law Review* 555–567.
Lambert, David K. (2014). Historical Impacts of Precipitation and Temperature on Farm Production in Kansas, 46 *Journal of Agricultural and Applied Economics* 439–456, DOI 10.22004/ag.econ.189144.
Landsea, Christopher W., Vecchi, Gabriel A., Bengtsson, Lennart & Knutson, Thomas R. (2010). Impact of Duration Thresholds on Atlantic Tropical Cyclone Counts, 23 (10) *Journal of Climate* 2508–2519, DOI 10.1175/2009JCLI3034.1.
Landsea, Christopher W. & Gray, William M. (1992). The Strong Association between Western Sahelian Monsoonal Rainfall and Atlantic Hurricanes, 5 (5) *Journal of Climate* 435–453, DOI 10.1175/1520-0442(1992)005<0435:TSABWS>2.0.CO;2.
Landy, Marc K., Robert, Marc J. & Thomas, Stephen R. (1994). *The Environmental Protection Agency: Asking the Wrong Questions Nixon to Clinton* (New York and Oxford: Oxford University Press).
Leena, G. & Hook, M. (2015). Assessing Rare Metal Availability: Challenges for Solar Energy Technologies, 7 (9) *Sustainability* 11818–11837, DOI 10.3390/su70911818.
Leggett, Jane A., Bruner, Emily & Lattanzio, Richard K. (2013, September). Federal Climate Change Funding from FY 2008 to FY 2014, Congressional Research Service Report R43227.
Lehner, Flavio, Born, Andreas, Raible, Christoph C. & Stocker, Thomas F. (2013). Amplified Inception of European Little Ice Age by Sea Ice–Ocean–Atmosphere Feedbacks, 26 (19) *Journal of Climate* 7586–7602, DOI 10.1175/JCLI-D-12-00690.1.
Lenton, Timothy M. (2000). Land and Ocean Carbon Cycle Feedback Effects on Global Warming in a Simple Earth System Model, 52 (5) *Tellus B: Chemical and Physical Meteorology* 1159–1188, DOI 10.3402/tellusb.v52i5.17097.
Levinson, Arik (2016, December). Energy Efficiency Standards Are More Regressive than Energy Taxes, NBER Working Paper No. 22956, available at http://www.nber.org/papers/w22956.

Lewis. Nicholas & Crok, Marcel (2014). A *Sensitive Matter: How the IPCC Buried Evidence Showing Good News about Global Warming*, Global Warming Policy Foundation.

Lewis, Nicholas & Curry, Judith (2018). The Impact of Recent Forcing and Ocean Heat Uptake Data on Estimates of Climate Sensitivity, 31 (15)*Journal of Climate* 6051–6071, DOI 10.1175/JCLI-D-17–0667.1.

Lewis, Nicholas & Curry, Judith (2015). The Implications for Climate Sensitivity of AR5 Forcing and Heat Uptake Estimates, 45 *Climate Dynamics* 1009–1023, DOI 10.1007/s00382-014–2342-y.

Li, Peng, Peng, Changhui, Wang, Meng, Li, Weizhong, Zhao, Pengxiang, Wang, Kefeng, Yang, Yanzheng & Zhu, Qiuan (2017). Quantification of the Response of Global Terrestrial Net Primary Production to Multifactor Climate Change, 76 *Ecological Indicators* 245–255, DOI 10.1016/j.ecolind.2017.01.021.

Lindzen, Richard S. (2007). Taking Greenhouse Warming Seriously, 18 (7–8) *Energy & Environment* 937–950.

Lindzen Richard, S., Chou, Ming-Dah & Hou, Arthur Y. (2001). Does the Earth Have an Adaptive Infrared Iris?, 82 (3) *Bulletin of the American Meteorological Society* 417–432.

Ling, Geoffrey & Bextine, Blake (2017, June 26). Precision Farming Increases Crop Yields, Scientific American.

Linton, J. (1991). Guest Editorial, The James Bay Hydroelectric Project: Issue of the Century, 44 (3) *Artic Institute of North America* iii–iv.

Lipton, Eric & Krauss, Clifford (2011, November 11). A *Gold Rush of Subsidies in Clean Energy Research*, New York Times.

Liu, Run, Liou, Kuo-Nan, Su, Hui, Gu, Yu, Zhao, Bin, Jiang, Jonathan H. & Liu, Shaw Chen (2017). High Cloud Variations with Surface Temperature from 2002 to 2015: Contributions to Atmospheric Radiative Cooling Rate and Precipitation Changes, 122 *Journal of Geophysical Research Atmospheres* 5457–5471, DOI 10.1002/2016JD026303.

Liu, Zhengyu (2012). Dynamics of Interdecadal Climate Variability: A Historical Perspective, 25 (6) *Journal of Climate* 1963–1995, DOI 10.1175/2011JCLI3980.1.

Liu, Zhengyu, Zhua, Jiang, Rosenthal, Yair, et al. (2014). The Holocene Temperature Conundrum, 111 (34) *Proceedings of the National Academy of Sciences* E3501–E3505, DOI 10.1073/pnas.1407229111.

Loss, Scott R., Will, Tom & Marra, Peter P. (2013). Estimates of Bird Collision Mortality at Wind Facilities in the Contiguous United States, 168 *Biological Conservation* 201–209, DOI 10.1016/j.biocon.2013.10.007.

Lourantou, Anna, Lavrič, Jošt V., Köhler, Peter, Barnola, Jean-Marc, Paillard, Didier, Michel, Elisabeth, Raynaud, Dominique & Chappellaz, Jérôme (2010). Constraint of the CO2 Rise by New Atmospheric Isotopic Measurements during the Last Deglaciation, 24 *Global Biogeochemistry Cycles* GB2015, DOI 10.1029/2009GB003545.

Luo, Jing-Jia & Yamagata, Toshio (2001). Long-Term El Nino-Southern Oscillation (ENSO)-Like Variation with Special Emphasis on the South Pacific, 106 *Journal of Geophysical Research* 22211–22212, DOI 10.1029/2011JD016690.

Lyman, John M. & Johnson, Gregory C. (2014). Estimating Global Ocean Heat Content Changes in the Upper 1800 m since 1950 and the Influence of Climatology Choice, 27 *Journal of Climate* 1945–1957.

MacDonald, Robert & Siegel, Daniel (1986). The Value of Waiting to Invest, 101 (4) *Quarterly Journal of Economics* 707–727, DOI 10.2307/1884175.

Maguire, Karen & Munasib, Abdul (2016). The Disparate Influence of State Renewable Portfolio Standards on Renewable Electricity Generation Capacity, 92 (3) *Land Economics* 468–490, DOI 10.3368/le.92.3.468.

Mahaffey, James (2009). *Atomic Awakening: A New Look at the History and Future of Nuclear Power*. (New York, Pegasus Books).
Mahmood, Razaul, Pielke, Roger A., Sr., Hubbard, Kenneth G., et al. (2014). Review: Land Cover Changes and Their Biogeophysical Effects on Climate, 34 *International Journal of Climatology* 929–953, DOI 10.1002/joc.3736.
Manabe, D. & Wetherald, R. T. (1975). The Effects of Doubling the Carbon Dioxide Concentration on the Climate of a General Circulation Model, 32 *Journal of Atmospheric Science* 3–15, DOI 10.1175/1520-0469(1975)032<0003:TEODTC>2.0.CO;2.
Mao, Hude, Wang, Hongwei, Liu, Shengxue, Zhigang, Li, Yang, Xiaohong, Yan, Jianbing, Li, Jiansheng, Tran, Lam-Son Phan & Qin, Feng (2015). A Transposable Element in a NAC Gene Is Associated with Drought Tolerance in Maize Seedlings, 6 *Nature Communications* 8326, DOI 10.1038/ncomms9326.
Maranz, S. & Weisman, Z. (2003). Evidence for Indigenous Selection and Distribution of the Shea tree, *Vitellaria paradoxa*, and Its Potential Significance to Prevailing Parkland Savanna Tree Patterns in Sub-Saharan Africa North of the Equator, 30 (10) *Agriculture* 1505, DOI 10.1046/j.1365-2699.2003.00892.x.
Maraun, Douglas (2016). Bias Correcting Climate Change Simulations – a Critical Review, 2 *Current Climate Change Reports* 211–220, DOI 10.1007/s40641-016-0050-x.
Marcott, Shaun A., Shakun, Jeremy D., Clark, Peter U. & Mix, Alan C. (2013). A Reconstruction of Regional and Global Temperature for the Past 11,300 Years, 339 (6124) *Science* 1198–1201, DOI 10.1126/science.1228026.
Marcott, Shaun A., Bauska, Thomas K., Buizert, Christo, et al. (2014). Centennial-Scale Changes in the Global Carbon Cycle during the Last Deglaciation, 514 *Nature* 616–620, DOI 10.1038/nature13799.
Markham, Penn N., Liu, Yilu & Young, Marcus (2013, July). Environmental Regulation Impacts on Eastern Interconnection Performance, Oak Ridge National Laboratory, Energy and Transportation Sciences Division.
Marsicek, Jeremiah, Shuman, Bryan N., Bartlein, Patrick J., Shafer, Sarah L. & Brewer, Simon (2018). Reconciling Divergent Trends and Millennial Variations in Holocene Temperatures, 554 *Nature* 92–96, DOI 10.1038/nature25464.
Marten, Alex L. (2011, October 28). Transient Temperature Response Modeling in IAM's: The Effects of Over Simplification on the SCC, 5 *Economics E-Journal* 2011–2018, DOI 10.5018/economics-ejournal.ja.2011-18.
Mashaw, Jerry L. & Harfst, David L. (1987). Regulation and Legal Culture: The Case of Motor Vehicle Safety, 4 *Yale Journal on Regulation* 257–316.
Massetti, Emanuele, Brown, Marilyn A., Lapsa, Melissa, Sharma, Isha, Bradbury, James, Cunliff, Colin & Li, Yufei (2017). Environmental Quality and the US Power Sector: Air Quality, Water Quality, Land Use and Environmental Justice, Oak Ridge National Laboratory of the US Department of Energy, ORNL/SPR-2016/772.
Matthews, Samuel W. (1976). What's Happening to Our Climate, 150 *National Geographic* 581.
Mauritsen, Thorsten, Stevens, Bjorn, Roeckner, Erich, et al. (2012). Tuning the Climate of a Global Model, 4 (3) *Journal of Advances in Modeling Earth Systems* MA00A01, DOI 10.1029/2012MS000154.
Mazor, Kathleen M., Clauser, Brian E., Field, Terry, Yood, Robert A. & Gurwitz, Jerry H. (2002). A Demonstration of the Impact of Response Bias on the Results of Patient Satisfaction Surveys, 37 (5) *Health Services Research* 1403–1417, DOI 10.1111/1475-6773.11194.
McGuire, Karen & Munasib, Abdul (2018). Electricity Price Increases in Texas: What Is the Role of RPS?, 69 *Environmental & Resource Economics* 293–316, DOI 10.1007/s10640-016-0079-2.

McIntyre, Stephen & McKitrick, Ross (2005). Hockey Sticks, Principal Components, and Spurious Significance, 32 (3) *Geophysical Research Letters* L03710, DOI 10.1029/2004GL021750.

McKitrick, Ross M. (2012). *Adversarial versus Consensus Processes for Assessing Scientific Evidence, in Institutions and Incentives in Regulatory Science* 55 (Lanham, MA, Lexington Books).

McKitrick, Ross M., McIntyre, Stephen & Herman, Chad (2010). Panel and Multivariate Methods for Tests of Trend Equivalence in Climate Data Series, 11 *Atmospheric Science Letters* 270–277, DOI 10.1002/asl.290.

McKitrick, Ross M. & Vogelsang, Timothy J. (2014). HAC Robust Trend Comparisons among Climate Series with Possible Level Shifts, 25 *Environmetrics* 528–547, DOI 10.1002/env.2294.

McKitrick, Ross M. & Christy, John (2018). A Test of the Tropical 200–300 hPa Warming Rate in Climate Models, 5 (9) *Earth & Space Science* 529–536, DOI 10.1029/2018EA000401.

McKitrick, Ross M. & Michaels, Patrick J. (2007). Quantifying the Influence of Anthropogenic Surface Processes and Inhomogeneities in Gridded Global Temperature Data, 112 *Journal of Geophysical Research* D24S09, DOI 10.1029/2007JD009465.

McKitrick, Ross M. & Neirenberg, Nicolas (2010). Socioeconomic Patterns in Climate Data, 35 *Journal of Economic and Social Measurement* 149–175, DOI 10.3233/JEM-2010-0336.

McLean, J. D., De Freitas, C. R. & Carter, R. M. (2009). Influence of the Southern Oscillation on Tropospheric Temperature, 114 *Journal of Geophysical Research* D14104, DOI 10.1029/2008JD011637.

McNider, R. T., Shi, Z., Friedman, M. & England, D. E. (1995), On the Predictability of the Stable Atmospheric Boundary Layer, 52 *Journal of Atmospheric Sciences* 1602–1614.

Meinshausen, M., Meinshausen, N., Hare, W., Raper, S., Frieler, K., Frame, D. & Allen, M. (2009). Greenhouse-Gas Emission Targets for Limiting Global Warming to 2C, 458 *Nature* 1158–1162.

Meko, David M., Woodhouse, Connie A., Baisan, Christopher A., Knight, Troy, Lukas, Jeffrey J., Hughes, Malcom K. & Salzer, Matthew W. (2007). Medieval Drought in the Upper Colorado River Basin, 34 (10) *Geophysical Research Letters* L10705, DOI 10.1029/2007GLR029988.

Menne, Matthew J., Williams, Claude N., Jr. & Vose, Russell S. (2009). The US Historical Climatology Network Monthly Temperature Data, Version 2, 90 (7) *Bulletin of the American Meteorological Society* 993–1007, DOI 10.1175/2008BAMS2613.1.

Mendelsohn, Robert, Nordhaus, William & Shaw, David (1994). The Impact of Global Warming on Agriculture: A Ricardian Analysis, 84 *American Economic Review* 753–771.

Mensing, Scott, Smith, Jeremy, Norman, Kelly Burkle & Allan, Marie (2008). Extended Drought in the Great Basin of Western North America in the Last Two Millennia Reconstructed from Pollen Records, 188 *Quaternary International* 79–89, DOI 10.1016/j.quaint.2007.06.009.

Metcalf, Gilbert E. (2019). The Distributional Impacts of US Energy Policy, 129 *Energy Policy* 926–929, DOI 10.1016/j.enpol.2019.01.076.

Metcalf, Gilbert E. (2009). Investment in Energy Infrastructure and the Tax Code, National Bureau of Economic Research Working paper 15429.

Michaels, Patrick J. & Knappenburger, Paul C. (2015). *Lukewarming: The New Climate Science That Changes Everything* 97–124 (Cato Institute).

Millar, Richard J., Fuglestvedt, Friedlingstein, Pierre, Rogelj, et al. (2017). Emission Budgets and Pathways Consistent with Limiting Warming to 1.5 C, 10 *Nature Geoscience* 740–748, DOI 10.1038/ngeo3031.

Miller, James A. (2011). Urban and Regional Temperature Trends in Las Vegas and Southern Nevada, 43 (1) *Journal of the Arizona-Nevada Academy of Science* 27–39, DOI 10.2181/036.043.0105.

Miller, Jonathan (2011). Double Absurdity: Regulating Greenhouse Gas under the Clean Air Act, 47 *Houston Law Review* 1389–1420.

Miller, Gifford H., Geirsdóttir, Áslaug, Zhong, Yafang, et al. (2012). Abrupt Onset of the Little Ice Age Triggered by Volcanism and Sustained by Sea-Ice/Ocean Feedbacks, 39 (2) *Geophysical Research Letters* L02708, DOI 10.1029/2011GL050168.

Minobe, Shoshiro (1997). A 50–70 Year Oscillation over the North Pacific and North America, 24 (6) *Geophysical Research Letters* 683–686, DOI 10.1029/97GL00504.

Minobe, Shoshiro (1999). Resonance in Bidecadal and Pentadecadal Climate Oscillations Over the North Pacific: Role in Regime Shifts, 26 *Geophysical Research Letters* 855–858, DOI 10.1029/1999GL900119.

Mitchell, J. Murray, Jr. (1977). The Changing Climate, in National Research Council, Energy and Climate: Studies in Geophysics 51–58.

Moffa-Sanchez, Poala & Hall, Ian R. (2017). North Atlantic Variability and Its Links to European Climate over the Last 3000 Years, 8 *Nature Communications* 1726, DOI 10.1038/s41467-017-01884-8.

Mohan, Manju & Kandya, Anurag (2015). Impact of Urbanization and Land-Use/Land-Cover Change on Diurnal Temperature Range: A Case Study of Tropical Urban Airshed of India Using Remote Sensing Data, 506–507 *Science of the Total Environment* 453–465, DOI 10.1016/j.scitotenv.2014.11.006.

Moore, Mark A., Boardman, Anthony E. & Vining, Aidan R. (2012). More Appropriate Discounting: The Rate of Social Time Preference and the Value of the Social Discount Rate, 4 (1) *Journal of Benefit-Cost Analysis* 1–16, DOI 10.1515/jbca-2012-0008.

Morales, Janin Guzman (2018). Santa Ana Winds of Southern California: Historical Variability and Future Climate Projections. PhD Dissertation, UC San Diego. ProQuest ID: GuzmanMorales_ucsd_0033D_17854. Merritt ID: ark:/13030/m5fj7dph, retrieved from https://escholarship.org/uc/item/6hm499nj.

Mortimore, Michael (2010). Adapting to Drought in the Sahel: Lessons for Climate Change, 1 *WIREs Climate Change* 134, DOI 10.1002/wcc.25.

Mortimore, Michael & Adams, William (2001). Farmer Adaptation, Change and 'Crisis' in the Sahel, 11 *Global Environmental Change* 49–57, DOI 10.1016/S0959-3780(00)00044-3.

Murray, William (2018, January 17). New Englanders Have Only Themselves to Blame for Energy Price Spikes, Real Clear Energy.

Myhre, Gunnar, Highwood, Eleanor J., Shine, Keith P. & Stordal, Frode (1998). New Estimates of Radiative Forcing due to Well Mixed Greenhouse Gases, 25(14) *Geophysical Research Letters* 2715–2718.

Nagle, John C. (2013). Green Harms of Green Projects, 27 *Notre Dame Journal of Law, Ethics and Public Policy* 59–102.

Nagy, R. Chelsea, Fusco, Emily, Bradley, Bethany, Abatzoglou, John T. & Balch, Jennifer (2018). Human-Related Ignitions Increase the Number of Large Wildfires across US Ecoregions, 1 *Fire* 4, DOI 103390/fire1010004.

National Research Council (1977). *Energy and Climate: Studies in Geophysics* (Washington, DC: The National Academies Press), DOI 10.17226/12024.

National Research Council (2006). *Surface Temperature Reconstructions for the Last 2,000 Years* (Washington, DC: The National Academies Press), DOI 10.17226/11676.

Nemani, Ramakrishna R., Keeling, Charles D. & Hashimoto, Hirofumi (2003). Climate-Driven Increases in Global Terrestrial Net Primary Production from 1982 to 1999, 300 *Science* 1560–1563.

NERC (2014, November 14) Potential Reliability Impacts of EPA's Proposed Clean Power Plan: Initial Reliability Review 18
Newman, Matthew, Alexander, Michael A., Ault, Toby R., et al. (2016). The Pacific Decadal Oscillation Revisited, 29 (12) *Journal of Climate* 4399–4427, DOI 10.1175/JCLI-D-15-0508.1.
Nevius, David (2020). History of the North American Electric Reliability Corporation 1–6, NERC.
Nicholson, S. E., Funk, Chris & Fink, Andreas H. (2018). Rainfall over the African Continent from the 19th through the 21st Century, 165 *Global and Planetary Change* 114–127, DOI 10.1016/j.gloplacha.2017.12.014.
Nielsen, R. L. (2017). *Historical Corn Grain Yields for the US*, Corny News Network.
Nielsen, R. L. (2018). *The Planting Date Conundrum for Corn*, The Corny News Network.
Nordhaus, William (2008). *A Question of Balanced: Weighing the Options on Global Warming Policies* 144 (Yale University Press) .
Nordhaus, William (2014). Estimates of the Social Cost of Carbon: Concepts and Results from the DICE-2013R Model and Alternative Approaches, 1 *Journal of the Association of Environmental and Resource Economists* 273–312, DOI 10.1086/676035.
Nordhaus, William & Boyer, Joseph (2000). *Warming the World: Economic Models of Global Warming* 69–98 (MIT Press).
Novak, William J. (1996). *The People's Welfare* 61 (Chapel Hill and London: University of North Carolina Press, 3rd Ed.).
Olmstead, Alan L. & Rhode, Paul W. (2008). *Creating Abundance: Biological Innovation and American Agricultural Development* (Cambridge University Press).
Oreskes, Naomi (2004) (corrected 2005, January Erratum). The Scientific Consensus on Climate Change, 306 *Science* 1686, DOI 10.1126/science.1103618.
O'Riordan, R. & Jager, J., eds. (1996). *Politics of Climate Change: A European Perspective* 346 (London and New York, Routledge).
Pacific Gas & Electric Company (2011) Smart Grid Deployment Plan 2011–2020, California Public Utilities Commission, Appendix A: PG&E's Smart Grid Deployment Plan 2
Pacific Gas & Electric Company (2015) Smart Grid Annual Report, California Public Utilities Commission.
Pacific Gas & Electric Company (2017) Smart Grid Annual Report, California Public Utilities Commission.
Pacific Gas & Electric Company (2018). PG&E Clean Energy Deliveries Already Meet Future Goals.
Palmer, M. D., Roberts C.D., Balmaseda, M., et al. (2017). Ocean Heat Content Variability and Change in an Ensemble of Ocean Reanalyse, 49 *Climate Dynamics* 909–930, DOI 10.1007/s00382-015-2801-0.
Palmer, Karen, Burtraw, Dallas, Bharvirkar, Ranjit & Paul, Anthony (2010). Restructuring and Cost of Reducing NOx Emissions in Electricity Generation, RFF Discussion Paper 01/10.
Paregoi, Ian M. (1998). Shocking Revelations at Hydro-Quebec: The Environmental and Legal Consequences of the Quebec–New York Power Line, 7 *Penn State International Law Review* 155–174.
Park, Jisung (2017, May). Will We Adapt? Labor Productivity and Adaptation to Climate Change, Harvard Environmental Economics Program, Discussion Paper 17–73.
Parrenin, F., Masson-Delmotte, V., Köhler, P., Raynaud, D., Paillard, D., Schwander, J., Barbante, C., Landais, A., Wegner, A. & Jouzel, J. (2013). Synchronous Change of Atmospheric CO2 and Antarctic Temperature during the Last Deglacial Warming, 339 *Science* 1060–1063, DOI 10.1126/science.1226368.

Past Interglacials Working Group of PAGES (2016). Interglacials of the Last 800,000 Years, 54 *Reviews of Geophysics* 162–219, DOI 10.1002/2015RG000482.

Pawa, Matthew F. (2005). Global Warming as a Public Nuisance: Connecticut v. American Electric Power, 16 *Fordham Environmental Law Review* 407–473.

Penn, Ivan & Eavis, Peter (2019, January 17). *PG&E Bankruptcy Could Deal Blow to Its Solar-Power Suppliers' Finances*, New York Times.

Percival, Robert V. (2006). Who's Afraid of the Precautionary Principle?, 23 *Pace Environmental Law Review* 21–47.

Pierce, Richard J., Jr. (1982). Natural Gas Regulation, Deregulation, and Contracts, 68 (1) *Virginia Law Review* 63–115, DOI 10.2307/1072705.

Pielke, Roger, Jr. (2007). *The Honest Broker: Making Sense of Science in Policy and Politics*, 2–7 (Cambridge University Press).

Pielke, Roger, Jr. (2000). Policy History of the US Global Change Research Program: Part I. Administrative Development, 10 (1) *Global Environmental Change* 9–25, DOI 10.1016/S0959-3780(00)00006-6.

Pielke, Roger, Jr. (1995). Usable Information for Policy: An Appraisal of the US Global Change Research Program, 28 (1) *Policy Sciences* 39–77, DOI 10.1007/BF01000820.

Pielke, Roger A., Sr., Davey, Christopher A., Niyogi, Dev, et al. (2007). Unresolved Issues with the Assessment of Multidecadal Global Land Surface Temperature Trends, 112 *Journal of Geophysical Research* D24S08, DOI 10.1029/2006JD008229.

Pielke, Roger, Sr. & Wilby, Robert L. (2012). Regional Climate Downscaling: What's the Point, 93 (5) *Eos* 52–53, DOI 10.1029/2012EO050008.

Pindyck, Robert S. (1991). Irreversibility, Uncertainty, and Investment, 26 (3) *Journal of Economic Literature* 1110–1148.

Pindyck, Robert S. (2011). Fat Tails, Thin Tails, and Climate Change Policy, 5 (2) *Review of Environmental Economics and Policy* 258–274, DOI 10.1093/reep/rer005.

Pindyck, Robert S. (2013). Climate Change Policy: What Do the Models Tell Us?, 51 *Journal of Economic Literature* 860–872, DOI 10.1257/jel.51.3.860.

Plastina, Alejandro & Hart, Chad (2014, Fall). *Crop Insurance in Iowa, CARD Agricultural Policy Review*, Iowa State University.

Polgreen, Lydia (2007, February 11). *In Niger, Trees and Crops Turn Back the Desert*, New York Times.

Pringle, Peter (2008). *The Murder of Nikolai Vavilov: The Story of Stalin's Persecution of One of the Great Scientists of the Twentieth Century, New York, London* (Sydney, Simon and Shuster).

Proett, Michael A. (1987). Cumulative Impacts of Hydroelectric Development: Beyond the Cluster Impact Procedure, 11 *Harvard Environmental Law Review* 77–146.

Pylant, Cortney L., Nelson, David M., Fitzpatrick, Matthew C., Gates, J. Edward & Keller, Stephen R. (2016). Geographic Origins and Population Genetics of Bats Killed at Wind-Energy Facilities, 26(5) *Ecological Applications* 1381–1395.

Quayle, Robert G., Easterline, David R., Karl, Thomas R. & Hughes, Pamela Y. (1991). Effects of Recent Thermometer Changes in the Cooperative Station Network, 72 (11) *Bulletin of the American Meteorological Society* 1718–1723, DOI 10.1175/1520-0477(1991)072<1718:EORTCI>2.0.CO;2.

Radeloff, Volker C., Helmers, David P., Kramer, H. Anu, et al. (2018). Rapid Growth of the US Wildland–Urban Interface Raises Wildfire Risk, 115 (13) *Proceedings of the National Academy of Sciences* 3314–3319, DOI 10.1073/pnas.1718850115.

Ramanathan, V. & Carmichael, G. (2008). Global and Regional Climate Changes due to Black Carbon, 1 *Nature Geoscience* 221, 222, DOI 10.1038/ngeo156.

Rand, Joseph T., Kramer, Louisa A., Garrity, Christopher P., Hoen, Ben D., Diffendorfer, Jay E., Hunt, Hannah E. & Spears, Michael (2020). A Continuously Updated, Geospatially Rectified Database of Utility-Scale Wind Turbines in the United States, 7 *Nature Scientific Data* 15, DOI 10.1038/s41597-020-0353-6.

Reich, P. F., Numbem, S. T., Almaraz, R. A. & Eswaran, H. (2014). Land Resource Stresses and Desertification in Africa, in Responses to Land Degradation. Proc. 2nd. International Conference on Land Degradation and Desertification, Khon Kaen, Thailand (E.M. Bridges et al., eds., New Delhi, India: Oxford Press)

Reifsnyder, S. D. (1992). The Policy of the USA on the Climate Change Convention, Seoul Symposium on UNCED and Prospects of the Environmental Regime in the 21st Century.

Ren, Guo-Yu (2015). Urbanization as a Major Driver of Urban Climate Change, 6 *Scipedia* 1–6.

Renewables Now (2020, January). Wind Meets Record 47% of Denmark's Power Demand in 2019.

Ring, Michael J., Lindner, Daniela, Cross, Emily F. & Schlesinger, Michael E. (2012). Causes of the Global Warming Observed since the 19th Century, 2 (4) *Atmospheric and Climate Science* 401–415, DOI 10.4236/acs.2012.24035.

Roberts, Michael J. & Schlenker, Wolfram (2011). The Evolution of Heat Tolerance of Corn: Implications for Climate Change, The Economics of Climate Change: Adaptations Past and Present 225, 239, 241 (Gary D. Libecap & Richard H. Steckel, eds.).

Roberts, Michael J. & Schlenker, Wolfram (2012). Is Agricultural Production Becoming More or Less Sensitive to Extreme Heat? Evidence from U.S Corn and Soybean Yields, in The Design and Implementation of US Climate Policy 271 (Don Fullerton & Catherine Wolfram, eds.).

Rochester, H., Jr., Lloyd, Thomas & Farr, Martha (1984). Physical Impacts of Small-Scale Hydroelectric Facilities and Their Effects on Fish and Wildlife, FWS/OBS-84/19.

Roe, Gerald H. (2007, September). Feedbacks, Timescales, and Seeing Red 15–18, Draft Paper.

Roe, Gerald H. & Baker, Marcia B. (2007). Why Is Climate Sensitivity So Unpredictable?, 318 (5850) *Science* 629–632, DOI 10.1126/science.1144735.

Roe, Gerald H. & Bauman, Yoram (2013). Climate Sensitivity: Should the Climate Tail Wag the Policy Dog?, 117 *Climatic Change* 647–662, DOI 10.1007/s10584-012-0582-6.

Rosenzweig, Mark & Udry, Christopher R. (2013, August). Forecasting Profitability, NBER Working Paper No 19334.

Rosewater, David & Williams, Adam (2015). Analyzing System Safety in Lithium-Ion Grid Storage, 300 *Journal of Power Sources* 460–471, DOI 10.1016/j.jpowsour.2015.09.068.

Rothman, Daniel (2002). Atmospheric Carbon Dioxide Levels for the Last 500 Million Years, 99 (7) *Proceedings of the National Academy of Sciences* 4167–4171, DOI 10.1073/pnas.022055499.

Rotstayn, Leon D., Collier, Mark A., Shindell, Drew T. & Boucher, Olivier (2015). Why Does Aerosol Forcing Control Historical Global-Mean Surface Temperature Change in CMIP5 Models?, 28 *Journal of Climate* 6608–6625.

Rubin, E. S., Davison, John E. & Herzog, Howard J. (2015). The Cost of CO_2 Capture and Storage, 40 *International Journal of Greenhouse Gas Control* 378–400, DOI 10.1016/j.ijggc.2015.05.018.

Rugh, David W. (2003). Clearer, but Still Toxic Skies: A Comparison of the Clear Skies Act, Congressional Bills, and the Proposed Rule to Control Mercury Emissions from Coal-Fired Power Plants, 28 *Vermont Law Review* 201–235.

Rule, Troy A. (2014). *Solar, Wind and Land: Conflicts in Renewable Energy Development* (London and New York, Routledge).

Sachs, Noah (2011). Rescuing the Strong Precautionary Principle from Its Critics. 2011 *University of Illinois Law Review* 1285–1338.
Sahagun, Louis (2016, September 2). This Mojave Desert Solar Plant Kills 6,000 Birds a Year. Here's Why That Won't Change Any Time Soon, Los Angeles Times.
Saikku, Reetta, Stott, Lowell & Thunell, Robert (2009). A Bi-polar Signal Recorded in the Western Tropical Pacific: Northern and Southern Hemisphere Climate Records from the Pacific Warm Pool during the Last Ice Age, 28 *Quarternary Science Review* 2374.
Sanderson, Michael G., Economou, Theo, Salmon, Kate H. & Jones, Sarah E. O. (2017). Historical Trends and Variability in Heat Waves in the United Kingdom, 8 (10) *Atmosphere* 191, DOI 10.3390/atmos8100191.
Santer, Benjamin D., Wigley, T. M. L., Mears, C., et al. (2005). Amplification of Surface Temperature Trends and Variability in the Tropical Atmosphere, 309 *Science* 1551–1556, DOI 10.1126/science.1114867.
Santer, Benjamin D., Thorne, P. W., Haimberger, L., et al. (2008). Consistency of Modelled and Observed Temperature Trends in the Tropical Troposphere, 28 *International Journal of Climatology* 1703–1722, DOI 10.1002/joc.
Santamaría-Gómeza, Alvaro, Gravelle, Médéric, Dangendorf, Sönke, Marcos, Marta, Spada, Giorgio & Wöppelmanna, Guy (2017). Uncertainty of the 20th Century Sea-Level Rise due to Vertical Land Motion Errors, 473 *Earth & Planetary Science Letters* 24–32, DOI 10.1016/j.epsl.2017.05.038.
Schimmelpfennig, David & Ebel, Robert (2016). Sequential Adoption and Cost Savings from Precision Agriculture, 41 (1) *Journal of Agricultural and Resource Economics* 97–115, DOI 10.22004/ag.econ.230776.
Schlenker, Wolfram, Hanemann, W. Michael & Fisher, Anthony C. (2005). Will US Agriculture Really Benefit from Global Warming? Accounting for Irrigation in the Hedonic Approach, 95 *American Economic Review* 395–406, DOI 10.1257/0002828053828455.
Schlenker, Wolfram & Roberts, Michael J. (2009). Nonlinear Temperature Effects Indicate Severe Damages to US Crop Yields under Climate Change, 106 *Proceedings of the National Academy of Sciences* 15594–15598, DOI 10.1073/pnas.0906865106.
Schmalensee, Richard & Stavins, Robert N. (2017). Lessons Learned from Three Decades of Experience with Cap and Trade, 11 (1) *Review of Environmental Economics and Policy* 59–79, DOI 10.1093/reep/rew017.
Schmidt, Gavin, Bader, David, Donner, Leo J., et al. (2017). Practice and Philosophy of Climate Model Tuning across Six US Modeling Centers, 10 *Geoscientific Model Development* 3207–3223, DOI 10.5194/gmd-10-3207-2017.
Schneider, Tapio (2006). The General Circulation of the Atmosphere, 34 *Annual Review of Earth and Planetary Sciences* 655–688, DOI 10.1146/annurev.earth.34.031405.125144.
Schnitkey, Gary (2016, August 2). Corn and Soybean Revenue Projections for 2016 and 2017, Weekly Farm Economics, 6 *Farmdoc Daily* 145.
Schober, Make (2011, July 11). *Yield Enhancer or Farmland Destroyer?*, Farm Journal Ag Web.
Schoengold, Karina, Ding, Ya & Headlee, Russell (2014). The Impact of Ad Hoc Disaster and Crop Insurance Programs on the Use of Risk-Reducing Conservation Tillage Practices, 97 *American Journal of Agricultural Economics* 897–919, DOI 10.1093/ajae/aau073.
Schwartz, John (2019, September 3). *How Has Climate Change Affected Hurricane Dorian?*, The New York Times.
Schwartz, Stephen E., Charlson, Robert J. & Rodhe, Henning (2007). Quantifying Climate Change, Quantifying Climate Change: Too Rosy a Picture?, 2 *Nature Climate Change* 23–24, DOI 10.1038/climate.2007.22.

Schwartz, Stephen E. (2008). Uncertainty in Climate Sensitivity: Causes, Consequences, Challenges, 1 *Energy & Environmental Science* 430–453, DOI 10.1039/B810350J.
Scott, Michael & Lindsey, Rebecca (2016. June 15). *Which Emits More Carbon Dioxide: Volcanoes or Human Activities?*, NOAA.
Seidel, Stephen & Keyes, Dale (1983, September). Can We Delay a Greenhouse Warming? The Effectiveness and Feasibility of Options to Slow a Build-up of Carbon Dioxide in the Atmosphere, Office of Policy and Resource Management.
Seigneur, Christian, Vijayaraghavan, Krish, Lohman, Kristen, Karamchandani, Prakash & Scott, Courtney (2004). Global Source Attribution for Mercury Deposition in the United States, 8 *Environmental Science and Technology* 555–569.
Seppänen, Olli, Fisk, William J. & Lei-Gomez, Quanhong (2006, July). Room Temperature and Productivity in Office Work, LBNL- 60952.
Seneviratne, Shinthaka & Ozansoy, C. (2016). Frequency Response due to a Large Generator Loss with the Increasing Penetration of Wind/PV Generation – A Literature Review, 57 *Renewable Energy and Sustainable energy Reviews* 659–668, DOI 10.1016/j.rser.2015.12.051.
Service, Robert F. (2008). Study Fingers Soot as a Major Player in Global Warming, 319 (5871) *Science* 1745, DOI 10.1126/science.319.5871.1745.
Shakun, Jeremy D., Clark, Peter U., He, Feng, Marcott, Shaun A., Mix, Alan C., Liu, Zhengyu, Otto-Bliesner, Bette, Schmittner, Andreas & Bard, Edouard (2012). Global Warming Preceded by Increasing Carbon Dioxide Concentrations during the Last Deglaciation, 484 (7392) *Nature* 49–54, DOI 10.1038/nature10915.
Shapiro, Carl R., Starke, Genevieve M., Meneveau, Charles & Gayme, Dennice F. (2019). A Wake Modeling Paradigm for Wind Farm Design and Control, 12 (15) *Energies* 2956, DOI 10.3390/en12152956.
Sheffield, Justin, Wood, Eric F. & Roderick, Michael L. (2012). Little Change in Drought over the Past 60 Years, 491 *Nature* 435–438.
Shellenberger, Michael (2018, May 23). If Solar Panels Are So Clean, Why Do They Produce So Much Toxic Waste, Forbes.
Sheridan, Scott & Dixon, P. Grady (2017). Spatiotemporal Trends in Human Vulnerability and Adaptation to Heat across the United States, 20 *Anthropocene* 61–73, DOI 10.1016/j.ancene.2016.10.001.
Sheridan, Scott C., Kalkstein, Adam J. & Kalkstein, Laurence S. (2009). Trends in Heat-Related Mortality in the United States, 1975–2004, 50 *Natural Hazards* 145–160.
Sherwood, Steven C. & Huber, Matthew (2010). An Adaptability Limit to Climate Change due to Heat Stress, 107 (21) *Proceedings of the National Academy of Sciences* 9552–9555, DOI 10.1073/pnas.0913352107.
Shi, Xingzhong, McNider, Richard T., Singh, M. P., England, David E., Friedman, Mark J., Lapenta, William M. & Norris, William B. (2005). On the Behavior of the Stable Boundary Layer and Role of Initial Conditions, 162 *Pure Applied Geophysics* 1811–1829, DOI 10.1007/s00024-005-2694-7.
Shiau, Ching-Shin Norman, Michalek, Jeremy J. & Hendrickson, Chris T. (2009). A Structural Analysis of Vehicle Design Responses to Corporate Average Fuel Economy Policy, 43 (9–10) *A Transportation Research Part* 814–828, DOI 10.1016/j.tra.2009.08.002.
Shindell, Drew & Faluvegi, Greg (2009). Climate Response to Regional Radiative Forcing during the Twentieth Century, 2 (4) *Nature Geoscience* 294–300, DOI 10.1038/ngeo473.
Skeie, R. B., Bernsten, T., Aldrin, M., Holden, M. & Myhre, G. (2014). A Lower and More Constrained Estimate of Climate Sensitivity Using Updated Observations and Detailed Radiative Forcing Time Series, 5 *Earth System Dynamics* 139–175.

Smagorinsky, Joseph (1977). *Modeling and Predictability in Energy and Climate*, 133–139 (Washington, DC: National Academy Press).
Smagorinsky, Joseph (1982). *Carbon Dioxide and the Climate: A Second Assessment* (Washington, DC: National Academy Press).
Smil, Vaclav (2017). *Energy and Civilization* (Cambridge, MA: MIT Press).
Smith, Irene (1978, April). Carbon Dioxide and the "Greenhouse Effect" – An Unresolved Problem, IEA Coal Research, Report Number ICTIS/ER 01.
Smith, Joshua Emerson (2019, January 31) Climate Change Should Tamp Down California's Wildfire-Fanning Santa Ana Winds, Study Finds, Los Angeles Times.
Smith, R. A. (1980), Golden Gate Tidal Measurements 1854–1978, Journal of the Waterways, Port Coastal and Ocean Division, Proceedings of the American Society of Civil Engineers 407–410.
Smith, Roger K., Montgomery, Michael T. & Vogl, Stefanie (2008). A Critique of Manuel's Hurricane Model and Potential Intensity Theory, 134 *Quarterly Journal of the Royal Meteorological Society* 551–561.
Smith, S. J., vanAardenne, J., Klimont, Z., Andres, R. J., Volke, A. & Delgado Arias, S. (2011). Anthropogenic Sulfur Dioxide Emissions, 1850–2005, 11 *Atmospheric Chemistry and Physics* 1101–1116, DOI 10.5194/acp-11-1101-2011.
Smith, Thomas M. & Reynolds, Richard W. (2004). Improved Extended Reconstruction of SST (1854–1997), 17 *Journal of Climate* 2466–2477, DOI 10.1175/1520-0442(2004)017<2466:IEROS>2.0.CO;2.
Spencer, Jack (2015, January 31). One Lawsuit Settled, but No Truce in Wind Energy Debate, Michigan Capitol Confidential.
Spencer, Roy W. (2010). *Climate Confusion: How Global Warming Hysteria Leads to Bad Science, Pandering Politicians and Misguided Policies That Hurt the Poor* (New York: Encounter Books).
Spurgeon, Anne (2006). Premnatal Methylmercury Exposure and Developmental Outcomes: Review of Evidence and Discussion of Future Directions, 14(2) *Environmental Health Perspectives* 307–312.
Stacy, Thomas F. & Taylor, George F. (2019). *The Levelized Cost of Electricity from Existing Generation Resources*, Institute for Energy Research.
Stebbing, E. P. (1935). The Encroaching Sahara: The Threat to the West African Colonies, 85 (6) *Geographical Journal* 506–519.
Steckel, Richard H. (1983). The Economic Foundations of East-West Migration during the 19th Century, 20 *Explorations in Economic History* 14–36, DOI 10.1016/0014-4983(83)90040-2.
Steelman, J. D., Jr. (1986, June 1). *Deregulation of the Natural Gas Industry*, Foundation for Economic Education.
Stella, Christina (2019, September 10) *Unfurling the Waste Problem Caused by Wind Energy*, NPR.
Stephens, Graeme L. (2005). Cloud Feedbacks in the Climate System: A Critical Review, 18 *Journal of Climate* 237–273, DOI 10.1175/JCLI-3243.1.
Stevens, Landon (2017, June). *The Footprint of Energy: Land Use of US Electricity Production*, Strata.
Stickler, Mercedes (2002, August). *Rights to Trees and Livelihoods in Niger*, Focus on Land in Africa.
Stickler, Mercedes (2012). Rights to Trees and Livelihoods in Niger, Focus on Land in Africa, August, available at https://allafrica.com/download/resource/main/main/idatcs/00091087:4d2765c88e422343f911288bee9dae81.pdf.

Stott, Peter A., Stone, D. A. & Allen, M. R. (2004). Human Contribution to the European Heatwave of 2003, 432 *Nature* 610–614, DOI 10.1038/nature03089.
Stammer, Detlef & Cazenave, Anny, eds. (2017). *Satellite Altimetry over Oceans and Land Surfaces*. CRC Press.
Stenhouse, Neil, Maibach, Edward, Cobb, Sara, Ban, Ray, Bleistein, Andrea, Croft, Paul, Bierly, Eugene, Seitter, Keith, Rasmussen, Gary & Leiserowitz, Anthony (2014, July). Meteorologists' Views about Global Warming: A Survey of American Meteorological Society Professional Members, 95 (7) *Bulletin of the American Meteorological Society* 1029–1040, DOI 10.1175/BAMS-D-13-00091.1.
Stephens, S. L. (2005). Forest Fire Causes and Extent on United States Forest Service Lands, 14 (3) *International Journal of Wildland Fire* 213–222, DOI 10.1071/WF04006.
Stephens, S. L. & Ruth, L. W. (2005). Federal Forest-Fire Policy in the United States, 15 (2) *Ecological Applications* 532–542, DOI 10.1890/04-0545.
Stott, Lowell, Timmermann, Axel & Thunell, Robert (2007). Southern Hemisphere and Deep-Sea Warming Led Deglacial Atmospheric CO_2 Rise and Tropical Warming, 318 (5849) *Science* 435–438, DOI 10.1126/science.1143791.
Sugimoto, Kota (2019). Does Transmission Unbundling Increase Wind Power Generation in the United States?, 125 *Energy Policy* 307–316, DOI 10.1016/j.enpol.2018.10.032.
Sullivan, Daniel & Von Wachter, Till (2009). Job Displacement and Mortality: An Analysis Using Administrative Data, 124 (3) *Quarterly Journal of Economics* 1265–1306, DOI 10.1162/qjec.2009.124.3.1265.
Sullivan, Daniel & Von Wachter, Till (2009). Average Earnings and Long-Term Mortality: Evidence from Administrative Data, 99 (2) *American Economic Review: Papers and Proceedings* 133–138, DOI 10.1257/aer.99.2.133.
Sunstein, Cass R. (2009). *The Laws of Fear* (New York: Cambridge University Press).
Sustainable Energy Authority of Ireland (2009). Renewable Energy in Ireland, Report.
Sutch, Richard (2011). *The Impact of the 1936 Corn Belt Drought on American Farmers' Adoption of Hybrid Corn in the Economics of Climate Change: Adaptations Past and Future* 195 (Gary Libecap & Richard H. Steckel, eds., NBER).
Sweet, Cassandra (2015, June 12). *High Tech Solar Projects Fail to Deliver*, Wall Street Journal.
Syphard, Alexandra D., Keeley, Jon E., Pfaff, Anne H. & Ferschweilera, Ken (2017). Human Presence Diminishes the Importance of Climate in Driving Fire Activity across the United States, 26(114) *Proceedings of the National Academy of Sciences* 3750–13755.
Taylor, F. W. (2005). *Elementary Climate Physics* (New York: Oxford University Press).
Thaxter, Chris B., Buchanan, Gaeme M., Carr, Jamie, Butchart, Stuart H. M., Newbold, Tim, Green, Rhys E., Tobias, Joseph A., Foden, Wendy B., O'Brien, Sue & Pearce- Higgins, James W. (2017). Bird and Bat Species' Global Vulnerability to Collision Mortality at Wind Farms Revealed through a Trait-Based Assessment, 284 *Proceedings of the Royal Society B* 20170829, DOI 10.1098/rspb.2017.0829.
Theobald, Daivd M. & Romme, William H. (2007). Expansion of the US Wildland–Urban Interface, 83 (4) *Landscape and Urban Planning* 340–354, DOI 10.1016/j.landurbplan.2007.06.002.
Thompson, Louis M. (1963). Weather and Technology in the Production of Corn and Soybeans 1–6, CAED Report 17, Center for Agricultural and Economic Development, Iowa State University.
Tielens, Piter & Van Hertem, Dirk (2016). The Relevance of Inertia in Power Systems, 55 *Renewable and Sustainable Energy Reviews* 999–1009, DOI 10.1016/j.rser.2015.11.016.
Timmerman, Axel, Timm, Oliver, Stott, Lowell & Menviel, Laurie (2009). The Roles of CO_2 and Orbital Forcing in Driving Southern Hemispheric Temperature Variations during the Last 21,000 Years, 22 *Journal of Climate* 1626–1640, DOI 10.1175/2008JCLI2161.1.

Tol, Richard S. J. (2002). Estimates of the Damage Costs of Climate Change: Part I: Benchmark Estimates, 21 *Environmental and Resource Economics* 47–73, DOI 10.1023/A:1014500930521.

Tol, Richard S. J. (2002). Estimates of the Damage Costs of Climate Change II: Dynamic Estimates, 21 *Environmental and Resource Economics* 135–160, DOI 10.1023/A:1014539414591.

Tol, Richard S. J. (2016). Comment on "Quantifying the Consensus on Anthropogenic Global Warming in the Scientific Literature," 11 *Environmental Research Letters* 048001, DOI 10.1088/1748-9326/11/4/048001.

Tra, Constant I. (2016). Have Renewable Portfolio Standards Raised Electricity Rates? Evidence from US Electric Utilities, 34 (1) *Contemporary Economic Policy* 184–189, DOI 10.1111/coep.12110.

Tubb, Katie (2019, March 13). *Making Nuclear Waste Disposal a Question of "How," Not "Where,"* The Washington Times.

Tung, Ka-Kit & Zhou, Jiansong (2013). Using Data to Attribute Episodes of Warming and Cooling in Instrumental Records, 110 *Proceedings of the National Academy of Sciences* 2058–2063, DOI 10.1073/pnas.1212471110.

Tushingham, A. M. & Peltier, W. R. (1991). Ice-3G: A New Global Model of Late Pleistocene Deglaciation Based upon Geophysical Predictions of Post Glacial Relative Sea Level Change, 96 (B3) *Journal of Geophysical Research* 4497–4523, DOI 10.1029/90JB01583.

Tyndall, John (1863, January 23). On Radiation through the Earth's Atmosphere, 4 *Professor of the Royal Institution of Great Britain* 204–205.

UK National Grid Electrical Systems Operator (2019, September) Technical Report on the Events of 9 August 2019.

University of Texas Energy Institute, The Full Cost of Electricity, Federal Financial Support for Electricity Generation Technologies 4.

US Global Change Research Program (2014). Climate Change Impacts in the United States: The Third National Climate Assessment, 28, DOI 10.7930/J0Z31WJ2.

Van Ulden, A. P. & Van Oldenborgh, G. J. (2005). Large-Scale Atmospheric Circulation Biases and Changes in Global Climate Model Simulations and Their Importance for Regional Climate Scenarios: A Case Study for West-Central Europe, 5 (4) *Atmospheric Chemistry and Physics Discussions, European Geosciences Union* 7415–7455, DOI 10.5194/acp-6-863-2006.

Van de Wiel, B. J. H., Moene, A. F., Ronda, R. J., DeBruin, H. A. R. & Holtslag, A. A. M. (2002). Intermittent Turbulence and Oscillations in the Stable Boundary Layer over Land, Part II: A System Dynamics Approach, 59 *Journal of Atmospheric Science* 2567–2581, DOI 10.1175/1520-0469(2002)059<2567:itaoit>2.0.CO;2.

Van Haren, Nathalie, Fleiner, Renate, Liniger, Hanspeter & Harari, Nicole (2019). Contribution of Community-Based Initiatives to the Sustainable Development Goal of Land Degradation Neutrality, 94 *Environmental Science and Policy* 211–219.

Van Vuuren, Detlef P., Edmonds, Jae, Kainuma, Mikiko, et al. (2011). The Representative Concentration Pathways: An Overview, 109 *Climatic Change* 5–31, DOI 10.1007/s10584-011–0148-z.

Vassell, Gregory S. (1991, January). Northeast Blackout of 1965, 11 *IEEE Power Engineering Review* 4–8, DOI 10.1109/MPER.1991.88621.

Vesterby, Marlow, Heimlich, Ralph E. & Krupa, Kenneth S. (1994, March) Urbanization of Rural Land in the United States, Resources and Technology Division, Economic Research Service, US Department of Agriculture, Agricultural Economic Report No. 673.

Vithayasrichareron, Peerapat, Riesz, Jenny & MacGill, Iain (2017). Operational Flexibility of Future Generation Portfolios with High Renewables, 206 *Applied Energy* 32–41, DOI 10.1016/j.apenergy.2017.08.164.

Vogelsang, Timothy J. & Franses, Philip H. (2005). Testing for Common Deterministic Trend Slopes, 126 *Journal of Econometrics* 1–24, DOI 10.1016/j.jeconom.2004.02.004.
Vogelsang, Timothy J. & Nawaz, Nasreen (2017). Estimation and Interference of Linear Trend Slope Ratios with an Application to Global Temperature Data, 38 (5) *Time Series Analysis* 640–667, DOI 10.1111/jtsa.12209.
Voosen, Paul (2019, April 16). *New Climate Models Predict a Warming Surge*, Science Magazine.
Vose, Russell S., Arndt, Derek, Banzon, Viva F., et al. (2012, November). NOAA's Merged Land-Ocean Surface Temperature Analysis, 93 (11) *Bulletin of the American Meteorological Society* 1677–1685, DOI 10.1175/BAMS-D-11-00241.1.
WAIS Divide Project Members (2013). Onset of Deglacial Warming in West Antarctica Driven by Local Orbital Forcing, 500 *Nature* 440–444, DOI 10.1038/nature12376.
Walker, W. Reed (2013). The Transitional Costs of Sectoral Reallocation: Evidence from the Clean Air Act and the Workforce, 128 (4) *Quarterly Journal of Economics* 1787–1835, DOI 10.1093/qje/qjt022.
Walters, Justin T., McNider, Richard T., Shi, Zinghong, Norris, William B. & Christy, John R. (2007). Positive Surface Temperature Feedback in the Stable Nocturnal Boundary Layer, 34(12) *Geophysical Research Letters* L12709, DOI 10.1029/2007GL029505.
Wang, Chien & Prinn, Ronald G. (2011). Potential Climate Impacts and Reliability of Large-Scale Offshore Wind Farms, 6 (2) *Environmental Research Letters* 025101, DOI 10.1088/1748-9326/6/2/025101.
Wang, Chien & Prinn, Ronald G. (2010). Potential Climatic Impacts and Reliability of a Very Large-Scale Wind Farm, 10 *Atmospheric Chemistry & Physics* 2053–2061, DOI 10.5194/acp-10-2053-2010.
Wang, Jianglin, Yang, Bao, Ljungqvistm, Fredrik Charpentier, Luterbacher, Jurg, Osborn, Timothy J., Briffa, Keith R. & Zorita, Eduardo (2017). Internal and External Forcing of Multidecadal Atlantic Climate Variability over the Past 1,200 Years, 10 *Nature Geoscience* 512–517, DOI 10.1038/ngeo2962.
Wang, Junhong, Dai, Aiguo & Mears, Carl (2016). Global Water Vapor Trend from 1988 to 2011 and Its Diurnal Asymmetry Based on GPS, Radiosonde, and Microwave Satellite Measurements, 29 (14) *Journal of Climate* 5205–5222, DOI 10.1175/JCLI-D-15-0485.1.
Wang, N. & Li, Z. (2013). *Wireless Sensor Networks (WSNs) in the Agriculture and Food Industries*, in *Robotics and Automation in the Food Industry* 171–199 (Woodhead Publishing), DOI 10.1533/9780857095763.1.171.
Wang, Xianglan, Wang, Hongwei, Liu, Shengxue, Ferjani, Ali, Li, Jiansheng, Yan, Jianbing, Yang, Xiaohong & Qin, Feng (2016). Genetic Variation in ZmVPP1 Contributes to Drought Tolerance in Maize Seedlings, 48 (10) *Nature Genetics* 1233–1241, DOI 10.1038/ng.3636.
Wang, Ye, Silva, Vera & Lopez-Botet-Zulueta, Miguel (2016). Impact of High Penetration of Variable Renewable Generation on Frequency Dynamics in the Continental Europe Interconnected System, 10 (1) *IET Renewable Power Generation* 10–16, DOI 10.1049/iet-rpg.2015.0141.
Washington, Warren M. & Parkinson, Claire L. (2005). *An Introduction to Three-Dimensional Climate Modeling* 49 (Sausalito, CA, University Science Books, 2nd ed).
Watson, Christopher S., White, Neil J., Church, John A., King, Matt A., Burgette, Reed J. & Legresy, Benoit (2015). Unabated Global Mean Sea-Level Rise over the Satellite Altimeter Era, 5 (6) *Nature Climate Change* 565–568, DOI 10.1038/nclimate2635.
Watt-Logic (2019, August). What Caused the UK's Power Blackout and Will It Happen Again?
Watts, Anthony, Jones, Evan, McIntyre, Stephen & Christy, John R. (2012). An Area and Distance Weighted Analysis of the Impacts of Station Exposure on the U.S. Historical

Climatology Network Temperatures and Temperature Trends, Preprint, available at https://wattsupwiththat.files.wordpress.com/2012/07/watts-et-al_2012_discussion_paper_webrelease.pdf.
Webster, Paul (2007, April 29). *Is It Time to Hand Global Warming to the Lawyers?*, The Toronto Star.
Wehrmann, Benjamin (2019, March 5). *Capacity Market Debate Resurfaces as Germany May Need Gas to Replace Coal*, Clean Energy Wire.
Weitzman, Martin (2009). On Modeling and Interpreting the Economics of Catastrophic Climate Change, 91 *Review of Economics & Statistics* 1–19, DOI 10.1162/rest.91.1.1.
Weiler, Conrad J. (2019, Summer). How "Commerce among the Several States" Became "Interstate Commerce," and Why It Matters, 34 *Constitutional Commentary* 329–400.
Wettengel, Julian (2020, February 11). *Gas Industry Calls for Capacity Market Debate as Germany Exists Nuclear and Coal*, Clean Energy Wire.
Wettengel, Julian (2018, June 25). *The Role of Gas in Germany's Energy Transition: Industry Bets on Gas as Last Trump Card in Energiewende*, Clean Energy Wire.
Westerling, A. L., Hidalgo, H. G., Cayan, D.R. & Swetnam, T.W. (2006). Warming and Earlier Spring Increase Western US Forest Wildfire Activity, 313 *Science* 940–943, DOI 10.1126/science.1128834.
Westervelt, Amy (2010, June 22). The Man Who Makes Greenhouse Polluters Face Their Victims in Court, *Attorney Matt Pawa Has Applied Tort Law to Global Warming and Provoked Groundbreaking Rulings*, InsideClimate News.
White, H. J. (1957). Fifty Years of Electrostatic Precipitation, 7 (3) *Journal of the Air Pollution Control Association* 166–177, DOI 10.1080/00966665.1957.10467797.
White, Sam (2015). Unpuzzling American Climate: New World Experience and the Foundations of a New Science, 106 (3) *Isis* 544–566, DOI 10.1086/683166.
White, Sam (2017). *A Cold Welcome* (Cambridge, MA: Harvard University Press).
Whitefoot, Kate S. & Skerlos, Steven J. (2012). Design Incentives to Increase Vehicle Size Created from the US Footprint-Based Fuel Economy Standards, 41 *Energy Policy* 402–411, DOI 10.1016/j.enpol.2011.10.062.
Wiener, Jonathan Baert (1999). On the Political Economy of Global Environmental Regulation, 87 *Georgetown University Law Journal* 749–792.
Wildavsky, Aaron (1997). *But Is It True? A Citizen's Guide to Environmental Health and Safety Issues*. Revised ed., Cambridge: Harvard University Press.
Wind Europe, Wind Energy in Europe in 2018: Trends and Statistics 7–10.
Wisser, Ryan, Mai, Trieu, Millstein, Dev, Barbose, Galen, Bird, Lori, Heeter, Jenny, Keyser, David, Krishnan, Venkat & Macknick, Jordan (2017). Assessing the Costs and Benefits of US Renewable Portfolio Standards, 12 *Environmental Research Letters* 094023, DOI 10.1088/1748-9326/aa87bd.
WMO (1975, August). Proceedings of the WMO/IMAP Symposium on Long-Term Climatic Fluctuations, WMO No. 421, Norwich, 18–23.
WMO (1977). Report of the Scientific Workshop on Atmospheric Carbon Dioxide, WMO Report No. 474.
World Nuclear News (2018, April 17). Report Highlights Impact of US Nuclear Plant Closures.
Wu, Ye, Wang, Shuxiao, Streets, David G., Hao, Jiming, Chan, Melissa & Jiang, Jingkun (2006). Trends in Anthropogenic Mercury Emissions in China from 1995 to 2003, 40 *Environmental Science and Technology* 5312–5318.
Wunsch, Carl, Ponte, Rui M. & Heimbach, Patrick (2007). Decadal Trends in Sea Level Patterns: 1993–2004, 20 (24) *Journal of Climate* 5889–5911, DOI 10.1175/2007JCLI1840.1.

Wunsch, Carl (2016). Global Ocean Integrals and Means, with Trend Implications, 8 *Annual Review Marine Science* 1–33, DOI 10.1146/annurev-marine-122414-034040.
Xiao, Yingjie, Liu, Haijun, Wu, Liuji, Warburton, Marilyn & Yan, Jianbing (2017). Genome-wide Association Studies in Maize: Praise and Stargaze, 10 *Molecular Plant* 359–374, DOI 10.1016/j.molp.2016.12.008.
Yandle, Bruce (2019, November 6). *Yes, Sen. Warren, the System Is Rigged – by Congress*, The Hill.
Zander, Joakim (2010). *The Application of the Precautionary Principle in Practice* (New York: Cambridge University Press).
Zhang, Tianyi, Lin, Xiaomao & Sassenrath, Gretchen F. (2015). Current Irrigation Practices in the Central United States Reduce Drought and Extreme Heat Impacts for Maize and Soybean but Not for Wheat, 508 *Science of the Total Environment* 331–342, DOI 10.1016/j.scitotenv.2014.12.004.
Zhang, Xuehai, Warbuton, Marilyn L., Setter, Tim, Liu, Haijun, Yadong, Xue, Yang, Ning, Yan, Jianbing & Xiao, Yingjie (2016). Genome-wide Association Studies of Drought-Related Metabolic Changes in Maize Using an Enlarged SNP Panel. 129 *Theoretical and Applied Genetics* 1449–1463, DOI 10.1007/s00122-016-2716-0.
Zheng, Hong-Ziang, Yan, Shi, Qin, Zhen-Dong & Jin, Li (2012). MtDNA Analysis of Global Populations Support That Major Population Expansions Began before Neolithic Time, 2 *Scientific Reports* 745, DOI 10.1038/srep00745.
Zhou, Jianson & Tung, Ka-Kit (2013). Deducing Multidecadal Anthropogenic Global Warming Trends Using Multiple Regression Analysis, 70 *Journal of Atmospheric Science* 3–8, DOI 10.1175/JAS-D-12-0208.1.
Zhu, Jiang, Poulson, Christopher J. & Otto-Bliesner, Better L. (2020). High Climate Sensitivity in CMIP6 Model Not Supported by Paleoclimate, 10 *Nature Climate Change* 378–379, DOI 10.1038/s41558-020-0764-6.
Zivin, Joshua Graff & Neidell, Matthew (2014, January). Temperature and the Allocation of Time: Implications for Climate Change, 32 (1) *Journal of Labor Economics* 1–26.

LIST OF LEGAL OPINIONS REFERENCED

Massachusetts v. EPA, 549 US 497 (2007).
Union Electric Co. v. EPA, 427 US 246 (1976).
Coalition for Responsible Regulation v. EPA, 684 F.3d 102 (D.C. Cir. 2012).
Ethyl Corp. v. EPA, 541 F.2d 1 (D.C. Cir. 1976).
In Utility Air Regulatory Group v. EPA, No. 01–1074 (D.C. Cir. 2001).
American Farm Bureau Federation v. EPA, 559 F.3d 512 (D.C. Cir. 2009).
Michigan v. E.P.A., 213 F.3d 663 (D.C. Cir. 2000), Appalachian Power Co. v. E.P.A., 249F.3d 1032 (D.C. Cir. 2001).
North Carolina v. EPA, 531 F.3d 896 (D.C. Cir. 2008), Reconsidered at, 550 F.3d 1176 (2008).
New Jersey v. EPA, 517 F. 3d 574 (D.C. Cir. 2008).
Del. Riverkeeper Network v. FERC, 753 F.3d 1304 (D.C. Cir. 2014).
Allegheny Defense Project v. FERC, 932 F.3d 940 (D.C. Cir. 2019).
Nuclear Energy Inst., Inc. v. EPA, 373 F.3d 1251 (D.C. Cir. 2004).
Public Utilities Commission of Rhode Island v. Attleboro Steam & Electric Company, 273 US 83 (1926).
US v PG&E, No. CR 14–0175 WHA, Document No. 1186 (N.D. Cal, April 29, 2020).

New Creek Mountain Sportsman's Club v. New Creek Wind, No.'s 2:18-cv-00111, 2:18-cv -00112, 2:18-cv-00113 (N.D. W.Va. 2018).
Shearwater v. Ashe, 2015 WL 4747881 (N.D Cal. 2015).
Attorney General ex rel Muskegon Booming Co. v. Evart Booming Co., 34 Mich. 462 (1876).
People v. Gold Run Ditch and Mining Co., 66 Cal. 138, 4 P. 1152, 56 Am.Rep. 80 (1884).
Wishart v. Newell et al., 4 Pa.C.C. 141 (1887).
People v. Gold Run Ditch and Mining Co., 66 Cal. 138, 153 (concurring opinion).
Pennsylvania v. Wheeling & B. Bridge Co., 13 How. 518, 14 L. Ed. 249 (1851).
International Paper v. Ouelette, 107 S.Ct. 805 (1987).
Missouri v. Illinois, 26 S.Ct 268, 200 US 496 (1906).
Georgia v. Tennessee Copper Co., 206 US 230 (1907).
New York v. New Jersey, 256 US 296 (1921).
City of Milwaukee v. Illinois and Michigan, 101 S.Ct. 1784, 1797 (1981).
Illinois v. Milwaukee, 731 F.2d 403 (7th Cir. 1984).
AEP v. Connecticut, 131 S.Ct. at 2540.
Native Village of Kivalina v. Exxonmobil Corp.,663 F. Supp.2d 863 (N.D.Cal.2009).
Native Village of Kivalina v. Exxonmobil Corp., 696 F.3d 849 (9th Cir. 2012).
Comer v. Murphy Oil USA, Inc., 839 F. Supp. 2d 849 (S.D. Miss. 2012).
City of New York v. BP PLC., 325 F. Supp.3d 466 (S.D.N.Y. 2018).
Kanuk v. State of Alaska Department of Natural Resources, 335 P.3d 1088 (Alaska 2014).
Juliana v. United States, 217 F.3d 1224 (D. Ore. 2016).
National Review, Inc. v. Michael E. Mann, Competitive Enterprise Institute et al. v. Michael E. Mann, 589 US __ (2019) (Justice Alito, dissenting).

Index